British Hotels & Inns

Dog-friendly Breaks in Britain

French Châteaux & Hotels

British Bed & Breakfast

Special Places to Stay

Ninth edition

Published in 2012
ISBN-13: 978-1-906136-57-4

Alastair Sawday Publishing Co. Ltd,
The Old Farmyard, Yanley Lane,
Long Ashton, Bristol BS41 9LR, UK
Tel: +44 (0)1275 395430
Email: info@sawdays.co.uk
Web: www.sawdays.co.uk

The Globe Pequot Press,
P. O. Box 480, Guilford,
Connecticut 06437, USA
Tel: +1 203 458 4500
Email: info@globepequot.com
Web: www.globepequot.com

A catalogue record for this book is available from the British Library. This publication is not included under licences issued by the Copyright Agency. No part of this publication may be used in any form of advertising, sales promotion or publicity.

We have made every effort to ensure the accuracy of the information in this book at the time of going to press. However, we cannot accept any responsibility for any loss, injury or inconvenience resulting from the use of information contained therein.

Cover photo credits
1. & 2. The Highlander Pub, entry 286
3. Newbridge On Usk, entry 719

Series Editor Alastair Sawday
Editor David Hancock
Editorial Assistance Joanne Hayers
Editorial Director Annie Shillito
Content & Publishing Manager Jackie King
Senior Editor Jo Boissevain
Production Coordinator Alex Skinner
Writing David Hancock, David Ashby, Jo Boissevain, Joanne Hayers, Mandy Wragg
Inspections David Hancock, David Ashby, Mandy Barnes, Maureen Flynn, Rebecca Harris, Mandy Wragg
Thanks also to others who did an inspection or two.
Marketing & PR
01275 395433

Alastair Sawday has asserted his right to be identified as the author of this work

Maps: Maidenhead Cartographic Services
Printing: Butler, Tanner & Dennis, Frome
UK distribution: Penguin UK, London
Production: Pagebypage Co. Ltd

Alastair Sawday's

Special Places

Pubs & Inns

of England & Wales

Contents

We have some extra gems for you at the back of the book – pubs numbered 745-944 and ordered by county – that haven't quite made a full entry. Perhaps they have just opened or changed hands or are simply on our radar as ones worth watching. They certainly merit a visit so why not drop in on them and let us know how you get on.

The news from the world of pubs has been gloom-laden for several years, but there is light at the end of the long, dark tunnel. In a nutshell: publicans are catching up, cottoning on, plugging in. Some are going out of business, it is true, but at a declining rate. The best of them are thriving, seeing that times are changing and that they need to move on.

The pub, like the rest of us, has to re-invent itself – and is doing so with startling creativity. They are not alone. As publishers we have to be especially creative to make sure we continue to please you and our owners; newspapers have embraced the digital world, in some cases brilliantly; kitchen designers, car-manufacturers, lawyers (even) have had to think again. Gardeners have had to learn about hot-climate planting, parents to find new ways of engaging their children when so many electronic gadgets compete; husbands of pleasing their wives, fishermen of catching their fish, vicars of finding their flocks and protecting their roofs. Little is the same any more – for publicans as well as the rest of us.

Here are a few examples of what our pubs are now doing:

- Creating their own micro-breweries within the pubs
- Selling 'beer flights' – three third pints, so the ale drinker can explore different tastes
- Embracing coffee culture, selling tea and cakes, staying open all day
- Erecting a deli-counter with homemade produce (stocks, jams, chutneys, eggs...)
- Having a cinema on Sunday evening, perhaps a film and a one-pot supper
- Operating a Bring Your Own Wine evening, with special three-course dinners on quieter nights
- Growing their own veg
- Setting up their own craft or food markets, or taking stalls at local markets for their own produce
- Creating the new Trek-Inn: accompanied walks with a breakfast, guided walk and afternoon tea
- Smoking their own fish, meats and cheeses
- Improving food quality generally – there were three new pubs with Michelin stars in 2011.

I could go on, but David will expand upon this theme in his own Introduction. All this is great news, and suggests that we may no longer have to lament the passing of the pub, but celebrate instead its gradual revival.

Alastair Sawday

Photo: Tom Germain

Welcome to Edition 9 – packed again with thriving locals, little-known freeholds and pubs of history, character and charm. Many are passionate about their beers and wines, others about their food – local, seasonal, organic. Others stand out for their pretty gardens, waterside settings, cosy bedrooms, sweeping views.

The result is a total of 944 pubs and inns, including over 200 with bedrooms. Some pubs have disappeared from the guide, others have moved sideways to 'Worth a Visit' and await re-inspection: landlords change, chefs move on.

Last year I lamented the speed at which pubs were closing, 50 a week as the recession took hold. In contrast, 2011, although clouded in economic malaise, has given the pub sector grounds for optimism. According to Christie & Co, fewer pubs were put up for sale than in 2010, and the number of pubs selling for alternative use has declined.

Many failing pubs are being sold on to enterprising entrepreneurs and small pub companies. In 2011, small groups like Flying Kiwi Inns, innovative Peach Pubs and upmarket Hillbrooke Hotels opened stunning new pubs or inns; all intend growing their portfolio during 2012.

The most successful operators and chef/patrons are the most enterprising. Many continue to focus on local foods, sometimes rearing their own livestock and growing their own produce, while good-value food offers and fixed-price menus have become ever more inventive. Some locals have become the hub of their community, doubling up as a space for quiz nights, film nights and exhibitions. Other recent trends aimed at boosting business include outdoor wood-fired ovens for pizzas; 'meet the supplier' dinners; day-time delis and cafés. And pubs with bedrooms continue to prosper.

Difficult times lie ahead, but many pubs are getting it right. Not only are they warm, vibrant, wonderful places to visit, they also offer great value. Please give them your support.

David Hancock

Photo: White Star Tavern & Dining Rooms, entry 245

Those who are familiar with our Special Places series know that we look for originality and authenticity, and disregard the anonymous and the banal. We also place great emphasis on the welcome – as important to us as the setting, the architecture, the atmosphere and the food.

The notion of 'special' is at the heart of what we do, and is highly subjective. We also recognise that one person's idea of special is not necessarily another's so there is a big variety of places in this book, from rural rustic to urban chic, from gastropub to cider house.

Inspections and subscriptions

We have visited every entry in this guide. We pick up those details that cannot be gleaned over the internet or by phone, and we write the descriptions ourselves, doing our best to avoid misinterpretation. If a pub is in, we think it's special, and the write-up should tell you if it's your sort of special.

Owners pay for their bedrooms to be mentioned but it is not possible for anyone to buy their way in; their fee goes towards the cost of the inspection process and includes a presence on our website.

Feedback

The pubs with rooms that appear in this guide are on our website, too. If you would like to tell us about your stay at any of these places, find them there and follow the link to the feedback form. For the non-rooms places, please email us with your feedback and tell us about your visit – the food, ales, staff and, crucially, the atmosphere. Write to info@sawdays.co.uk.

A lot of the new entries in each edition are recommended by our readers, so keep telling us about new places you've discovered, too.

Disclaimer

We make no claims to pure objectivity in choosing these places. They are here simply because we like them. Our opinions and tastes are ours alone and we hope you will share them. We have done our utmost to get our facts right but apologise unreservedly for any mistakes that may have crept in.

You should know that we don't check such things as fire alarms, kitchen hygiene or any other regulation with which owners of properties receiving paying guests should comply. This is the responsibility of the owners.

Finding the right place for you

Drink, eat, sleep A growing number of pubs and inns combine atmosphere with good food and bedrooms to match – and at lower prices than many hotels. It's true that some pubs are virtually indistinguishable from some small hotels, but a lively bar serving real beer should put them into the classic inn category. Some pubs with rooms are more modest village affairs where the enthusiasm to get things right in the bar extends upstairs.

Photo: The Sands End entry 351

Bar Snacks
Rock Oysters...£1.50 (ea)
Mixed Olives...£3.45
fried White Bait w/ lemon aioli...£4.00
Chipolatas w/ Mustard...£4.00
Pork Spare Ribs w/ Black Bean Sauce...£4.50
Sands End Crackling...£3.50
Spicy Chicken Wings w/ Coriander Yoghurt £5
Sundried tomato, olive & pesto pastry...£2.75
Scotch Egg...£2.80
Sausage Roll

(If you are worried about noise at weekends, you can ask for a room at the back or a room across the way.) So the next time you take a weekend or business break, dismiss those roadside lodges and impersonal hotels in favour of a friendly country inn.

Gastropubs and country dining pubs

Our best pubs are luring foodies away from pricier restaurants as a wave of casual dining enfolds the nation. Many backstreet boozers have been transformed, the fruit machines and beer-stained carpet being replaced by chalked-up menus and chunky tables. In the countryside, too, old-fashioned locals are being rejuvenated by landlords and chefs who believe that gastronomy is rooted in the soil and that food should be fresh, seasonal and sourced from the best local suppliers.

Photo: The Highlander Pub, entry 286

Our favourite food pubs in England and Wales are described within these pages; all strike a happy balance between restaurant and pub. (Note that booking is not always a given and you may have to take your chance with a table.)

Maps and directions

The maps at the front of the book show the approximate position, via a series of coloured flags, of each of our pubs and inns. Red flags indicate pubs with rooms, gold flags the award winners, dark grey flags the Worth a Visits. The maps are for guidance only; use a detailed road map or you could lose yourself down a tangle of lanes. There are directions on each guide entry, but these are also for guidance only.

Symbols

Below each entry you will see a line of symbols, which are explained at the very back of the book. They are based on the information given to us by the owners but things do change, so use the symbols as a guide rather than an absolute statement of fact. Please note that the symbols do not necessarily apply to the bedrooms. Double-check anything that is important to you. A fuller explanation of some symbols is given below. On our website, where you will find all our pubs with rooms, the symbols apply to 'staying' rather than just visiting.

Children – The symbol is given to pubs that accept children of any age. That doesn't mean that they can go everywhere in the pub, or that highchairs and special menus or small portions are provided. Nor does it mean that children should be anything less than well-behaved! Call to check details such as separate family rooms, whether children are allowed in the dining room and whether there is play equipment in the garden.

Dogs – The symbol is given to places where your dog can go into some part of the pub, generally the bar and garden. It is unlikely to include eating areas.

Wheelchairs – We use the symbol if we've been told those in wheelchairs can access the bar and a wc. The symbol does not apply to accommodation.

Pub awards

Every year we choose those pubs that we think deserve a special mention. Our categories are: pubs serving local, seasonal and organic produce; authentic pubs; community pubs; and pubs with rooms. More details are given on pages 14-15, and all the award winners have been stamped.

Opening times

We list the hours pubs are closed during the afternoon and whether or not they are closed during particular lunchtimes and evenings. We do advise that you check before setting out, especially in winter.

Meals and meal prices

We give the approximate cost of main courses in the bar and/or restaurant. Note that some pubs charge extra for side dishes, which significantly increases the main course price. Note that many pubs do fixed-price Sunday lunches, and that prices in general may change. Check when booking. We also state days or sessions when no food is served.

Bedrooms, bathrooms and breakfasts

If you're thinking of staying the night in a simple pub or inn, bear in mind that an early night may not be possible if folk are carousing below. A few bedrooms do not have en suite bathrooms – please ask on booking – and pub room check-ins are often late, eg. from 6.30pm. Breakfasts are generally included in the room price, and most places serve breakfast between 8am and 10am.

Bedroom prices

Prices are per room for two people sharing. If a price range is given, then the

Photo: The Tobie Norris, entry 338

lowest price is for the least expensive room in low season and the highest for the most expensive room in high season. The single room rate (or the single occupancy of a double room) generally follows. Occasionally prices are for half board, ie. they include dinner, bed and breakfast. Do check.

Bookings and cancellations

Tables – At weekends, food pubs are often full and it is best to book a table well in advance; at other times, only tables in the dining rooms may be reserved. Tables in the bar may operate on a first-come, first-served basis. Some of the best gastropubs do not take reservations at all, wanting to hold on to their pubby origins. We applaud that, but it does mean you need to be super-organised and arrive early to bag a space. Always phone to double-check meal times.

Rooms – Most pubs and inns will ask for a credit card number and a contact phone number when you telephone to book a room. They may take a deposit at the time of booking, either by cheque or credit/debit card. If you cancel – depending on how much notice you give – you can lose all or part of this deposit unless your room is re-let. Ask the pub to explain their cancellation policy before booking so you understand where you stand; it may avoid a nasty surprise.

Payment

Those places that accept credit or debit cards are marked with a credit card symbol.

Tipping

It is not obligatory but it is appreciated, particularly in pubs with restaurants.

Photo above: The Victoria Inn, entry 192
Photo right: The Crown Inn, entry 683

Local, seasonal & organic produce award

A passion for actively sourcing seasonal foods from high-quality local suppliers now extends to deli counters by the bar, farmers' markets in pub car parks and poly-tunnels and vegetable plots bursting with home-grown produce. Hearts soar when our inspectors find menus promoting regional, seasonal produce: farm meats, village-baked bread, locally shot game, fish from local catches, organic wines and local brewery ale. Our champions are:

The Lazy Toad Inn
Devon
entry 175

The Sun at Northaw
Hertfordshire
entry 287

The Fox
Wiltshire
entry 618

Authentic pub award

We have visited scores of simple, authentic, unadulterated pubs and they are a diminishing breed. Those that we found particularly special are:

Two Brewers
Berkshire
entry 26

Blacksmiths Arms
Cumbria
entry 118

The Stag
Sussex
entry 565

Pubs with rooms award

Our eclectic bunch of inns-with-rooms get full-page entries and include bedrooms that range from swish suites with plasma TVs to simple but good rooms overlooking the sea. With an increasing number of pubs wishing to promote their rooms above the bar – or in the converted barn, coach-house or stables across the way – our inspectors have visited more bedrooms than ever for this edition. Our winners are good 'all-rounders', too, serving excellent food, beers and wines.

The Wheatsheaf Inn
Gloucestershire
entry 212

The Beckford Arms
Wiltshire
entry 607

Cross Foxes
Gwynedd
entry 718

Community pub award

Within these pages you will find some great little locals run by enterprising, hard-working landlords who have succeeded in making their pub the hub of the community. Our shining examples are:

Five Bells Inn
Kent
entry 302

The Full Moon
Nottinghamshire
entry 427

The Crown Inn
Yorkshire
entry 683

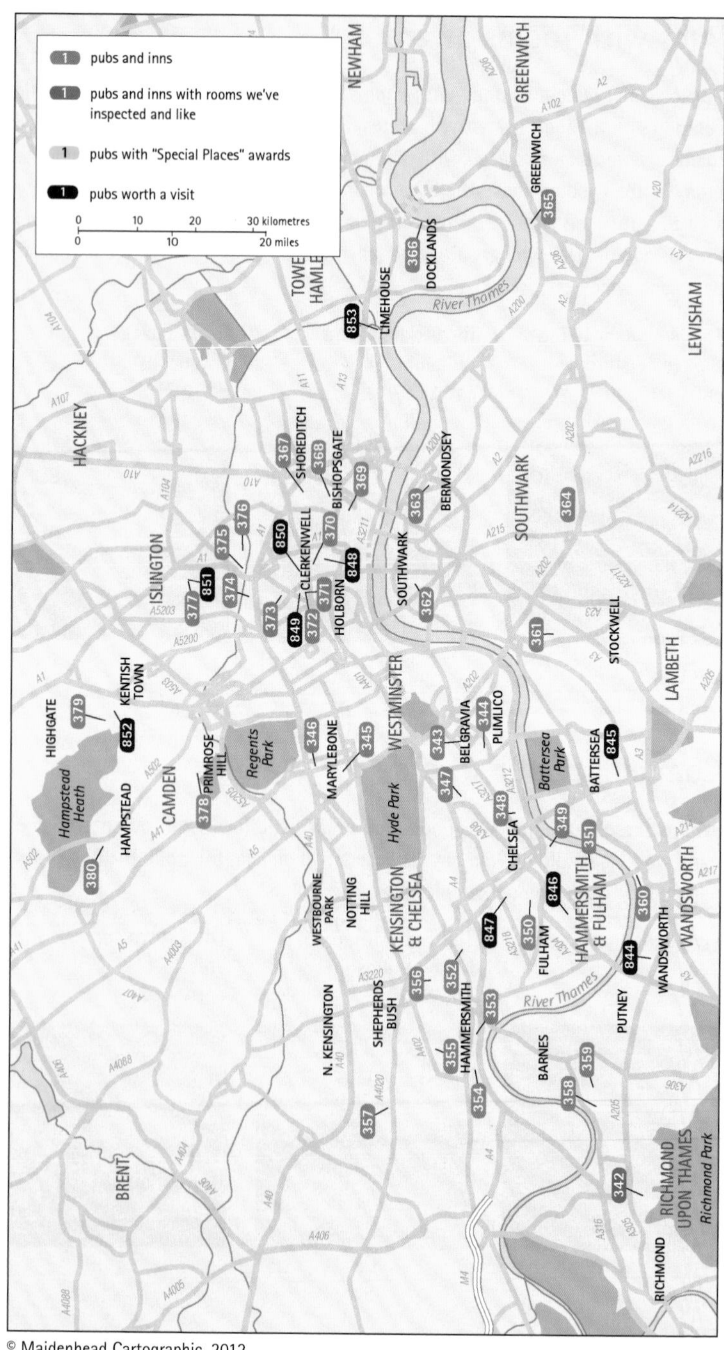

1 pubs and inns
1 pubs and inns with rooms we've inspected and like
1 pubs with "Special Places" awards
1 pubs worth a visit
0 10 20 30 kilometres
0 10 20 miles
HACKNEY
ISLINGTON
CAMDEN
HIGHGATE
HAMPSTEAD
Hampstead Heath
KENTISH TOWN
PRIMROSE HILL
Regents Park
MARYLEBONE
WESTMINSTER
Hyde Park
KENSINGTON & CHELSEA
NOTTING HILL
WESTBOURNE PARK
N. KENSINGTON
SHEPHERDS BUSH
HAMMERSMITH
BRENT
BARNES
PUTNEY
FULHAM
HAMMERSMITH & FULHAM
CHELSEA
BELGRAVIA
PLIMLICO
Battersea Park
BATTERSEA
WANDSWORTH
RICHMOND
RICHMOND UPON THAMES
Richmond Park
LAMBETH
STOCKWELL
SOUTHWARK
BERMONDSEY
HOLBORN
CLERKENWELL
SHOREDITCH
BISHOPSGATE
LIMEHOUSE
DOCKLANDS
TOWER HAMLETS
NEWHAM
GREENWICH
LEWISHAM
River Thames

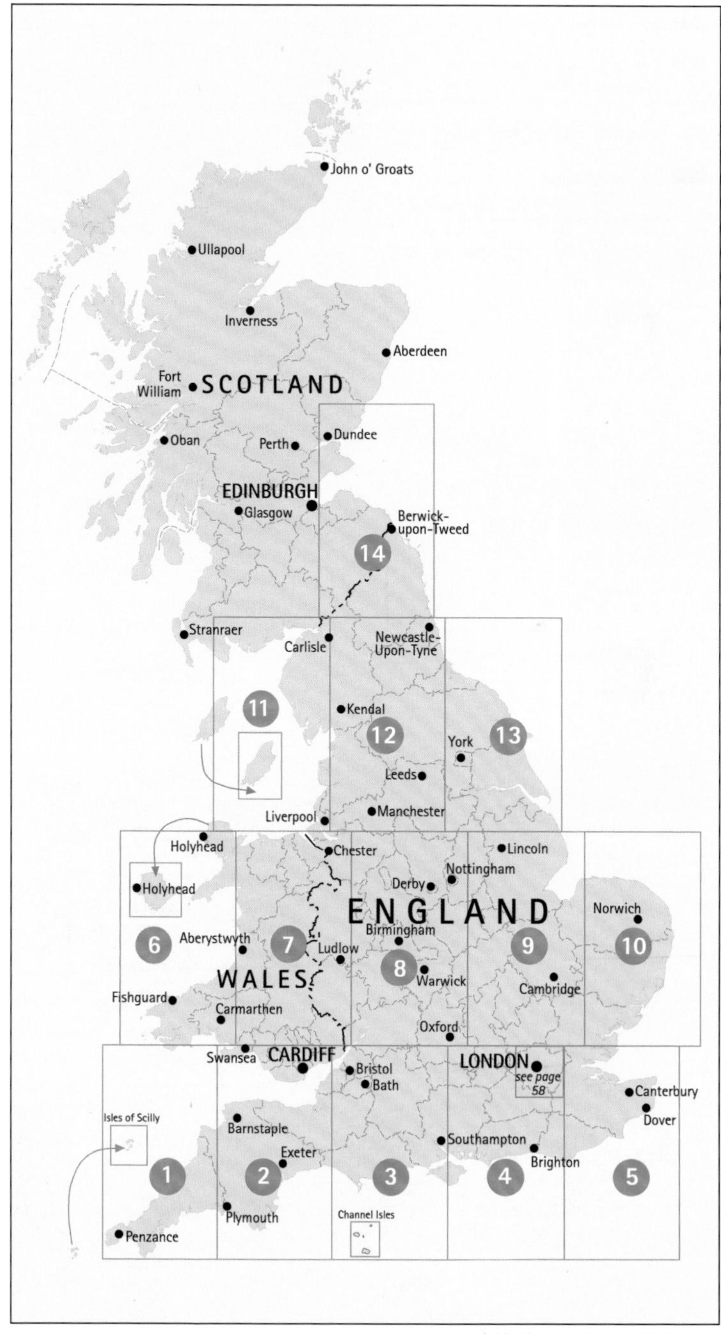
John o' Groats
Ullapool
Inverness
Aberdeen
Fort William
SCOTLAND
Oban
Perth
Dundee
EDINBURGH
Glasgow
Berwick-upon-Tweed
14
Stranraer
Carlisle
Newcastle-Upon-Tyne
11
Kendal
12
York
13
Leeds
Liverpool
Manchester
Holyhead
Chester
Lincoln
Holyhead
Nottingham
Derby
ENGLAND
Norwich
Birmingham
6
Aberystwyth
7
Ludlow
8
9
10
WALES
Warwick
Fishguard
Cambridge
Carmarthen
Oxford
Swansea
CARDIFF
Bristol
LONDON
see page 58
Bath
Canterbury
Isles of Scilly
Dover
Barnstaple
Southampton
Exeter
Brighton
1
2
3
4
5
Plymouth
Channel Isles
Penzance

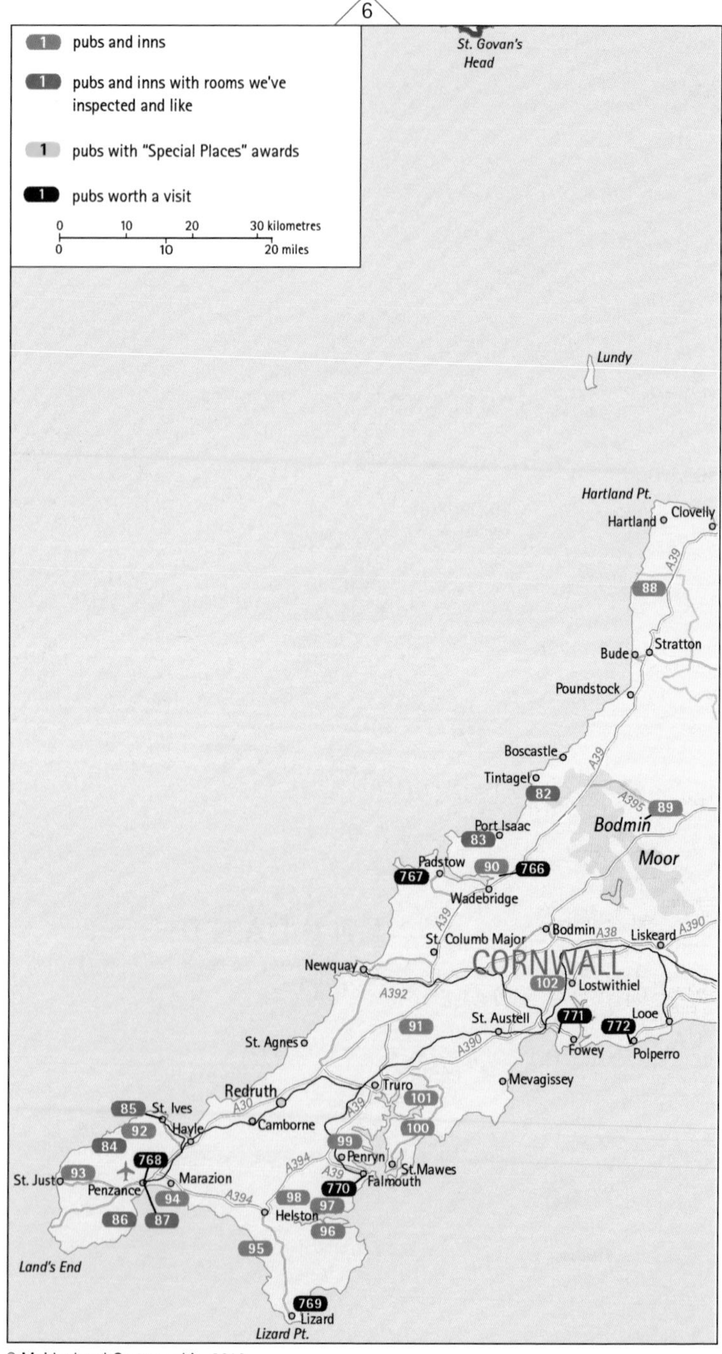
6
1 pubs and inns
1 pubs and inns with rooms we've inspected and like
1 pubs with "Special Places" awards
1 pubs worth a visit
0 10 20 30 kilometres
0 10 20 miles
St. Govan's Head
Lundy
Hartland Pt.
Hartland
Clovelly
A39
88
Bude
Stratton
Poundstock
Boscastle
Tintagel
82
A395
89
Bodmin
Moor
Port Isaac
83
Padstow
767
90
766
Wadebridge
A39
St. Columb Major
Bodmin
A38
Liskeard
A390
CORNWALL
Newquay
A392
102
Lostwithiel
St. Austell
771
772
Looe
91
A390
Fowey
Polperro
St. Agnes
Mevagissey
Redruth
Truro
101
85
St. Ives
A30
A39
Camborne
100
92
Hayle
84
768
99
Penryn
A394
St. Mawes
St. Just
93
Marazion
A39
Falmouth
Penzance
94
A394
98
770
97
Helston
86
87
96
95
Land's End
769
Lizard
Lizard Pt.

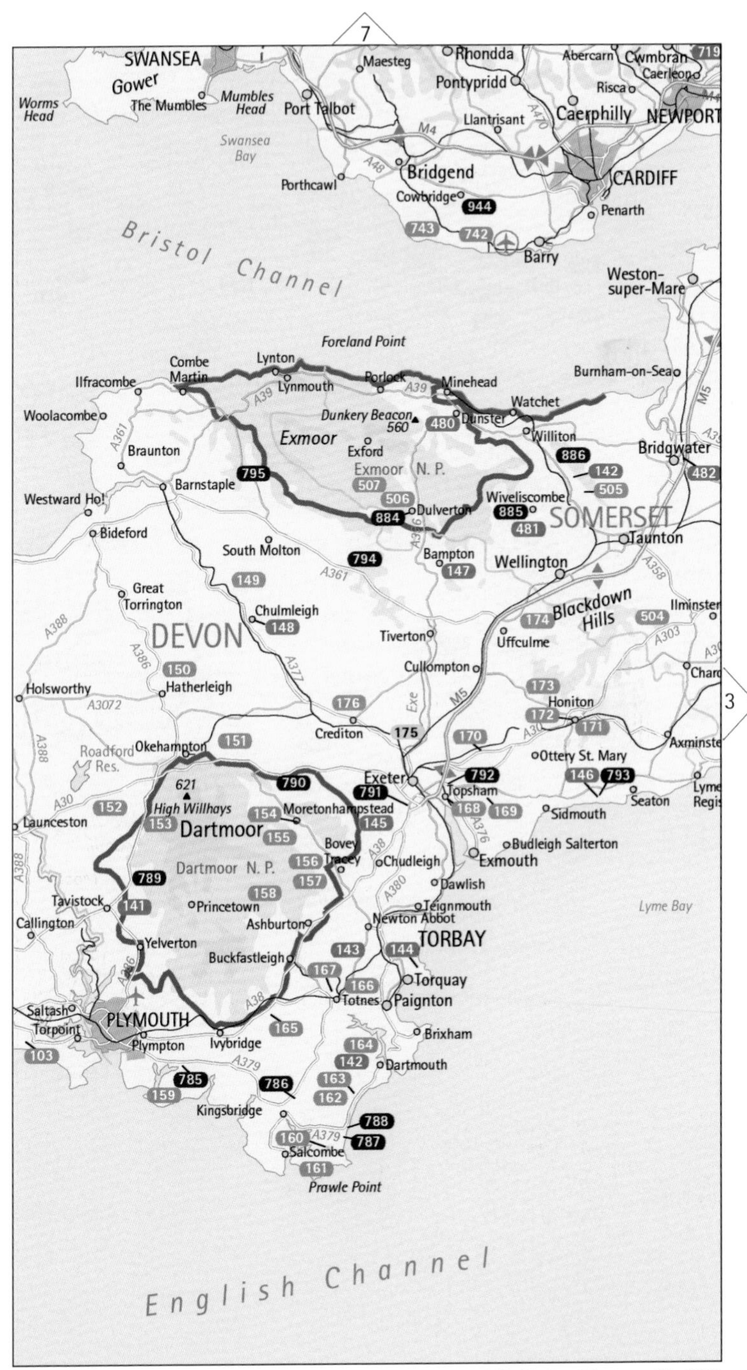
7
SWANSEA
Gower
Worms Head
The Mumbles
Mumbles Head
Swansea Bay
Port Talbot
Maesteg
Rhondda
Pontypridd
Abercarn
Cwmbran
Caerleon
Risca
Caerphilly
NEWPORT
Llantrisant
Bridgend
Porthcawl
Cowbridge
CARDIFF
Penarth
Barry
Bristol Channel
Weston-super-Mare
Foreland Point
Lynton
Lynmouth
Combe Martin
Ilfracombe
Woolacombe
Porlock
Minehead
Watchet
Dunster
Williton
Burnham-on-Sea
Bridgwater
Dunkery Beacon 560
Exmoor
Exford
Exmoor N. P.
Braunton
Barnstaple
Westward Ho!
Bideford
Dulverton
Wiveliscombe
SOMERSET
Taunton
South Molton
Bampton
Wellington
Great Torrington
DEVON
Chulmleigh
Tiverton
Uffculme
Blackdown Hills
Ilminster
Chard
Cullompton
Holsworthy
Hatherleigh
Honiton
Crediton
Okehampton
Roadford Res.
Axminster
Ottery St. Mary
Exeter
Topsham
Seaton
Lyme Regis
Sidmouth
621
High Willhays
Dartmoor
Moretonhampstead
Launceston
Bovey Tracey
Chudleigh
Budleigh Salterton
Exmouth
Dartmoor N. P.
Dawlish
Tavistock
Princetown
Teignmouth
Lyme Bay
Callington
Ashburton
Newton Abbot
TORBAY
Yelverton
Buckfastleigh
Torquay
Totnes
Paignton
Saltash
Torpoint
PLYMOUTH
Plympton
Ivybridge
Brixham
Dartmouth
Kingsbridge
Salcombe
Prawle Point
3
English Channel

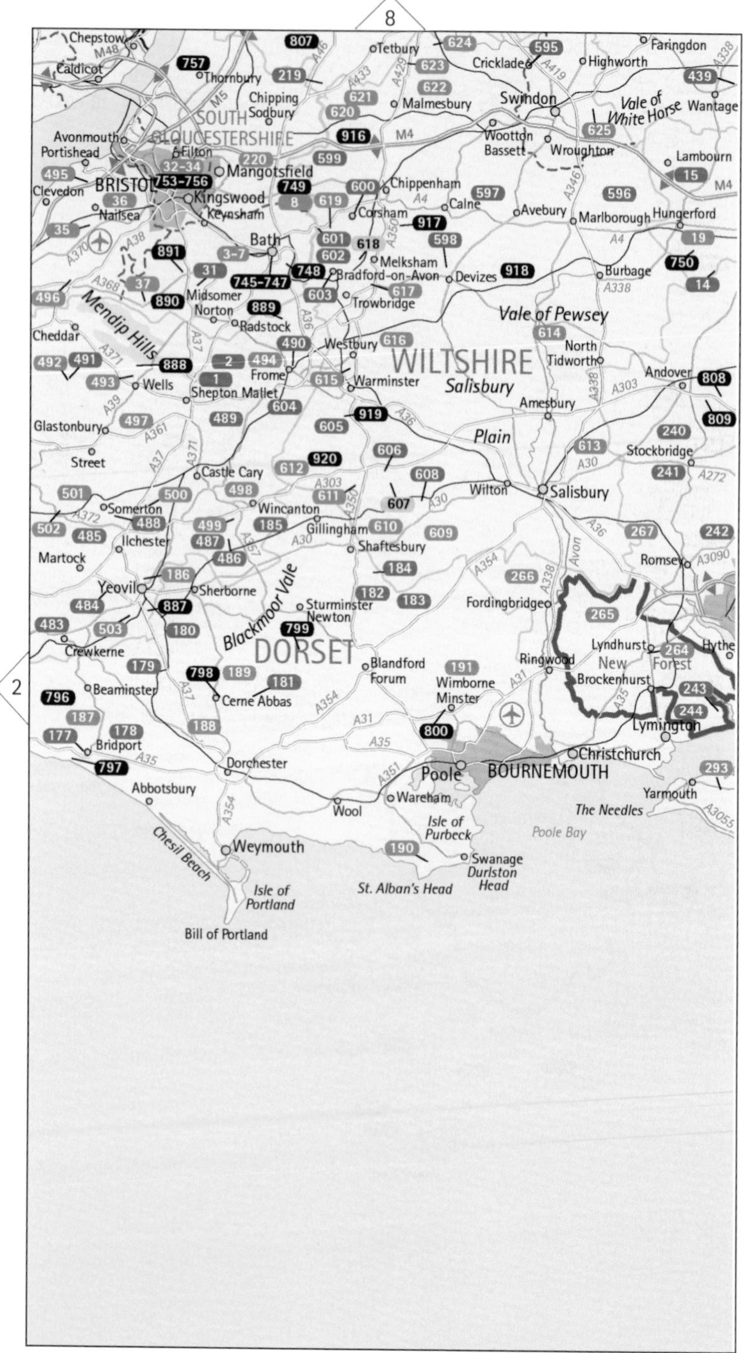
8
2
Chepstow
Caldicot
Thornbury
Chipping Sodbury
Tetbury
Malmesbury
Cricklade
Highworth
Faringdon
Swindon
Vale of White Horse
Wantage
Avonmouth
Portishead
Filton
BRISTOL
Mangotsfield
Kingswood
Keynsham
Clevedon
Nailsea
Wootton Bassett
Wroughton
Lambourn
Chippenham
Corsham
Calne
Avebury
Marlborough
Hungerford
Bath
Melksham
Bradford-on-Avon
Devizes
Trowbridge
Burbage
Midsomer Norton
Radstock
Mendip Hills
Vale of Pewsey
Cheddar
Westbury
WILTSHIRE
North Tidworth
Frome
Wells
Shepton Mallet
Warminster
Salisbury Plain
Andover
Amesbury
Glastonbury
Street
Stockbridge
Castle Cary
Wilton
Salisbury
Somerton
Wincanton
Gillingham
Shaftesbury
Ilchester
Martock
Romsey
Yeovil
Sherborne
Blackmoor Vale
Sturminster Newton
Fordingbridge
Crewkerne
DORSET
Lyndhurst
Hythe
New Forest
Ringwood
Brockenhurst
Blandford Forum
Wimborne Minster
Beaminster
Cerne Abbas
Lymington
Bridport
Christchurch
Poole
BOURNEMOUTH
Dorchester
Abbotsbury
Wareham
Wool
Yarmouth
The Needles
Isle of Purbeck
Poole Bay
Weymouth
Chesil Beach
Swanage
Durlston Head
Isle of Portland
St. Alban's Head
Bill of Portland

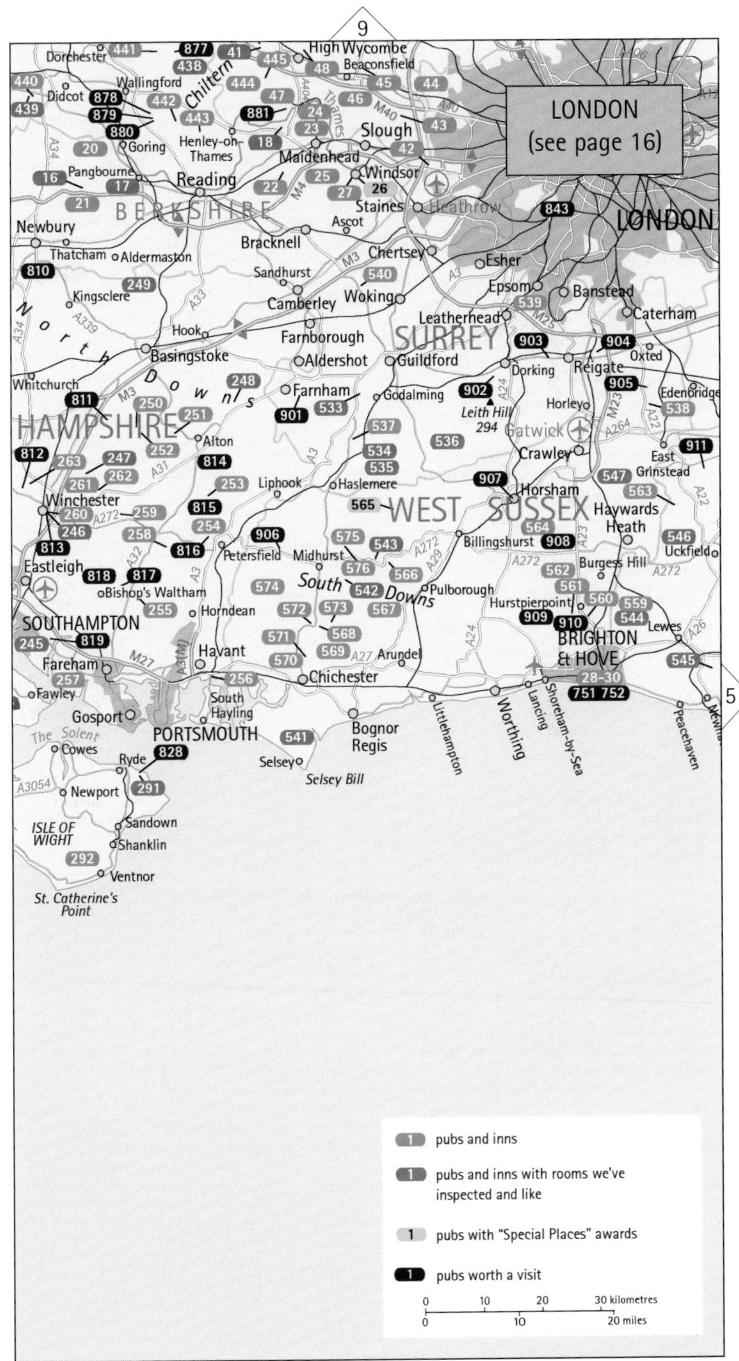
LONDON
(see page 16)
pubs and inns
pubs and inns with rooms we've inspected and like
pubs with "Special Places" awards
pubs worth a visit
30 kilometres
20 miles

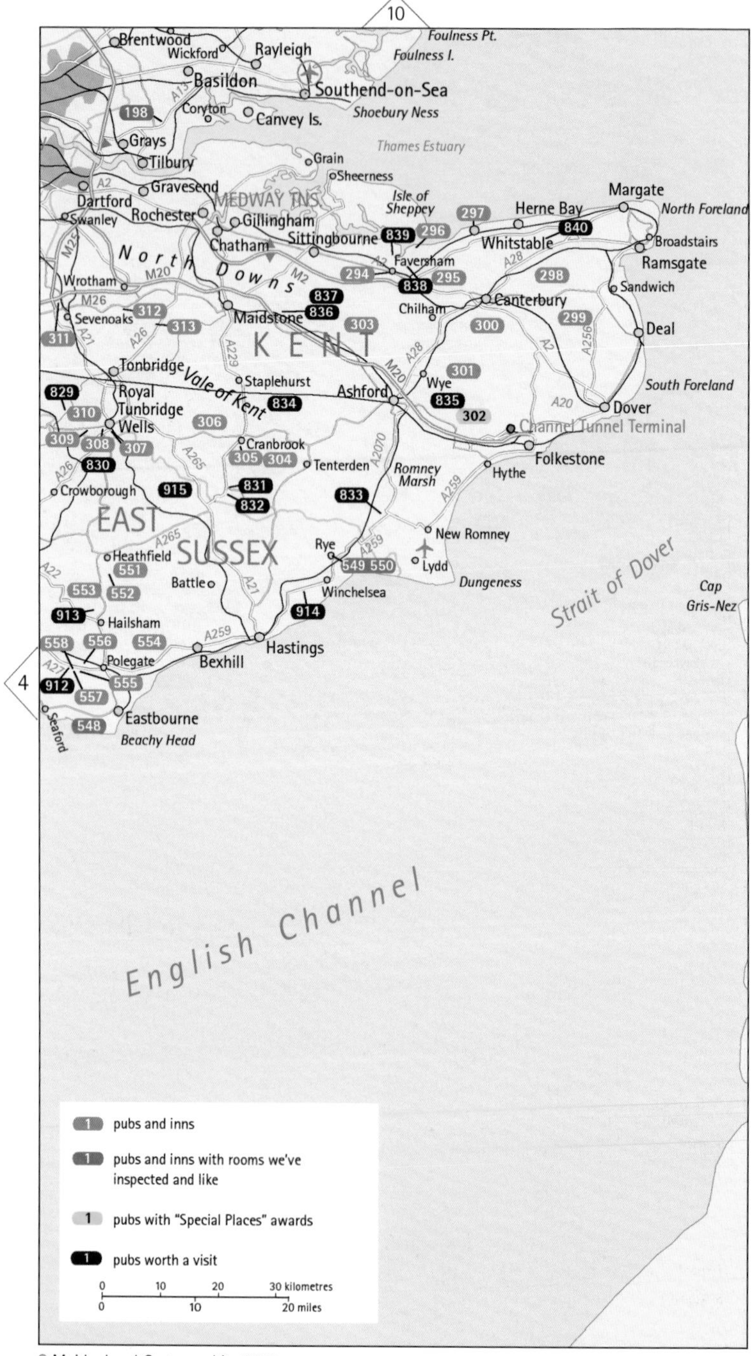

10
4
Brentwood
Wickford
Rayleigh
Foulness Pt.
Foulness I.
Basildon
Southend-on-Sea
Coryton
Canvey Is.
Shoebury Ness
Grays
Tilbury
Thames Estuary
Grain
Sheerness
Gravesend
Dartford
MEDWAY TNS
Isle of Sheppey
Margate
Herne Bay
North Foreland
Swanley
Rochester
Gillingham
Chatham
Sittingbourne
Whitstable
Broadstairs
Ramsgate
North Downs
Faversham
Wrotham
Sandwich
Canterbury
Sevenoaks
Chilham
Maidstone
Deal
KENT
Tonbridge
Vale of Kent
Staplehurst
Ashford
Wye
South Foreland
Royal Tunbridge Wells
Dover
Channel Tunnel Terminal
Cranbrook
Tenterden
Folkestone
Romney Marsh
Hythe
Crowborough
EAST SUSSEX
New Romney
Heathfield
Rye
Lydd
Battle
Winchelsea
Dungeness
Strait of Dover
Cap Gris-Nez
Hailsham
Polegate
Bexhill
Hastings
Eastbourne
Seaford
Beachy Head
English Channel
198 311 312 313 829 310 309 308 307 830 306 305 304 915 831 832 833 834 835 836 837 838 839 840 294 295 296 297 298 299 300 301 302 303 549 550 551 552 553 554 555 556 557 558 548 912 913 914
pubs and inns
pubs and inns with rooms we've inspected and like
pubs with "Special Places" awards
pubs worth a visit
0 10 20 30 kilometres
0 10 20 miles

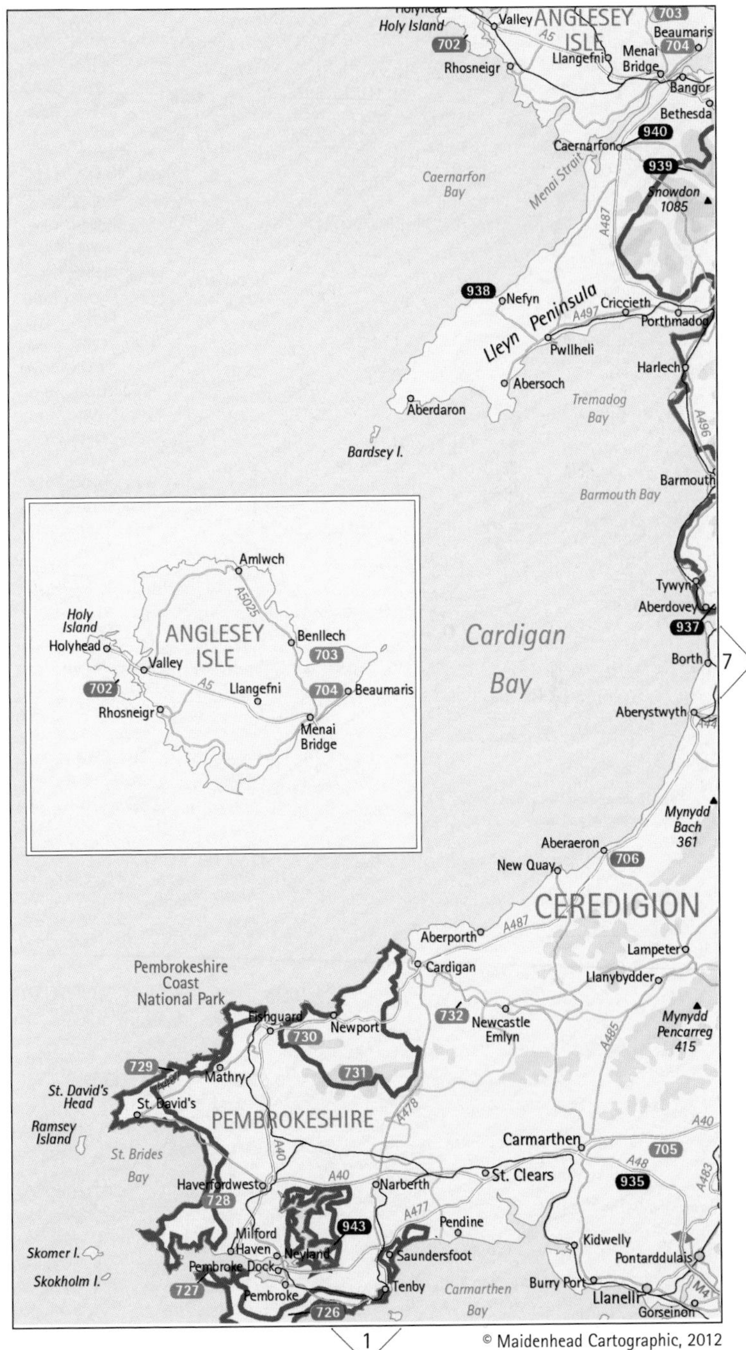
Holy Island
Valley
ANGLESEY ISLE
703
Beaumaris
702
704
Menai Bridge
Llangefni
Rhosneigr
Bangor
Bethesda
940
Caernarfon
939
Caernarfon Bay
Menai Strait
Snowdon 1085
A487
938
Nefyn
Lleyn Peninsula
A497
Criccieth
Porthmadog
Pwllheli
Harlech
Abersoch
Tremadog Bay
Aberdaron
A496
Bardsey I.
Barmouth
Barmouth Bay
Amlwch
A5025
Holy Island
Holyhead
ANGLESEY ISLE
Benllech
703
Valley
702
A5
Llangefni
704
Beaumaris
Rhosneigr
Menai Bridge
Tywyn
Aberdovey
937
Cardigan Bay
Borth
7
Aberystwyth
Mynydd Bach 361
Aberaeron
706
New Quay
CEREDIGION
Aberporth
A487
Lampeter
Cardigan
Pembrokeshire Coast National Park
Llanybydder
732
Newcastle Emlyn
Fishguard
Newport
730
Mynydd Pencarreg 415
A485
729
731
Mathry
St. David's Head
St. David's
PEMBROKESHIRE
A478
Ramsey Island
A40
Carmarthen
St. Brides Bay
705
A48
Haverfordwest
A40
Narberth
St. Clears
935
728
A477
Pendine
943
Milford Haven
Neyland
Kidwelly
Skomer I.
Saundersfoot
Pontarddulais
Pembroke Dock
Skokholm I.
727
Tenby
Carmarthen Bay
Burry Port
Pembroke
726
Llanelli
Gorseinon
1

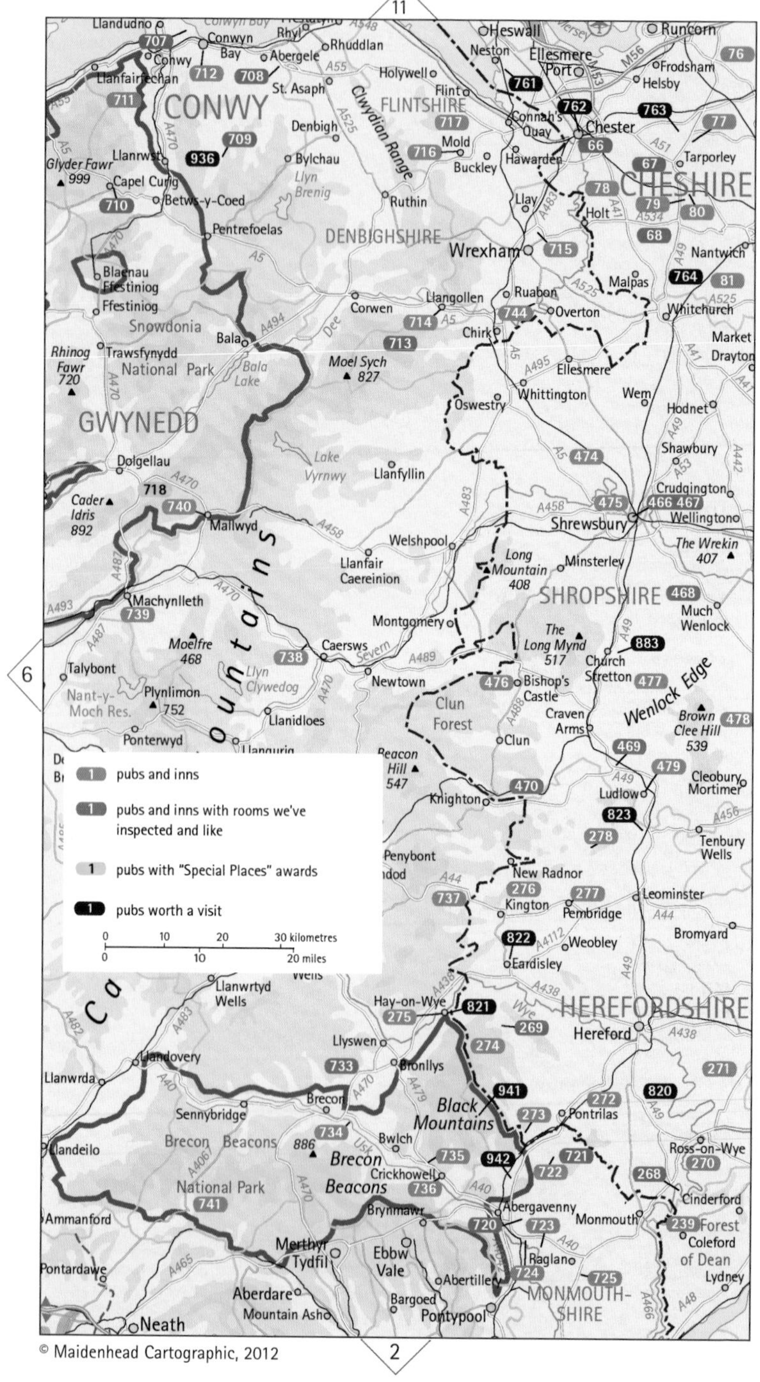
pubs and inns
pubs and inns with rooms we've inspected and like
pubs with "Special Places" awards
pubs worth a visit
0 10 20 30 kilometres
0 10 20 miles
CONWY
FLINTSHIRE
DENBIGHSHIRE
CHESHIRE
GWYNEDD
SHROPSHIRE
HEREFORDSHIRE
MONMOUTHSHIRE
Chester
Wrexham
Shrewsbury
Hereford
Brecon Beacons National Park
Snowdonia National Park
Black Mountains
Clun Forest
Wenlock Edge
Forest of Dean

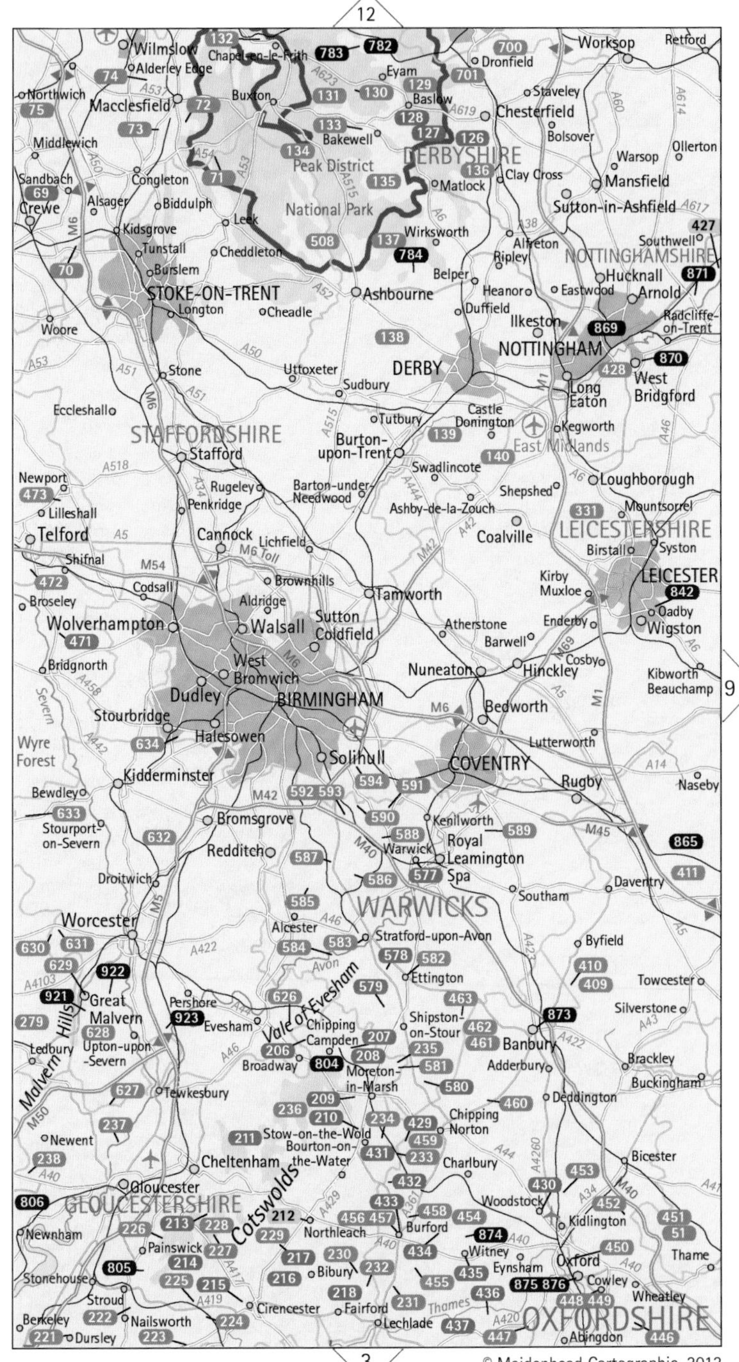
12
Wilmslow
Alderley Edge
Chapel-en-le-Frith
Eyam
Dronfield
Worksop
Retford
Northwich
Macclesfield
Buxton
Baslow
Staveley
Chesterfield
Bolsover
Middlewich
Bakewell
DERBYSHIRE
Warsop
Ollerton
Peak District
National Park
Clay Cross
Mansfield
Sandbach
Congleton
Matlock
Crewe
Alsager
Biddulph
Sutton-in-Ashfield
Kidsgrove
Leek
Wirksworth
Tunstall
Cheddleton
Alfreton
Southwell
Ripley
NOTTINGHAMSHIRE
Burslem
Belper
Hucknall
STOKE-ON-TRENT
Ashbourne
Heanor
Eastwood
Arnold
Longton
Cheadle
Duffield
Ilkeston
Radcliffe-on-Trent
Woore
NOTTINGHAM
Stone
Uttoxeter
DERBY
Long Eaton
West Bridgford
Sudbury
Eccleshall
Tutbury
Castle Donington
Kegworth
STAFFORDSHIRE
Burton-upon-Trent
East Midlands
Stafford
Swadlincote
Newport
Loughborough
Rugeley
Barton-under-Needwood
Shepshed
Lilleshall
Penkridge
Ashby-de-la-Zouch
Mountsorrel
Telford
Cannock
Lichfield
Coalville
LEICESTERSHIRE
Shifnal
Birstall
Syston
Brownhills
Kirby Muxloe
LEICESTER
Codsall
Tamworth
Broseley
Aldridge
Oadby
Wolverhampton
Walsall
Sutton Coldfield
Atherstone
Enderby
Wigston
Barwell
Bridgnorth
West Bromwich
Cosby
Nuneaton
Hinckley
Kibworth Beauchamp
Dudley
BIRMINGHAM
9
Severn
Stourbridge
Bedworth
Halesowen
Lutterworth
Wyre Forest
Solihull
COVENTRY
Kidderminster
Rugby
Naseby
Bewdley
Kenilworth
Bromsgrove
Stourport-on-Severn
Royal Leamington Spa
Warwick
Redditch
Droitwich
Daventry
Southam
WARWICKS
Worcester
Alcester
Stratford-upon-Avon
Byfield
Avon
Ettington
Towcester
Great Malvern
Pershore
Vale of Evesham
Silverstone
Malvern Hills
Evesham
Chipping Campden
Shipston-on-Stour
Banbury
Ledbury
Upton-upon-Severn
Broadway
Moreton-in-Marsh
Adderbury
Brackley
Buckingham
Tewkesbury
Deddington
Chipping Norton
Newent
Stow-on-the-Wold
Bourton-on-the-Water
Cheltenham
Cotswolds
Charlbury
Bicester
Gloucester
GLOUCESTERSHIRE
Woodstock
Kidlington
Newnham
Northleach
Burford
Painswick
Witney
Thame
Eynsham
Oxford
Stonehouse
Bibury
Cowley
Wheatley
Stroud
Cirencester
Fairford
Thames
Berkeley
Nailsworth
Lechlade
OXFORDSHIRE
Dursley
Abingdon
3

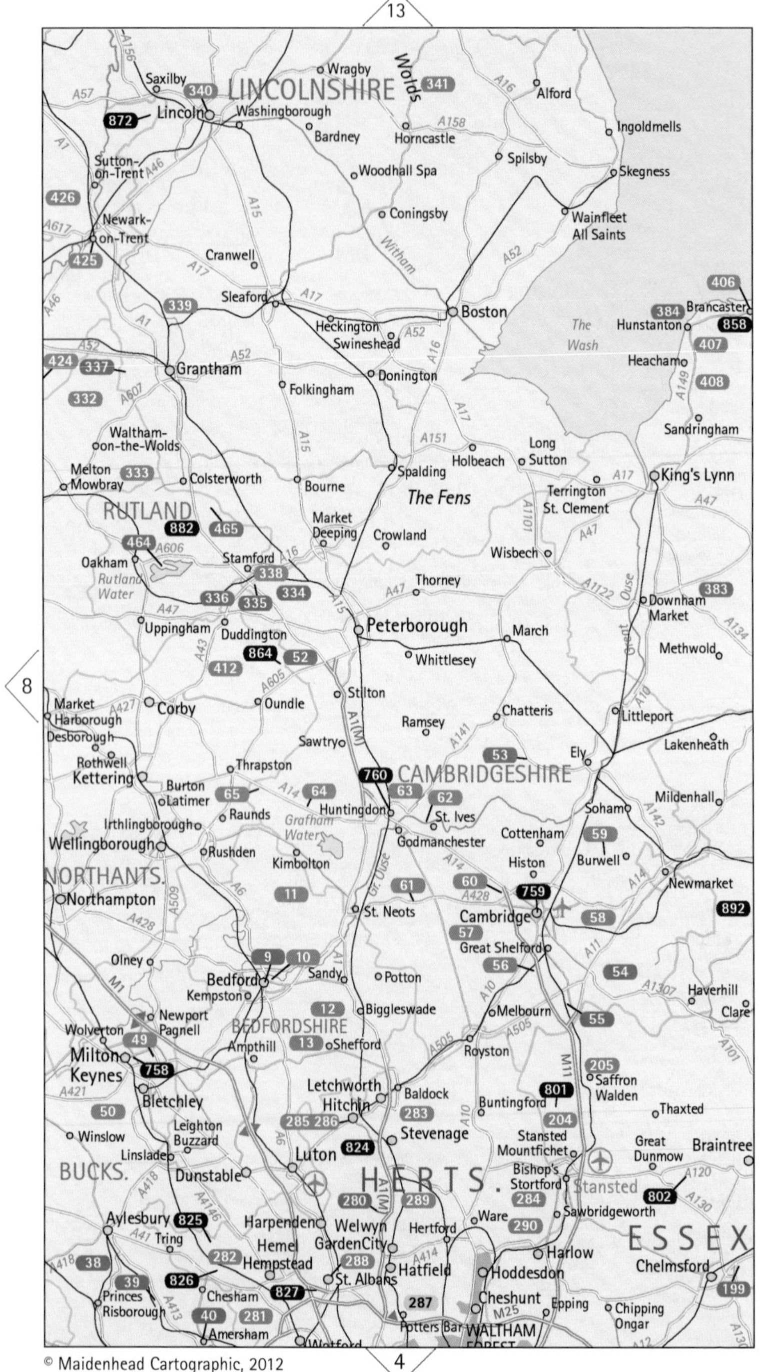
13
8
4
LINCOLNSHIRE
Wolds
Saxilby
Lincoln
Washingborough
Wragby
Bardney
Horncastle
Alford
Ingoldmells
Spilsby
Skegness
Woodhall Spa
Coningsby
Wainfleet All Saints
Sutton-on-Trent
Newark-on-Trent
Cranwell
Sleaford
Boston
Heckington
Swineshead
Witham
The Wash
Hunstanton
Brancaster
Heacham
Grantham
Folkingham
Donington
Sandringham
Waltham-on-the-Wolds
Melton Mowbray
Colsterworth
Bourne
Spalding
Holbeach
Long Sutton
King's Lynn
The Fens
Terrington St. Clement
RUTLAND
Market Deeping
Crowland
Wisbech
Oakham
Rutland Water
Stamford
Thorney
Downham Market
Uppingham
Duddington
Peterborough
March
Methwold
Whittlesey
Market Harborough
Corby
Oundle
Stilton
Chatteris
Littleport
Ramsey
Lakenheath
Desborough
Rothwell
Kettering
Sawtry
Ely
Thrapston
CAMBRIDGESHIRE
Burton Latimer
Huntingdon
St. Ives
Soham
Mildenhall
Raunds
Grafham Water
Irthlingborough
Wellingborough
Godmanchester
Cottenham
Burwell
Rushden
Kimbolton
Histon
Newmarket
NORTHANTS.
Northampton
St. Neots
Cambridge
Great Shelford
Olney
Bedford
Sandy
Potton
Kempston
Haverhill
Clare
Newport Pagnell
Biggleswade
Melbourn
Wolverton
BEDFORDSHIRE
Ampthill
Shefford
Royston
Milton Keynes
Saffron Walden
Letchworth
Baldock
Bletchley
Hitchin
Buntingford
Thaxted
Winslow
Leighton Buzzard
Stevenage
Stansted Mountfichet
Great Dunmow
Braintree
Linslade
Luton
BUCKS.
Dunstable
HERTS.
Bishop's Stortford
Stansted
Aylesbury
Harpenden
Welwyn Garden City
Hertford
Ware
Sawbridgeworth
Tring
Hemel Hempstead
Hatfield
Harlow
ESSEX
Chelmsford
St. Albans
Hoddesdon
Princes Risborough
Chesham
Cheshunt
Epping
Chipping Ongar
Amersham
Watford
Potters Bar
WALTHAM FOREST
A156
A57
A1
A46
A617
A15
A17
A158
A16
A52
A607
A151
A149
A47
A606
A1101
A1122
Ouse
Great Ouse
A134
A43
A605
A427
A10
A141
A14
A142
A1(M)
Gr. Ouse
A428
A509
A6
M1
A11
A1307
A505
M11
A101
A421
A418
A4146
A41
A413
A414
M25
A120
A130
A12
872
340
341
426
425
339
424
337
332
333
882
465
464
338
334
336
335
406
384
858
407
408
383
864
52
412
53
760
63
62
64
65
59
60
759
61
11
58
57
892
56
54
9
10
12
55
205
801
204
13
49
758
50
283
285 286
824
802
280
289
284
290
825
282
288
38
826
827
287
39
40
281
199

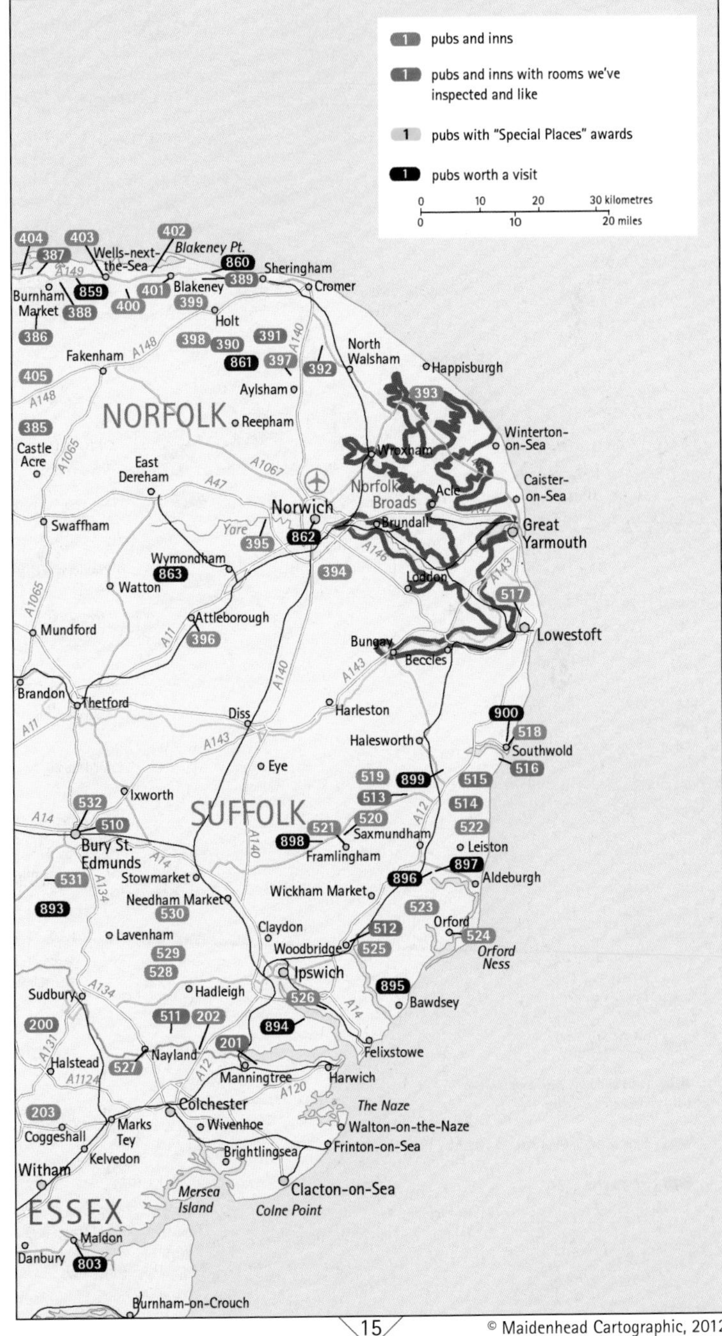
pubs and inns
pubs and inns with rooms we've inspected and like
pubs with "Special Places" awards
pubs worth a visit
0 10 20 30 kilometres
0 10 20 miles
NORFOLK
SUFFOLK
ESSEX
Wells-next-the-Sea
Blakeney Pt.
Sheringham
Cromer
Blakeney
Holt
Burnham Market
Fakenham
North Walsham
Happisburgh
Aylsham
Reepham
Castle Acre
East Dereham
Winterton-on-Sea
Wroxham
Caister-on-Sea
Norfolk Broads
Acle
Norwich
Brundall
Great Yarmouth
Swaffham
Yare
Wymondham
Watton
Loddon
Attleborough
Mundford
Lowestoft
Bungay
Beccles
Brandon
Thetford
Diss
Harleston
Halesworth
Southwold
Eye
Ixworth
Saxmundham
Leiston
Bury St. Edmunds
Framlingham
Stowmarket
Aldeburgh
Needham Market
Wickham Market
Orford
Lavenham
Claydon
Woodbridge
Orford Ness
Ipswich
Hadleigh
Sudbury
Bawdsey
Felixstowe
Nayland
Halstead
Manningtree
Harwich
Colchester
The Naze
Marks Tey
Wivenhoe
Walton-on-the-Naze
Coggeshall
Frinton-on-Sea
Kelvedon
Brightlingsea
Witham
Clacton-on-Sea
Mersea Island
Colne Point
Maldon
Danbury
Burnham-on-Crouch
404 403 402 387 860 389 859 401 400 399 388 386 398 390 391 861 397 392 405 393 385 395 862 394 863 517 396 900 518 516 519 899 515 513 514 520 521 898 522 532 510 897 896 531 893 530 523 512 524 525 529 528 895 526 511 202 200 894 201 527 203 803
A149 A148 A140 A1065 A1067 A47 A146 A143 A11 A140 A12 A14 A134 A131 A1124 A120

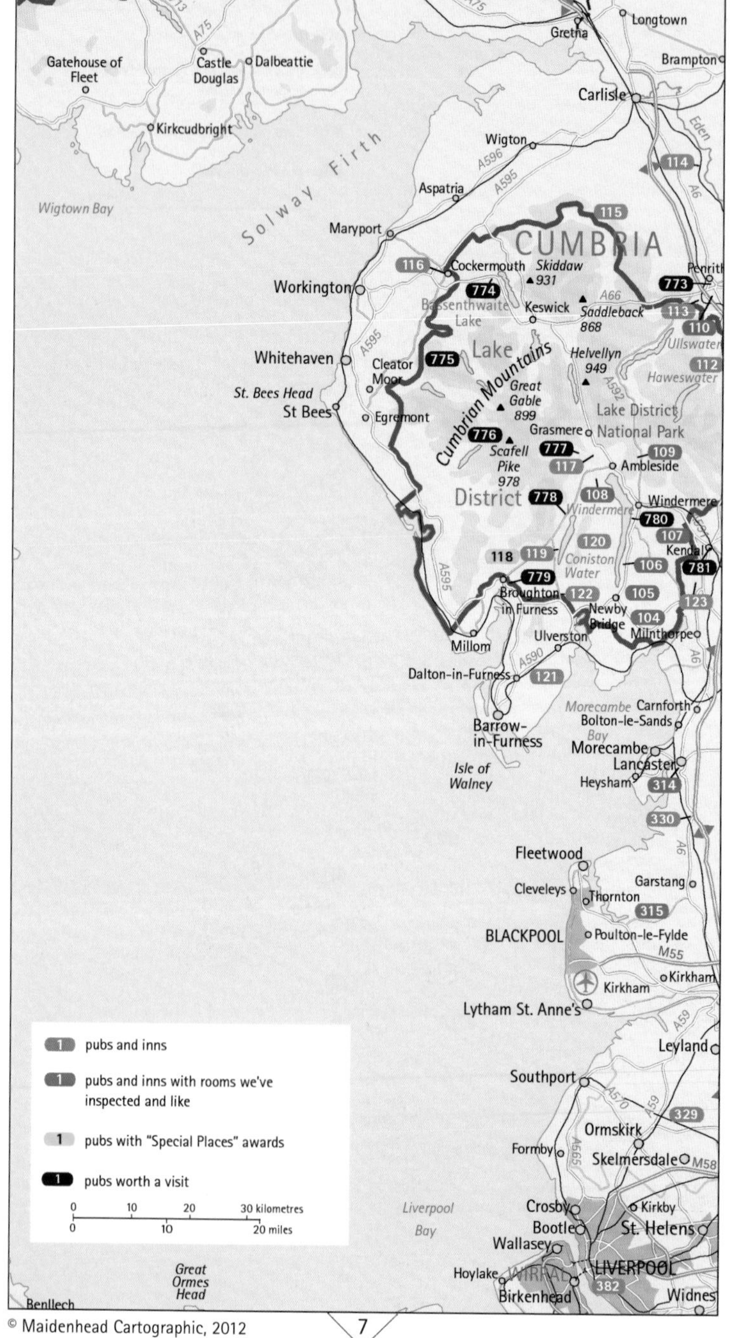
Longtown
Gretna
Brampton
Gatehouse of Fleet
Castle Douglas
Dalbeattie
Carlisle
Kirkcudbright
Solway Firth
Wigton
Aspatria
Wigtown Bay
Maryport
CUMBRIA
Cockermouth
Skiddaw 931
Penrith
Workington
Bassenthwaite Lake
Keswick
Saddleback 868
Ullswater
Whitehaven
Cleator Moor
Lake District
Cumbrian Mountains
Helvellyn 949
Haweswater
St. Bees Head
St Bees
Egremont
Great Gable 899
Lake District National Park
Grasmere
Scafell Pike 978
Ambleside
Windermere
Kendal
Coniston Water
Broughton-in-Furness
Newby Bridge
Milnthorpe
Millom
Ulverston
Dalton-in-Furness
Morecambe Bay
Carnforth
Bolton-le-Sands
Barrow-in-Furness
Morecambe
Lancaster
Isle of Walney
Heysham
Fleetwood
Cleveleys
Thornton
Garstang
BLACKPOOL
Poulton-le-Fylde
Kirkham
Lytham St. Anne's
Leyland
Southport
Ormskirk
Formby
Skelmersdale
Liverpool Bay
Crosby
Kirkby
Bootle
St. Helens
Wallasey
Hoylake
WIRRAL
LIVERPOOL
Birkenhead
Widnes
Great Ormes Head
Benllech
1 pubs and inns
1 pubs and inns with rooms we've inspected and like
1 pubs with "Special Places" awards
1 pubs worth a visit
0 10 20 30 kilometres
0 10 20 miles

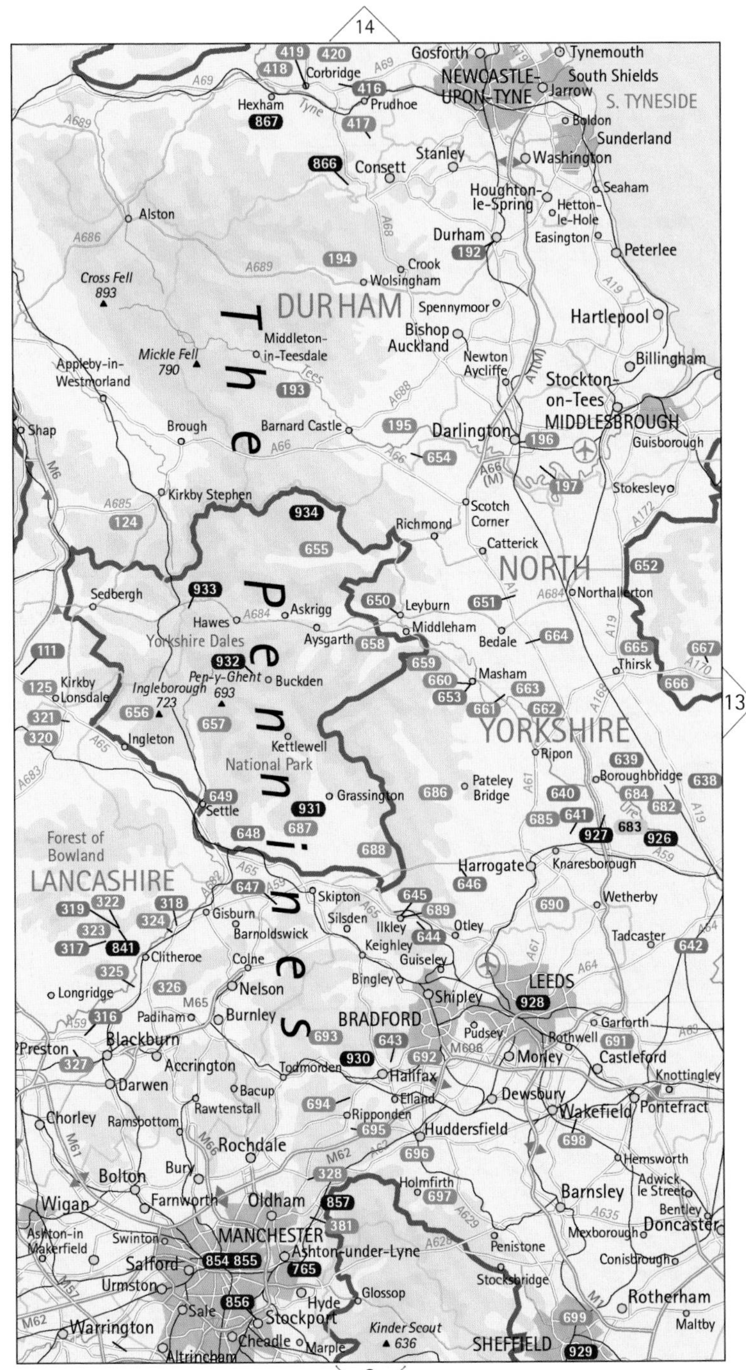
14
13
8
The Pennines
DURHAM
NORTH
YORKSHIRE
LANCASHIRE
S. TYNESIDE
NEWCASTLE-UPON-TYNE
MIDDLESBROUGH
LEEDS
BRADFORD
MANCHESTER
SHEFFIELD
Yorkshire Dales
National Park
Forest of Bowland
Cross Fell 893
Mickle Fell 790
Ingleborough 723
Pen-y-Ghent 693
Kinder Scout 636
Hexham
Corbridge
Prudhoe
Gosforth
Tynemouth
South Shields
Jarrow
Boldon
Sunderland
Washington
Stanley
Consett
Seaham
Houghton-le-Spring
Hetton-le-Hole
Durham
Easington
Peterlee
Alston
Crook
Wolsingham
Spennymoor
Bishop Auckland
Hartlepool
Middleton-in-Teesdale
Newton Aycliffe
Billingham
Appleby-in-Westmorland
Stockton-on-Tees
Shap
Brough
Barnard Castle
Darlington
Guisborough
Kirkby Stephen
Stokesley
Scotch Corner
Richmond
Catterick
Sedbergh
Leyburn
Northallerton
Hawes
Askrigg
Aysgarth
Middleham
Bedale
Thirsk
Kirkby Lonsdale
Buckden
Masham
Ingleton
Kettlewell
Ripon
Boroughbridge
Pateley Bridge
Grassington
Settle
Harrogate
Knaresborough
Wetherby
Skipton
Gisburn
Barnoldswick
Silsden
Ilkley
Otley
Keighley
Tadcaster
Clitheroe
Colne
Guiseley
Bingley
Longridge
Nelson
Shipley
Padiham
Burnley
Garforth
Pudsey
Rothwell
Preston
Blackburn
Morley
Castleford
Accrington
Todmorden
Halifax
Knottingley
Darwen
Bacup
Elland
Dewsbury
Rawtenstall
Ripponden
Wakefield
Pontefract
Chorley
Ramsbottom
Huddersfield
Rochdale
Hemsworth
Bury
Bolton
Holmfirth
Adwick le Street
Wigan
Farnworth
Oldham
Barnsley
Bentley
Ashton-in-Makerfield
Swinton
Mexborough
Doncaster
Penistone
Salford
Ashton-under-Lyne
Conisbrough
Urmston
Stocksbridge
Glossop
Hyde
Rotherham
Sale
Stockport
Maltby
Warrington
Cheadle
Marple
Altrincham
A69
A689
A686
A68
A688
A66
A66(M)
A1(M)
A1
A19
A172
A684
A685
A65
A683
A682
A59
A61
A168
A170
A64
A63
A6068
A62
A628
A629
A635
A56
M6
M65
M66
M61
M62
M57
M606
M1
Tyne
Tees
Ure
419
420
418
416
417
867
866
192
194
193
195
196
654
197
124
934
655
933
652
650
651
111
658
664
665
667
932
659
125
656
660
653
663
666
321
320
657
661
662
639
638
649
686
640
684
682
931
685
641
927
683
926
648
687
688
646
647
645
690
319
322
318
689
323
324
317
841
644
642
325
326
928
316
693
643
691
327
930
692
694
695
698
696
328
857
697
381
854
855
765
856
699
929

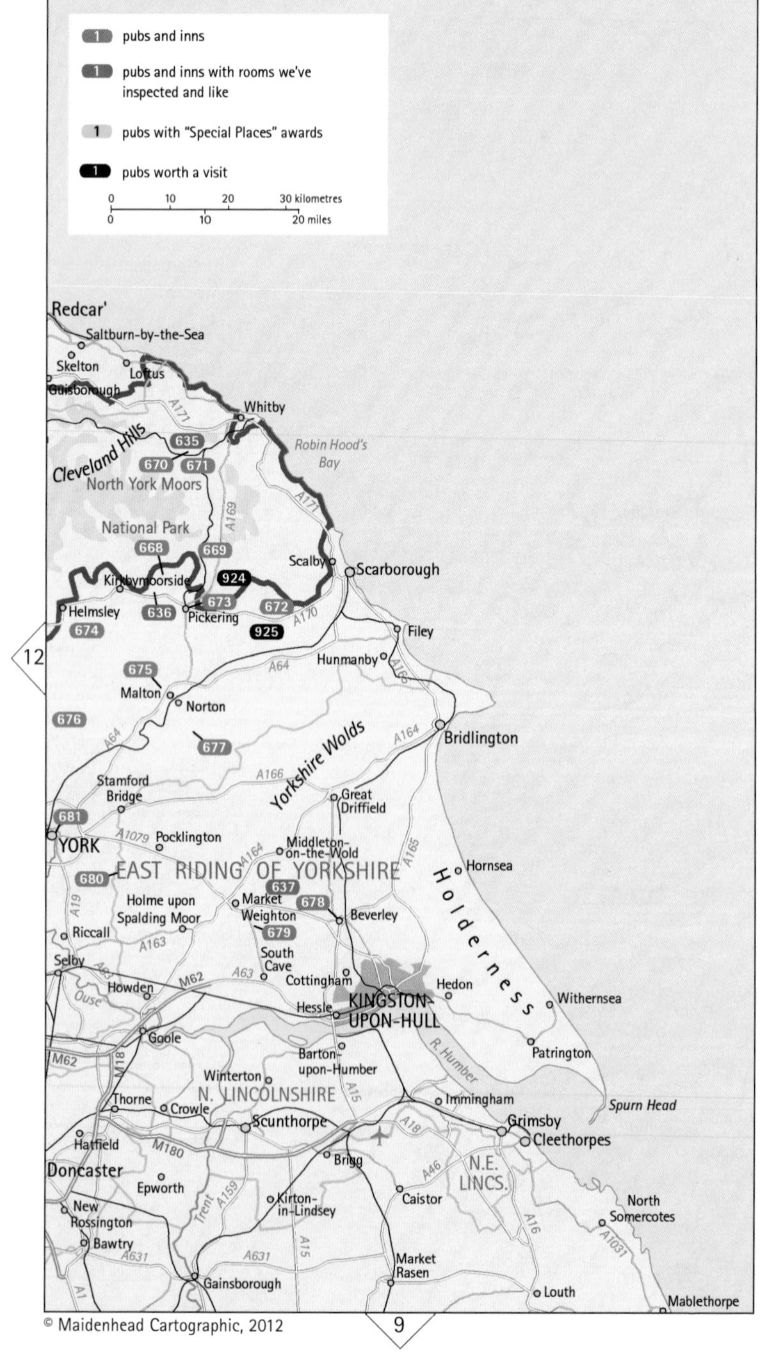
1 pubs and inns
1 pubs and inns with rooms we've inspected and like
1 pubs with "Special Places" awards
1 pubs worth a visit
0 10 20 30 kilometres
0 10 20 miles
Redcar
Saltburn-by-the-Sea
Skelton
Loftus
Guisborough
Whitby
Robin Hood's Bay
Cleveland Hills
North York Moors
National Park
635
670
671
668
669
924
Kirkbymoorside
636
673
Pickering
672
925
Scalby
Scarborough
Helmsley
674
Filey
Hunmanby
12
675
Malton
Norton
676
677
Bridlington
Yorkshire Wolds
Stamford Bridge
Great Driffield
681
YORK
Pocklington
Middleton-on-the-Wold
EAST RIDING OF YORKSHIRE
680
Hornsea
Holderness
637
678
Holme upon Spalding Moor
Market Weighton
Beverley
679
Riccall
South Cave
Selby
Cottingham
Hedon
Howden
Withernsea
Hessle
KINGSTON-UPON-HULL
Ouse
Goole
Barton-upon-Humber
Patrington
R. Humber
Winterton
N. LINCOLNSHIRE
Thorne
Crowle
Immingham
Spurn Head
Scunthorpe
Grimsby
Cleethorpes
Hatfield
Brigg
Doncaster
N.E. LINCS.
Epworth
Kirton-in-Lindsey
Caistor
North Somercotes
New Rossington
Trent
Bawtry
Market Rasen
Gainsborough
Louth
Mablethorpe
A171
A169
A170
A64
A165
A164
A166
A1079
A19
A163
A63
M62
M18
M180
A18
A46
A159
A15
A16
A1031
A631
A1
9

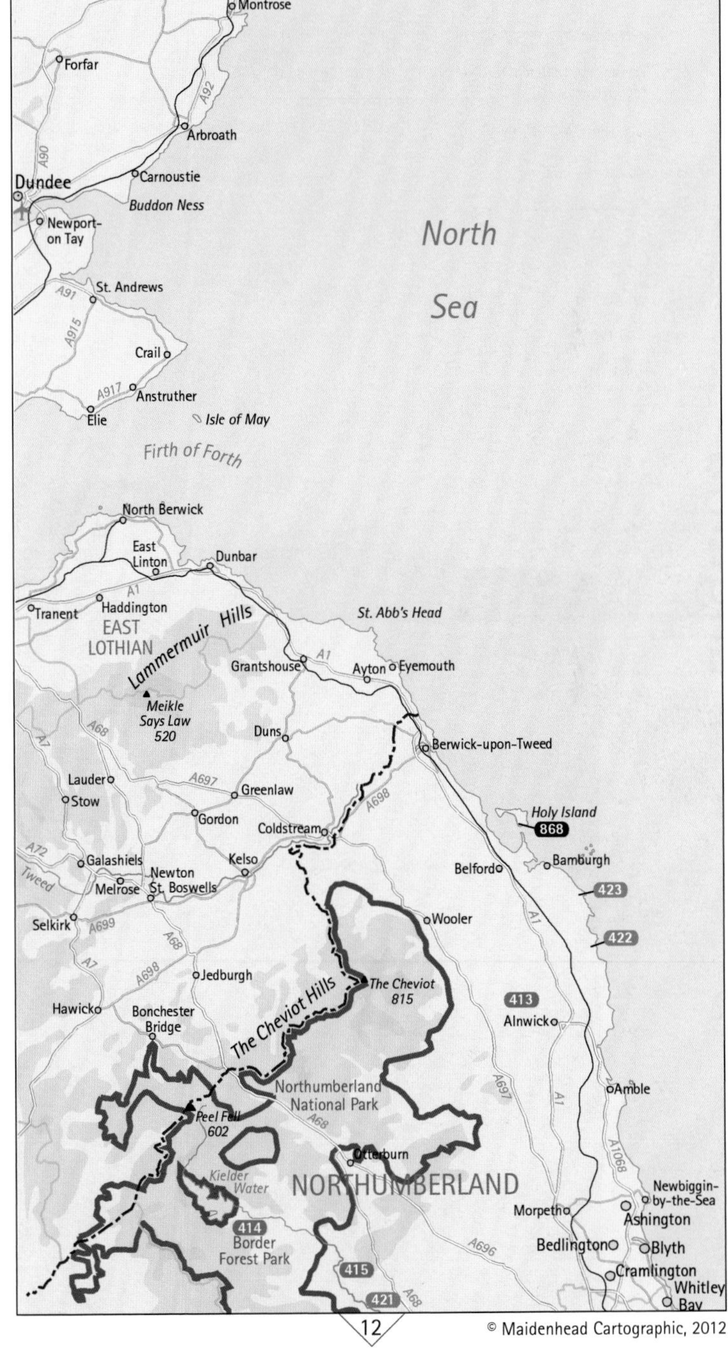

© Maidenhead Cartographic, 2012

England

Photo: Alec Studerus

Oakhill Inn

Oakhill

The Digneys, owners of the inimitable King William and the Garrick's Head in Bath, have given the old village inn a sympathetic brush up and a fresh look since they took over in 2007. Expect rugs on bare boards, bold red and green walls lined with local artwork, old sofas and rustic tables, a cosy corner by the blazing log fire. Now families and food and ale-lovers flock in for the raft of local ales from the likes of Newmans and Stonehenge breweries, and the well-priced menu of robust British dishes. Tuck into rump steak and horseradish sandwiches; beef and ale stew with curly kale; pot-roast partridge; beer-battered pollock and triple-cooked chips; and the most comforting of comfort puddings – warm treacle tart and winter nut crumble with custard... served seasonally, of course. The eclectic, very individual feel extends upstairs – the purple-painted master bedroom sports a big brass bed, crisp linen, bold lamps, a feature fireplace, quirky paintings and old furnishings, and a wood-floored bathroom with claw-foot bath, candles, thick towels, and a walk-in shower. A cracking inn.

Price	£90-£120. Suite £180. Single £77.50. Extra bed £18.
Rooms	5: 4 doubles, 1 twin/double (2 rooms connect to create suite).
Meals	Lunch from £10.95. Bar meals from £6.95. Dinner from £11.95. Sunday lunch, 3 courses, £23.95.
Closed	3pm-5pm. Open all day Sat & Sun.
Directions	Just off A367 between Bath & Shepton Mallet, 3 miles north of Shepton Mallet.

Charlie & Amanda Digney
Oakhill Inn
Fosse Road, Oakhill,
Radstock BA3 5HU

Tel +44 (0)1749 840442
Web www.theoakhillinn.com

Holcombe Inn

Holcombe

If you're looking for a country hideaway south of Bath, then this striking 17th-century inn tucked down twisting lanes will fit the bill. Revitalised with passion by Julie Berry, the classy cream-painted building is chock full of charm, with stone-flagged floors, old beams and settles in the bar, and a cosy lounge where fat candles, magazines, squashy sofas and a blazing log fire entice you to linger. Colourful orchids, pots of basil on old dining tables, daily newspapers, local ales and snug nooks and crannies add to the relaxed but smart feel. Appealing menus combine pub classics with inventive dishes – we loved the Elm Farm lamb rump with sweetbreads, mustard mash and rosemary jus. Gorgeous, individually designed bedrooms are Julie's pride and joy. 'Champagne' has a French feel with its rich fabrics and big brass bed; 'Africa' lives up to its name: a leather sleigh bed, quirky artefacts, a gold-painted roll top by the bed, a wet room with rain shower. All have crisp linen and fabulous views across open fields towards the Mendips Hills or Downside Abbey. A treat.

Price	£80-£100. Singles from £75.
Rooms	8: 7 doubles, 1 twin.
Meals	Lunch & bar meals from £5.95. Dinner from £9.95.
Closed	3pm-6pm (Mon-Thurs).
Directions	Holcombe is signposted off A361 at Stratton-on-the-Fosse south of Radstock; 12 miles south of Bath.

Julie Berry
Holcombe Inn
Stratton Road, Holcombe,
Radstock BA3 5EB
Tel +44 (0)1761 232478
Web www.holcombeinn.co.uk

The Garricks Head

Bath

The famous pub by the Theatre Royal, a refuge for actors and a theatre since 1720, has become a second success story for the proprietors of the King William. Enter a lovely lazy sofa'd bar, with a chic utilitarian dining room to the side. The drinking side of things is important still but the food is something special. Owner Charlie used to work at the Anchor & Hope in Waterloo so the style is robust English. Top produce and seasonality are paramount and the dishes pay a debt to Clerkenwell's celebrated St John's: in one critic's words, "a paragon of everything British eating is heading towards." Just try the snails with braised oxtail and mash, and the rib of beef with goose fat chips. The beers change all the time with the emphasis on small breweries and the cider comes from Julian Temperley at Burrow Hill. Great value.

Meals	Lunch from £10.95. Bar meals from £6.45. Dinner from £10.95. Sunday lunch, 2 courses, £18.95.
Closed	Open all day.
Directions	5-minute walk from Bath railway & bus stations, next to Bath Theatre Royal.

Charlie & Amanda Digney
The Garricks Head
8 St John's Place, Bath BA1 1ET
Tel +44 (0)1225 318368
Web www.garricksheadpub.com

Entry 3 Map 3

The Old Green Tree

Bath

Right in the centre, the cosy pub, whose staff are fanatical about ale (at least six guest beers chalked up on the board), hums with life even before midday. Deep in conversation, old regulars clutch pint jars to their chests as you squeeze through the narrow planked bar into a cabin-like room. Undecorated since the panelling was installed in 1928, the pub is part of our heritage and has no intention of changing – Tim and Nick refuse any form of modernisation, and it's all the better for it. In three little, low-ceilinged rooms, a mosaic of foreign coins are stuck up in frames behind the bar – along with artists' work. The menu includes hearty old English dishes and a daily chef's special; homemade chutneys and pâtés too. They have a devoted following and drink is not limited to beer: there are malts, wines and hot toddies.

Meals	Lunch & dinner £5.50-£10.
Closed	Open all day.
Directions	Green Street, off Milsom Street. Bath city centre.

T Bethune & F N Luke
The Old Green Tree
12 Green Street,
Bath BA1 2JZ
Tel +44 (0)1225 448259

Entry 4 Map 3

The Marlborough Tavern

Bath

The old down-at-heel boozer, a pint's throw from the Royal Crescent, was rescued by Cussens and Sleath in 2006. Now it is one of Bath's best food pubs. An airy, high ceilinged room with a central bar, the 18th-century tavern ticks all the gastropub boxes with its sage green paintwork, velvety wallpapers, standard lamps, sofas and village hall furniture. Wines include a fashionable palette of rosés, perfect for sipping in the garden. As for the food, it is driven by the produce, so seasonal and local are the buzzwords and producers and provenance are listed. There's Chew Valley smoked salmon, Neston Park Farm beef, local woodland pork and fruit and veg from seventh generation Eades, just up the road. Fish arrives daily from Cornwall and Devon, Sunday lunches are the stuff of legend and booking is pretty much essential.

Meals	Lunch from £4.95. Dinner from £9.50.
Closed	Open all day.
Directions	2-minute walk from the Royal Crescent, pub is on the corner of Marlborough Buildings opposite Approach Golf Course.

Joe Cussens
The Marlborough Tavern
35 Marlborough Buildings,
Bath BA1 2LY

Tel +44 (0)1225 423731
Web www.marlborough-tavern.com

Entry 5 Map 3

Bath & N.E. Somerset

The Star Inn

Bath

Listed on the National Inventory of Historic Pubs, a serious boozer and museum piece wrapped into one. A pub since 1760, it is partitioned off into three numbered rooms, each with rough planks, panelled walls, ancient settles and opaque toplights. A real coal fire pumps out the heat and you can still get a free pinch of snuff from the tins on the ledge above the wall... you can almost imagine the Victorian regulars pressing their lips to their pewter tankards. To this day Bass is served in four-pint jugs which you can take away for a small deposit. There are no meals, just the odd bap from a basket on the bar. What counts is the beer, so much so that Alan has started his own brewery and has since scaled the heady heights of the real ale world to win several awards for his Bellringer tipple. A jewel.

Meals	Rolls from £2.20.
Closed	2.30pm-5.30pm. Open all day Sat & Sun.
Directions	On A4 (London Road) in Bath.

Alan Morgan
The Star Inn
23 Vineyards,
Bath BA1 5NA

Tel +44 (0)1225 425072
Web www.star-inn-bath.co.uk

Entry 6 Map 3

King William

Bath

It's tiny and candlelit, smiley and friendly, "a gastropub to bring a tear to your eye." Named after the king who was on the throne when the Duke of Wellington passed his Beer Act (in a bid to wean people off foreign spirits), the little corner pub known as the King Billy has a chilled café/bar feel and a terrific range of wines and beers. They get into gastropub gear at lunch and dinner, and the food's so wonderful they've created extra space in the dining room upstairs (booking advised). It's Slow food sourced in season, and dishes are simple, rustic and modern – smoked venison with beetroot and apple salad, wild bass with roast fennel, local unpasteurised cheeses with homemade quince jelly. Bare boards, village hall furniture and background soul pull in an art-funky, Walcot Street crowd. And the staff couldn't be nicer.

Meals	Lunch from £5. Bar meals from £6. Dinner from £12. Sunday lunch, 3 courses, £25. Not Monday or Tuesday lunch.
Closed	3pm-5pm. Open all day Sat & Sun.
Directions	Short walk from Walcot Street, off London Road.

Charlie & Amanda Digney
King William
36 Thomas Street,
Bath BA1 5NN
Tel +44 (0)1225 428096
Web www.kingwilliampub.com

Entry 7 Map 3

Bath & N.E. Somerset

White Hart

Widcombe Hill

A short walk from Bath Spa Station, in sought-after Widcombe, this large detached pub has a pleasant courtyard garden and a backpackers' hostel above. Despite its reputation as one of the best places to eat in town, it still feels pubby, with a jolly bar, a pleasingly plain dining room and a mixed bag of tables. On rugby day it heaves, as pints of Butcombe Bitter and RCH Pitchfork are downed. Chef Rupert Pitt has worked in some of Bath's best restaurants and his menu is short and to the point, with five starters and six mains. The food, well-priced and following the seasons, is delicious. Try the marinated feta with Mediterranean bulgur wheat salad, the baked sea bass with lemon and saffron butter, and the tender slow-braised pork belly with mashed potato and cider gravy.

Meals	Lunch & dinner £10-£13. Sunday lunch, 3 courses, £23. Not Sunday eve.
Closed	Open all day. Closed Sun eves in winter.
Directions	Where A3604 becomes Claverton Street, pub on right, at Widcombe Hill & Prior Park Road junc.

Jo Parson
White Hart
Widcombe Hill,
Bath BA2 6AA
Tel +44 (0)1225 338053
Web www.whitehartbath.co.uk

Entry 8 Map 3

The Embankment

Bedford

Peach Pubs snapped up this town-centre hotel in 2008; now it's their flagship inn. The strikingly timbered neo-Tudor building overlooks the leafy embankment of the Great Ouse. The style of its late-Victorian heyday has been recreated inside, so there are period fireplaces, big mirrors, wooden floors, leather wall benches and a semi-retro feel, from the airy front bar to the dining rooms at the back. Now a vibrant inn (you won't find a residents' lounge here!) with a buzzy, laid-back bar and a modern all-day menu, the Embankment draws a lively crowd; prepare to drink, eat and make merry. You can drop in for breakfast (very cosy in front of the fire); order a delicious coffee and cake; graze from the tempting deli board menu; or chomp your way through the daily roast. The retro styling extends to the bedrooms, with bold wall coverings, leather chairs and huge comfy beds topped with crisp linen; Room 101 has river views and a grand bathroom (soak in the tub, splash in the shower). There's a super heated and semi-covered area outside at the front, and the riverside walks are gorgeous.

Price	£85-£125.
Rooms	20: 5 doubles, 15 twins/doubles.
Meals	Lunch & bar meals from £5. Dinner from £11. Dinner from £10. Sunday lunch, 2 courses, £13.50.
Closed	Open all day.
Directions	On the Embankment by the River Great Ouse, east of the town centre.

Kelly McKenzie
The Embankment
6 The Embankment,
Bedford MK40 3PD
Tel +44 (0)1234 261332
Web www.embankmentbedford.co.uk

The Park

Bedford

In a residential suburb near the park, the uninspiring 1900s exterior conceals an interior with a funky feel, following an inspired refurbishment by a small and passionate pub company. Traditional fireplaces, flagstones, beams and wood panelling blend effortlessly with quirky fabrics and furnishings in trendy-retro dining rooms that converge on a wraparound bar; lounge on a cool leather sofa or nurse a pint at the bar. The kitchen delivers great pub food: duck liver pâté with quince jelly, slow-cooked shoulder of lamb, baked ricotta and lemon cheesecake, while the market-fresh fish and daily specials are listed on a brown paper roll on the wall. Tip-top ales from Bedford's Charles Wells brewery and a verdant heated patio garden area complete a very promising picture.

Meals	Lunch & dinner £9.50-£15. Sunday lunch, 2 courses, £16.95. Not Sunday eve.
Closed	Open all day.
Directions	On the junction of Kimbolton Road, with Park Avenue and Polhill Avenue.

Steve Wilkins
The Park
98 Kimbolton Road,
Bedford MK40 2PA
Tel +44 (0)1234 273929
Web www.theparkbedford.co.uk

Entry 10 Map 9

Bedfordshire

The Plough at Bolnhurst

Bolnhurst

A tavern has stood here since the 1400s, but nearly 20 years ago the last one burnt down; tradition lives on in this happy reincarnation. The Plough holds on to its heritage, with reclaimed blackened beams and cast-iron chimney. Overlaying this is a modern touch – stripped boards, hewn-wood bar and crisp white walls. Food is equally sophisticated; chef-patron Martin Lee's grounding was with Raymond Blanc. Crab risotto with chilli and parsley, Denham Estate venison, caramel soufflé with armagnac ice cream… "gutsy flavours but restrained formulation" are the order of the day, and, going by the heaving crowd of happy foodies, they've got it right. Come to dine rather than pop in for a pint – the wines are impressive, though the well-kept Village Bike bitter also slips down a treat. A bright light in the desert that is Bedfordshire.

Meals	Lunch & dinner £13.50-£25. Bar meals £7.50-£12.95. Sunday lunch from £14.95.
Closed	3pm-6.30pm. Sun eves & Mon.
Directions	On B660 north of Bedford; pub in village centre.

Martin & Jayne Lee & Michael Moscrop
The Plough at Bolnhurst
Kimbolton Road, Bolnhurst,
Bedford MK44 2EX
Tel +44 (0)1234 376274
Web www.bolnhurst.com

Entry 11 Map 9

Hare & Hounds

Old Warden

The food may be fabulous but the Hare & Hounds is first and foremost a pub. There's always a welcome and a buzz, you can drop by for a glass of wine and the aromas from the kitchen mingle irresistibly with the woodsmoke from the fire. The beer's good too (Eagle Bitter, Young's Bitter). On a Sunday in summer, when they fly a Shuttleworth Spitfire from the grass airstrip next door, you could find the ice rattling in your G&T; otherwise the garden is blissfully quiet. No barbecues, just a few drinkers' tables and a smokers' gazebo. Inside are low timbered ceilings and four distinct areas: a funky snug with sofas, two rooms for eating, and a family room beyond. Game and poultry come from the village estate, veg and herbs from the allotment, cheeses are proudly British and the puddings are a treat.

Meals	Lunch & dinner £10-£18. Not Sunday eve.
Closed	3pm-6pm. Mon (except bank hols).
Directions	Off B658 & A6001 3 miles west of Biggleswade; next to village hall.

Jane & Jago Hurt
Hare & Hounds
The Village, Old Warden,
Biggleswade SG18 9HQ

Tel +44 (0)1767 627225
Web www.hareandhoundsoldwarden.co.uk

Entry 12 Map 9

Bedfordshire

The Black Horse

Ireland

In Ireland – in Bedfordshire – is a wonderfully welcoming gastropub. Stone dogs guard the front door, bollards linked by ships' rope divide terrace from car park and the door opens to a sweep of open-plan, split-level space. There's floor to ceiling glass at one end – looking out to palms, sculptures and ferns – and more formal dining areas at the other. The bar top is solid slate, smart banquettes edge tables both sides of a wood-burning stove but, in spite of the modernity, traditional features remain: fireplaces in excellent order and refurbished beams from which downlighters shine. More geared towards dining than casual drinking, the food ranges from chicken on the griddle to pollock with a tiger prawn brochette, the puddings are superlative and Michael Winner, we are told, loved his Sunday roast.

Meals	Lunch from £6.25. Bar meals from £4.95. Dinner from £9.95. Sunday lunch, 3 courses, £22.95.
Closed	3pm-6pm. Sun eves.
Directions	Pub signed from the A600 Shefford to Bedford road.

Darren Campbell
The Black Horse
Ireland,
Shefford SG17 5QL

Tel +44 (0)1462 811398
Web www.blackhorseireland.com

Entry 13 Map 9

Crown & Garter

Inkpen

An unreformed country local hidden down lanes beneath Inkpen Beacon, run with passion by Gill Hern. Gamekeepers and village footballers drop by for a pint of London Pride or Good Old Boy, cockerels crow in the fields and in summer life spills onto a stone terrace and into a pretty garden. Inside are wooden floors, thick red curtains and a huge settle by the fire. There's a small restaurant serving whole grilled Cornish sole with new potatoes, fillet steak with pepper sauce and steak and kidney pudding; tuck in here, or in the bar, or, on sunny days, on the patio. James II is said to have visited, on his way to meet one of his mistresses. Bedrooms, in a single-storey annexe built around a garden with a pergola and fish pond, are spacious and airy and have painted floorboards, blended voiles and brass or wooden beds. Two rooms interconnect for families, piping hot water flows in super little bathrooms. You can walk from the front door, try your luck at Newbury Races or watch the early morning gallops at Lambourn. Gill and her team are most welcoming.

Price	£99. Singles £79.50.
Rooms	9: 6 doubles, 2 twins, 1 single.
Meals	Bar meals from £6.95. Lunch & dinner from £9.95. Sunday lunch £22. Not Sun eves or Mon/Tues lunch.
Closed	3pm-5.30pm (5pm-7pm Sun). Mon & Tues lunch.
Directions	A4 from Hungerford to Newbury. After 2 miles left for Kintbury & Inkpen. In Kintbury left at corner shop onto Inkpen Road; inn on left after 2 miles.

Gill Hern
Crown & Garter
Great Common, Inkpen,
Hungerford RG17 9QR
Tel +44 (0)1488 668325
Web www.crownandgarter.co.uk

The Queen's Arms
East Garston

Deep in horse training country, so expect to rub shoulders with owners, trainers, jockeys and locals. The main bar is steeped in character and warmth, the wood-burner glows, candles flicker and walls are stylish with well-chosen prints. Plonk yourself on a wicker sofa on the heated outdoor terrace and consider the menu while sipping something nurturing from the witty wine list; or a real ale. Bar snacks are not tiny – ploughman's, steak sandwich, fresh fish and hand-cut chips; hungrier folk can eat royally in the Shaker-red restaurant. Try oysters with sweet and sour red onions, local pheasant with a jug of gravy, and rice pudding with quince. Gun dogs and pooches are welcome throughout, adding to the country feel. Follow bridleways and footpaths to woods and water meadows, return to cosy bedrooms with seagrass floors and friendly antiques, checked rugs, soft lights and feathery beds; the most delightful are in the main pub. Spoil yourself in toasty warm bathrooms with slate tiled floors, walk-in showers, thick towels; if you want space, and a bath, choose 'Hardy'.

Price	£80-£139.
Rooms	8 doubles.
Meals	Lunch from £7. Dinner, 3 courses, about £25.
Closed	Open all day.
Directions	Inn 10 minutes from J14 off M4; inn signed off A338 Wantage to Hungerford road at Great Shefford.

Adam Liddiard
The Queen's Arms
Newbury Road, East Garston,
Newbury RG17 7ET

Tel +44 (0)1488 648757
Web www.queensarmshotel.co.uk

The Royal Oak

Yattendon

Handsome centrepiece of a handsome village, the Royal Oak sits at its crossroads – the quintessential country Inn. The bar is a back-in-time proposition of original checkerboard tiles, beams, brick and panelling, four hearths ablaze, offering superb pints of Good Old Boy and Mr Chubbs from the indubitable West Berkshire Brewery. But time has not stood still. The lobby's leather sofas and gleaming wooden floors made homely by patterned rugs project a smartness that carries through to the restaurant's terracotta reds and chunky beech furnishings where the likes of venison Wellington, beef cheeks with Chantenay carrots and duck egg on toast reflect an inventive use of local ingredients. Stay over and snuggle down in big comfy bedrooms, some classically kitted out with antiques and rich fabrics, others more contemporary in style; all have pretty views across the village square or the walled garden. A garden ringed with herbs, shrubs and pretty trellises includes smart wicker seating as a boon for summer. Pub quizzes and family suppers underlie links to the community.

Price	£85-£120.
Rooms	7: 5 doubles, 2 twins/doubles.
Meals	Lunch & dinner £11-£16.
Closed	Open all day.
Directions	M4, junc. 13, A34 south for under 1 mile. Take 1st left passed petrol station, then 1st left again onto B4009. Continue through Hermitage, then branch right to Yattendon.

Rob McGill
The Royal Oak
The Square,
Yattendon RG18 0UF
Tel +44 (0)1635 201325
Web www.royaloakyattendon.co.uk

The Elephant at Pangbourne

Pangbourne

Elephants everywhere – all benign, including those in the Ba-bar. This is a super hotel on the edge of town, renovated in unremitting style, with huge sofas in front of the fire, a tongue-and-groove bar for Sunday brunch, a cocktail lounge where candles flicker and a deeply elegant restaurant. It's a big hit with the locals, with much to draw them in: a supper club on Thursday nights (delicious food and a glass of wine for a song), a game menu on Monday nights in season. Eclectic bedrooms come fully loaded and spin you round the world in style: an Indian four-poster in Viceroy; collage wallpaper in Charlestown; colonial chic in Rangoon. Beds are dressed in crisp cotton, there are custom-made soaps and bubblebaths, perhaps leather sofas, regal colours and rugs on stripped floors; bathrooms are mostly in charcoal grey. Back downstairs eat informally in the bar (wild mushrooms on toast; game pie, sweet carrots and mashed potato) or in the restaurant for something fancier, perhaps pork and apricot pâté, slow-cooked duck leg, white chocolate parfait with amaretto.

Price	£155-£175. Singles from £115.
Rooms	22: 18 doubles, 2 twins, 2 singles.
Meals	Lunch from £9.95. Bar meals £5.50-£20. Dinner £11.95-£25.
Closed	Open all day.
Directions	M4 junc. 12, A4 south, then A340 north. In village on left at roundabout.

Dominic Bishop
The Elephant at Pangbourne
Church Road, Pangbourne,
Reading RG8 7AR
Tel +44 (0)118 984 2244
Web www.elephanthotel.co.uk

The Olde Bell
Hurley

This very old inn near the Thames Path opened its doors in 1135 – as a guest house for visitors to the priory. Rescued from chain-hotel ownership, serenely restored by the Dhillon Group, it marries history with simplicity and charm. Step back centuries in the bar, to rugs on worn terracotta tiles, limewashed beams, board games and crackling fires. In the rustic-chic dining rooms are fur rugs on Ercol chairs, Welsh blankets on old settles, fresh flowers in pewter pots and a modish antler chandelier; glorious thick rafters and inglenooks, too. Full-flavoured British food, washed down with local Marlow ales, draws on local produce and the inn's kitchen garden. Try wild mushroom soup, baked duck leg, grilled lemon sole with leeks and mussels, sticky toffee pudding. Rooms in the main inn have a cool, rustic feel: wonky walls, sloping floors, huge beds, natural materials and quirky-elegant touches like red Roberts radios and rocking chairs. Stylish bathrooms throughout; some with roll top baths, and there are newly refurbished rooms (Bell Lodge) by the Tithe Barn. The garden is dreamy, replete with wildflower meadow and summer kitchen. Lovely.

Price	£150-£350.
Rooms	49: 38 doubles, 11 suites.
Meals	Lunch & dinner £12-£29.50. Bar meals £2-£10.50.
Closed	Open all day.
Directions	From Maidenhead take A4 dir. Reading. At Thicket r'bout merge onto A404 then take A4130. Turn onto Hurley High St. The inn is half mile on the right.

Alan Dooley
The Olde Bell
High Street, Hurley,
Maidenhead SL6 5LX
Tel +44 (0)1628 825881
Web www.theoldebell.co.uk

Pheasant Inn

Shefford Woodlands

The spruced-up Pheasant is still a cracking old pub with a reputation among the horse-racing set – and old-school landlord Johnny Ferrand is still at the helm. The much-loved shabby gentility (rustic tiling, blood red walls, big mirrors, pine tables, heavy drapes) has been retained and the TV remains tuned into the racing – often drowned out by the hubbub of jockeys and trainers. Loddon Hoppit and Wadworth 6X help charge the atmosphere, backed up by several wines by the glass. As for food, good ingredients are used in comfortingly familiar ways. A short menu delivers simple but careful home cooking: game terrine with homemade piccalilli and excellent meaty burgers; local partridge with tomato and pancetta jus, halibut with pea and mint risotto, vanilla panna cotta. It's the best M4 pit-stop for miles.

Meals	Lunch & dinner £11.50-£19.50.
Closed	Open all day.
Directions	400 yards from M4 exit 14; A338 towards Wantage; 1st left onto B4000 for Lambourn; inn on right.

John Ferrand
Pheasant Inn
Ermin Street, Shefford Woodlands,
Hungerford RG17 7AA
Tel +44 (0)1488 648284
Web www.thepheasant-inn.co.uk

Entry 19 Map 3

Berkshire

The Bell Inn

Aldworth

The Bell has the style of village pubs long gone and has been in the Macaulay family for over 250 years. Plain benches, venerable dark-wood panelling, settles and an outside gents: it's an unspoilt place that visitors love. There's an old wood-burning stove in one room, a more impressive hearth in the public bar, and early evening drinkers cluster around the unique glass hatched bar. Fifty years ago the regulars were agricultural workers; today piped music and mobile phones are fervently opposed. The food fits the image and they keep it simple: choose from hearty warm rolls filled with thick slices of home-baked ham, ox tongue or good old cheddar, treacle sponge and winter soups of the day. Drink prices are another draw; the ales come from the local Arkell's and West Berkshire breweries. There's also a great big garden.

Meals	Bar meals £2.80-£6.50.
Closed	3pm-6pm (7pm Sun). Mon (except bank hols).
Directions	Off B4009, 3 miles west of Streatley.

H E Macaulay
The Bell Inn
Aldworth,
Reading RG8 9SE
Tel +44 (0)1635 578272

Entry 20 Map 4

The Pot Kiln

Frilsham

TV chef Mike Robinson drank his very first pint in this remote and determinedly old-fashioned ale house – and jumped at the chance to buy it. A sprucing up of the scrubbed pine tables has not altered the character a jot, and you still find thirsty agricultural workers crowding the tiny, basic bar (bare tables, dartboard) for foaming pints of Brick Kiln Bitter and a venison burger. Perfectly lovely in summer – the front garden looks onto fields – it's also a treat in winter, when log fires and a menu strong on game come into their own. In the restaurant it's "European country cooking": fallow deer (most likely shot by Mike) with peppercorn sauce; roast partridge with braised lentils and cider sauce; passionfruit soufflé. The wine list is serious and affordable and the service is all it should be.

Meals: Lunch & dinner £12.50-£16. Bar meals £3.95-£10. Not Tuesdays.
Closed: 3.30pm-6pm. Open all day Sat & Sun.
Directions: In Yattendon, on main road through village, pick up sign for Frilsham and The Pot Kiln; continue for 0.5 miles, over motorway, continue for 0.5 miles.

Mike & Katie Robinson
The Pot Kiln
Frilsham,
Thatcham RG18 0XX
Tel: +44 (0)1635 201366
Web: www.potkiln.org

Entry 21 Map 4

Berkshire

The Bell Inn

Waltham St Lawrence

Owned by Waltham St Lawrence village, deep in rural Berkshire, is a rare all-rounder of a pub, a very atmospheric 14th-century Wealden house, beamed inside and out with low ceilings, creaking fireplaces, wattle and daub walls, a mishmash of furniture and candelabra lighting. It's a haven for ale fiends, five pumps rotating superbly kept local brews and a further six cask ciders held in cellar. A menu mounted above the hearth at midday and at 7pm offers one delicious constant – 'Bambi burger', minced on site from venison shot by a regular – alongside other dishes (mallard with duck leg fritter, rösti potato, braised chard and elderberry sauce; juniper marinated venison with mash, cavolo nero and onion gravy) dictated daily by season and produce. Regulars are a crew of colourful eccentrics, preventing this great little place from ever becoming too serious.

Meals: Lunch & dinner £10-£16.
Closed: 3pm-5pm (Mon-Fri).
Directions: A4 between Reading and Maidenhead; turn off at Hare Hatch and follow signs to Waltham St Lawrence.

Iain Ganson
The Bell Inn
The Street, Waltham St Lawrence,
Twyford RG10 0JJ
Tel: +44 (0)1189 341788
Web: www.thebellwalthamstlawrence.co.uk

Entry 22 Map 4

Hind's Head

Bray

When the Tudor tavern across the road from Heston Blumenthal's legendary Fat Duck came on the market, Heston snapped it up. Now the old Hind's Head is the poshest of village pubs (polished panelling, wing-back armchairs, open fires) with one striking difference: terrific food. Expect a short slate of British classics... pea and ham soup, potted shrimps with watercress salad, wild boar and apple sausages, the trademark thrice-cooked chips, and revivals of historic puds (Quaking Pudding, Eton mess). Kevin Love heads the kitchen and never loses the focus: to maximise the taste of the finest materials. Side dishes are extra so it ain't cheap; bar food includes Scotch quail eggs, coffee comes with chocs. Book if you want a table in the restaurant, or a private room, suitable for parties.

Meals	Lunch & dinner £12.95-£19.50. Bar meals £1.50-£7.50
Closed	Open all day.
Directions	On B3028 in Bray.

Heston Blumenthal
Hind's Head
High Street, Bray,
Maidenhead SL6 2AB

Tel +44 (0)1628 626151
Web www.thehindsheadhotel.com

Entry 23 Map 4

Berkshire

The White Oak

Cookham

Henry and Katherine snapped up the former Spencers by the common, in atmospheric, upmarket Cookham. Transformed in 12 weeks, the White Oak (sibling to the Greene Oak near Windsor) soon passed muster with the local foodies and now chef Clive Dixon is part of the team. Wooden floors, oak beams, heritage colours, bold artwork, big mirrors and cool jazz set the mood for some seriously good cooking: duck leg confit with roasted root vegetables; braised blade of beef with roast garlic and pearl barley risotto; pan-fried cod with tiger prawns and lemon and herb gnocchi. Dreamy chocolate brownies and ice cream, impeccable wines and friendly service complete the picture. Take a coffee to a leather wing chair by a crackling fire, then walk off your indulgence with a Thames path stroll.

Meals	Lunch & dinner £12-£22.
Closed	Sunday evenings.
Directions	West side of Cookham Common and village on B4447 towards Maidenhead.

Henry & Katherine Cripps
The White Oak
The Pound, Cookham,
Maidenhead SL6 9QE

Tel +44 (0)1628 523043
Web www.thewhiteoak.co.uk

Entry 24 Map 4

The Royal Oak

White Waltham

Modest at first glance, it has star quality inside. Nick Parkinson (son of Michael) may have given this small inn a contemporary and stylish lift, but he has cleverly managed to keep much of the traditional character. There are scrubbed wooden floors and stripped beams, timbers and panelling, the occasional music night. The bar is cosy and inviting, with solid wooden furniture, an open fire and a couple of armchairs. The dining room's food, beautifully cooked by Dominic Chapman, is modern and classy, with a good choice of wines. Tuck into pickled South Devon mackerel with beetroot and watercress, peppered haunch of venison and creamy spinach, Yorkshire rhubarb trifle. And you can get a lovely pint of London Pride. The Royal Oak is friendly and well-run, opening its door to drinkers and diners with equal enthusiasm.

Meals	Lunch & dinner £12.50-£24.
Closed	3pm-6pm. Sun eves.
Directions	On B3024 west of Paley Street, between A330 south of Maidenhead & Twyford.

Nick Parkinson
The Royal Oak
Littlefield Green, White Waltham,
Maidenhead SL6 3JN

Tel +44 (0)1628 620541
Web www.theroyaloakpaleystreet.com

Entry 25 Map 4

Berkshire

Two Brewers

Windsor

In Royal Windsor, next to the Cambridge Gate and the magnificent Long Walk, is a charming pub whose small quaint rooms meander around a panelled bar. One room with big shared tables has deep red walls and matching ceilings; the others have intimate seating areas. There are magazines to dip into and walls crammed with posters, press-cuttings, pictures and mirrors; on a blackboard above the fire, anecdotes commemorating each day are chalked up in preference to menu specials. It's massively popular but reserve a table and you won't go hungry: the compact menu follows a steady pub line, with daily specials, roasts on Sundays, and tapas on Friday and Saturday nights. Choose between beer, champagne, fine wines… and a sprinkling of pavement tables to tempt you after the rigours of the Big Tour. Dogs are welcome – but no under-18s.

Meals	Lunch & dinner £11-£19.50. Sunday lunch £12.50.
Closed	Open all day.
Directions	Off High Street, by Cambridge Gate entrance to the Long Walk.

Authentic pub

Robert Gillespie
Two Brewers
34 Park Street,
Windsor SL4 1LB

Tel +44 (0)1753 855426
Web www.twobrewerswindsor.co.uk

Entry 26 Map 4

The Greene Oak

Windsor

With a background in London gastropubbery, Henry and Katherine Cripps could not fail at their first solo venture, a swishly renovated dining pub close to Windsor, Ascot and foodie Bray. Enter an interior of wood and slate floors and soft green hues, antique French light fittings and big country mirrors. Most people come to eat and the style is traditional with a contemporary twist, a mix of British classic dishes and fashionable modern. Lunch may include pheasant and pistachio terrine with chilli jam and Caesar salad, or homemade beefburger with tomato and chilli relish. In the evening, potted crab and brown shrimp, roast belly pork with wok-fried Asian greens, fillet steak with béarnaise – polished off by a Valrhona chocolate pot with mascarpone. Service, wines and beers are as elegant as the rest.

Meals	Lunch & dinner £13.50-£24. Bar meals from £7. Set lunch £15 & £19. Sunday lunch £21 & £25.
Closed	Open all day.
Directions	On B3383 south of A308, 2 miles west of Windsor.

Henry & Katherine Cripps
The Greene Oak
Dedworth Road,
Windsor SL4 5UW

Tel +44 (0)1753 864294
Web www.thegreeneoak.co.uk

Entry 27 Map 4

The Chimney House

Brighton

The Victorian corner boozer in arty Seven Dials has become a gastropub of note and Helen and Andrew Coggings are keeping it that way. Taking its stylish lead from the bistro pubs of London it has not lost its community feel, so settle in to leather armchairs, scrubbed tables and an open kitchen from which classic British dishes flow. As you might expect, the produce is local and well-sourced, the sort of place where the ketchup is homemade. From the daily menu, tuck into butternut squash soup, sea bass with creamy chorizo sauce, and a prune and pecan nut crumble. Or pop in at lunchtime for a hot beef and horseradish sandwich – or just a bowl of hand-cut chips to soak up the excellent Harveys ale. Tables are filled on a first come, first-served basis in the bar area – but you can reserve one in the restaurant!

Meals	Lunch from £4.95. Dinner from £10.50. Sunday lunch £12.50.
Closed	3pm-5pm (Tues-Thurs). Mon.
Directions	In the Seven Dials area, on the corner of Upper Hamilton Road & Exeter Street.

Helen & Andrew Coggings
The Chimney House
28 Upper Hamilton Road,
Brighton BN1 5DF

Tel +44 (0)1273 556708
Web www.chimneyhousebrighton.co.uk

Entry 28 Map 4

The Ginger Pig

Hove

Everyone loves this smart pub minutes from the beach. The décor is fresh, contemporary and open-plan, and the food is consistently brilliant. Whether it's poached skate wing terrine or a blackboard special of slow-braised shoulder of lamb with spiced cabbage and garlic mash (or a simple chargrilled rib-eye with hand-cut chips) this is a serious destination for those who love real British food. In spite of clear gastropubby leanings, the friendly team has created a balanced mix of drinking bar frequented by locals and cool dining area decked with modern art. It's all down to experienced restaurateur Ben McKeller who, in transforming this building, has created the first in a proposed mini pub empire (note too The Ginger Fox, Albourne). The paved, sheltered garden is a little oasis.

Meals	Lunch & dinner £9.50-£18.
Closed	Open all day.
Directions	Southern end of Hove Street which runs between Church Road and the Kingsway (A259).

Ben McKeller
The Ginger Pig
3 Hove Street,
Hove BN3 2TR

Tel +44 (0)1273 736123
Web www.gingermanrestaurants.com

Entry 29 Map 4

Brighton & Hove

The Foragers

Hove

The laid-back Forager in residential Hove combines the conviviality of a boozer with classy food from a talented team – you can glimpse the chefs at work from the front bar. Blackboard specials and printed menus are dependent on the seasons and raw materials are sourced from Sussex producers. There's a definite preference for organic, especially concerning meat (the Sunday roast always is). Everything bursts with flavour, from braised wild rabbit with buttered greens to Jerusalem artichoke and mushroom suet pudding; mash might be truffled or roast onion'd. There are sandwiches too, perhaps salt beef with dill pickle or steak with mayo, and Sussex Best Bitter to wash it all down. The interior revamp has created two distinct rooms with a relaxed, casual air – and the smart, decked all-weather garden is a popular draw.

Meals	Lunch £6-£14. Bar meals £4-£8. Dinner £19-£14. Sunday lunch, 3 courses, £21. Not Sunday eve.
Closed	Open all day.
Directions	From A259 turn into Hove Street, cross Church Road (B2066) and second right into Stirling Place.

Paul Hutchison
& Sara Rottner Hutchison
The Foragers
3 Stirling Place, Hove BN3 3YU

Tel +44 (0)1273 733134
Web www.theforagerspub.co.uk

Entry 30 Map 4

The Hunters Rest Inn

Clutton

Astride Clutton Hill with fine views over the Cam valley the inn began life in the 1750s – as a hunting lodge. Eighty years later it became a smallholding and tavern. It's a big place, rambling around a large central bar, part wood, part stone, its bar topped with copper. There's plenty of jostling space so get ready to order from the Butcombe, Otter and guest ales and the Original Broad Oak and Pheasant Plucker ciders. Get cosy amongst the old oak and pine settles, the odd sofa and the tables to fit all sizes, the quirky wine-label wallpaper, the horse and country paraphernalia, the fires crackling away. Food is hale and hearty: shepherd's pie, pickled beetroot, crusty bread, wild mushroom risotto. Children are well looked after and there's a miniature railway in the garden. The fun continues upstairs with rooms that range from traditional four-poster with antiques to contemporary chic. All are distinctive, all have views, several look south to the Mendips; others have private terraces. Stylish bathrooms have bold tiles, roll top baths and thick towels. A most enjoyable 'sprack and spry' Somerset hideaway.

Price	£95-£130. Singles £67.50-£77.50.
Rooms	5: 4 doubles, 1 twin.
Meals	Lunch & dinner £8.25-£17.95.
Closed	Open all day.
Directions	A37 south from Bristol. At r'bout with A368, left for Bath; next right (100m), then at T-junction left to top of hill.

Paul Thomas
The Hunters Rest Inn
King Lane, Clutton Hill, Clutton,
Bristol BS39 5QL

Tel	+44 (0)1761 452303
Web	www.huntersrest.co.uk

Kensington Arms

Bristol

Tucked away at the end of a quiet street in leafy Redland, this Victorian corner pub with its decked front terrace – abuzz in summer, from lunch till late – is a popular place with well-heeled locals and a youthful crowd. Stylish and unpretentious, its painted panelling and plain planked floor are complimented by big mirrors and quirky touches. Fresh flowers and daily-printed menus sit on scrubbed tables so tuck into swordfish carpaccio in the bar – accompanied by delicious warm bread – or settle down to several scrumptious courses in the restaurant. This is modern food of the best kind, with a focus on provenance: pan-fried duck livers with bone marrow toast and persillade, home-smoked salmon fishcakes, pumpkin and pinenut gnocchi, hot chocolate fondant. Everything about the 'Kenny' is lovely, and that includes the staff.

Meals	Lunch & dinner £9.50-£14.
Closed	Open all day.
Directions	From B4468 Redland Hill, 2nd exit at r'bout; right at Clyde Road; left at Elliston Road. On to Stanley Road, pub on left.

Kensington Arms
35-37 Stanley Road,
Redland,
Bristol BS6 6NP

Tel +44 (0)117 9446444
Web www.thekensingtonarms.co.uk

Entry 32 Map 3

Bristol

Robin Hood's Retreat

Bristol

An ordinary red-brick pub on bustling Gloucester Road; inside is special. Owner and chef Nathan Muir started his career working under Simon Hopkinson at Bibendum and his beautifully executed food is delivered from a broom cupboard-sized kitchen at the back. The refurb is classy, the cuisine modern European with occasional Asian influences, the menus driven by the seasons and the best produce available. Muir majors on bold flavours, often conjured from the humblest of ingredients, be they lambs' tongues with salsa verde or slow-braised mutton. Desserts include a much-loved treacle tart with English custard. Accompany these with a pint of real ale from a constantly changing selection of up to a dozen, mainly from West Country breweries, or an excellent wine. Sunday lunches are fabulous.

Meals	Set lunch £12.50 & £15.50. Dinner from £11.90. Sunday lunch £17.95 & £20.95. Tasting menu £65.
Closed	Open all day.
Directions	North of the city centre on the main Gloucester Road.

Nathan Muir
Robin Hood's Retreat
197 Gloucester Road, Bishopston,
Bristol BS7 8BG

Tel +44 (0)117 9248639
Web www.robinhoodsretreat.co.uk

Entry 33 Map 3

The Lion

Bristol

On one of the steep narrow roads in the lovely little community of Clifton Wood is a family run pub that the locals love. Mum and daughter are in the kitchen, brother is behind the bar, Grandad's on a barstool chatting and keeping a friendly watchful eye. Bath Ales and Tribute are on tap and the food's very popular; tucking into Welsh lamb stew with dauphinoise potatoes next to the winter's fire is a warming, comforting thing. The risottos and steaks are good, too, and Sunday lunch is legendary – come with the keenest appetite. Find Irish music in the back bar on Fridays (you can hire this room for meetings), a pub quiz on Wednesdays, and a happy throng: families, couples, groups, dogs. There's a terrace to the side and a little community park for children next door. Perfect!

Meals	Lunch from £4.75. Dinner from £7.25. Sunday lunch £9.50.
Closed	Open all day.
Directions	Enter Bristol on A4, left off Hotwell Road onto Ambra Vale. Up steep hill; right at bend at top; straight on to junc., bear left.

Fiona & Charity Vincent
& David Waddilove
The Lion, 19 Church Lane,
Clifton Wood, Bristol BS8 4TX
Tel +44 (0)117 9268492
Web www.thelionclifton.com

Entry 34 Map 3

Bristol

The New Inn

Backwell

In a sought-after commuter village between Bristol and the Mendips is the New Inn, Backwell's oldest pub. In 2009 it received the full gastro makeover as chef Nathan Muir, of Bristol's Robin Hood's Retreat, took over the reins. In the main bar: sage tongue and groove, slate flagstone floors, smart leather sofas. In the smaller drinking area: a real fire and high stools. In the stone-walled restaurant: farmhouse tables, church candles and a mocha carpet. Now the pub attracts locals in for a pint of Butcombe ale and city dwellers escaping for lunch or dinner – and Muir has been sensible enough to offer comforting bar food alongside the full-on à la carte. Pop in for potted beef and a pint or stay longer for rib-eye of Clevedon beef with duck fat-fried chips, and prune and armagnac tart. The food is fabulous.

Meals	Set lunch £10 & £13.50. Bar meals from £2.50. Dinner £13-£20. Sunday lunch £17 & £20.
Closed	Open all day.
Directions	A370 far south side of main road. Opposite the Rising Sun.

Nathan Muir
The New Inn
86 West Town Road, Backwell,
Bristol BS48 3BE
Tel +44 (0)1275 462199
Web www.newinn-backwell.co.uk

Entry 35 Map 3

The Battleaxes

Wraxall

Originally an alcohol-free meeting place for Tyntesfield estate workers, this pub – free of temperance shackles since WWI – has been refurbished in a playful Victorian country house style. Reclaimed pine from an old Welsh chapel paves your way around an open-plan bar area with scrub top tables, chapel chairs and old leather armchairs. Prints and oil paintings adorn the walls along with reclaimed crystal and brass light fittings. The painted bar is imaginatively stocked and features their own Flatcappers ale and other local brews. The Club Room – once the village hall – is the main dining area where menus are a traditional-modern mix, from hearty rib-eye steaks and ale-battered cod with fat chips to pork chops and butterbean and leek cassoulet. Grazing boards for those not up to a full meal are fun and convivial.

Meals	Lunch & dinner from £6.95. Sunday lunch, 3 courses, £19.95.
Closed	See website for details.
Directions	On B3130 in Wraxall.

Pierre Woodford
The Battleaxes
Wraxall,
Bristol BS48 1LQ

Tel	+44 (0)1275 857473
Web	www.flatcappers.co.uk

Entry 36 Map 3

Bristol

The Pony & Trap

Knowle Hill

Just outside pretty Chew Magna, a short drive from Bristol and Bath, is one of the best little gastropubs in the country. Josh Eggleton, who earned his spurs in France, Sicily and America, has won his first Michelin star. Provenance is all; from the blue cheese panna cotta to the fillet of pork with celeriac purée, almost every ingredient has travelled only a few miles to the plate. Deer is bought from a local marksman, eggs are from the chickens in the garden, berries from the hedges and perfect spears of asparagus straight from the patch. As for the views, they're stunning, and both the conservatory-style dining room and the large sloping garden – dine out on a summer's day – have them. For winter the bar is the place to be – super-cosy with wood panelling, old cider flagons and a cast-iron range.

Meals	Lunch from £7.50. Dinner £10.50-£18.50. Sunday lunch from £10.95.
Closed	Mon (except bank hols & Dec). Open all day Sun.
Directions	From A37, right on A368 for Weston-super-mare at Chelwood r'bout, right after 1.5 miles, signed Chew Magna; pub 1 mile on right.

Josh Eggleton
The Pony & Trap
Knowle Hill,
Chew Magna BS40 8TQ

Tel	+44 (0)1275 332627
Web	www.theponyandtrap.co.uk

Entry 37 Map 3

The Dinton Hermit

Ford

A listed local in a peaceful hamlet with long lawns that run down to the road and fields which stretch out beyond. Hanging baskets and wooden tubs add colour to the garden, while inside, both bar and restaurant are small but sweet, a cosy contemporary kingdom that comes complete with timber-framed walls, roaring fire, the odd wooden pillar and a fine settle. Here you eat great food served off a short menu, perhaps homemade fishcakes with a sweet chilli sauce, venison stew with roasted vegetables, Bramley apple crumble with clotted cream. Breakfasts are delicious. Bedrooms are scattered about the place: those in the main house are bigger but more traditional (two have four-posters) while those in the refurbished barn have a clean, contemporary style (suede headboards, neutral colours, pretty fabrics, robes in bathrooms). The gardens draw a crowd in summer and Sunday lunch is popular with locals. Further afield, bridle paths lead into the hills and Oxford's spires are close. The Aylesbury Vale cycle route passes outside so expect a few cyclists in summer.

Price	£95. Four-posters £135. Singles from £70.
Rooms	13: 11 doubles, 2 four-posters.
Meals	Lunch from £6.50. Dinner from £8.95. Sunday lunch from £11.95.
Closed	Open all day.
Directions	M40, junc. 7, then A418 for Aylesbury. Through Thame, then right after a mile for Haddenham. Through village, right after a mile for Ford. On left in village.

Wendy Kinnair
The Dinton Hermit
Ford,
Aylesbury HP17 8XH

Tel	+44 (0)1296 747473
Web	www.dintonhermit.co.uk

The Nags Head Inn

Little Kingshill

This was Roald Dahl's local – it features in *Fantastic Mr Fox*, half a mile out of Great Missenden. It's a beautiful old building built of red brick and flint under bright red pantiles, framed by the rolling hills of the Chilterns. At the back is a vast garden with plenty of trees under which to dream and picnic tables with umbrellas. Inside, a classic refurbishment from owner Alvin Michaels of the award-winning Bricklayers Arms, with food to match: the beloved 15th-century boozer has become a great dining pub. Now low dark beams and big inglenook blend with modern oak and lemon hues, there are salt and pepper mills on shining tables and boxed shelves guarding armagnacs. Our meal was faultless: various smoked fish with lemon coriander butter, and a trio of pheasant in a red wine and shallot sauce. Drinks cover every aspect of the grape and globe, plus London Pride, and young staff are attentive. Bedrooms above are equally good, their creams and whites complementing ancient timbers. There are ironing boards, toiletries and full-length mirrors, and the bed linen is delicious.

Price	£90-£130.
Rooms	5: 3 doubles, 2 twins.
Meals	Lunch & dinner from £10.95. Sunday lunch, 3 courses, £23.95.
Closed	Open all day.
Directions	A413 Amersham to Aylesbury. Left onto London Road, past the Children's Hospital.

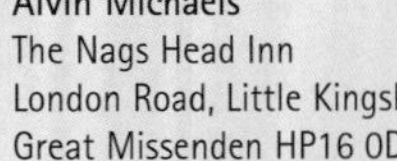

Alvin Michaels
The Nags Head Inn
London Road, Little Kingshill,
Great Missenden HP16 0DG
Tel +44 (0)1494 862200
Web www.nagsheadbucks.com

The Crown Inn

Amersham

Celebrated designer Ilse Crawford has reinvented the English inn. Behind the beautiful timber framework of this 16th-century building is an understated new look, Shaker-simple and full of personality. In the classic bar and timbered dining areas, old planked floors, thick beams, inglenook fireplaces and charming furniture blend with soft muted colours, fur rugs on Ercol windsor chairs, fresh flowers in pewter pots and Welsh blankets on ancient settles. For summer: a cobbled courtyard grill. Now home to a Josper Oven, the Crown boasts a chop house style menu specialising in grilled meats. Daily menus burst with local produce and the pub even grows its own veg out the back. As for the bedrooms, a labyrinth of corridors leads to wonky beamed rooms with sloping oak floors and a décor that is elegant, contemporary, rustic, understated: big beds with crisp linen and Jakob's wool blankets, Robert's radios, seagrass mats. Modern bathrooms have vast walk-in showers and Room 12 has a 16th-century hand-painted wall; the modern-build bedrooms are a tad more traditional. A chic Chiltern's bolthole for city escapees.

Price	£109-£250.
Rooms	37: 29 doubles, 8 suites.
Meals	Lunch & dinner £12-£21.50. Bar meals £3-£9.50.
Closed	Open all day.
Directions	Leave M40 at junc. 2 signs Beaconsfield.

David Hodgson
The Crown Inn
16 High Street,
Amersham HP7 0DH

Tel	+44 (0)1494 721541
Web	www.thecrownamersham.co.uk

Three Horseshoes Inn

Radnage

London may only be an hour's drive, but this is lost down a leafy lane. Red kites circle a deep bowl of countryside, smoke curls from cottages below, and the inn surveys the idyllic scene from on high. Inside are flagstones and an open fire in the tiny bar, and exposed timbers and pine settles in the restaurant. Simon, chef turned patron, has cooked at Le Gavroche and all the best places; dinner is delectable and the homemade piccalilli worth the trip alone. Come for lunch and baked camembert with garlic and rosemary, stay for dinner and tiger prawns, roasted sea bass, bread and butter pudding with marmalade ice cream. If you're here for the night, private stairs lead to super attic rooms (and more in the annexe) with silky quilts, goose down pillows, deluge showers, funky furniture and Farrow & Ball walls. Breakfast indulgently, drink in the views, hike in the hills, walk by the Thames. There's jazz and tapas once a month and in summer you can eat on the terrace at the back while ducks circle a sunken phone box in the pond. Great value set lunches, and sandwiches for passing walkers.

Price	£90-£150.
Rooms	6: 2 doubles, 2 garden rooms, 2 suites.
Meals	Lunch from £6.50. Bar meals from £7.50. Dinner from £15. Sun lunch £27.50. Not Sun eves or Mon lunch.
Closed	3pm-6pm. Mon lunch. Tues after bank hols & Sun after 6pm.
Directions	M40 junc. 5, A40 south thro' Stokenchurch, left for Radnage. After 2 miles left to Bennett End. Sharp right, up hill, on left.

Simon Crawshaw
Three Horseshoes Inn
Horseshoe Road, Radnage,
High Wycombe HP14 4EB

Tel +44 (0)1494 483273
Web www.thethreehorseshoes.net

The Ostrich

Colnbrook

Smartened up a few years back, the Ostrich is an ancient, rambling place, within a mile of the motorways. The wonky timbered façade remains, but step through the huge glass doors and you enter a world in which old blends vibrantly with new. There's a glittering scarlet and steel bar that picks up the colour in the original stained glass, while the floors are slate-tiled and the furniture chunky. There are sandblasted beams, standing timbers and, in the atmospheric dining room, bowed, putty-coloured walls. Food is modern British and the menu wide-ranging, so pitch up for salads and sandwiches, chicken and lobster sausages with creamed leeks, and braised pork cheeks with vegetables. Take a peek upstairs at the lofty, tightly raftered function room (comedy nights) or enjoy a Sunday roast and a pint of Doom Bar.

Meals — Lunch & dinner £8.75-£16.75.
Closed — 3pm-5pm.
Directions — Colnbrook is signed off M4 (junc. 5) & A4 east of Slough.

Phillippe de Azevedo
The Ostrich
High Street, Colnbrook,
Slough SL3 0JZ
Tel +44 (0)1753 682628
Web www.theostrichcolnbrook.co.uk

Entry 42 Map 4

The Black Horse

Fulmer

A hop from London, the Black Horse is the hub of Fulmer, a sleepy conservation village between Gerrards Cross and Slough. Made up of three 17th-century cottages that housed the craftsmen working on the church next door, the pub is a warren of tiny character-steeped rooms. It's warm, cosy, a charming mix of brocante finds, rich fabrics and heritage colours, while outside is a large garden and a peaceful terrace. Look forward to hand-pulled beers, European wines and robust 'British Colonial' cooking: try grilled mackerel fillet with horseradish blini; Buckinghamshire pheasant with white pudding and apple parcel; local wild plum and frangipane tart. Explore the nearby heathland of Stoke Common. Black Park – a mile away and 530 acres – is perfect for tiring out children and dogs, and walking off all that lovely food!

Meals — Lunch & dinner £4.75-£18.75.
Closed — Open all day.
Directions — From A40, east of Gerrards Cross, take turn dir. Fulmer & Wexham Park. 1.5 miles on left in centre of village.

David & Becky Salisbury
The Black Horse
Windmill Road, Fulmer,
Gerrards Cross SL3 6HD
Tel +44 (0)1753 663183
Web www.blackhorsefulmer.co.uk

Entry 43 Map 4

The Swan Inn

Denham

Swap the bland and everyday for the picture-book perfection of Denham village and the stylish Swan. Georgian, double-fronted, swathed in wisteria, the building has had a makeover by David and Becky (of the Alford Arms, the Old Queens Head, the Royal Oak and the Black Horse). It has been transformed by rug-strewn boards, chunky tables, cushioned settles, a log fire and a fabulous terrace for outdoor meals. Food is modern British. If pressed for time, choose from the 'small plates' list – ham hock ballotine with pease pudding and mustard focaccia. If you've nothing to rush for, linger over barbary duck breast with duck hash croquette and parsnip purée, with a pint of Rebellion IPA or one of 22 wines by the glass. The owners have thought of everything, and the gardens are large enough for the kids to go wild in.

Meals	Lunch, bar meals & dinner, all £11.75-£19.25.
Closed	Open all day.
Directions	From A412 (M25 junc. 17 or M40 junc. 1) follow signs for Denham Village.

David & Becky Salisbury
The Swan Inn
Village Road, Denham,
Uxbridge UB9 5BH
Tel +44 (0)1895 832085
Web www.swaninndenham.co.uk

Entry 44 Map 4

Buckinghamshire

The Jolly Cricketers

Seer Green

If you can't find the pub you want, start your own. When the Jolly Cricketers came on the market, longtime Seer Green residents Chris Lillitou and Amanda Baker couldn't resist. Three years on and what a transformation. Now pretty plants clamber up the brickwork outside, while behind the bar optics have been replaced by sweet shop jars of roasted nuts, olives and lollipops – a picture of individuality matched by a freehouse ale selection that showcases the best of local breweries. Ornate fireplaces, oddment-cluttered shelves and quirky vegetable artwork create an unpretentious backdrop for cider-braised ham, crispy poached egg, pineapple chutney and triple-cooked chips; or beef rump, tongue and cheek with potato purée. Coffee mornings, book signings and pub quizzes contribute to a community spirit but do nothing to dilute this pub's new found dining status.

Meals	Lunch from £6.50. Bar meals from £10.50. Dinner from £14.50. Sunday lunch, 3 courses, £28.50. Not Sunday or Monday.
Closed	Mon until 5pm.
Directions	M40 junc. 2; at r'bout head towards Beaconsfield; take 1st left A40 to Amersham, 2nd exit on to A355. 1st right to Seer Green, pub opposite church.

Amanda Baker & Chris Lillitou
The Jolly Cricketers
24 Chalfont Road, Seer Green,
Beaconsfield HP9 2YG
Tel +44 (0)1494 676308
Web www.thejollycricketers.co.uk

Entry 45 Map 4

The White Horse

Hedgerley

In tiny Hedgerley village, a surprise only ten minutes from Slough, is a perfectly preserved slice of unspoiled pubbery. Whitewashed brick, horseshoes and cartwheels peer from burgeoning shrubbery and window baskets, illuminated by ancient gas lamps on both street and façade. Inside, exposed wood is overlaid by time-worn carpet, while endless beams and supports for low ceilings are festooned with a magpie's nest of artefacts. As a serious ale house, seven ever-changing beers are drawn direct from cask and served via a hatch, the selection rotating on a seasonal basis. Food is from a pre deep-fryer age with ploughman's, quiches, cold meats and baps displayed at a chilled deli counter alongside the odd hot option of chunky lamb broth or maybe pheasant Wellington. A busy garden and marquee are a treat in summer – and an aviary of finches.

Meals	Lunch £6-£10.
Closed	2.30pm-5pm. Open all day Sat & Sun.
Directions	M40 to junc 2; take A355 and first turning left, following Hedgerley lane to the village.

Doris Hobbs & Kevin Brooker
The White Horse
Village Lane,
Hedgerley,
Slough SL2 3UY
Tel +44 (0)1753 643225

Entry 46 Map 4

Buckinghamshire

The Royal Oak

Bovingdon Green

The old whitewashed cottage stands in a peaceful hamlet on the edge of the common – it's hard to believe that Marlow is just a mile away. It's one of a thriving small group of dining pubs owned by David and Becky Salisbury (The Alford Arms, Hertfordshire; The Swan Inn, The Black Horse and The Old Queens Head, Buckinghamshire). Beyond the terrace is a stylish, open-plan bar, cheerful with terracotta walls, rug-strewn boards, cushioned pews and crackling log fires. Order a pint of local Rebellion ale or one of the 22 wines available by the glass and check out the daily chalkboard or printed menu. Innovative pub grub comes in the form of 'small plates' (local venison cottage pie) and main meals (roast Cornish mullet with parsley gnocchi and savoy cabbage): fresh and delicious. The sprawling gardens are perfect for summer.

Meals	Lunch & dinner £11.75-£21.75.
Closed	Open all day.
Directions	From Marlow A4155; right signed Bovingdon Green.

David & Becky Salisbury
The Royal Oak
Frieth Road, Bovingdon Green,
Marlow SL7 2JF
Tel +44 (0)1628 488611
Web www.royaloakmarlow.co.uk

Entry 47 Map 4

The Old Queens Head

Penn

David and Becky's mini-empire contains this pub by the green. Dating from 1666 it has character and charm while inside, old beams and timbers in the rambling bar and dining areas blend perfectly with a stylish and contemporary décor – rug-strewn flags, polished boards, classic fabrics, lovely old oak. Innovative seasonal menus and chalkboard specials mix classic pub recipes with modern British flair. Choices range from 'small plates' – seared pigeon breast with celeriac rösti and warm blueberry vinaigrette – to big dishes of roast butternut squash gnocchi with wild mushrooms and toasted pine nuts. For those who have room left there are a tempting selection of puddings including apple brandy syllabub. There's a glorious summer garden and, to top it all off, there are walks nearby in the ancient beech woodlands of Common and Penn Woods.

Meals	Lunch, bar meals & dinner, all £11.75-£19.25.
Closed	Open all day.
Directions	From High Wycombe (M40 junc. 4), A40 towards Beaconsfield, then left for 1.5 miles into Hammersley Lane; pub on right, opposite church.

David & Becky Salisbury
The Old Queens Head
Hammersley Lane, Penn,
High Wycombe HP10 8EY

Tel +44 (0)1494 813371
Web www.oldqueensheadpenn.co.uk

Entry 48 Map 4

Swan Inn

Milton Keynes Village

A 13th-century beauty in the heart of a sprawling New Town; across roundabouts and through housing estates you arrive at the clearly signed 'Milton Keynes Village'. Spruced up in gastropub style, keeping its beams, fireplaces and layout, the Swan has cool colours, scatter cushions and pews, chic chairs in its snug and a glowing wood-burner in its bar. In the cosy dining room – wooden floors, chunky tables, open-to-view kitchen – Italian cured meats with chutney and homemade bread are on the menu alongside English pot-roasted chicken and cottage pie. Some produce comes from local allotments (in return for a pint or two), while imaginative evening meals include the likes of venison carpaccio with sweet onion jam. In summer you may eat outside, on the covered sun terrace or in the orchard garden.

Meals	Lunch & dinner £7-£16. Sunday lunch £11.95.
Closed	Open all day.
Directions	Follow signs to Milton Keynes Village off V11 between junctions H6 & H7, 5 mins from town centre.

Tyrone Bentham
Swan Inn
Broughton Road, Milton Keynes
Village, Milton Keynes MK10 9AH

Tel +44 (0)1908 665240
Web www.theswan-mkvillage.co.uk

Entry 49 Map 9

The Crooked Billet

Newton Longville

The twin talents of a former Sommelier of the Year, John Gilchrist, and head chef Emma have put the 16th-century pub on the county's culinary map. With innovative menus and a 400-bin wine list (all, astonishingly, available by the glass), you may imagine it's more restaurant than pub but it's an exemplary local with a great bar, weekly-changing ales, a log-fired inglenook and a great pubby atmosphere. Munch sandwiches, salads or steak and chips in the beamed bar at lunch; or pan-fried turbot fillet, Palourde clams and artichokes, goat's cheese and tomato soufflé and apple spotted dick in the restaurant – inviting with its deep red walls, candles and country prints. Delicious cheeses come with fig and walnut cake and Emma's seasonal menus make full use of produce from first-class suppliers, villagers included.

Meals: Lunch & dinner £10-£20. Bar meals £5.75-£10. Sunday lunch, 3 courses, £26. Not Sunday eve.
Closed: 2.30pm-5.30pm & Mon lunch.
Directions: From Milton Keynes A421 for Buckingham, left for Newton Longville.

John & Emma Gilchrist
The Crooked Billet
2 Westbrook End, Newton Longville,
Milton Keynes MK17 0DF
Tel +44 (0)1908 373936
Web www.thebillet.co.uk

Entry 50 Map 9

Buckinghamshire

The Mole & Chicken

Long Crendon

Midsomer Murders was filmed here: it's in the middle of nowhere, hardish to find and absurdly picturesque. Come on a damp Sunday and settle in for the day; in summer there's a decked area with fabulous views, a big barbecue and a children's play area. Inside, lovely low beams, a vast fire and squishy leather sofas: a perfect pub for a dog. It's that sort of a bolthole, relaxed, pubby, with ales on tap and 12 wines by the glass. The restaurant feel takes over in several little rooms with chunky pine tables, 60s art and gleaming glasses, and we hear great reports of the food: woodland mushroom risotto with poached egg and truffle oil; grilled plaice with caper and parsley butter; a superb Sunday roast (thick tender beef, fiery horseradish sauce, creamy celeriac, the best Yorkshire pudding).

Meals: Lunch & dinner £5-£30.
Closed: 3pm-6.30pm. Open all day Sun.
Directions: North from Thame on B4011 to Long Crendon. Right on main street opp. the Gurkha, signed Chilton. Left at T-junction; pub on left after 0.5 miles.

Steve Bush
The Mole & Chicken
Easington Terrace, Long Crendon,
Aylesbury HP18 9EY
Tel +44 (0)1844 208387
Web www.themoleandchicken.co.uk

Entry 51 Map 8

The Crown Inn

Elton

Conkers, hundreds of them, harden to a deep russet brown in the late summer sun by the front door and under the towering chestnut tree, beneath which huddles The Crown; the setting is idyllic. The ancient sandstone inn looks across the green of this Wolds village that harbours the equally beautiful Elton Hall. The bar, beamed, and painted in pastel hues, with a huge oak mantel and grate, is the epitome of Old England. Here you may enjoy a pint of Golden Crown and a light meal. In the 'snug', seated by the big log fire on a wintery night, what nicer than to settle in and try chicken liver and brandy parfait with homemade chutney or fillets of sea bass and red mullet with prawn and courgette risotto. For something more traditional, there's ale-battered haddock and chips, beef, ale and mushroom pie. Weekend dining is in the circular conservatory, which opens to a large decked area, great for summer. As for the bedrooms, they're gorgeous (plantation-style shutters for privacy, king-size beds, great lighting) with snazzy en suites. Three are tucked upstairs beneath the thatch, two at the rear in the courtyard.

Price	£95. Singles from £65.
Rooms	5 doubles.
Meals	Lunch & dinner £7-£25. Restaurant closed first week in January.
Closed	Mon lunch (bar open in eves).
Directions	A1(M), junc. 17, then A605 west for 3 miles. Right on B671 for Elton. In village left, signed Nassington.

Marcus Lamb
The Crown Inn
8 Duck Street, Elton,
Peterborough PE8 6RQ
Tel +44 (0)1832 280232
Web www.thecrowninn.org

The Anchor Inn

Sutton Gault

A real find, a 1650s ale house on Chatteris Fen, run by good people. Wedged between the bridge and the raised dyke, the little inn was built to bed and board the men conscripted to tame the vast watery tracts of swamp and scrub. These days cosy luxury infuses every corner. There are low beamed ceilings, timber-framed walls, raw dark panelling and terracotta-tiled floors. A wood-burner warms the bar, so stop for a pint of cask ale, then pick from a menu that is light, imaginative and surprising: hand-dressed crabs from Cromer in spring, asparagus and Bottisham hams in summer, wild duck from the marshes in winter. Breakfast is equally indulgent. Four rooms up the narrow stairs fit the mood exactly: not posh, supremely comfy, with trim carpets, wicker chairs, crisp white duvets, Indian throws, candles by the bath. The suites have a sofabed each and three rooms have fen and river views. Footpaths flank the water; stroll down and you might see mallards or whooper swans, even a seal – the river is tidal to the Wash. Don't miss Ely (the bishop comes to eat).

Price	£79.50-£99. Suites £115-£155. Singles from £59.50. Extra bed £20.
Rooms	4: 1 double, 1 twin/double, 2 suites.
Meals	Lunch, 2 courses, £13.95. Dinner, 3 courses, £25-£30. Sunday lunch from £11.50.
Closed	3pm-7pm (6.30pm Sat & Sun).
Directions	From Ely A142 west. In Sutton left on B1381 for Earith. Right in southern Sutton, signed Sutton Gault. 1 mile north on left at bridge.

Adam Pickup & Carlene Bunten
The Anchor Inn
Bury Lane, Sutton Gault,
Ely CB6 2BD
Tel +44 (0)1353 778537
Web www.anchorsuttongault.co.uk

The Black Bull Inn

Balsham

Buoyed by the success of the Red Lion at Hinxton, Alex has snapped up the 16th-century Black Bull in nearby Balsham. Unloved for years, it is firmly back on track as a pretty thatched pub. The beamed and timbered bar is spruced up, a new bar servery has been added, wooden floors gleam and there's a smart mix of old dining tables and deep leather sofas fronting the glowing log fire; so cosy up with a pint of Rusty Bucket on a winter evening. The ancient, high-raftered and adjoining barn has been restored and refurbished to perfection and is the place to sit and savour some cracking pub food; try the lamb shank with roasted garlic mash and rosemary jus, or the smoked haddock with tarragon foam. In the bar, tuck into roast beef and horseradish sandwiches or a plate of Suffolk ham, plus eggs and hand-cut chips. Comfortable rooms in the annexe across the yard sport oak floors and hand-made furniture, rich fabrics, and down duvets on king-size beds. Super tiled bathrooms come with bath and shower. A peaceful backwater bolthole, handy for the A11/M11, and Cambridge and the Newmarket Races.

Price	£99-£119. Singles £79.
Rooms	5 twins/doubles.
Meals	Lunch & dinner from £12. Bar meals from £6.
Closed	Open all day.
Directions	Balsham is on B1052 Linton to Newmarket road, signed off A11 south west of Newmarket; pub in village centre.

Alex Clarke
The Black Bull Inn
27 High Street, Balsham,
Cambridge CB21 4DJ
Tel +44 (0)1223 893844
Web www.blackbull-balsham.co.uk

Red Lion Inn

Hinxton

In pretty, peaceful Hinxton, close to Cambridge, the rambling Red Lion is a popular stopover in an area deprived of good inns. And its secluded garden, replete with dovecote, arbour and patio, overlooks the church: a lovely spot for peaceful summer sipping. Another draw is the buzzy atmosphere Alex has instilled in the beamed bar with its deep green chesterfields, worn wooden boards, cosy log fire and ticking clock. Ales from City of Cambridge, Adnams and Woodforde's add to the appeal, as do eclectic menus that list a range of classic pub dishes and more inventive specials, all at good prices. Pop in for a beef and horseradish sandwich or linger over venison with blackberry jus or wild mushroom fettuccine; tuck into delicious roast Norfolk chicken on Sunday. Puddings are to die for: sticky toffee pudding with caramel sauce, lemon tart with mango coulis. Named after local beers and ciders, new-build rooms are comfortable and smart with a fresh, contemporary feel – lightwood furniture, wooden floors, crisp cotton on top-quality beds, fully tiled bathrooms. Breakfasts are a serious treat.

Price	£115. Singles £90.
Rooms	8: 3 doubles, 5 twins/doubles.
Meals	Lunch & dinner £11-£25. Bar meals £4.50-£10.50. Sunday lunch £12.
Closed	3pm-5.30pm (4.30pm-7pm Sun). Open all day Fri & Sat.
Directions	See website.

Alex Clarke
Red Lion Inn
32 High Street, Hinxton,
Saffron Walden CB10 1QY
Tel +44 (0)1799 530601
Web www.redlionhinxton.co.uk

The Queen's Head

Newton

David and Juliet have run the legendary pub for nearly half a century and are joined by son Robert. There's a timeless appeal in the almost spartan main bar where clattering floorboards, plain wooden tables and aged paintings are watched over by a vintage clock that keeps the beat; a tiny carpeted lounge with dark beams and well-worn furniture is a cosier alternative when its fire is blazing. The whole interior is unusual and utterly unspoilt, a perfect backdrop for shove ha'penny, cribbage and beef dripping on toast. Yes, the food is simple, but deliciously so: rare roast beef sliced wafer-thin, ripe stilton sandwiches, ham on the bone, a mug of rich brown soup – dispensed with slow deliberation and accompanied by Adnams ales tapped straight from the barrel. A real pub with a loyal following.

Meals	Bar meals £3.50-£6.
Closed	2.30pm-6pm (7pm Sun).
Directions	M11 junc. 11; A10 for Royston; left on B1368.

David, Juliet & Robert Short
The Queen's Head
Fowlmere Road,
Newton,
Cambridge CB22 7PG
Tel +44 (0)1223 870436

Entry 56 Map 9

The Willow Tree

Bourn

A quirky, funky, foodie haven. Kitchen and front of house are run by a young lively couple backed by a well-trained, welcoming team – and rural Cambridgeshire flocks. You enter via a raised terrace at the back – magically storm lantern-lit at night – to find an unexpectedly theatrical décor with French rococo flourishes. It's not large but it's glamorous, the bar packed with curvy chairs, gilt mirrors and two sofas; the longer restaurant is aglow with candles, candelabras and log fires, one at each end. Best of all is the menu, vibrant and rounded. Settle into seared scallops with beetroot panna cotta and crisp parsley, or roasted lamb rump with root vegetables; or just walk away with a pizza. There are three ales served and bar shelves stocked with high-end stuff, from Black Sheep to Belvoir juices, there are summer balls and New Year's parties and live jazz twice a month.

Meals	Lunch & dinner from £7.50. Sunday lunch from £9.95.
Closed	Open all day.
Directions	Bourn is signed off A428 west of Cambridge; pub in village centre.

Craig & Shaina Galvin-Scott
The Willow Tree
29 High Street,
Bourn CB23 2SQ
Tel +44 (0)1954 719775
Web www.thewillowtreebourn.com

Entry 57 Map 9

Hole in the Wall

Little Wilbraham

Hiding down a hundred lanes, this pretty village pub is now in the hands of Masterchef winner 2010, chef Alex Rushmer. It's clearly well-loved. Regulars drop by for a swift half in the big timbered bar, and gather for lunch in the country-style restaurant at the back. In the bar are horse brasses and country prints, junk-shop find tables and several log fires. In contrast to all this old-fashioned rusticity the food is decidedly modern: ingredients are as local and as organic as can be and the chalkboard specials change regularly. Alex's cooking embraces many ideas: potted ham hock with piccalilli and spiced roasted cauliflower; lamb leg and shoulder with caponata, couscous and dates; halibut with smoked haddock and bacon chowder; Sunday roast rib of beef with all the trimmings. On summery days, the front garden is glorious.

Meals	Lunch & dinner £10.50-£17.50.
Closed	3pm-6.30pm. Sun eves & Mon.
Directions	Take the Stow cum Quy turn off A14, then A1303 Newmarket road & follow signs to Little Wilbraham.

Alex Rushmer
Hole in the Wall
Primrose Farm Road,
Little Wilbraham, Cambridge CB1 5JY
Tel +44 (0)1223 812282
Web www.holeinthewallcambridge.co.uk

Cambridgeshire

Dyke's End

Reach

In a community hamlet in Fen country is a "splendid pub" (to quote the Prince of Wales), rescued from closure by its regulars in 1997. Now privately owned, the former 17th-century farmhouse is a lovely old place, with rug-strewn bare boards, glowing log fires, high-backed settles, scrubbed pine tables and a relaxing vibe in two refurbished candlelit bars. Settle in for a pint of Devil's Dyke Bitter or No 7, brewed in the microbrewery at the back, and try one of the seasonal specialities from the oft-changing lunch and dinner menus. Choose from linguini with scallops, black pepper and truffle oil; pork belly with chorizo and cannellini beans; local sausages and mash; chocolate mousse with sloe gin jelly. Book for memorable Sunday roasts. Al fresco dining on the lawn overlooks the village green.

Meals	Lunch from £6.95. Dinner from £10.95. Sunday lunch, 3 courses, £19.95. No food Mon.
Closed	2pm-6pm & Mon lunch. Open all day Sat & Sun.
Directions	Take B1102 from A14 (junc. with A1103) to Swaffham Prior, then follow signs to Reach.

Simon Owers
Dyke's End
8 Fair Green, Reach,
Cambridge CB25 0JD
Tel +44 (0)1638 743816
Web www.dykesend.co.uk

Three Horseshoes

Madingley

From the outside, the thatched pub is old; push the door and you embrace the new. It is simple, stylish, open, with pale wooden floors and chocolate and cream paintwork; there is lightness and space yet the familiar features remain. The bar has Adnams bitter and a guest ale on tap, a modern open log fire and a menu packed with Italian country dishes and imaginative combinations – chargrilled lamb with cavolo nero and braised beans; roast pork belly with fagioli beans, lemon and spinach; white chocolate, mascarpone and pistachio cheesecake. Relaxed but excellent service matches the atmosphere of the busy bar while formality and white linen come together in the conservatory dining room, popular with business lunchers. In both rooms the choice of wines is superb – pity the designated driver.

Meals	Lunch & dinner £12-£25. Bar meals from £4. Sunday lunch, 3 courses, £26.
Closed	3pm-6pm. Open all day Sat & Sun in summer.
Directions	Off A1303, 2 miles west of Cambridge; 1 mile from M11 & A14.

Richard Stokes
Three Horseshoes
High Street, Madingley,
Cambridge CB23 8AB

Tel +44 (0)1954 210221
Web www.threehorseshoesmadingley.co.uk

Entry 60 Map 9

Cambridgeshire

The Eltisley

Eltisley

Lucky locals. The Eltisley – once a grubby old boozer – looks across the green of this deeply peaceful village but now the style is individual and quirky. The bar has an industrial late-Victorian feel with mock gas lamps, distressed paintwork and brick and flag floors; the restaurant is all shimmering chandeliers, high backed leather chairs and pale walls. You will eat the freshest, most local produce: meat, poultry and eggs from nearby farms, freshly baked bread, fish from sustainable sources. Starters include mussels with vindaloo sauce and pan-fried mackerel fillet with fennel and orange salad; wild boar and local rabbit are braised slowly, and you can polish it all off with quince and almond tart. Sup a pint of the real stuff, or good wine by the glass; spill into the garden in summer, and listen to jazz on monthly Sundays.

Meals	Lunch & dinner £9.95-£20. Bar meals from £4.95 (lunch only).
Closed	3pm-6pm. Sun eves & Mon. Open all day Sat.
Directions	In village centre just off A428 between Cambridge and St Neots.

John Stean
The Eltisley
2 The Green, Eltisley,
St Neots PE19 6TG

Tel +44 (0)1480 880308
Web www.theeltisley.co.uk

Entry 61 Map 9

The Cock

Hemingford Grey

Oliver and Richard have stripped the lovely 17th-century village pub back to its original simplicity. Step directly into an attractive bare-boarded bar, cosy with low beams and log-burner, and sup four real ales from local breweries. For food, move into the airy restaurant where buttermilk walls and modern prints sit beautifully with wooden floors and tables. The menu is strong on pub classics – braised beef cheek with celeriac mash and horseradish gravy, sticky toffee pudding – and the chef makes his own sausages, served with a choice of delicious sauces (wild mushroom, wholegrain mustard). Pheasant and port pithivier is a favourite winter starter, while fish and game dishes reveal a refreshing, modern view, all delicious. The British and continental cheeses should not be missed, and Sunday lunch is much praised.

Meals	Lunch & dinner £11-£18.
Closed	3pm-6pm (4pm-6.30pm Sun).
Directions	From A14 south for Hemingford Grey; 2 miles south of Huntingdon.

Oliver Thain & Richard Bradley
The Cock
47 High Street, Hemingford Grey,
Huntingdon PE28 9BJ
Tel +44 (0)1480 463609
Web www.thecockhemingford.co.uk

Entry 62 Map 9

Cambridgeshire

The Crown Inn

Broughton

There's been a pub cum saddler's shop in this peaceful hamlet since medieval times; villagers saved the Crown from residential conversion back in 2001 and now you find one of Cambridgeshire's best gastropubs. Huge terracotta floor slabs, oak beams, a long lightwood bar aimed at drinkers, with a large selection of whites, reds and sparkling for wine lovers. Round the side of the chimney breast is a bright open dining room with fresh blooms, a mixture of old and new – all very 21st-century. If the game and cranberry terrine with red onion and juniper marmalade, loin of venison with baby roast potatoes and port jus, and the sticky toffee pudding are anything to go by then the food, refined and unshowy, is worth travelling for. Children have capacious lawns to play on in summer, and conkers from majestic chestnuts to plunder.

Meals	Lunch £6.50-£15.95. Bar meals £6.50-£10.95. Dinner £6.95-£17.50. Sunday lunch, 3 courses, £18.45.
Closed	3pm-6pm Mon-Sat. Open all day Sun.
Directions	Broughton is signed off A141 north east of Huntingdon.

Mark Burrell
The Crown Inn
Bridge Road, Broughton,
Huntingdon PE28 3AY
Tel +44 (0)1487 824428
Web www.thecrowninnrestaurant.co.uk

Entry 63 Map 9

The George Inn

Spaldwick

The rambling building – 500 years old – overlooks the village green. Inside, wonky walls are hung with prints and big mirrors, leather sofas and chunky wood tables speak 'modern brasserie', old timbers are exposed and boards are bare. This uncluttered styling blends beautifully with the history of the place. Modern variations on traditional dishes fit the bill – chicken liver parfait with tomato chutney, smoked haddock and lemon fishcakes with lemon butter sauce, duck leg confit with braised red cabbage and rosemary jus, pear and cinnamon tart: simple, robust dishes based on first-rate produce. The relaxed feel extends from the several eating areas in the rambling bar – this is a genuine village local – to the magnificent high-raftered restaurant. To drink there's Adnams, Greene King, and 25 wines by the glass.

Meals	Lunch & dinner £7.95-£21.50. Bar meals £6.95-£13.95.
Closed	Open all day.
Directions	Beside A141, off junc. 18 A14, 5 miles west of Huntingdon.

Leanne Langman
The George Inn
7 High Street, Spaldwick,
Huntingdon PE28 0TD

Tel +44 (0)1480 890293
Web www.thegeorgespaldwick.co.uk

Entry 64 Map 9

Cambridgeshire

The Pheasant

Keyston

This textbook country outpost does beams, open fires and comfy sofas better than anyone, yet never forgets it's a pub; two or three guest ales are always on hand pump. John Hoskins bought the Pheasant in early 2012 and chef/patron Simon Cadge is at the helm. The menu is English, the cooking is restorative, the meat is reared in the village, and if the mushroom man turns up with a colony of particularly flavoursome fungi, then the menu will announce them. Add an enterprising list of wines and expertly kept ales and you have the Pheasant to a T. Expect a good-value set menu and, if you don't want a full-blown meal – carpaccio of venison with parsley root purée, wild sea bass with crab and cockle chowder, steamed orange pudding – there's bar food instead. And beautiful unpasteurised British cheeses.

Meals	Lunch & dinner from £15. Sunday lunch £12.95 & £16.50.
Closed	Open all day.
Directions	Keyston off A14, halfway between Huntingdon & Kettering.

Simon Cadge
The Pheasant
Village Loop Road, Keyston,
Huntingdon PE28 0RE

Tel +44 (0)1832 710241
Web www.thepheasant-keyston.co.uk

Entry 65 Map 9

Albion Inn

Chester

Chester's last unspoilt Victorian corner pub. Many a young man would have spent his shilling in the public bar, before he left to sign up for King and Country. The Albion is dedicated to the memory of those who fought. To a background of William Morris wallpaper, leather sofas and soft glowing lamps there is Great War memorabilia aplenty – and a 1928 Steck Player piano that occasionally entertains. There are four cask ales, a flurry of malts, decent wines and 'Trench Rations' in un-trench-like portions – lamb's liver with bacon and onions in cider gravy, monkfish, prawn and chorizo casserole, beef stew. Yummy Staffordshire oatcakes from Tunstall with all sorts of fillings are a house special; desserts include spiced apple sponge and custard. Do stay: the bedrooms at the top, with a separate entrance, are compact, cosy and en suite, with good antique furniture and super-comfortable beds. You are very welcome to bring the dogs (cold water and sausages available) but not the children. Michael the landlord has been at the helm for 40 years, the Albion is that rare thing: a traditional city pub with an individual streak.

Price	£85. Singles £70.
Rooms	2: 1 double, 1 twin.
Meals	Lunch & dinner £6.20-£9.70. Not Sunday eve.
Closed	3pm-5pm (6pm Sat, 7pm Sun).
Directions	Opp. city walls between The Newgate & River Dee.

Michael Mercer
Albion Inn
Park Street,
Chester CH1 1RN
Tel +44 (0)1244 340345
Web www.albioninnchester.co.uk

The Pheasant Inn

Tattenhall

After a hike along the Sandstone Trail, stand before the largest fireplace in Cheshire with a pint of Weetwood Old Dog. Out on the terrace, you can gaze across the Cheshire Plain all the way to Liverpool. Gloriously positioned up in the Peckforton Hills, the Pheasant has been stylishly revamped. The old laid-back feel has survived the smartening up of big beamed bars where food is informally served; there's a restaurant, too. Duck terrine with confit root vegetables, battered haddock with mushy peas and tartare sauce, game pie with red wine jus, and mulled fruit cheesecake should satisfy the most ravenous walker, while the deli boards and all-day hot beef sandwiches are equally hearty. Just perfect for weary walkers and comfort-seekers are the flurry of traditional and contemporary bedrooms, split between the inn and the quieter ivy-clad stables; go for one with a view. Beams and exposed stone abound as do fine oak and traditional darkwood furnishings, stylish fabrics, sumptuous beds and bathrooms with thick towels and indulgent toiletries.

Price	From £85. Singles from £65.
Rooms	12 twins/doubles.
Meals	Lunch & dinner £8.50-£18.95. Bar meals £3.95-£8.50. Sunday lunch £12.95.
Closed	Open all day.
Directions	Follow A5115 Christleton Road; at r'bout, 2nd exit onto A41. Left at Chester Road, left at Burwardsley Road, then left at Harthill Road. Pub on left.

Andrew Nelson
The Pheasant Inn
Higher Burwardsley, Tattenhall,
Chester CH3 9PF
Tel +44 (0)1829 770434
Web www.thepheasantinn.co.uk

The Cholmondeley Arms

Cholmondeley

As prim and proper as a Victorian schoolmistress on the outside, as stylish as Beau Brummell within: the sandblasted brick walls of this old school house rise to raftered, vaulted ceilings and large windows pull natural light into every corner. Shelves of wine hover above fat radiators, cartoons and photos nestle amongst old sporting paraphernalia, and oriental rugs sprawl beneath an auction lot of tables, pews and chairs. The glorious carved oak bar dominates the main hall and apart from the malted charms of Weetwood's Ambush and Merlin's Gold there are a staggering 55 varieties of ruinously good gin to discover, with the aid of a well-thumbed guide or one of the many charming staff. And when the dinner bell goes study the menus on antique blackboards and opt for potted rabbit and pheasant with doorstep toast and heritage piccalilli. Followed by baked cod with brown shrimps and lemon butter, and a spicy sausage and butternut squash hash cake. Rooms in the old headmaster's house behind are calm and civilised with all the comfort you need. Seldom has going back to school been this much fun.

Price	£60-£100.
Rooms	6: 5 doubles, 1 twin.
Meals	Lunch & dinner £7.25-£17.95. Not Christmas Day.
Closed	Open all day.
Directions	On A49, 6 miles north of Whitchurch.

Tim Bird & Mary McLaughlin
The Cholmondeley Arms
Cholmondeley,
Malpas SY14 8HN

Tel +44 (0)1829 720300
Web www.cholmondeleyarms.co.uk

The Bear's Paw

Warmingham

Tucked into a pretty village is a dazzlingly refurbished 19th-century inn. There's an almost baronial feel to the Bear's Paw, thanks to the polished oak panelling, the huge fireplaces, the sweeping floors, the leather bucket chairs, bookshelves and old prints and vintage photos. No stuffiness here, just cheery staff making sure you are well-watered and well-fed. Six cask ales, several from Weetwood, all local, take centre stage on the bar; there are also premium brand spirits, 12 malts and an excellent wine list. At well-spaced wooden tables are menus that blend classics with modern twists. Try game and root vegetable pie served with hand-cut chips and pickled red cabbage; vegetarian lasagne with wild mushrooms, spinach and toasted pine nuts; posh poached egg with truffle sabayon. There are deli boards and fabulous sandwiches too. Staying the night? You have 17 superb bedrooms to choose from, each boutiquey, each flaunting funky fabrics, contemporary wallpapers, media hubs and designer fittings. Bathrooms are sleek with granite tops, rain showers, and the softest towels and robes.

Price	£99-£140.
Rooms	17 doubles.
Meals	Lunch & dinner £8.95-£17.95.
Closed	Open all day.
Directions	Village signed off A530 south of Middlewich.

Andrew Nelson
The Bear's Paw
School Lane, Warmingham,
Sandbach CW11 3QN
Tel +44 (0)1270 526317
Web www.thebearspaw.co.uk

The White Lion

Barthomley

An inn since 1614 and a siege site in the Civil War, the character-oozing White Lion – wonky black and white timbers, thick thatched roof – stands beside a cobbled track close to a fine sandstone church. Step in to three gloriously unspoilt rooms, all woodsmoke and charm, wizened oak beams, ancient benches and twisted walls, tiny latticed windows and quarry-tiled floors. No music or electronic wizardry, just the crackling of log fires and a happy hubbub. Lunchtime food is listed on chalkboards as walkers and locals settle down on ancient settles at scrubbed wooden tables for hot beef and onion baguettes with chips, hearty ploughman's and Sunday roasts, washed down with well-kept pints of Marstons and Jennings real ale. Summer seating is at picnic benches on the cobbles, with pretty views onto the village.

Meals	Lunch & dinner £4.75-£7.95.
Closed	Open all day.
Directions	M6 junc. 16; 3rd exit for Alsager; left for Barthomley.

Laura Condliffe
The White Lion
Barthomley,
Crewe CW2 5PG

Tel +44 (0)1270 882242
Web www.whitelionbarthomley.com

Entry 70 Map 8

Cheshire

The Ship Inn

Wincle

You're on the edge of the Peaks so the walks stretch in every direction; the pub provides a great little guide. Michael and Cathy are friendly and professional and know what makes a good pub tick; this one is a winner all round. The two little taprooms are pleasingly simple, one with an oak-topped bar, the other with stone flags and a cast-iron range. Tuck into a hot roast pork sandwich with apple sauce or a crusty ploughman's, or choose from a broad and daily-changing menu in the dining room extension; deep-fried squid, baby clams with spaghetti, pheasant in red wine, mixed game casserole, chocolate truffle torte. Much of the produce is locally sourced and all of it is delicious. There's a designated family and hikers' room, and the pub is loved too for its beers – try a pint of J W Lees. The neat little beer garden is shaded by mature trees.

Meals	Lunch & dinner £9.45-£13.95. Not Sunday eve or Monday (except bank hols).
Closed	3pm-6pm. Mon (except bank hols).
Directions	At A54/A523 junc. at Congleton & Macclesfield take A54 for Buxton for 3 miles; right at Clulow Cross via Barlow Hill for Wincle, 1.5 miles.

Michael Hazelton & Cathy Dean
The Ship Inn
Wincle,
Macclesfield SK11 0QE

Tel +44 (0)1260 227217

Entry 71 Map 8

Sutton Hall Inn

Sutton

A grand place set in expansive grounds, this astonishing pub has been fashioned from the 480-year-old family home of the Earls of Lucan and a former convent. Inside are dark oak floors and furniture, beams and Indian rugs, crossed swords and racks of muskets – and everywhere pictures, eye-catching and interesting. Charming staff whir between seven different dining areas with effortless efficiency and smiles. Six cask ales will please all, with Flower's Original and Wincle Lord Lucan. Honest and unfussy modern British menus deliver in spadefuls: slow-roasted belly pork with baked apple, braised potatoes and whole grain mustard sauce or pan-fried sea bass with a pea and spring onion potato cake and marjoram butter. A toasty place, with log fires in winter and view-filled terraces in summer; hugely friendly, too.

Meals	Lunch & dinner £7.95-£16.95. Bar meals from £4.95.
Closed	Open all day.
Directions	See website.

Syd Foster
Sutton Hall Inn
Bullocks Lane, Sutton,
Macclesfield SK11 0HE

Tel +44 (0)1260 253211
Web www.suttonhall.co.uk

Entry 72 Map 8

Cheshire

Harrington Arms

Gawsworth

This red-brick building started life as a farmhouse in 1663 and could still be part of a working farm. The outside may have grown but the inside has barely changed – and it wasn't long ago that they were serving beer here just from the cask. Off the passageway are a bar and a quarry-tiled snug – big enough to fit a settle, a table and an open fire. Then three more public rooms: the traditionally furnished Top Parlour, the Garden Room with its magnificent baking range and the Tap Room where Friday's folk club sessions take place. The Wightmans took over in 2006 and have changed little. That includes the quality of the ale: it's said you won't get a finer pint of Robinson's than at the Harrington. Home-cooked meals are locally sourced and range from soup to sirloin steak; look out for homemade wild boar pie from the specials board.

Meals	Bar meals £3.95-£11.25. Sunday lunch £8.25. Not Sunday eve.
Closed	3pm-5pm (4pm-7pm Sun).
Directions	Off A536 at junc. with Church Lane, 2.5 miles from Macclesfield.

Andy & Caroline Wightman
Harrington Arms
Church Lane, Gawsworth,
Macclesfield SK11 9RJ

Tel +44 (0)1260 223325
Web www.harringtonarms.co.uk

Entry 73 Map 8

The Wizard

Nether Alderley

The old coaching inn is backed by magnificent leafy National Trust woodland – and there's a wizard's well out there with a legend to match. You're a world away from bustling Alderley Edge and this large rambling pub has many good things to offer: stone floors with Indian rugs, scrubbed wooden tables, an eclectic mix of prints, paintings and photos, great fare. It's a cosy and intimate place run by a bright and cheery staff. Ales come in the form of Thwaite's Original or an award-winning Storm Brewery's beer (Silk of Amnesia and Looks Like Rain Dear being just two); all are magic in a glass. Foodies won't be unhappy either; we found Gillian Pugh's roast pork belly, served with mashed potato and apple compote, and followed by deep-filled treacle tart with vanilla ice cream, a big treat. There's also a pretty sheltered patio for warm days.

Meals Lunch & dinner £7-£13.95.
Closed 3pm-5.30pm. Open all day Sat & Sun.
Directions On B5087 1.5 miles before Alderley Edge.

Martin Ainscough
The Wizard
Macclesfield Road, Nether Alderley,
Macclesfield SK10 4UB
Tel +44 (0)1625 584000
Web www.ainscoughs.co.uk

Cheshire

The Duke of Portland

Lach Dennis

A recent refurbishment has created something of a style journey at the Duke. Wander between a 1920s Parisian bistro, an arty club lounge – worn leather sofas, a futuristic stone fire – and Victorian formality... before pulling up in front of a glorious carved oak bar to order a pint of Jenning's Cocker Hoop or Ringwood Best. Menus are hearty and inventive and the provenance is impeccable. Start with naturally smoked mackerel pâté flavoured with whisky, parsley and double cream before moving on to Glyn Arthur lamb, its gravy infused with tomato, basil and slow roasted garlic, its accompaniment Cheshire potatoes and spring greens. A solid wine list complements it all and there's freshly ground Illy coffee. Under the lofty dining roof is a village pub with a great sense of style and hospitality.

Meals Lunch & dinner £9.95-£18.95.
Closed 3pm-5pm (Mon-Wed).
Directions On B5082 in village centre.

Mathew Mooney
The Duke of Portland
Penny's Lane, Lach Dennis,
Northwich CW9 7SY
Tel +44 (0)1606 46264
Web www.dukeofportland.com

Chetwode Arms

Lower Whitley

The 400-year-old, Cheshire-brick roadside inn hides a warren of small rooms and passageways. There's the bar room itself, tiny, with an open coal fire, and four more; the snuggest may be used as a private dining room. Expect low ceilings, exposed brick and beams, fresh flowers and mirrors, oodles of atmosphere and tasty food. In the dining room – opening onto a terrace that overlooks the pub's own bowling green – contented locals tuck into local game pie, confit duck with black cherry jus and rosemary mash, chilli crab cakes, roast pork knuckle, and steaks cooked on hot rocks. There are lunchtime sandwiches, salads and ploughman's, four changing guest ales on tap and the wine list favours some top vineyards from Richard's home country – South Africa. Great for judicious drinkers of wine and beer, and a super dining pub.

Meals	Lunch & dinner £12.50-£32. Sunday lunch £9.95.
Closed	3.30pm-5.30pm & all day Mon in winter. Open all day Sat & Sun.
Directions	On A49 2 miles from M56 junc. 10.

Richard Sharnok
Chetwode Arms
Street Lane, Lower Whitley,
Warrington WA4 4EN
Tel +44 (0)1925 730203
Web www.chetwodearms.org

Entry 76 Map 7

The Fox & Barrel

Cotebrook

Legend has it that a kind former landlord allowed a pursued fox to escape to the cellar. Whatever the name, this busy roadside pub buzzes with drinkers and diners in equal measure. Inside, life centres on a large bar ringed by terracotta tiles; beyond, acres of oak boards are dotted with Indian rugs. A brick fire is stacked with logs, pictures and prints fill the walls and there are plenty of snug corners in which to sup a Deuchars IPA or a Weetwood cask ale such as Wags to Witches. Convivial Gary chooses a mean wine list with his monthly favourites on the board; Aspinall's cider is soon to arrive. Generous, crowd-pleasing menus include a fish pie of smoked haddock, salmon and prawns, and Cumberland sausage with bubble and squeak mash and onion gravy. Hearty sandwiches too if time is short. There's a smart patio and pub benches on lawns with pleasant rural views. Tally-ho!

Meals	Lunch & dinner £7.95-£16.95. Sunday lunch from £9.95.
Closed	Open all day.
Directions	On A49 near Oulton Park.

Gary Kidd & Richard Cotterill
The Fox & Barrel
Forest Road, Cotebrook,
Tarporley CW6 9DZ
Tel +44 (0)1829 760529
Web www.thefoxandbarrel.com

Entry 77 Map 7

The Grosvenor Arms

Aldford

Pretty Aldford – all prim cottages and farms with barleysugar-twist chimneys and chequerboard brickwork. Not far from the old church and castle is an imposing Victorian brick and half-timber village local rejuvenated by Brunning & Price – their flagship pub. There's something for everyone in this relaxing and classy pastiche: a traditional taproom and snug with log fire, tiled floor, dozing dogs and a old photo of drunks in the stocks; an imposing part-panelled Library Room; a verdant conservatory. Find rustic kitchen tables on boards, tiles and rugs, mismatched chairs, heaps of books and a dark-wood bar with hand pumps for local beers. The menu carries something for everyone, from game pie to Thai red seafood curry, and you can eat in summer on huge tree-shaded lawns next to the village cricket pitch. Lovely.

Meals Lunch & dinner £7.95-£22.50.
Closed Open all day.
Directions 6 miles south of Chester on B5130 to Farndon & Holt.

Tracey Owen
The Grosvenor Arms
Chester Road, Aldford,
Chester CH3 6HJ
Tel +44 (0)1244 620228
Web www.grosvenorarms-aldford.co.uk

Entry 78 Map 7

Cheshire

The Yew Tree

Spurstow

Enthusiastic owners Jon and Lindsey have identified a need for their talents in this pretty corner of Cheshire. Step in to find a fresh interior with an eclectic mix of old and new and several quirky touches – including a wall and ceiling entirely papered in tartan, dedicated to the life of the Queen. There are several areas for eating and drinking including handsome snugs and everyone's welcome. The children's menu is typical of the overall level of care: not just sausages and mash but roasted vegetable pasta too – and Eton mess for pud! Beautifully kept ales (Mobberley Whirly Bird, Stone House Station Bitter) and ten wines from the glass accompany some skilled cooking – our creamy smoked haddock and salmon pie was spot on, and the sourcing is impeccable. There's a private paddock for marquee events and summer beer festivals.

Meals Lunch & bar meals from £5.95. Dinner from £9.50. Not Christmas Day.
Closed Open all day.
Directions From A49 at Bunbury turn left onto Long Lane Spurstow. 500m on left.

Jon & Lindsay Cox
The Yew Tree
Long Lane, Spurstow,
Bunbury CW6 9RD
Tel +44 (0)1829 260274
Web www.theyewtreebunbury.com

Entry 79 Map 7

The Dysart Arms

Bunbury

It is one of those rare places – all things to all people. And, with separate areas clustered round a central bar, it feels open and cosy at the same time. The 18th-century brick building protects a listed interior of scrubbed floorboards, good solid tables and chairs, pictures, prints, plants, and French windows opening to terrace and garden. There's an inglenook packed with logs, a dining area in a library, and the beers and wines are superb. They're proud, too, of their food, and rightly so: chicken liver parfait with spiced fruit chutney; seafood paella; roast lamb with herb stuffing; strawberry Eton mess. The cheeses are taken as seriously as the cask ales (try the local Weetwood or Eastgate Bitter) and the wines are thoughtfully chosen. Warm, intimate, friendly… the place runs on well-oiled wheels.

Meals	Lunch from £4.50. Bar meals £4.50-£10.25. Dinner £7.95-£16.95.
Closed	Open all day.
Directions	Off A49, 3.5 miles from Tarporley; opposite the church in Bunbury.

Gregory Williams
The Dysart Arms
Bowes Gate Road, Bunbury,
Tarporley CW6 9PH

Tel	+44 (0)1829 260183
Web	www.dysartarms-bunbury.co.uk

Entry 80 Map 7

Cheshire

Bhurtpore Inn

Aston

The extended old Cheshire-brick village farmhouse trumpets eleven real ales, countless bottled continental beers, one hundred malts, and farmhouse ciders and perry. Whatever you choose, you can soak it up with something excellent from the ever-changing menu. The pub was named after an Indian city besieged by a local army commander, and multitudinous maps, paintings and ephemera spread through the warren of rooms vividly recall this deed. Low beams sag beneath myriad water jugs, and open fires crackle in the cosy lounge, where a mongrel-mix of furniture and seating, settles, a longcase clock and absorbing local bric-a-brac add tremendous character. The home-cooked food is really tasty, with local produce at the fore, the portions generous, the choice vast, and there are curries – galore! One great little place.

Meals	Lunch & bar meals from £5.50. Dinner from £8.50. Sunday lunch, 3 courses, £18. Not Fri 2pm-6.30pm.
Closed	2.30pm-6.30pm. Open all day Fri-Sun.
Directions	Off A530, 5 miles south west of Nantwich. Follow signs for Wrenbury from turn in Aston near pottery.

Simon George
Bhurtpore Inn
Wrenbury Road, Aston,
Nantwich CW5 8DQ

Tel	+44 (0)1270 780917
Web	www.bhurtpore.co.uk

Entry 81 Map 7

The Mill House Inn

Trebarwith

You coast down a steep winding lane to the 1760s mill house in its woodland setting, with Trebarwith's spectacular beach – all surf and sand a ten-minute walk away. It's quite a setting. Back at the inn, the bar combines the best of Cornish old and Cornish new: big flagged floor, wooden tables, chapel chairs, two leather sofas by a wood-burning stove. The swanky dining room overlooking the burbling mill stream is light, elegant and very modern. Settle down to fish chowder; rib-eye steak with wild mushroom and pink peppercorn fricassée; rose, jasmine and orchid panna cotta. Bar meals are more traditional, they do lovely barbecues in summer and, be warned, a band often plays at the weekend. In keeping with the peaceful seaside setting, simple bedrooms are uncluttered with a fresh feel, and the smaller standard rooms have good shower rooms. Room character and comfort have been raised following some essential upgrading. Coastal trails lead to Tintagel, official home of the Arthurian legends. Walking, biking, surfing, crabbing... you couldn't possibly be bored.

Price	£75-£130.
Rooms	8: 7 doubles, 1 family room.
Meals	Lunch from £7.50. Dinner from £12. Sunday lunch, 3 courses, £17.85.
Closed	Open all day.
Directions	From Tintagel, B3263 south, following signs to Trebarwith Strand. Inn at bottom of steep hill.

Mark & Kep Forbes
The Mill House Inn
Trebarwith,
Tintagel PL34 0HD
Tel +44 (0)1840 770200
Web www.themillhouseinn.co.uk

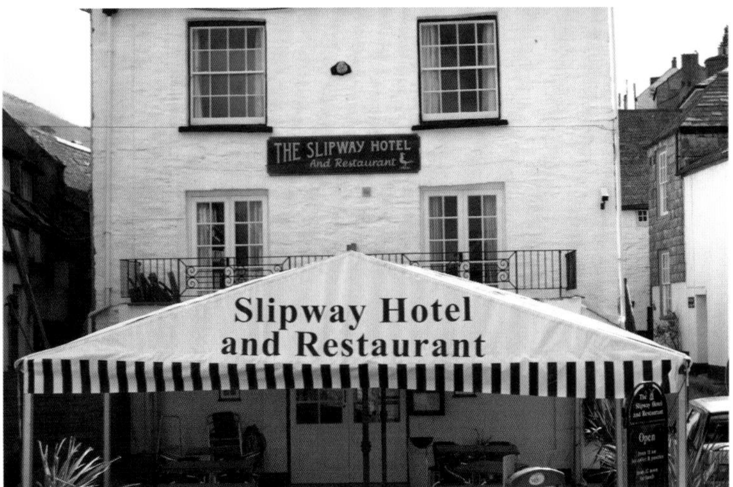

Slipway Hotel

Port Isaac

Leave your car at the top and approach on foot. To arrive unflustered (the streets are narrow) is the best way to appreciate this charming Cornish fishing village. At the Slipway, a modest bar area plays second fiddle to the front terrace with its prime views of the working harbour, beach and sea. Sup Sharp's ales as seagulls wheel overhead before tucking into the freshest of fresh crab sandwiches (we're talking 'food yards' here, not miles!). If walking the coast path or surfing drums up more of an appetite then move into the galleried restaurant – once a chandlery – for some serious fishiness. You could start with local scallops with pancetta and black pudding salad before diving into sea bass on crayfish and chilli tagliatelle with garlic and rocket dressing. If your appetite is hearty, finish with lemon tart with clotted cream, or a Cornish cheese board with red onion chutney. Bedrooms, little havens of modernity with stylish bathrooms and wooden furniture – some with sloping floors, some at the back – offer true shelter from a storm. Ask for a balcony and a sea view.

Price	£90-£140. Family suites £130-£180. Singles £67.50-£97.50.
Rooms	10: 8 twins/doubles, 2 family suites.
Meals	Lunch from £6.25. Dinner from £13.25.
Closed	Open all day.
Directions	Opposite harbour & beach in village centre.

Mark & Kep Forbes
Slipway Hotel
Middle Street,
Port Isaac PL29 3RH
Tel +44 (0)1208 880264
Web www.portisaachotel.com

The Gurnard's Head

Zennor

The coastline is magical and the hike to St Ives hard to beat. Secret beaches appear at low tide, cliffs tumble down to the water and wild flowers streak the land pink in summer. As for the pub, you couldn't hope for a better base. It's earthy, warm, stylish and friendly, with airy interiors, colourwashed walls, stripped wooden floors and log fires at both ends of the bar. Maps and local art hang on the walls, books fill every shelf; if you can't finish one, take it home and post it back. Rooms are warm and cosy, simple and spotless, with superb mattresses, throws over armchairs, Roberts radios and, in the suite, a lovely big tub. Downstairs, super food, all homemade, can be eaten wherever you want: in the bar, in the restaurant or out in the garden in good weather. Snack on rustic delights – confit duck, grilled figs – or tuck into more substantial treats: sole with muscat grapes and new potatoes, braised beef with colcannon, spiced chocolate soup with hazelnut meringue. Picnics are easily arranged, there's bluegrass folk music in the bar most Mondays, and the St Ives-Penzance bus runs right outside – a huge plus.

Price	£95-£165. Singles from £75. Half-board from £70 p.p.
Rooms	7: 4 doubles, 3 twins/doubles.
Meals	Lunch from £16.50. Dinner, 3 courses, from £26.50. Sunday lunch, 3 courses, £21.
Closed	Open all day.
Directions	On B3306 between St Ives & St Just, 2 miles west of Zennor, at head of village of Treen.

Charles & Edmund Inkin
The Gurnard's Head
Zennor,
St Ives TR26 3DE

Tel +44 (0)1736 796928
Web www.gurnardshead.co.uk

The Queen's Hotel

St Ives

It rises from the roadside in magnificent granite blocks, hung with flowers in season. A fresh wind has blown through this pub, at the heart of wonderful St Ives: now the interior is open-plan and upbeat. Perch on a red bar stool at the impressive white marble-topped bar and choose from St Austell's fine ales – HSD will see you reeling – or some good old Cornish Rattler cider. Pick a 45 to spin on Neythan's vintage jukebox and head to a well-scrubbed candlelit table, or a tartan bench seat by the fireplace. Matt Perry's menus are constantly evolving and have big flavours based on rustic French and Italian recipes alongside sturdy old-fashioned English offerings: try lamb faggot with crispy belly pork, carrot purée, cabbage and bacon and onion gravy; finish with orange posset, marmalade ice cream and shortbread. When you feel sleep beckons, you have eight light, cosy, modern bedrooms to choose from, each with vintage furniture and a local coastal theme. Bathrooms are simple but spotless. Awake refreshed and ready to stride south, along some of the finest coastline in Cornwall.

Price	£60-£150.
Rooms	8: 6 doubles, 2 triples.
Meals	Lunch & bar meals from £5. Dinner from £8. Sunday lunch, 3 courses, £14. Not Mon eves (Jan-Feb).
Closed	Open all day.
Directions	Sent on booking.

Neythan Hayes
The Queen's Hotel
High Street,
St Ives TR26 1RR

Tel +44 (0)1736 796468
Web www.queenshotelstives.com

The Old Coastguard

Mousehole

The Old Coastguard hugs the coast and gazes east towards St Michael's Mount and the Lizard peninsula. The lush palm-filled garden has lawns that run down to the harbour wall and just offshore lies St Clement's Isle, former home to an ancient hermit. But things are far from spartan here now and Charles and Edmund are bringing their unique style and experience to this large Victorian building. Views flood in to bar and restaurant via floor to ceiling glass windows and there's an effortless informality to the airy interiors. You can also expect food of the highest and freshest calibre: sardines on toast, cod with carrots and parsley sauce, and vanilla panna cotta with pink rhubarb. A well-chosen wine list, plus local ales, ciders and much more. Upstairs are fourteen uncluttered, light and stylish bedrooms of great variety and all with views of sea or Mousehole and its boat-filled harbour: many have balconies for that first al fresco sortie in the morning to watch the sun rise. The Penwith peninsular beckons so head west for the Minack theatre, then north to Zennor and St Ives. Wonderful.

Price	£110-£195. Half-board £150-£235. Ask about seasonal offers.
Rooms	14: 10 doubles, 2 twins/doubles, 1 family room, 1 suite.
Meals	Set lunch from £14. Dinner, 3 courses, from £25. Sunday lunch, 2 courses, £17.50.
Closed	Open all day.
Directions	Take A30 to Penzance then Land's End. Signs to Newlyn & Mousehole. Hotel on left immed. as you enter Mousehole. Limited parking or public car park next door; £2 on departure.

Charles & Edmund Inkin
The Old Coastguard
The Parade, Mousehole,
Penzance TR19 6PR

Tel	+44 (0)1736 731222
Web	www.oldcoastguardhotel.co.uk

The Coldstreamer

Gulval

The Coldstreamer dates from 1895 and stands in the middle of the village opposite the church. It has one foot in the country and one foot in town – Penzance is a short drive or a good walk. There's a terrace at the front where you can catch the morning sun, a wood-burner in the bar for winter nights. Inside, the colour is red in honour of the Coldstream guards. You can order a pint of Betty Stoggs at the bar, grab the daily papers, browse a fine collection of Penzance photographs, try your hand at bagatelle. Excellent food – as important as the beer – waits in the snug restaurant (low ceilings, smart colours, exposed stone walls). Meat is from Cornwall, fish landed at Newlyn, vegetables from a local farm shop, so dig into cauliflower soup with truffle oil, seared venison with juniper, fish stew with saffron mash, tarte tatin with bay leaf ice cream. Rooms above have a warm feel – smart carpets, crisp linen, comfy beds, excellent bathrooms – and the English breakfast is superb. St Michael's Mount, St Ives, The Lizard and the coast all wait; the heliport for the Scillies is tantalisingly close.

Price	£70-£85. Half board £50-£60 p.p.
Rooms	3: 2 doubles, 1 twin/double.
Meals	Lunch from £8. Dinner from £11. Sunday lunch, 3 courses, £16.50.
Closed	Open all day.
Directions	B3311 to St Ives; 1 mile north east of Penzance. Opposite church.

Richard Tubb
The Coldstreamer
Gulval,
Penzance TR18 3BB
Tel +44 (0)1736 362072
Web www.coldstreamer-penzance.co.uk

The Bush Inn

Morwenstow

After a blowy walk along the cliffs, what better than to come home to this fine little place? Once a monastic rest house, its oldest parts date back to AD950; note the Celtic piscina carved from serpentine in one wall. Slate-flagged floors, a huge stone fireplace and lovely old wooden furnishings in the bar preserve the timeless character of an immutable place. Food is served all day in two charming contemporary dining rooms with old pine tables and yellow-washed walls, and picture windows for views of farmland and sea. Menus include beef and lamb from neighbouring farms, Cornish seafood and vegetables from the kitchen garden; venison, pork and juniper terrine, sea bass with red onion, fennel and parmesan risotto. Weary walkers are revived by excellent beers, robust snacks and a lively buzz.

Meals	Lunch & dinner £8-£18.
Closed	Open all day.
Directions	Follow signs for Morwenstow off A39, 9 miles north of Bude.

Rob & Edwina Tape
The Bush Inn
Crosstown, Morwenstow,
Bude EX23 9SR
Tel +44 (0)1288 331242
Web www.bushinn-morwenstow.co.uk

Entry 88 Map 1

Cornwall

The Rising Sun Inn

Altarnun

Beginning life as a farm on the edge of Bodmin Moor in the 1600s, the property later became a 'hole in the wall'. The main bar is all no-nonsense Delabole flagstones and oak floors surrounded by wall settles with long padded cushions; add guns and prints, archaic needlework verse, beams, plenty of woodchip and delicately tobacco tinged paint tones – the smugglers' breath perhaps? Things are all very local hereabouts, the barman brews the Penpont Ale just a mile away and there's also Skinner's Spriggan or Betty Stoggs. Next door in the old cattle shed is a more contemporary dining area, its exposed stone walls hung with local art. After a blow on the moors the oxtail and root vegetable broth with rosemary suet dumplings followed by sticky toffee pudding will put the colour back in your cheeks. Hard to leave? There's even a campsite.

Meals	Lunch £4-£14. Bar meals £4-£10. Dinner £4-£20. Sunday lunch, 3 courses, £20.
Closed	2pm-6pm. Open all day Sat, Sun & bank hols.
Directions	Off A30 in Altarnun village, through with church on left; at T-junc. left (pub signed).

Andy Mason
The Rising Sun Inn
Altarnun PL15 7SN
Tel +44 (0)1566 86636
Web www.therisingsuninn.co.uk

Entry 89 Map 1

St Kew Inn

St Kew

Lost down a maze of lanes in a secluded wooded valley, the St Kew is a grand old inn originally built in the 15th-century for the masons working on the church. It is an irresistibly friendly, chatty place with a huge range and a warming fire, a dark slate floor, winged settles and a terrific unspoilt atmosphere – no pub paraphernalia here, but do look out for the resident ghost who has been spotted in the past. Meat hooks hang from a high ceiling and earthenware flagons embellish the mantelpiece in the bar. Local St Austell ales are served in the traditional way, straight from the barrel, and the food is bang up-to-date. Try mussels with cider, cream and chives, fish and chips with pea purée and tartare sauce, warm coconut Bakewell tart. In summer, the big streamside garden is the place to be.

Meals	Lunch & bar meals from £5.50. Dinner from £9.50. Sunday lunch, 3 courses, £19.50.
Closed	3pm-6pm.
Directions	From Wadebridge for Bude on A39 for 4 miles; left after golf club. 1 mile to St Kew Churchtown.

Sarah Allen
St Kew Inn
St Kew, Bodmin PL30 3HB
Tel +44 (0)1208 841259
Web www.stkewinn.co.uk

The Plume of Feathers

Mitchell

It was an inspired move to transform the old 16th-century coaching inn where John Wesley once preached into a warm and stylish pub-restaurant. The imaginative cooking draws an appreciative crowd and in summer food is available all day. Low stripped beams, half-panelled walls hung with modern art, fresh flowers, candle-studded pine tables and soothing lighting make this place a pleasure to walk into; it feels novel and fun. Delightful staff serve Scottish beef and local vegetables and fish at sensible prices – take Cornish fishcakes with sweet chilli sauce and dressed leaves, or grilled Dover sole with lemon butter. There are thick bacon sandwiches at lunch and delicious puddings, perhaps chilled vanilla rice pudding with spiced pineapple. The central bar is lively with TV, piped music and Sharp's Doom Bar on tap. Great value.

Meals	Lunch & bar meals from £10. Dinner from £15. Sunday lunch, 3 courses, £21.
Closed	Open all day.
Directions	Off junction of A30 & A3076 south of Newquay. In centre of Mitchell village.

Pete & Jaqui Fair
The Plume of Feathers
Mitchell, Newquay TR8 5AX
Tel +44 (0)1872 510387
Web www.theplume.info

Tinner's Arms

Zennor

Under landlords Grahame and Richard, one of Cornwall's most historic pubs thrives in the wilds of West Penwith. Close to the church in the coastal hamlet of Zennor, the 13th-century inn is pretty unspoilt with its flagstone floors, whitewashed walls and fabulously long, well-stocked bar. The food and drink have moved sharply up a gear, with lunch and evening menus changing daily – rabbit stew, roast pork belly, venison with red wine jus, hake with red pepper sauce, ales from St Austell and Sharp's. The Tinner's Arms, bursting with character and open log fires, will always be a popular stop for walkers heading for the nearby coastal paths. It's packed in summer, so spill out in the lovely large garden overlooking the sea; off-season, it could be you and the dog alone in the bar. Worth the walk from St Ives.

Meals	Lunch & bar meals from £5.25. Dinner from £9.50. Not Monday eves in winter.
Closed	3.30pm-6.30pm. Open all day April-November.
Directions	Off B3306 St Ives-St Just road, 4 miles west of St Ives.

Grahame Edwards
& Richard Motley
Tinner's Arms
Zennor, St Ives TR26 3BY
Tel +44 (0)1736 796927
Web www.tinnersarms.co.uk

Entry 92 Map 1

The Star Inn

St Just

Entrenched in the wild landscape close to Land's End is the "last proper pub in Cornwall". This 18th-century beauty, owned by the ex-mayor of St Just and its oldest and most authentic inn, proudly shirks the trappings of tourism and remains a drinkers' den. Bands of locals sink pints of Tinners Ale in the low-beamed, spick-and-span bar, old pub games thrive and the place is the hub of the local folk scene, with live music at least ten nights a month, singalongs and joke-telling all part of the Monday evening entertainment. The dimly-lit bar is jam-packed with interest and walls are littered with seafaring and mining artefacts; coals glow in the grate on wild winter days. Come for St Austell ale and the 'craic'. A free juke box, mulled wine in winter and that pub rarity: a great family room.

Meals	No food served.
Closed	Open all day.
Directions	A3071 from Penzance. On right-hand side of square in centre.

Johnny McFadden
The Star Inn
1 Fore Street, St Just,
Penzance TR19 7LL
Tel +44 (0)1736 788767
Web www.thestarinn-stjust.co.uk

Entry 93 Map 1

The Victoria Inn

Perranuthnoe

With glorious Mount's Bay (beach and coastal path) down the lane, this striking pink-washed village inn draws the crowds. Arrive early and bag a seat in the stone-walled bar sprinkled with seafaring and fishing memorabilia, or in the sunny sunken garden. Chef-landlord Stewart is making waves locally, using the best Cornish ingredients to produce some delicious pub food. For ale-lovers there's Doom Bar on tap, a perfect match for a lunchtime crab sandwich or haddock and chips. Cooking moves up a gear in the evenings, so start with a seafood and shellfish soup, move on to crispy belly of St Buryan pork with chorizo and haricot beans, and finish with a rhubarb and ginger crumble – or a plate of artisan cheeses. Built to house the masons extending the church in the 12th century, this old, old pub later became a safe house for the clergy.

Meals	Lunch & dinner £8.95-£16.75.
Closed	Sun eves. Mon (Nov-Mar).
Directions	Pub and village signed off A394 Penzance to Helston road, 4 miles east of Penzance.

Stewart & Anna Eddy
The Victoria Inn
Perranuthnoe,
Penzance TR20 9NP
Tel +44 (0)1736 710309
Web www.victoriainn-penzance.co.uk

Entry 94 Map 1

Halzephron Inn

Gunwalloe

An opera singer running a pub in a remote smuggler's inn – irresistible and only in Cornwall. Looking out across Mount's Bay towards Land's End, the rugged whitewashed inn has been taking in guests (and smuggler's: there's an underground passage) for 500 years. Come for low ceilings, stone walls, log fires and polished brass in numerous cosy eating areas around the bar. There are sea views from the roadside terrace, a lively courtyard for summer afternoons, and a small garden overlooking fields. Lunch on hearty homemade food – perhaps cheese soufflé, seafood risotto or fish pie, baked American cheesecake (there's a tempting menu for juniors, too) – then walk it all off on a clifftop walk to Gunwalloe's 13th-century church down beside the sand. Angela, exuberant and charming, runs this popular coastal inn with aplomb.

Meals	Lunch from £5.95. Dinner from £10.50. Bar meals from £5.95. Sunday lunch, 3 courses, £22.50.
Closed	2.30pm-6pm (6.30pm in winter).
Directions	From Helston, A3083, signed The Lizard. Pass Culdrose air base, then right, signed Gunwalloe. 2 miles and inn on left after houses.

Angela Thomas
Halzephron Inn
Gunwalloe,
Helston TR12 7QB
Tel +44 (0)1326 240406
Web www.halzephron-inn.co.uk

Entry 95 Map 1

The New Inn

Manaccan

Genuinely unspoilt country pubs in tourist-trade Cornwall are hard to find, but this rustic thatched cottage close to The Lizard is a treasure. Access is via tortuously narrow lanes, which gives Penny's pub that rare 'lost in the old country' feel. Many opt to stroll over from Helford for heart-warming pub grub, refreshing pints of Doom Bar and a natter with the locals. Don't be fooled by the new thatch and a lick of whitewash, the bar remains delightfully unspoilt, with its beam and plank ceiling, built-in wall settles, walls hung with local art, crackling log fire, and time-honoured pub games. Refuel on lunchtime sandwiches or bowls of moules marinière with crusty dipping bread; steak and ale pie or blackboard-listed smoked haddock risotto and lamb shank with redcurrant jus. Head for the rose-filled garden when the sun shines.

Meals Lunch & dinner £4.50-£14.
Closed Open all day.
Directions Manaccan signed off B3293 between Helston and St Keverne. Follow signs and narrow lanes through Mawgan; pub in village centre.

Penny Williams
The New Inn
Manaccan,
Helston TR12 6HA
Tel +44 (0)1326 231323
Web www.newinnmanaccan.co.uk

Entry 96 Map 1

Cornwall

The Ferryboat Inn

Helford Passage

The position is unbeatable. You're bang on the water with boats to hire or the ferry on hand to whisk you across the magical Helford river. It's one of those rare spots that has resisted the urge to enter the 21st century, and is all the more popular for it. Inside you find rugs on slate floors, a fire that burns every day, a smart restaurant tucked into the corner and an oyster bar that hums with life in summer (the pub is owned by local oyster farmers). Outside, the allure of a watery view draws a happy crowd to the terrace, and even in late October the place was buzzing. St Austell ales are on tap for your pleasure, there's a good selection of wines by the glass and local nourishment to fortify walkers and boatmen alike: French onion soup, fish pie, west country cheeses. Come for Sunday lunch or live music in summer.

Meals Lunch & dinner from £8.50.
Closed Sun eves & Mon in winter.
Directions See website.

Ben Wright & Robin Hancock
The Ferryboat Inn
Helford Passage,
Falmouth TR11 5LB
Tel +44 (0)1326 250625
Web www.wrightbros.eu.com/ferryboatinn

Entry 97 Map 1

Trengilly Wartha Inn

Constantine

Well tucked down steep and twisting lanes, in the verdant heaven that is the Helford estuary, is this friendly Cornish inn. Grab a pint of Skinner's Trengilly Gold or St Austell HSD and enjoy a stroll in the six acres of old orchard with pond – and a gravelled pergola with ingenious underfloor heating. The main bar is a cracker with a wealth of mini-snugs formed by mid-height wooden settles, beer mats tacked to beams, cricketing memorabilia, local black and white photos, local paintings, and a display of some of the over 150 wines on offer; there are 40 malts too. Chef Nick Tyler has 20 years under his belt here and keeps it fresh, local and seasonal; a shame not to try the Falmouth River mussels with onion, white wine, cream and chips, or the crab thermidor that comes with homemade granary bread.

Meals	Lunch from £4.80. Bar meals & dinner from £7.20. Sunday lunch, 3 courses, £20.
Closed	3pm-6pm.
Directions	Approaching Falmouth on A39, follow signs to Constantine. On approach to village, inn signed left, then right.

Lisa & William Lea
Trengilly Wartha Inn
Constantine,
Falmouth TR11 5RP
Tel +44 (0)1326 340332
Web www.trengilly.co.uk

The Pandora Inn

Mylor Bridge

Yachtsmen moor at the end of the pontoon that reaches into the creek. The building itself is special: thatched, 13th-century, and rebuilt following a recent devastating fire. Originally The Passage House, the pub was renamed in memory of the *Pandora*, a naval ship sent to Tahiti to capture the mutineers of Captain Bligh's *Bounty*. The pub keeps its traditional layout on several levels, along with a few panelled walls, polished flagged floors, snug alcoves, log fires, maritime mementoes, and amazingly low wooden ceilings. The bar food has something to please everyone, with fresh seafood dominating the specials board. Arrive early in summer – by car or by boat; the place gets packed and parking is tricky. On winter weekdays it's blissfully peaceful; the postprandial walking along wooded creekside paths is a delight.

Meals	Lunch & dinner £8.50-£14.95.
Closed	Open all day.
Directions	A39 from Truro; B3292 for Penryn & follow Mylor Bridge signs; descend steeply to Restronguet.

John Milan
The Pandora Inn
Restronguet, Mylor Bridge,
Falmouth TR11 5ST
Tel +44 (0)1326 372678
Web www.pandorainn.com

The Roseland Inn

Philleigh

Beside a peaceful parish church, two miles from the King Harry Ferry, a cob-built Cornish treasure with its own microbrewery (their Gull-able is award winning). The front courtyard is bright with blossom in spring and climbing roses in summer. Indoors: old settles with scatter cushions, worn slate floors, low black beams and winter log fires. Local photographs, gig-racing memorabilia and a corner dedicated to rugby trophies scatter the walls. Spotlessly kept, it attracts locals and visitors in search of good food – such as local farm meats and fish landed at St Mawes. Dishes range from decent sandwiches to scallops with belly pork and white onion sauce, and roast duck with raspberry jus. Staff are full of smiles – even when the pub doubles as the Roseland Rugby Club clubhouse on winter Saturday nights.

Meals	Lunch & dinner £8.50-£13.95. Sunday lunch £9.95.
Closed	3pm-6pm. Open all day weekends & in summer.
Directions	Off A3078 St Mawes road or via King Harry Ferry from Truro (Feock) to Philleigh.

Phil & Debbie Heslip
The Roseland Inn
Philleigh,
Truro TR2 5NB
Tel +44 (0)1872 580254
Web www.roselandinn.co.uk

Entry 100 Map 1

Cornwall

The Kings Head

Ruanlanihorne

A pub with a heart. Niki and Andrew are warm, friendly and love what they do. Find pine-backed stools, a comfy sofa, a real fire. An impressive collection of tea cups hangs from the ceiling, a window sparkles with coloured bottles and all is quirky and fun. Off the main bar is a second dining room with hunting prints and wood-burner and a friendly carpeted dining room with gleaming tables and Windsor chairs. Ales are from Skinners in Truro, fish from St Mawes. Tuck into crab pâté, the famous Ruan slow-roasted duck with pepper sauce, a duo of local sausages and a fabulous Cornish sirloin of beef with tip-top Yorkshire pudding on Sunday. The quiet little village has a church with a Norman font and a creek that is a haven for waders and waterfowl… behind is the Roseland countryside; perfect for walkers and watersporters.

Meals	Lunch from £5.15. Dinner from £9.95. Sunday lunch, 3 courses, £21.60.
Closed	2.30pm-6pm. Sun eves & Mon all day in winter.
Directions	Village signed off A3078 Tregony-St Mawes road.

Andrew & Niki Law
The Kings Head
Ruanlanihorne, Ruan High Lanes,
Truro TR2 5NX
Tel +44 (0)1872 501263
Web www.kingsheadruan.co.uk

Entry 101 Map 1

The Crown Inn

Lanlivery

You are on the bucolic Saint's Way, along which Irish drovers used to 'fat walk' the cattle from Padstow to Fowey before setting sail for France. Walkers still stop by for sustenance. Most of the 12th-century longhouse's flagged floors have been carpeted, but the deep granite-lined clome oven remains and a country mood prevails – the Crown is the hub of the village. Three areas ramble: the largest for dining, the conservatory for the sun, and the classic, granite-floored bar for foaming pints of Betty Stoggs or Knocker Ale. Tasty food comes courtesy of fine Cornish produce, and is cooked to order: mackerel pâté with toasted organic bread, crab gratin, braised shoulder of local lamb, Cornish rump steak with pepper sauce and all the trimmings. There's a decent wine list and the pretty garden has a view of the church tower.

Meals	Lunch & dinner £8.95-£14.95. Bar meals £3.95-£10.95.
Closed	Open all day.
Directions	Signed off A390 between Lostwithiel & St Blazey. Pub opp. church.

Andy Brotheridge
The Crown Inn
Lanlivery,
Bodmin PL30 5BT
Tel +44 (0)1208 872707
Web www.wagtailinns.com

The Finnygook Inn

Crafthole

A treat awaits those who climb up to this quirky inn. Built into the hill with a modest façade, you don't expect what you find within: five-mile views over hill and water back to Plymouth. But the Finnygook has more than just its top vantage point. Stylish interiors, friendly staff, super food and local ales all combine to ensure you go home happy. The back room has the old-world charm – a roaring fire that burns both sides, low beams, stripped floors – while the front room takes in the vista and has walls of books curling around you. You can pluck weighty tomes from the shelves to browse while you dig into a good lunch, perhaps carrot and coriander soup, local plaice with new potatoes, pancakes with bananas and maple syrup. Afterwards, repent on the beach at Freathy or pick up the coastal path and drink in the sea air.

Meals	Lunch from £9.95. Bar meals from £5. Dinner from £10.50. Sunday lunch, 3 courses, £20.95.
Closed	Mon in winter.
Directions	From Torpoint A374 to Antony. After 5 miles turn left, then right at T-junc. 3 miles, left and pub on right.

Bruce Brunning
The Finnygook Inn
Crafthole,
Torpoint PL11 3BQ
Tel +44 (0)1503 230338
Web www.finnygook.co.uk

The Derby Arms

Witherslack

There's been a fresh lick of paint for this traditional local, and its façade now shines. Behind lies a hugely comfortable and very individual pub. Step into a stylish series of candlelit rooms, aglow with rug-strewn floors, cream and red walls, some rather grand paintings, polished period furniture, merry log fires, old stone fireplaces, dogs and booted walkers. The central bar heaves with hand pumps dispensing Cumbrian microbrewery ales (including Dent Aviator), hand-pressed juices from Witherslack, and heaps of wines by the glass. Bag a seat by the fire and settle in for supper; the changing menu announces a crowd-pleasing mix of traditional and modern pub dishes, much prepared from fresh local produce. Start with own-smoked duck breast, follow with sirloin steak with peppercorn sauce or butternut squash risotto, end with sticky toffee pudding. It's super civilised yet nicely laid-back, so stay the night. Upstairs are six refurbished bedrooms with old brass beds, period furnishings, crisp linen, slate-tiled bathrooms, a couple of claw-foot baths, and peaceful country views. After continental breakfast, explore the southern Lakes.

Price	£65-£85.
Rooms	6 doubles.
Meals	Lunch & dinner £8.95-£15.25.
Closed	3pm-5.30pm. Open all day Fri-Sun.
Directions	Witherslack is signed off A590 midway between Kendal and Grange-over-Sands.

Adam Thorpe
The Derby Arms
Witherslack,
Grange-over-Sands LA11 6RN

Tel	+44 (0)15395 52207
Web	www.ainscoughs.co.uk

The Hare & Hounds

Bowland Bridge

Immerse yourself in the glorious Winster Valley to find a 17th-century coaching inn delightfully restored. Kerry Parsons and her team have worked miracles, unearthing stone flagged floors, beams, and cosy fireplaces. They welcome you warmly and on chilly days the wood-burner belts out the heat. Eat in one of the comfortable bars or the elegant private dining room; enjoy a pint of Hare of the Dog while you choose what to have for lunch. The seasonal menu might include a pork, sweet chilli and black pudding terrine, followed by homemade beef and ale pie and steamed vegetables; most ingredients come from the farm around the corner or elsewhere in the valley. Homemade puddings may include delicious sticky chocolate parfait with a tangy orange sauce... it's just as well this is hearty walking country. If you're going to make a night of it, settle down in cosy bedrooms – not huge, but bursting with fabulous fabrics; some have roll top baths. There are pretty outside eating areas with long views over the fells, and you are a short drive from the shores of Lake Windermere – and bustling Bowness.

Price	£85-£145.
Rooms	3 doubles.
Meals	Lunch, 2 courses, £10. Bar meals from £5. Dinner from £10.25. Sunday lunch, 2 courses, £12.95.
Closed	Open all day.
Directions	Sent on booking.

Kerry Parsons
The Hare & Hounds
Bowland Bridge LA11 6NN
Tel +44 (0)1539 568333
Web www.hareandhoundsbowlandbridge.co.uk

Masons Arms

Cartmel Fell

A perfect Lakeland inn tucked away two miles inland from Lake Windermere. You're on the side of a hill with huge views across lush fields to Scout Scar in the distance. In summer, all pub life decants onto a spectacular terrace – a sitting room in the sun – where window boxes and flower beds tumble with colour. The inn dates from the 16th century and is impossibly pretty. The bar is properly traditional with roaring fires, flagged floors, wavy beams, a cosy snug… and a menu of 70 bottled beers to quench your thirst. Rustic elegance upstairs comes courtesy of stripped floors, country rugs and muted walls in the first-floor dining room – so grab a window seat for fabulous views and order delicious food, anything from a sandwich to Cumbrian duck. Suites are contemporary and gorgeous, with cool colours, fabulous beds, gleaming bathrooms and Bang & Olufsen TVs. Self-catering cottages, equally immaculate, come with fancy kitchens (breakfast can be served in the bar or hampers can be arranged); best of all, you have your own private terrace, so order a meal in the restaurant and they'll bring it to you here.

Price	£75-£140. Cottages £110-£165.
Rooms	5 + 2: 5 apartments. 2 self-catering cottages: 1 for 2-4, 1 for 2-6.
Meals	Breakfast hampers £15-£25. Lunch from £6.95. Bar meals from £9.95. Dinner from £14.95.
Closed	Open all day.
Directions	M6 junc. 36; A590 west, then A592 north. 1st right after Fell Foot Park. Straight ahead for 2.5 miles. On left after sharp right-hand turn.

John & Diane Taylor
Masons Arms
Cartmel Fell,
Grange-over-Sands LA11 6NW
Tel +44 (0)15395 68486
Web www.strawberrybank.com

The Punch Bowl Inn

Crosthwaite

You're away from Lake Windermere in a small village encircled by a tangle of lanes that defeat most tourists. A church stands next door; the odd bride ambles out in summer, bell ringers practise on Friday mornings. But while the Punch Bowl sits in a sleepy village lost to the world and doubles up as the local post office, it is actually a seriously fancy inn. It was rescued from neglect and after a top-to-toe renovation it now sparkles. Outside, honeysuckle climbs on old stone walls, inside four fires keep you warm in winter. A clipped elegance runs throughout: leather sofas in a beamed sitting room, candles in vases on dining room tables, an old farmhouse table in the restaurant crammed with brandies and malts. Dine on succulent roast Cumbrian lamb with duck-fat potatoes, creamed leeks and a mint jus, finish with a perfectly executed chocolate fondant pudding, then retire to a fabulous room with bold fabrics, flat-screen TV, Roberts radio and a bathroom with a heated floor. Four rooms have huge views down the Lyth valley. It's a townie's dream of what a country inn should be.

Price	£95-£235. Suite £225-£305. Singles from £75.
Rooms	9: 5 doubles, 1 twin/double, 2 four-posters, 1 suite.
Meals	Lunch from £5. Dinner, 3 courses, £30-£35.
Closed	Open all day.
Directions	M6 junc. 36, then A590 for Newby Bridge. Right onto A5074, then right for Crosthwaite after 3 miles. Pub on southern flank of village.

Abigail Lloyd
The Punch Bowl Inn
Crosthwaite,
Kendal LA8 8HR

Tel +44 (0)15395 68237
Web www.the-punchbowl.co.uk

Drunken Duck Inn

Barngates

Afternoon tea can be taken in the garden, where lawns run down to Black Tarn and Greek gods gaze upon jumping fish. You're up on the hill, away from the crowds, cradled by woods and highland fell. Huge views from the terrace shoot off for miles to towering Lakeland peaks. Roses ramble on the veranda, stone walls double as flower beds and burst with colour. As for the Duck, she may be old, but she sure is pretty, so step into a world of airy interiors: stripped floors in a beamed bar, timber-framed walls in the restaurant. Wander at will and find open fires, grandfather clocks, rugs on the floor, exquisite art. They brew their own beer, have nine bitters on tap and the food is utterly delicious: diver-caught scallops, roasted and served with slow confit of pork; fillet of monkfish with crab risotto and sauce gribiche. Bedrooms are dreamy, smartly dressed in crisp white linen, with colours courtesy of Farrow & Ball and peaty water straight off the fell. Rooms in the main house are snug in the eaves; those across the courtyard are crisply uncluttered and indulgent.

Price	£95-£285. Singles from £71.25.
Rooms	17: 15 doubles, 2 twins.
Meals	Lunch from £5. Dinner, 3 courses, £30-£35.
Closed	Open all day.
Directions	West from Ambleside on A593, then left at Clappersgate for Hawkshead on B5286. After 2 miles turn right, signed. Up hill to inn.

Stephanie Barton
Drunken Duck Inn
Barngates,
Ambleside LA22 0NG

Tel +44 (0)15394 36347
Web www.drunkenduckinn.co.uk

Queens Head Hotel

Troutbeck

Nowhere are the views as majestic as on the Kirkstone pass – and there's woodsmoke in the air as you approach this classic old Lakeland inn. Inside: a warren of fascinating rooms and a flagged bar created from a carved Elizabethan four-poster – reputed to have come through the ceiling and never returned. Old instruments hang above beams, stuffed birds and beasts gaze down from mantelpieces, ramblers tuck into their suppers and dogs recover before blazing fires. The dining area is newer but it's the food that is a major draw: earthy, dependable and chalked up on the boards each day; homemade black pudding; fish pie, slow-braised lamb shank; sticky toffee pudding. There are fine beers, eight wines by the glass, plenty of choice, small portions for kids (sausages, mussels), and desserts for hearty hikers. At the front are splendid views; the bedrooms are a treat, too, some peacefully positioned in the barn opposite. Neat, compact, refurbished with an elegant farmhouse feel, they sport four-posters, relaxing colours, unusual fabrics, and wind-up alarm clocks so you don't miss breakfast!

Price	£120-£150. Singles £75-£90. Half-board from £80 p.p.
Rooms	15: 3 doubles, 2 twins/doubles, 5 four-posters. Barn: 4 doubles, 1 four-poster.
Meals	Lunch from £7.50. À la carte from £11.95. Dinner, 3 courses, £20.
Closed	Open all day.
Directions	Exit M6 at junc. 36, A591 dir. Ambleside. At mini r'bout right on A592 signed Ullswater/ Kirkstone Pass. 3 miles, on left.

Ian Dutton
Queens Head Hotel
Town Head, Troutbeck,
Windermere LA23 1PW

Tel +44 (0)15394 32174
Web www.queensheadtroutbeck.co.uk

George and Dragon

Clifton

Charles Lowther has found a chef who does perfect justice to the slow-grow breeds of beef, pork and lamb produced on the Lowther Estate – and you'll find lovely wines to match, 16 by the glass. Ales and cheeses are local, berries and mushrooms are foraged, vegetables are home-grown… and his signature starter, twice-baked cheese soufflé with a hint of spinach – is divine. As for the long low coaching inn, it's been beautifully restored by craftsmen using wood, slate and stone, and painted in colours in tune with the period. Bare wooden tables, comfy sofas, intimate alcoves and crackling fires make this a delightful place to dine and unwind; old prints and archive images tell stories of the 800-year-old estate's history. Outside is plenty of seating and a lawned play area beneath fruit trees. Upstairs are ten bedrooms of varying sizes (some small, some large and some above the bar), perfectly decorated in classic country style. Carpeting is Cumbrian wool, beds are new, ornaments come with Lowther history, showers are walk-in, baths (there are two) are roll top, and breakfast is fresh and delicious.

Price	£90-£145. Singles from £70.
Rooms	10 twins/doubles.
Meals	Lunch & dinner from £11.50.
Closed	Open all day.
Directions	On A6 at end of Clifton village, just south of Penrith and M6 (junc. 40).

Juno & Charles Lowther
George and Dragon
Clifton,
Penrith CA10 2ER
Tel +44 (0)1768 865381
Web www.georgeanddragonclifton.co.uk

The Plough

Kirkby Lonsdale

This rambling 19th-century roadside inn has had mixed fortunes down the years but now it's back with innumerable bells and whistles. Outside is a pleasant paved patio with chunky furniture for lunch on a good day; inside is a vast open space full of comfortable corners. Expect nicely battered vintage furniture, polished oak floors, colourful rugs and wood-burning stoves. An interesting menu offers 'small plates' alongside pub classics, that include salt and pepper squid with soy and sesame dressing, crispy fried whitebait, mussels with black bean sauce and lamb koftas – perfect mini-bites to accompany a well-kept pint of Kirkby Lonsdale bitter. On the specials board, you might find confit duck leg, hash browns and damson sauce. Upstairs, five glamorous and spacious bedrooms await, dressed with pale carpets, fat mattresses and crisp linen; many have lovely views over the fells. Bathrooms are stunning, all with claw-foot roll top baths; the spectacular 'Torsin' flaunts a double monsoon shower, double sinks and toasty warm tiles. An irresistible addition to accommodation in the Lakes!

Price	£115-£165. Suites £165-£195.
Rooms	5: 3 doubles, 2 suites.
Meals	Lunch from £8.95. Bar meals from £5.95. Dinner from £10.50.
Closed	Open all day.
Directions	See website.

Abigail Lloyd
The Plough
Cow Brow, Lupton,
Carnforth LA6 1PJ

Tel +44 (0)15395 67700
Web www.theploughatlupton.co.uk

Mardale Inn

Bampton

Though close to the M6 at Shap, this area east of the Lakes is much overlooked, with its high fells and romantic Haweswater. The hub of the village is its pub – all modern stone flags, exposed stone and brickwork, beams and open fireplaces, nifty lighting and good use of space. Chunky wooden tables and chairs encourage a look at the menu: try potted Morecambe Bay shrimps or sea bass on lemon and coriander mash. Finish with toffee pudding and caramel sauce, or a local cheese platter – nothing a dose of harsh fell walking wouldn't put right. Sebastian oversees proceedings and the feeling is modern, but this is still 'the local' to folk nearby so you'll be rubbing shoulders with Cumbrians quaffing great local beers. Walk the dog to Haweswater where a golden eagle soars high above its dark surface.

Meals	Lunch & dinner £9.95-£19.25.
Closed	Open all day.
Directions	Bampton is signed from A6 at Shap or B5320 south of Penrith.

Seb Hindley
Mardale Inn
Bampton, Penrith CA10 2RQ
Tel +44 (0)1931 713244
Web www.mardaleinn.co.uk

Entry 112 Map 11

Cumbria

The Yanwath Gate Inn

Yanwath

It was built as a toll gate in 1683 – hence the name. Known to locals as the Yat, the old pub has gained a reputation for its food, locally sourced and served in hearty portions. The place is immaculate, the young staff are attentive and the landlord remains loyal to the pub's roots, so you may eat anywhere, including the sunny sheltered patio at the back. Walk in to a characterful, dimly-lit bar, all cosy corners and crackling fire, background music and happy chatter. Beyond is a light, airy and raftered dining room. The menu depends on fresh deliveries every day including Cumbrian meat and plenty of fish, and there's homemade food for children, from pizza to beefburgers and fishcakes. Wines come from an excellent merchant's in Kendal, beers include the fruity and full-flavoured Doris's 90th Birthday Ale.

Meals	Lunch & dinner £12-£25.
Closed	Open all day.
Directions	On B5320 south-west of A6 & Penrith; 2.5 miles from M6 junc. 40.

Matt Edwards
The Yanwath Gate Inn
Yanwath, Penrith CA10 2LF
Tel +44 (0)1768 862386
Web www.yanwathgate.com

Entry 113 Map 11

Highland Drove

Great Salkeld

Yards from the Norman church with its keep-like tower (protection against marauding Scots), the old wooden front door leads you into a flagged bar – cosy, warm, civilised. There's a bar-dining area with easy leather chairs and pine tables, and a popular games room with pool. With open log fires, tartan, brick and timber, this is a spruce, 21st-century inn that pleases drinkers, diners and walkers. Named after the rugged cattle that were brought down from Scotland by drovers to market, the dining room has a Highland lodge feel, its great windows gazing to the lush Pennines. Tuck into wild game terrine, Lakeland venison Wellington with red wine jus, or steak and ale pie, followed by sticky toffee pudding. Beers are from the cask, wines are well-chosen. Or keep things simple with a fresh baguette in the bar.

Meals	Lunch & dinner £7.95-£18.95. Sunday lunch £9.95.
Closed	2.30pm-6pm & Mon lunch (except bank hols). Open all day Sat & Sun.
Directions	Just off B6412 in Great Salkeld, off A686 north east of Penrith.

Donald & Paul Newton
Highland Drove
Great Salkeld, Penrith CA11 9NA

Tel +44 (0)1768 898349
Web www.highland-drove.co.uk

Entry 114 Map 11

Cumbria

Old Crown

Hesket Newmarket

In a dreamy village and with porter on tap! The old pub is owned by a cooperative of 147 souls and is run by Keith and Edna. Its tiny front room with bar, settles, glowing coals, thumbed books, pictures and folk music (the first Sunday of the month) squeezes in a dozen; a second room houses darts and pool; a third and fourth are dining rooms. Not only is this the only pub where you can sample all of Hesket Newmarket's beers brewed in the barn at the back – ask about tours – but it is the focal point of the community, even supporting the post office whose postmistress repays in puddings and pies. The Old Crown is also known for its fine curries and Sunday roasts. Its authenticity draws people from miles around, Prince Charles dropped by (twice) to launch the *Saving Your Village Pub* guide, walkers come for the Caldbeck Fells.

Meals	Lunch & dinner £6-£13. Bar meals £2.50-£6.50.
Closed	2.30pm-5.30pm Fri-Sun. Open from 5.30pm Mon-Thurs.
Directions	M6 junc. 41 for Wigton on B5305. 6.5 miles turn for Hesket Newmarket.

Keith & Edna Graham & Joanne Richardson
Old Crown, Hesket Newmarket,
Wigton CA7 8JG

Tel +44 (0)1697 478288
Web www.theoldcrownpub.co.uk

Entry 115 Map 11

Kirkstile Inn

Loweswater

Hard to imagine a more glorious setting than that of the Kirkstile Inn, tucked among the fells, next to an old church and a stream, a half mile from the lakes of Loweswater and Crummock. The whole place is authentic, traditional, well looked after: whitewashed walls, low beams, solid polished tables, cushioned settles, a well-stoked fire, plants, flowers and the odd horse harness to remind you of the past. Come for afternoon tea, or settle down with an unforgettable pint of Loweswater Gold or Melbreak Bitter or one of the Cumbrian Legendary Ales, brewed by Roger in Esthwaite Water near Hawkshead. Expect local produce and unfussy traditional dishes such as steak and ale pie, chicken breast stuffed with Cumberland sausage with an onion sauce, and sticky toffee pudding, leaving room for a plate of excellent local cheeses.

Meals: Lunch & dinner £8.95-£18.95. Bar meals from £5.95. Sunday lunch, 3 courses, £18.

Closed: Open all day.

Directions: Lorton road from Cockermouth; follow signs to Loweswater.

Roger Humphreys
Kirkstile Inn
Loweswater,
Cockermouth CA13 0RU
Tel +44 (0)1900 85219
Web www.kirkstile.com

Entry 116 Map 11

Cumbria

Britannia Inn

Elterwater

Being everyone's secret, this pub is always busy, with happy punters spilling out onto the terrace, garden and maple-shaded village green. At the centre of lovely Elterwater, with Great Langdale beck tumbling past into the tarn close by, it's a brilliant starting point for walkers. Drink and dine to your heart's delight in low-ceilinged rooms, corridors and little snug, amid old settles, oak seats, open fires and homely touches. A fine range of real ales is always on tap (they organise their own Champion Beers festival in November) while menus offer satisfying lunchtime soups and sandwiches, and tasty steak and ale pie. In the evening, tuck into confit duck leg with port reduction, Lakeland lamb marinated in mint and spices, and delicious vanilla cheesecake.

Meals: Lunch from £5. Dinner from £11.50.

Closed: Open all day.

Directions: A593 for 3 miles; right at Skelwith Bridge onto B5343, after a mile cross cattle grid. Next left is Elterwater; in middle of village.

Clare Woodhead
Britannia Inn
Elterwater,
Ambleside LA22 9HP
Tel +44 (0)15394 37210
Web www.britinn.co.uk

Entry 117 Map 11

Blacksmiths Arms

Broughton Mills

In the land of rugged hills and wooded valleys, the approach is down a winding lane between high hedges; once round the final bend, the low-slung farmhouse-inn comes into view. Welcome to an utterly unspoilt little local. Inside are four small slate-floored rooms with beams and low ceilings, long settles and several log fires, and the bar is strictly for drinking – indeed, there's not much room for anything else. There are three cask ales (two local, one guest) and traditional cider in summer. Across the passage: a room serving proper fresh food – snacks or full meals – and two further dining rooms sparkling with glass and cutlery. The blackboard advertises dishes with a contemporary slant, plus beef and Herdwick lamb reared in the valley. The food is seriously good so it gets busy; in summer you can wander onto the flowery terrace.

Meals	Lunch & dinner £8.50-£13.95. Bar meals from £3.95.
Closed	2.30pm-5pm Tues-Fri & Mon lunch (except bank hols). Open all day Sat & Sun.
Directions	Off A593 Broughton-Coniston road.

Authentic pub

Michael & Sophie Lane
Blacksmiths Arms
Broughton Mills,
Broughton-in-Furness LA20 6AX

Tel +44 (0)1229 716824
Web www.theblacksmithsarms.com

Entry 118 Map 11

Cumbria

Church House Inn

Torver

Michael Beaty arrived in 2006 and injected life into a historic pub, while keeping the best of original features and 15th-century charm. Ceilings are low and heavy beamed, there are slate floors and wood panelling, and locals and visitors steam together by the ever-stocked log fires, swapping tips on the merits of the various ales – perhaps a pint of Whitehaven or Hawkshead before a light lunch? Then set off for a walk: the iconic Coniston Old Man peak surveys the inn, and makes a stunning backdrop to the beer garden, replete with fruit trees and children's play area in summer. Ingredients are as local as can be, and all is made from scratch; join friends for dinner and share a hotpot or game pie between four or more before devouring a platter of puddings – white chocolate mousse, crème brûlée; there's always room.

Meals	Lunch & dinner £11.95-£17.95.
Closed	Open all day. Closed Mon & Tue lunch in winter.
Directions	Beside A593 Ambleside to Broughton-in-Furness road; in village 2 miles south of Coniston.

Michael Beaty
Church House Inn
Torver,
Coniston LA21 8AZ

Tel +44 (0)15394 41282
Web www.churchhouseinntorver.com

Entry 119 Map 11

Tower Bank Arms

Sawrey

Just across from the ferry, next to Hilltop – Beatrix Potter's farm – is Jemima Puddleduck's inn. (She may not have caroused here, but she did waddle by.) Today the National Trust are its sympathetic custodians. Jumbles of whitewashed buildings make up the legendary village of Sawrey; a courteous staff handles the summer crowds. Enter a slate-flagged bar with a grand open range that throws out the heat on chilly days; further in it is carpeted and cosy. Flowers and shining bits and bobs make the place homely; the oak-floored dining room is set with white linen napkins and polished cutlery. Five local ales accompany dishes to please walkers: beef casseroled in ale, Woodall's Cumberland sausages and Cumbrian lamb. The puddings are scrumptious and the cheeses reflect Cumbria's producers. Special.

Meals	Lunch from £4. Dinner from £11.50. Sunday lunch, 3 courses, £17.65.
Closed	3pm-5pm in winter. Open all day Sat & Sun & in summer.
Directions	On B5285 2 miles south east of Hawkshead; towards the Windermere Ferry.

Anthony Hutton
Tower Bank Arms
Sawrey,
Ambleside LA22 0LF

Tel +44 (0)15394 36334
Web www.towerbankarms.co.uk

Entry 120 Map 11

Cumbria

General Burgoyne

Great Urswick

In a little-known part of the Lake District, this handsome 17th-century inn was a proper old local boozer, complete with flagged floors, open fires and beams. Two years ago it had a spruce-up (though they kept the best bits, including Hartley's ales); Craig has worked in Michelin star restaurants in Cumbria and brings his skills to a menu that promises a bit more than standard pub grub. You'll find fish pie and homemade burgers but you can treat yourself to roulade of smoked salmon and prawns with citrus salad, too, or roast rump of Duddon Valley lamb with dauphinoise potatoes, roast garlic beans and rosemary gravy. Follow with 'Peanuts and a Pint'; Chocolate Tom jelly, vanilla panna cotta, and salted caramel and peanut parfait... then plan a big walk over the fells and down to the coast! A real find.

Meals	Lunch from £4.95. Dinner £9.95-£20. Sunday lunch, 2 courses, £12.95.
Closed	Mon & Tue lunch. Open all day Wed-Sun.
Directions	See website.

Craig & Louise Sherrington
General Burgoyne
Church Road, Great Urswick,
Ulverston LA12 0SZ

Tel +44 (0)1229 586394
Web www.generalburgoyne.com

Entry 121 Map 11

White Hart Inn

Bouth

The main counter drips with brass, hops and beer pumps; walls and shelves are strewn with clay pipes, sepia photos, taxidermy and tankards. It's a sleepy-snoozy village local, friendly too, where regulars cheerfully mingle with visitors over pints of Coniston and Hawkshead Bitter, decent wines and a delicious, no-nonsense menu: rare-breed meat from Aireys of Ayside; steak and Guinness pie; vegetarian chilli; and mallard and pheasant from the shooting parties that gather in the pub car park on winter Saturdays. They source locally, and – yes! – do small portions for children. A sloping flagged floor reflects the light from the window; black leather sofas front stoves at each end, log-fuelled in cold weather. The walking's marvellous and the village fits snugly into the ancient landscape of wooded valleys and tight little roads.

Meals	Lunch & dinner £10.75-£15.75.
Closed	Open all day.
Directions	Off A590 Barrow road after Lakeside & Haverthwaite Steam Railway.

Nigel & Kath Barton
White Hart Inn
Bouth,
Ulverston LA12 8JB

Tel +44 (0)1229 861229
Web www.whitehart-lakedistrict.co.uk

Entry 122 Map 11

Strickland Arms

Sizergh

Right beside the gates to Sizergh Castle, this old pub was desperate for attention. Now it is jointly run by Martin Ainscough and the National Trust. Behind the stark stone exterior are two civilised rooms decked out in best NT style: earthy Farrow & Ball colours, rugs on slate and wooden floors, an eclectic mix of antiques. Order a pint of Barngates Red Bull Terrier, pick a seat by a glowing coal fire, peruse the papers while you wait, then tuck into delicious food that bears no resemblance to normal pub fare. From local and organic ingredients come potted Morecambe Bay shrimps, lamb hotpot with red cabbage and crusty bread, lemon sole with rosemary and chive butter. Don't miss the Thursday fish nights and live music on Sunday afternoons. There's a lovely flagged front terrace for summer with pretty views.

Meals	Lunch & dinner £10.95-£15.95. Bar meals £5.50-£10.95 (lunch only).
Closed	3pm-5.30pm. Open all day Sat & Sun & May-Sept.
Directions	Just off A590 north of Kendal, by Sizergh Castle gates.

Helen & Martin Ainscough
Strickland Arms
Sizergh,
Kendal LA8 8DZ

Tel +44 (0)15395 61010
Web www.thestricklandarms.com

Entry 123 Map 11

The Black Swan

Ravenstonedale

Duck under hanging baskets to find a good mix of people in the busy main bar, cosy with red plush stools, exposed stone and soft lighting. Or nip through to the public bar with TV, games of scrabble and newspapers to read. A small lounge is quieter, with comfy seating at bay windows and an open fire. Wherever you land you are looked after by energetic, efficient staff; choose from a simple sandwich to a three-course blow out (try the pie of the day topped with shortcrust pastry, slow roasted belly pork with cider gravy, poached smoked haddock with creamy mash and spinach,). Meat comes from known local farms, the eggs are home-laid, the vegetables are fresh from Kirkby Stephen; visit the thriving village shop and take home some local produce. You are deep in the Eden valley and it would be a crime not to explore it!

Meals	Lunch from £3.95. Dinner, 3 courses, £20-£30.
Closed	Open all day.
Directions	Off A685 between M6 junc. 38 & A66 at Brough.

Alan & Louise Dinnes
The Black Swan
Ravenstonedale,
Kirkby Stephen CA17 4NG
Tel +44 (0)15396 23204
Web www.blackswanhotel.com

Cumbria

The Sun Inn

Kirkby Lonsdale

Set in a narrow street, with the historic parish church in view, the Sun is a fine example of an old inn. Step under the ancient portico and into a low-ceilinged bar of warmth, soft colours and a jolly mix of tables and chairs. Food is lavish, so push the boat out and sit in the smart brasserie-style dining room for potted mackerel pâté with rhubarb chutney, monkfish with herb gnocchi, clams, squid and butter sauce, steak and kidney pudding... and rhubarb crumble tart or a plate of cheese. All of it is delicious. There are cask ales to keep serious beer drinkers happy, the wine list is sublime (there are organic choices too) and the staff are wonderful. Pootle around Kirkby Lonsdale with its interesting shops or strike out further for some grand walking in the Yorkshire Dales National Park. Sublime.

Meals	Lunch from £8.95. Dinner from £14.95. Not Monday lunch.
Closed	Mon lunch.
Directions	M6 junc. 36 then A65 for 5 miles following signs for Kirkby Lonsdale. In town centre.

Mark & Lucy Fuller
The Sun Inn
6 Market Street, Kirkby Lonsdale,
Carnforth LA6 2AU
Tel +44 (0)1524 271965
Web www.sun-inn.info

Red Lion & Peak Edge Hotel

Stone Edge

Beside the road that snakes its way to Chatsworth and the Peak District National Park, this sprawling stone building tells a story: of a 16th-century pub that has had a dramatic makeover. At heart the Red Lion remains a local with its open fires, leather sofas, beamed ceilings and wooden tables – and, from brewery Peak Ales, Chatsworth Gold and Swift Nick on handpump. The mood is cheerful, the stone walls exposed. Saunter across to the new-build hotel and enter another world – firmly, swishly, 21st century. Here wait big beds, crisp sheets, fat pillows, free WiFi, flat-screen TVs and bathrooms bright with rain showers. Back in the bar a list of suppliers is on show: owner Damian Dugdale is a stickler for seasonality (and grows salads and herbs in the back garden). Allotment vegetables, game from local shoots and beef and lamb from the locality are championed ... so tuck into game terrine, slow-braised lamb shank, a plate of belly pork with black pudding, sausage croquette, crackling and cider sauce, and warm frangipane Bakewell tart. You won't do better in Derbyshire!

Price	£150-£300.
Rooms	27 doubles.
Meals	Lunch from £8. Bar meals from £7. Dinner from £10. Sunday lunch, 2 courses, £16.
Closed	Open all day.
Directions	Sent on booking.

Damian Dugdale
Red Lion & Peak Edge Hotel
Darley Road, Stone Edge,
Chesterfield S45 0LW
Tel +44 (0)1246 566142
Web www.redlionpubandbistro.com

The Devonshire Arms at Beeley

Beeley

Classic Peak District scenery surrounds Beeley's stone cottages and this public house. Converted from three cottages in 1747, it became a coaching inn – once visited by Edward VII – and is popular now for its proximity to great Chatsworth House. Ever a civilised lunch spot for well-heeled locals, it now verges on the opulent. Along with the beams, the log fires and the settles are candy-stripe tub chairs in vibrant hues and cushions tucked into cosy crannies: irresistible. In a room where floor-to-ceiling windows overlook the beck are snazzy bar stools, a glass-fronted wine store and yet more enticing colours. Bar and brasserie serve traditional and modern food and meat from the estate (try lamb rump with parsley pesto and spinach and rocket jus); all is delicious and the wine list is worth exploring. In the stone-flagged tap room, walkers are refreshed with expertly kept ales. Bedrooms upstairs – and in Brookside House next door – are equally stylish and understated, full of comfort and joy. The staff are lovely and breakfast's eggs come courtesy of the Duchess's own hens.

Price	£114-£207.
Rooms	8: 4 doubles, 3 twins/doubles, 1 suite.
Meals	Lunch & bar meals from £9.95. Dinner, 3 courses, about £25.
Closed	Open all day.
Directions	North from Matlock on A6, then right onto B6012 for Chatsworth and Beeley. Right in village; pub on right.

Alan Hill
The Devonshire Arms at Beeley
Beeley,
Matlock DE4 2NR
Tel +44 (0)1756 718111
Web www.devonshirebeeley.co.uk

The Devonshire Arms at Pilsley

Pilsley

A stroll from the Chatsworth Farm Shop and the legendary mansion, the Devonshire Arms at Pilsley is the second estate-owned pub to have been spruced up by the Duchess of Devonshire. Although very much a pub at heart – loved by walkers, estate-workers and Chatsworth visitors – the eye-catching interiors cleverly combine traditional wood and rustic stone with bright richly upholstered wall benches, bold wall coverings and quirky lamps. Making excellent use of farm shop produce and estate-reared meats, the classic pub menu announces steak and kidney pudding, lamb's liver with onion sauce and mash, farm-shop faggots with autumn vegetables, a roast-of-the-day, and new takes on old-fashioned puds like treacle tart with fruit compote. All well-priced and best washed down with a pint of home-brewed Chatsworth Gold. The Duchess's eye for colour and detail is also on display in the stylish and immaculate bedrooms. Treat yourself to big beds topped with feather down and delightful fabrics and throws; real coffee, country magazines and very high-spec bathrooms. There are wonderful walks right from the door.

Price	£89-£114.
Rooms	7 doubles.
Meals	Lunch, bar meals & dinner from £4.95.
Closed	Open all day.
Directions	From A619 at Baslow, B6012, signs to Chatsworth, then 2nd right for Pilsley. In village centre.

Alan Hill
The Devonshire Arms at Pilsley
High Street, Pilsley,
Bakewell DE45 1UL
Tel +44 (0)1756 718111
Web www.devonshirepilsley.co.uk

The Chequers Inn

Froggatt

The setting is almost alpine in its loveliness – impossible to pass this pub by. Once four stone-built cottages going back to the 16th century, the Tindall's ancient whitewashed inn has been sympathetically modernised and refurbished and is full of homely touches. Wooden floorboards, pine and country prints, cottage furniture and interesting objets give character to rooms that radiate off a stone-walled, timber-ceilinged bar. While blackboards promise modern bistro-style dishes – seafood risotto, calves' liver with mash, pancetta and fruit chutney, lamb shank with braised winter vegetables – the standard menu lists doorstep sandwiches and traditional casseroles and pies. From the raised garden behind, a path leads straight up through woods to stunning Froggatt Edge; the walking is marvellous.

Meals	Lunch, bar meals & dinner from £13. Sunday lunch £14.
Closed	Open all day.
Directions	On A625 8 miles northwest of Chesterfield, 9 miles southwest of Sheffield.

Jonathan & Joanne Tindall
The Chequers Inn
Froggatt Edge, Froggatt,
Hope Valley S32 3ZJ
Tel +44 (0)1433 630231
Web www.chequers-froggatt.com

Entry 129 Map 8

Derbyshire

Three Stags Heads

Wardlow

As you weave your way across the limestone plateau, you could easily miss this Derbyshire longhouse, modest home to a pottery and a pub. The pub is a gem inside, and couldn't be plainer: two small rooms, one heated by a fire, the other by a coal-burning kitchen range. So settle into a pint of Abbeydale's Black Lurcher, the house bitter with an 8% ABV, named in memory of one of the dogs. The menu really is a case of what is available from the surrounding countryside, it changes with the week and the season, and features a lot of game (it has been known for squirrel to have gone into the pot). Opening times are restricted depending on whether you're here for pottery or a pint, and a plate of something hot and wholesome from the blackboard. Soaked in history it's no museum – the hosts and the dogs see to that!

Meals	Lunch & dinner £7.50-£12.50.
Closed	Mon-Thur all day & Fri until 7pm. Open all day weekends & bank hols.
Directions	At junction of A623 & B6465 south east of Tideswell.

Geoff & Pat Fuller
Three Stags Heads
Wardlow,
Buxton SK17 8RW
Tel +44 (0)1298 872268

Entry 130 Map 8

The Red Lion

Litton

Stunning walks start and end at this picture-perfect pub, standing prettily on the oak-dappled village green. You'll like the interiors, too, all stone floors, open fires and wood panelled rooms. Staff are lovely, dishes are honest, good value for money, and the beer is great. Absolution from Sheffield's Abbeydale Brewery is a favourite, as is Oakwells Barnsley Bitter. Pub classics include fish and chips, beef stew, ham and eggs; puds continue the homely theme, with treacle sponge and custard and a historic sticky toffee pudding. This is pub as hub – a happy ship full of locals, who help organise several summer carnivals, winter fairs and a weekly fund-raising quiz that attracts so many that you should arrive early if you fancy a seat by the fire. In the spring, a million daffodils fringe the green – enjoy a pint before striking out again.

Meals	Lunch & dinner £5.95-£9.95.
Closed	Open all day Friday-Sunday. Check erratic opening hours.
Directions	One mile east of Tideswell, off A623.

Susie Turner
The Red Lion
Litton,
Tideswell SK17 8QU

Tel	+44 (0)1298 871458
Web	www.theredlionlitton.co.uk

Entry 131 Map 8

Derbyshire

The Old Hall Inn

Chinley

Welcome to a glorious stone-built 16th-century coaching inn and Elizabethan manor house, family-run and with reclaimed flagstones, chunky furniture, padded pews, real fires and local maps, blueprints and archive photos. Find cask ales from Thornbridge and Abbeydale amongst others, and their own to arrive shortly – once Dan has perfected the brew. Helpful staff will guide you through a multitude of bottled lagers and ciders, great wines, malts and cognacs. Food ranges from pub classics to more gourmet choices and the provenance is impeccable. Try locally shot game pie with braised red cabbage and handmade chips; the cheese board is good, too. Eat in the main bar area or for a treat next door, in the old hall where you dine beneath a beamed minstrels' gallery. The garden has peak views: pure Derbyshire.

Meals	Lunch from £5.50. Bar meals & dinner from £8. Sunday lunch, 3 courses, £18.50.
Closed	Open all day.
Directions	Signed off B6062 in centre of Chinley.

Daniel Capper
The Old Hall Inn
Whitehough, Chinley,
Chapel en le Frith SK23 6EJ

Tel	+44 (0)1663 750529
Web	www.old-hall-inn.co.uk

Entry 132 Map 8

Derbyshire

The Bull's Head
Ashford in the Water

Lovely carved settles, cushions, clocks and country prints – this is pub heaven. There are newspapers and magazines to read, light jazz hums in the background, coals glow in the grate. The busy Bull's Head has been in Debbie Shaw's family for half a century and she and Carl have been at the helm for the past 12 years. Carl cooks, proudly serving "bistro food, not a laminated menu"; even the bread and the cheese biscuits are homemade. With a strong emphasis on local and seasonal produce, there could be a full-flavoured chicken and pistachio terrine, beef and Guinness sausages with celeriac mash and red wine gravy, monkfish ragoût, sticky toffee pudding with black treacle sauce. Service is swift and friendly and, this being a Robinson's pub, Unicorn Best Bitter, Old Stockport and Double Hop are on hand pump – a brilliant place.

Meals	Lunch & dinner £9.95-£17.50. Not Thursday eve in winter.
Closed	3pm-6pm (7pm Sun).
Directions	Off A6, 2 miles north of Bakewell. 5 miles from Chatsworth.

Debbie Shaw
The Bull's Head
Church Street,
Ashford in the Water,
Bakewell DE45 1QB
Tel +44 (0)1629 812931

Entry 133 Map 8

Derbyshire

The Royal Oak
Hurdlow

Consigned to the scrap heap, this old boozer has been rescued by business partners Paul and Justin, who have slowly, tenderly returned it to life. They haven't ripped the heart out of the place and, in the old bar, have improved on all the good things – beams, open fires, exposed stone walls and comfortable seating; and there's an extra room, with scrubbed wooden tables and views over fields. Honest, straightforward pub grub flows from a spanking new kitchen, and everything's homemade and wholesome. Expect hand-raised pork and chicken pie; lamb chops with leek mash; goat's cheese and red onion tart. Local beers include Hartingtons, Pedigree and the award-winning Thornbridge ales. For walkers and cyclists the stunning Tissington Trail is on the doorstep – just as well if you're going the whole hog and choose apple crumble and custard to finish.

Meals	Lunch from £6.95. Bar meals & dinner from £8.95. Sunday lunch, 2 courses, £15.25.
Closed	Open all day.
Directions	From A515 Buxton-Ashbourne, junction for Hurdlow. 400m, on left.

Rachel Clark & Justin Heslop
The Royal Oak
Hurdlow,
Buxton SK17 9QJ
Tel +44 (0)1298 83288
Web www.peakpub.co.uk

Entry 134 Map 8

The Druid Inn

Birchover

A strange enticing countryside of tors, crags, wooded knolls and stone circle-strewn moors erupts high above Matlock. In the midst of this morphological mayhem stands the Druid Inn, its mellow stone exterior disguising a chic gastropub, and a menu combining traditional British with the best of European. Try game terrine with fig chutney, Chatsworth venison stew, sea bream with clams and mussels, baked ginger parkin with spiced syrup, and Wensleydale and ale pickle sandwiches. Shadows of the old village local remain – a quarry-tiled snug with an open fire, antique seats, and beers brewed by Leatherbritches – but the general atmosphere is that of bistro-in-the-country with a minimalist décor in the split-level restaurant rooms. Suntrap patios deliver village views, ramblers rub shoulders with epicures.

Meals	Lunch & dinner £9-£21.
Closed	Open all day.
Directions	From A6; B5056; signs for Birchover.

Nick Buchanan & Lee Hawksworth
The Druid Inn
Main Street,
Birchover DE4 2BL

Tel	+44 (0)1629 650302
Web	www.thedruidinn.co.uk

Entry 135 Map 8

Derbyshire

Old Poets' Corner

Ashover

Old Poets' Corner has something for everyone and it has been achieved with effortless style. Inside this mock-Tudor village-centre inn, ideally placed for forays into the Peaks and Dales, is a whirlwind of activity that pulls together live music, eight real ales, one perry, an ever-changing range of five ciders and an Arts and Crafts interior. And, living up to its name, there's a regular poets' night for local rhymesters. From good hefty farmhouse settles and pine tables, music-loving regulars sup ale brewed in the pub's own microbrewery and ciders such as Broadoak Moonshine (8.4% ABV)... And with that in mind the menu is more than substantial, trumpeting chillis, pastas, pies, casseroles and a carvery on Sundays. Sit back, relax and be entertained by the energy and good vibes surrounding you.

Meals	Lunch & dinner £6.50-£14. Bar meals £3.25-£9.50. Sunday lunch £8.25.
Closed	Open all day.
Directions	Ashover is just off B6036, between Kelstedge & Woolley Moor.

Kim & Jackie Beresford
Old Poets' Corner
Butts Road, Ashover,
Chesterfield S45 0EW

Tel	+44 (0)1246 590888
Web	www.oldpoets.co.uk

Entry 136 Map 8

Ye Olde Gate Inne

Brassington

One of the most exquisite pubs in Derbyshire, built from timber salvaged from the wrecks of the Armada. Furnishings are plain: ancient settles, rush-seated chairs, gleaming copper pans, a clamorous clock, a collection of pewter. In winter a fire blazes in the blackened range that dominates the quarry-tiled bar. In the dim yet wonderfully atmospheric snug are a glowing range and flickering candlelight. There's a daily specials board and traditional tucker: baguettes, a hearty and memorable steak and Guinness pie, liver and onions, beer-battered fish and chips, homemade bread and butter pudding. Come too for superbly kept Marston's Pedigree on hand pump and a number of malts. Mullioned windows look onto a sheltered back garden – perfect for warm summer evenings.

Meals	Lunch from £7.95. Bar meals from £4.25. Dinner from £8.95. Sunday lunch, 2 courses, from £12.75. Not Sunday eve.
Closed	2.30pm-6pm (7pm Sun). Mon (except bank hols) & Tues lunch.
Directions	Midway between Ashbourne & Wirksworth off B5035.

Peter Scragg
Ye Olde Gate Inne
Well Street,
Brassington,
Matlock DE4 4HJ
Tel +44 (0)1629 540448

Entry 137 Map 8

Derbyshire

Saracen's Head

Shirley

A pearl of a pub in unsung South Derbyshire. Renowned chef Robin Hunter and wife Terri have brought bags of gastropub style to this historic village, while cleverly holding on to an authentic country pub feel. Slate floors give way to smart carpeting, light wood chairs are cushioned, an open roof space is stylishly decorated and fires crackle in cast-iron surrounds at either end. Greene King ales greet you at the bar and there's a well-chosen wine list. Linger over the menus as the smell of freshly baked breads waft from the kitchen: modern English food and the best local and seasonal ingredients hold sway here, and you can bring your own produce in to barter! Try rack of lamb with chorizo mash and olive and garlic jus, then lemon meringue roulade with summer berries and vanilla bean ice cream – fit for Saladin himself.

Meals	Lunch & dinner from £9.25.
Closed	3pm-6pm (Mon-Sat). Open all day Sun.
Directions	Take sign to Shirley off A52 between Derby and Ashbourne.

Robin & Terri Hunter
Saracen's Head
Church Lane, Shirley,
Ashbourne DE6 3AS
Tel +44 (0)1335 360330
Web www.saracens-head-shirley.co.uk

Entry 138 Map 8

The Bulls Head

Repton

Once a derelict shell, this pub was brought back to life by Richard and Loren Pope, with the best of the original features brought to the fore. The downstairs bar is a jumble of connected rooms with wooden floors, stone flags, stripped timbers and designer quirks: chairs upholstered in black and white cow hide, bulls heads made from bicycles, driftwood sculptures, steel pillars. The main restaurant has huge 1930s gilt mirrors that hang on either side of a gas-effect fire; it all works. Energetic staff flit hither and thither to bring you serious dinners or a casual real ale: start with Indonesian fishcakes, follow with seafood chowder, cannon of lamb with tomato and black olive salsa and red wine sauce, or a wood-fired pizza, and finish with apple, pear and blueberry crumble. A great kids menu, too.

Meals	Lunch & dinner £8.95-£22.95. Sunday lunch £8.95.
Closed	Open all day.
Directions	Repton is signed off A38 between Derby & Burton-upon-Trent. Pub in High Street.

Richard & Loren Pope
The Bulls Head
84 High Street, Repton,
Derby DE65 6GF

Tel +44 (0)1283 704422
Web www.thebullsheadrepton.co.uk

Entry 139 Map 8

Derbyshire

Three Horseshoes

Breedon on the Hill

Opposite the old 'village lock up', a listed village inn. Ian Davison and Jenny Ison have revitalised the old place and introduced a relaxed modern feel with a menu to match. Expect painted brickwork, seagrass matting, antique tables, Windsor chairs, eclectic pictures and masses of space. Smaller rooms include a simple quarry-tiled bar and an intimate red dining room with three tables, while pride of place goes to a handsome Victorian bar counter picked up years ago, now groaning with chocolates and wine. Dishes are chalked up on boards in the bar and the award-winning formula includes monkfish with capers and spinach, and pork and cider casserole. Marston's Pedigree on hand pump should satisfy those in for a swift half, while foodies can check out the farm shop, and the chocolate workshop across the yard.

Meals	Lunch & dinner £8.95-£26.50. Bar meals £4.95-£10.95.
Closed	2.30pm-5.30pm & Sun from 3pm.
Directions	Follow signs off A42 between Ashby de la Zouch & Castle Donington.

Ian Davison & Jenny Ison
Three Horseshoes
44-46 Main Street,
Breedon on the Hill, Derby DE73 8AN

Tel +44 (0)1332 695129
Web www.thehorseshoes.com

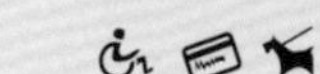

Entry 140 Map 8

The Elephant's Nest Inn
Horndon

Overseas visitors will give a rapturous smile as they enter the main bar, all polished oak beams, flagstone floors and crackling fires... you almost imagine a distant Baskerville hound baying. This is an atmospheric inn that serves properly home-cooked food – very local, very seasonal and British with a twist: perhaps antipasto of pastrami, rosette saucisson and Black Forest ham, or South Devon sirloin with mushrooms, vine tomatoes and French fries; sweet tooths will surely drool over Mrs Cook's fabulous lemon posset with blueberry compote. When suitably sated, slip off to the annexe and a nest of your own in one of three rather fun, wonderfully quiet and extremely comfortable rooms. Wake to a pretty garden with views to Brentor church and Dartmoor, an exceptional breakfast and even, perhaps, a cricket match to watch: the pub has its own ground and club. Settle back to the thwack of willow on leather with a pint of Palmer's IPA – or Doom Bar, Jail Ale from Princetown, and guest ales from, Otter, Cotleigh, Teignworthy and Butcombe. What's more, the pub is as dog-friendly as they come.

Price	£87.50.
Rooms	3 twins/doubles.
Meals	Lunch & dinner £8.95-£19.95.
Closed	3pm-6.30pm.
Directions	Signed off A386 Okehampton-Plymouth road at the Mary Tavy Inn in Mary Tavy; follow signs for Horndon.

Hugh & Denise Cook
The Elephant's Nest Inn
Horndon, Mary Tavy,
Tavistock PL19 9NQ

Tel +44 (0)1822 810273
Web www.elephantsnest.co.uk

Normandy Arms

Blackawton

After a day on rugged moor or windswept sea you can't do better than anchor here for the night. This continental looking pub stands smack in the middle of a pretty Devon village, looking south towards the church. Inside all is effortlessly stylish: leather armchairs glow by the wood-burner, slate tiles flow beneath solid wooden tables, original local art provides splashes of colour, walls are of exposed stone, or painted in calm colours. Firmly at the helm is charming Nick, there to help you choose from a seriously quaffable wine list as you scan the menu of once-Michelin-feted chef, Roger Hawkshaw. Start with deep-fried soft shell crab in spicy batter with organic yogurt and cucumber and ginger relish, move on to grilled fillets of fresh red mullet, potato gnocchi, ratatouille and basil pesto. There are good spirits and liqueurs and if a pint is all you're after, Dartmoor Legend will fit the bill. Upstairs are four hugely comfortable bedrooms with pampering bathrooms, calm and deeply restful with Nantucket colours, goose down duvets and L'Occitane toiletries. Our inspector did not want to leave.

Price	£95.
Rooms	4: 3 doubles, 1 twin.
Meals	Lunch & bar meals from £5. Dinner, 2 courses, £12.50. Sunday lunch, 2 courses, £15.90.
Closed	4pm-6pm (3.30pm-6.30pm in winter).
Directions	A381 Totnes to Kingsbridge, turn onto A3122 at Halwell towards Dartmouth, right at Forces Tavern.

Nick Crosley
Normandy Arms
Blackawton,
Dartmouth TQ9 7BN

Tel +44 (0)1803 712884
Web www.normandyarms.co.uk

Bickley Mill Inn

Stoneycombe

The microclimate of the English Riviera is never more apparent than in the garden of this 13th-century flour mill. The stylish cosy interiors are enticing, too: wooden floors, stone walls, hessian rugs, cushioned sofas. Three fires burn in winter, there are Swedish benches, colourful art and a panelled breakfast room in creamy yellow. Everywhere you look something lovely catches the eye, be it a huge sofa covered with mountainous cushions, old black and white photos framed on the walls or the sweet private seating corners outside, perfect for a pint – or more – in the summer sun. Bedrooms (including one ideal for families, large, light and up in the loft) are stylish, with upbeat art and sculptures, crisp linen and jazzy fabrics. Bathrooms are immaculate and, at these prices, quite a steal. Downstairs you'll find wonderful staff, local ales and some delicious food, from light bites to three-course feasts; tuck into baked field mushrooms, devilled kidneys, salmon fishcakes, banana and toffee pancakes… there's a menu for children and baby chairs, too. A small inn full of good things.

Price	£85-£130. Family room £130-£140. Singles £67.30.
Rooms	10: 8 doubles, 1 twin, 1 family room.
Meals	Lunch from £5. Dinner from £11.
Closed	3pm-6pm.
Directions	South from Newton Abbot on A381. Left at garage in Ipplepen. Left at T-junction after 1 mile. Down hill, left again, pub on left.

Tricia Smith
Bickley Mill Inn
Stoneycombe,
Newton Abbot TQ12 5LN
Tel +44 (0)1803 873201
Web www.bickleymill.co.uk

The Cary Arms at Babbacombe Bay

Babbacombe

The Cary Arms hovers above Babbacombe Bay with huge views of water and sky that shoot off to Dorset's Jurassic coast. It's a cool little place – half seaside pub, half dreamy hotel – and it makes the most of its spectacular position: five beautiful terraces drop downhill towards a small jetty, where locals fish. The hotel has six moorings in the bay, you can charter a boat and explore the coast. Back on dry land the bar comes with stone walls, wooden floors, rustic-chic tables and a fire that burns every day. In good weather you eat on the terraces, perhaps seared Brixham scallops, roast partridge, elderflower and lime crème brûlée. Dazzling bedrooms come in New England style. All but one opens onto a private terrace or balcony (perfect for dogs!), you get decanters of sloe gin, flat-screen TVs, fabulous beds, super bathrooms (one has a claw-foot bath that looks out to sea). Back outside, you can snorkel on mackerel reefs or hug the coastline in a kayak. If that sounds too energetic, either head to the treatment room (do pre-book) or sink into a deck chair on the residents' sun terrace.

Price	£170-£270. Suite £320-£370. Cottages £900-£2,995 pw.
Rooms	8 + 4: 6 doubles, 1 twin/double, 1 family suite. 4 self-catering cottages for 2-8.
Meals	Lunch from £7.95. Dinner £25-£35.
Closed	Open all day.
Directions	From Teignmouth south on A379; 5 miles to St Mary Church, thro' lights, left into Babbacombe Downs Rd. Follow road right; left downhill.

Jen Podmore
The Cary Arms at Babbacombe Bay
Beach Road, Babbacombe,
Torquay TQ1 3LX
Tel +44 (0)1803 327110
Web www.caryarms.co.uk

Nobody Inn

Doddiscombsleigh

Thankfully, little has changed since the current owners arrived in 2007. The wine and whisky lists remain 200-strong, and the Devon cheeseboard continues to draw rural winers and diners from afar. Settles and tables are crammed into every corner, horse brasses brighten low beams, there's an inglenook glowing with logs and part of the bar dates from Tudor times. Start with a bowl of Exmouth mussels, move on to rack of lamb with redcurrant and rosemary jus, finish with treacle tart. Or try something from the bar menu, perhaps fish pie, ham, egg and chips, that famous board of cheeses. To wash all this down: Nobody Bitter served in old pint glasses. A rare dram of Islay malt might be an excellent nightcap before retiring to one of five refurbished rooms upstairs, colour-themed according to name: Violet, Rose, Bluebell, Lily and Primrose. Quirky, fun, variously sized and extremely comfortable, they have soft carpets, super beds and decanters of sherry; bathrooms are, bar one, en suite. The village is buried down a maze of lanes but is certainly worth the detour.

Price	£60-£95. Singles £45-£70.
Rooms	5: 3 doubles, 1 twin/double; 1 double with separate shower.
Meals	Lunch & bar meals from £9.95. Dinner from £14.95. Sunday lunch, 3 courses, £24.95.
Closed	Open all day.
Directions	Off A38 at Haldon Racecourse exit, then 3 miles; following pub signs.

Sue Burdge
Nobody Inn
Doddiscombsleigh,
Exeter EX6 7PS
Tel +44 (0)1647 252394
Web www.nobodyinn.co.uk

Masons Arms

Branscombe

Approach meandering Branscombe down narrow lanes to this creeper-clad inn. The 14th-century bar has a traditional feel with dark ship's timbers, stone walls, slate floor and a fabulous fire that cooks spit-roasts to perfection. Quaff pints of Branscombe Vale by the fire or head for the suntrap terrace. Nothing is too much trouble for the staff, whose sole aim is for you to unwind. Local produce, including crab and lobster landed on Branscombe's beach, is the focus of the modern British menu. There's Ruby Red beef casserole with horseradish mash and line-caught sea bass, roast leg of organically reared lamb with pancetta and tomato jus, and crab ploughman's; the set menu is great value. No need to drive home – bed down instead in a room upstairs, or climb the steps to one of the cottages behind. No room is the same but the doubles are comfortably traditional and the suites are characterful and vast – four-posters, deep sofas, thick carpets, antiques. The pebbly beach is a 15-minute stroll across National Trust land and coastal path walks reward the adventurous. All who visit love the Masons Arms.

Price	£75-£145. Suites £165-£180.
Rooms	21: 8 doubles, 6 twins/doubles, 6 four-posters, 1 family room.
Meals	Lunch from £7.50. Bar meals from £9.95. Dinner, 3 courses, £20-£25. Sunday lunch from £9.95.
Closed	Open all day.
Directions	Branscombe is signed off A3052 between Seaton & Sidmouth. In village.

John McKitterick
Masons Arms
Branscombe,
Seaton EX12 3DJ

Tel +44 (0)1297 680300
Web www.masonsarms.co.uk

The Quarryman's Rest

Bampton

There's something for everyone here, at this lively market town inn. Real ale for beer buffs, a dining room for foodies, a fruit machine for gamblers, pool for the football team, and a shelter with cushions in the garden for the smokers. The garden is lovely, and overlooks fields. Back in the pub, it's spacious, with dark panelling and sofas in one area, lightness and sunshine in another, and a separate carpeted dining room for quiet meals. All the produce is local, from the beer and cider (heady Sam's from Winkleigh) to the beef, and you can see the cows from the window. (It's not unheard of for regulars to swap a pheasant or a box of tomatoes for a pint.) Along with the art on the walls – for sale – you get proper steak and kidney pudding, braised lamb shank with rosemary gravy, roast beef on Sunday – fantastic food, well priced. Upstairs, tucked away at the rear, are three homely bedrooms sporting trendy wallpapers, the big double boasts leather sleigh bed, huge plasma screen and bathroom with a corner bath, a walk-in shower and Arran Aromatics. Wild Exmoor walks are on the doorstep.

Price	£65-£85. Singles £50-£60.
Rooms	3 doubles.
Meals	Lunch & dinner £9.50-£13.95. Sunday lunch £8.95.
Closed	Open all day.
Directions	From A396 follow signs to Bampton; pub just as you enter the village.

Paul & Donna Berry
The Quarryman's Rest
Briton Street, Bampton,
Tiverton EX16 9LN
Tel +44 (0)1398 331480
Web www.thequarrymansrest.co.uk

Red Lion Hotel

Chulmleigh

A short trip from the Taw valley and you reach this lively village in the heart of Devon. The pub has welcomed man, horse and coach since the 17th century and is the sort of place you can march into from a gale and not worry about your waterproofs dripping on the slate flags. Plenty of blazing log fires to roast in front of too, with a zesty pint of local cider or a Cornish ale like Tribute. In the bar take your pick from rustic wooden settles to well-worn leather wingbacks: take care when a darts match is in progress! The TV is for major sporting events only. The restaurant is chicly utilitarian, with sparkling-lit wooden tables, painted stone walls and more new flagstones. Things take an Italian twist in the kitchen: handmade pizzas cooked in a stone-based oven and pasta specials; but dishes closer to home make an appearance too: homemade pork and pear pie served with hand-cut chips and seasonal vegetables, and heavenly puddings with clotted cream. Bedrooms upstairs and across the road at the old Globe pub are über-stylish with glowing oak floors, designer mirrors, super beds and bathrooms to linger in. Gorgeous.

Price	£60-£80.
Rooms	5: 2 doubles, 2 four posters, 1 twin.
Meals	Lunch & bar meals from £5. Dinner from £7.50. Dinner, 2 courses, £12.50. Not Tues lunch.
Closed	Monday.
Directions	Sent on booking.

Josie Russell
Red Lion Hotel
East Street,
Chulmleigh EX18 7DD
Tel +44 (0)1769 580384
Web www.theredlionchulmleigh.co.uk

The Grove Inn

Kings Nympton

The pub is in the heart of old Kings Nympton: a 'natural sacred grove'. A place of celebration for our pagan ancestors, you should raise a glass to your good fortune in being here. There are paintings of the superb countryside by local artists, a picture gallery of faces past and present, beams hung with bookmarks, stone walls, a slate floor and a wood-burner. Old and new combine with understated ease. Robert is the perfect host, Deborah his wife uses the freshest local produce to create her menus. Try roast May's Farm beef or Brewers Farm lamb for Sunday lunch, smoked trout with horseradish sauce, wild rabbit stew with mash, fish pie, white chocolate cheesecake with Patrick's blackcurrants. Ales are from local breweries, ciders are Sam's Dry and Poundhouse, wine & champagnes all come by the glass, over 50 single malts. A truly super local.

Meals	Lunch & dinner £7-£17. Sunday lunch, 3 courses, £16.40. Not Sunday eves.
Closed	3pm-6pm. Mon lunch (except bank hols). Sun eves.
Directions	Off B3226 south of South Molton; pub in village centre.

Deborah & Robert Smallbone
The Grove Inn
Kings Nympton EX37 9ST

Tel +44 (0)1769 580406
Web www.thegroveinn.co.uk

Entry 149 Map 2

Duke of York

Iddesleigh

One small room, one big fire, one pub packed with attitude. This is the pub that defines the phrase 'defiantly uninterested in prevailing fashions.' It stands next to the church in a tiny village marooned in Devon's glorious hinterland, as fine a spot as any in the country. Outside, a couple of benches catch the afternoon sun and locals bring their sheep to the door and stop for a pint. Inside, an inherent scruffiness is part of the Duke's DNA; it's rustic and enchanting, just like the food. You tuck into the heartiest home cooking: tureens of homemade soup, steak and kidney pudding, lamb chops with rosemary and garlic gravy. The locals treat the bar as their sitting room and they come and go, followed by their dogs. Walls are hung with old photos of village life, the ale is mostly local. Not for the faint-hearted.

Meals	Bar meals £4.50-£14.
Closed	Open all day.
Directions	On B3217 between Exbourne & Dolton, 3 miles north east of Hatherleigh.

John Pittam
Duke of York
Iddesleigh,
Winkleigh EX19 8BG

Tel +44 (0)1837 810253
Web www.dukeofyorkdevon.co.uk

Entry 150 Map 2

Tom Cobley Tavern

Spreyton

They come by the hundreds to drink the ales at this shrine to the hop, and the front room – 1930s trapped in aspic – must qualify as one of the finest spots in the land to sample intoxicating potions. Roger treats his ales the way most of us treat our children, nurturing them with love before sending them out into the world. You'll find more than twenty waiting, all from the south west, all brilliantly named: Bitter and Twisted, Druid's Fluid, Proper Job, Black Pearl; you're even asked which type of glass you'd like when ordering. Fishermen, hash runners and shooting parties drop by for a meal and dig into excellent, warming homemade pies and stews – the no-nonsense cooking goes down a treat. There's a garden, a thatched roof, Felix the cat. As for Tom Cobley, he set off for Widecombe Fair from this very building.

Meals	Lunch & dinner £7.95-£15.95.
Closed	3pm-6pm.
Directions	Exit A30 at Whiddon Down and follow signs to Spreyton. In middle of village.

Roger & Carol Cudlip
Tom Cobley Tavern
Spreyton,
Crediton EX17 5AL
Tel +44 (0)1647 231314

Entry 151 Map 2

Devon

The Harris Arms

Portgate

You are welcomed on the way in and thanked on the way out. The passion Andy and Rowena have for food and wine is infectious and the awards they are gathering is proof of their commitment. Expect a long bar, a wood-burner at one end, a patterned carpet, maroon walls and a big strawberry blond cat named Reg. A large decked area at the back has rich rolling views. The Whitemans are members of the Slow Food movement so real food is their thing: cheeses are the West Country's finest, fish, meat, vegetable and dairy produce come from exemplary local suppliers, and wines are chosen from small growers. Flavoursome food is what the chefs deliver and whether it be roast belly pork with cider jus, fish and chips or Devon lamb steak with roasted vine tomatoes and balsamic jus, it is consistently good. Great value, too.

Meals	Lunch £7.95-£9.95. Dinner £12.50-£17.95. Sunday lunch, 3 courses, £18.
Closed	3pm-6.30pm. Sun eves & Mon.
Directions	On old A30 between Lewdown & Lifton; leave A30 at Broadwoodwidger exit dir. Lifton then follow signs to Portgate.

Andy & Rowena Whiteman
The Harris Arms
Portgate,
Lewdown EX20 4PZ
Tel +44 (0)1566 783331
Web www.theharrisarms.co.uk

Entry 152 Map 2

The Dartmoor Inn

Lydford

There aren't many inns where you can sink into Zoffany-clad winged armchairs in the dining room or shop for Swedish tableware as you wait for the wild sea bass to crisp in the pan. Here you can: the Dartmoor Inn is the template of deep-country chic, a fairytale inn dressed as a country local. Walkers and dogs stride in from the moors and squeeze into the bar, for Dartmoor Best Bitter and organic bottled cider, fish and chips, hearty steak sandwiches, pork belly with celeriac purée and pepper and thyme sauce, chocolate and hazelnut torte... The walls are coated in textured wallpaper, the settles are smartly sandblasted, the gilded mirrors hang above smouldering fireplaces. And the moors are on your doorstep (nearby is the thrilling Lydford Gorge). So walk in the wind, then eat, drink and unwind.

Meals	Lunch & dinner £10-£19.50. Sunday lunch £26. Not Sunday eve or Monday lunch.
Closed	2.30pm-6.30pm. Sun eves & Mon lunch.
Directions	North from Tavistock on A386. Pub on right at Lydford turn-off.

Karen & Philip Burgess
The Dartmoor Inn
Lydford,
Okehampton EX20 4AY
Tel +44 (0)1822 820221
Web www.dartmoorinn.com

Entry 153 Map 2

Devon

White Horse Inn

Moretonhampstead

The back room doubles as an art gallery, folk bands play once a month, a fabulous courtyard catches the summer sun. The White Horse is all things to all men: a community centre, a great little restaurant, the sort of local you'd move to the village for. This year sees the arrival of a deli offering homemade delights; smoked charcuterie, bread, cakes and pastries. Nigel and Malene escaped London for the country and have transformed an old biker's boozer into a foodie's joy. The front bar teems with rustic charm – stripped boards, painted panelling, old settles, a hungry wood-burner. Follow the flagstones south past the open kitchen to a high-ceilinged dining room. You can spoil yourself variously with strong coffee, sparkling wine, local ales and crispy pizzas. A great place to wash up after a day on the moors, the welcome is second to none.

Meals	Lunch from £9.50. Bar meals from £4.95. Dinner from £10.95. No food Monday.
Closed	Tues-Sun lunch in winter.
Directions	Village centre, on The Square on B3212.

Nigel Hoyle & Malene Graulund
White Horse Inn
George Street, Moretonhampstead,
Newton Abbot TQ13 8PG
Tel +44 (0)1647 440242
Web www.whitehorsedevon.co.uk

Entry 154 Map 2

Ring of Bells

North Bovey

You'd be hard pressed to find a better inn on Dartmoor. First, there's the village, utterly unspoilt and lost in green hills. Then there's the pub, set back from the village, with a sun-trapping terrace that welcomes you at the front. New owners have given the place a smart lick of paint but the feel remains traditional as befits a venerable old hostelry. Inside you get a little time travel – timber frames, ancient walls, original flagstones – as you weave through cosy rooms, ducking to avoid low beams, sliding past open fires that burn brightly. Order a pint of local ale and head back onto the terrace, or seek out the dining room and tuck into super local food; suppliers are listed on the back of the menu with meat coming from the fields around you and fish fresh from nearby ports. Brilliant walking waits, dogs are very welcome.

Meals	Lunch from £8.95. Bar meals from £6.50. Dinner from £8.95. Sunday lunch, 2 courses, from £15.
Closed	Open all day.
Directions	5-minute drive from Chagford & Moretonhampstead, off B3212.

Karen Kitshoff
Ring of Bells
The Village, North Bovey,
Newton Abbot TQ13 8RB

Tel +44 (0)1647 440375
Web www.ringofbells.net

Entry 155 Map 2

Devon

The Cleave Inn

Lustleigh

It's too pretty for words, this 15th-century longhouse on the edge of Dartmoor National Park. The main bar is classic to the core, with a granite fireplace and leather armchairs and Windsor chairs forming cosy huddles on red and gold carpeting, and a no-nonsense planked bar dispensing Otter Ales and local guests such as Yellowhammer. The head chef brings passion to the kitchen so menus are blessed with regional, seasonal produce. Bar meals don't get much better than the Cleave Inn pie with vegetables, or the venison with sweet potato mash, fish stew and lamb tagine. There are scrumptious pork pies and sandwiches for walkers, and good wines poured by cheerful staff. Plenty of dining tables at the back, but arrive early in summer: seats are like gold dust outside at the front.

Meals	Lunch & dinner £7.50-£12. Sunday lunch £9.95-£15.95.
Closed	Open all day.
Directions	Off A382 halfway between Bovey Tracey and Moretonhampstead; pub signed. In village centre, opposite church.

Ben Whitton
The Cleave Inn
Lustleigh,
Newton Abbot TQ13 9TJ

Tel +44 (0)1647 277223
Web www.thecleavelustleigh.com

Entry 156 Map 2

The Rock Inn

Haytor Vale

Originally an ale house for quarrymen and miners, the 300-year-old Rock Inn stands in a tiny village in a sheltered vale on Dartmoor's windswept slopes. Run by the same family for over 20 years, this civilised haven oozes character; there are polished antique tables and sturdy settles on several levels, a grandfather clock, pretty plates and fresh flowers, cosy corners and at least two fires. Settle down with a pint of Dartmoor Best in the beamed and carpeted bar and peruse the supper menu that highlights local, often organic, produce. All that fresh Dartmoor air will have made you hungry, so tuck into Devon rump steak with garlic butter and chunky chips, then caramelised lemon tart with ginger ice cream. Lunchtime meals range from soup and sandwiches to local sausages in onion gravy. There's a pretty beer garden, too.

Meals	Lunch & dinner £7.50-£18.
Closed	Open all day.
Directions	At Drumbridges roundabout A382 for Bovey Tracey; B3387 to Haytor. Left at phone box.

Christopher & Susan Graves
The Rock Inn
Haytor Vale,
Newton Abbot TQ13 9XP
Tel +44 (0)1364 661305
Web www.rock-inn.co.uk

Entry 157 Map 2

Rugglestone Inn

Widecombe in the Moor

Beside open moorland, within walking distance of the village, is a 200-year-old stone pub whose two tiny rooms lead off a stone-floored passageway. Few of the daytrippers who descend on this idyllic village in the middle of Dartmoor make it to the Rugglestone. Low beams fill the old-fashioned parlour with its simple furnishings and deep-country feel. Both rooms are free of modern intrusions, the locals preferring cribbage, euchre and dominoes. The tiny bar serves local farm cider; Teiqnworthy Moor Beer and Dartmoor Brewery Legend are tapped from the cask. From the kitchen comes proper home cooking, from ploughman's lunches and soups to lamb shanks and fresh fish. Across the babbling brook at the front is a lawn with benches and peaceful moorland views. A little piece of heaven.

Meals	Lunch & dinner £6.95-£10.95. Bar meals from £3.75.
Closed	3pm-6pm. Open all day Sat & Sun.
Directions	250 yards from centre of Widecombe; signed.

Richard & Vicki Palmer
Rugglestone Inn
Widecombe in the Moor,
Newton Abbot TQ13 7TF
Tel +44 (0)1364 621327
Web www.rugglestoneinn.co.uk

Entry 158 Map 2

The Ship Inn

Noss Mayo

At the head of a tidal inlet, a 16th-century pub remodelled with a nautical twist. While visiting boats can tie up alongside (with permission!), high-tide parking is trickier. When the tide is in, you enter via the back door on the first-floor level; when out, it's a quick stroll over the 'beach' and in at the front. Downstairs are plain boards, a wooden bar, solid wood furniture and walls heaving with maritime prints. Open fires, books and newspapers add to the easy feel. Upstairs the Galley, Bridge and Library areas have views and a happy, dining buzz. The menu strikes a modern chord: shank of Devon lamb with rosemary and garlic sauce and pan-fried duck breast alongside pumpkin and pea risotto and chocolate mousse. Take your drink to the sunny patio at octagonal tables and relish the watery views.

Meals	Lunch & dinner £9.75-£17.95. Bar meals £5.25-£11.95. Sunday lunch, 3 courses, £20.
Closed	Open all day.
Directions	South of Yealmpton, on Yealm estuary.

Charles & Lisa Bullock
The Ship Inn
Noss Mayo,
Plymouth PL8 1EW
Tel +44 (0)1752 872387
Web www.nossmayo.com

Entry 159 Map 2

Devon

The Millbrook Inn

South Pool

Arrive before the boats do. They drop anchor a step away and their first port of call is this inn. The atmosphere is charming, the food is quite something, and perfect ingredients are worshipped in best seasonal style. Tuck into Start Bay crab, confit of duck leg with chorizo cassoulet, and rhubarb and apple crumble – and look out for the lively 'guest chef' nights. In winter, a log fire warms the immediate bar area while padded settles and wheelback chairs cluster comfortably around tables in several snugs. The stream-side terrace is tiny but assures entertainment in summer once the Aylesbury ducks are at play, so sit back and watch with a pint of Red Rock IPA. The owners have ambition and integrity and succeed in delivering some of the best bounty in the area; visit the Veg Shed and stock up on produce from village allotments.

Meals	Lunch from £5.50. Dinner from £10.
Closed	Open all day.
Directions	From Frogmore on A379 east of Kingsbridge follow signs south to South Pool; pub in village centre.

Ian Dent & Diana Hunt
The Millbrook Inn
South Pool,
Kingsbridge TQ7 2RW
Tel +44 (0)1548 531581
Web www.millbrookinnsouthpool.co.uk

Entry 160 Map 2

Pig's Nose Inn

East Prawle

Winding lanes with skyscraper hedges weave from the main road to the edge of the world. There are an awful lot of porcine references round these parts (South Hams, Gammon Head, Piglet Stores) and the Pig's Nose is Devon's most southerly pub. Filled with character, a wood-burner and quirky ephemera, it has an atmosphere all of its own. A pie, pint and a paper at lunchtime can give way at night to the entire pub joining in a singalong; Peter's connections entice legendary acts – The Yardbirds, Wishbone Ash – to play in the adjacent hall. Innovations include a flurry of fur 'smoking jackets' hanging in the porch and random pots of knitting inviting punters to 'do a line'. Your hosts have a terrific sense of fun and faithful visitors return again and again. A one-off in a sea-view village that has barely changed since the thirties.

Meals	Lunch & dinner £6.50-£12.50.
Closed	2.30pm-6pm (7pm in winter). Sun eves & Mon all day in winter.
Directions	A379 Kingsbridge-Dartmouth; at Frogmore, right over bridge opp. bakery; signs to East Prawle. Pub by green.

Peter & Lesley Webber
Pig's Nose Inn
East Prawle,
Kingsbridge TQ7 2BY
Tel +44 (0)1548 511209
Web www.pigsnoseinn.co.uk

The Tower Inn

Slapton

A southern belle, loved by all who visit: despite the drawbacks of hidden access and tricky parking, this 14th-century inn attracts not just locals but visitors from Slapton Sands. Standing beside the ivy-clad ruins of a chantry tower, it's a flower-bedecked classic outside. As for the low-beamed and stone-walled interior – all rustic dark-wood tables, old pews and fine stone fireplaces, it is hugely atmospheric by night, thanks to the flickering light from candles and fires. Golden, bitter-sweet St Austell Brewery Proper Job from the handpumps could be accompanied by a plateful of seabass with braised fennel and crab dumplings; local beef; trio of duck or rabbit and chorizo pie; do book at weekends. A lovely, sleepy village setting – and a super landscaped garden at the back with views of the parish church and the tower.

Meals	Lunch from £5. Dinner from £10. Sunday lunch, 3 courses, £22. Not Sunday eve in winter.
Closed	3pm-6pm Sun eves in winter.
Directions	Off A379 between Torcross & Dartmouth. Signed.

Thea Butler, Dan Cheshire & Kevin Tweddell
The Tower Inn
Slapton, Kingsbridge TQ7 2PN
Tel +44 (0)1548 580216
Web www.thetowerinn.com

Kings Arms

Strete

Tempting to visit on a dark and rainy night – but a shame to miss the glorious views of Start Bay. Rob Dawson has revitalised the Edwardian hotel-turned-pub, bringing a natural warmth and a fine menu. A modest bar and a few tables greet you, then up the pine stair to a mezzanine dining room. Delicious smells waft from the kitchen – of seared scallops with pea mousse and serrano ham, brill with red wine glaze and garlic confit, poached pears with Devon Blue ice cream and port jelly. Oysters are gathered from the river Dart, lobsters and crabs come from the bay, the cheeses are local and the wines are wide-ranging with an excellent number by the glass. The Kings Arms and its garden fill up at summer weekends as holiday-cottagers get wind of the place, and return – for the food, the friendliness and the views.

Meals	Lunch & dinner £9.50-£19.95.
Closed	2.30pm-6pm (3pm-7pm Sun). Call ahead for winter opening times.
Directions	Between Dartmouth & Torcross on the A379.

Rob Dawson
Kings Arms
Strete, Dartmouth TQ6 0RW

Tel +44 (0)1803 770377
Web www.kingsarms-strete.co.uk

Entry 163 Map 2

Devon

The Ferry Boat Inn

Dittisham

The only inn right on the river, it used to serve the steamers plying between Dartmouth and Totnes – you can still arrive by boat. Big windows show off the view to the wooded banks of the Greenway Estate (once Agatha Christie's home, now owned by the NT: shake the bell and catch the ferry). Arrive early for the best seats in the rustic, unspoilt little bar with its bare boards, crackling log fire, nautical bric-a-brac and all-important 'high tides' board; if you've missed the village car park, negotiated the steep lane and parked on the 'beach', then check the board before ordering your pint. Similarly, the tide dictates whether or not you can dine outside in summer. Expect a rousing welcome, live music sessions and decent home-cooked pub food. Gents can 'spray and pray' next door in the converted chapel.

Meals	Lunch & dinner £6.95-£14.50.
Closed	Open all day.
Directions	Off A3122, 2 miles west of Dartmouth.

Ray Benson
The Ferry Boat Inn
Manor Street, Dittisham,
Dartmouth TQ6 0EX

Tel +44 (0)1803 722368
Web www.ferryboatinndittisham.co.uk

Entry 164 Map 2

Turtley Corn Mill

Avonwick

The mill, revamped in 2005, has six acres sloping down to the lake – space for a multitude of picnic tables: order your hampers in advance. Ducks too... and boules, croquet, Jenga and a ginormous chess set. Inside has been transformed to create a series of spacious inter-connected areas: the bar with its dark slate floors and doors to the garden; the wooden-floored 'library' lined with books; the mill room (turning wheel right outside) with wood-burner, prints on pristine white walls, oriental rugs and newspapers to read. The food is traditional and homemade, be it local game terrine, braised beef in red wine or sea bass with minted pea sauce. There's Princetown Jail Ale on tap and a raft of wines by the glass. The South Hams is close as are the Dartmoor tors; it's also the perfect A38 stopover!

Meals	Lunch & dinner £7.50-£17.95.
Closed	Open all day.
Directions	A38 eastbound, turn for South Brent/Avonwick; 1st right to Avonwick, on B3372. Bear left following signs for Totnes; pub 100m on left.

Samantha & Scott Colton
Turtley Corn Mill
Avonwick,
South Brent TQ10 9ES

Tel	+44 (0)1364 646100
Web	www.turtleycornmill.com

Entry 165 Map 2

Devon

The Church House Inn

Marldon

The old village pub is a civilised place, popular with retired locals and ladies that lunch. With a welcoming bar, several dining areas and a lovely sloping garden, it's a proper all-rounder. The feel is one of a well-crafted, rustic elegance – stonework and beams, original bell-shaped windows, crisp table settings and smiling service. The central bar has been partitioned into three areas, plus one four-tabled candlelit snug, perfect for a party. Food is modern British and locally sourced: baked hake with butterbean and chorizo ragoût, Dartmouth smoked fish platter, bramble Bakewell tart with blackberry compote. Others come just for a pint of well-kept Dartmoor Best and a chat by the fire. The pub originally housed the artisans who worked on Marldon Church, and its ancient tower overlooks the hedged garden.

Meals	Lunch & dinner £9-£19.95. Sunday lunch £11.95.
Closed	2.30pm-5pm (3pm-5.30pm Sun).
Directions	Marldon off Torquay-Brixham ring road. Pub at bottom of village, signed.

Julian Cook
The Church House Inn
Marldon,
Paignton TQ3 1SL

Tel	+44 (0)1803 558279
Web	www.churchhousemarldon.com

Entry 166 Map 2

The White Hart

Dartington

Down a long, long drive past farmland and deer, Dartington Hall finally peeps into view: the college, conference centre, arts centre, dairy farm and 14th-century hall built for a half-brother of Richard II. Tucked into the corner of the courtyard – dotted with picnic tables in summer – is the White Hart. The bar and restaurant is informally 21st-century, with chunky beams, York stone floor, log fires, round light-oak tables and Windsor chairs. Organic and local produce are the mainstay of the menus, from soups to sea bass with sauce vierge. In the trestled dining hall: game terrine with baby figs; chargrilled rump steak with horseradish butter; local cheeses. Beers are from Otter Brewery, there are excellent wines and organic juices and ciders. Walk off a fine lunch with a stroll through the parkland that borders the Dart.

Meals	Lunch & dinner £9.50-£15.50.
Closed	Open all day.
Directions	Off A385, 2 miles north west of Totnes on the outskirts of Dartington village.

John Hazzard
The White Hart
Dartington Hall, Dartington,
Totnes TQ9 6EL

Tel	+44 (0)1803 847111
Web	www.dartingtonhall.org

Entry 167 Map 2

Devon

The Bridge Inn

Topsham

Unchanged for most of the century – and in the family for as long – the 16th-century Bridge is a must for ale connoisseurs. And for all who love a pub furnished in the old-style: just high-back settles, ancient floors, a simple hatch. (The Queen chose the Bridge for her first official 'visit to a pub'.) Years ago it was a brewery and malthouse; Caroline's great-grandfather was the last publican to brew his own here. This is beer-drinker heaven, with up to ten real ales served by gravity from the cask. There's cider and gooseberry wine, too. Cradle your pint to the background din of local chatter in the Inner Sanctum, or out in the garden by the steep river bank. With bread baked at the local farm, home-cooked hams, homemade chutneys and Devon cheeses, the sandwiches, pork pies and ploughman's are first-class.

Meals	Lunch from £3.20. Bar meals £3.20-£7.
Closed	2pm-6pm (7pm Sun).
Directions	M5 exit 30; A376 to Exmouth; 2 miles, right to Topsham; Elmgrove Road into Bridge Hill.

Caroline Cheffers-Heard
The Bridge Inn
Bridge Hill, Topsham,
Exeter EX3 0QQ

Tel	+44 (0)1392 873862
Web	www.cheffers.co.uk

Entry 168 Map 2

Digger's Rest

Woodbury Salterton

A 500-year-old, fat-walled former cider house built of stone and cob – surely the quintessential thatched Devon inn. A good-looking makeover has revived the timbered interior: mellow walls and an eclectic mix of old dining tables, subtle wall lighting, tasteful prints. Arrive early to bag the sofa by the log fire. In addition to the local Otter and guest ales, the good list of wines and the relaxing atmosphere, there are organic soft drinks, Italian Gaggia coffee, soothing piped jazz, baby-changing facilities, newspapers and a one-hour lunch promise. The brilliant pub menu employs the best local produce, so treat yourself to wild sea bass with pea and mint risotto, fine West Country beef and local Kenniford Farm pork, roasted for Sunday lunches; little ones have a menu all of their own. A beautifully landscaped patio garden, too.

Meals	Lunch & dinner £7.95-£16.95. Bar meals £4.75-£16.95.
Closed	3pm-5.30pm. Open all day Sat & Sun in summer.
Directions	Off A3052, 3 miles east of Exeter & 3 miles from M5 junc. 30.

Ben Thomas
Digger's Rest
Woodbury Salterton,
Exeter EX5 1PQ
Tel +44 (0)1395 232375
Web www.diggersrest.co.uk

Entry 169 Map 2

The Jack in the Green

Rockbeare

Bustle and buzz in the dark wood bar, and good local brews on tap – Otter Ale, Doom Bar, Butcombe Bitter. But this is more restaurant than pub: "For those who live to eat," reads the sign. In a series of smart, brightly lit, blue-motif carpeted rooms Matthew Mason's bar menu goes in for modern and mouthwatering variations of tried and trusted favourites: braised faggot with creamed potato, steamed venison pudding with port and juniper jus... More ambition on display in the restaurant, with chef Matthew Downing winning South West Chef of the Year in 2010. Seared fillet of salmon with sorrel and hollandaise sauce and roasted Creedy Carver duck breast with liqueur-soaked cherries make for succulent seasonal choices. Paul Parnell has been at the helm for years and he and his staff do a grand job.

Meals	Lunch & dinner £11.50-£19.50. Bar meals from £4.95.
Closed	3pm-5.30pm (6pm Sat). Open all day Sun.
Directions	5 miles east of M5 (exit 29) on old A30 just past Exeter Airport.

Paul Parnell
The Jack in the Green
Rockbeare,
Exeter EX5 2EE
Tel +44 (0)1404 822240
Web www.jackinthegreen.uk.com

Entry 170 Map 2

The Holt

Honiton

So named (a holt = the lair of an otter) because the McCaig family own the Otter Brewery in the Blackdown Hills. Young Joe and chef Angus run the pub, and Otter brews (Bitter, Ale, Bright and Head) from a new underground eco-cellar are showcased. But the spruced-up boozer on Honiton's high street is much more than the brewery 'tap', the vibrant bar and contemporary-styled dining room upstairs playing host to live music and film nights when food is off the menu. Angus delivers modern pub food from an open-plan kitchen, the emphasis being on local produce – farm meats, estate-shot game, smoked meats and fish from the on-site smokehouse. On seasonal menus are beefburgers, confit duck leg and sandwiches for lunch; for dinner, bream with crab and coriander cream sauce, lamb shank with herb dumplings, chocolate brownies. A superb A30 pit-stop.

Meals: Lunch from £5.50. Dinner from £12.50.
Closed: 3pm-5.30pm & all day Sun & Mon.
Directions: Exeter end of Honiton High Street. Public car park on Dowell Street.

Joe & Angus McCaig
The Holt
178 High Street,
Honiton EX14 1LA
Tel: +44 (0)1404 47707
Web: www.theholt-honiton.com

Entry 171 Map 2

Devon

The Railway

Honiton

A gem of a pub, tucked just off the High Street in this vibrant market town. Built by GWR workers en route to Cornwall it has seen plenty of action; now a calmer vibe rules. The bar area is lounge style with long bench seats, Indian flagstones and café tables on which to sit a pint of Branscombe Brannoch or Dragon Tears cider. The dining area beyond is upbeat and quirky with brightly painted pulley wheels and tools, and lots of local art. Gorgeous food and an engaging atmosphere are matched with an authentic bistro-brasserie style, courtesy of vivacious Jean Sancey who serves a wide-ranging menu: zucchini fritti, pressed ham hock terrine of local pedigree pork, fragrant chicken Vietnamese salad, traditional Louisiana jambalaya, pan-seared scallops, and bucatini puttanesca – dazzling. Be sure to make this a stop on your eating timetable.

Meals: Lunch from £5.95. Bar meals from £9.95. Dinner from £12.95.
Closed: Open all day.
Directions: From A30, A35 to Dorchester. Right at mini r'bout. Left signed station. Left opp. Star Inn, follow round to right, pub on left.

Jean Sancey
The Railway
Queen Street,
Honiton EX14 1HE
Tel: +44 (0)1404 47976
Web: www.therailwayhoniton.co.uk

Entry 172 Map 2

The Drewe Arms

Broadhembury

Taking pride of place at the crossroads of this pretty cob and thatch Devon village, the low and wide hallway of this 15th-century pub draws you in to a blend of old and new. Golden oak floors lead to a smart well-stocked bar, and there's a calm, leather-chaired dining room in which to enjoy the much talked about food, such as roasted guinea fowl with lentils, bacon, lemon and thyme, and, from the bar menu, ham hock with buttered vegetables, mashed potato and piccalilli. Even if you're just settling down with a paper by the log-fired inglenook for a pint of Otter Bitter, Hanlon's Yellowhammer or one of three ciders you'll be well looked after by Anthony and his team. All wines are by the glass, and many dishes come with fruit, vegetables and herbs from their own plot. Outside is a dreamy garden overlooked by the village church: pure Devon soul.

Meals	Lunch, bar meals & dinner, all £6-£15. Sunday lunch, 3 courses, £21.
Closed	3pm-6pm. Mon. Open all day Sat & Sun.
Directions	M5 junc. 28; A373 Honiton to Cullompton; follow signs to Broadhembury; pub in village centre

Anthony Russell
The Drewe Arms
Broadhembury,
Honiton EX14 3NF

Tel +44 (0)1404 841267
Web www.thedrewearms.com

Entry 173 Map 2

Devon

Culm Valley Inn

Culmstock

Richard Hartley's old pub by the lovely river Culm may not be posh but it's warm, easy and charming: deep pink-washed walls, glowing coals, flickering oil lamps and candles. From bar stools the locals sample microbrewery beers while the gentry drop by for unusually good food. Easy-going chef-patron Richard and his merry band make this place zing. Look to the chalkboard for south coast seafood – cod with langoustine broth, halibut with mussels and pesto – Ruby Red Devon beef from nearby farms, tea-smoked venison with tomato relish, spicy Balinese pork, and tapas. From the English elm bar you can order from a fantastic array of rare and curious spirits, French wines from specialist growers and up to ten local beers tapped from the cask. In the words of one reader: "Fantastic host, great wine, superb homemade everything..."

Meals	Lunch & dinner £7-£20. Bar meals £6-£10.
Closed	3pm-7pm in winter. Open all day Sat & Sun.
Directions	On B3391, 2 miles off A38 west of Wellington.

Richard Hartley
Culm Valley Inn
Culmstock,
Cullompton EX15 3JJ

Tel +44 (0)1884 840354
Web www.culmvalleyinn.co.uk

Entry 174 Map 2

The Lazy Toad Inn

Brampford Speke

Stroll the banks of the river Exe, then, with appetite enhanced, return to this smart listed inn in a tranquil village. Slate tiles polished to a pewter hue gleam on floors around the bar where ales from Otter, Exe Valley and St Austell vie for attention, farming implements dot one wall, bistro style art another, and an eclectic mix of tables and chairs add pizzazz. Settle into the wicker rocking chair by the fire and study Mo and Ian's daily changing menus, featuring much of their own produce and meat and fish from their smokery. How about roasted Kent cob nuts, Sharpham brie and fresh fig salad, followed by local wild rabbit loin wrapped in pancetta with roast almonds, rabbit leg and shoulder stew... prepare to be spoiled! There's a great little menu for kids, a lovely walled cobbled courtyard outside, and more garden at the back.

Meals: Lunch from £5.10.
Bar meals from £10.95..
Dinner from £14.00.
Sunday lunch, 3 courses, £25.

Closed: Sun eves & Mon.

Directions: See website.

Local, seasonal & organic produce

Mo Walker
The Lazy Toad Inn
Brampford Speke,
Exeter EX5 5DP
Tel +44 (0)1392 841591
Web www.thelazytoadinn.co.uk

Entry 175 Map 2

Devon

The Lamb Inn

Sandford

Animal paintings brighten the bar, the chef is passionate about provenance and Bob and Tiny (the dogs) are a delight. The old posting inn is the hub of the village. There are three open fires in winter and carpeting for cosiness, stubby white candles on plain tables, tankards filled with roses and, upstairs, a long window seat that looks onto the village below. (Skittles and darts too, a free cinema for films and sporting events, and a brilliant open mic night once a month.) The unplush décor is matched by a blackboard menu free of affectation, the scrumptious-sounding dishes ranging from a platter of West Country cheeses to a Mediterranean cassoulet (and you can round it all off with banoffee pie and clotted cream). All is locally sourced and made from scratch, and that includes the soups, the pastas and the breads.

Meals: Lunch from £8.
Dinner, 3 courses, £15-£25.

Closed: Open all day.

Directions: A377 north from Exeter. 1st right in Crediton, left, signed Sandford. 1 mile up & in village.

Mark Hildyard
& Katharine Lightfoot
The Lamb Inn
Sandford, Crediton EX17 4LW
Tel +44 (0)1363 773676
Web www.lambinnsandford.co.uk

Entry 176 Map 2

The Bull Hotel

Bridport

Urban-chic meets rural simplicity at Richard and Nikki's Regency-style coaching inn. Funky and fun sums up this vibrant place and you feel good the moment you step through the door. Escape Bridport's bustle, kick off your shoes, plonk yourself down on a squashy sofa with a pint of Lyme Gold. The bar is open all day, for hearty English breakfasts, cappuccino and cake, for lunchtime sandwiches and high tea. For seriously good food, there's a candlelit restaurant; for summer lunches, a Victorian courtyard. Enjoy live music in the Hayloft, take a turn in the ballroom, order a cocktail in the sumptuous lounge. Daily menus are contemporary and work with the seasons while organic ingredients are locally sourced: lamb cutlets with red wine, stone-baked pizza, vanilla rice pudding, handmade cheeses. And the bedrooms... classic period features mix serenely with modern pieces and antiques, there are Designer Guild fabrics, Milo sofas, big comfy beds, Tivoli radios, white waffle robes, roll top tubs and Neal's Yard delights. A boon for arty Bridport – and the fantastic Jurassic coast is a mile away.

Price	£85-£195. Four-poster £155-£195. Family room £170-£210. Singles £75-£115. Suite £205-£265.
Rooms	19: 10 doubles, 1 twin, 3 four-posters, 3 family rooms, 1 single, 1 suite.
Meals	Lunch, 2 courses, from £12. Dinner, 3 courses, around £30. Sunday lunch £19.
Closed	Open all day.
Directions	On main street in town. Car park at rear.

Nikki & Richard Cooper
The Bull Hotel
34 East Street,
Bridport DT6 3LF

Tel	+44 (0)1308 422878
Web	www.thebullhotel.co.uk

The Three Horseshoes

Powerstock

On the site of a former smithy this Victorian pub sits in the drowsiest Dorset countryside: hollow ways, Iron Age forts and steeply wooded valleys surround the village. Walk up an appetite on Eggardon Hill, then beat a path to this timeless little pub with its cosy interior of stripped pine, thatched bar and stone fireplace. Arrive hungry: the scene is set for some seriously good food. From Karl's kitchen flow hand-dived scallops with Bath chaps and sauce gribiche; warm salad of crispy rabbit leg and smoked eel with homemade salad cream and baby gem – inspired. There are pub classics too, the homemade bread and butter are a meal in itself, the cheese board is a local marvel and the hand-cut chips the best we've had. Ales are from Palmers, there are well-chosen wines and a local cider in summer to carry out to the patio at the back and soak up the views. In an annexe, overlooking the village school and the valley, are two light modern rooms with feature beds, signature wallpaper and smart oak furniture. Rural bliss – and food worth travelling a long distance for.

Price	£75-£95.
Rooms	3 doubles.
Meals	Lunch from £10. Bar meals from £6. Dinner £10-£25. Not Mon lunch in winter.
Closed	3pm-6.30pm.
Directions	Village signed off A3066 Bridport-Beaminster road.

Karl Bashford & Zuzana Prekopova
The Three Horseshoes
Powerstock,
Bridport DT6 3TF
Tel +44 (0)1308 485328

The Acorn Inn
Evershot

Perfect Evershot and rolling countryside lie at the door of this 400-year-old inn deep in Thomas Hardy country. Hardy called the inn the Sow and Acorn and let Tess rest a night here; had he visited today he might have let her stay longer. Red Carnation Hotels, under the guidance of Alex and chef Jack, are reviving its fortunes. This is very much a traditional inn: as much a place for locals to sup pints of Otter Ale and swap stories by the fire in the flagstoned bar, as for foodies to sample some good food sourced within 25 miles. Walk through to the dining room and the atmosphere changes to rural country house with smartly laid tables, terracotta tiles, soft lighting and elegant fireplaces; food is taken seriously, take scallops with pumpkin and vanilla purée and chorizo dressing and roast pork belly with sherry vinegar jus, or a rare roast beef and horseradish sandwich in the bar. Bedrooms creak with age and style; uneven floors, antiques, bright fabric wall-coverings, beautiful draperies to soften grand four-posters, and smart new bathrooms. Hardy would approve.

Price	£99-£119. Four-posters £119-£149. Suite £149-£194. Singles £79-£149.
Rooms	10: 3 doubles, 3 twins, 3 four-posters, 1 suite.
Meals	Lunch & dinner £4.95-£21.95. Bar meals from £4.95. Sunday lunch, 3 courses, £20.
Closed	Open all day.
Directions	Evershot 1 mile off A37 midway between Yeovil & Dorchester.

Jack Mackenzie
& Alex Armstrong-Wilson
The Acorn Inn
Evershot,
Dorchester DT2 0JW
Tel +44 (0)1935 83228
Web www.acorn-inn.co.uk

The Chetnole Inn

Chetnole

A cream-painted pub reached by leafy lanes south of Sherborne, half an hour from the wonderful Dorset coast. Opposite the parish church, the updated inn has not lost touch with its roots; there's a snug bar area with a wood-burning stove; a stone-floored, hop-hung lounge bar; a restaurant beyond, similarly attractive; and a beer garden with giant rabbits. Dishes range from straightforward, for children, to imaginative, and Mike sources ingredients as locally as possible. A memorable meal might include pan-fried breast of pigeon with puy lentils, black pudding and pancetta followed by duo of duck with red cabbage and redcurrant jus, and an orange and cardamom crème brûlée to round things off. If staying over you'll be comfortable in one of the smart, pale-carpeted bedrooms; all look towards the church, all are prettily dressed. Beds are inviting with thick duvets and feather pillows, so too are the homemade biscuits, the real coffee and the magazines. Gleaming bathrooms have bathrobes and Molton Brown treats. As winner twice of the Best Dining Pub in the Taste of Dorset Awards, the Chetnole is hard to fault!

Price	From £95. Singles £70.
Rooms	3: 2 doubles, 1 twin/double.
Meals	Lunch & dinner £9-£16. Bar meals from £5. Sunday lunch from £9.50.
Closed	3pm-6.30pm. Sun eves & Mon (Oct-Apr).
Directions	Chetnole is signed off A37 between Yeovil and Dorchester, 7 miles south of Yeovil, 7 miles south west of Sherborne.

Mike Lewin
The Chetnole Inn
Chetnole,
Sherborne DT9 6NU
Tel +44 (0)1935 872337
Web www.thechetnoleinn.co.uk

Brace of Pheasants

Plush

In a sleepy hamlet surrounded by downland, this thatched brick and flint building is Dorset's prettiest pub – or a close contender. Originally two 16th-century cottages linked to the smithy, it became an inn in the 1930s and displays an unusual sign: a brace of pheasants in a glass case. Beyond the latch door, the traditional low-beamed main bar has charm and character, with an inglenook big enough to plonk yourself down in, a second impressive fireplace with a winter log fire, and an assortment of tables and chairs. Foaming pints of Doom Bar and Copper Ale are tapped from the cask to accompany plates of warming seasonal food – maybe lambs' kidneys with mustard cream sauce; roasted Lyme Bay sole; treacle tart to finish. Super-smart rooms lie upstairs under the thatch, and in the converted skittle alley overlooking the garden; all come with dramatic lamps, ornate drapes and splashes of colour (striking headboards, fancy bed throws, piles of cushions). Expect leather sofas, ceiling speakers and vast tiled bathrooms, too – and great walks from the door.

Price	£99. Singles £89.
Rooms	8 twins/doubles.
Meals	Lunch & dinner £9-£16. Bar meals from £6. Sunday lunch, 2 courses, £14.
Closed	Open all day.
Directions	Plush is signed off B3143 Dorchester-Sherborne road, just north of Piddletrenthide. In village on left.

Phil & Carol Bennett
Brace of Pheasants
Plush,
Dorchester DT2 7RQ

Tel +44 (0)1300 348357
Web www.braceofpheasants.co.uk

The Fontmell

Fontmell Magna

After a year-long refurbishment, the former Crown opened up shop in 2011 – with a change of name and a stylish new feel. Colourful cushions and striped bar stools, striking red and blue walls, deep leather sofas and a table laden with magazines and games combine to create a super-cosy feel. Quaff Keystone Brewery's Mallyshag Bitter and mussels and chips at scrubbed tables – or follow glass-enclosed corridors across babbling Collyer's Brook to the dining room, furnished in relaxed country-house style. Jazzy rugs, old tables, a wall of shelves stacked with wine bottles and books create an easy mood, so settle down and enjoy chef Tom Shaw's imaginative cooking. Dishes include treats such as crab and armagnac soup, classic oxtail suet pudding, Moroccan duck leg tagine and banana tarte tatin. Delve into the wines – the list is eclectic – and stay the night. Fabulous rooms, named after 'butterfly' in six languages, ooze comfort and warmth. Rich colours and fabrics, fine linen and goose down, swish bathrooms and quirky details are there to seduce you; the best, Mallyshag, has a fashionable roll top tub in the room.

Price	£85-£140. Singles £75-£130.
Rooms	6: 5 doubles, 1 twin/double.
Meals	Lunch, bar meals & dinner from £9.50. Sunday lunch, 2-3 courses, £17-£23.
Closed	Open all day.
Directions	On A350 between Shaftesbury & Blandford Forum.

Tom Shaw
The Fontmell
Fontmell Magna,
Shaftesbury SP7 0PA
Tel +44 (0)1747 811441
Web www.thefontmell.com

The Museum Inn

Farnham

In a village with roses round every door is one of the finest inns in England, built by the father of modern archaeology (his museum, the Pitt Rivers, is in Oxford). Today, James Harrison and his team keep the atmosphere warm and happy. Bedrooms – big in the main house, smaller in the stables, all super smart – have cool colours, crisp linen, fancy bathrooms (and hi-tech gadgetry in most), while the self-contained Moles Cottage is aimed at family groups in summer and shooters in season. The big 17th-century bar has a period feel – all flagstones, inglenook, fresh flowers and a fashionable mismatch of tables and chairs. There are cosy alcoves to hide in, a book-filled drawing room to browse and a smart white-raftered dining room. The head chef's dishes range from pork belly with braised red cabbage and mustard mash to roasted local-estate venison with butternut squash mash and sour cherry jus, all sourced from the freshest ingredients; iced apple parfait comes with apple and cinnamon tarte tatin. The inn, popular with the barbour-and-dog set, fabulous all year round, is quietest out of season.

Price	£110-£150. Four-poster £170-£180. Cottage from £140.
Rooms	8 + 1: 5 doubles, 2 twins/doubles, 1 four-poster. Self-catering cottage for 8.
Meals	Lunch from £8.50. Bar meals from £6.75 (lunch only). Dinner from £14. Sunday lunch, 2 courses, £21.
Closed	3pm-6pm (7pm Sun).
Directions	From Blandford, A354 for Salisbury for 6.5 miles, then left, signed Farnham. Inn on left in village.

James Harrison
The Museum Inn
Farnham,
Blandford Forum DT11 8DE

Tel +44 (0)1725 516261
Web www.museuminn.co.uk

The King John Inn

Tollard Royal

You're on the Dorset/Wiltshire border, lost in blissful country, with paths that lead up into glorious hills. Tumble back down to this super inn. Alex and Gretchen have refurbished every square inch and the place shines. Expect airy interiors, a smart country feel, a sun-trapping terrace and a fire that crackles in winter. Originally a foundry, it opened as a brewery in 1859 and, when beer proved more popular than horseshoes, the inn was born. You'll find three local ales on tap but great wines too – Alex loves the stuff and has opened his own shop across the courtyard – take home a bottle if you like what you drink. As for the food, it's as local as can be with game straight off the Rushmore estate and meat from over the hill; the sausages are a thing of rare beauty. Country-house bedrooms are the final treat. Some are bigger than others, three are in the Coach House, all come with wonderful fabrics, padded headboards, crisp white linen and super bathrooms (one has a slipper bath). In summer, a terraced lawn gives views over a couple of rooftops onto the woods. A perfect spot.

Price	£120-£170.
Rooms	8: 6 doubles, 2 twins/doubles.
Meals	Lunch from £7.95. Bar meals from £8.95. Dinner from £13.95. Sunday lunch, 3 courses, £30.
Closed	3pm-6pm.
Directions	South from Salisbury on A354, then right onto B3081 at roundabout after 8 miles. In village on right.

Alex & Gretchen Boon
The King John Inn
Tollard Royal,
Salisbury SP5 5PS
Tel +44 (0)1725 516207
Web www.kingjohninn.co.uk

Stapleton Arms

Buckhorn Weston

An inn with a big heart. There are no pretensions here, just kind, knowledgeable staff committed to running the place with informal panache. A facelift has brought a streak of glamour back to this old coaching inn, and a delightful garden at the back. Downstairs are sofas in front of the fire, a piano for live music in the bar and a restaurant in Georgian blue with shuttered windows and candles in the fireplace. You can eat wherever you want. Pork pies (to eat in or take out), serrano ham and scotch eggs all wait at the bar, but if you want a three-course feast you must book – it gets packed out. There are salmon and crab fishcakes, home-baked Dorset ham, banana tarte tatin, even a beer menu; ale matters here. On Sundays groups can order their own joint of meat, and there's always a menu for kids. Rooms above are soundproofed to ensure a good night's sleep. They're comfy-chic with Egyptian linen, fresh flowers, happy colours, perhaps a claw-foot bath. Also: maps and picnics, wellies if you want to walk, games for children, DVDs for all ages. Wincanton is close for the races.

Price	£80-£120. Singles £72-£96.
Rooms	4: 3 doubles, 1 twin/double.
Meals	Lunch from £5.50. Bar meals from £7.50. Dinner from £9.50.
Closed	3pm-6pm. Open all day Sat & Sun.
Directions	A303 to Wincanton. Into town right after fire station, signed Buckhorn Weston. Left at T-junction after 3 miles. In village, pub on right.

Rupert & Victoria Reeves
Stapleton Arms
Church Hill, Buckhorn Weston,
Gillingham SP8 5HS

Tel	+44 (0)1963 370396
Web	www.thestapletonarms.com

Rose & Crown Trent

Trent

In a sleepy estate village is a 15th-century pub – stone-built, thatched and peacefully hidden away next to the church down the lane. Owned by Wadworth and spruced up by tenant Heather, with help from managers Neven and Angela, it remains refreshingly simple, with a rug-strewn stone floors, winter log fires, soothing colours, glowing church candles on scrubbed tables, ticking grandfather clock, books and newspapers. Expect four gleaming handpumps (try the Bishops Tipple), squashy sofas, impressive artwork in the conservatory dining room and sylvan views from the bar... and a wagging welcome from Archie the spaniel. Food is simple, hearty and home-cooked and made from local ingredients – mussels with cider and chive cream, game casserole with thyme-roasted root vegetables, sticky toffee and walnut pudding, and excellent Sunday roasts.

Meals	Lunch from £7.95. Dinner from £9.95. Sunday lunch, 3 courses, from £19.95. Not Sun eves or Mon.
Closed	3pm-6pm Tues-Fri. Sun eves & Mon. Open all day Sat.
Directions	Just off the A30 between Sherborne and Yeovil.

Heather Kirk
Rose & Crown Trent
Trent,
Sherborne DT9 4SL
Tel +44 (0)1935 850776
Web www.roseandcrowntrent.co.uk

Entry 186 Map 3

The Half Moon

Melplash

Local boy-turned-chef Dan Clarke had already wowed customers at some of Dorset's best food pubs; now, with wife Jenny, he's taken on and spruced up this pretty, thatched roadside pub. Initial fears of a quiet winter in a seasidey area were soon dispelled as local foodies tracked him down and descended in hordes. Driven by passion and a desire to succeed on their own has seen this pair through several frantic early months, delivering charm and big smiles to the traditionally furnished bar alongside consistently good food. Dive into Lyme Bay scallops with celeriac purée and smoked pancetta, venison loin with confit shoulder and beetroot fondant, and posh fish pie. Just the ticket after a breezy downland stroll or a day fossil-hunting on the Jurassic coast – and there's a pretty garden with views.

Meals	Lunch & dinner £10-£16.50. Not Sunday eve or Monday.
Closed	Sun eves & Mon.
Directions	On A3066 Bridport to Beaminster road, 2 miles south of Beaminster.

Dan & Jen Clarke
The Half Moon
Melplash,
Bridport DT6 3UD
Tel +44 (0)1308 488321

Entry 187 Map 3

The Greyhound

Sydling St Nicholas

It's hard to fault this fabulous inn. It sits in one of Dorset's loveliest villages, lost in a lush valley with views that shoot uphill. Outside, roses, clematis and lavender add the colour; inside, rustic rooms have a warm traditional feel. Find stone walls, old flagstones, gilt mirrors and a wood-burner to keep things cosy. There's a lively locals' bar where you can grab a pint of Butcombe and sink into a chesterfield, and a lovely little restaurant with old beams and curios where you can dig into delicious food. The feel here is delightfully relaxed and you can eat wherever you want, so spin onto the terrace in good weather and feast on local food; try seared Lyme Bay scallops, pork belly with smoked hock hash, whole baked plaice. The Cerne Abbas giant is close, the walking is exceptional.

Meals	Lunch & dinner £11-£18.
Closed	2.30pm-6pm & from 3pm Sun.
Directions	Village signed off A37, 6 miles north of Dorchester.

Helena Boot & Alice Draper
The Greyhound
26 High Street, Sydling St Nicholas,
Dorchester DT2 9PD

Tel +44 (0)1300 341303
Web www.dorsetgreyhound.co.uk

Entry 188 Map 3

Dorset

Gaggle of Geese

Buckland Newton

Mark and Emily took on the forlorn Gaggle, deep in the Dorset downs, in 2009 – and worked their magic. Squashy sofas by the fire, bookcases and big flowers, church candles on old pine tables and a lick of Farrow & Ball did the trick in the bar; red walls and rugs soften the rambling dining room. Come for pints of Butcombe and modern pub food – goose leg hash, organic rump steak with pepper sauce, jam rolypoly. Meat comes from Mark's family farm at Cattistock, and allotment vegetables and game are delivered by locals – in return for a pint or two. Skittle evenings, lunch clubs, the village fête, Remembrance dinners, charity goose auctions, takeaway fish and chips... it's the village's adopted hub. Plans for five acres include a kitchen garden, rare-breed livestock and bedrooms.

Meals	Lunch from £4.50. Dinner from £10.
Closed	3.30pm-5.30pm. Open all day Sat & Sun.
Directions	In village centre off B3143, 10 miles north of Dorchester.

Mark & Emily Hammick
Gaggle of Geese
Buckland Newton,
Dorchester DT2 7BS

Tel +44 (0)1300 345249
Web www.thegaggle.co.uk

Entry 189 Map 3

The Square & Compass

Worth Matravers

The name honours those who cut stone from the nearby quarries. This splendid old pub has been in the family for generations and remains wonderfully unchanged; a narrow, and rare, drinking corridor leads to two hatches from where Palmer's Copper Ale and guest ales are drawn from the cask. With a pint of farmhouse cider and a homemade pastie, you can chat in the flagged corridor or settle in the parlour; find painted wooden panels, wall seats and local prints and cartoons, and a wood-burner to warm you on a wild night. The stone-walled main room has live music; there's cribbage and shove ha'penny and a fossil museum (the family's) next door. Gazing out across fields to the sea this pub and its sunny front terrace – dotted occasionally with free-ranging hens – is a popular stop for coastal path hikers. A national treasure.

Meals	Pasties £3.
Closed	3pm-6pm. Open all day Sat & Sun & every day July-Sept.
Directions	B3069 east of Corfe Castle; through Kingston; right for Worth Matravers.

Charlie Newman & Kevin Hunt
The Square & Compass
Worth Matravers,
Swanage BH19 3LF

Tel	+44 (0)1929 439229
Web	www.squareandcompasspub.co.uk

Entry 190 Map 3

Dorset

The Bull

Wimborne St Giles

In sleepy Wimborne St Giles, in the heart of the Cranborne Chase, is Mark's beautifully refurbished Bull. The open-plan bar-dining room is kitted out with old dining tables, decorative ceiling lights and grand paintings, along with leather armchairs and an old chesterfield by the cosy log fire; peruse the papers over a pint. Booking is advisable if you hope to eat: the food, from chef Ian Craddock, is the main draw, and the chefs are on display in the open kitchen. Choose from such delights as confit wild duck; whole bream with couscous and romesco sauce. Pudding lovers should leave room for a baked almond and pistachio filo! Wash it all down with a local ale or one of 18 well-chosen wines by the glass. There's also a peaceful rambling garden for simple summer drinking, just the thing after a great downland walk.

Meals	Lunch from £6.50. Dinner, 3 courses, £25-£30.
Closed	3pm-6pm.
Directions	M27 and A31 west, then B3081 north. Village signed left 1 mile south of Cranborne.

Mark Thornton
The Bull
Wimborne St Giles,
Wimborne BH21 5NF

Tel	+44 (0)1725 517300
Web	www.bullinnwsg.com

Entry 191 Map 3

The Victoria Inn

Durham

In the centre of lovely old-fashioned Durham – all cobbled streets, riverside walks, cathedral – is a Victorian public house with small rooms, high ceilings, marble fireplaces, three coal fires, etched and cut glass and a collection of Victoriana. Once upon a time, shawled ladies would pop in for a porter or an errant husband, now it's frequented by builders, students, academics and beer lovers. Virtually unaltered since it was built in 1899, The Vic has been in the Webster family for years and has a strong local following. The three traditional bar rooms are spick and span; above the servery is an unusual gallery with shining figurines and ornaments of Queen Victoria and the Prince Consort. Simple snacks are available but it is the Big Lamp and other local and Scottish beers, the whiskies and the camaraderie that makes this place enticing. Just-refurbished bedrooms and bathrooms are warm, comfortable and good value, with free WiFi; breakfasts are relaxed and generous and there's limited off-street parking and garaging. Original, timeless, welcoming – and five minutes to Durham Castle.

Price	£68-£70. Family room £65-£75. Singles £49-£68.
Rooms	6: 4 doubles, 1 twin, 1 family room.
Meals	Toasted sandwiches £1.50.
Closed	Open all day.
Directions	5-minute walk over Kingsgate Bridge from university, cathedral, castle & market place.

Michael Webster
The Victoria Inn
86 Hallgarth Street,
Durham DH1 3AS

Tel	+44 (0)191 386 5269
Web	www.victoriainn-durhamcity.co.uk

Rose & Crown

Romaldkirk

An idyllic village of mellow stone where little has changed in 200 years. The Rose and Crown dates from 1733 and stands on the green, next to the village's Saxon church. Roses ramble above the door in summer, so pick up a pint and search out the sun on the gravelled forecourt. Inside is just as good. You can sit at settles in the tiny locals' bar and roast away in front of the fire while reading the *Teesdale Mercury*, or seek out sofas in the peaceful sitting room and tuck into afternoon tea. Bedrooms are lovely. Those in the converted barn are less posh but have padded headboards and tumble with colour; those in the main house come with stylish furnishings and vibrant colours; all have Bose sound systems, quietly fancy bathrooms and lots of other extras. Delicious food can be eaten informally in the brasserie (smoked salmon soufflé, confit of duck, sticky toffee pudding) or grandly in the panelled dining room (farmhouse ham with fresh figs, grilled sea bass, honey and whisky ice cream). High Force waterfall and Hadrian's Wall are close and there's a drying room for walkers.

Price	£150-£190. Suites £210-£225. Singles from £95. Half-board from £110 p.p.
Rooms	12: 6 doubles, 4 twins, 2 suites.
Meals	Lunch & bar meals from £12. Dinner, 3 courses, from £35. Sunday lunch £18.95.
Closed	Open all day.
Directions	From Barnard Castle B6277 north for 6 miles. Right in village towards green. Inn on left.

Christopher & Alison Davy
Rose & Crown
Romaldkirk,
Barnard Castle DL12 9EB
Tel +44 (0)1833 650213
Web www.rose-and-crown.co.uk

Black Bull Inn

Frosterley

An enticing village pub run as its owners like it. It is atmospherically lit, with solid tables and high-back settles cushioned for comfort, stone flags, ticking clocks, glowing ranges, warmth and good cheer. No lagers, but coffee and scones from 10.30am, cider from the cask and beers from a few villages away. The hop is treated with reverence here – dark malty porter from Wylam Brewery, bitter from Allendale – and the good value food is a joy. Rather than devising a menu then searching for suppliers, Diane and Duncan source the produce first: local if possible, and in tune with the seasons. A herb-crusted lamb shoulder with apricot stuffing, served with three root dauphinoise and rosemary jus is the sort of thing they do well here. Regular classical, folk and jazz sessions, too... hey, this place even has its own peal of bells.

Meals	Lunch £7.95-£12.95. Dinner £11.95-£18.95. Sunday lunch from £9.95.
Closed	Sun from 5pm. Mon & Tues.
Directions	Beside A689 in Weardale between Wolsingham & Stanhope, next to Frosterley steam railway station.

Duncan & Diane Davis
Black Bull Inn
Bridge End, Frosterley,
Bishop Auckland DL13 2SL

Tel +44 (0)1388 527784
Web www.blackbullfrosterley.com

Entry 194 Map 12

Durham

Bridgewater Arms

Winston

A Victorian schoolhouse with views rising across fields to distant woods: an unusual setting for a stylish modern bar and restaurant. The memory of the old school is carefully retained in the bar, with its high ceiling, decorative leaded windows, shelves of books and photos of pupils past; the names of the children that took part in 1957's *Jack and the Beanstalk* are inscribed above the bar, adding charm and a touch of history. Adjoining half-panelled dining rooms are warmly decorated and furnished in contemporary style. Blackboards and daily printed menus place firm emphasis on fresh, local supplies with a strong emphasis on fish and game in season – roast grouse with game gravy, sea trout with herb butter sauce – cooked by Paul Grundy, former head chef at the renowned Black Bull in Moulton.

Meals	Lunch & dinner £10-£20.
Closed	2.30pm-6pm. Sun & Mon.
Directions	Just off A67 between Darlington & Barnard Castle; at entrance to village on Staindrop crossroad.

Paul Grundy
Bridgewater Arms
Winston,
Darlington DL2 3RN

Tel +44 (0)1325 730302
Web www.thebridgewaterarms.com

Entry 195 Map 12

Number Twenty 2

Darlington

It is young, yet it is Darlington's most classic pub. Just off the town centre, the Victorian-styled "Traditional Alehouse & Canteen" looks no different from the neighbouring shop fronts. Inside, a high ceiling and raised areas in the front bays give a vault-like impression; Number Twenty 2 is licensed for the sale of ales, wines and a limited range of spirits. There are up to eleven changing guest ales alongside four house beers, nine continental beers on tap, and a good choice of wines chosen for easy quaffing; it's a civilised place favoured by local business folk, and the staff know their stuff. At the back of the long bar is a seating area known as the 'canteen' at lunchtimes, and the food is good and uncomplicated. It may be closed on Sundays, but for the rest of the week Darlington has a very fine local.

Meals	Lunch & dinner £6-£12.
Closed	Sun.
Directions	Just west of Darlington town centre. Coniscliffe Road leads into A67 to Barnard Castle.

Ralph Wilkinson
Number Twenty 2
22 Coniscliffe Road,
Darlington DL3 7RG

Tel	+44 (0)1325 354590
Web	www.villagebrewer.co.uk

Entry 196 Map 12

The Bay Horse

Hurworth

A pretty, bow-fronted building, painted cream under red pantiles, which sits happily at the end of a terrace with open countryside beyond. Inside is nicely pubby: comforting button-back wall seating, polished oak floor boards, local prints and soft wall lamps, quiet background jazz. At least two good cask ales are served (in dimpled tankards), and truly stunning food from chef Marcus Bennett is brought to you by friendly folk in crisp aprons; you eat in a dining room with antique tables and proper linen napkins. Try wild duck and pistachio terrine with fig chutney, smoked bacon, scrambled egg and toasted mushroom and onion brioche – the eggs come in a shell with a soldier! Puddings are irresistible – try caramelised rice pudding with spiced autumn berries, even the bread is home baked and there are private dining rooms upstairs.

Meals	Lunch from £12.95. Bar meals from £6.95. Dinner from £13.95. Sunday lunch, 3 courses, £21.95.
Closed	Open all day.
Directions	Hurworth is signed off A167, 2 miles south of Darlington at Croft. Pub is 1 mile in village centre.

Marcus Bennett & Jonathan Hall
The Bay Horse
45 The Green, Hurworth,
Darlington DL2 2AA

Tel	+44 (0)1325 720663
Web	www.thebayhorsehurworth.com

Entry 197 Map 12

The Bell Inn & Hill House

Horndon-on-the-Hill

A 600-year-old timber-framed coaching inn, as bustling today with contented locals as it was when pilgrims stopped on their way to Canterbury. Everything here is a delight: hanging lanterns in the courtyard, stripped boards in the bar, superb staff in the restaurant, copious window boxes bursting with colour. This is a proper inn, warmly welcoming, with thick beams, country rugs, panelled walls and open fires. Stop for a pint of cask ale in the lively bar, then potter into the restaurant for top food, perhaps stilton ravioli, grilled Dover sole, orange and passionfruit tart. Christine grew up here, John joined her years ago; both are much respected in the trade, as is Joanne, Master sommelier and loyal manager of many years. An infectious warmth runs throughout this ever-popular inn. As for the bedrooms, go for the suites above: cosily inviting, individual, quite fancy. In the morning stroll up the tiny high street to breakfast with the papers at elegant Hill House, where further bedrooms, some snazzily refurbished, lie. Then head north into Constable country, or east to the pier at Southend. Wonderful.

Price	£50-£60. Suites £85.
Rooms	15: 5 suites. Hill House: 7 doubles, 3 twins.
Meals	Lunch from £11.95. Bar meals from £8.95. Dinner, à la carte, £27. Not bank holidays.
Closed	2.30pm-5.30pm (3pm Sat. 4pm-7pm Sun).
Directions	M25 junc. 30/31. A13 dir. Southend for 3 miles; B1007 to Horndon on the Hill. On left in village.

Christine & John Vereker
The Bell Inn & Hill House
High Road, Horndon-on-the-Hill,
Stanford-le-Hope SS17 8LD
Tel +44 (0)1375 642463
Web www.bell-inn.co.uk

The Lion Inn

Boreham

On the A12, in need of sustenance or a comfortable bed? Look no further than the Lion. Money has been lavished on the old roadside pub, now dwarfed by its restaurant and B&B extensions, rolling back to a decked terrace and a secluded herb garden. It may look big and brash but the tardis-like interior has been cleverly kitted out in eclectic style. Expect the unexpected: a long bar with gleaming beer fonts, old signs and a distinctly French feel, a bustling open-plan kitchen, a vast dining area filled with old tables, leather armchairs and standard lamps; a floor-to-ceiling wine rack covers one wall. Beyond, in the original pub, are cosy beamed dining rooms and a new conservatory. Modern menus list sharing platters and pasta meals alongside classic grills and specials like Irish stew and fish pie. Smart air-conditioned bedrooms, named after French villages are adorned with old French prints, dark repro antiques, big down-topped beds, fresh coffee; bathrooms sport rain showers, Damana lotions and the odd splash of marble. A super-duper bolthole in Essex's heart.

Price	£89-£150.
Rooms	15 doubles.
Meals	Lunch from £7.95. Bar meals from £6.25. Dinner from £9.95. Sunday lunch, 2-3 courses, £17-£22.
Closed	Open all day
Directions	On B1137 between Chelmsford & Hatfield Peverel, 0.5 mile east of A12 (junction 19).

Julie Mirams
The Lion Inn
Main Road, Boreham,
Chelmsford CM3 3JA
Tel +44 (0)1245 394900
Web www.lioninnhotel.co.uk

The Pheasant

Gestingthorpe

Smack on the Essex/Suffolk border, with serene views over the Stour valley, the Pheasant thrives under former garden designer James Donoghue and wife Diana, who have transformed it from a run-down boozer to a popular food-led community pub. The two cosy, countrified bars draw village folk in for quiz nights, wine tasting events, bonfire night revels, a monthly supper club, and the Thirsty Thursday Club, when locals gather for drinks and complimentary snacks. Well-informed foodies help swell the numbers, attracted by James's seasonal monthly menus and dishes like potted crab, lamb and smoked mushroom pie, and apple, pear and quince crumble. James also finds time to smoke fish, seafood and cheeses , maintain his award-winning Chelsea show garden (beautifully re-created outside), and both oversee five super new rooms in the Coach House. Named after local historical characters and all with a different feel, they have big comfortable beds, smart bathrooms, mini-fridges, fresh coffee and flat-screens. The Constable room has a four-poster, double shower, and a view that takes in 22 churches.

Price	£90-£150.
Rooms	5: 2 doubles, 2 twins/doubles, 1 four-poster.
Meals	Dinner from £10. Bar meals from £5.95. Sunday lunch, 3 courses, £18.50.
Closed	Open all day.
Directions	Sent on booking.

James & Diana Donoghue
The Pheasant
Gestingthorpe,
Halstead CO9 3AU
Tel +44 (0)1787 461196
Web www.thepheasant.net

The Mistley Thorn
Mistley

In Constable land: an unexpectedly chi-chi village where Georgian cottages gather around a river estuary with wide, light views of water, bobbing boats and green hills beyond. David and Sherri (who have a cookery school next door) run the place beautifully: staff are young and very good, there are plenty of locals tossed into the mix downstairs and some impeccably behaved children too. The mood is laid-back city wine bar rather than roadside country pub. Colours are soft and easy, the tables are of various shapes, candles flicker, modern art rubs along well with the odd antique and food is taken seriously but with no grim reverence. There's lots of good local fish and seafood – squid with chilli, garlic and lemon oil, crab cakes with mayonnaise, gurnard with black olive tapenade, brilliant chips – and a pudding list that includes cheesecake from Sherri's mum. Bedrooms are calm with cream carpets, big beds and pale green paintwork; ask for a room with a view over the river. Bathrooms have a Turkish feel with tiny beige and cream tiles, spotless white baths and overhead showers. It's all entirely charming.

Price	£90-£120. Singles from £75.
Rooms	7: 4 doubles, 3 twins/doubles.
Meals	Lunch from £6.25. Set lunch £11.95 & £14.95. Dinner, 3 courses, about £25.
Closed	3pm-6.30pm. Open all day Sat & Sun.
Directions	From A12 Hadleigh/East Bergholt exit north of Colchester. Thro' East Bergholt to A137; signed Manningtree; continue to Mistley High St. 50 yards from station.

David McKay & Sherri Singleton
The Mistley Thorn
High Street, Mistley,
Manningtree CO11 1HE
Tel +44 (0)1206 392821
Web www.mistleythorn.co.uk

The Sun Inn

Dedham

These days you can hire boats on the river, so order a picnic at the inn, float down the Stour, and tie up on the bank for lunch al fresco. You're in Constable country here, in an idyllic village made rich by mills in the 16th century and you couldn't hope to wash up in a better place. Step in to find log fires in grand grates, board games on old tables, stripped floors and an easy elegance. A panelled lounge comes with sofas and armchairs, the bar is made from a slab of local elm and the dining room is beamed and airy. Settle in for delicious food that's inspired by Italy: celeriac and black cabbage soup; pasta with red mullet, tomatoes, olives, thyme and chilli; hake baked with tomatoes, fennel and parsley; pork chop with cannellini beans and salsa verde. The cheeses are local and children may have portions of whatever they fancy.

Meals	Lunch & dinner from £12. Bar meals from £6.85. Sunday lunch £24.
Closed	Open all day.
Directions	A12 north past Colchester. 2nd exit, signed Dedham. In village opposite church.

Piers Baker
The Sun Inn
High Street, Dedham,
Colchester CO7 6DF

Tel +44 (0)1206 323351
Web www.thesuninndedham.com

Entry 202 Map 10

Essex

The Compasses at Pattiswick

Pattiswick

Jono and Jane Clark's transformation of this old pub is a huge success. Slick and sophisticated bars mix flagstones with floorboards, modern furniture and soft lights with creams and sages. At heart it remains a local, with plenty of space for drinkers in for a pint of Woodforde's Wherry or Abbot Ale. Yet the food is the major draw, served in the bar or the elegantly beamed and spacious restaurant. Old favourites such as British Excellence bangers with mash and onion gravy are founded on well-sourced raw materials, for the kitchen cultivates a network of small local producers. More modern dishes might include grilled sea bass and minted jersey royals with pepperonata or chicken chorizo with roasted red pepper terrine; for pudding, who could resist sticky toffee pudding with hot toffee sauce? Outside: a terrace and an adventure play area so children may romp.

Meals	Lunch from £6.75. Dinner from £11.95. Sunday lunch from £12.95. Not Sun eves.
Closed	Open all day.
Directions	B1024 towards Coggeshall from A12, then left on A120 towards Braintree & take 2nd right for Pattiswick.

Jono & Jane Clark
The Compasses at Pattiswick
19 Compasses Road, Pattiswick,
Braintree CM77 8BG

Tel +44 (0)1376 561322
Web www.thegreatpubcompany.co.uk

Entry 203 Map 10

The Cricketers Arms

Rickling Green

Having snapped up the Cricketers in 2011, Leanne Langman is working her magic and restoring the fortunes of this striking 200-year-old red-brick inn. The setting is tranquil and gorgeous, overlooking a vast village green and cricket pitch; arrive early on a summer Sunday to bag a bench and watch an innings or two with a foaming pint of Wherry. Rickling Green became *the* venue for London society cricket matches in the 1880s and it's still taken seriously. There's a contemporary feel to the rambling bar and dining areas – old beams and timbers, wood and stone floors, chunky tables, colourful cushions on banquettes, sofas and easy chairs in front of a crackling log fire. Hungry? Tuck into grazing boards, risottos, fishcakes, lamb and mint pies, dry-aged steaks and sticky toffee puddings – best enjoyed on the terrace on warm days.

Meals	Lunch & dinner £9.50-£16.95.
Closed	Open all day.
Directions	Rickling Green is signposted off B1383 midway between Saffron Walden & Bishops Stortford; pub overlooks the green.

Leanne Langman
The Cricketers Arms
Rickling Green,
Saffron Walden CB11 3YG
Tel +44 (0)1799 543210
Web www.thecricketersarmsricklinggreen.co.uk

Essex

The Eight Bells

Saffron Walden

Leanne's first 'Cosy Pub' is a beautifully restored 16th-century wool merchant's house tucked away on a street lined with wonky timbered and painted houses, an easy stroll from the town centre. Find bowed beams, old wall timbers, crackling logs in a big brick fireplace, polished wooden floors, Farrow & Ball colours and chesterfield armchairs in cosy corners; the relaxing bars are perfect for quaffing pints of Taylor Landlord and sharing a charcuterie grazing board. Arrive early to bag a table in the historic barn at the back, replete with vaulted ceiling and painted timbers. With two wood-burners keeping things toasty, tuck into baked camembert with rustic breads, lamb shank with redcurrant and rosemary jus, and Blackberry Eton Mess; or come on Sunday for a classic roast. Outside is a swish summer terrace.

Meals	Lunch & bar meals from £10. Dinner from £20. Sunday lunch, 2 courses, £13.50.
Closed	Open all day.
Directions	On B184 just north of the town centre.

Leanne Langman
The Eight Bells
18 Bridge Street,
Saffron Walden CB10 1BU
Tel +44 (0)1799 522790
Web www.8bells-pub.co.uk

Seagrave Arms

Weston Subedge

Locked and unloved for nearly two years, this classic Cotswold coaching inn has been snapped up by Kevin and Sue and restored to its former Georgian glory. Worn flagstones draw you into the cosy, wood-floored bar, where leather armchairs by the inglenook provide the perfect spot to cradle a pint of Hooky, or to ponder Kevin Harris's mouthwatering modern menu. Served at old dining tables in two warm and inviting candlelit rooms, a delicious meal may kick off with Lighthorne lamb sweetbreads with pumpkin and sage ravioli, be followed by partridge with roasted marrow and game sauce, and finished with crème brûlée and poached fruits – or a slate of Cotswold cheeses. Meat and game are sourced from local farms and shoots; everything, including the breads, chutneys and the lunchtime burgers, is freshly prepared. Immaculate, well-designed bedrooms are the icing on the cake. Look forward to top-notch linen and down, fresh coffee, homemade cookies, and high-spec bathrooms with Ren soaps and walk-in showers. Just 20 minutes from Stratford-upon-Avon and Cheltenham, strolling distance from Chipping Campden and the Cotswold Way.

Price	£95-£125.
Rooms	7: 6 doubles, 1 suite.
Meals	Lunch & dinner from £10.95.
Closed	Tues-Fri 3pm-5pm & all day Mon. Open all day Sat & Sun.
Directions	London-Oxford M40 junc. 8; A44 to Broadway/Evesham; B4632 towards Stratford-upon-Avon.

Kevin & Sue Davies
Seagrave Arms
Friday Street, Weston Subedge,
Chipping Campden GL55 6QH

Tel +44 (0)1386 840192
Web www.seagravearms.co.uk

Ebrington Arms

Ebrington

The glorious gardens at Hidcote Manor and Kiftsgate Court are a ramble across fields from the Ebrington Arms. This is a relaxed and rustic Cotswold stone pub that has been restored and revived by Claire and Jim. Little has changed in the 17th-century bar, hub of the community, cosy with low beams and roaring fires. Bag a seat and share pints of Purity with the regulars, or seek out the fun dining room next door. Worn stone floors, fresh flowers and a delightful mishmash of tables and chairs set the scene for some terrific pub food cooked from mostly local produce. Dishes are simple yet full of flavour, so dive in to scallops with celeriac purée and black pudding, calves' liver with garlic mash and caramelised onion jus, and apple, strawberry and ginger crumble. No need to negotiate the route home when you can bed down here; bedrooms (up steepish stairs) are full of charm, with chunky wooden beds, colourful throws and plump pillows, deep window seats with village or country views, and smart new bathrooms. A properly unpretentious pub, run by the nicest people.

Price	£80-£125. Min. 2 nights at weekends.
Rooms	5 doubles.
Meals	Lunch & dinner £9-£17.50. Limited menu Sunday eve.
Closed	Open all day.
Directions	West from Shipston-on-Stour on B4035. Across A429. After a mile, bear right at sharp left-hand bend; village signed, pub signed.

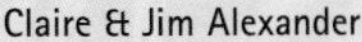

Claire & Jim Alexander
Ebrington Arms
Ebrington,
Chipping Campden GL55 6NH
Tel +44 (0)1386 593223
Web www.theebringtonarms.co.uk

The Churchill Arms

Paxford

On the edge of a pretty village, next to a tiny church and fields of sheep, is this authentic Cotswold pub. Polished wooden tables, chairs and cushioned pews sit beneath a beamed ceiling, a wood-burner warms the flagstones, and from behind the neat bar, charming staff pull a well-kept pint of Hook Norton. Sit down, settle in, and look forward to the arrival of unfussy food with wonderful flavours. Our braised pork belly with roast butternut squash and morel jus was divine, while the Bramley apple and blackberry compote with nutmeg crème brûlée and shortbread was a beautiful Anglo-Gallic melange. On the blackboard are bar snacks such as sardines on toast and crab bruschetta with lemon and coriander; expect top local cheeses and interesting wines, too. Four bedrooms upstairs, three with postcard views, have a contemporary/traditional take with a mix of beams, mullion windows, elm boards, original art and antique furniture. In the garden, lively teams play traditional Aunt Sally in summer. In short, a near-perfect pub tucked just off the tourist trail – arrive early!

Price	From £80-£95. Singles £60-£75.
Rooms	4 doubles.
Meals	Lunch & dinner £9.50-£17.95.
Closed	3pm-6pm.
Directions	From Moreton-in-Marsh N on A429; 2 miles, left signed Paxford. Follow lane then left on B4479 down hill to Paxford.

Richard Shore
The Churchill Arms
Paxford,
Chipping Campden GL55 6XH

Tel	+44 (0)1386 594000
Web	www.thechurchillarms.com

Horse & Groom

Bourton-on-the-Hill

You're at the top of the hill, so grab the window seats for views that pour over the Cotswolds. This is a hive of youthful endeavour, with brothers at the helm; Will cooks, Tom pours the ales, and a cheery conviviality flows. Refurbished interiors mix the old (open fires, stone walls, beamed ceilings) with the new (halogen lighting, crisp coir matting, a cool marble bar), making this a very fine place in which to hole up for a night or two. There are settles and boarded menus in the bar, stripped wooden floors and old rugs in the dining room. Food goes way beyond the pub norm, so tuck into fillet of Loch Duart salmon baked in pastry with currents, ginger and hollandaise, Cornish mackerel, Longhorn steak. Sit back in summer under the shade of damson trees with a mellow pint of Goff's Jouster and watch the chefs raid the kitchen garden – for raspberries, strawberries, broad beans, herbs and more. Bedrooms are nicely plush, smart but uncluttered; those at the front are soundproofed to minimise noise from the road. The deluxe room is huge and comes with a king-sized bed, the garden room has doors that open onto the terrace.

Price	£115-£165. Singles £80. Half-board from £70 p.p.
Rooms	5 doubles.
Meals	Lunch & dinner from £11.50. Not Sunday eve.
Closed	3pm-6pm. Sun eves.
Directions	West from Moreton-in-Marsh on A44. Climb hill in Bourton-on-the-Hill; pub at top on left. Moreton-in-Marsh railway station 2 miles away.

Tom & Will Greenstock
Horse & Groom
Bourton-on-the-Hill,
Moreton-in-Marsh GL56 9AQ

Tel	+44 (0)1386 700413
Web	www.horseandgroom.info

White Hart Inn

Stow-on-the-Wold

Stow's famous old market square goes all the way back to 1107 and was built on the orders of Henry I. The White Hart stands on its northern flank and has an experienced new pair at the helm, Peter and Louise, owners of the very delightful Old Butchers restaurant down the road. Inside, beautifully refurbished interiors sit perfectly amid old walls and it's all very relaxing. The front bar comes in period colours with stripped floorboards, shuttered windows and an open fire, while a cool rustic chic pours through the dining room. Here you dig into Peter's delicious food, perhaps tarragon potted shrimps followed by chicken, leek and crayfish pie, plaice with lemon butter sauce, apple and blackberry crumble. Bedrooms come in different shapes and sizes with fabulous little shower rooms. The small ones are perfect for a night or two, but if you're staying longer, go for the Stag which overlooks the square; it has a wonderful roll top bath in its room. All share the same country style: low ceilings, wonky floors, cool colours, papered walls. And the friendly young staff are lovely.

Price	£80-£120. Singles from £60.
Rooms	5 doubles.
Meals	Lunch from £6.25. Bar meals from £5.25. Dinner from £9.75. Sunday lunch, 3 courses, £22.
Closed	Sunday evenings.
Directions	M4 junc. 15, A419 north, then A429 for Stow. On the square in town.

Peter & Louise Robinson
White Hart Inn
The Square,
Stow-on-the-Wold,
Cheltenham GL54 1AF
Tel +44 (0)1451 830674

The White Hart Inn

Winchcombe

A stroll from Sudeley Castle is a 16th-century village pub for trekkers of the Cotswold Way – and all who love the Cotswolds. Ongoing changes by the owner are slowly returning the old place to its coaching inn roots so, although gastrofied, there are still quarry tiles, scrubbed pine tables and framed cricketing memorabilia in the pubby front bar. Eat in here or in the intimate little dining room (just five tables); the food is a treat. Start with a pint of Goffs Jouster or one of 20 exceptional wines by the glass, move on to devilled lambs' kidneys, pork belly with cider gravy, nut roast, venison stew, spiced apple crumble. The menu is awash with local produce, and lists its suppliers. Refurbishment is ongoing upstairs, with most of the 11 rooms upgraded – including the simple Ramblers Rooms at the top – so look forward to Farrow & Ball colours, antique pine, chunky wooden beds and super slate-floored bathrooms. Another brilliant touch: if you dine in, there's an organic wine shop that allows you to choose your bottle at cost price, plus corkage. Winchcombe is wonderfully quaint.

Price	£40-£115.
Rooms	11: 8 twins/doubles en suite; 3 ramblers rooms sharing bathroom.
Meals	Lunch & dinner £9.95-£16.95. Bar meals from £3.95. Sunday lunch, 3 courses, £17.50.
Closed	Open all day.
Directions	From Cheltenham, B4632 to Winchcombe. Inn on right.

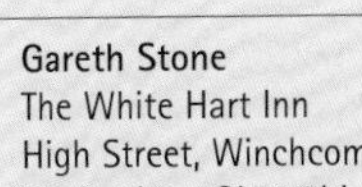

Gareth Stone
The White Hart Inn
High Street, Winchcombe,
Cheltenham GL54 5LJ

Tel +44 (0)1242 602359
Web www.whitehartwinchcombe.co.uk

The Wheatsheaf Inn

Northleach

A well-kept Cotswold secret, this small former wool market town is tucked between pretty hills on a crossroads of the Roman Fosse Way. Big smiles from a young staff greet you and a pint of fresh local bitter will be in your hand before you know it. The wonderfully worn flagstones in the very well-stocked bar separate two well-proportioned and coordinated dining areas, aglow with wooden floors, striking Asian rugs and armchairs fronting crackling fires. Expect a mix of traditional English fare of unpretentious goodness and impeccable provenance, from steak frites and garlic butter to cod with roast Jerusalem artichoke, chorizo and crayfish. Wine from the best of the old world has been carefully chosen to suit all budgets. Retire to rooms in contemporary-retro style, some newly refurbished and each one a treat, with huge beds, eclectic paintings, calm colours, wall coverings. Swish bathrooms too, with roll top baths or storm showers and dressing gowns to wrap up in. A brilliant little bolthole to return to after a day out exploring the High Wold countryside and villages, with a youthful buzz.

Price	£130-£200.
Rooms	14 doubles.
Meals	Lunch & dinner £7-£17. Bar meals from £5.
Closed	Open all day.
Directions	In village centre, off A429 between Stow & Burford.

Pub with rooms

Sam & Georgina Pearman
The Wheatsheaf Inn
West End, Northleach,
Cheltenham GL54 3EZ
Tel +44 (0)1451 860244
Web www.cotswoldswheatsheaf.com

Green Dragon

Cowley

Hidden down a sleepy lane somewhere off the A435, this mellow Cotswold stone building, festooned with honeysuckle and hanging baskets, was a cider house three centuries ago. It's still beautifully traditional inside. So settle down with a pint of Butcombe in the stone-flagged bar, all warm mustard walls and glowing candles, logs crackling in the inglenook, rustic beams and blackboard menus. Furnishings are hand-crafted by 'Mouseman' Thompson (look for the mouse trademark signature) and the food is comforting, fresh and delicious. Tuck into a bowl of chilli or haddock in lemon batter, or, in winter, something more substantial, a hearty mutton stew or a steak and kidney pudding with minted mushy peas. The pick of the courtyard-annexe bedrooms – most compact, kitted out in contemporary style and named after Gold Cup winners – is the St George's Suite above the former stables, a vast room with deep leather sofas and a king-size bed, a flat-screen TV, books, magazines and a huge tiled bathroom with free standing bath and walk-in shower. Wonderful walks start from the front door.

Price	£95-£150. Singles £70.
Rooms	9: 8 twins/doubles, 1 suite.
Meals	Lunch & dinner £7.50-£18.95.
Closed	Open all day.
Directions	Cockleford is signed off A435 at Elkstone south of Cheltenham.

Simon & Nicky Haly
Green Dragon
Cockleford, Cowley,
Cheltenham GL53 9NW
Tel +44 (0)1242 870271
Web www.green-dragon-inn.co.uk

Bathurst Arms

North Cerney

James has worked hard to breathe new life into this handsome inn on the Bathurst Estate. The once neglected 17th-century building now exudes warmth and energy as locals, walkers and travellers drop in for pints of Hooky and unpretentious, delicious pub food. The stone-flagged bar is the hub of the place, warmed by a crackling log fire. Eat here or head next door to James's pride and joy, the revamped restaurant, with open kitchen and a sitting area that displays the wine list – just choose a bottle from the shelf. Allotment vegetables, Cerney goat's cheese, game from Withington and local farm beef are championed, so tuck into rabbit and hare pie, pork loin with gratin dauphinoise and roasted onion jus, pumpkin torte with garden-grown quince, banana and lime cheesecake with gingerbread ice cream. It's the best of British and the set menu is a steal. Spruced-up bedrooms, two with white four-posters, provide a homely base for city folk escaping to the Cotswolds: clean, comfortable, freshly painted and TV-free. Room 2 is compact; ask for a room with a view.

Price	From £80. Singles from £60.
Rooms	7: 5 doubles, 2 twins.
Meals	Lunch & dinner £10.95-£16.95. Bar meals £3.95-£8.95.
Closed	Open all day.
Directions	Beside A435 Cirencester-Cheltenham road, 4 miles north of Cirencester.

James Walker
Bathurst Arms
North Cerney,
Cirencester GL7 7BZ

Tel	+44 (0)1285 831281
Web	www.bathurstarms.com

The Fleece at Cirencester

Cirencester

Charles II once stayed at this coaching inn – posing as a manservant, the story goes. Now it's had a serious refurb, in classic English style. By Easter 2012, bar, lounge and restaurant will glow; bedrooms already do so, spreading across three floors. Open all day, the Fleece has quite a buzz. Drop by for a wake-up coffee and eggs on toast; choose a deli board at lunchtime and a pint of Thwaites. There are daily specials and Sunday roasts – our beef steak with chips was delicious. As for the staff, they're charming, well-trained and smartly turned out. Set off into the Cotswolds for a hike with the dog, browse the antique shops and the chic little delis, then come back to the Fleece for the night. The 'Character' rooms, with their beamy, up-in-the-roof feeling, are the best, but all are top-notch, with plush carpets and dark boards, beds antique and new, coordinated cushions, feature wallpapers, plump pillows and Crabtree & Evelyn soaps... face the famous market square and watch the world go by, or settle quietly into a room at the back. The Fleece is a crowd-pleaser from start to finish.

Price	£75-£150.
Rooms	28: 24 doubles/suites, 3 twins/doubles, 1 family room.
Meals	Lunch from £6.95. Bar meals from £4.95. Dinner from £8.95. Sunday lunch, 2 courses, £11.95.
Closed	Open all day.
Directions	Cirencester on A417. From London Road, turn right onto The Waterloo, car park end of road on left.

Rebecca Smith
The Fleece at Cirencester
Market Place,
Cirencester GL7 2NZ

Tel +44 (0)1285 658507
Web www.thefleececirencester.co.uk

The Village Pub

Barnsley

An old favourite of locals and faithfuls from far and wide, this civilised Cotswold bolthole has been given a gentle facelift by Calcot Health & Leisure – owners of Barnsley House, the country-house hotel across the road. Expect seasonal food based on the best local produce, good-quality Hook Norton ale and decent wines. There's even a service hatch to the heated patio at the back, so you can savour the sauvignon until the sun goes down. Cotswold stone and ancient flags sing the country theme; past bar and open fires, quiet alcoves provide a snug setting that entices you to stay. If you do, tuck into crab and leek tart, rib-eye steak with béarnaise sauce, or whole plaice with crab and parsley butter; sweet tooths will love the warm ginger cake with rum and raisin ice cream. Classy, spruced-up rooms are equally cosy and inviting, with soothing colours, stylish fabrics, plasma screens and iPod docks. Two stunning four-poster rooms have big bathrooms with claw-foot baths, walk-in showers, posh toiletries. Roman Cirencester and gorgeous Bibury are close by; this is classic Cotswold country.

Price	£125-£150.
Rooms	6: 4 twins/doubles, 2 four-posters.
Meals	Lunch & bar meals from £6. Dinner from £12.50. Sunday lunch, 3 courses, £28.
Closed	Open all day.
Directions	From M4 exit junc. 15. A419 for Gloucester; right onto B4425 for Bibury; village 2 miles.

Michele Mella
The Village Pub
Barnsley,
Cirencester GL7 5EF

Tel +44 (0)1285 740421
Web www.thevillagepub.co.uk

Inn at Fossebridge

Fossebridge

Here, on the old Roman road, rusticity and elegance achieve the perfect balance at this gorgeous 17th-century coaching inn run with aplomb by the Jenkins family. Stone archways divide the bar, which is as authentic as they come with flagstone floors, stone walls, open fires, beamed ceilings and a real hubbub at lunchtime. Throw in real ales, roast lunches and a welcome for all and you have somewhere worth going out of your way for. The Georgian style dining room pulls in lovers of good food for local venison haunch steak, celeriac dauphinoise, braised red cabbage and bitter chocolate jus with lavender crème brûlée to finish. The pub gardens is one of the largest and most attractive in the Cotswolds with a two-acre lake, mature trees, barbecues in summer, a tyre swing and wooden tractor and train for children. Bedrooms, country-smart, and decorated in Georgian style, range from smallish to spacious, with coordinated fabrics, striped walls, L'Occitane goodies, flat-screen TVs. There's also an elegant residents sitting room. Walk from the pub up the River Coln valley and revel in glorious countryside.

Price	£89-£170. Ask about mid-week offers.
Rooms	9: 8 twins/doubles, 1 family suite for 3.
Meals	Lunch & dinner £11.00-£21.50. Bar meals £4.50-£9.50. Sunday lunch £14.
Closed	Open all day.
Directions	Beside A429 between Cirencester & Northleach.

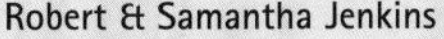

Robert & Samantha Jenkins
Inn at Fossebridge
Fossebridge,
Cheltenham GL54 3JS
Tel +44 (0)1285 720721
Web www.fossebridgeinn.co.uk

The New Inn at Coln

Coln St Aldwyns

The New Inn is old – 1632 to be exact – but well-named nonetheless. The pub stands in a handsome Cotswold village with ivy roaming on original stone walls and a sun-trapping terrace where roses bloom in summer. Owner Christoph Brooke has injected his quirky trademark Indian Empire feel into the refurbished inn – see the Bath Arms, Wiltshire and The Elephant at Pangbourne, Berks. Airy interiors have low ceilings, painted beams, flagged floors and fires that roar – perfect for supping pints of real ale with roast beef and horseradish sandwiches, or lingering over seared scallops, pan-roasted duck and baked lemon tart, served in red-walled dining rooms by thoroughly delightful staff. Bedrooms are a treat, all warmly elegant with soft carpets, swish bed throws, perfect white linen in good little bathrooms (a couple with claw-foot baths). There are wonky floors and the odd beam in the main house, while those in the Dovecote come in bold colours and have views across water meadows to the river; walks start from the door. Bibury, Burford and Stow are all close, so spread your wings.

Price	£140-£160. Singles from £130. Half-board from £90 p.p.
Rooms	14 doubles.
Meals	Lunch from £5.95. Dinner, 3 courses, about £30. Sunday lunch from £12.50.
Closed	Open all day.
Directions	From Oxford A40 past Burford, then B4425 for Bibury. Left after Aldsworth to Coln St Aldwyns.

Stuart Hodges
The New Inn at Coln
Main Street, Coln St Aldwyns,
Cirencester GL7 5AN
Tel +44 (0)1285 750651
Web www.new-inn.co.uk

The King's Arms Inn

Didmarton

The spruced-up roadside village inn sports slate floors, stone lintels, mellow walls and oak settles in the bar, and a cheekily bright front room adorned with lithographs of the area. In the dining room are terracotta walls, carved panels and smart high-backed chairs. There's a big old fireplace for winter, darts and dominoes for fun, a walled garden for summer and a boules pitch that people travel some way for. For a light lunch consider a wholemeal sandwich of Wiltshire ham and coleslaw, or rare roast beef and horseradish. 'Classics' on the menu might include home-cooked ham, Sherston free-range eggs and chips and steak and kidney pie, while daily dishes could highlight monkfish with tiger prawn and tomato risotto – all delicious. 'If they don't serve beer in heaven, then I'm not going', reads the sign behind the bar, so Uley Bitter stands alongside guest ales. Rooms upstairs are cosy, stylish and inviting, with colourful throws on comfortable beds and spotless shower rooms; the self-catering cottages are in the coaching stable. A perfect place in the Cotswolds.

Price	£75. Singles from £55. Cottages from £90.
Rooms	6 + 2: 1 double, 3 twins/doubles, 1 single, 1 family room. 2 self-catering cottages for 4-8.
Meals	Lunch from £9.95. Bar meals from £8.95. Dinner from £10.95. Sunday lunch, 2 courses, £17.
Closed	Open all day.
Directions	M4 junc. 18, A46 north, then A433 for Tetbury. In village on left.

Steve & Sue Payne
The King's Arms Inn
The Street, Didmarton,
Badminton GL9 1DT
Tel +44 (0)1454 238245
Web www.kingsarmsdidmarton.co.uk

The Bull Inn

Hinton

A deep-cut Cotswold lane brings you to this solid stone 17th-century pub in a peaceful village. In good weather, sit on the sunny south-facing terrace and enjoy Wadworth's Bishop's Tipple or Henry's IPA, or wander round to the ample play area at the back where you can see the vegetables and Gloucester Old Spots growing – low food miles indeed. The menus are traditional with a French flavour, the Royal Gloucester steak and ale pie with horseradish pastry has won awards, and the 'trio of French bread and butter pudding' is made from pain au chocolat, croissant and brioche; try it with Marshfield Farm's chocolate ice cream if you dare. Inside the large, beamed and flagged bar are a stone fireplace and some super big oak tables and pews around which to tuck in and chat away an evening. A family run pub with personality.

Meals	Lunch & dinner £8.75-£15.95.
Closed	Mon lunch.
Directions	5 minutes from junc 18 on the M4; A46 to Bath, first right to Hinton

David & Elizabeth White
The Bull Inn
Hinton,
Chippenham SN14 8HG

Tel +44 (0)117 9372332
Web www.thebullathinton.co.uk

Entry 220 Map 3

The Old Spot

Dursley

Nudged by a car park and Dursley's bus station is the old and lovely Old Spot. Built in 1776 as a farm cottage, the pub has since gained national recognition among ale buffs who make pilgrimages to sample the brews. Indeed, the Old Spot has become something of a showcase for the beers of Uley Brewery, including Pig's Ear and Old Ric, the latter named after a former landlord. Real ciders include Weston's and Ashton Press. For a pub named after a rare-breed pig it comes as no surprise that there are porcine figurines and pictures dotted around the place, as well as a few old prints and posters. Food is simple and pubby – BLT sandwiches, bangers and mash, home-baked pies with shortcrust pastry lids. Friendly, no-nonsense, traditional, and on the Cotswolds Way. For ale-lovers, sheer joy.

Meals	Bar meals £3.45-£9.25. Sunday lunch, 3 courses, £16.45.
Closed	Open all day.
Directions	100 yards from Dursley town centre.

Steve Herbert
The Old Spot
2 Hill Road,
Dursley GL11 4JQ

Tel +44 (0)1453 542870
Web www.oldspotinn.co.uk

Entry 221 Map 8

The Old Lodge

Minchinhampton

Lording it on a high and ancient piece of common ground is this former hunting lodge to Henry VIII. The cattle roam free; you too can wander and gaze on the views of five valleys. Outside is traditional, inside is striking. Expect bold art, classical columns, acres of smooth oak and honey-coloured stone walls; sofas sprawl around low coffee tables, fireplaces crackle, the conversation is lively. Still with a pub feel, albeit an up-to-the-minute one, the bar serves Budding from Stroud Brewery alongside Abbotts, IPA and Otter. In the restaurant, large and open plan with floor-to-ceiling windows for the view, an eco-chic bar made from reclaimed wine barrels, and locally sourced delights on daily menus: chicken liver parfait, confit duck leg with mash, savoy cabbage and red wine jus, spicy pear and plum crumble.

Meals	Lunch & dinner £10.95-£17.95. Sunday lunch £10.95.
Closed	Open all day.
Directions	In the middle of Minchinhampton Common - 300 yds off common road - signed.

Craig Daly
The Old Lodge
Minchinhampton,
Stroud GL6 9AQ

Tel +44 (0)1453 832047
Web www.food-club.com

Entry 222 Map 8

Gloucestershire

The Trouble House

Tetbury

Forget civil war skirmishes and rural riots over the introduction of new machinery; the only thing you have to worry about at this 18th-century pub today is deciding what to eat and drink. In the quarry-tiled bar Shane will pull you a pint of Wadworth's ale and describe the daily specials created by chef Liam, who worked here with the previous tenants, and at Calcot Manor. The food is seriously good; take the roast Cornish hake with chorizo, the white bean and parsley casserole, the braised blade of beef with confit garlic mash and black cabbage. Expect too fine British cheeses, well-chosen wines, delicious coffees and teas. There are two dining areas with painted stone walls, low beams, real fires and scrubbed pine tables and chairs. It's smart yet wonderfully cosy with lovely friendly people and a very personal approach.

Meals	Lunch from £12. Bar meals from £8.50. Dinner from £12. Sunday lunch, 3 courses, £23. Not Sunday or Monday lunch (except bank hols).
Closed	3pm-6.30pm.
Directions	On A433, 2 miles north-east of Tetbury.

Shane and Liam Parr
The Trouble House
Cirencester Road,
Tetbury GL8 8SG

Tel +44 (0)1666 502206
Web www.troublehousetetbury.co.uk

Entry 223 Map 8

The Tunnel House Inn

Coates

Emerge via the portico tunnel of the Severn & Thames Canal to find a gracious Cotswold stone house in the clearing; it was built in the 1780s to house the canal workers. Its latest conversion has been well considered. There's lots to like here: landlord Rupert, the laid-back hospitality, the beef and horseradish sandwiches, the Uley Bitter and Hook Norton to keep ale fans happy, and the quirky décor: scrubbed tables and huge faded sofas in front of a fire, a cacophony of bric-a-brac in the bar (most on the ceiling!), an Ogygian juke box with decent tunes. In the dining room choose from a seasonal menu: Old Spot sausages with mash and red onion marmalade, crab and watercress tart, roast belly pork on root vegetable mash. Outside, a rather smart terrace, a big garden with open-field views – great for kids – and wild camping in Hailey Wood.

Meals	Lunch & dinner £8-£14.95.
Closed	Open all day.
Directions	Off A433 Cirencester to Tetbury road; follow brown signs to the pub.

Rupert Longsdon
The Tunnel House Inn
Coates,
Cirencester GL7 6PW
Tel +44 (0)1285 770280
Web www.tunnelhouse.com

Entry 224 Map 8

Gloucestershire

The Bell at Sapperton

Sapperton

This elegant pub attracts wine-lovers, foodies, ramblers and riders. Inside is a spacious but intimate décor that spreads itself across several levels – stripped beams and wood-burners, modern art on stone walls, old settles and church chairs, fresh flowers and newspapers. Sup on local Uley Old Spot or Otter Amber Bitter, dine on fresh local produce and rare-breed meats. Specials are chalked up above the fireplace and the food is generous in its range: pan-fried Madgetts Farm duck breast, lamb from Butts Farm, warm apple crumble crème brûlée with blackberry ice cream, goat's cheese called Rachel. Not a typical family pub but Sunday roast lunches are hugely popular and the wine list is expertly considered to match the clientele. Summer eating can be outside on the well-tended terrace and spills over into the sun-trapping 'Mediterranean' courtyard.

Meals	Lunch from £9.95. Bar meals from £4.95. Dinner from £10.95. Sunday lunch, 3 courses, £29.
Closed	2.30pm-6.30pm (3pm-7pm Sun). Open all day Sat (& Sun in summer).
Directions	Off A419, 6 miles west of Cirencester. Follow signs to Sapperton Village.

Paul Davidson & Pat Le Jeune
The Bell at Sapperton
Sapperton,
Cirencester GL7 6LE
Tel +44 (0)1285 760298
Web www.foodatthebell.co.uk

Entry 225 Map 8

The Butcher's Arms

Sheepscombe

Tracking down this delightful local involves an "are you sure this is the right road?" adventure down narrow winding lanes – to tiny Sheepscombe, one of Laurie Lee's favourite places. If the weather's fine, and you haven't had one too many pints of Otter Bitter, find the most level spot you can in the sloping garden and relish the views. Inside: flowery curtains at mullioned windows, beams, brasses and bentwood chairs. Grab a perch by the wood-burning stove or a table in the tiny dining room and tuck into flavoursome food made from local ingredients – a roast rib of Beech Farm beef, a homemade pie. At weekends you'll rub shoulders with walkers, cyclists and locals. Inside or out, a place to savour. No plans for trendification, just a friendly down-to-earth place doing the thing it does best.

Meals	Lunch, bar meals & dinner, all from £7.95. Sunday lunch, 3 courses, £19.
Closed	3pm-6pm. Open all day Sat & Sun.
Directions	Off A46 north of Painswick.

Mark & Sharon Tallents
The Butcher's Arms
Sheepscombe,
Stroud GL6 7RH

Tel	+44 (0)1452 812113
Web	www.butchers-arms.co.uk

Entry 226 Map 8

Gloucestershire

The Colesbourne Inn

Colesbourne

If it's authenticity you seek then look no further: this handsome Cotswold stone coaching inn dates back to 1827 and oozes country pub atmosphere with horsey tack, country scene prints and old books, bottles and willow pattern plates. A bar billiard table is tucked in a corner and there are three real log fires to warm you after a tramp in the glorious surroundings. Sip ales from Wadworths and good wines by the glass as you study a modern pub menu that starts with duck liver and orange pâté with cranberry and kumquat chutney before Scottish salmon, wilted baby spinach and tarragon cream sauce. Eat in the bar beneath stone mullioned windows or the light-filled restaurant with its vibrant oriental rugs. On sunny days you can laze in the super garden with its heavenly views across the valley. A hale and hearty pub indeed.

Meals	Set menu, 2-3 courses, £9.95-11.95. Sunday lunch from £10.95.
Closed	Open all day.
Directions	Sent on booking.

Trevor & Liz
The Colesbourne Inn
Colesbourne,
Cheltenham GL53 9NP

Tel	+44 (0)1242 870376
Web	www.thecolesbourneinn.co.uk

Entry 227 Map 8

Five Mile House

Duntisbourne Abbots

In 300 years the interior has changed not a jot. Here are planked floors, glowing log fires, two curving settles, a sunny lounge bar, newspapers, darts and cribbage. There's a flagstoned 'poop deck' of a snug for locals and a galley a few steps below; a more genteel wardroom – once the owner's private parlour – stands across the hall. Deserving more consideration than the proverbial swift half, the beer, which includes guests and Taylor's Landlord, is seriously good. Food is no longer available to soak up a few pints – traditional snacks like crisps and nuts will have to do! Children and dogs are welcome, there are serene views to the valley below and, above, a busy main road, mercifully concealed by a bank and burgeoning hedgerows. You can hardly go wrong.

Meals	No food served.
Closed	3pm-6pm (4pm-7pm Sun).
Directions	On A417, turn at Duntisbourne Abbots Services; pub down the road past the petrol station.

Jo & Jon Carrier
Five Mile House, Old Gloucester Rd,
Duntisbourne Abbots,
Cirencester GL7 7JR
Tel +44 (0)1285 821432
Web www.fivemilehouse.co.uk

Entry 228 Map 8

Gloucestershire

Seven Tuns Inn

Chedworth

In 1610, and for a few centuries after that, the Seven Tuns was a simple snug; then they diverted the river and built the rest. Part-creepered on the outside, it rambles attractively inside, past open fires, aged furniture, antique prints and a skittle alley with darts. After a gentle walk to Chedworth's Roman Villa, buried in the wooded valley nearby, there's no finer place to return to for a pint of Young's Bitter. Mingle with cyclists, walkers and locals in the little lounge or rustic bar. If you're here to eat you can do so overlooking the garden through gorgeous mullioned windows in the country-style dining rooms; across the road is a raised terrace by a waterwheel, babbling brook and boule court. Pub grub is listed on daily menus, from ham, eggs and chips to rack of lamb. This is still the village hub, just as it should be.

Meals	Lunch & dinner £7.95-£14.95.
Closed	3pm-6pm. Open all day Sat & Sun in winter, every day in July & Aug.
Directions	Off A429, north of Cirencester.

Alex Davenport-Jones
Seven Tuns Inn
Queen Street,
Chedworth,
Cheltenham GL54 4AE
Tel +44 (0)1285 720242

Entry 229 Map 8

The Victoria Inn

Eastleach Turville

The golden-stoned Victoria pulls in the locals – whatever their age, whatever the weather – propping up the bar, welly-clad with dogs or indulging in home-cooked grub by the log fire. A simple village hostelry on the outside, it's deceptively spacious inside. The Richardsons, in spite of opening up the interior, have kept much of the character and cosiness intact. The low-ceilinged and flagstoned bar offers darts, conversation and pints of Arkells 3B, while the L-shaped dining room is the setting for delicious platefuls of freshly prepared food: salmon fishcakes; pork and leek sausages; slow-roasted lamb shank with garlic potatoes and red wine sauce. There are picnic tables out at the front, from where you can look down onto the pretty stone cottages of two villages. A lovely spot for a country stroll.

Meals	Lunch & dinner £7.95-£14.75.
Closed	3pm-7pm.
Directions	Off A361 between Burford & Lechlade.

Stephen & Susan Richardson
The Victoria Inn
Eastleach Turville,
Cirencester GL7 3NQ
Tel +44 (0)1367 850277

Entry 230 Map 8

Gloucestershire

The Five Alls

Filkins

Duncan Ray's CV makes impressive reading: he's cooked at the legendary Fat Duck, and at the Latymer Restaurant of Pennyhill Park Hotel. Keen to go it alone, he and partner Manoli Gonzalez landed at this gorgeous Cotswold pub in 2011 and haven't looked back. The old 18th-century coaching inn is tucked into a picture-postcard village close to Burford, Thames-path walks and Buscot Park, and Duncan's exciting cooking is drawing the locals back. At painted tables in the rustic bar you can enjoy tapas-style bar bites (whitebait with garlic mayo, duck-fat chips) with a pint of Brakspear, or go the whole hog in the dining room – to a backdrop of beams, slate, fat candles and modern art. There's red onion tart with goat's cheese and mint pesto, sea bass with gem lettuce and clam chowder, and salted butter caramel with dark chocolate ice cream. All of it's delicious.

Meals	Lunch & dinner from £12. Set lunch £15 & £19. Sunday lunch £16.
Closed	Open all day.
Directions	Filkins is signposted off A361 between Lechlade & Burford, 3 miles north of Lechlade; pub in village centre.

Duncan Ray & Manoli Gonzalez
The Five Alls
Filkins,
Lechlade GL7 3JQ
Tel +44 (0)1367 860875
Web www.thefivealls.com

Entry 231 Map 8

The Swan at Southrop

Southrop

A roaring log fire, a sober décor, a relaxed mood and a skittle alley for locals – this is the village inn on the village green that everyone dreams of, and restaurateurs Sebastian and Lana Snow were happy to leave their Shepherd's Bush restaurant for this Cotswolds' treasure. The handsome Georgian inn has a much-loved bar but is still a foodie haven. Menus are seasonal and unshowy: a crab, saffron and tomato tart, roast rump of Southrop lamb, Kelmscott pork belly with mushroom fricassée, elderflower panna cotta with autumn raspberries. An excellent wine list matches a tasty selection of local real ales, accompanied by scrumptious bar snacks like ham, egg and chips, beef bourguignon and ploughman's. Come for the great value weekday set lunches. Faultless service comes with a big smile.

Meals	Lunch & dinner £12.50-£17.
Closed	2.30pm-7pm (3pm-7pm Sat & Sun). Closed from 10pm every day.
Directions	2 miles west off A361 between Burford & Lechlade.

Sebastian & Lana Snow
The Swan at Southrop
Southrop,
Lechlade GL7 3NU
Tel +44 (0)1367 850205
Web www.theswanatsouthrop.co.uk

Gloucestershire

The Horse & Groom Village Inn

Upper Oddington

Cotswold stone, hanging baskets, hefty beams and flagstone floors, chunky logs around the double fireplace... is this the pub from central casting? It's 500 years old and Simon and Sally have rejuvenated without losing the traditional charm. There's a good selection of guest ales, some from nearby microbreweries, including Wye Valley Best, Prescott Hill Climb and Chuffin Ale. Cider and lager, including Cotswold Premium, come from the Cotswold Brewing Co. ten minutes away. The menu takes a cook's tour of Europe, with a good serving of traditional English; shin of beef and root vegetable casserole, fillet of haddock topped with chorizo, lime and parmesan crust, game from the Adlestrop Estate. Produce is organic and local whenever possible, breads and puddings are all homemade. No fewer than 25 wines are available by the glass.

Meals	Lunch & bar meals from £5.95. Dinner from £12.95. Sunday lunch, 3 courses, £25.
Closed	3pm-5.30pm.
Directions	Village signed off A436 east of Stow-on-the-Wold.

Simon & Sally Jackson
The Horse & Groom Village Inn
Upper Oddington,
Moreton-in-Marsh GL56 0XH
Tel +44 (0)1451 830584
Web www.horseandgroom.uk.com

The Fox Inn

Lower Oddington

Amid the grandeur of old Cotswold country houses, the Fox evokes a wonderful sense of times past. Low ceilings, worn flagstones, a log fire in winter, good food and an exemplary host… people love it here. The comfortably stylish bar has scrubbed pine tables topped with fresh flowers and candles; newspapers, magazines and ales are on tap; rag-washed ochre walls date back years; no wonder the locals are happy. Eat here or in the elegant, rose-red dining room, or on the terrace, heated on cool nights, of the pretty cottage garden. Imaginative, sometimes elaborate dishes include goat's cheese and roasted red pepper tart, carrot, coriander and ginger soup, sirloin steak with garlic butter, dark chocolate torte. Before you leave, explore the honey-stone village and 11th-century church, known for its magnificent frescos.

Meals	Lunch & dinner £10.95-£16.25.
Closed	3.30pm-6pm (5pm-7pm Sun).
Directions	From Stow-on-the-Wold, A436 for Chipping Norton for 3 miles, then 2nd right after VW garage, for Lower Oddington. Inn 500 yds on right.

Ian McKenzie
The Fox Inn
Lower Oddington,
Moreton-in-Marsh GL56 0UR

Tel +44 (0)1451 870555
Web www.foxinn.net

Entry 234 Map 8

Gloucestershire

The Farriers Arms

Todenham

A treasure: a couple of tables in front, a private dining room in the 'library', a restaurant for 25 – and smart tables in the landscaped rear garden, one of many improvements made by Nigel and Louise. It's cosy, cheerful and reassuringly old-fashioned. Polished flagstones, hop-hung beams and an inglenook with a wood-burner; add great beers, real cider, an enjoyable blackboard menu that changes every day and you have one special little pub. The Farriers is jam-packed on Sundays (lunch must be booked), and the draw is the high quality pub food: fresh local ingredients with tasty sauces. There are fresh soups, local sirloin steaks and the likes of apricot and stilton tart, roast duck with rösti and redcurrant sauce, and salmon and spinach Wellington. Colouring books welcome kids, and the mellow-stone village is as pretty as the pub.

Meals	Lunch from £8.95. Bar meals from £4.95. Dinner from £10.95. Sunday lunch, 3 courses, £19.85.
Closed	3pm-6pm. (3pm-6.30pm Sun & every day in winter)
Directions	Signed from Moreton-in-Marsh & from A3400.

Nigel & Louise Kirkwood
The Farriers Arms
Todenham,
Moreton-in-Marsh GL56 9PF

Tel +44 (0)1608 650901
Web www.farriersarms.com

Entry 235 Map 8

The Plough Inn

Temple Guiting

Horses from the local stables gallop past, local shoots lunch here, race-goers dine. The pub's rustic walls are lined with photographs of meetings at Cheltenham: this place is dedicated to country pursuits. Cheltenham week is bedlam (a marquee is erected in the garden) but every week is busy. The cooking has a following, the dining room is famous for its asparagus suppers and the Aberdeen Angus fillet in its brandy and black peppercorn sauce tastes as good as it looks. There are local beers, real ciders and well-chosen wines. The building has been an inn since the 16th century and was once a courthouse, so bars are darkly cosy with low beams, flagstones and smouldering fires. In spite of its success, The Plough still pulls in the locals. Children will make a bee-line for the play fort in the garden.

Meals	Lunch & dinner £8.95-£17.95.
Closed	Open all day.
Directions	B4077 between Stow-on-the-Wold & Tewkesbury.

Craig & Becky Brown
The Plough Inn
Ford, Temple Guiting,
Cheltenham GL54 5RU
Tel +44 (0)1386 584215
Web www.theploughinnatford.co.uk

Gloucestershire

The Boat Inn

Ashleworth

This extraordinary, tiny pub has been in the family since Charles II granted them a licence for liquor and ferry – about 400 years ago! It's a gem – a peaceful, unspoilt red-brick cottage on the banks of the Severn and an ale-lover's paradise. The choice of beer changes regularly and small, local brewers are preferred. Settle back with a pint of Beowulf, Church End or Archer's in the gleaming front parlour – colourful with fresh garden flowers, huge built-in settle and big scrubbed deal table fronting an old kitchen range – or in the spotless bar. On sunny summer days you can laze by the languid river. Adjectives are inadequate: this place is cherished. Real ale straight from the cask, Weston's farm cider, a bar of chocolate, a packet of crisps... There's no 'jus' here; lunchtime meals are fresh filled rolls with homemade chutney.

Meals	Filled rolls only.
Closed	2.30pm-7pm (3pm-7pm Sat & Sun). Wed lunch & Mon.
Directions	On A417 1.5 miles from Hartpury, between Gloucester & Ledbury.

Ian Lock
The Boat Inn
The Quay, Ashleworth,
Gloucester GL19 4HZ
Tel +44 (0)1452 700272
Web www.boat-inn.co.uk

The Glasshouse Inn

May Hill

If you are a fan of Fuller's London Pride and Butcombe, Weston's ciders and all good, nature-blessed produce, come here. Ramshackle tables and open log fires are considered modern at this converted 15th-century brick cottage where glass was once blown in wood-fired ovens and cider pressed in the shed. Guinness adverts, cartoons and horse racing prints decorate the place as do autographed England rugby shirts – and the chiming clock never serves as an invitation to leave. Say landlords Steve and Gill: "We buy the best available produce locally, so chefs can provide our customers with generous portions of tasty, interesting, homemade food." Expect authentic Thai curries or pork fillet stuffed with apricots with a cider sauce, a lovely calm atmosphere, a terrific little garden for summer sipping and super local walks.

Meals	Lunch from £4.50. Dinner from £9.50. Sunday lunch, 2 courses £13.95.
Closed	3pm-6.30pm. Sun eves.
Directions	North off A40 between Gloucester & Newent at Longhope, signed Cliffords Mesne: through Glasshouse, pub at bottom of hill on right.

Steve & Gill Pugh
The Glasshouse Inn
Glasshouse Hill,
May Hill,
Longhope GL17 0NN

Tel +44 (0)1452 830529

Entry 238 Map 8

The Ostrich Inn

Newland

In the village of Newland the Ostrich is where the beer drinkers go to sample eight changing ales. Across from All Saints Church, that 'Cathedral of the Forest', you'll mix with all sorts before a log fire. Huntsmen and trail bikers pile in for the massive portions of delicious food, from the Newland bread and cheese platter to rack of Welsh lamb with lashings of marsala sauce. The nicotine-brown ceiling that looks in danger of imminent collapse is supported by a massive oak pillar in front of the bar where the locals chatter and jazz CDs keep the place swinging. The weekly menu, served throughout the pub, takes a step up in class, and is excellent value. Energetic Kathryn and her team, including Alfie the pub dog, aide the buzzing atmosphere. To the back is a walled garden – and the loos, 'just by there', beyond the coal sacks.

Meals	Lunch & dinner £12.50-£18.50. Bar meals £5.50-£10.50.
Closed	3pm-6.30pm (6pm Sat).
Directions	Signed on lane linking A466 at Redbrook & at Clearwell between B4228 Coleford & Chepstow road.

Kathryn Horton
The Ostrich Inn
Newland,
Coleford GL16 8NP

Tel +44 (0)1594 833260
Web www.theostrichinn.com

Entry 239 Map 7

The Peat Spade

Longstock

Hampshire is as lovely as any county in England, deeply rural with lanes that snake through verdant countryside. As if to prove the point, the Peat Spade serves up a menu of boundless simplicity and elegance. First there's this dreamy thatched village in the Test valley, then there's the inn itself, packed to the gunnels with lip-licking locals for Sunday lunch in early February (and there's a 4pm sitting to satisfy demand). Behind the lozenge-paned windows a Roberts radio on the bar brings news of English cricket, gilt mirrors sparkle above smouldering fires, candles illuminate chunky tables, and fishing rods hang from the ceiling; note there's a handy fishing tackle shop on site. There's a horseshoe bar, a roof terrace for summer breakfasts and three bedrooms above the bar. The rest are in Peat House next door, and are as lovely as you'd expect. Fired Earth colours, sisal matting, big wooden beds, top mattresses, crisp white linen – the works. There's no space left to describe how fabulously wonderful the food is, but be assured it is.

Price	From £130.
Rooms	6: 2 doubles, 1 twin. Peat House: 3 doubles.
Meals	Lunch & dinner £5-£25.
Closed	Open all day.
Directions	A3057 north from Stockbridge, then left after a mile for Longstock. In village.

Paula Righton
The Peat Spade
Longstock,
Stockbridge SO20 6DR

Tel	+44 (0)1264 810612
Web	www.peatspadeinn.co.uk

The Greyhound
Stockbridge

Civilised, one-street Stockbridge is England's fly-fishing capital, and the colourwashed Greyhound reels in fishing folk and foodies. The 15th-century coaching inn is a dapper, food-and-wine-centred affair run with charm and panache by Susie Fiducia. Chef Alan Haughie produces modern dishes based on skill and impeccable produce, served by charming staff. Try smoked haddock scotch eggs, slow-braised cheek and crispy belly of Greenfield Farm pork with celeriac, chorizo and saffron chowder, Palourde clams and crispy squid. Bar meals might see Greyhound fishcake with poached egg and chive beurre blanc or wild mushrooms on toast with hollandaise sauce. In the lounge are low dark beams, modern armchairs and sofas and a big inglenook; in the open-plan dining area, wooden floors, solid trestle-style tables, contemporary leather chairs, more beams. Upgraded bedrooms manage to blend comfort with character, so you'll find spotlights alongside auction antiques, classy bathrooms, books, pictures and mohair throws. A garden at the back overlooks the Test; rest here awhile with a glass of chablis – or cast a line.

Price	£95-£125. Singles £70.
Rooms	7: 3 twins, 3 doubles, 1 single.
Meals	Lunch & dinner £16.50-£20. Bar meals £4.20-£14.50. Not Sunday eve.
Closed	Open all day.
Directions	A303, A34 south, then A30 into Stockbridge. Pub on right on west end of High Street.

Susie Fiducia
The Greyhound
31 High Street,
Stockbridge SO20 6EY

Tel +44 (0)1264 810833
Web www.thegreyhound.info

The King's Head
Hursley

Five local farmers bought this inn to guarantee a good pint after a day in the fields. Sensibly, they asked their wives to oversee the interior design; the place now shines. It dates to 1810, stands opposite the church, and was once a coaching inn linking London to the New Forest. These days the feel is half country pub, half country house. You find armchairs in front of roaring fires, shuttered windows in a Georgian dining room and, in the bar, excellent ales on tap – and not just for thirsty farmers. Elegant bedrooms are a treat. Two have slipper baths, all have warm colours, fancy bathrooms, soft carpeting and comfy beds. Some are smaller, as is reflected in the price; a couple have space for sofas. Back downstairs, delicious rustic fare awaits in bar and restaurant alike, perhaps ox cheek and kidney pie or pheasant breast and confit leg with pancetta potatoes and wild mushrooms; puds include lemon tart with raspberry sorbet. You get film nights, book clubs, skittles every now and then, and wine tastings in a vaulted cellar. Richard Cromwell, Oliver's son, lived in the village.

Price	£89-£114. Singles from £59.
Rooms	7: 4 doubles, 2 twins/doubles, 1 single.
Meals	Lunch from £6. Dinner, 3 courses, about £25.
Closed	Open all day.
Directions	South from Winchester on A3090. In village on left.

Jimmy Hajiantoni
The King's Head
Main Road, Hursley,
Winchester SO21 2JW
Tel +44 (0)1962 775208
Web www.kingsheadhursley.co.uk

The Master Builder's House Hotel

Bucklers Hard

The position here is faultless: lawns roll down to the Beaulieu river, curlews race across the water, a vast sky hangs overhead. The house, built in 1729, was home to shipwrights who served the British fleet and Nelson's favourite vessel, *Agamemnon*, was built here. More hotel than inn, the Master Builder mixes contemporary flair with classical design. Expect earthy colours and a roaring fire in the yachtsman's bar, then huge sofas and watery views in the sitting room. Bedrooms in the main house are nothing short of gorgeous: huge beds, pots of colour, fabulous views, super bathrooms. Those in the annexe are simpler, but cosy, and getting the same treatment. Back downstairs, the dining room swings to an informal beat. You get wooden booths, smart rugs and doors that open onto a terrace which looks the right way. You can eat here in summer or barbecue on the lawn, perhaps New Forest asparagus, a rib-eye steak, then custard tart with nutmeg ice cream. Stride out on the footpaths that sweep along the river, dive into the forest to cycle and ride or lose yourself in acres of silence.

Price	£130-£205. Singles from £120. Half-board from £100 p.p.
Rooms	28: 5 doubles, 3 suites. Annexe: 13 doubles, 5 twins/doubles. Cottage: 1 double, 1 single.
Meals	Lunch from £7.50. Dinner, 3 courses, £25-£30.
Closed	Open all day.
Directions	From Lyndhurst B3056 south past Beaulieu turn-off. 1st left, signed Bucklers Hard. Hotel signed left after 1 mile.

Damir Terzic
The Master Builder's House Hotel
Bucklers Hard, Beaulieu,
Brockenhurst SO42 7XB
Tel +44 (0)1590 616253
Web www.themasterbuilders.co.uk

The East End Arms

East End

No London boozer but a good little local hidden down New Forest lanes, winningly unpretentious and owned by John Illsley of Dire Straits. Walkers, wax jackets and locals congregate in the small, rustic Foresters Bar with its chatty community vibe; walls come lined with the famous. The carpeted-cosy dining room, all cottagey furniture and roaring log fire, cocks a snook at gastropub remodelling, but the menus change twice daily and make the best of seasonal produce. Try seafood casserole with peppers, fennel, saffron potatoes and sauce aïoli, or wild mushroom risotto. A paved terrace invites al fresco drinking, while bedrooms on the back add va-va-voom. Clean-lined and comfortable, in fashionably neutral tones that bring the forest indoors, they sport roman blinds and coordinated soft furnishings. Stylish bathrooms and paintings by John Illsley add warmth and class; fine breakfasts are the cherry on the cake. A great little find for anyone who loves the New Forest – neither new nor a forest, but fine open heathland nonetheless and excellent hiking terrain.

Price	£98.50-£120.
Rooms	5 twins/doubles.
Meals	Lunch from £8.50. Dinner from £10.50. Not Sunday eves.
Closed	3pm-6pm. Open all day Sun.
Directions	Off B3054 signposted Beaulieu; follow signs for Isle of Wight ferry, bear left onto South Baddesley Rd; 2 miles, pub on right.

John Illsley & Jeremy Willcock
The East End Arms
Lymington Road, East End,
Lymington SO41 5SY

Tel +44 (0)1590 626223
Web www.eastendarms.co.uk

White Star Tavern & Dining Rooms

Southampton

The old seafarers' hotel has been revived. Large etched windows carry the White Star logo, while a cluster of lounges at the front come decked with funky seating and chesterfields. The place is stocked with a modish mix of real ales, continental lagers, premium spirits and cocktails. Around the big darkwood bar, to a backdrop of original wood panelling, is crescent-shaped seating for casual dining; wide floorboards and original chandeliers add to the cosmopolitan mood. The more formal dining area comes with a lighter, softer approach: stylish wallpaper and sophisticated lighting. The cooking hits all the fashionable notes, with a novel, all-day selection of 'small plates' as well as à la carte; dishes include the likes of mussel and watercress velouté and grey mullet fillet with potato fondant and organic rainbow chard. Bedrooms above – named after White Star Line ships or America's Cup yachts – are individually styled and continue the upbeat theme, while bathrooms are decked out with roll tops and big showers. And there's a guests' sundeck, too. Young and fun.

Price	£89-£179.
Rooms	13: 11 doubles, 2 twins/doubles.
Meals	Lunch & dinner £9.50-£19. Bar meals £4.50-£11.
Closed	Open all day.
Directions	M271 into town. Past Ikea, down to docks. Join one-way system & left to Terminus Terrace. 2nd left into Bernard St. 3rd left into Oxford St. Ask about parking.

Matthew Boyle
White Star Tavern & Dining Rooms
28 Oxford Street,
Southampton SO14 3DJ
Tel +44 (0)2380 821990
Web www.whitestartavern.co.uk

The Old Vine

Winchester

You are in a small square overlooking the cathedral and mature trees. This red-bricked Georgian building has sash windows and pretty hanging baskets – all tickety-boo and smart. Walk straight into the bustling bar with its beamed ceiling, upright timbers, open fires and a partly covered outdoor terrace for sunny days where a cheerful team of local staff serve two permanent ales (Ringwood Best and Timothy Taylor) and two guests on rotation; the wine list has helpful comments and some organic choices, and more on the specials board. If you get peckish after all the quaffing, you can have anything from a hearty sandwich (Hampshire pork sausages and red onion relish) to confit of duck with port and black cherry sauce, then homemade sticky toffee pudding and custard or some excellent local cheese. Stumble upstairs to a rather posh bedroom; all are generous, with a mix of antique-looking and contemporary furniture. Colour schemes are muted with splashes of bold on throws and cushions, mahogany sleigh beds are deep and comfortable and you can splash about in spoiling bathrooms with fluffy towels and gleaming taps.

Price	£100-£195.
Rooms	5: 4 doubles, 1 twin/double.
Meals	Lunch & dinner £9.90-£14.50.
Closed	Open all day.
Directions	Located opposite Winchester Cathedral green and the City Museum, just a short walk from the high street. Permit parking available.

Ashton Gray
The Old Vine
8 Great Minster Street, Winchester
SO23 9HA

Tel +44 (0)1962 854616
Web www.oldvinewinchester.com

The Woolpack Inn

Northington

Brian and Jarina have revived the fortunes of the old drovers' inn in the Candover valley. In the bar are rugs on wood and tiled floors, logs in a stone fireplace, fat church candles on pine tables, newspapers and the *Tatler*. The vibe is laid-back – dogs doze, walkers and cyclists down pints of Flower Pots Bitter, shooting parties drop by in season, foodies are happy. The smart dining room, replete with striped banquettes and high-backed leather chairs, is the setting for hearty pub classics from Brian's open-to-view kitchen... simple ham, duck egg and hand-cut chips; shepherd's pie; roast rib of beef on Sundays. Or the more inventive pork and pistachio terrine, slow-cooked lamb with red wine sauce, chocolate and orange tart. Explore the local footpaths, visit The Grange for summer opera, drop into Winchester over the hill. Then return to refurbished cottages out the back, whose contemporary rooms, named after game birds, have exposed brick and flint walls, darkwood and leather furnishings, big beds and gun cupboards; bathrooms come with storm showers and posh smellies.

Price	£85-£105. Family suite £145.
Rooms	7 doubles.
Meals	Lunch & dinner £5-£30. Sunday lunch from £13.50.
Closed	Open all day.
Directions	On B3046 between Alresford and Basingstoke, 4 miles north of Alresford.

Brian & Jarina Ahearn
The Woolpack Inn
Totford, Northington, Alresford
SO24 9TJ
Tel +44 (0)8452 938066
Web www.thewoolpackinn.co.uk

The Anchor Inn

Lower Froyle

A super-smart country inn, renovated in imperious style. The house is Edwardian with 14th century roots, and its treasure-trove interiors are full of beautiful things: timber frames, wavy beams, oils by the score, trumpets and pith helmets, a piano in the bar. Old photographs of Charterhouse School cover the walls, there are winged chairs by the fire in the panelled bar and candles and deep green walls in the cosy restaurant, where you dine on proper English food: game terrine; pork shoulder with mash, cabbage and bacon; vanilla rice pud. Doors open onto a gorgeous new terrace with country views, so come in summer for lunch in the sun. Bedrooms upstairs are seriously indulging. Expect beautifully upholstered armchairs, seagrass matting, fine linen on comfy beds, flat-screen TVs. There are power showers, huge towels and bathrobes, too. One room is open to the rafters; another has an enormous window that opens onto a private balcony with views across open fields. Don't come looking for a gastropub; do come looking for good ales, sublime food and old-world interiors. A treat!

Price	From £120.
Rooms	5: 4 doubles, 1 suite.
Meals	Lunch & dinner £6.50-£20.
Closed	Open all day.
Directions	Leave A31 for Bentley, 4 miles west of Farnham. West through village, north for Lower Froyle. Inn on left in village.

Amy Greener
The Anchor Inn
Lower Froyle,
Alton GU34 4NA
Tel +44 (0)1420 23261
Web www.anchorinnatlowerfroyle.co.uk

The Wellington Arms

Baughurst

Lost down a web of lanes, the 'Welly' draws foodies from miles around. Cosy, relaxed and decorated in style – old dining tables, crystal decanters, terracotta floor – the newly extended bar-dining room fills quickly, so make sure you book to sample Jason's inventive modern British cooking. Boards are chalked up daily and the produce mainly home-grown or organic. Kick off with home-grown courgette flowers stuffed with ricotta, parmesan and lemon zest, follow with rack of home-reared lamb with root vegetable mash and crab apple jelly, finish with elderflower jelly, strawberries and raspberry sorbet. Migrate to the huge garden for summer meals and views of the pub's small holding: bees, four Tamworth pigs, Longwool sheep and 120 rarebreed chickens; the eggs can be bought at the bar. Stay over and cosy up in either the gorgeous New or Old room, housed in the former wine store and pig shed. Expect exposed brick and beams, vast Benchmark beds topped with goose down duvets, fresh flowers, coffee machines, mini-fridges, and slate tiled bathrooms with underfloor heating and walk-in rain showers. Breakfast is a real treat.

Price	£130.
Rooms	2 doubles.
Meals	Set lunch £15.75 & £18.75. Dinner £11-£21. Not Sun eves.
Closed	3pm-6.30pm. Sun eves.
Directions	Baughurst is signed off A340 at Tadley, or A339 east of Kingsclere.

Jason King & Simon Page
The Wellington Arms
Baughurst Road,
Baughurst RG26 5LP
Tel +44 (0)118 982 0110
Web www.thewellingtonarms.com

The Purefoy Arms

Preston Candover

The owners at this upmarket dining pub in the charming Candover Valley know a thing or two about running an inn. Their previous venture was in Mayfair but they've clearly taken to village life with this gentle remodelling of a 19th-century inn: it's warm, light and contemporary with its traditional framework intact. Hand-written menus tick the requisite local-and-seasonal boxes and draw a loyal band. Expect big-hearted dishes like venison and mushroom pie with kale and onions, or the lighter veal Holstein with frites and watercress, and some very comforting desserts like apple crumble and ginger parkin. The separate rare-breed steak menu includes chateaubriand for two, with a wine list to match. Hand-pump ales at the bar keep the traditionalist happy; for sunny days there's a well-kept terrace and garden at the back.

Meals	Lunch from £6.50. Bar meals from £3. Dinner from £10. Sunday lunch £13.95.
Closed	Sun eves & Mon all day.
Directions	On B3046 between Alresford and Basingstoke; pub in village centre.

Andres & Marie-Louise Alemany
The Purefoy Arms
Preston Candover,
Alresford RG25 2EJ
Tel +44 (0)1256 389777
Web www.thepurefoyarms.co.uk

Hampshire

The Sun Inn

Bentworth

Timothy Taylor's Landlord, Hog's Back Tea, Andwell's Resolute, Ringwood Best, Fuller's London Pride... a parade of hand pumps pulls the punters in. There's charm, too: this friendly, flower-decked local was once a pair of 17th-century cottages. Surprisingly little has changed. On ancient bricks and bare boards is a rustic mix of scrubbed pine tables and oak benches and settles; beams are hung with brasses, walls adorned with prints and plates; there are fresh flowers, candelight and newspapers. Cosy, log-fired inglenooks warm the interlinking rooms. Food is mostly perfect English: steak and ale pie, calves' liver and bacon with peas and onion gravy, Sunday roasts, warming puddings. Hidden down a tiny lane on the edge of a village in deepest Hampshire, the Sun could scarcely be more rural. Footpaths radiate from the door.

Meals	Lunch & dinner £8.95-£15.95. Sunday lunch £10.95.
Closed	3pm-6pm. Open all day Sun.
Directions	Off A339, 2 miles from Alton.

Mary Holmes
The Sun Inn
Bentworth,
Alton GU34 5JT
Tel +44 (0)1420 562338
Web www.thesuninnbentworth.co.uk

The Yew Tree

Lower Wield

Tim Gray has totally revitalised this hard-to-find but worth-tracking-down inn. The re-worked, stone-flagged and beamed bar is immediately welcoming: a winter fire, a chiming clock, walls festooned with character prints, a happy mishmash of furniture. There's a slightly more formal note to the dining area off to one side. As for Tim, he is "fuelled by passion and fun." On summer weekends it's especially buzzy as beer flows and the local cricket team play on the pitch opposite; if cricket's not your thing, bag a seat in the peaceful front garden, in the shade of the eponymous yew. Good fresh dishes are chalked up daily, so be cheered by a warm halloumi, chorizo, celery and red onion salad, fillet steak with a brandy, peppercorn and cream sauce, and maybe a Yew tree white choc pot for pudding.

Meals	Lunch & dinner £8.95-£17.95.
Closed	3pm-6pm. Mon. Open all day Sun.
Directions	4.5 miles north of Alresford, off B3046, on a small lane between villages of Upper and Lower Wield.

Tim Gray
The Yew Tree
Lower Wield,
Alresford SO24 9RX

Tel +44 (0)1256 389224
Web www.the-yewtree.org.uk

Hampshire

The Hawkley Inn

Hawkley

In a sleepy village at the end of plunging lanes, a friendly mix of locals, farmers and walkers fill this genuine old inn. The Hawkley's front bars remain delightfully scruffy (a 'listed' carpet, nicotine-stained walls, bare boards, a mad moose head above the log fire) while the rear extension adds a touch of modernity, yet stays true to its roots thanks to sagging old sofas. So bag one of the rustic scrubbed tables and quaff amazing local beers – Ballards Best, Bowmans Swift One – or enjoy some country food. Arrive early at weekends – it's a popular place. Food ranges from soups and ploughman's to sea bream with caper butter and mash, and there are Sunday roasts and hearty weekend breakfasts too (do book). Worth the detour, once you've found it. Chawton, famous for Jane Austen's house, is nearby.

Meals	Lunch & dinner £7.50-£13.50. Sunday lunch £10.
Closed	3pm-5.30pm. Open all day Sat & Sun.
Directions	After A3/B3006, thro' Burgates, right into Hawkley Road & back over A3; 2 miles to hairpin bend; next left is Pococks Lane.

Simon Hawkins
The Hawkley Inn
Pococks Lane, Hawkley,
Liss GU33 6NE

Tel +44 (0)1730 827205
Web www.hawkleyinn.co.uk

Harrow Inn

Steep

The 16th-century Harrow is a gem. Unspoilt, brick-and-tiled, it hides down a country lane that dwindles into a footpath by a little stream (not easy to find!). It has been in Claire and Nisa McCutcheon's family since 1929 and they keep it very much as it must always have been. Where nicer to sup a pint than within these two small rooms with their timbered walls, scrubbed elm tables and brick inglenook fireplace aglow in winter. Behind a hatch-like serving counter, barrels of local ale rest on racks, bundles of drying hops hang above. There's a small, wild orchard garden – only the distant hum of the hidden A3 disturbs the bucolic calm. Food is limited to generously filled sandwiches, fresh soups, homemade quiches, a ploughman's platter, treacle tart – served with a smile. Loos are a quick dash across the lane.

Meals	Bar meals £4.50-£14. Not Sun eves.
Closed	2.30pm-6pm (3pm-6pm Sat, 3pm-7pm Sun) & Sun eves Oct-May.
Directions	Off A3 signed Midhurst; left at roundabout; 1st left Inmans Lane; left at church; cross A3 to reach pub.

Claire & Nisa McCutcheon
Harrow Inn
Steep,
Petersfield GU32 2DA

Tel +44 (0)1730 262685
Web www.harrow-inn.co.uk

The Bakers Arms

Droxford

Set in the attractive Meon Valley, this small, unprepossessing pub is a bit of a find for lovers of generous British cooking. For locals, there's the added plus of Droxford's Bowman Ales – and the village stores parked on the side. Inside has a relaxed, traditional charm and a winter fire. The L-shaped, opened-up space is light and cheery, the customary miscellany of old wooden furniture sitting alongside a couple of modish leather sofas, but the décor is no slave to fashion. The kitchen's chalkboard menu pleases all with its use of prime local produce and seasonal dishes with punchy flavours and, in this rolling countryside, the local meats are a forte; organic Hyden Farm pork belly with smoked eel from the River Test, Hampshire sausages served with crowd-pleasing mash and shallot gravy. An excellent meeting place.

Meals	Lunch & dinner £10.95-£17.95.
Closed	Sun eves & Mon all day.
Directions	In village centre beside A32, 5 miles north of Wickham.

Adam & Anna Cordery
The Bakers Arms
High Street, Droxford,
Southampton SO32 3PA

Tel +44 (0)1489 877533
Web www.thebakersarmsdroxford.com

The Royal Oak

Havant

Twitchers beat a path to the door of this waterside pub. The views across Chichester Harbour are stunning, of moored boats and rare birds. From your bench by the water's edge you can watch the tide ebb and flow and study the waders in the mudflats; at spring tide the water laps at the front door. The pub, licensed since 1725, was once a row of 16th-century cottages lived in by workers at Langstone Mill next door; they used to have a 'tidal licence' allowing travellers a drink while waiting for the tide to ebb. When inclement weather forces you in and away from the view you'll discover rambling rooms with flagstone and pine floors, beams and an open fire. There are real ales, standard pub grub, roasts on Sundays and sandwiches all day. But it's the view that's the draw here – magical on a summer's eve.

Meals — Lunch & dinner £6.95-£14.95. Sunday lunch £7.95.
Closed — Open all day.
Directions — Beside Chichester harbour, off A3023 before bridge to Hayling Island. Parking can be tricky.

Kevin Buck
The Royal Oak
19 Langstone High Street,
Havant PO9 1RY
Tel +44 (0)23 9248 3125
Web www.royaloak-havant.com

Entry 256 Map 4

Hampshire

The Bugle

Hamble

Hamble's famous pub, celebrated by yachtsmen the world over, was saved in 2005 by those behind Southampton's White Star Tavern. Using traditional materials and methods they have remodelled the Bugle's 16th-century heart – so you find new-and-old oak beams and standing timbers, stripped-back brick fireplaces and open fires, natural flagstone floors and polished boards. The atmosphere is relaxed, the bar throngs with drinkers and diners on sailing days, there's a simply adorned dining area for escaping the bustle and a private room upstairs. A wide-ranging clientele informs the style of the food. Sit at the bar with a pint of Bowmans Swift One and tapas-style dishes, or go the whole hog and order mussels and chips or pork belly with bubble and squeak and cider gravy. Or slip off to the super front terrace for views of bobbing boats on the Hamble.

Meals — Lunch £5-£15. Bar meals £3.50-£8. Dinner £10-£16. Sunday lunch, 3 courses, £19.
Closed — Open all day.
Directions — M27 junc. 8; signs to Hamble, right at Hamble Square & follow cobbled street down to riverside car park.

Matthew Boyle
The Bugle
High Street, Hamble,
Southampton SO31 4HA
Tel +44 (0)23 8045 3000
Web www.buglehamble.co.uk

Entry 257 Map 4

The Thomas Lord

West Meon

Named after the founder of Lord's, this unpretentious rural gem groans with cricketing paraphernalia. The darkly beamed and half-panelled walls are decorated with old bats, caps, pads and associated prints, while well-used sofas and the odd leather armchair draw up to a fire in winter. There's an endearing miscellany of weathered wooden furniture, big fat candles, drinkers, dogs and a small back room weighed down by books. It's a busy, friendly pub loved by a loyal crowd and the daily menus are crammed with local produce including vegetables and herbs from the pub's own large veg patch; try Grange Farm lamb shoulder with rosemary sauce. A choice of Hampshire ales direct from the cask follows the local theme, while a smart garden and outdoor wood-fired kitchen beckon on sunnier days. A great, rustic country inn.

Meals	Lunch & dinner £9.95-£15.
Closed	3pm-6pm. Open all day Sat & Sun.
Directions	Just off A32 between Alton & Wickham. Signed.

Richard Taylor
The Thomas Lord
West Meon,
Petersfield GU32 1LN
Tel +44 (0)1730 829244
Web www.thethomaslord.co.uk

The Flower Pots Inn

Cheriton

Ramblers and beer enthusiasts beat a path to Pat and Jo Bartlett's door, where award-winning pints of Flower Pots Bitter, Goodens Gold and Perridge Pale are brewed in the brewhouse across the car park. Open fires burn in two traditional bars: one a wallpapered parlour, the other a quarry-tiled public bar with scrubbed pine and an illuminated, glass-topped well. Ales are tapped from casks behind the counter hung with hops, and drunk to the accompaniment of happy chat; music and electronic games would be out of place here. In keeping with the simplicity of the place, the menu is short and straightforward: baps with home-cooked ham, sandwiches toasted or plain, home-cooked hotpots, spicy chilli with garlic bread, hearty winter soups, all served with a smile from a very happy staff.

Meals	Lunch & dinner £5-£10. Not Sunday or bank holiday eves.
Closed	2.30pm-6pm (3pm-7pm Sun).
Directions	Village signed off A272 east of Winchester; pub off B3046 in village centre.

Joanna & Patricia Bartlett
The Flower Pots Inn
Cheriton,
Alresford SO24 0QQ
Tel +44 (0)1962 771318
Web www.flowerpots-inn.co.uk

The Black Boy

Winchester

Quirky pubs with personality, real ale and fine food are worth tracking down. Winchester's example is best reached on foot – following the riverside path from the NT's Winchester Mill. The landlord has created an unassuming tavern that is pleasingly off the wall. Fascinating paraphernalia ranges from fire buckets and old signs to a 'library' crammed with books; oddities greet the eye at every turn. It's the easiest place in the world to while away an hour or three. Choose a pint of Flower Pots Bitter (one of five hand-pumped ales) and a cosy corner with a deep sofa and a log fire to relish it in. Lunchtime peckish? Tuck into beer-battered cod, shepherd's pie or sandwiches. In the evening, pop across the road to the Michelin-starred Black Rat restaurant (also owned by David) and splash out on something a touch more inventive.

Meals	Lunch & dinner £5.50-£8.50. Sunday lunch, 2 courses, £12.50. Not Sunday eve, Monday or Tuesday lunch.
Closed	Open all day.
Directions	Head south out of city along Chesil Street; Wharf Hill 1st road on right; parking off Chesil Street.

David Nicholson
The Black Boy
1 Wharf Hill,
Winchester SO23 9NQ

Tel	+44 (0)1962 861754
Web	www.theblackboypub.com

Entry 260 Map 4

Hampshire

Chestnut Horse

Easton

In the beautiful Itchen valley, this rather smart 16th-century dining pub is in the capable hands of Karen Wells and the standards of food and service are high. A decked terrace leads to a warren of snug rooms around a central bar, warmed by log fires. At night it is cosy and candlelit; you can eat either in the low beamed 'red' room, with its wood-burning stove, cushioned settles and mix of dining tables, or in the panelled and memorabilia-filled 'green' room. Try the two-course menu (smoked mackerel pâté, sea bream with pesto dressing, apple and walnut pie – all good value). Or tuck into beer-battered fish and chips, lamb shank with broad bean risotto, or rib-eye steak with hand-cut chips and béarnaise. There are great local ales, decent wines and champagne by the glass. A cracking food pub.

Meals	Lunch & dinner £10-£18, 2 courses, £12. Sunday lunch £12.
Closed	Monday. Thurs 3.30pm-5.30pm. Open all day Fri-Sun.
Directions	1 mile off B3047 (Winchester to Alresford), 4 miles east of Winchester.

Karen Wells
Chestnut Horse
Easton,
Winchester SO21 1EG

Tel	+44 (0)1962 779257
Web	www.thechestnuthorse.com

Entry 261 Map 4

Bush Inn

Ovington

Down a meandering lane alongside the clear-running waters of the Itchen, a 17th-century jewel in Hampshire's crown. In winter the bar is dark and atmospheric: a roaring log fire, candles on tables, walls gas lamp-lit. In summer, what nicer, in the words of a visitor, than to sit on the bridge with a pint, the evening sun pouring through the trees, the trout hiding in the reeds below. The setting and the cottagey garden are blissful in summer, and you can stroll along the river. Cottage furniture and high-backed pews fill a series of small rooms off the bar; walls are hung with fishing and country paraphernalia. City dwellers come for the atmosphere: cosy and peaceful (though busy in summer). The kitchen is driven by fresh local produce and presents a modern menu, and there are old favourites, too.

Meals	Lunch & dinner £11.50 & £18.50; sandwiches from £6.75. Weekday menu £15 & £17.50.
Closed	3pm-6pm. Open all day Sat & Sun and Jul & Aug.
Directions	Off A31 between Winchester & Alresford.

Nick & Cathy Young
Bush Inn
Ovington,
Alresford SO24 0RE
Tel +44 (0)1962 732764
Web www.thebushinn.co.uk

Entry 262 Map 4

Hampshire

The Wykeham Arms

Winchester

The old Wykeham is English to the core, full of its own traditions and neatly hidden away between the cathedral and the city's famous school. Ceilings drip with memorabilia and bow-tied regulars chat, pints in hand. It's grand too, a throwback to the past and brimming with warm colours and atmosphere. There are small red-shaded lamps on graffiti-etched desks (ex-Winchester College), three roaring fires and two dining rooms. At heart it remains a pub, but it's easy to mistake it for something smarter. Food is not cheap, but certainly reliable, from posh sandwiches and cottage pie at lunch to daily-changing evening dishes, perhaps herb-crusted rack of lamb and fillet steak with pepper sauce. The Fuller's Gales ales are good, the wine list is interesting (20 by the glass), and the staff young and laid-back.

Meals	Lunch £7-£15. Bar meals £7-£10. Dinner £15-£24. Sunday lunch, 3 courses, £23.
Closed	Open all day.
Directions	Immediately south of Cathedral between Winchester College & Cathedral. Access via Southgate Street & Canon Street; parking tricky.

Jon Howard
The Wykeham Arms
75 Kingsgate Street,
Winchester SO23 9PE
Tel +44 (0)1962 853834
Web www.fullershotels.com

Entry 263 Map 4

The Oak Inn

Bank

Aptly named (among the forest oaks), this 18th-century pub, with its double-bay frontage and red phone box outside, is a friendly and traditional little place. It's popular not just with locals but also with walkers and cyclists who pour in at weekends to feast on generous portions of hearty pub grub – much of which has been reared or caught within the New Forest; note the symbols on the menu. Others drop in for a pint of Gales Seafarers in the low-beamed bar, or the little garden sheltered by a big yew. Blackboard specials might include whole baked John Dory or local venison sausages; doorstep sandwiches and homemade steak and ale pie catch the eye of hungry walkers. Come for winter fires, cottagey furniture, old-fashioned comfort, dark red walls and endearing touches like milk-urn bar stalls: everyone loves The Oak.

Meals	Lunch & dinner £8.95-£16.95.
Closed	3.30pm-6pm. Open all day Sat & Sun.
Directions	Bank is signed off A35 1 mile SW of Lyndhurst.

Martin Sliva & Zuzana Slivova
The Oak Inn
Pinkney Lane, Bank,
Lyndhurst SO43 7FE

Tel +44 (0)23 8028 2350
Web www.fullers.co.uk

Hampshire

The Royal Oak

Fritham

Small, ancient, thatched and secluded is this ale-lover's retreat. No fruit machines, just old-fashioned bonhomie. Locals exchange stories around the bar; ramblers and dogs drop by. Huge fires crackle through the winter, demanding you linger. Neil and Pauline McCulloch believe in local produce and deliver honest and unpretentious pub lunches: ploughman's with homemade pâté, French-dressed local crab, sausages from a local butcher, no chips. Though rustically simple, the three small rooms are perfect, with pale boards, solid tables and spindleback chairs, darts, dominoes and cribbage, and homely touches. Five local beers are drawn straight from the cask, including Hop Back Summer Lightning and Royal Oak by Bowman ales. And there's more: a large garden for barbecues and a beer and food festival in September. Pub heaven.

Meals	Lunch & dinner £4.50-£9.
Closed	3pm-5.30pm. Open all day Sat & Sun. Open all day Jul-Sept.
Directions	M27 junc. 1; B3078 to Fordingbridge; turn for Fritham after 2.5 miles. Follow signs.

Neil & Pauline McCulloch
The Royal Oak
Fritham,
Lyndhurst SO43 7HJ

Tel +44 (0)23 8081 2606

The Rose & Thistle

Rockbourne

Rockbourne is the kind of village where you might find Miss Marple trimming a rose bush. The pub is dreamy too, and, like many, started life as two thatched cottages – the two huge fireplaces should be no surprise. It is a great mix of oak beams and timbers, carved benches, flagstones and tiles. Add country-style fabrics and tables strewn with magazines and you have an enchanting place to return to after visiting Rockbourne's Roman villa. Kerry Dutton makes use of fresh local produce: estate game in season, pork with champ and black pudding and cider gravy, veal with béarnaise sauce. In summer you can dine in the garden, perhaps smoked trout and scrambled eggs or classic steak and kidney pudding. The changing chalkboard menu favours Cornish fish, such as monkfish wrapped in pancetta.

Meals	Lunch & dinner £9.50-£19.50. Bar meals from £5.
Closed	3pm-6pm (Sun from 8pm Nov-Mar).
Directions	3 miles north west of Fordingbridge, off B3078.

Kerry Dutton
The Rose & Thistle
Rockbourne,
Fordingbridge SP6 3NL

Tel	+44 (0)1725 518236
Web	www.roseandthistle.co.uk

Entry 266 Map 3

Hampshire

The Kings Arms

Lockerley

Lucy Townsend and Paul Wigg have breathed new life into the 18th-century Kings Arms, in a sleepy village close to Romsey and the glorious Test Valley. Soft lamplight, flickering candles and glowing log fires pull drinkers and diners into a classily refurbished bar. The floor is stone-tiled, the walls carry an eclectic range of paintings, there's Ringwood Bitter on tap and 12 wines by the glass. In the dining room next door: cool grey hues, local art on panelled walls, gleaming glasses on old dining tables. It's civilised and the food fits the setting, short menus promising smoked trout pâté, rib-eye steak with watercress, chips and tarragon butter, and Bakewell tart with almond ice cream. Heating dining pods (with WiFi) in the garden add a stylish touch; be sure to book. All this two miles from Mottisfont Abbey and its heavenly roses.

Meals	Lunch & dinner £10.95-£18.95.
Closed	Open all day.
Directions	Lockerley is signposed off B3084 at Awbridge, 5 miles north of Romsey.

Lucy Townsend & Paul Wigg
The Kings Arms
Romsey Road, Lockerley,
Romsey SO51 0JF

Tel	+44 (0)1794 340332
Web	www.kingsarmsatlockerley.co.uk

Entry 267 Map 3

The Saracens Head

Symonds Yat

This is an adventure before you've booked in. The bar staff still, obligingly, run the old, hand-cranked ferry across the lovely limpid river. The old inn dates from the 16th century and became a pub in the 18th but has a 21st-century buzz now, thanks to its friendly young staff and its big choice of dining tables. Dishes are chalked up on the blackboard by the bar – exotic sandwiches and bruschettas, pheasant terrine, wild boar with chive mash, Welsh goat's cheese panna cotta, crème brûlée – all so delicious that people travel from far away for the experience. The terraces by the water attract a crowd in summer and lend a seaside-holiday feel; sit back with your Theakston's Old Peculier and watch the canoeists float by. In winter, the public bar is a warm haven; sit and roast by the wood burner while watching the trippers come for Symonds Yat. A shame not to stay: upstairs and in The Boathouse next door are a flurry of bedrooms, some oak-floored, some carpeted with smart bathrooms. Ask for a room with a view up *and* down the river. Breakfast is one of the best.

Price	£89-£138. Singles from £59.
Rooms	10: 8 doubles, 2 twins.
Meals	Lunch & dinner £9.50-£19.95. Bar meals £4.50-£16.95. Sunday lunch £9.95-£15.
Closed	Open all day.
Directions	A40 Ross-on-Wye to Monmouth; exit at South Hereford Motorcaravan Centre; signs for Symonds Yat East.

Chris & Peter Rollinson
The Saracens Head
Symonds Yat,
Ross-on-Wye HR9 6JL
Tel +44 (0)1600 890435
Web www.saracensheadinn.co.uk

The Pandy Inn

Dorstone

Built in 1185... a half-timbered Herefordshire delight, a contender for 'oldest pub in the land'. Heavy beams, worn flagged floors, smoke-smudged stone and a vast oak lintel over the old log grate. This is the country of Golden Valley and Butty Bach ales and 'cloudy' scrumpy – no wonder there's a happy buzz. On the menus are organic Hereford beef steaks and delicious seasonal specials: try Welsh lamb shank with redcurrant and red wine sauce, hearty baguettes, walkers' soups, homemade fish pie and first-class bread. Families and dogs are welcome here and children can spin into a garden with picnic tables and a play area in summer. The garden also sees a spanking new arrival: an eco-friendly mountain chalet built according to traditional Polish methods but with a clean-cut modern design. Inside are five well-sized en suite rooms in lustrous pale spruce, light, airy, comfortable and with a minimalist feel; two have private balconies and wooded hill views. You are in the 'Golden Valley' so set off for Abbey Dore and Arthur's Stone, or bookish Hay-on-Wye, a short drive. Special place, special people.

Price	From £80. Singles from £70.
Rooms	5 twins/doubles.
Meals	Lunch from £4.95. Dinner from £10.95. Sunday lunch £10.95.
Closed	3pm-6pm (6.30pm Sun). Mon in winter (except bank hols). Open all day Sat.
Directions	Signed from B4348 Hereford to Hay-on-Wye, 5 miles from Hay.

Bill & Magdalena Gannon
The Pandy Inn
Dorstone,
Hereford HR3 6AN

Tel +44 (0)1981 550273
Web www.pandyinn.co.uk

The Mill Race

Walford

As the 'ecclesiastical' door swings open, prepare yourself for a stainless steel kitchen glistening behind a granite-topped bar; this is a stylish place. A wood-burner divides eating areas and there are counter-style bar tables and leather armchairs for aperitifs. A food provenance blackboard shows how seriously food is taken here: the kitchen team choose the meat and the game from their 1,000 acre farm and estate and help dig the vegetables; they'll even catch the trout for the table. Linger long over roast red leg of partridge with mash, bread sauce and watercress, or roast Gower pollock with crushed potatoes, wild mushrooms and parsley oil. A new carbon-neutral wood fired pizza oven, lit on certain days only, sits on the rear terrace. Look across the Wye to the ruins of Goodrich Castle, sip ales from the same valley. Fabulous.

Meals	Lunch from £5. Bar meals from £5. Dinner from £9.50. Sunday lunch, 3 courses, £16.
Closed	3pm-5pm. Open all day Sat & Sun.
Directions	B4234 out of Ross-on-Wye towards Kerne Bridge. Pass village hall on left, pub on right.

Luke Freeman
The Mill Race
Walford,
Ross-on-Wye HR9 5QS

Tel +44 (0)1989 562891
Web www.millrace.info

The Butchers Arms

Woolhope

Chef Stephen Bull was one of the architects of the modern British food revolution in the 1980s, and he continues to draw foodies to The Butchers Arms, a short drive from Hereford. A splendid 16th-century half-timbered pub tucked down a winding lane in walking country, it is noted for its low beams and smouldering log fires. Bull is in the kitchen as much as he is pulling pints of Wye Valley ale, local ciders, perries and well-chosen wines. The ingredients-driven seasonal menu reads like a 'greatest hits' from his London restaurant days and makes delectable use of local produce: the signature dish of twice-baked cheese soufflé; pork chop with apples, sage and calvados; warm ginger cake with treacle toffee ice cream. In the summer, enjoy the peace of the sheltered garden with its babbling stream.

Meals	Lunch & dinner £9.50-£16.
Closed	3pm-6pm. Sun eves & Mon.
Directions	Off B4224 between Hereford & Ross-on-Wye.

Stephen Bull
The Butchers Arms
Woolhope,
Hereford HR1 4RF

Tel +44 (0)1432 860281
Web www.butchersarmswoolhope.com

The Kilpeck Inn

Kilpeck

Kilpeck – known for its Norman church – has a second string to its bow: a super little country inn with a facelift. It stands on the edge of the village overlooking beautiful fields, ten miles south of Hereford. Outside, smart white walls sparkle in the sun. Inside: old stone, slate floors and a warm contemporary feel. Find darts in the locals' bar, alongside the daily papers and a smouldering fire, and original beams, candle lanterns and painted panelling in the airy restaurant. Dig into the sort of food you'd hope to find in a country inn: fillet of beef, lemon sole, steak and mushroom pie, fruit crumble. It's as local as possible and serious green, what with low food miles, a wood-pellet boiler, hi-spec insulation and a rainwater tank. Walkers rejoice: the Black mountains and Offa's Dyke are close.

Meals: Lunch & bar meals from £5.95. À la carte dinner £9.95-£17.95. Sunday lunch, 3 courses, £15.95. Not Sun eves.
Closed: Open all day.
Directions: South from Hereford on A465. Village signed left after about 7 miles.

Neil Wadelin
The Kilpeck Inn
Kilpeck,
Hereford HR2 9DN
Tel +44 (0)1981 570464
Web www.kilpeckinn.com

Entry 272 Map 7

Herefordshire

Carpenter's Arms

Walterstone

A little chapel-side pub in the middle of nowhere, hard to find but worth it, superb in every way. Vera has been dispensing Wadworth 6X and Breconshire Golden Valley from behind the corner hatch for years and everyone gets a welcome: locals, walkers, families, babies. Through an ancient oak doorway is a tiny bar with a log-fired range and a dining area to the side. Floors are Welsh slate, settles polished oak, tables cast iron, walls open stone; it's as cared for as can be. On the menu are beef and Guinness pie, faggots, mash, mushy peas and onion gravy, bread and butter pudding – proper homemade food, some organic, at great prices. Beer is served from the drum, cider and perry from the flagon. In summer, spill into the grassy garden and gaze up at the Skirrid, then pull on the hiking boots and climb it.

Meals: Lunch & dinner £10.95-£14.95. Bar meals from £5.
Closed: Open all day.
Directions: Village signed from Pandy; Pandy signed from A465 from Abergavenny.

Vera Watkins
Carpenter's Arms
Walterstone,
Hereford HR2 0DX
Tel +44 (0)1873 890353

Entry 273 Map 7

Bull's Head

Craswall

It's often said that getting there is half the fun… and the road to Craswall will delight you as it snakes up beneath the brooding bulk of the Black Hill of Bruce Chatwin fame. At this old drovers' inn, rusticity rules in a bar of scrubbed-top tables, old pews and vintage Laura Ashley wallpaper barely clinging to crumbling plaster. Wye Valley ale or Gwatkins farmhouse cider comes at you through a 'hole in the wall' and is the perfect tonic after a hike. Up steps to a flagstoned dining area and an open fire where the enchanting Mackintoshes bring a dash of the Mediterranean to their unfussy and flavoursome dishes; a pie here is a proper wedge of goodness, with vegetables good enough to eat on their own. In season you can sample Black Mountain wimberry tart and double cream. And there's a garden and a field for camping. Heaven!

Meals	Lunch & dinner £10.50-£19.50.
Closed	3pm-6pm. Mon-Weds & Sun eves. Call for winter opening times.
Directions	From Hay-on-Wye take Capel-y-ffin road south; bear left to Craswall. Pub on left before village.

Charles & Kathryn Mackintosh
Bull's Head
Craswall,
Hay-on-Wye HR2 0PN
Tel +44 (0)1981 510616
Web www.thebullsheadcraswall.co.uk

Entry 274 Map 7

Herefordshire

Old Black Lion

Hay-on-Wye

Heaven for historians, book lovers and foodies in equal measure. Oliver Cromwell lodged here while laying siege to Hay Castle – the main building heaves with oak beams, ancient artefacts and conspiratorial nooks and crannies. Dolan Leighton has changed little at this popular dining pub, where cheerful staff pull pints of the eponymous Black Lion bitter. Seasonal bar favourites keep the kitchen working through every session as diners feast on creamy peppered venison casserole with cabbage mash. In the evening, pick a table in the cosy 20-seat restaurant to sample a warm salad of pigeon and smoked bacon and roast salmon with red pesto and mushroom sauce. There's a well-priced wine list and a good list of halves. Don't miss the 13th-century Mappa Mundi in Hereford Cathedral – or the town's 30 bookshops.

Meals	Lunch from £4.95. Dinner from £12.95. Bar meals from £10.45. Sunday lunch £12.95.
Closed	Open all day.
Directions	2-minute walk from centre of Hay.

Dolan Leighton
Old Black Lion
26 Lion Street, Hay-on-Wye,
Hereford HR3 5AD
Tel +44 (0)1497 820841
Web www.oldblacklion.co.uk

Entry 275 Map 7

The Stagg Inn

Titley

In a Herefordshire village lies the first British pub to have been awarded a Michelin star. Gavroche-trained Steve Reynolds took it on and, defying all odds, ended up a Herefordshire food hero. As for provenance: the only thing you're not told is the name of the bird from which your pigeon breast (perfectly served on herb risotto) came. Most of the produce is very local, some is organic, with fresh fruit and vegetables from the kitchen garden or Titley Court next door. Seductive and restorative is the exceptional food: goat's cheese and fennel tart, saddle of venison with horseradish gnocchi and kummel, bread and butter pudding with clotted cream, a cheese trolley resplendent with 15 regional cheeses. The intimate bar is perfect and dog-friendly, there's beer from Hobsons, cider from Dunkerton's and some very classy wines.

Meals	Lunch & dinner from £25. Bar meals £9.80. Sunday lunch, 3 courses, £19.30.
Closed	3pm-6.30pm. Sun eves & Mon.
Directions	On B4355 between Kington & Presteigne.

Steve & Nicola Reynolds
The Stagg Inn
Titley,
Kington HR5 3RL
Tel +44 (0)1544 230221
Web www.thestagg.co.uk

Entry 276 Map 7

Herefordshire

The New Inn

Pembridge

Perfect for English heritage lovers with big appetites. The food is generously portioned, the building is as old as can be (1311), and Pembridge is a remarkable survivor; its market hall (where you can sup pints in the summer) could be in deepest France. It is a simple but great pleasure to amble in to this ancient inn, order a drink and squeeze into the curved back settle in the flagstoned bar; when the fireplace logs are lit, it's heaven. This is the most timeless of old locals, with photos of village shenanigans up on the wall and a darts board put to good use. Upstairs has floral carpets, books and sofa; it's a reassuring spot in which to tuck into hearteningly familiar smoked chicken and avocado salad, steak and ale pie and seafood stew. Jane Melvin is happy doing what she does best.

Meals	Lunch & dinner £6.95-£12. Bar meals £5.95-£8.50. Dinner from £15. Sunday lunch, 3 courses, £16.
Closed	3pm-6pm.
Directions	Just off A44 in Pembridge. In centre next to Market Square.

Jane Melvin
The New Inn
Market Square,
Pembridge,
Leominster HR6 9DZ
Tel +44 (0)1544 388427

Entry 277 Map 7

The Riverside Inn

Aymestrey

Edward IV had a celebratory noggin here after a decisive incident in the Wars of the Roses. He was declared King soon afterwards. It is much altered: to an easy mix of antiques, fresh flowers, hops and pine. Menus change with the seasons and the seductive dishes include Herefordshire guinea fowl with fondant turnip and wild mushroom sauce, and local venison with juniper and red wine jus. Wander from the bar into linked rooms with log fires; order an award-winning pint of Wye Valley from Stoke Lacy or a house wine from Sicily, Chile, Germany. And look for the map of the kitchen gardens from which so much of the fruit and vegetables come. The setting is bucolic, tucked back from a stone bridge over the river Lugg, alive with river trout, waterside seats and a lovely terraced garden. The Mortimer Trail passes the front door.

Meals	Lunch from £8.50. Bar meals from £5.95. Dinner from £14.95. Sunday lunch, 3 courses, £19.95. Not Sunday eves.
Closed	3pm-6pm. Sun eves & Mon all day in winter (closed Mon lunch in summer).
Directions	On A4110 18 miles north of Hereford.

Richard & Liz Gresko
The Riverside Inn
Aymestrey,
Leominster HR6 9ST
Tel +44 (0)1568 708440
Web www.theriversideinn.org

Entry 278 Map 7

The Oak Inn

Staplow

Just west of the Malvern Hills this freehouse dating from the 1600s has been very sympathetically refurbished. Farmhouse tables and chairs jostle together on polished flagstones, hops hang from beams and wood burners crackle in exposed brick hearths – country pub to the core. There are ales from Bathams and Wye Valley and, as you'd expect, good ciders like Robinson's Flagon and Weston's Perry. Traditional home-cooked food with modern twists are the order of the day; try slow-cooked pork belly with 'boozy' mustard mash or braised venison casserole with spiced red cabbage. There are also deli boards and sandwiches made with their own bread. The pretty garden is backed by apple orchards, while inside the fires and candles in the bar, two snugs and dining area are kept glowing by a bright and attentive team. A super little pub.

Meals	Lunch from £4.25. Dinner £11.50.
Closed	3pm-5.30pm (Mon-Sat). 3pm-7pm (Sun).
Directions	On B4214 2 miles north of Ledbury.

Hylton Haylett & Julie Woollard
The Oak Inn
Staplow,
Ledbury HR8 1NP
Tel +44 (0)1531 640954
Web www.oakinnstaplow.co.uk

Entry 279 Map 8

The Brocket Arms

Ayot St Lawrence

Welcome to a splendid medieval pub in an equally splendid village, close to Shaw's Corner; George Bernard lived here for 40 years (pull out your National Trust cards). Little has changed over the centuries, although new owner Bhupen Solanki has spruced up the classic three-roomed interior, with its atmospheric dark oak beams and timbers, blazing fire in the inglenook, rustic benches and bar tables, and tiled and parquet floors. In the bar, tuck into roast beef and horseradish sandwiches or ham, egg and chips, perfect with a pint of Adnams Broadside. Or choose from the set menu in the restaurant; there's potted crab with cucumber chutney, braised rabbit with mustard cream, warm chocolate and chestnut torte. Stay the night to get your full quota of historic charm. Three bedrooms have wonky timbered walls, sloping floors, leaded windows, new brass beds and old fireplaces, and modern-day comforts abound – crisp linen, posh toiletries. The four-poster room may have an amazing vaulted ceiling but the simpler rooms in the converted stable block are as comfortable. And there's a super walled garden.

Price	£95-£125.
Rooms	6: 5 doubles, 1 twin.
Meals	Bar meals £4.95-£12.95. Set menu £19.95 & £24.95.
Closed	Open all day.
Directions	From Wheathampstead, follow signs to Shaw's Corner.

Bhupen Solanki
The Brocket Arms
Ayot St Lawrence,
Welwyn AL6 9BT
Tel +44 (0)1438 820250
Web www.brocketarms.com

The Bricklayers Arms

Flaunden

Tucked away at a remote crossroads in the exotically named Hogpits Bottom ('hog' is local dialect for shale) is a pretty, ivy-covered 18th-century building with low beams, blazing winter fires and timbered walls. Once a row of cottages and shops, and an ale house since 1832, this listed building has recently been refurbished by the Michaels family, currently in their ninth year. Now it's rammed with diners daily and Alvin's staff are run off their feet. French chef Claude Pallait turns out local rare-breed fillets of pork with apple compote and cider jus; Little Missenden lamb with a pea flan; home-smoked fish; good old steak and kidney pie. All are delicious, all are prepared from locally sourced or organic ingredients where possible. There's an excellent range of ales, and over 140 wines, ports and Armagnacs.

Meals	Lunch & dinner £9.95-£24.95. Bar meals from £8.95.
Closed	Open all day.
Directions	M25 junc. 20; A41; 1st left to Chipperfield; 1st right to Flaunden.

Alvin Michaels
The Bricklayers Arms
Hogpits Bottom, Flaunden,
Hemel Hempstead HP3 0PH
Tel +44 (0)1442 833322
Web www.bricklayersarms.com

Entry 281 Map 9

Hertfordshire

The Alford Arms

Frithsden

It isn't easy to find, so be armed with a detailed map or precise directions before you set out – David and Becky Salisbury's gastropub is worth any number of missed turns. It's in a hamlet enfolded by acres of National Trust common land. Inside, two interlinked rooms, bright, airy, with soft colours, scrubbed pine tables on wooden or tiled floors. Food is taken seriously and ingredients are as organic, free-range and delicious as can be. On a menu that divides dishes into small plates and main meals, there is salt 'n' pepper squid with Asian slaw, local game and caramelised onion pie with crushed neeps and mulled plum jus, homemade mulled rosé sorbet. Wine drinkers have the choice of 22 by the glass, while service is informed and friendly. Arrive early on a warm day to take your pick of the teak tables on the sun-trapping front terrace.

Meals	Lunch, bar meals & dinner, all £11.75-£19.75.
Closed	Open all day.
Directions	A4146 Hemel Hempstead to Water End; 2nd left after Red Lion to Frithsden; left after 1 mile at T-junction, then right; on right.

David & Becky Salisbury
The Alford Arms
Frithsden,
Hemel Hempstead HP1 3DD
Tel +44 (0)1442 864480
Web www.alfordarmsfrithsden.co.uk

Entry 282 Map 9

The Fox

Willian

Cliff and James's village pub has a fresh, contemporary feel and a foodie menu that showcases British ingredients, including seafood from the Norfolk coast and local farm meats. It could beat many neighbourhood restaurants into a cocked hat but part of its charm is that it is still a place where beer drinkers are welcome – try a pint of one of the Brancaster ales from the Nye family brewery. A cool, formal dining room sits astride a relaxed bar where Brancaster oysters in sesame tempura add glamour to a menu that includes a beef and pork burger with sweet onion and chilli relish. The restaurant is a mix of French bistro and British pub: cod with spring onion and tiger prawn risotto, venison with braised red cabbage and blackberry jus, chocolate orange fondant. This Fox is one you'd do well to hunt down.

Meals	Lunch & bar meals from £9.95. Dinner from £12.25. Sunday lunch, 3 courses, £26.40. Not Sunday eves.
Closed	Open all day.
Directions	A1 junc 9 for Letchworth; 1st left into Baldock Lane; pub 0.5 miles.

Cliff & James Nye
The Fox
Willian,
Letchworth Garden City SG6 2AE

Tel +44 (0)1462 480233
Web www.foxatwillian.co.uk

Entry 283 Map 9

Hertfordshire

The Hoops Inn

Perry Green

Recently spruced up by the Henry Moore Foundation (Henry used to drop by every Sunday) who bought the place in 1990, this old whitewashed pub thrives as a dining venue. Visitors to Moore's Sculpture Garden and Studios opposite fill the low-beamed and open-plan interior, decorated in contemporary style with Moore-inspired artefacts and touches. For sunny days there's a garden and terrace for a glass of red and a beef sandwich, or a plate of whitebait from the summer al fresco menu. Expect tasty, wholesome British cooking from Mark Williams, seasonal set menus brimming with locally sourced produce: smoked haddock and leek broth with homemade bread, lamb with spring greens and minted cucumber, cheddar and potato pie with garlic purée. Leave room for rhubarb bakewell tart and clotted cream, and don't miss the September food festival.

Meals	Lunch from £3.95. Dinner, 2 courses, £25. Not Sun eves.
Closed	Open all day.
Directions	See website.

Mark & Lowri Williams
The Hoops Inn
Perry Green,
Much Hadham SG10 6EF

Tel +44 (0)1279 843568
Web www.hoops-inn.co.uk

Entry 284 Map 9

Hermitage Rd.

Hitchin

Anglian Country Inns opened its fourth dining venue in 2011 and what a surprise: a former ballroom and nightclub in the heart of Hitchin. From the street and the coffee bar (all-day cakes, pasties, sandwiches), stairs lead up to the cavernous bar and dining room, elegantly stripped back in New York style, with exposed brick walls, acres of oak floor, cool subtle lighting, floor-to-ceiling arched windows and a state-of the-art, open-to-view kitchen. Chill out with a cocktail or a pint of Brancaster brew and share a charcuterie board at high tables, or watch your food being cooked from your dining table – steaming Brancaster mussels; rack of sticky pork ribs; beetroot, mint and baby spinach risotto; sirloin steak from the grill; roast cod with clam, bacon and potato chowder. Everyone is beating a path to Hermitage Rd. – please book!

Meals	Lunch & dinner from £9. Bar meals from £3. Sunday lunch, 2 courses, £18.50.
Closed	Open all day.
Directions	On Hermitage Road in town centre, between train station and market square.

Howard Nye
Hermitage Rd.
21 Hermitage Road,
Hitchin SG5 1BT
Tel +44 (0)1462 433603
Web www.hermitagerd.co.uk

Entry 285 Map 9

Hertfordshire

The Highlander Pub

Hitchin

The Prutton family have been running this wonderful pub for over 30 years. Now the new generation – the Anglo-French partnership of Charlotte and Eric, back from several years in the Alps – add youthful energy and culinary skill to the family provenance. This is an unpretentious local that moves with the times and there's an informal Gallic bistro feel to the place. Stand over your pint at the bar, or settle back into one of the settles; read the papers, peruse the menu. Behind the immaculate bar, all aubergine and white, wines are enticingly displayed beneath old-fashioned beer mugs hanging from beams; a touch of nostalgia. Eric's delicious food fuses the best traditions of France and England, from tasty ploughman's to beef bourguignon with creamy mash – and Sunday lunches worth missing breakfast for.

Meals	Lunch from £4.10. Dinner from £5.65.
Closed	2.30pm-6pm (7pm Sun). Open all day Fri & Sat.
Directions	On the A505 almost in the centre of Hitchin.

Charlotte Prutton & Eric Ransinangue
The Highlander Pub
45 Upper Tilehouse Street,
Hitchin SG5 2EF
Tel +44 (0)1462 454612
Web www.highlanderpubhitchin.co.uk

Entry 286 Map 9

The Sun at Northaw

Northaw

The 16th-century pub overlooking Northaw's pretty green shines in this north-of-London culinary desert. Passionate about food provenance, Oliver ensures his menus bristle with fabulous produce and, as the menu food map shows, most of it is from Hertfordshire and neighbouring Essex. Find biodynamic, organic, outdoor-reared and artisan goodies, all delicious. There's 'rose' (welfare-friendly) veal chop with celeriac and crab apple mash; local wood pigeon with brussel sprout tops, bacon and salsify; a classic beer-battered haddock with chips and mushy peas. Kids are looked after with organic, guilt-free portions of their own. The rustic-chic interior oozes charm and atmosphere: soothing green hues, period fireplaces, board and stone floors, smart antique tables, and crates of fruit and vegetables dotted around the bar and dining rooms.

Meals: Lunch & dinner £9.50-£19.50. Sunday lunch, 3 courses, £16.50.
Closed: Sun eves from 7pm & Mon all day.
Directions: M25 junc 24, take A111 to Potters Bar, then right A1000 along High Street and take B156 right signed to Northaw. Pub on left by green.

Local, seasonal & organic produce

Oliver Smith & Sarah Doyle
The Sun at Northaw
1 Judges Hill, Northaw,
Potters Bar EN6 4NL
Tel +44 (0)1707 655507
Web www.thesunatnorthaw.co.uk

Entry 287 Map 9

Hertfordshire

The Blue Anchor

St Albans

While the boxy exterior is no visual delight, Paul Bloxham's cooking makes the Blue Anchor worth seeking out. Far from being an ego-fuelled indulgence for this exuberant chef, here is modern pub food at its best – top quality ingredients, generous portions and fair prices. Scotch duck-egg conceals juicy sausage and a warm gush of gooey yolk, while a wing of ray with cockles, caper butter, mash and kale dwarfs its substantial plate. There's a daily changing 'grill board' and a bargain lunch menu that might include hake brandade, or pork loin with apples, mash and cabbage. Beers come courtesy of McMullens with Rusty Anchor brewed exclusively for the pub; wine rotates a less than predictable list of landlords' favourites. Visually, the dining room may lack character, but bright nautical art, a diminutive hearth and chunky mismatched tables add a certain homeliness.

Meals: Lunch & dinner £10-£15.
Closed: Monday.
Directions: See website.

Paul Bloxham
The Blue Anchor
145 Fishpool Street,
St Albans AL3 4RY
Tel +44 (0)1727 855038
Web www.theblueanchorstalbans.co.uk

Entry 288 Map 9

The Tilbury

Datchworth

Standing on the village crossroads, the old Tilbury was known as the Inn on the Green. Now smart downlighters illuminate pastel walls and chic wallpaper, there are inglenook fires and chalkboard menus, leather dining chairs and gilt mirrors; this is a sanctuary for ladies that lunch. A fabulous place, too, for a special dinner: the food is a major attraction. Celebrity chef Paul Bloxham and his crew are dedicated to sourcing the very best of local produce and that means free-range pork from Great Dunmow, ducks from Saffron Walden, oysters from Colchester and watercress from Whitwell. So tuck in to red mullet escabeche, fillet Rossini and autumn fruit crumble. You can take home pickles, preserves and terrines as mouthwatering reminders. Coming up for summer: barbecues for the big garden with picnic tables and parasols.

Meals	Lunch & dinner £11-£17. Set market menu £12 & £17.
Closed	3pm-6pm. Sun eves.
Directions	A1 to Stevenage, then A602 for Hertford; follow signs to Datchworth, then Datchworth Green.

Paul Bloxham
The Tilbury
Watton Road, Datchworth,
Knebworth SG3 6TB
Tel +44 (0)1727 855038
Web www.thetilbury.co.uk

Entry 289 Map 9

Hertfordshire

The Fox & Hounds

Hunsdon

London chefs quitting fabulous establishments to transform country boozers are almost two a penny, but few have managed it with the aplomb of James Rix. Enter a comfy laid-back bar with a log fire, leather sofas, the daily papers, local ales on tap and a menu that changes twice daily. Tuck into something simple like a plate of Spanish charcuterie or tender calves' liver with mash with bacon. Things step up a gear in the country-house-on-a-shoestring dining room that throws together polished old tables and a crystal chandelier: a funky backdrop to peppered venison steaks with beetroot and port sauce, tagliolini with clams, garlic and chilli, and apple and amaretti tart. Even the focaccia is homemade. It is a treat to see an old pub in the right hands, and booking is recommended.

Meals	Lunch & dinner £9-£22. Bar meals £4.95-£16.50. Sunday lunch, 3 courses, £27.50. Not Sun eves or Mon.
Closed	4pm-6pm. Sun eves & Mon (except bank hol lunches).
Directions	Off A414 between Harlow & Hertford on B1004.

James Rix
The Fox & Hounds
2 High Street, Hunsdon,
Ware SG12 8NH
Tel +44 (0)1279 843999
Web www.foxandhounds-hunsdon.co.uk

Entry 290 Map 9

Seaview Hotel
Seaview

Everything here is a dream. You're 50 yards from the water in a small seaside village that sweeps you back to a nostalgic past. Locals pop in for a pint, famished yachtsmen float in for a meal, those in the know drop by for a luxurious night in indulging rooms. The bar has nautical curios nailed to its walls, the terrace buzzes with island life in summer, the restaurants hum with the contented sighs of happy diners. The whole show is orchestrated by Andrew and a battalion of kind staff, who book taxis, carry bags, send you off in the right direction. Interior designer Graham Green oversaw the fabulous refurbishment; some rooms come in smart country-house style (upholstered four-posters, padded headboards), others are contemporary (cool colours, fancy bathrooms). Three new apartments have blossomed from a converted bank next door, another is on the way. Don't miss the food. The hotel has its own farm – home-reared meat, home-grown vegetables, home-laid eggs, while the crab ramekin is an island institution. There's a treatment room, too, for expert pampering.

Price	£125-£255. Suites £295.
Rooms	29: 14 twins/doubles, 3 four-posters. New wing: 4 doubles, 3 twins/doubles, 5 family suites.
Meals	Lunch & dinner £5-£35.
Closed	Open all day.
Directions	From Ryde B3330 south for 1.5 miles. Hotel signed left.

Andrew Morgan
Seaview Hotel
High Street,
Seaview PO34 5EX
Tel +44 (0)1983 612711
Web www.seaviewhotel.co.uk

The Taverners

Godshill

A pub for all seasons: in summer take your pint (Taverners Own or a good guest beer) out into a pretty rear garden with petanque, picnic tables, vegetable beds and roaming chickens; in winter hunker down by the front bar with its warming fire, flagstone floor and wooden tables. There's a couple of sofas too for after lunch snoozers, if they can ignore the jazzy background music. Food is straightforward, fresh and local, skilfully cooked by Roger who used to head the kitchen team at The Haymarket Hotel in London; the family room has been converted into a shop selling home-baked goodies and island food stuffs. Lovely to see hand-raised free-range pork pie, homemade pickles, and 'My Nan's lemon meringue pie' on a simple menu; the wine list is short but well chosen, and there's freshly-squeezed orange juice and real hot chocolate too.

Meals	Lunch & dinner £8-£13.50.
Closed	Sun eves from 5pm (except bank hols, school hols & high summer).
Directions	On A3020 in village centre, opposite model village.

Roger Serjent
The Taverners
High Street, Godshill,
Ventnor PO38 3HZ

Tel	+44 (0)1983 840707
Web	www.thetavernersgodshill.co.uk

Entry 292 Map 4

Isle of Wight

The New Inn

Shalfleet

Built in 1746, this old fishermen's haunt is worth more than a passing nod – especially if you are on the 65-mile coastal path trail. Or have got here by boat and moored at Shalfleet Quay. The place now draws a cheery mix of tourists, walkers and sailors to a spick-and-span bar with 900-year-old flagstones, beams and old fireplaces, and a series of pine-tabled dining rooms decked with nautical bits and bobs. Refreshment includes pints of island-brewed ales and fabulously fresh seafood marked up on the daily-changing chalkboard. The huge platter is a treat; other fish choices might include sea bass cooked with lemon or simply grilled plaice. The crab sandwiches are memorable, and carnivores are not forgotten, with prime steak, game in season and traditional pub grub. There's a decked garden too for summer al fresco supping.

Meals	Lunch & dinner £6-£20.
Closed	Open all day.
Directions	On A3054 between Yarmouth & Newport.

Martin Bullock
The New Inn
Main Road, Shalfleet,
Newport PO30 4NS

Tel	+44 (0)1983 531314
Web	www.thenew-inn.co.uk

Entry 293 Map 3

The Three Mariners

Oare

After a ramble across Oare marshes, welcome to a hideaway full of good things. Food, sourced locally from farms and day boats, is excellent value and it's the sort of place where you want to try everything that goes by. Potted crab, fish soup, and roast widgeon with red cabbage and parsnip potato cake represent contemporary pub classics, but a straightforward slow-cooked leg of lamb (for six to share at Sunday lunch) has a reassuringly timeless appeal. This 400-year-old pub comes with a laid-back medley of furniture and a double-sided log fire, cleverly dividing the bar from the dining room. It's simple and understated with a pleasant informality and lots of bare wood – a place to treasure; many do. There are Shepherd Neame ales and a modest but thoughtful selection of wines.

Meals	Lunch & dinner £11.00-£17.50. Bar meals from £4.
Closed	3pm-6pm & all day Mon. Open all day Sat & Sun.
Directions	From A2, take B2045 for Oare, left at T-junction; pub on right in 200 yds.

John O'Riordon
The Three Mariners
2 Church Road, Oare,
Faversham ME13 0QA
Tel +44 (0)1795 533633
Web www.thethreemarinersoare.co.uk

Entry 294 Map 5

The Dove

Dargate

Who could resist a country pub in the gloriously named Plum Pudding Lane? Enter through a series of small rooms with bare floorboards, scrubbed tables and solid chairs, the bar invariably propped up by drinkers with pints of Shepherd Neame's Late Red or Spitfire. Everyone else is here for the food. A decade ago Phillip MacGregor worked here as a trainee chef; now he has returned as proprietor and chef, and cooks with great skill and imagination. On the lunchtime menu you may find slip sole with herb butter, or a smoked bacon and rocket baguette, or bavette of beef with potato gratin; only the best ingredients are used, and roasted stuffed saddle of Romney Marsh lamb flies the local flag on the carte. Good for both a special meal and a relaxing country lunch, especially in summer when the garden is a draw.

Meals	Lunch & dinner £13-£21. Bar meals £3-£10.
Closed	Monday.
Directions	Off A299, 4 miles south west of Whitstable signed Yorkletts, Dargate, Waterham.

Phillip & Sarah MacGregor
The Dove
Plum Pudding Lane, Dargate,
Faversham ME13 9HB
Tel +44 (0)1227 751360
Web www.doveatdargate.co.uk

Entry 295 Map 5

The Sportsman

Seasalter

Brothers Steve and Phil Harris's pub is a gastronomic haven amid marshland, beach huts and caravan sites with the North Sea somewhere behind. The blackboard menu, short and sweet, promises everything seasonal and local. Meat comes from farms within sight of the front door, Whitstable is just down the road. Order a native oyster or two to slurp while waiting for smoked mackerel with Bramley apple jelly or pork terrine. Roast chicken with bacon, sprouts and bread sauce is an old fashioned treat; apple sorbet and burnt cream makes a stunning finale. There's a tasting menu (book in advance), delicious bread, hams cured in the beer cellar, they churn their own butter and make their own salt. You eat at large chunky tables made from reclaimed wood in any of three airy rooms with marsh views. Exceptional.

Meals	Lunch & dinner £17.95-£22.95. Tasting menu £65. Not Sun eve or Mon.
Closed	3pm-6pm.
Directions	On coast road between Faversham & Whitstable.

Phil & Stephen Harris
The Sportsman
Faversham Road, Seasalter,
Whitstable CT5 4BP

Tel	+44 (0)1227 273370
Web	www.thesportsmanseasalter.co.uk

Entry 296 Map 5

Kent

Pearson's Arms

Whitstable

TV chef Richard Phillips is the man behind the mood of warmth in this listed 18th-century seaside pub. Into the sprawling ground-floor bar he's injected a stylish but traditional pubby feel, and he takes his ales seriously: locally brewed Gadds and Hopdaemon accompany the kitchen's short selection of Kent-sourced dishes... girolle soup, whitebait, prawns, baked brill, beer-battered ling, even deep-fried pig's ear. With its log fire lit in the winter, warm planked floors, clever trompe l'oeil of shelves of books, slouchy leather sofas and local art, this is fast becoming a jewel in Whitstable's crown. The pricier, light-filled restaurant-with-views upstairs provides a ringside seat for a Whitstable sunset as you tuck into the likes of ham hock ballotine; roast saddle of hare; autumn vegetable gratin; battered cod, fat chips and mushy peas.

Meals	Lunch & dinner £11.95-£15.95.
Closed	Open all day.
Directions	From centre of Whitstable walk 150 yds down Horsebridge Road to Sea Wall.

Richard Philips
Pearson's Arms
The Horsebridge, Sea Wall,
Whitstable CT5 1BT

Tel	+44 (0)1227 272005
Web	www.pearsonsarmsbyrichardphillips.co.uk

Entry 297 Map 5

The Red Lion

Stodmarsh

Down rutted lanes that wind through bluebell woods is an enchanting village and a 15th-century pub with tiny rooms. Walk into an interior of bare boards, log fires, draped hops, prints, menus, old wine bottles, milk churns, trugs, baskets, candles on every table and one bossy cat. Charlotte may have taken over from her father, the legendary Robert Whigham, but expect few changes. A basket of freshly laid eggs (chickens roam the garden, of course), chutney and a sign for the sale of locally smoked ham add to the rustic, rural feel. Greene King IPA and Old Speckled Hen are tapped from barrels behind the bar and everyone here is a regular, or looks like one. The blackboard menu changes according to what arrives from the farms and shoots, food arrives on huge painted plates and the quality is high. It doesn't get much better than this.

Meals	Lunch & dinner £10.95-£20.95.
Closed	Open all day.
Directions	Off A257 Canterbury to Sandwich road.

Charlotte Whigham
The Red Lion
Stodmarsh,
Canterbury CT3 4BA
Tel +44 (0)1227 721339

Entry 298 Map 5

Kent

The Griffin's Head

Chillenden

Dominated by a log fire in the tiny flagstoned central bar, this is a superb winter pub. Parts of the Wealden Hall House are 13th century so timbers and beams abound, ceilings are low and a maze of beer mugs hangs above the bar. Lovers of fizz know they've come home the moment they step in and spot the blackboard's roll call of champagne. But then long-standing landlord Jeremy Copestake takes his wines seriously; he even offers a chance to taste before committing. Back to back with its doppelganger hearth is a restaurant where good traditional home cooking rules; whether you choose ham, egg and chips or a seasonal partridge casserole, it'll be a perfect match for this simple, affable country pub. While the interior is not suitable for children, they are more than welcome in the gorgeous garden come summer.

Meals	Lunch & dinner £8.95-£20.
Closed	Open all day. Closed Sun eves.
Directions	A2 from Canterbury; left on B2068 for Wingham; Chillenden signed.

Jeremy Copestake
The Griffin's Head
Chillenden,
Canterbury CT3 1PS
Tel +44 (0)1304 840325

Entry 299 Map 5

The Granville

Street End

From the same stable as the Sportsman in Seasalter, the Granville mirrors its older sibling, straddling the divide between restaurant and pub. Rugs are strewn, leather sofas fill one corner and there's a big beer garden outside. It's a pleasure to sit back in this laid-back place, downing rock oysters with shallot vinegar and a pint of stout (or a well-chosen wine). Overseeing it all is Gabrielle Harris, aided by chef Jim Shave heading an open-to-view kitchen that deals in modern uncontrived dishes. Chalked up on blackboards are tried-and-trusted favourites like whole roast wild sea bass with garlic and rosemary. There's homemade bread to dip, and a flourless chocolate cake that will charm those even without allergies. Ingredients are impeccably sourced. Great for walkers, foodies, families – and the Channel tunnel.

Meals	Lunch & dinner £11.95-£19.95.
Closed	3pm-5.30pm. Open all day Sun.
Directions	On B2068 just outside Canterbury.

Phil & Gabrielle Harris
The Granville
Faussett Hill, Street End,
Canterbury CT4 7AL

Tel +44 (0)1227 700402

Entry 300 Map 5

Kent

Froggies at the Timber Batts

Bodsham

Winding lanes lead, finally, to Bodsham, and glorious views of the North Downs. Wander into the splendidly rural Timber Batts – built in 1485 – and you are in for a surprise. Along with the bar menu is a slateboard of British and Gallic specialities, chalked up in French – and the Loire house wine comes from the vines of the owner-chef's cousin. Sit yourself down at an old pine table and be cheered by platefuls of local game, delicious cheeses, Hythe Bay fish, free-range eggs and crispy thin French fries, confit de canard, roast rack of lamb with herbs, café liègeois and a temptingly golden crème brûlée. In winter, nurse a whisky by one of three fires, in summer enjoy the garden with its Kentish views. Lush downland walks radiate from the front door.

Meals	Lunch & dinner £15-£23. Sunday lunch £20 & £25.
Closed	3pm-6.30pm.
Directions	B2068 for Canterbury; left for Wye & Bodsham; 1st left fork; 1.5 miles; right for Wye; right for Bodsham; 300 yds up on top of hill.

Joel Gross
Froggies at the Timber Batts
School Lane, Bodsham,
Ashford TN25 5JQ

Tel +44 (0)1233 750237
Web www.thetimberbatts.co.uk

Entry 301 Map 5

Five Bells Inn

East Brabourne

Looking for somewhere that's quirky, full of character, champions local produce and has a huge community spirit? Seek out this 15th-century village inn tucked beneath the North Downs. Alison and John revamped the building in 2011 and there's much to delight the eye: hop-adorned beams, wood and tiled floors, exposed bricks walls, eclectic furnishings, blazing fires, and individual touches – candles in upturned wine bottles, posh unisex loos. There's a local-produce shop in the bar, and the bar-cum-deli counter displays tip-top Kent ales and cider, olives, cheeses and Wye Bakery bread. Menus bristle with farm foods – Alkham beef and lamb, Potton Farm fruit and vegetables, estate game. Downland walkers and lucky locals love the place, dropping by for breakfast from 9am, acoustic music, farmers' markets, craft fairs, and harvest supper. A perfect little local.

Meals	Breakfast £5-£8. Lunch & dinner £10-£15.
Closed	Open all day.
Directions	Brabourne is signposted off A20, 3 miles east of Ashford.

Community pub

Alison Rogers
Five Bells Inn
The Street, East Brabourne,
Ashford TN25 5LP
Tel +44 (0)1303 813334
Web www.fivebellsinnbrabourne.com

The Plough

Stalisfield Green

Wonderful walks, Swale estuary views, a raft of lagers, ciders and Kentish ales, and land-rustic country cooking – just a few reasons for seeking out this 15th-century hall house hidden in a hamlet high on the North Downs. Beamed bars have wooden floors, old scrubbed pine tables, green and terracotta hues and glowing log fires. Doors in the light airy garden room can wander onto a peaceful patio for a pint of Hopdaemon ale or a heady Biddenden cider. Menus brim with local produce – saltmarsh lamb, rare-breed pork, delicious Angus beef from surrounding farms – while chef Alex makes the bread, ice cream, pickles, sausages and home-smoked goodies. Typically, tuck into pork terrine with piccalilli, suet-crusted Romney mutton pie and apple and quince crumble. It's quite a find!

Meals	Lunch & dinner £10.95-£18.95.
Closed	Open all day.
Directions	Follow signs for Stalisfield off the A20, 2 miles east of Charing.

Robert Lloyd
The Plough
Stalisfield Green,
Faversham ME13 0HY
Tel +44 (0)1795 890256
Web www.stalisfieldgreen.co.uk

The Bull

Benenden

Overlooking Benenden's large and lovely green, complete with cricket pitch and parish church, the 17th-century Bull draws an appreciative crowd, especially on match days. Behind the unusual paned windows, the appeal is obvious in this rustic-chic bar, all stripped wooden floors, fat church candles, scrubbed tables, cushioned old settles, and a blazing fire in the inglenook. The dining room is equally informal and relaxed. Come for the local heady Biddenden cider or a cracking pint of Old Dairy Red Top, brewed along the road at Hole Park. Come for the craic – the monthly music nights heave – and for the hearty, locally sourced food. Employing local farm meats and Rye Bay seafood, the menu promises scallops with sweet chilli butter, fish pie, wild rabbit and bacon casserole, treacle tart, and some rather good sandwiches.

Meals	Lunch from £6.95, bar meals from £9.50, Dinner from £10.50. Sunday lunch £11.50. Not Sunday eve.
Closed	Open all day.
Directions	Centre of Benenden village on B2086 between Cranbook and Tenterden.

Mark & Lucy Barron-Reid
The Bull
Benenden,
Cranbrook TN17 4DE
Tel +44 (0)1580 240054
Web www.thebullatbenenden.co.uk

Entry 304 Map 5

The George Hotel

Cranbrook

Casual and understated, the pale woods and soft colours of the interior complement 13th-century origins; it may look like a brasserie but The George is Cranbrook's favourite local. While a network of local producers has been assiduously encouraged to add a sense of local identity, it is the consistently high standards that keep the place not just afloat but thriving. The kitchen moves deftly through a repertoire of modern dishes – rump of lamb with horseradish mash and aubergine and tomato confit, sea bass with roast fennel and salsa verde – while the odd pub classic is thrown in: Spitfire beer-battered cod and chips, braised red wine and venison sausages. Well kept Shepherd Neame ales make a matchless accompaniment to a steak and onion ciabatta sandwich. And Sissinghurst's gardens are gloriously close.

Meals	Lunch, bar meals & dinner all from £8.95.
Closed	Open all day.
Directions	On the main village street.

Martin Lyall
The George Hotel
Stone Street,
Cranbrook TN17 3HE
Tel +44 (0)1580 713348
Web www.thegeorgehotelkent.co.uk

Entry 305 Map 5

The Three Chimneys

Biddenden

Ramble through tiny, unspoilt rooms of stripped brick, faded paintwork, ancient timber and smouldering fires. During the Napoleonic wars French officers imprisoned nearby were allowed to wander as far as the point where the three paths meet (the 'trois chemins' – hence the name)... so, nothing to do with chimneys, of which there are only two. There's farm cider and Adnams Best Bitter drawn straight from the cask, and the cooking is modern and tasty; parmesan and herb-crusted loin of lamb may be followed by chocolate and praline torte with pistachio ice cream. You can eat in the bars (though not the public one) as well as the charming restaurant, replete with a stylish conservatory extension, or on the sheltered patio. They pretty much get the balance right between pub and restaurant here, so prop up the bar for as long as you like.

Meals	Lunch & dinner £11.95-£18.95. Bar meals £3.95-£8.95.
Closed	3pm-5.30pm (3.30pm-6pm Sun).
Directions	On A262 2 miles west of Biddenden.

Craig Smith
The Three Chimneys
Hareplain Road, Biddenden,
Ashford TN27 8LW

Tel +44 (0)1580 291472
Web www.thethreechimneys.co.uk

Entry 306 Map 5

Kent

The Black Pig

Tunbridge Wells

Rustic menus brimming with organic and biodynamic foods put Julian Leefe-Griffiths's George & Dragon on Kent's culinary map. Keen to replicate the success, he took on the Orson Welles in 2007, spruced it up in his own eclectic style and re-named it after a tasty rare-breed pig. Now there's a relaxed informality and a funky feel. In the bar are leather chairs, contemporary wall coverings and a chandelier; in the dining areas, earthy colours and planked floors. From the open-to-view kitchen flow pork sausages with mash and onion gravy, slow-roasted belly pork with roasted vegetables and Three Little Pigs, a board laden with English, Italian and Spanish hams. Non-porcine dishes include crab and scallop fettuccine and rump of Sussex Red beef, and there are 13 wines by the glass. Pig heaven in Tunbridge Wells.

Meals	Lunch from £7.50. Dinner from £10.50.
Closed	Open all day.
Directions	Town centre; Grove Hill Road is almost opposite the railway station entrance, to the right of Hoopers Store.

Julian Leefe-Griffiths
The Black Pig
18 Grove Hill Road,
Tunbridge Wells TN1 1RZ

Tel +44 (0)1892 523030
Web www.theblackpig.net

Entry 307 Map 5

The Beacon

Rusthall

Everything ticks over beautifully at the Beacon. The spacious late-Victorian interior is a work of art, resplendent with oak panelling, stained glass and ornate plaster ceilings. Good beers, an impressive range of wines by the glass and open fires lure drinkers to the clubby bar; in summer, you can take to the terrace with its famed panorama of the Weald of Kent – stunning. In every season, the food, served in the bar or the formal dining room, draws people from far and wide. Whether you are here for the Sunday roast, a fillet of plaice battered in Harveys Ale or a three-course feast – layered pork and chicken liver terrine with home-grown grape and apple chutney, slow-braised Kentish lamb shoulder, sticky toffee pudding with butterscotch sauce – you will go home happy.

Meals	Lunch & dinner £9.95-£18.
Closed	Open all day.
Directions	Tea Garden Lane signed off A264 1 mile west of Tunbridge Wells.

John Cullen
The Beacon
Tea Garden Lane, Rusthall,
Tunbridge Wells TN3 9JH
Tel +44 (0)1892 524252
Web www.the-beacon.co.uk

Entry 308 Map 5

The Hare

Langton Green

As you negotiate the town green and the surrounding area in the quest for somewhere to park, you'll see that The Hare is Kent's least well-kept secret. Don't be put off. It may be mighty but it's relaxed and friendly too and the food is some of the best in the area. Large light rooms display gleaming, well-spaced tables on polished boards, and character in old prints, paintings and books. The blackboard menu trumpets pub classics like haddock and chips and posh sandwiches and wraps (try sausage with onion jam), plus more ambitious dishes such as pork fillet with herb and mushroom sauce and slow-cooked beef with garlic and thyme gravy. Chirpy staff dispense Greene King Abbot Ale and guest beers such as Ridley's Witchfinder. Wine is taken seriously too, the well-balanced list announcing 17 by the glass.

Meals	Lunch & dinner £9.75-£18.50. Bar meals £6.50-£10.50.
Closed	Open all day.
Directions	On A264 3 miles west of Tunbridge Wells.

Robert Broadbent
The Hare
Langton Road, Langton Green,
Tunbridge Wells TN3 0JA
Tel +44 (0)1892 862419
Web www.hare-tunbridgewells.co.uk

Entry 309 Map 5

George & Dragon

Speldhurst

"We buy from people not companies,'" says Julian Leefe-Griffiths – before launching into an exuberant description of the produce he finds in the local woods and the beers that come from Chiddingstone. Meat, game and vegetables are local and often organic; cheeses come mostly from Sussex. Rescuing one of the oldest inns in southern England from years of mediocrity is no easy task, but they've made a fine start. It's a characterful old pub, loved for its massive flagstones, doors, inglenook and beams. Gutsy food is the biggest treat: crisp, salty sea purslane cooked with creamy soft scallops, wood sorrel with seared local wood pigeon breast, smoked eel on toast with poached duck egg and confit garlic, Valrhona chocolate tart. The atmosphere is easy, the staff friendly, and there's a lovely rear garden.

Meals	Lunch & dinner £9.50-£15.50. Bar meals £5.50-£9.50.
Closed	Open all day.
Directions	In centre of village opposite church.

Julian Leefe-Griffiths
George & Dragon
Speldhurst Hill, Speldhurst,
Tunbridge Wells TN3 0NN

Tel +44 (0)1892 863125
Web www.speldhurst.com

Entry 310 Map 5

The George & Dragon

Chipstead

Julian Leefe-Griffiths and Ben James snapped up this once failing boozer in upmarket Chipstead in 2009. Spruced up with style, minutes from Sevenoaks and the M25, it's a 16th-century timbered gem resplendent with log fires, ancient beams and timbers, happy locals and great wines, and a classy daily menu bristling with fresh produce from the larders of Kent and Sussex. At lunch, accompany a pint of Westerham Grasshopper Ale with a steak sandwich or share a deli-board of cured meats, cheeses and chutneys. At dinner, tuck into such delights as pigeon and pancetta salad, seared Chart Farm 'sika' venison, roast chicken breast with butterbeans and chorizo; vegetarians are looked after with Blue Monday, pear and walnut salad and wild mushroom risotto with truffle oil. Shun the motorway services – this is the best pit-stop for miles.

Meals	Lunch & dinner £9-£18.50.
Closed	Open all day.
Directions	2 mins from junc. 5 on M25; off A25, on High Street, in centre of Chipstead.

Julian Leefe-Griffiths
The George & Dragon
39 High Street, Chipstead,
Sevenoaks TN13 2RW

Tel +44 (0)1732 779019
Web www.georgeanddragonchipstead.com

Entry 311 Map 5

The Harrow

Ightham

The continuing hands-on approach of John Elton and Claire Butler is reaping rewards. Their Kent ragstone country pub looks the part: cottage garden flowers outside, candlelight and winter fire within. The cooking is based on sound supplies, from local game to wild mushrooms, and the food adds enough spice to provoke interest without being overpowering: citrus sauce with salmon and chive fishcakes, calves' liver and bacon with mash and onion gravy. Some of the starters might make a meal in themselves: spicy vegetable and lentil soup comes with bread, and tomato and anchovy salad is a great heaped pile. A separate restaurant, spreading into a small conservatory, has a more formal feel to match the starched white cloths on the bookable tables. It's first-come, first-served for tables in the bar – and this is a popular place.

Meals	Lunch & dinner £9.50-£18.50.
Closed	3pm-6pm. Sun eves & Mon.
Directions	Ightham Common signed off A25.

John Elton & Claire Butler
The Harrow
Common Road,
Ightham,
Sevenoaks TN15 9EB
Tel +44 (0)1732 885912

Entry 312 Map 5

Kent

The Swan on the Green

West Peckham

West Peckham may be the back of beyond – a well-heeled beyond – but there's nothing backward about Gordon Milligan's pub. People are drawn by its reputation for good food and its beer from the microbrewery at the back. The décor is fresh, contemporary and open-plan: blond wood, rush-seated chairs, modern black and white photographs. Under the Swan Ales label, half a dozen brews are funnelled from the central bar: Ginger Swan, Swan Mild, Trumpeter Best, Fuggles, Bewick, Cygnet. Menus are a compendium of updated pub classics and the likes of tomato and root vegetable chowder, red mullet with mussel broth, and crispy duck confit with red wine jus. Gordon and his team have created a balanced mix of drinking bar and dining areas in a 16th-century pub. You may even borrow a rug and eat on the village green.

Meals	Lunch & dinner £9.95-£15.95. Bar meals £5.65-£12.95. Not Sunday or Monday eve.
Closed	3pm-6pm. Check Sun eves in winter.
Directions	From A26 north east of Tonbridge, north on B2106; 1st left for West Peckham; pub by green & church.

Gordon Milligan
The Swan on the Green
The Village Green, West Peckham,
Maidstone ME18 5JW
Tel +44 (0)1622 812271
Web www.swan-on-the-green.co.uk

Entry 313 Map 5

Penny Street Bridge

Lancaster

This grand old city pub-hotel has had a chequered past but its facelift is bound to impress. High ceilings, stained-glass windows, huge Art Deco lights (yes, the originals) and ornate plasterwork abounds. And the elegant dining room with its vintage mismatch of furniture and gleaming parquet is a pleasing space from which to ponder a varied menu; scallops with crab, apple and chilli is a typically good-looking dish. In the bar, sandwiches are packed with the likes of Lancashire cheese and chutney; for something more substantial, go for a light crispy stone-baked pizza – we're told they're going down a treat. Well-kept Thwaites cask beers await, and there's a selection of wines by the glass. Contemporary bedrooms of different shapes and sizes pick up on the period mood, and are comfortable and quiet, with drenching showers and triple-glazed windows, plasma TVs, snowy white linen; one has a beautiful listed wardrobe! Breakfast is full Lancashire – the works, and delicious. In short, a lovely friendly pub-hotel, and a fine place for a spot of retail therapy, slap in the throbbing heart of historic Lancaster.

Price	£70-£105. Singles from £64.
Rooms	28 doubles.
Meals	Lunch from £6.95. Bar meals from £5.95. Dinner from £8.95. Sunday lunch, 2 courses, £11.95.
Closed	Open all day.
Directions	M6 junc. 33. Follow signs for city centre. Past Hospital. Pub on left after river bridge.

Paul Spencer
Penny Street Bridge
Penny Street,
Lancaster LA1 1XT

Tel +44 (0)1524 599900
Web www.pennystreetbridge.co.uk

The Cartford Inn

Little Eccleston

Ten miles inland from the bling of Blackpool stands a handsome 17th-century pub on the banks of the river Wyre. Once 'Dirty Annie' ruled the roost; now stylish Patrick and Julie reign. Enter the etched glass and oak door to find an airy, open-plan space filled with fabulous open fires, polished floors and the bold use of statement wallpaper. Contemporary black and white photographs, candles and huge vases of flowers add to the vibe; locally sourced ingredients shine through the menu. Try Lytham prawns in chilli, lime, garlic and coriander, or leek and creamy Lancashire tartlets. Fleetwood fish pie makes the most of the catch; oxtail and beef in real ale with suet pudding, mash potato and green beans, served with a cold beetroot salad, is richly dense. Stunning boutiquey bedrooms have carved French beds dressed in crisp linen, the Beaume's signature wallpapers and sumptuous textured fabrics, and little chandeliers. The penthouse suite has its own rooftop terrace with far-reaching views. Bathrooms are bronze-tiled and dramatic; roll top baths and walk-in showers. Quite a place.

Price	£100-£120. Twin £100. Suites £110-£400. Family rooms £140-£160. Suite £220. Singles from £65 (Sun-Thurs only).
Rooms	14: 6 doubles, 1 twin, 4 suites for 2-6, 3 family rooms for 3-4.
Meals	Lunch from £8.50. Dinner, 3 courses, £20-£30.
Closed	Open all day.
Directions	M6 junc. 32, M55 junc 3, then A585 north. Right at T-junc. onto A586 for Garstang. Little Ecclestone signed left.

Patrick & Julie Beaume
The Cartford Inn
Cartford Lane, Little Eccleston,
Preston PR3 0YP
Tel +44 (0)1995 670166
Web www.thecartfordinn.co.uk

Millstone Hotel

Mellor

Modern meets traditional – this time, in a handsome 18th-century coaching inn in a pretty village on the edge of the Ribble valley. There's a welcoming glow in the bar, with its oak beams and panelling, richly patina'd furniture, grandfather clocks and smart carpeting. Get cosy by the roaring fire with a pint of local Thwaites Bitter and a crispy duck spring roll. Or eat in the stylish new dining room with its warm wood-panelled walls. Local ingredients are carefully sourced – poultry from Goosnargh, lamb from Pendle, shrimps from Morecambe Bay. The food is wholesome and unpretentious, including the chutney that bursts with fruit from Balderstone, served with Eccles cake and crumbly cheese. Then there's Ribblesdale goat's cheese and avocado salad, spiced salmon fishcakes with chilli jam and grilled lime, and Farnsworth of Whalley sausages with black pudding, mash and onion gravy. Bedrooms ooze comfort: sumptuous fabrics and luxurious linen, Roberts radios and plasma TVs, top-spec bathrooms, padded coat hangers, umbrellas for wet days. A marvellously popular inn.

Price	£95-£125. Singles £109-£124.
Rooms	23 twins/doubles.
Meals	Lunch & dinner £8.95-£16.95.
Closed	Open all day.
Directions	M6 junc. 31; A59 dir. Clitheroe past British Aerospace; right at r'bout signed Blackburn/Mellor; signs to Mellor.

Anson Bolton
Millstone Hotel
Church Lane, Mellor,
Blackburn BB2 7JR
Tel +44 (0)1254 813333
Web www.millstonehotel.co.uk

Red Pump Inn

Bashall Eaves

Down meandering lanes in the stunning Ribble valley is this handsome roadside pub, its south-facing terrace tumbled with flowers. In the bar: stone floors, an open fire, richly worn oak settles and tables, books scattered here and there, shuttered windows with green views – Jonathan and Martina have transformed the old place into a great country inn. Beers include Moorhouses and Timothy Taylor; pints are downed by the local shoot during the season. For lunch there are two rooms to choose from: one cosy with dark red walls, the other with bare oak tables and settles next to the wood burner. In the evening, sit in the large, beamed, candlelit restaurant. The menu is big in season on local game (with a rare sighting of jugged hare!). There's homemade faggots with parsley mash and cabbage, rich rabbit casserole with seasonal veg, and their own sausages made with herbs from the garden, served with delicious champ and minted gravy. White-painted bedrooms have golden silk bedspreads, luxurious linens, spic and span bathrooms with thick snowy towels. And those glorious views.

Price	£75-£115. Singles £65-£95.
Rooms	3 twins/doubles.
Meals	Lunch & dinner £9.50-£17.95. Bar meals from £4.50.
Closed	2.30pm-6pm & Mon (except bank hols). Open all day Sun.
Directions	From Clitheroe, B6243 following signs to Edisford Bridge. Cross bridge & turn right, signed Bashall Eaves.

Jonathan & Martina Myerscough
Red Pump Inn
Clitheroe Road, Bashall Eaves,
Clitheroe BB7 3DA
Tel +44 (0)1254 826227
Web www.theredpumpinn.co.uk

The Spread Eagle

Sawley

With the river Ribble winding its winsome way along one side, and the Cistercian Sawley Abbey 100 yards down the other, the reborn Spread Eagle must be a contender for the 'loveliest location' gong. Martin Clarkson's eye for design has created a pleasing combo of old and new: reclaimed flagged floors, carved settles and antique sofas, kitschy curtains, crushed velvet, funky tartan and a bold wallpaper of books. Retro posters on Farrow & Ball walls proclaim 'Eat your greens', but there's nothing vintage about the menu. To start: air-dried ham with blue cheese panna cotta and quince paste. To follow: wild mushroom, broccoli, smoked garlic and shallot tagliolini with basil cream. And we cannot omit the warm parkin with treacle sauce (just walk it all off later...). Seven striking and stunning bedrooms above have fabulous views over river or abbey. Be seduced by sumptuous textiles and lavish linen, big beds and fat mattresses, cutting-edge showers and a scarlet bathtub in one room. And delightful touches like knitted Arran wool hot water bottle covers. The senses are tickled at every turn.

Price	£80-£99. Suite £120. Singles from £70.
Rooms	7: 4 doubles, 2 twins/doubles, 1 suite.
Meals	Lunch & bar meals from £8.95. Dinner from £9.95
Closed	Open all day.
Directions	A59 north past Clitheroe. Sawley & Sawley Abbey signed left after 2 miles.

Kate & Gary Peill
The Spread Eagle
Sawley,
Clitheroe BB7 4NH
Tel +44 (0)1200 441202
Web www.spreadeaglesawley.co.uk

The Waddington Arms
Waddington

The old stone coaching inn stands beside a babbling stream, overlooking the parish church of famously pretty Waddington. End up in this rustic rambling bar after a day's discovery of the Trough of Bowland and you'll find it impossible to leave. The bar is the hub of the village, bustling with locals, bursting with character. Logs blaze in stone fireplaces, there are old settles and big pine tables on wood and stone floors, fat lamps, framed posters, original paintings and vast mirrors on painted or quirkily papered walls. Food is hearty, full-flavoured and fabulous: try ham hock and black pudding terrine, duck with potato gratin, smoked bacon and savoy cabbage, plaice with mussel and leek stew – and proper traditional sticky toffee pudding. Ale lovers are spoiled with Tirril Nameless Ale and Bowland Sawley Tempted – and more. Bedrooms are warm, cosy, well-equipped and attached to smart new bathrooms. Some combine country-house fabrics with antique beds, others have painted and pine furniture. And breakfasts set you up for moorland walks of the most invigorating kind.

Price	£75. Singles £55.
Rooms	6: 4 doubles, 2 twins.
Meals	Lunch, 2 courses, £10.35. Dinner from £9.45.
Closed	Open all day.
Directions	2 miles from A59 east-west trunk road. 1.5 miles north of Clitheroe, in centre of village.

Phil Glynn
The Waddington Arms
Waddington,
Clitheroe BB7 3HP
Tel +44 (0)1200 423262
Web www.waddingtonarms.co.uk

The Lunesdale Arms

Tunstall

A soft, wide, undulating valley, the Pennines its backdrop – this is the setting of The Lunesdale Arms. A traditional pub with a fresh, modern feel: Pimm's in the summer, mulled wine in the winter, good ales and good cheer. Comfort is deep: big sofas and wood-burning stoves, cushioned settles, newspapers to browse and oil paintings to consider – even to buy. A big central bar separates drinkers (three local cask ales, whiskies and wines) from diners. Sit down to locally reared produce, home-baked bread and seasonal, often organic, vegetables at tables away from the bar. Chef Richard Price delivers wholesome food full of flavour – spinach, pea and mint soup with home-baked bread, roast Cumbrian smoked ham hock with mash and parsley sauce, chocolate brownie – and encourages children to have small portions.

Meals	Lunch & dinner £9-£16.95. Bar meals £4.95-£14.50. Sunday lunch, 3 courses, £19.95.
Closed	Monday (except bank hols).
Directions	M6 junc. 34; A683 for Kirkby Lonsdale.

Emma Gillibrand
The Lunesdale Arms
Tunstall,
Carnforth LA6 2QN
Tel +44 (0)1524 274203
Web www.thelunesdale.co.uk

Entry 320 Map 12

Lancashire

The Highwayman

Burrow

Hot on the heels of the Three Fishes at Mitton, the Highwayman was the second pub for Ribble Valley Inns. In this stylishly revamped old stone inn in the beautiful Lune valley, Nigel Haworth raids the rich borderlands of Cumbria and Yorkshire in his continuing pursuit of good produce; his regional heroes are showcased on the menus and the walls. So look forward to heather-reared lamb Lancashire hotpot, Lake District 10oz sirloin steak, warm Flookburgh shrimps, and caramel sticky toffee pudding. There are a raft of classy wines by the glass and Thwaites Lancaster Bomber on tap. Knowledgeable staff add attentive service to a gloriously informal country interior of stone and wooden floors, eclectic old tables and cosy corners with crackling log fires. For summer: a fantastic terrace and garden.

Meals	Lunch & dinner £9.95-£19.75. Sunday lunch, 3 courses, £19.50.
Closed	Open all day.
Directions	20 mins from junc. 34 on M6; less than 10 mins from junc. 36.

Nigel Haworth & Craig Bancroft
The Highwayman
Burrow,
Carnforth LA6 2RJ
Tel +44 (0)1524 273338
Web www.highwaymaninn.co.uk

Entry 321 Map 12

The Lower Buck

Waddington

Look for the church as you enter the village and you'll find an 18th-century treasure tucked behind – peaceful and unspoiled. Andrew Warburton took over the stone pub in 2005 and, while gently upgrading, has preserved the traditional layout and atmosphere beautifully. Devoid of machines and music, each of the three original rooms off the slate-tiled lobby has polished rug-strewn floors, cream walls, old prints and big mirrors, feature fireplaces and glowing coal fires, and a mix of dark wood dining tables. Banter with the locals over a pint of Bowland Hen Harrier or Sawley Tempted at the bar, or order from a menu that's chock full of pub classics made from local ingredients, including meat and vegetables from Longridge farms. Dive into black pudding with mustard sauce, Lancashire hotpot, game pie, fish and chips. Perfect after a Ribble Valley ramble.

Meals Lunch & dinner from £9.95.
Closed Open all day.
Directions Take B6478 north from Clitheroe for 1.5 miles to Waddington, then turn left by church; pub on right.

Andrew Warburton
The Lower Buck
Edisford Road, Waddington,
Clitheroe BB7 3HU
Tel +44 (0)1200 423342
Web www.lowerbuckinn.co.uk

Lancashire

The Inn at Whitewell

Whitewell

The old deerkeeper's lodge sits just above the river Hodder with views across parkland to rising fells in the distance. Merchants used to stop by and fill up with wine, food and song before heading north through notorious bandit country. Now barbours and muddy dogs mix with posh frocks and suits. You can eat in the bar but the long restaurant and the outside terrace drink in the view – which will only increase your enjoyment of Bowland lamb with cassoulet of beans and root vegetables, homemade ice cream and fine wines (including their own well-priced Vintner's). In the bar, antiques, bric-a-brac, peat fires, old copies of *The Beano*, fish and chips, warm crab cakes and local bangers. At weekends it gets packed; if you want a table, the more formal restaurant takes bookings. A perfect place.

Meals Bar meals from £8.
Dinner £25-£35.
Closed Open all day.
Directions M6 junc. 31A, B6243 east through Longridge, then follow signs to Whitewell for 9 miles.

Charles Bowman
The Inn at Whitewell
Dunsop Road, Whitewell,
Clitheroe BB7 3AT
Tel +44 (0)1200 448222
Web www.innatwhitewell.com

Duke of York

Grindleton

In the magnificent Ribble Valley Michael Heathcote's roadside pub sits in the shadow of Pendle Hill. In the bar are oak floors, wood-burning stoves and beams – and a gloriously kitsch velvet candelabra. This reformed boozer is littered with quirky touches; a full-length mirror above a leather banquette; designer chairs upholstered in raspberry pink chenille. Heathcote is largely self-taught, and his touch is inspired. Lamb shank potato cake with watercress salad is perfectly judged, a homemade peach chutney offsetting its robust earthiness; poached haddock tagliolini is full of flavour and sublimely silky – the sort of dish you'd choose as a last supper. New season's English plum clafoutis with lavender and honey ice cream makes a strong finish. So, a seriously talented chef in an appealing village – beat a path to his door!

Meals	Lunch from £11.99. Bar meals from £7.50. Dinner from £12.99. Sunday lunch, 3 courses, £18.50. Not Monday (except bank hols).
Closed	3pm-6pm. Monday.
Directions	A59 Clitheroe to Skipton; exit for Chatburn and turn left at post office onto Ribble Lane; Grindleton in 1 mile.

Michael Heathcote
Duke of York
Grindleton,
Clitheroe BB7 4QR
Tel +44 (0)1200 441266
Web www.dukeofyorkgrindleton.com

Entry 324 Map 12

Lancashire

The Three Fishes

Mitton

Lancashire is a hotbed of food artisans, and the producers, suppliers and growers are the heroes of this venture; they are listed on the back of every menu. The 17th-century village pub in the lovely Ribble Valley has taken gastropubbery to a mouthwatering level. The long whitewashed public house has been restyled in rustic-smart 21st-century fashion and is vast: up to 130 inside, a further 60 out. Walls are pale brick, floors stone, furniture sober, lighting subtle and winter logs glow. Wines are gorgeous, local pints and real ciders are served and the beer-friendly food includes ignored but once-popular British delicacies. Delicious are the game terrine with pear chutney, the Lancashire hotpot with braised red cabbage, the chocolate tart with honeycomb. The places heaves with diners – arrive early, especially on Sunday.

Meals	Lunch & dinner £9-£17.95. Sunday lunch £15 & £19.50.
Closed	Open all day.
Directions	From M6 junc. 31 onto A677, then follow A59 into Whalley; B6246 for Great Mitton.

Nigel Haworth & Craig Bancroft
The Three Fishes
Mitton Road, Mitton,
Clitheroe BB7 9PQ
Tel +44 (0)1254 826888
Web www.thethreefishes.com

Entry 325 Map 12

Freemasons at Wiswell

Wiswell

This old village pub has had a facelift; pots, plantings and a gravel drive swish it up. Inside, antique rugs on stone-flagged floors, gleaming oak furniture and beams, leather wing chairs, fires and fresh flowers. A series of rooms upstairs promise more sophisticated dining at antique refectory tables set with white linen and candelabra. Back down in the bar, Pride of Pendle and Blonde Witch are cask conditioned, whilst a staggering cellar (250 wines) awaits. Local lad 'done good' (most recently at Cassis at Stanley House), Steven Smith produces dishes bursting with seasonal ingredients: poached and roast wood pigeon, pressed leeks and hazelnuts, steamed game pudding. Organic salmon is cooked in vanilla oil with Morecambe Bay mussels, fennel and saffron; to finish, Magners cider granita with hot cinnamon doughnuts rounds everything off.

Meals	Lunch & dinner £10.95-28.95. Seasonal set menu £13.95 & £15.95. Tasting menu £55.
Closed	Open all day.
Directions	From A59, 2 miles south of Clitheroe, take A671 to Blackburn. After 0.5 miles, 1st left to Wiswell.

Steven Smith
Freemasons at Wiswell
8 Vicarage Fold, Wiswell,
Clitheroe BB7 9DF
Tel +44 (0)1254 822218
Web www.freemasonswiswell.co.uk

Entry 326 Map 12

Lancashire

The Clog and Billycock

Blackburn

Following the success of the Three Fishes and the Highwayman, Nigel Haworth and Craig Bancroft have another winner. Now the old boozer in a leafy village close to Blackburn has crackling fires, gleaming oak furniture and an eye-catching beamed atrium: a sensitively-lit showcase for a collection of black and white photographs of the pub's esteemed growers and producers. The colour scheme is subtle and calming yet there's a great buzz to the place, as staff ferry beautiful food to cosy tables. Tuck into heather-fed lamb hotpot with pickled red cabbage, then jam roly poly with custard for a traditional dessert. With a great outside space, an inspiring children's menu, very helpful staff and fine wines and ales, this gloriously named pub is one to get excited about.

Meals	Lunch & dinner £8.95-£19.75. Sunday lunch, 3 courses, £19.50.
Closed	Open all day.
Directions	From M6 junction 3, follow A677 towards Blackburn, then right in 5 miles to follow Billinge End Road to Pleasington. 1 mile; pub on left.

Nigel Haworth & Craig Bancroft
The Clog and Billycock
Billinge End Road,
Blackburn BB2 6QB
Tel +44 (0)1254 201163
Web www.theclogandbillycock.com

Entry 327 Map 12

The Rams Head Inn

Denshaw

You're on the border here and the views are glorious. High on the moors between Oldham and Ripponden, this inn is two miles from the motorway but you'd never know. Unspoilt inside and out, there's an authentic, old-farmhouse feel. Small rooms, cosy with winter log fires, are carpeted, half-panelled and beamed, and filled with interesting memorabilia. Until recently beer was served straight from the cask; there's still an old sideboard behind the bar to remind you of former days. Menus announce a heart-warming selection of tasty and well-priced food (note the set menu at £16.95 & £19.95): game and venison in season, seafood specialities, great steaks and puddings like treacle tart with ice cream. A wonderfully isolated Lancashire outpost, staffed by people who care, and with a farm shop, a deli and a tea room to boot.

Meals	Lunch & dinner £9.50-£17.95. Deli prices from £2.50.
Closed	2.30pm-6pm Tue-Sat. Sun from 8.30pm & Mon eves.
Directions	M62 junc. 22 for Oldham & Saddleworth; 2 miles on right.

G R Haigh
The Rams Head Inn
Ripponden Road, Denshaw,
Oldham OL3 5UN
Tel +44 (0)1457 874802
Web www.ramsheaddenshaw.co.uk

The Eagle & Child

Bispham Green

There's an old-fashioned pubbiness here *and* a sense of style – an informality touched with zing. The candlelit main bar welcomes you in with its rug-strewn flagged floors, hop-decked beams and open fire; another room, just as cosy, has a cast-iron fireplace. Hand pumps line the bar (with beers from lesser-known brewers like Beartown Brewery) while the shelves parade an army of malts and the wine cellar has some fine offerings. The staff seem to enjoy themselves as much as the customers and the food has won awards; there's Lancashire hotpot, roast suckling pig with apple and cider gravy, partridge with porcini and Madeira sauce. The pub's reputation lies, too, with its cask ales, and the beer festival in May packs the place out. Don't forget to stock up in next door's farm shop before you leave.

Meals	Lunch & dinner £10-£16.50. Bar meals £3.75-£10.
Closed	3pm-5.30pm. Open all day Sat & Sun.
Directions	From M6 junc. 27, A5209 for Parbold; right along B5246; left for Bispham Green. Pub in 0.5 miles.

Helen & Martin Ainscough
The Eagle & Child
Malt Kiln Lane, Bispham Green,
Ormskirk L40 3SG
Tel +44 (0)1257 462297
Web www.ainscoughs.co.uk

Bay Horse Inn

Bay Horse

The Wilkinsons have been in the saddle for a number of years and son Craig takes full advantage of the marvellous Lancashire produce in his modern British cooking – tuck into fish pie with cheese mash, Bowland lamb hotpot with pickled red cabbage, and roast Lune Valley venison with honey sauce. Although the Bay Horse takes its food seriously and is dedicated to quality (right down to its home-grown herbs and veg) it has not lost sight of its pubbiness, so the atmosphere is easy and Moorhouses Pendle Witches Brew and Black Sheep are on tap. Interconnecting areas are comfortably furnished with a mix of old chairs and cushioned seating in bay windows, the dining room sparkles and the red-walled bar is warm and inviting. Gentle background jazz, quirky ephemera and two crackling fires add to the mood.

Meals	Lunch & dinner £11.95-£20.95. Sunday lunch £17.50 & £21.50. No food Sun eve.
Closed	3pm-6.30pm. Mon.
Directions	From M6 junc. 33; A6 for Preston, 2nd left; pub on right.

Craig Wilkinson
Bay Horse Inn
Bay Horse,
Lancaster LA2 0HR

Tel +44 (0)1524 791204
Web www.bayhorseinn.com

Entry 330 Map 11

The Curzon Arms

Woodhouse Eaves

In the village of Woodhouse Eaves is a pub that ticks almost every box. No matter there are few real ales and no ciders of note: the Curzon attracts a marvellously diverse crowd – suits and locals, friends and office parties, families at weekends, horses in summer and walkers en route. Newly refurbished in traditional style, with leather banquette seating and heritage colours, the interiors are warm and appealing. Painted beam ceilings and prints on the walls, a Chesterfield sofa, a big box of toys, two log-burners belting out the heat. There are a 'pie of the day' and a 'catch of the day,' too, a cheese platter with tasting notes, wines to satisfy most, and chips crisp and hot. Local and seasonal are the watchwords and the British menu changes monthly. The terrace is attractive even on a winter's day and the garden is big enough to play in.

Meals	Lunch from £5.95. Dinner from £10.25.
Closed	Open all day.
Directions	See website.

Ben Moore
The Curzon Arms
44 Maplewell Road,
Woodhouse Eaves LE12 8QZ

Tel +44 (0)1509 890377
Web www.thecurzonarms.com

Entry 331 Map 8

Red Lion Inn

Stathern

Quirky stylishness and cheerful service. The rambling Red Lion feels like a home, with its books and papers, deep sofas and open fires; gamekeepers frequent the flagstoned bar. A trusted network of growers and suppliers fills the kitchen with game from the Belvoir estate, cheeses from the local dairy, fruits and vegetables from nearby farms. Menus are on blackboards, with a choice that leaps between fashion and tradition: shell on prawns and garlic aïoli; village-made sausages with mustard mash; braised fillet of brill, tarragon mash, mushroom fricassée; treacle tart, blackberry compote, clotted cream ice cream. The set Sunday lunch is great value. The wine list is imaginative; beers include village-brewed Brewsters Hophead and children have homemade lemonade.

Meals	Lunch & dinner from £9.95. Bar meals from £5.50. Sunday lunch, 3 courses, £18.50. Not Sunday eve.
Closed	3pm-6pm. Sun from 6.30pm. Open all day Fri & Sat.
Directions	Off A607 north east of Melton Mowbray; through Stathern; past Plough; pub signed on left.

Ben Jones & Sean Hope
Red Lion Inn
2 Red Lion Street, Stathern,
Melton Mowbray LE14 4HS
Tel +44 (0)1949 860868
Web www.theredlioninn.co.uk

Leicestershire

The Berkeley Arms

Wymondham

In the middle of the village of Wymondham is an exemplary pub. Enter a low-beamed, pine-tabled, light-filled room, with the original terracotta tiled floor and a fire at the carpeted end. It's a wonderfully intimate place to drink and eat, and if you prefer to be slightly more formal, there's a stylish dining room too. Owners Louise and Neil met at Hambleton Hall so the food is special and the suppliers are lovingly listed: pigeons, tomatoes and rhubarb come from Ray and Pam Elsome; mint, marrows and flowers from Ken Hill. We tried the pâté of rabbit, pork and prune; the pasta with pickled walnuts, reblochon cheese and truffle oil; the pear and ginger crumble with pear sorbet. All were exquisite. In summer you can stroll in the garden, take in the pretty views, retreat to the smokers' shelter. Staff are friendly, polite, perfect.

Meals	Lunch from £14.95. Bar meals from £10. Dinner from £25. Sunday lunch, 2 courses, £17.95.
Closed	Sun eves & Mon lunch.
Directions	Sent on booking.

Neil & Louise Hitchen
The Berkeley Arms
59 Main Street, Wymondham,
Melton Mowbray LE14 2AG
Tel +44 (0)1572 787587
Web www.theberkeleyarms.co.uk

The White Hart

Ufford

This much-forgotten slip of England is prettier than most imagine. Wash up at the White Hart and join the locals who come for a traditional bar with atmosphere. The ales are good too: Ufford's own, brewed 50 paces from the beer tap. Farmers gather on Fridays, the cricket team drops by on Sundays, in summer life spills onto the terrace. Flags, floorboards and a crackling fire continue the rustic feel; railway signs, wooden pitch forks and hanging station lamps add colour. You can eat simply or more grandly, anything from a ploughman's to a three-course feast, much is seasonal and meat comes from the family farm; there are great cheese boards, too. Walk through to a conservatory-style dining area, furnished with Lloyd Loom furniture for comfortable dining all year round. Bedrooms (four above the bar, two out by the microbrewery) are simple, spotless and carry an honest price. White is... white, airy and lovely, with period lounge chairs and views across the fields to the church. One has a four-poster bed while all have crisp white linen and feather pillows.

Price	From £90. Singles from £80.
Rooms	6: 3 doubles, 2 twins, 1 four-poster.
Meals	Lunch & dinner £10-£15. Bar meals £5.25-£8.75. Sunday lunch, 3 courses, £19.50. Not Sun eve.
Closed	Sun eves from 9pm. Open all day.
Directions	A1, then east on A47 four miles south of Stamford. Ist left, thro' Southorpe & keep right for Ufford.

Michael Thurlby & Sue Olver
The White Hart
Main Street, Ufford,
Stamford PE9 3BH
Tel +44 (0)1780 740250
Web www.whitehartufford.co.uk

The Bull & Swan

St Martins

A magical renovation, an ancient inn that stands a short walk from the middle of glorious Stamford. It's part of the Burghley estate – and the Order of Little Bedlam, a 17th-century aristocratic drinking club, would almost certainly have popped in for the odd snifter. Not that they had it this good. Step inside to find varnished wood floors, golden stone walls, fires smouldering all over the place and newspapers hanging on poles. At the bar venison Scotch eggs are impossible to resist, as are a raft of local ales and splendid wines. You eat wherever you want, here or in the dining room across the coach arch, where leather-backed settles take the strain and regal oils adorn the walls. As for beautiful bedrooms, they come in country-house style with huge beds, fabulous linen, warm colours and super-funky bathrooms. Most are big, all are delightful, two interconnect for families, and mattresses are divine. Back downstairs, delicious food waits, perhaps stilton on toast, Burghley game pie, apple and blueberry crumble. And don't miss Burghley, a five-minute stroll, one of Britain's finest houses.

Price	£95-£105. Half-board from £72.50 p.p.
Rooms	7: 5 doubles, 2 twins.
Meals	Lunch from £6. Dinner, 3 courses, £25-£30.
Closed	Open all day.
Directions	On the Old London Road, just south of the river and town centre, heading south towards the A1.

Ben Larter
The Bull & Swan
St Martins,
Stamford PE9 2LJ
Tel +44 (0)1780 766412
Web www.thebullandswan.co.uk

The Exeter Arms

Easton on the Hill

The Exeter Arms is a smashing place serving wonderful food. Discreetly, stylishly modernised, it keeps its pubby feel – an open fire in the narrow bar and well-kept Ufford Ales on handpump. Soft coffee and cream colours, gentle lighting, exposed stone and polished wooden tables set the restaurant apart, but for a change of mood head for the elegant conservatory with views onto the large, smart terrace; it has the same regularly changing menu and a sunny, contemporary feel. The cooking is classy yet simple, the kitchen moving deftly through a repertoire of modern dishes and pub classics: fish and chips or homemade sausages and creamy mash; chicken liver parfait; pheasant casserole with Aspalls cider; slow-braised loin of lamb; rice pudding mousse with caramelised plums. Praise, too, for fair prices, stone-baked pizzas and a good, sensible children's menu. Always a treat to stay the night and there are six cosseting rooms upstairs – serene and softly modern with big beds, crisp white duvets, plump pillows and spotless bathrooms. Stamford and Burghley House are close.

Price	£75-£140.
Rooms	6 doubles.
Meals	Lunch & bar meals from £11. Dinner from £12.50. Sunday lunch, 3 courses, £18.95.
Closed	Sunday after 6pm.
Directions	Join A43 signed towards Kettering. Pub on left as you enter village.

Michael Thurlby & Sue Olver
The Exeter Arms
21 Stamford Road, Easton on the Hill,
Stamford PE9 3NS
Tel +44 (0)1780 756321
Web www.theexeterarms.net

The Chequers Inn

Woolsthorpe

Though it started life as a bakery, the Chequers has been an inn for 200 years, and is neatly tucked off the road that passes through a small estate village. With its exposed timbers, rug-strewn bar, Farrow & Ball colours and flurry of open fires, it marries old-fashioned charm with rustic comfort and chic. They have two ales on hand pump, plenty of wines by the glass, 50 malt whiskies, 30 gins and a humidor behind the bar, all backing up a well-deserved reputation for good service and food across three rooms. Robust dishes are a satisfying mix of traditional and modern, taking in ham hock terrine, rib of beef and great burgers, as well as seared scallops with sweet potato purée and cod with chorizo and potato; vegetarians could try roasted vegetable pasta; the weekday evening menu is a steal (three courses for £16.50). Four good-sized bedrooms in the stable block are as comfy as can be – one with a super-king bed – and fine breakfasts complete the treat. In summer the pub hosts the village cricket team on its three-acre pitch. The vale of Belvoir and its grand castle are as beautiful as they sound.

Price	£70-£85. Singles from £50.
Rooms	4: 3 doubles, 1 family room.
Meals	Lunch & dinner £9.50-£19. Bar meals £4.95-£8.95. Sunday lunch £11.95.
Closed	3pm-5.30pm. Open all day Sat & Sun.
Directions	Off A52, west of Grantham. Follow signs to Belvoir Castle.

Justin & Joanne Chad
The Chequers Inn
Main Street, Woolsthorpe,
Grantham NG32 1LU
Tel +44 (0)1476 870701
Web www.chequersinn.net

The Tobie Norris

Stamford

Built in 1280, remodelled in 1663 and again, superbly, in 2006, the Tobie Norris draws you in to a warren of stunningly atmospheric rooms and takes you back to the old days – Cromwellian at least. Huge stone flags, oak settles and the smell of woodsmoke assail you as you leave the bustling pavements behind, the weekly market in full flow. Between the main rooms is a staircase leading to three more, each one oozing character and style, with vast exposed timbers, little recesses and cupboard-like doors. Find a church pew or a nice leather armchair and sit back with your Ufford Ales and Adnams – or a tasty wine from a list of 21, each available by the glass. Dogs doze on bare boards, perfect staff ferry pizzas and plates of smoked salmon linguine, there are rotating ales on tap and you could stay here all day.

Meals	Lunch, bar meals & dinner from £9.95. Not Sunday eve.
Closed	Open all day.
Directions	South on B6403; right at A1. Take A427/A43 exit, left at Kettering Rd. Left at A16, left at St Paul's St; pub on right.

Michael Thurlby & Will Fry
The Tobie Norris
12 St Paul's Street,
Stamford PE9 2BE
Tel +44 (0)1780 753800
Web www.tobienorris.com

Entry 338 Map 9

Brownlow Arms

Hough-on-the-Hill

Standing proudly in the centre of a hilltop village, this magnificent building is said to have been the servants' quarters to the Manor. Now it has the feel of an intimate country house. Winged Queen Anne chairs in autumnal hues invite you to settle in by the open fire amid deep rich oak beams and polished panelling, and regulars sup Marstons Burton ale as chatter flows around the central bar. In the intimate restaurant, the food, revealing a French classical influence, is accomplished as befits such a setting – soufflés, parfaits, lamb with red wine jus, plaice with scallops and chive beurre blanc. Desserts range from refreshing lemon crème brûlée to comforting sticky toffee pudding. It's blowy up here with idyllic open countryside all around, but there is a sheltered, landscaped terrace for a quiet pint and an early supper.

Meals	Lunch & dinner £14.95-£22.50.
Closed	Tues-Sat lunch. Sun eves & Mon.
Directions	On A607 6 miles north of Grantham.

Paul & Lorraine Willoughby
Brownlow Arms
High Road, Hough-on-the-Hill,
Grantham NG32 2AZ
Tel +44 (0)1400 250234
Web www.thebrownlowarms.com

Entry 339 Map 9

Wig & Mitre

Lincoln

Sandwiched between the cathedral and the castle, this famous inn draws an eclectic clientele, from journeymen and judges to barristers and bishops. Downstairs has a French café feel: old oak boards, exposed stone, sofas to the side – a civilised spot for late breakfast and the papers. Upstairs, a cosy series of plush carpeted dining rooms. In the Seventies it was hard to find decent food in a pub, let alone one in Lincoln. Valerie's kitchen became one of the most exciting in the area, serving a mix of dishes years before the term 'gastropub' was born. Today you'll find the likes of salt cod with celeriac purée and roast lamb with cabbage and bacon. More restaurant than pub, there are also some top of the market wines – available by the case from the Hope's shop next door.

Meals	Lunch & dinner from £12.50. Bar meals from £5.95. Sunday lunch, 3 courses, £14.95.
Closed	Open all day.
Directions	On Steep Hill between Lincoln Cathedral and Lincoln Castle.

Michael & Valerie Hope
Wig & Mitre
32 Steep Hill,
Lincoln LN2 1LU
Tel +44 (0)1522 535190
Web www.wigandmitre.com

Entry 340 Map 9

Lincolnshire

The Bluebell

Belchford

High in the Wolds, amid the vast openness of the Lincolnshire farms, is the Bluebell in Belchford – warmth and cosiness hit you as you enter. To a traditional backdrop of deep polished oak is a bar sporting chintz curtains with neat ties, comfy sofas and wing-back chairs; in one of two dining areas are gilt-framed oil paintings on deep red walls, in the other, an airy modernity. They're proud of their food here, and so they should be: almost all the produce is locally sourced (Lincolnshire Red beef, fish from Grimsby). At lunch there are filled ciabattas and beef and Guinness pie, while things step up a gear at dinner with dishes such as charred calves' liver with roast garlic mash. It's as friendly as can be and as cosy as a steamed sponge pudding with custard – and you might tuck into one of those, too.

Meals	Lunch from £5.95. Bar meals from £8.95. Dinner from £10.95. Sunday lunch, 3 courses, £18.50.
Closed	3pm-6.30pm. Sun eves & Mon.
Directions	Village signed off A153 between Horncastle & Louth.

Darren & Shona Jackson
The Bluebell
1 Main Road, Belchford,
Horncastle LN9 6LQ
Tel +44 (0)1507 533602
Web www.bluebellbelchford.co.uk

Entry 341 Map 9

The Victoria

Richmond

On a leafy, secluded street in the smart suburb of Richmond with a church and Sheen Common as neighbours, this has been a well established pub for many years, but Greg Bellamy and acclaimed chef Paul Merrett have swept through the inside and created two stylish bar areas and a modern conservatory restaurant. The atmosphere is busy, purposeful and fun: find wooden floors, some open brickwork and sofas to flop on while you decide on the bar menu (muffin with smoked salmon, Jersey rock oysters) or, if you are really hungry, cured Teruel ham with pan-fried manouri cheese, cumin-rubbed lamb loin, then maybe greengage crumble with baked egg custard. The wine list, chosen by Olly Smith, bursts with passion and helpful notes, so it would be a shame not to allow yourself to be led. In an adjacent building are simple, modern bedrooms, with white walls, light carpets and splashes of colour from pictures and cushions. Bathrooms are smart, fully tiled and well lit. You are within striking distance of a lovely stroll through Sheen Common or Richmond Park, and ten minutes from Twickenham if rugby is your passion.

Price	£125. Singles £115.
Rooms	7: 5 doubles, 2 twins/doubles.
Meals	Lunch & bar meals from £6. Dinner from £13.50. Sunday lunch, 2 courses, £25.
Closed	Open all day.
Directions	Mortlake station on line from Waterloo. Buses: 33, 337, 493. Tube: Richmond or East Putney. Private car park at rear of hotel.

Paul Merrett & Greg Bellamy
The Victoria
10 West Temple Sheen,
Richmond, London SW14 7RT

Tel +44 (0)20 8876 4238
Web www.thevictoria.net

The Thomas Cubitt

Belgravia

As well-upholstered as Belgravia itself, the ground-floor bar has high ceilings, oak-block floors, tall windows that open to tables in the street and a bit of panelling thrown in for good measure. A cords and cashmere crowd is drawn by the classic country-house feel, the real ales, the superb wines, and the kitchen, which puts more thought into what it produces than many a full-blown restaurant. In the bar is a reassuring selection of pub favourites – organic beef burgers, grilled sausages with roasted red onion gravy and buttery mash – and the organic Sunday roasts are great. In the elegant dove-grey dining room upstairs the food is fiercely modern (take grilled tuna with red pepper and pearl barley and langoustine bisque). It's popular, and the friendliness of the staff, even under pressure, is a pleasure.

Meals	Lunch from £10.50. Bar meals from £8.50. Dinner from £17. Sunday lunch, 3 courses, from £31.
Closed	Bar open all day. Restaurant closed Sun.
Directions	Nearest tube: Victoria; Sloane Square.

Ryan Moses
The Thomas Cubitt
44 Elizabeth St, Belgravia,
London SW1W 9PA
Tel +44 (0)20 7730 6060
Web www.thethomascubitt.co.uk

Entry 343 Map 15

London

The Orange Public House & Hotel

Belgravia

Discover tall sash windows, lofty ceilings, and elegant limed tables that give the bar an intimate feel. There's a cosy corner with a gas fire blazing, and candlelight and panelling in keeping with Georgian origins. Upstairs and downstairs this is one stylish rabbit warren, divided by cheerful seagrass landings and a basement full of chatter and luscious cooking smells. Helpful young staff ferry rustic dishes to and fro, from a zippy menu that changes with the seasons: poussin, chorizo, Bellecourt salmon, Carlingford Lough oysters, ale-braised venison, wood-fired pizzas, homemade ice creams. Not forgetting muffins for breakfast from 8am to 11am. In the heart of pretty Pimlico, dispensing mulled wines and cocktails, The Orange is more gastro than pub, but the office workers love it and the ales are tip top – from Meantime of London to Harveys of Sussex.

Meals	Lunch from £6.50. Bar meals from £5. Dinner from £10.50. Sunday lunch, 3 courses, £30.
Closed	Open all day.
Directions	Nearest tube: Victoria; Sloane Square.

Ryan Moses
The Orange Public House & Hotel
37 Pimlico Road, Belgravia,
London SW1W 8NE
Tel +44 (0)20 7881 9844
Web www.theorange.co.uk

Entry 344 Map 15

The Grazing Goat

Marylebone

Where goats once grazed, smart boutiques flourish, but you barely know you're in the heart of London. Step inside, to a serene space of sage green walls and low lighting, sturdy wooden floors, limed tables and gas log fires, and a wall of glazed doors opening to benches in summer. There are a few heads of African beasts mounted on walls (collecting is the owner's passion) but don't let this put you off: the food is tasty. You could have eggs Benedict at breakfast, and a Bloody Mary; an organic beef burger with a black fig salad at lunch; Scottish halibut with lemon butter at dinner. What's good about this intimate pub (little sister to the more characterful Thomas Cubitt and The Orange) is that it attracts a well-mixed crowd, including tourists on leave from Oxford Street. Ales include Doom Bar, juice is freshly squeezed, breakfasts are superb.

Meals	Lunch £9.50. Bar meals from £8. Dinner from £15.50. Sunday lunch, 3 courses, £30.
Closed	Open all day.
Directions	Nearest tube: Marble Arch.

Ryan Moses
The Grazing Goat
6 New Quebec Street, Marylebone,
London W1H 7RQ
Tel +44 (0)20 7724 7243
Web www.thegrazinggoat.co.uk

The Beehive

Marylebone

In 2008 restaurateur Claudio Pulze – creator of Aubergine, Zafferano and Brasserie St Jacques – took on one of London's earliest boozers, and accommodated the wishes of the regulars in his first foray into the pub world. Now the quality of the food and drink are a match for civilised Marylebone. The beers are his own – Brew Wharf microbrewery ales – and the wine list a delight to explore. As for the food, it is striking in its simplicity and available all day. Steak sandwiches; burgers with bacon, cheese and egg; Caesar salads; fish and chips with tartare sauce (homemade). In the plain wood-floored bar room the old Edwardian bar remains, and parasoled picnic benches wait outside. A friendly, youthful, Baker Street refuge.

Meals	Lunch from £10.90. Bar meals from £4.90. Dinner from £13.90.
Closed	Open all day.
Directions	Just off Baker Street at the Marylebone Road end.

Claudio Pulze
The Beehive
126 Crawford Street, Marylebone,
London W1U 6BF
Tel +44 (0)20 7486 8037
Web www.thebeehive-pub.co.uk

Admiral Codrington

Chelsea

It may be hiding down a Chelsea back street, but the savvy beat a path to The Cod. Opened up and remodelled, the Victorian-style central bar is rich in dark woods (panelling, floorboards, furniture) while pale yellow walls are hung with prints, and banquettes, sofas and subtle lighting add softness. The restaurant, by contrast, is a light contemporary space with a retractable glass skylight (a wow in summer), salmon high-backed chairs and wall banquettes, and fishy prints to reflect the nautical name. Tuck into three-cheese macaroni with crispy bacon and a pint of Black Sheep Bitter on the small all-weather terrace, or braised lamb hotpot and ever-popular beer-battered fish and chips in the restaurant. Or even West Mersea rock oysters and Devon crab cake, accompanied by a chilled bottle of Sancerre.

Meals	Lunch & dinner £12.75-£46.
Closed	Open all day.
Directions	Nearest tube: Sloane Square; South Kensington.

Alexander Langlands Pearse
Admiral Codrington
17 Mossop Street, Chelsea,
London SW3 2LY
Tel +44 (0)20 7581 0005
Web www.theadmiralcodrington.co.uk

Entry 347 Map 15

London

The Pig's Ear

Chelsea

Off the King's Road, a great little corner pub serving Uley Pig's Ear on tap and a zippy Bloody Mary – drinking is encouraged. In the chattering bar (this is Chelsea) are high ceilings, planked floors, big mirrors, a zinc-top bar and formica tables; upstairs, a cosy sash-windowed dining room with twinkly lights and not a touch of Victoriana. Staff are knowledgeable, casually dressed and perky, in keeping with the spirit of the place. Cooking is rousingly rustic – part French, part English. The beef brisket and ox cheek casserole, topped with robust Jerusalem artichoke crisps, was deep flavoured and succulent; the orange panna cotta smooth, citrusy and decorated with a perfect sesame tuile. There are cured herrings and rock oysters, and most nights it's rammed.

Meals	Lunch from £8.50. Bar meals from £5.50. Dinner form £14. Sunday lunch, 3 courses, £26.
Closed	Open all day.
Directions	Nearest tube: Sloane Square; South Kensington.

Simon Cherry
The Pig's Ear
35 Old Church Street, Chelsea,
London SW3 5BS
Tel +44 (0)20 7352 2908
Web www.turningearth.co.uk/thepigsear

Entry 348 Map 15

Chelsea Ram
Chelsea

A quiet residential street off the Lots Road seems an unlikely place to find a corner pub bursting with bonhomie. It used to be a junk shop; now the arched etched-glass shop windows are complemented by soft greens and terracottas, a green wooden bar and local art. A carpeted area to the back has small alcoves, soft lighting and thumbed books, and makes an intimate spot for some enticing food. Salmon fishcakes with crab and citrus bisque, perhaps, or confit duck leg on roasted garlic mash and braised red cabbage – it's all great value. Scrubbed tables see lively card games (bring your own) over coffee, chirpy staff run a fast-paced bar. Close to the large storage depot of Bonhams the auctioneers, this much-loved pub is worth the few minutes' walk from the end of the King's Road.

Meals	Lunch & dinner £9.95-£16.50.
Closed	Open all day.
Directions	Nearest tube: Fulham Broadway; Sloane Square.

James Symington
Chelsea Ram
32 Burnaby Street, Chelsea,
London SW10 0PL
Tel +44 (0)20 7351 4008

Entry 349 Map 15

London

The Harwood Arms
Fulham

Hard to believe you're a pint's throw from the mayhem of Fulham Broadway. There's an easy-on-the-eye modernity to this big-windowed gastropub on the corner, well-dressed in pastels and pine boards with a Shaker-ish feel. Now there's a Michelin star. Menus, driven by seasonality and provenance, revel in an intelligent simplicity, with game a speciality. The chef is Barry Fitzgerald (ex Arbutus and Wild Honey) so you're in mighty good hands. Expect to book days (even weeks) in advance – for game 'tea' served with a venison sausage roll; pheasant Kiev with champ and turnips glazed with mead and rosemary; warm Bramley apple doughnuts with spiced sugar; sweet egg custard tart with drunk golden raisins. Hand-pump ales, well-chosen wines, tasty bar snacks and a laid-back but informed staff make this a most civilised bolthole.

Meals	Lunch & dinner £16-18. Bar snacks £3-£8.
Closed	Mon lunch.
Directions	Nearest tube: West Brompton; Fulham Broadway.

Brett Graham & Mike Robinson
The Harwood Arms
Walham Grove, Fulham,
London SW6 1QP
Tel +44 (0)20 7386 1847
Web www.harwoodarms.com

Entry 350 Map 15

The Sands End

Fulham

Down a residential street off Wandsworth Bridge Road the faithful flock. It might have something to do with the fact that one of the business partners was formerly an equerry to the Prince of Wales (sightings of the young Princes are not unfounded) but more of a certainty is the menu, market-based, changing daily and pleasingly affordable. The food zings with flavour – queen scallops with spinach and smoked gubbeen; braised beef, onion and mushroom pie; chocolate brownie – and complements the modern urban rusticity of scrubbed tables, bare boards and displays of bottled produce. While half the place is restaurant, the rest is old-fashioned bar, serving beers, good wine and slices of hand-raised pork pie. Word has spread: at weekends you book. Staff are friendly and attitude-free.

Meals	Lunch & dinner £12-£18. Bar meals from £3.
Closed	Open all day.
Directions	Off A127 (Wandsworth Bridge Road), second turning on left before bridge, heading south.

Eamonn Manson & Mark Dyer
The Sands End
135-137 Stephendale Road,
Fulham, London SW6 2PR
Tel +44 (0)20 7731 7823
Web www.thesandsend.co.uk

Cumberland Arms

Hammersmith

The Cumberland hits the mark, when Olympia's full on. It's also a favourite with the locals. Old planked floors and wooden panelling, mellow furniture and candles in the evening: beyond the exuberant baskets and the bright blue exterior there's a lovely down-to-earth feel. A treat to sit next to the fire with a big glass of wine (many to choose from, each enticingly described) or a pint of Timothy Taylor's (four hand pumps on the bar). You don't have to eat here but it would be a shame not to: the food is tasty, affordable, the specials change daily and the staff are friendly. The mackerel fillet en escabeche is subtly soused, and comes with a spicy potato and spring onion salad; Tuscan sausages too, and oxtail casserole with gremolata. Outside is a handful of tables; a small park at the back adds a leafy feel.

Meals	Lunch & dinner £10-£15.50.
Closed	Open all day.
Directions	Nearest tube: Kensington Olympia.

Richard & George Manners & Susan Tugwell
Cumberland Arms, 29 North End Rd,
Hammersmith, London W14 8SZ
Tel +44 (0)20 7371 6806
Web www.thecumberlandarmspub.co.uk

The Hampshire Hog
Hammersmith

The little painted pig flies proudly out the front of this 'pantry-pub' fighting its quirky corner, opposite the likes of 'Kings Kebabs and Pizzas'. This is a beacon on the Hammersmith/Ravenscourt border, a light bright refuge to which locals are drawn, from chatty office workers to breakfasting babies; at weekends, families descend. Wooden floors have been stripped and walls painted cream, wicker chairs have sheepskin throws, chandeliers twinkle and flowers top tables. To the left of the bar is the Pantry, its walls lined with lagers, wines, chutneys, breads, coffees and jams, its tables bright with fresh organic dishes. (Our rare chargrilled beef with shaved vegetables, green papaya and pomegranate salad was delicious.) The bar fronts an open-hatch kitchen; the dining area opens to a pretty garden. One for foodies.

Meals	Lunch £7-£23. Bar meals from £4.50. Dinner £14-£23. Sunday lunch £15-£18.
Closed	Open all day.
Directions	See website.

Eddie Francis
The Hampshire Hog
227 King Street, Hammersmith,
London W6 9JT
Tel +44 (0)20 8748 3391
Web www.thehampshirehog.com

Entry 353 Map 15

The Carpenter's Arms
Hammersmith

An unexpected find: an extraordinary distillation of gastropub and local in a charming backwater between King Street and the Great West Road (aka the A4). The glorious single bar has fashionably bare boards, plain tables, a fire that glows on chilly days and doors giving onto a sheltered little garden. And it's done well for itself, being a popular spot for a discerning mix while managing (just) to hold on to its pubby feel, in spite of the emphasis on dining. An ever-changing seasonal menu sees inventive dishes popping up every day. So you get seared scallops with butterbeans, pine nuts and saffron; rib-eye steak with fries and Café de Paris butter; apple tart 'fine' with nutmeg ice cream. Service is exuberant and warm, the atmosphere is laid back. It's a satisfying place to dine.

Meals	Lunch & dinner £8-£16.95.
Closed	Open all day.
Directions	Off King Street between Ravenscourt Park & Stamford Brook.

Simon Cherry & Matt Jacomb
The Carpenter's Arms
91 Black Lion Lane, Hammersmith,
London W6 9BG
Tel +44 (0)20 8741 8386
Web www.carpentersarmsw6.co.uk

Entry 354 Map 15

The Anglesea Arms
Hammersmith

Everyone loves Hammersmith's long-running Anglesea – home to the well-heeled and the young at heart. Find an opened-up space and an endearingly shabby-chic interior, a log fire, a chesterfield, retro furniture and banquette seating. It's high octane but convivial, the bar delivering four ales and a score of wines by glass. As for the cooking, it's fabulous, ferried from an open theatre kitchen to a relaxed sky-lit dining area. Ticking all the local-and-seasonal boxes, dishes, chalked up on a daily-changing menu, are uncomplicated and flavour-driven: skate with butterbean casserole and salsa verde; panna cotta with winter berries; steamed orange pudding and custard. You can dine wherever you like, including the cordoned-off front terrace in summer. Lovely!

Meals	Lunch from £10. Dinner from £14. Sunday lunch from £15.50.
Closed	Open all day.
Directions	Nearest tube: Ravenscourt Park; Goldhawk Road.

Michael Mann
The Anglesea Arms
35 Wingate Road, Hammersmith,
London W6 0UR

Tel +44 (0)20 8749 1291
Web www.anglesea-arms.com

Entry 355 Map 15

London

Havelock Tavern
Shepherd's Bush

Local and seasonal isn't easy in London but chef James goes to farmers' markets when he can and even likes a good forage (try the roast field mushroom soup with truffle oil). In a modest street near Brook Green, the Havelock is a place where beer and food meet head to head and the food is so gorgeous it's packed to the gills. Everyone and anyone is welcome here: mums with babies in papooses, a granddad out with his grandson for lunch, business folk, friends catching up with their dogs. The floor is planked, there's a mish mash of tables, the sun peeks through adding a sparkle and a small fire crackles away. The menu changes twice a day and the food is traditional British with Asian touches; the bread, we are told, is mouthwatering. Real ales, great wines, hot toddies, good coffee… a special pub that back on track.

Meals	Lunch from £8.50. Dinner from £10.
Closed	Open all day.
Directions	Nearest tube: Shepherd's Bush; Hammersmith; Kensington Olympia.

Helen Watson & Andrew Cooper
Havelock Tavern
57 Masbro Road, Shepherd's Bush,
London W14 0LS

Tel +44 (0)20 7603 5374
Web www.thehavelocktavern.co.uk

Entry 356 Map 15

The Princess Victoria
Shepherd's Bush

Once a Georgian gin palace, then an Irish boozer, now a big, light-filled, parquet-floored pub, with a curve of bar selling cask ales and shelves stacked with wines to the ceiling. Despite this the focus of the Princess lies in the dining room beyond, a beautiful room of French grey panelled walls and high ceilings, candelabras, mirrors, old oils... and stuffed animals; you could almost be dining in a country house. People travel far and wide for the food and James McLean likes to keep it British; they even have an on-site charcuterie. Friendly staff ferry luscious dishes to big tables, from crispy pig cheeks to rock oysters. Obviously it's more restaurant than pub, but note the blackboard of guest beers, and ongoing support of local producers like Sipsmith Gin.

Meals	Lunch from £10. Bar meals from £9.50. Dinner from £12.50.
Closed	Open all day.
Directions	Nearest tube: Shepherd's Bush Market.

James McLean
The Princess Victoria
217 Uxbridge Road,
Shepherd's Bush, London W12 9DT
Tel +44 (0)20 8749 5886
Web www.princessvictoria.co.uk

Entry 357 Map 15

The Idle Hour
Barnes

Where else in London would you find an Alaska crab barbecue on the back terrace? Continued local support for this intimate haven in Barnes says it all. Tucked down an alley – one of many – it's a proper local boozer, as popular with foodies as it is with those who come to prop up the bar (perhaps with dog in tow). Pistachio walls, fat candles, purple sofa, little fire, a pint of Adnams, a collection of clocks, a pretty cat – what more can you ask? Sundays are legendary, with a whole roast chicken or a leg of lamb brought to the table, and goose fat roasted potatoes to boot. The meat comes from Liz Hurley's organic farm in Gloucestershire, the crabs (six-footers) from Alaska, the edible flowers and micro herbs from Covent Garden. Staff are lovely but thin on the ground – don't come if you're in a hurry.

Meals	Lunch & dinner £8.95-£12.95. Bar meals £4.95-£8.95.
Closed	Weekday lunchtimes. Open all day Sunday.
Directions	Nearest rail: Barnes; Barnes Bridge.

Stephen Thorp
The Idle Hour
62 Railway Side, Barnes,
London SW13 0PQ
Tel +44 (0)20 8878 5555
Web www.theidlehour.co.uk

Entry 358 Map 15

The Brown Dog
Barnes

Set the satnav to find a small, friendly, neighbourhood gem, hiding down the streets of pretty Barnes 'village' – great after a Richmond Park romp. A recent makeover has delivered an easy-on-the-eye modernity; it's opened-up and pared-back, a well-heeled local. Copper lights dangle from the red ceiling over the bar, there are floorboards, banquette seats and solid-wood furniture. Not a lot of passing trade here, just regulars with their families and their pooches – pig's ears are stocked behind the bar. It's as much gastro as pub, the kitchen driven by top seasonal ingredients and a light modish touch. Try the classics – shepherd's pie – or the posh: roasted monkfish tails with baked pumpkin, curly kale and sage pesto. Local-brewery cask ales and well-selected wines up the ante, while a rear terrace keeps al fresco lovers on board.

Meals	Lunch & dinner £8.25-£17.
Closed	See website for details.
Directions	Close to Barnes Bridge Railway Station.

Jamie Prudhom
The Brown Dog
28 Cross Street, Barnes,
London SW13 0AP
Tel +44 (0)20 8392 2200
Web www.thebrowndog.co.uk

Entry 359 Map 15

The Ship
Wandsworth

Drinking a pint of Young's Special next to a concrete works doesn't sound enticing, but the riverside terrace by Wandsworth Bridge is a dreamy spot. Chilly evenings still draw the crowds to this super old pub, cosy inside with its warm-red and sage-green walls, and its conservatory with central chopping-board table and wood-burning stove. Chef Shaun Harrington sources fresh ingredients to create his seasonal menus. Try braised pork belly braised with caramelised white cabbage, fondant potato with bacon and herb dumpling; parsnip, tomato and goat's cheese gratin; Jerusalem artichoke and chestnut mushroom fricassée. The Ship opens its arms to all, there are live acoustic duos, Irish music on Tuesdays, quiz nights, and families and friends gather merrily in summer.

Meals	Lunch & dinner £9.95-£19.95.
Closed	Open all day.
Directions	Nearest rail: Wandsworth.

Oisin Rogers
The Ship
41 Jews Row, Wandsworth,
London SW18 1TB
Tel +44 (0)20 8870 9667
Web www.theship.co.uk

Entry 360 Map 15

Canton Arms

Stockwell

In one of London's less salubrious zones is a big, high-ceilinged, screen-dominated bar – aimed at those in for a pint. Beyond: cosy ox-red panelled walls with Edwardian mirrors, leaded windows, fat candles and merry eaters of all ages. No bookings, it's first come first served, and you can linger as long as you like; note the teapots and the piles of books. Trish Hilferty, "unsung heroine of the gastropub scene", heads the kitchen. The foie gras toasties are legendary and the menu changes daily with lunch smaller than dinner: three starters, three mains, big rustic flavours and a special way with meat. Chomp your way through slow-cooked Hereford beef shoulder with roasties, swoon over panna cotta, grappa and quince. Drinks range from Bloody Mary to Black Sheep from Yorkshire to marvellous wines. A pub driven by passion, and good value. Give it a whirl.

Meals	Lunch from £8.80. Dinner from £14. Bar meals from £2.80. Sunday lunch £14. Not Sun eve or Mon lunch.
Closed	Mon until 5pm.
Directions	Nearest tube: Stockwell.

Trish Hilferty
Canton Arms
177 South Lambeth Road,
Stockwell, London SW8 1XP
Tel +44 (0)20 7582 8710
Web www.cantonarms.com

Entry 361 Map 15

Anchor & Hope

Southwark

Come for some of the plainest yet gutsiest cooking in London; chef Jonathan Jones attracts droves. The food is described as 'English bistro', and give or take the odd foreign exception (a chorizo broth, a melting pommes dauphinoise), it is just that. The menu is adventurous yet striking in its simplicity: warm snail and bacon salad, smoked herring with fennel and orange, slip soles with anchovy butter, rabbit with pearl barley and sherry, homemade liqueurs, blackberry meringue. The beer comes from Charles Wells, the wine list has 18 by the glass. Staff are youthful – and may be rushed. Décor is 1930s sober and the restaurant area glows by candlelight. No bookings bar Sunday lunch and a legend in the making – but arrive early (or late) and you may get a table.

Meals	Lunch & dinner £10-£20. Sunday lunch £30.
Closed	Mon lunch & Sun eves. Open all day Tues-Sat.
Directions	Nearest tube: Southwark; Waterloo.

Robert Shaw
Anchor & Hope
36 The Cut,
Southwark,
London SE1 8LP
Tel +44 (0)20 7928 9898

Entry 362 Map 15

The Garrison Public House
Bermondsey

The kitchen is open, staff are laid-back, decibels are high, tables are crammed. Forget hushed conversation: the Garrison bounces with bonhomie, more eaterie than pub. What's more, it has the confidence to be different: traditional benches and French boutique chairs, pistachio paintwork and quirky objets and the vegetables for the kitchen displayed in crates by the hatch. Earthy food reflects the décor (steak sandwich, chickpea and pumpkin tagine, Morecombe Bay potted shrimps) – classic British with a continental twist, most of it, from apricots to Orkney mussels, coming from the market down the road. Accompany a bottle of St Peter's with a rib-eye steak with watercress and roquefort butter. Arrive for breakfast, stay for dinner and a movie: there's a cinema downstairs and free screenings every Sunday.

Meals	Lunch & dinner £9.50-£15.90.
Closed	Open all day.
Directions	Nearest tube: London Bridge.

Clive Watson & Adam White
The Garrison Public House
99 Bermondsey Street, Bermondsey,
London SE1 3XB
Tel +44 (0)20 7089 9355
Web www.thegarrison.co.uk

The Crooked Well
Camberwell

Set up by a group of friends sharing a love of great food (and a training at Le Gavroche and Hotel du Vin) this new-wave neighbourhood pub stands between vibrant Camberwell and leafy-smart Grove Lane. The commitment is to rustic British food, with the emphasis on locally sourced produce, shared dishes (eg. rabbit and bacon pie) and family-roast platters on Sundays. On Matt's menu find scallop and squid ink risotto, Torbay sole with capers, anchovy and broad beans, and treacle tart with orange mascarpone. Basking in natural light, the elegant bar-dining room has a laid-back feel, with comfy armchairs in one corner and, in the stylish dining section, Art Deco wallpaper and candles on eclectic tables. Cocktails, wine by the carafe, jazz nights, BYO wine dinners and fish-and-chip Fridays complete this pleasing picture.

Meals	Lunch & dinner £8.75-£17.90.
Closed	Open all day.
Directions	Nearest train station: Denmark Hill (10 mins).

Hector Skinner & Jen Aries
The Crooked Well
16 Grove Lane, Camberwell,
London SE5 8SY
Tel +44 (0)20 7252 7798
Web www.thecrookedwell.com

The Old Brewery
Greenwich

A total one-off on the bank of the Thames, a brewery founded in 1717 – when beer was drunk in favour of water. Not only is the interior cavernous, listed and unique, it's a shrine to the world's beers: you are actively encouraged to taste before choosing your pint. Beyond are the restaurant and tea room, doubling up as a brewing area with vast gleaming tanks and funky beer bottle chandeliers. All is rich to reflect the warmth of the beers: dark woods, deep reds, terracottas; they even hold classes for aspiring brewers. Great staff are passionate about all things beer, but food is taken seriously too, and the best of traditional British is served: fish from Billingsgate, meat from rare breeds, cheese from Neal's Yard; there's raspberry beer for jelly terrines and the spent brewing grain is used to make the bread. Glorious.

Meals	Lunch & dinner from £10. Bar meals from £5.50.
Closed	Open all day.
Directions	Nearest tube: Greenwich.

Alastair Hook
The Old Brewery, The Pepys Building,
The Old Royal Naval College,
Greenwich, London SE10 9LW
Tel +44 (0)20 3327 1280
Web www.oldbrewerygreenwich.com

The Gun
Docklands

Fiendishly difficult to find, but persevere. The front room, dominated by a dark panelled bar, is hugely atmospheric – a planked floor, settles, battered leather sofas, the smell of truffles in the air. The restaurant area is pristine, and a loose nautical theme runs through the prints and paintings. Bag a table by the fire; settle in till the sun sets over the river, on a candlelit terrace. In the bar is a reassuring selection of pub favourites – fish pie, beef shin burger with fat chips – while the restaurant menu is fiercely modern: scallops with samphire, wild garlic and hot butter; roast saddle of wild rabbit with black pudding and shoulder Scotch broth. Weekend brunch from 11.30am to 1pm is too popular not to book; Portuguese barbecues employ Billingsgate fish. Wow.

Meals	Lunch & dinner £11.95-£18. Bar meals from £4.50.
Closed	Open all day.
Directions	Just off A1206 (Prestons Road); turn into Managers Street; right turn at the end.

Tom & Ed Martin
The Gun
27 Coldharbour, Docklands,
London E14 9NS
Tel +44 (0)20 7515 5222
Web www.thegundocklands.com

The Fox

Shoreditch

It may be tucked away from the main drag of Shoreditch but it's still filled with bright young things; no room for wallflowers here. Upstairs: a dining room with large windows, plain wooden chairs and tables, silver candlesticks and an open fire, and modern British food that makes the best of local/rare -breed suppliers. Try small but delicious tapas (chorizo cooked in red wine, anchovies marinated with almonds) or tuck into a rare-breed 'bacon chop' with cloves, russet apples, cider and mash, followed by spiced pear and almond cake. The wine list is long and ales include guests like Otter and Harvey's Best. A lovely sturdy Victorian pub with a big central bare-boarded bar that rocks for a special occasion; further up the narrow staircase is a cosy private dining room, quite opulent with sparkling glasses and Chinese wallpaper.

Meals	Lunch & dinner from £9.
Closed	Open all day (Mon-Fri). Open from 6pm Sat. Closed from 5pm Sun.
Directions	Nearest tube: Old Street.

Amanda Pritchard
The Fox
28 Paul Street, Shoreditch,
London EC2A 4LB
Tel +44 (0)20 7729 5708
Web www.thefoxpublichouse.co.uk

London

The White Horse

Bishopsgate

The setting is great: above Liverpool street station and all its hubbub. Seats outside the pub on Exchange Square overlook the glorious arches of the station roof; fun to watch with a pint of Mad Goose or Doom Bar. Inside is a 'rustic hits the city' feel, with limed benches, colourful cushions, leather sofas, stripy poufs and chic bar stools. Against avocado-tiled walls hang huge salamis, garlic and meats; the bar counter is piled high with fat pork pies and sausage rolls; grab one in a hurry (the 'plat rapide') or opt for something slower – from breakfast to dinner. Try Jersey rock oysters, slow-roast veal, braised faggots and mash with mushy peas, apple and pear crumble; wash it down with mulled Pimm's or a good wine. There's a modern open fire too – a taste of home for busy city workers. Just make sure you don't miss your train.

Meals	Lunch & dinner from £8.95.
Closed	Open all day.
Directions	Nearest tube: Liverpool Street.

Celene Berman
The White Horse
2 Exchange Square, Appold Street,
Bishopsgate, London EC2M 2QS
Tel +44 (0)20 7377 9958
Web www.geronimo-inns.co.uk/thewhitehorse

The White Swan

Holborn

It had spent the previous ten years as the Mucky Duck; then, in 2003, brothers Tom and Ed transformed the old journalists' den. The bar evokes a classic, cramped, city pub feel; at plain tables on unpolished boards, City traders knock back real ales and fine wines. Upstairs is a smart restaurant with some delightfully good food – modern European – that ranges from the robust (roast leg of rabbit with tomato compote, herb dumplings and mustard cream sauce) to the subtle (baked halibut with Savoy cabbage, clams and white wine sauce). Cheese and wine lists are encyclopaedic and regulars get lockers to store their unfinished spirits. The daily bar menu takes in pub classics, perhaps Denham Estate pork sausages with mash and onion gravy, open steak sandwich, brilliant fish and chips.

Meals	Lunch & dinner £15-£18. Bar meals from £8-£15.
Closed	Open all day Mon-Fri. Private parties only Sat & Sun.
Directions	Nearest tube: Chancery Lane.

Tom & Ed Martin
The White Swan
108 Fetter Lane, Holborn,
London EC4A 1ES

Tel +44 (0)20 7242 9696
Web www.thewhiteswanlondon.com

Entry 369 Map 15

Jerusalem Tavern

Clerkenwell

There's so much atmosphere here you could bottle it up and take it home – along with one of the beers. Old Clerkenwell has reinvented itself and the quaint little 1720 tavern epitomises all that is best about the place. Its name is new, acquired when the St Peter's Brewery of Suffolk took it over and stocked it with their ales and fruit beers. Step in to a reincarnation of a nooked and crannied interior, candlelit at night with a winter fire; come before six if you'd like a table. Lunchtime food is simple and English – bangers and mash, a roast, a fine platter of cheese – with ingredients from Smithfield Market down the road. Staff are friendly and know their beer, and the full range of St Peter's ales is all there, from the cask or the specially designed bottle. Heaven.

Meals	Lunch £5-£10.
Closed	Sat & Sun. Open all day Mon-Fri.
Directions	Nearest tube/rail: Farringdon.

Dave Hart
Jerusalem Tavern
55 Britton Street, Clerkenwell,
London EC1M 5UQ

Tel +44 (0)20 7490 4281
Web www.stpetersbrewery.co.uk/london

Entry 370 Map 15

The Gunmakers
Clerkenwell

Who'd not fall in love with this pub, lost down a Clerkenwell lane? Ex-city boy Jeffrey Bell, was smitten on his first visit; now he pulls the pints. Soft lights, wheat walls, Victorian mirrors, chalked menus and guest beers (they get their own blackboard) entice you in to the long narrow bar, while the little conservatory at the back – all bright velvet banquettes and sumptuous aromas – is a foodie haven. It's also the sort of place where the staff are as passionate about the drink, the food and the buzz as are the regulars – architects, media folk and old chaps in for a pint of Purity Mad Goose, Woodforde's Wherry, Redemption Fellowship Porter, or a selection of the guest beers. The menu is short, simple and fresh; the community spirit is palpable. The downside? It's not open at weekends.

Meals	Lunch, bar meals & dinner, all from £8.
Closed	Sat & Sun.
Directions	Nearest tube: Farringdon.

Jeffrey Bell
The Gunmakers
13 Eyre Street Hill, Clerkenwell,
London EC1R 5ET
Tel +44 (0)20 7278 1022
Web www.thegunmakers.co.uk

Entry 371 Map 15

London

Coach & Horses
Clerkenwell

Gone are the days when the Edwardian pub was a corner boozer; now it fills with a media crowd. Enjoy a pint of London Pride in the small panelled bar as you check out the tempting blackboard menu. British dishes are devised with enthusiasm and ingredients burst with flavour: venison and partridge terrine with chutney; sea bream with lentils, fennel and salsa verde; quince and almond tart with clotted cream. Rare-breed meats are reared at Elwy Valley in Wales, fish is delivered daily; there's a selection of charcuterie and cheese too. The bar specialises in malt whiskies and attentive staff lay on nibbles of toasted pumpkin seeds in keeping with the pub's logo, a pumpkin pulled by four mice. Note: most tables have a reserved sign on them on busy nights. Best book.

Meals	Lunch & dinner £10.75-£14. Bar meals £4-£8.
Closed	Open all day. Closed Sat lunch & Sun eves.
Directions	Nearest tube: Farringdon; Chancery Lane.

Giles Webster
Coach & Horses
26-28 Ray Street, Clerkenwell,
London EC1R 3DJ
Tel +44 (0)20 7278 8990
Web www.thecoachandhorses.com

Entry 372 Map 15

The Easton
Clerkenwell

Home from home for the Amnesty International crowd, whose headquarters are down the street, this corner pub may look like the classic London pub but inside is airy and modern. Bare boards, plain windows, a long bar topped with fresh flowers, funky wallpaper at the far end… drinkers and diners mingle over pints of Timothy Taylor and global house-white and wonder what to pick from the ever-changing board. The kitchen goes in for rustic portions of chargrilled lemon and thyme pork chops; roast tomato and chorizo stew; Springbok sausages with spring onion champ, braised red cabbage and pancetta gravy. It's a godsend for the area, with pub tables spilling onto the pavement and a genuinely local feel. Staff are charming, even on Fridays when the drinkers descend, and hearty dishes are replaced with tapas.

Meals — Lunch & dinner £9-£16.
Closed — Open all day.
Directions — Nearest tube: Farringdon.

Jeremy Sutton & Andrew Veevers
The Easton
22 Easton Street, Clerkenwell,
London WC1X 0DS
Tel +44 (0)20 7278 7608
Web www.theeastonpub.co.uk

Entry 373 Map 15

The Compass
Islington

A Victorian pub in trendy Islington, so settle by the sunny pavement tables for an ale and a scrumpy, or dive inside for a traditional feel: dark furniture, cream walls, soft jazz, happy chat. Upstairs is an elegant sage-green dining room. The focus rests equally on food and drink here, in fact the open kitchen is an extension of the bar: watch chefs beavering at one end and smiley staff pulling pints at the other. Blackboards list a good wine selection, delicious specials and a cheese of the day. The kitchen team source locally, bake on-site and make all their sauces and chutneys from scratch. The community spirit is kept alive with evening events: comedy and film nights, political discussions and more. It's an old pub with a beating heart, hugely popular with both the locals and the 'drink on the way back from work' crew.

Meals — Lunch from £5. Dinner from £9. Sunday lunch from £8.50.
Closed — Open all day.
Directions — Nearest tube: Angel.

Summa Grierson
The Compass
58 Penton Street, Islington,
London N1 9PZ
Tel +44 (0)20 7837 3891
Web www.thecompassn1.co.uk

Entry 374 Map 15

Charles Lamb Public House

Islington

Everyone's welcome at Camille and Hobby's small pub, hidden down a tangle of Georgian streets behind Camden Passage. It's a dear little place that keeps its pubby feel, with two unshowy bar rooms and well-kept hand-pump beer. So the blackboard menu – fresh, short, ever-changing – is a surprise. Eat informally at plainly set tables in either bar, on serrano ham with celeriac remoulade, or Lancashire hotpot; Camille is French so there may be duck confit too. Best of all is Sunday's all-day roast beef and Yorkshire pudding with all the trimmings. It's good home-cooked food and you need to get here early: tables cannot be booked. Walk it all off with a stroll along the bosky banks of the Regent's Canal; seek out the house where essayist and poet Charles Lamb lived, two streets away.

Meals	Lunch & dinner £9-£12. Sunday lunch £10.50-£12.
Closed	Open all day (open from 4pm Mon & Tues).
Directions	Nearest tube: Angel.

Hobby & Camille Limon
Charles Lamb Public House
16 Elia Street, Islington,
London N1 8DE
Tel +44 (0)20 7837 5040
Web www.thecharleslambpub.com

Entry 375 Map 15

London

The Duke of Cambridge

Islington

Thanks to pioneering Geetie Singh, 'organic' and 'sustainable' are the watchwords at Britain's first organic pub. British-rustic is the style. Wines, beers, spirits are certified organic and they buy as locally as they can to cut down on food miles. Most of the beers are brewed around London, meat comes from two farms, and fish is Marine Conservation Society-approved; impeccable produce and menus that change twice a day. It's a sprawling airy space with a comfortable, easy atmosphere; you could be alone happily here. Sit back and take your fill of lentil and pancetta soup, mussels with chorizo, fennel and chives, game pie with braised red cabbage, venison steak with redcurrant jus, crusty bread, fruity olive oil, quince crumble and cream – in here, or in the large restaurant. Justifiably rammed.

Meals	Lunch & dinner £9-£22.
Closed	Open all day.
Directions	Nearest tube: Angel.

Geetie Singh
The Duke of Cambridge
30 St Peter's Street, Islington,
London N1 8JT
Tel +44 (0)20 7359 3066
Web www.dukeorganic.co.uk

Entry 376 Map 15

Drapers Arms
Islington

The name implies a drapery connection, but you'll find few flounces at this new gastropub in Islington. Reborn in 2009, the pared-back, opened-up Georgian building has high ceilings, bare boards and an eclectic mix of tables and chairs; there's a relaxed, community vibe. The kitchen, under chef James de Jung, fits the mood and ethic to a tee. Gutsy no-nonsense British dishes appear on twice-daily changing menus: grilled ox tongue with split peas and ham hock; grilled quail with braised chard and aïoli; lentils with roast shallots, roast butternut squash and goat's curd. Room should be left for the lardy cake with crème fraîche or a generous plate of British cheeses. Hand-pump ales, enterprising wines, a cooly decorative dining room upstairs and a courtyard garden top a super-charged act.

Meals	Lunch from £9.50. Bar meals from £4.50. Dinner from £11.50. Sunday lunch, 3 courses, £24.
Closed	Open all day.
Directions	Nearest tube: Highbury & Islington; Angel.

Nick Gibson
Drapers Arms
44 Barnsbury Street, Islington,
London N1 1ER
Tel +44 (0)20 7619 0348
Web www.thedrapersarms.com

Entry 377 Map 15

London

The Lansdowne
Primrose Hill

It's buzzing, laid-back, open-plan and atmospherically lit, with big wooden tables and a dark blue décor. Upstairs is an elegant charming 60-seat restaurant where a cool crowd is treated to tempting aromas from the pizza oven and the open kitchen hatch; downstairs is abuzz. Couples come for late breakfasts, young families for early roast lunch, and everyone for the in-house muffins. There's deep-fried whitebait with tahini, semolina gnocchi with roast squash and mozzarella, old-fashioned ginger pudding. On offer are two draught ales and one real cider but really this is a wine, lager and olives place; the wines are good and don't cost the earth. Outside in summer is a little oasis to which you can retreat and leave the city behind.

Meals	Lunch & dinner £11.50-£16. Bar meals £5-£7.50.
Closed	Open all day.
Directions	Nearest tube: Chalk Farm.

Amanda Pritchett
The Lansdowne
90 Gloucester Avenue,
Primrose Hill, London NW1 8HX
Tel +44 (0)20 7483 0409
Web www.thelansdownepub.co.uk

Entry 378 Map 15

Dartmouth Arms

Highgate

Sitting unobtrusively in a Highgate side street, the Dartmouth Arms may look smartly unexceptional but inside is another story. There's personality in the front bar, wooden tables are junk-shop simple and the flat-screen TV attracts fans for the footie. The back room, where champagne bottles hang from a chandelier, is a more peaceful space. Come for three perfectly kept cask ales, loads of small-producer ciders, several wines by the glass and a modern British menu displayed on boards – landlord Nick is passionate about food and beer. Expect something for everyone here: wild mushroom soup, sausages with tomato sauce and mash, steaks, Sunday roasts, croque monsieur, big salads. The background music is noisy at times, there are quizzes on Tuesdays and a lively crowd.

Meals	Lunch & dinner from £7.50.
Closed	Open all day.
Directions	Nearest tube: Tufnell Park; Kentish Town.

Nick May
Dartmouth Arms
35 York Rise, Dartmouth Park,
Highgate, London NW5 1SP

Tel +44 (0)20 7485 3267
Web www.dartmoutharms.co.uk

Entry 379 Map 15

London

Holly Bush

Hampstead

Down a Hampstead cul-de-sac, the stables once owned by painter George Romney have become a hugely loved pub. It's one of the most Dickensian places you could go for Sunday lunch in London: a labyrinth of corridors leading to treacle-coloured rooms, cosy corners, painted settles, tables set with board games, potted ferns on the bar. Ale rules at the Holly Bush, where the chef cooks not with wine but with beer: through the open kitchen, the aromas of beef and Harveys pie prove a temptation for drinkers to become diners. Adnams rarebit or a pint of prawns – followed by hot chocolate, marmalade and malt whisky fondant – will educate the beer lover's palate. Upstairs in the dining room, all pistachio walls and wooden floors, the celebration of all things British continues. The staff are as happy as the punters here. One of the best.

Meals	Lunch & dinner £8-£15. Bar meals £3.50-£6.
Closed	Open all day.
Directions	Nearest tube: Hampstead.

Jesus Anorve
Holly Bush
22 Holly Mount,
Hampstead,
London NW3 6SG

Tel +44 (0)20 7435 2892

Entry 380 Map 15

The White Hart
Lydgate

Decay was setting in at this 18th-century ale house overlooking Saddleworth Moor when Charles Brierley took it over a decade or so ago. It has since been transformed into a charming restaurant-pub. Relax in the bar with a glass of Timothy Taylor's Landlord, toast your toes by the wood-burning stove and admire the décor – a sleek backdrop for British cheeses, platters of oysters, 'Saddleworth' sausages. Move to the restaurant, where delicacy combines with robustness in some unusually fine cooking: roast pork belly with black pudding and mustard mash, sea bass with smoked bacon and mussel risotto, braised beef with horseradish dumplings. Finish with Granny Smith trifle or hot chocolate fondant. This is a beautiful village and, on a fine day, you can stretch your eyes all the way to the distant Cheshire Plain.

Meals	Lunch & bar meals from £6. Dinner from £12.50. Sunday lunch, 3 courses, £19.95.
Closed	Open all day.
Directions	From Oldham east on A669 for 2.5 miles. Before hill right onto A6050; 50 yds on left.

Charles Brierley
The White Hart
51 Stockport Road, Lydgate,
Oldham OL4 4JJ

Tel	+44 (0)1457 872566
Web	www.thewhitehart.co.uk

Entry 381 Map 12

The Philharmonic
Liverpool

The Phil was built by Liverpool brewers Robert Cain & Co in the style of a gentlemen's club: a place for bodily refreshment after the aesthetic excitements of the Philharmonic Hall opposite. There's ornate Victorian extravagance at every turn, high ceilings, elaborate embellishment, etched glass; the gents is decked in marble and mosaic, its porcelain fittings of historical importance. Sweep through the columned entrance into the imposing central bar, gawp at the scale. Beyond, a succession of small rooms and snugs separated by mahogany partitions, then a Grand Lounge with a stately frieze and table service for lunch: settle down to baked potatoes or fish and chips. Very popular with students, the Philharmonic is a great pub serving excellent beers, wines and whiskies and a huge dose of cheer.

Meals	Lunch & dinner £3.95-£10.
Closed	Open all day.
Directions	City centre; between the cathedrals at corner of Hardman Street.

Marie-Louise Wong
The Philharmonic
36 Hope Street,
Liverpool L1 9BX

Tel	+44 (0)1517 072837

Entry 382 Map 11

The Berney Arms
Barton Bendish

In a peaceful estate village in open country, by the village green, is a spruced-up inn with candy-coloured tables out front. The sleek feel continues within, and there is much to love, from the the bar areas with their beautiful fires and beams, settles, comfy leather chairs and cheeky Pirelli posters, to the bright restaurant with its linen tablecloths and stylish French-country feel. The menu is good-looking and tempting and attracts Norfolk foodies, so look forward to stilton and pear tart, estate venison with red wine jus, chocolate truffle torte with toffee ice cream. Friendly staff, under landlords the Hirsts, bustle efficiently, while the atmosphere tempts one to linger, as does the promise of afternoon tea. The conversion of the old stables, forge and carriage house is impressive, and holds five stylish rooms and some original features; the suite sports a splendid brick forge. Expect gleaming dark wood floors and clean lines, chunky wood and brass beds, good bathrooms and private terraces – every room has one. Off the beaten track but well worth knowing if visiting the north Norfolk coast.

Price	£75-£95. Singles £57.50.
Rooms	5: 4 doubles, 1 twin.
Meals	Lunch & dinner from £8.50-£19.95.
Closed	Open all day.
Directions	Barton Bendish signed off A1122 between A47 west of Swaffham and Downham Market.

Phil & Sue Hirst
The Berney Arms
Church Road, Barton Bendish,
King's Lynn PE33 9GF
Tel +44 (0)1366 347995
Web www.theberneyarms.co.uk

The Orange Tree
Thornham

The Orange Tree knows what a modern food pub should be. From the wicker fencing fronting the garden to the sage-splashed front, the approach says it all; owners Mark and Jo have made subtle changes to a coastal treasure off the village green. Step inside, to polished wood floors, cosy mulberry walls and log-stuffed fireplaces. Snuggle up at a cheeky *table à deux* in the bar, or retire to one of two relaxed dining rooms. This is a fabulous area for food, the pub sources locally and well and there's something for everyone on Philip Milner's innovative menu. Try lamb and apricot hotpot; beer-battered haddock with lemon and caper mayonnaise; salmon, chilli and crayfish cakes with ginger and soy dressing; garlic roasted halibut with passionfruit jus... and the odd delightful whacky touch. Money and thought has been lavished on the chalet rooms at the back, which, although small, are cosy and comfortable with wooden floors, Farrow & Ball colours, coffee-makers and super wet rooms. Come for urban chic, divine food and a happy feel – and, if you're a birdwatcher, for Titchwell Nature Reserve.

Price	From £85.
Rooms	6: 5 twins/doubles, 1 family room.
Meals	Lunch & dinner £10-£22.
Closed	Open all day.
Directions	On A149 in village centre; from Hunstanton, pub on left-hand side.

Mark & Jo Goode
The Orange Tree
High Street, Thornham,
Hunstanton PE36 6LY
Tel +44 (0)1485 512213
Web www.theorangetreethornham.co.uk

The Dabbling Duck
Great Massingham

After a tireless campaign by the villagers to buy their local in 2006, the neglected Rose & Crown became the Dabbling Duck and the pub was revived with panache. The duck egg-blue inn stands prettily by the green and… the dabbling-duck pond. Business has been brisk, the draw being the wonderful food and the beers from the barrel – well-kept Adnams and Woodforde's. As for the mood, it is warmly endearing. The bar has been cut from a single slice of ancient Norfolk oak, there are high-backed settles by a blazing log fire, sober hues, rug-strewn floors, chunky candles on scrubbed tables, and shelves lined with books and board games. Views are to the village. The food includes bowls of Brancaster mussels, roast sea bass with caper butter, sirloin steaks from the Holkham Estate, local-rabbit casserole. The care and attention to detail extends to gorgeous bedrooms with big brass beds, colourful cushions and throws, plasma screens, Roberts radios and wood-floored bathrooms; cookies and fresh coffee on tap. All this, 20 minutes from the beach and the bird-rich saltmarshes. Superb!

Price	£80. Singles £55.
Rooms	6: 5 twins/doubles, 1 single.
Meals	Lunch from £5.75. Bar meals from £5. Dinner from £10.
Closed	Open all day (from 12pm).
Directions	Village signed south off A148 at Harpley between King's Lynn & Fakenham.

Mark & Jess Lapping, Dominic Symington & Steve Kilham
The Dabbling Duck
11 Abbey Road, Great Massingham,
King's Lynn PE32 2HN

Tel	+44 (0)1485 520827
Web	www.thedabblingduck.co.uk

The Duck Inn
Stanhoe

The Stanhoe Crown morphed into the Duck in 2010, and now Sandy and Berni, owners of the Wiveton Bell along the coast, have taken on this much extended and spruced up village local. Enter from the car park a slate-floored bar, with barrels of Elgood's ale racked behind glass, and simple tables and benches for those who appreciate a tip-top pint of Black Dog. Cosy dining rooms beyond are rustic-smart with their wood and slate floors, wood-burning stoves, candles on scrubbed tables, and stunning local art adorning the walls. Expect to find seasonal dishes and fresh fish on the menu, perhaps game terrine with piccalilli, big bowls of Brancaster mussels, sea bass with bacon braised puy lentils and parsnip purée, or a warming beef bourguignon. Leave room for sticky toffee pudding or a plate of local cheeses. Bedrooms have a contemporary feel, with thick down duvets on big comfy beds, leather sofas, plasma screens, fresh coffee, and swish bathrooms with baths and walk-in showers. You are close to trendy Burnham Market, Brancaster Beach and the famous saltmarshes.

Price	£95-£125. Singles £75-£105.
Rooms	2: 1 twin, 1 double.
Meals	Lunch from £6.95. Dinner from £11.25. Sunday lunch £12.95.
Closed	3pm-6pm.
Directions	On B1155 3 miles west of Burnham Market; pub by pond as you enter Stanhoe from Burnham Market.

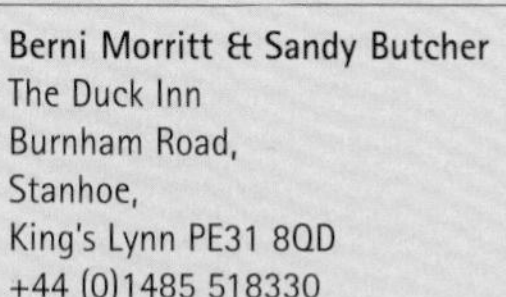

Berni Morritt & Sandy Butcher
The Duck Inn
Burnham Road,
Stanhoe,
King's Lynn PE31 8QD

Tel +44 (0)1485 518330
Web www.duckinn.co.uk

The White Horse
Brancaster Staithe

The setting is magical. Fabulous views reach across the marshes and the boat-bobbed water; dinghies sail on the evening high tide. The coastal path starts right outside this neat inn and the garden provides the perfect spot for a post-stroll pint. Inside the fishy theme continues, but in a modern, crisp way: seascape colours, natural materials, pictures of boats, bowls of pebbles and shells, and big windows for the views. Simple, stylish bedrooms reflect the seaside feel to a tee, and all have gleaming new bathrooms. Those upstairs capture the ever-changing light; those on the ground floor have flower-filled terraces leading to the marshes and a New England feel. A perfect place for bird-spotting, especially geese in winter – bring the binoculars. Later, dine by candlelight on mussels and oysters, mullet with a bean, chorizo and tomato ragout, blade of beef with thyme jus; all of it as local and seasonal as possible, served with a great big smile. Huge sunsets, great food, great breakfasts and a welcome for children and dogs… there's nothing to stop you staying the night!

Price	£96-£170.
Rooms	15: 11 doubles, 4 twins.
Meals	Lunch & bar meals from £8.95. Dinner £12.95-£17.75. Sunday lunch, 3 courses, £26.15.
Closed	Open all day.
Directions	Midway between Hunstanton & Wells-next-the-Sea on A149.

Cliff & James Nye
The White Horse
Brancaster Staithe,
King's Lynn PE31 8BY

Tel	+44 (0)1485 210262
Web	www.whitehorsebrancaster.co.uk

The Hoste Arms
Burnham Market

Lord Nelson was once a local, now it's farmers, fishermen and film stars who jostle at the bar and roast in front of the fire. In its 300-year history the Hoste has been a court house, a livestock market, a gallery and a brothel; these days it's more a cosy social hub and even on a grey February morning buzzes with life – the locals in for coffee, the residents polishing off leisurely breakfasts. The place has a genius of its own with warm bold colours, armchairs to sink into, panelled walls, an art gallery plus a new beauty spa. Fancy food can be eaten anywhere and anytime, so dig into local oysters or mussels, braised pork cheeks with sautéed wild mushrooms and spiced sweet potato and vegetable cake with fenugreek sauce and bok choi. In summer, life spills out onto tables at the front or you can dine on the terrace in the garden at the back. Rooms are all different, the quietest away from the bar: a tartan four-poster, a swagged half-tester, leather sleigh beds in the Zulu Wing, luxury boutique rooms in Vine House, across the village green. The sandy beaches of the north Norfolk coast are on the doorstep.

Price	£122-£213. Half-board from £91 p.p.
Rooms	49 + 3: 34 twins/doubles & suites. Vine House: 7 doubles. Railway Inn: 7 doubles, 1 railway carriage for 2. 3 self-catering cottages.
Meals	Lunch from £5.50. Bar meals from £9.25. Dinner, 3 courses, from £25. Sunday lunch, 3 courses, £25.
Closed	Open all day.
Directions	On B1155 for Burnham Market. By green & church in village centre.

Emma Tagg
The Hoste Arms
Market Place, Burnham Market,
King's Lynn PE31 8HD
Tel +44 (0)1328 738777
Web www.hostearms.co.uk

The Wiveton Bell

Wiveton

The pull of the great outdoors led Berni and Sandy, Nottingham-based restaurateurs, to a pretty pub with a backdrop of a village green and church. The setting may be bucolic but Wiveton is no backwater; on highdays and holidays these coastal outposts of North Norfolk get livelier than the King's Road. City escapees, with or without children in tow, will find much to enjoy, for a rustic-chic makeover has transformed the interior of this charming whitewashed inn – all beams, chunky tables and polished plank floors – that fits the bistro-pub bill down to the ground. The menu is seductive, ranging from pork belly with black pudding mash and cider jus to hearty bowls of Morston mussels with shallots, white wine and cream, to simple haddock and chips. It's all so lovely you'll want to stay the night – and why not? Four opulent bedrooms in shabby-chic style – three with furnished terraces – come with antique beds and goose down pillows, mini CD players, iPod docks and books; cosy bathrooms have bathrobes and top toiletries. Staff are wonderfully relaxed and fresh croissants are delivered to the door.

Price	£95-£140.
Rooms	4 doubles.
Meals	Lunch from £6.95. Dinner, 3 courses, around £30.
Closed	Open all day.
Directions	Wiveton signed south off A149 at Blakeney; pub on the green.

Berni Morritt & Sandy Butcher
The Wiveton Bell
Blakeney Road,
Wiveton, Holt NR25 7TL

Tel +44 (0)1263 740101
Web www.wivetonbell.com

The Pigs
Edgefield

This gutsy gastropub stands for all we love. "Pig in charge" Tim Abbott, along with fellow foodie entrepreneurs, fights the corner for real food locally sourced, and is ever on the look out for suppliers; you can barter your produce for a pint. This is the retro village pub of your dreams – decent ales, great wines and a menu that delivers tastes long forgotten. Try the potted rabbit with redcurrant jelly, the venison burgers on toasted muffins, the slow-roast lamb shoulder with fresh thyme, the caramelised rice pudding. Kids will love the new adventure play area, the indoor play room full of toys, and the little menu for 'piglets', served with in-house lemonade. Bar 'iffits' (Norfolk tapas), homemade pork scratchings and mixed pickle pots are further enticements, as are quiz nights and pub games. And if you long for a sumptuous breakfast à la Pigs, then you must stay the night. Their innovative take on rustic country style extends into three fabulous bedrooms upstairs, the Tamworth, the Saddleback and the Pig Sty – possibly the only room in Norfolk with an eight-foot bed!

Price	£130.
Rooms	3 doubles.
Meals	Lunch & dinner £9.95-£14.50.
Closed	3pm-6pm (Mon-Sat).
Directions	Edgefield is on B1149, 3 miles south of Holt; pub south side of village.

Tim Abbott
The Pigs
Norwich Road, Edgefield,
Melton Constable NR24 2RL
Tel +44 (0)1263 587634
Web www.thepigs.org.uk

Saracens Head
Wolterton

Lost in the lanes of deepest Norfolk, an English inn that's hard to beat. Outside, Georgian red-brick walls ripple around, encircling a beautiful courtyard where you can sit for sundowners in summer before slipping into the restaurant for a good meal. Tim and Janie came back from the Alps, unable to resist the allure of this inn. A sympathetic refurbishment has brightened things up, but the spirit remains the same: this is a country-house pub with lovely staff who go the extra mile. Downstairs the bar hums with happy locals who come for Norfolk ales and good French wines, while the food in the restaurant is as good as it ever was, perhaps Morston mussels, pork belly with mustard mash, whole sea bass with ginger and spring onions, and seasonal game. Upstairs you'll find a sitting room on the landing, where windows frame country views, and six cosy bedrooms. All have smart carpets, pale wood furniture, soothing colours, comfy beds and sparkling new bathrooms. Breakfast sets you up for the day, so explore the coast at Cromer, play golf on the cliffs at Sheringham, or visit Blickling Hall, a Jacobean pile. Blissful.

Price	From £95. Singles £65.
Rooms	6: 5 twins/doubles, 1 family room.
Meals	Lunch & dinner £6.50-£20. Not Mon & Tues lunch Sept-June.
Closed	3pm-6pm. Mon (except bank hols) & Tues lunch (Oct-Jun).
Directions	From Norwich A140 past Aylsham, then 3rd left for Erpingham. Right into Calthorpe, through village, straight out the other side (not right). On right after about 0.5 miles.

Tim & Janie Elwes
Saracens Head
Wolterton, Norwich NR11 7LZ
Tel +44 (0)1263 768909
Web www.saracenshead-norfolk.co.uk

The Gunton Arms
Thorpe Market

Click open the latch gate and enter Gunton Park. The beautifully restored Gunton Arms overlooks one thousand acres of lush and historic parkland – the setting is stunning. Art dealer Ivor Braka has lavished money on the once faded hotel and the results are impressive... who would not love the relaxed country-house feel? Be seduced by warm red hues, wooden floors, a blazing log fire in the traditional bar (dogs welcome too) and elegant lounges with pretty views of deer from every window. Quaff pints of Wherry alongside gamekeepers and gentry; tuck into rib of beef cooked over the fire in the vaulted dining room. Stuart (ex-Mark Hix) champions locally sourced ingredients, so look forward to mixed grill of estate fallow deer served with crab apple jelly; Brancaster mussels and chilli tossed in linguine; Cromer crab in summer. Super inviting rooms ooze country-house charm: find antiques, gorgeous fabrics, Persian rugs, classic wallcoverings, old prints and paintings and indulgent marble-tiled bathrooms, some with deep tubs and walk-in showers... wake to parkland views. A delicious, unusual find.

Price	£95-£150.
Rooms	8 doubles.
Meals	Lunch & dinner from £9.50. Bar meals £1.50-£5.50.
Closed	Open all day.
Directions	Off A149 between North Walsham and Cromer; pub just south of Thorpe Market.

Simone Baker & Stuart Tattersall
The Gunton Arms
Cromer Road, Thorpe Market,
Norwich NR11 8TZ
Tel +44 (0)1263 832010
Web www.theguntonarms.co.uk

The Ingham Swan
Ingham

An away-from-the-crowds inn in a wilderness of lanes. Perfectly positioned between the fashionable coast and the Broads, the ancient Swan pleases foodies and lovers of Woodforde's Best. Chef Daniel is a Norfolk boy made good through hard work and talent; note the innovative and seasonally driven menu. Come for Cromer crab and pink grapefruit salad, crispy brie beignets with olive jam, fillet of beef with sautéed wild mushrooms, fillet of sea bass with muscat grapes and samphire, vanilla crème brûlée with raspberry sorbet and almond tuile. The drinks shelf is the perfect justification for a taxi home – very gentleman's club; the staff are engaging, attentive and on the ball. Add a dining room of brick, flint, beams, wood-burners, suave leather chairs and just the right level of lighting, and a cosy sofa'd snug in the bar and you have the perfect gastro inn.

Meals: Lunch & dinner £9.95-£24. Sunday lunch, 3 courses, £20.95.
Closed: 3pm-6pm.
Directions: From Happisburgh take B1159 to Sea Palling, turning right to Ingham. From A149 at Stalham, take the Ingham road.

Daniel Smith
The Ingham Swan
Sea Palling Road, Ingham,
Norwich NR12 9AB
Tel: +44 (0)1692 581099
Web: www.theinghamswan.co.uk

Norfolk

The Wildebeest Arms
Stoke Holy Cross

In the 1990s Henry Watt introduced good food to this country inn – a rarity then. Today the Wildebeest is one of the most popular dining pubs in Norfolk. The 19th-century building may be no great shakes on the outside but the atmosphere is special. Modernised to create one long room split by a central bar, there are rich yellow walls, dark oak beams, a winter fire and an African safari lodge feel to match the pub's name. Ales include Woodforde's Wherry, there's an impressive list of wines and the food is up-to-the-minute and freshly made. Tuck into the delights of smoked haddock and saffron chowder, beef fillet with onion marmalade and wild mushroom jus, pistachio parfait... or opt for good old English favourites like sausage and mash and sticky toffee pudding. Then head for Norwich for some city bustle or don your wellies and explore.

Meals: Lunch from £5.95. Dinner from £6.50. Sunday lunch, 3 courses, £19.50.
Closed: 3pm-6pm.
Directions: Off A140, 3 miles south of Norwich.

Henry Watt
The Wildebeest Arms
82-86 Norwich Road,
Stoke Holy Cross, Norwich NR14 8QJ
Tel: +44 (0)1508 492497
Web: www.thewildebeest.co.uk

King's Head
Bawburgh

After 28 years as a thriving village local, there's no snoozing in front of the wood-burners for Anton and his team as they work together with ever more enthusiasm to raise the profile of their own special slant of Norfolk-ness. The feel is still of slowly evolving, scuffed-around-the-edges nostalgia, all low beams, horse brasses and old maps – now joined by new leatherette sofas near the fire and blackboards enticing you to local seasonal specials. The menu brims with pride for their "very important producers", chef Dan Savage and his team create dishes from the East Coast and Norfolk larders; try Norfolk moules frites with local Brancaster mussels… outstanding. Bustle, background music, a heated terrace at the back – there's lots of love. Pop in for a pint, take home fish and chips wrapped in proper paper. A fiver well spent!

Meals	Lunch from £6. Dinner from £11. Sunday lunch, 3 courses, £20. Not Sunday eve (Nov-Apr).
Closed	Open all day.
Directions	Off B1108 (Watton Road) west of Norwich, 1 mile from A47.

Anton Wimmer
King's Head
Harts Lane, Bawburgh,
Norwich NR9 3LS
Tel +44 (0)1603 744977
Web www.kingshead-bawburgh.co.uk

Entry 395 Map 10

Norfolk

The Mulberry Tree
Attleborough

Urbane, contemporary and soothing, this is just perfect for ladies (or shy gentlemen) who lunch, and it wouldn't matter if you arrived alone at this sophisticated pub in the middle of a sleepy market town. There are lots of seating areas in the bar, along with bay windows, high ceilings, huge church candles in glass lanterns and dark leather sofas to guarantee comfort. There's good food, too. Choose from the daily changing bar menu (Suffolk ham with free-range eggs and hand-cut chips) or go the whole hog in the restaurant (potted Cromer crab, pan-fried sea bass). Gooey chocolate squares with butterscotch sauce and vanilla ice cream could finish you off. In summer, simple seating with parasols are set up behind the bar area with its big windows. Forests, beaches, market towns and nature reserves are near to explore.

Meals	Lunch from £7. Dinner, 3 courses, £25-£30.
Closed	Sun. Open all day Mon-Sat.
Directions	On one-way system around town centre at junction with Station Road.

Philip & Victoria Milligan
The Mulberry Tree
Station Road,
Attleborough NR17 2AS
Tel +44 (0)1953 452124
Web www.the-mulberry-tree.co.uk

Entry 396 Map 10

Buckinghamshire Arms

Blickling

A Jacobean coaching inn that was originally the estate builder's house for Blickling Hall; it stands close to the grand gates and was fully done up during the winter of 2011/2012. Like the Hall, it is owned by the National Trust but functions as a self-contained inn, serving the locals in the winter and the crowds in the summer, when the big lawn and sheltered courtyard have an outside servery. Tuck into bangers and mash with red onion gravy, pork pie ploughman's and a pint of Woodforde's Wherry. In the evening: perhaps duck and pistachio terrine, Gunton Park venison casserole, treacle tart. Bars are charming, a cosy red or bold green, with log fires, leaded windows, scrubbed tables, and a super-snug bar at the front. Take a trot in the park to admire the lake, the Gothic folly and the pyramidal mausoleum; the Hall is open April to October.

Meals	Lunch from £8.95. Dinner from £9.25.
Closed	3pm-6pm. Open all day in summer.
Directions	From Aylsham B1354; pub opp. Hall.

Pip Wilkinson
Buckinghamshire Arms
Blickling,
Norwich NR11 6NF

Tel +44 (0)1263 732133
Web www.bucks-arms.co.uk

The Hunny Bell

Hunworth

The extended 18th-century pub sits by Hunworth's idyllic green in the glorious Glaven Valley. Animal Inns snapped up this little North Norfolk beauty five years ago – an upmarket eaterie to add to their collection. Follow a breezy saltmarsh stroll with lunch at long oak tables in the rustic-chic, slate-floored bar. Stuffed owls peer out of cubby-holes by the wood-burner, walls are honey-coloured and flourish country prints, the snug has modish walls and winged chairs, and posh loos wear bee motif wallpapers. Food is fresh, imaginative and locally sourced, so enjoy your potted King's Lynn brown shrimps, steaming Brancaster mussels, Norfolk Wherry beer-battered cod with hand-cut chips, and steak and watercress sandwiches; even the bread is homemade. Illy coffee, Norfolk ales (try a pint of Wolf), and a sweet secret side garden add to the charm.

Meals	Lunch & dinner £7.25-£16.95. Bar meals from £5.25.
Closed	3pm-5.30pm (4pm-6.30pm Sun).
Directions	From Norwich B1149 to Saxthorpe, B1354 to Briston, signposted right for Hunworth. 2 miles, on left of village green.

Henry Watt
The Hunny Bell
The Green, Hunworth,
Melton Constable NR24 2AA

Tel +44 (0)1263 712300
Web www.thehunnybell.co.uk

The Kings Head
Letheringsett

Flying Kiwi Inns – Chef Chris's mini pub empire – may be expanding along the Norfolk coast, but the Kings Head is his most impressive makeover. In family-happy gardens close to Holt, this rambling manor-like building has been revamped with panache. The mood is rustic-chic: rugs on wooden boards or terracotta, fat table lamps, bookcases crammed with books to browse, big mirrors, warm hues and feature fireplaces fronted by squashy leather; there's a civilised feel. Adnams and Woodforde ales, decent wines and classy pub food are further enticements, as menus salute the region's fishermen, farmers and traders. Enjoy smoked duck breast and chicory salad, roast halibut with wild rocket pesto, plum and almond Bakewell with crème anglaise, and Norfolk cheeses. There are cows in the field (theirs) and a willow maze in the garden.

Meals	Lunch from £6.95. Dinner from £13.95. Sunday lunch, 2-3 courses, £15.95-£19.95.
Closed	Open all day.
Directions	Just off A148 Holt to Fakenham road, 1 mile west of Holt.

Chris Coubrough
The Kings Head
Holt Road, Letheringsett,
Holt NR25 7AR
Tel +44 (0)1263 712691
Web www.kingsheadnorfolk.co.uk

Entry 399 Map 10

Norfolk

The Three Horseshoes
Warham

An atmospheric treasure in a rural backwater. This former row of 18th-century cottages hides a mile from the coastal path and glorious saltmarshes. Inside, three utterly plain, unspoilt rooms have barely changed since the Thirties – gas lights, rough deal tables, Victorian fireplaces and a pianola that performs.... once in a while. Vintage entertainment includes an intriguing American Mills one-armed bandit converted for modern coins and a rare Norfolk 'twister' set into the ceiling – for village roulette, apparently. The food is in keeping, just traditional English dishes based emphatically on Norfolk produce – locally shot game, hearty casseroles, shortcrust pastry pies – enhanced by great pints of Wherry straight from the cask. Alternatively, sample local cider or homemade lemonade.

Meals	Lunch from £4.20. Bar meals & dinner from £7.80. Sunday lunch £8.20.
Closed	2.30pm-6pm.
Directions	Warham off A149 between Wells-next-the-Sea & Stiffkey; 2 miles east of Wells.

Iain Salmon
The Three Horseshoes
69 The Street,
Warham,
Wells-next-the-Sea NR23 1NL
Tel +44 (0)1328 710547

Entry 400 Map 10

White Horse Hotel
Blakeney

The smart hub of this small coastal village attracts its share of switched-on custom; Blakeney is the jewel in north Norfolk's crown. The lamp-lit windows of the bar beckon, and Adnams ales are served to those in for a pint. But stay for more: hot soups, filled ciabattas and fish and chips are traditional favourites, while Morston mussels, rib-eye steak, pan-roast partridge and a plate of local cheeses are given a contemporary treatment. All are served in served in the polished bar and the sunny-coloured restaurant. With its airy conservatory and sheltered courtyard, this friendly inn, bought by Adnams Brewery in 2011, is a pleasant place to rest weary limbs following a bracing coast path walk. At the bottom of the steep, narrow high street are marshes of sea lavender, natural mussel beds and seals a ferry ride away.

Meals — Lunch & dinner £8.95-£19.95.
Closed — Open all day.
Directions — Just up from quay, in village; off A149 10 miles west of Sheringham.

Francis Guildea
White Horse Hotel
4 High Street, Blakeney,
Holt NR25 7AL
Tel +44 (0)1263 740574
Web www.blakeneywhitehorse.co.uk

Entry 401 Map 10

Norfolk

Red Lion
Stiffkey

Tucked into the side of a hill, overlooking the meadows where beef cattle graze, is a cosy inn that's a pleasure to step into: a warren of three small rooms with bare floorboards and 17th-century quarry tiles, 'clotted cream' walls, open log fires and a mix of stripped wooden settles, old pews and scrubbed tables. The pub attracts a loyal crowd for its fresh seafood – crab from Wells boats, mussels from Mark Randall in the village, beer battered cod – or roast partridge with braised red cabbage, and first-rate ales from local brewers: Woodforde's, Yetmans. Locals rub shoulders with booted walkers and birdwatchers recovering from the rigours of the Peddars Way path and Stiffkey's famous marshes. After a day on the beach the large and airy conservatory is popular with families; dogs, too, are welcomed.

Meals — Lunch, bar meals & dinner from £9.95. Sunday lunch, 3 courses, £20.
Closed — Open all day.
Directions — From Wells, 2 miles along coast road towards Cromer.

Stephen Franklin
Red Lion
44 Wells Road, Stiffkey,
Wells-next-the-Sea NR23 1AJ
Tel +44 (0)1328 830552
Web www.stiffkey.com

Entry 402 Map 10

The Crown Hotel

Wells-next-the-Sea

The interior of Chris's handsome 16th-century coaching inn has been neatly rationalised yet is still atmospheric with its open fires, bare boards, bold colours and easy chairs. Order pub food at the bar and eat it in the lounges or the lovely modern conservatory: a hearty serving of Brancaster mussels, roast venison with pumpkin and ginger risotto, bread and butter pudding. Or, more simply, the battered haddock with hand-cut chips and tartare sauce and a pint of Adnams Bitter. Modern art and attractively laid tables give life to the restaurant where local ingredients are translated into global ideas: bubble-and-squeak and apple purée; Thai marinated duck breast with seared scallops and chilli jam. Beaches and bracing saltmarsh walks are mere minutes away and the geese wheel above: this is birdwatching country!

Meals	Lunch & dinner from £11.25. Set menu £12.95-£15.95. Sunday lunch £10.95.
Closed	Open all day.
Directions	Wells-next-the-Sea is on B1105, 10 miles north of Fakenham; pub by the green south of town centre.

Chris Coubrough
The Crown Hotel
The Buttlands,
Wells-next-the-Sea NR23 1EX
Tel +44 (0)1328 710209
Web www.thecrownhotelwells.co.uk

Entry 403 Map 10

Norfolk

The Jolly Sailors

Brancaster Staithe

Cliff and James Nye have revived a 200-year-old coastal treasure. 'Eat, Drink and be Jolly' says it all: not only is this a community boozer geared to locals and families but it attracts all those who flock to Brancaster's beach, which lies just across the road. In the classic bar, replete with beams, tiled floor, settles and a wood-burner pumping out the heat, dads can enjoy pints of home-brewed Brancaster ales while kids can watch the pizzas being baked in the open-to-view oven. Hearty traditional pub dishes using fresh local produce include mussels cooked in wine, onion, garlic and cream; lamb and mint pie; gammon, egg and chips; and good ol' fish and chips (delicious). It's may be less classy than the Nyes' White Horse Inn down the road, but the Sailors is a great little pit-stop for families, beach bums and walkers.

Meals	Lunch & bar meals from £8.50. Dinner from £9.50. Sunday lunch, 3 courses, £20.
Closed	Open all day.
Directions	In village centre on A149 coast road, midway between Hunstanton and Wells-next-the-Sea.

Cliff & James Nye
The Jolly Sailors
Brancaster Staithe,
King's Lynn PE31 8BJ
Tel +44 (0)1485 210314
Web www.jollysailorsbrancaster.co.uk

Entry 404 Map 10

The Crown Inn

East Rudham

Kiwi TV chef Chris Coubrough bought his second Crown in 2008 (his first is at Wells-next-the-Sea). Right by the A148, overlooking the village green, it's a handy spot to rest and refuel while exploring the North Norfolk coast. For beyond the charming and spruced-up exterior lies a lovely big open-plan bar with low beams, rug-strewn tiles, fresh contemporary colours, shelves full of books and an assortment of well-scrubbed dining tables. Fishermen and farmers supply the produce for modern dishes listed on daily printed menus – and it's hard not to be tempted by Houghton Hall venison with braised red cabbage, sea bass with saffron and spring onion risotto, a slate of crayfish, prawns, cockles and brown shrimp (to share), and delicious warm apricot tart. It's all so relaxing and quietly pleasing.

Meals	Lunch from £7.95. Dinner from £11.95. Sunday lunch, 2 courses, £16.95.
Closed	Open all day.
Directions	Beside A148 between Fakenham and King's Lynn; by village green.

Chris Coubrough
The Crown Inn
The Green, East Rudham,
King's Lynn PE31 8RD
Tel +44 (0)1485 528530
Web www.thecrowneastrudham.co.uk

Entry 405 Map 10

Norfolk

The Ship Inn Hotel

Brancaster

The swanky Ship is smack on the coast road and a ten-minute walk from Brancaster beach. Once a grim boozer, ignored by most, this cosy coastal bolthole is now the first port of call for post-beach drinks and tucker; kids and dogs are welcome. Grab a pint of Adnams and a crab sandwich, or linger over scallops with pea purée and pancetta… temptingly followed by pork belly with champ and cider jus, or chocolate brownie with vanilla ice cream. The bar is stylish, the food is locally sourced and the atmosphere in the dining areas is relaxed and informal. Be wowed by a quirky-chic décor: jute blinds, driftwood lights, slate-topped tables, striped fabrics, antique mirrors, objets d'art, and map-of-Norfolk wallpaper in the Map Room. It's a fun place to end an outdoorsy day, a brilliant refuge for happy beach bums.

Meals	Lunch from £6.95. Dinner from £12.45. Sunday lunch, 2-3 courses, £15.95-£19.95.
Closed	Open all day.
Directions	On A149 between Hunstanton and Wells-next-the-Sea.

Chris Coubrough
The Ship Inn Hotel
Brancaster,
King's Lynn PE31 8AP
Tel +44 (0)1485 210333
Web www.shiphotelnorfolk.co.uk

Entry 406 Map 9

Gin Trap Inn

Ringstead

An actor and a lawyer run this old English Inn. Steve and Cindy left London for the quiet life and haven't stopped since, adding a conservatory dining room at the back and giving the garden a haircut. The Gin Trap dates to 1667, while the horse chestnut tree that shades the front took root in the 19th century. A smart whitewashed exterior gives way to cosy beamed bars with traditional brasses, rustic tables and crackling fires, and a smartly dressed restaurant. It's a comfortable haven for walkers on the Peddars Way but most come for the food: Norfolk mussels, scallops with black pudding, bream with crayfish and lemon ravioli, steak and kidney pudding, ginger cake with toffee sauce. Ringstead – a pretty village lost in the country – is two miles inland from the coastal road, Sandringham is close and fabulous beaches beckon.

Meals	Lunch from £7. Dinner from £20.
Closed	2.30pm-6pm. Open all day in summer.
Directions	North from King's Lynn on A149. Ringstead signed right in Heacham. Pub on right in village.

Steve Knowles & Cindy Cook
Gin Trap Inn
6 High Street, Ringstead,
Hunstanton PE36 5JU
Tel +44 (0)1485 525264
Web www.gintrapinn.co.uk

Entry 407 Map 9

The Rose & Crown

Snettisham

Roses round the door and twisting passages within, it is gloriously English. Holkham sausages, mash and onion gravy and gammon, eggs and hand cut chips should please the traditionalists; more adventurous diners can tuck into smoked haddock chowder. It's great value. In spite of 30 wines on the list, half available by the glass, the Rose and Crown is still proud to be a pub; fine beers on hand pump and a hands-on feel. The walled garden was once the village bowling green and children will enjoy the wooden play fort. Inside are a warren of rooms with low ceilings and uneven floors, old beams and log fires, and a family-friendly garden room. Golfers have Brancaster and Hunstanton, shoppers Burnham Market, birdwatchers Snettisham and Titchwell. For walkers and families the North Coast beaches of Holme and Holkham are stupendous.

Meals	Lunch & dinner £8.50-£14.50.
Closed	Open all day.
Directions	Village signed off A149 10 miles north of King's Lynn. Turn right at r'bout into village & then 1st left, pub 100yds on left.

Anthony & Jeannette Goodrich
The Rose & Crown
Old Church Road,
Snettisham, King's Lynn PE31 7LX
Tel +44 (0)1485 541382
Web www.roseandcrownsnettisham.co.uk

Entry 408 Map 9

Royal Oak
Eydon

Everyone's welcome at this small unpretentious pub with a Sunday papers-and-a-pint feel. Walkers drop by to refuel, children are happy, dogs amble freely. No music, just the hum of contented eaters: the menu – fresh, locally sourced ingredients and regularly changing – is a big attraction. You may find braised beef with root vegetables and mash, salmon supreme with hollandaise, spiced bread and butter pudding with custard, and delicious bar meals (Thai chicken curry; haddock and chips). The pretty 17th-century pub has old flagstones, exposed stone walls, a wood-burner in the inglenook. The long bar is propped up by ale-quaffing old-timers, the rest is made over to three small eating areas and a games room in the old stable. There are picnic seats out in front and the village – seven miles from the motorway – feels as remote as can be.

Meals	Lunch £4.45-£12. Dinner £16.
Closed	2.30pm-6pm (3pm-7pm Sun) & Mon lunch.
Directions	Off A361 midway between Banbury & Daventry.

John Crossan
Royal Oak
6 Lime Avenue, Eydon,
Daventry NN11 3PG
Tel +44 (0)1327 263167
Web www.theroyaloakateydon.co.uk

Northamptonshire

The Red Lion
Culworth

Culworth has it all: thatched stone cottages, pretty green and church, grand manor – and the Red Lion, a classic old local revived by chef Justin Lefevre who has carefully restored the once boarded-up boozer. The unlovely 70s décor has gone; the stone and wood floors, the timbers and the fireplaces have been rediscovered; and there's a fresh rustic-chic feel. Diners mingle with locals, booted walkers quaff pints of Landlord in the bar, and dogs doze. In keeping, the food is hearty and unpretentious, the lunch and monthly-changing dinner menus featuring everyone's favourites – lamb burgers, ham, egg and chips, rump steak with all the trimmings, seafood risotto, sea bass with lemon cream sauce. The garden is huge and has village views.

Meals	Lunch & dinner £8.50-£16.
Closed	3pm-6pm. Monday.
Directions	Village signed off A361 and B4525 NE of Banbury.

Justin Lefevre
The Red Lion
High Street,
Culworth,
Banbury OX17 2BD
Tel +44 (0)1295 760050

The Althorp Coaching Inn
Great Brington

Near Althorp House – home of the Spencers – the pub was once known as the Fox & Hounds. Decked with flowers inside and out, resting in the heart of an multi-thatched estate village, it is a popular place. There's an enclosed courtyard within earshot of the cricket green, a nice spot for a pint of Langton Bowler (alongside many other wonderful ales) and, when the nights draw in, the fires burn brightly in the restaurant and bar, glowingly traditional with its floorboards, flagstones and plentiful bric-a-brac. The regulars appreciate the good value meals and the baguettes from the bar, while the restaurant serves beef and game from the farm estate, cooked in an unfussy manner. Major sporting events – Silverstone is up the road – are shown (discreetly) in the bar, and Tuesday evenings see live music.

Meals	Lunch & dinner £9.25-£16.75.
Closed	Open all day.
Directions	From Northampton, A428; then 1st left after Althorp; pub near Althorp Hall.

Phillippa Payne-Roberts & Julie Gidley
The Althorp Coaching Inn
Main Street, Great Brington,
Northampton NN7 4JA

Tel +44 (0)1604 770651
Web www.althorp-coaching-inn.co.uk

Entry 411 Map 8

Northamptonshire

The Queen's Head
Bulwick

A mellow old stone pub opposite the church in a lovely village – you'll wish it was your local. The simple beamed and flagstoned bar rambles into country-styled dining rooms that deliver atmosphere and charm, their thick beams and timbers and wonderfully wonky walls expressing a history that goes back 600 years. New landlords took over in 2011 and intend to keep things simple. Nor do they want to lose the village pub feel: bell ringers still head across the road every Wednesday evening. There's a stone oven on the decked summer terrace, and you can look forward to traditional pub food with a modern twist – devilled lambs' kidneys, saddle of lamb with sun-dried tomato and rosemary crust, apple and caramel tart. A cracking pit-stop if you find yourself in need of refreshment on the A43.

Meals	Lunch & dinner £9.95-£19.95.
Closed	3pm-6pm (5pm-7pm Sun) & Mon all day.
Directions	Just off A43, between Stamford & Corby.

Julie Barclay
The Queen's Head
Bulwick,
Corby NN17 3DY

Tel +44 (0)1780 450272
Web www.thequeensheadbulwick.co.uk

Entry 412 Map 9

The Tankerville Arms

Eglingham

Fancy exploring the rolling acres between Northumberland's dramatic coastline and the wild Cheviot Hills? Charming Eglingham has the best inn for miles, a hospitable bolthole personably run by George and Mary. The long stone-built tavern, a boon for ramblers and cyclists, cheerfully mixes traditional and new. In the lounge and bar are carpeted and stone-flagged floors, blackened beams, log fires and plush seating. In the kitchen is a traditional British approach, all seasonal menus and chalkboard specials featuring fresh local ingredients – game and wild mushroom terrine, salmon with tomato and basil risotto, steak and ale pie, blackcurrant and cinnamon pavlova – as well as hearty sandwiches and Sunday lunchtime roasts. Drinkers can sample Northumbrian brews, or choose from a well-balanced list of wines. Three sumptuous bedrooms range from the small and cosy French room with painted furniture, to the large and striking suite with a super king-size bed, a stylish leather seating area, top-notch electronic wizardry and a swish bathroom with a walk-in shower. Bliss.

Price	£90-£130. Singles from £55.
Rooms	3 doubles.
Meals	Lunch & dinner from £12. Bar meals from £6.
Closed	Open all day.
Directions	On B6346 towards Wooler, 7 miles north-west of Alnwick.

George & Mary Elliott
The Tankerville Arms
15 The Village, Eglingham,
Alnwick NE66 2TX
Tel +44 (0)1665 578444
Web www.tankervillearms.com

The Pheasant Inn
Stannersburn

A super little inn run with an instinctive understanding of its traditions. The stone walls carry old photos of the community: from colliery to smithy, a record of its past. The bars are wonderful: brass beer taps glow, anything wooden has been polished to perfection and the clock above the fire keeps perfect time. The house ales are expertly kept – Timothy Taylor's, Wylam Gold Tankard – and Robin cooks with relish, nothing too fancy, but more than enough to keep a smile on your face: slow-roasted Northumbrian lamb; fish simply grilled, no chips; brioche and marmalade bread and butter pudding. As for Sunday lunch, it was once voted one of the best in the North. Bedrooms in the old hay barn are simple and tidy, not grand but cosy and newly refurbished (most with flat-screen TVs) and you'll get a piping hot breakfast the next morning – accompanied maybe by a view of the sheepdogs bringing the flock in for shearing. This is the glorious Northumberland National Park – no traffic jams, no rush – and don't miss the sculpture at Kielder. Then hire bikes and cycle round the lake, or saddle up on a pony and take to the hills.

Price	£90-£100. Singles £50-£65. Half-board from £70 p.p.
Rooms	8: 4 doubles, 3 twins, 1 family room.
Meals	Bar meals from £8.95. Dinner, 3 courses, £18-£22.
Closed	3pm-6.30pm (7pm Sun). Mon & Tues Nov-Mar.
Directions	From Bellingham follow signs west to Kielder Water & Falstone for 9 miles. Hotel on left, 1 mile short of Kielder Water.

Walter, Irene & Robin Kershaw
The Pheasant Inn
Stannersburn,
Hexham NE48 1DD

Tel	+44 (0)1434 240382
Web	www.thepheasantinn.com

Battlesteads Hotel

Wark

In the land of castles, stone circles and fortified towers is Battlesteads, an old inn given a fresh lease of life by owners who aim to go as 'green' as possible. The boiler burns wood chips from local sustainable forestry, a poly-tunnel produces the salads, the waste composting involves the local school; no wonder the Slades have won a bevy of awards including Considerate Hotel of the Year and a Green Tourism gold. Enter a large, cosy, low-beamed and panelled bar with a wood-burning stove and local cask ales on hand pump. A step further and you find a spacious dining area: leather chairs at dark wood tables and a conservatory dining room that reaches into a sunny walled garden. The menus show a commitment to sourcing locally and the food is flavoursome. The Northumbrian fillet steak with Cumbrian blue cheese is meltingly tender, specials like hake with leek fondue and spiced pea purée are scrummy. Exemplary is the housekeeping so bedrooms are spotless – and spacious, carpeted and comfortable. The newest are mini-suites, and there's wheelchair access on the ground floor. Hadrian's Wall is marvellously close.

Price	£105-£135. Singles £60-£85.
Rooms	17: 16 twins/doubles, 1 single.
Meals	Lunch & dinner from £7.95. Sunday lunch, 3 courses, £14.50.
Closed	Open all day.
Directions	From A69 at Hexham, A6079 to Chollerford, then A6320 for Bellingham; Wark is halfway.

Richard & Dee Slade
Battlesteads Hotel
Wark, Hexham NE48 3LS
Tel +44 (0)1434 230209
Web www.battlesteads.com

The Duke of Wellington
Newton

The village inn has been transformed. Now, at the back, is a generous L-shaped space for diners: exposed stone walls and sleek wooden floors keep things rural, white paintwork, crisp curtains and immaculate furniture add style, and French windows open to a big, sheltered, south-facing terrace with views across the valley. But it's still a pub at the front, with its smart stone-flagged bar, glowing log-burner and good old English darts. As for the food, expect traditional British comfort food from seasonal produce: slow-cooked pork shoulder with sage and onion boulangère potatoes, locally produced sausages with mustard mash. Food-lovers come for roast cod fillet with smoked haddock brandade; crispy parma ham and leek velouté; roast duck breast with butter roasted roots, fondant potato and wholegrain mustard; families can tuck into roast sirloin of Northumbrian beef – "served pink" – on Sundays. Bedrooms excel; nothing has been overlooked. Enjoy top beds and bed linen, beams, baths and skylights with remote controls, and scatter rugs on polished wood floors. Only the best for innkeeper Rob Harris.

Price	£95-£125.
Rooms	7: 6 doubles, 1 twin.
Meals	Lunch & dinner from £9.95. Sunday lunch £11.95.
Closed	Open all day.
Directions	Newton is signposted off A69 between Newcastle and Hexham, 3 miles east of Corbridge.

Rob Harris
The Duke of Wellington
Newton, Corbridge NE43 7UL
Tel +44 (0)1661 844446
Web www.thedukeofwellingtoninn.co.uk

The Feathers Inn
Hedley on the Hill

Helen and Rhian have worked hard to develop the Feathers' reputation as a destination for good food, yet this pub keeps its old-fashioned pubby feel. It is a rare treat west of Newcastle to find such an authentic little place. In the two bars are old beams, exposed stone, simple furnishings, open fires and a cottagey feel; you're as much at home browsing the papers here as enjoying a fireside chat. Beer is excellent, with four cask beers from local or microbreweries; wines are taken as seriously. The delicious food – grilled mackerel with grain mustard butter and crispy shallots, black pudding stuffed local rabbit with cider cream sauce, wild cherry and kirsch Bakewell tart – is cooked with skill and passion by Rhian from locally sourced produce, she'll even let you in to the secrets of some of her recipes! A star in the making.

Meals	Lunch £9-£12. Dinner £11-£18. Sunday lunch, 3 courses, £20.
Closed	Mon lunch (except bank hols).
Directions	From Newcastle cross at Scotswood Bridge; take A695 through Balydon towards Prudhoe. B6315 signed Greenside; right in Greenside towards Chopwell along lead road. Continue to village of Hedley.

Helen Greer & Rhian Cradock
The Feathers Inn
Hedley on the Hill,
Stocksfield NE43 7SW
Tel +44 (0)1661 843607
Web www.thefeathers.net

Entry 417 Map 12

Northumberland

Rat Inn
Anick

Tucked into the south-facing hillside, overlooking the Tyne Valley, this hard-to-find old drovers' inn has an irresistible appeal. The bar is cosy, with gleaming dark oak, flagged floor, simple tables and chairs, a roaring fire: sup a pint of something local or a good glass of wine while you toy with the idea of nibbles or a sandwich (try honey roast ham and pease pudding) to appease your rumbling tum. Those who have yomped heartily to get here may be hungrier, so look to the blackboard and its excellent, mostly regional delights: roast Northumberland rib of beef with watercress and golden chips for two is delicious, and maybe rice pudding afterwards. The sun room has grand views of the spectacular valley, and on warm days you can spill out into the little garden with its benches and pretty shrubs.

Meals	Lunch & dinner £8.95-£18.95. Bar meals from £1.95. Sunday lunch £8.95.
Closed	3pm-6pm (Mon). Open all day Tues-Sun.
Directions	Off A69 between Corbridge & Hexham, 2 miles east of Hexham.

Phil Mason & Karen Errington
Rat Inn
Anick,
Hexham NE46 4LN
Tel +44 (0)1434 602814
Web www.theratinn.com

Entry 418 Map 12

The Angel
Corbridge

Even older than Hadrian's Wall, quaint Corbridge is a pretty place with the 17th-century Angel, full of history and character, at its heart. Step straight into the splendid panelled lounge, cosy with its leather armchairs, heavy drapes, big open fire and newspapers to browse. Off to the left, another more modern lounge with deep sofas; to the right, the bar, a big room simply decorated in brasserie style with a bright and contemporary feel. To the rear, the oak-beamed dining room opens onto a sun-trap courtyard. Five cask beers are available and the menu announces chorizo and black pudding risotto and navarin of lamb as well as more traditional dishes – lamb's liver with bacon and champ, and the Angel's legendary Yorkshire puddings. A comfortable stopover on the long journey from north to south.

Meals	Lunch & dinner £9.95-£16.95.
Closed	Open all day.
Directions	In Corbridge, 2 miles off A69.

John Gibson
The Angel
Main Street,
Corbridge NE45 5LA

Tel +44 (0)1434 632119
Web www.theangelofcorbridge.com

Entry 419 Map 12

Queens Head Inn
Great Whittington

A warm refuge in a wild country of moors, sheep and vast skies. The mellow bar is charming, its 1930s hunting mural satisfactorily yellowed by open fires. Gleaming beer engines disperse High House Farm Brewery ale from down the road; hunting prints hint at local interests; a background tape plays. Toast your toes from the carved oak settle before the fire, then up steps to a traditional lounge and another log-filled grate for those bitter Northumbrian days. Claire Murray greets all who enter from the cold, staff are still gently charming and people come for the food; chef Steven Murran uses the best available produce, including local beef and lamb. Daily menus may include seared red mullet with coriander and lime dressing, crisp pork belly with apple and cider jus, and dark chocolate steamed pudding.

Meals	Lunch & dinner £8.95-£15.50. Bar meals £7.95-£15.50.
Closed	3pm-5.30pm. Open all day Fri-Sun (closes 10.30pm Sun).
Directions	Off B6318, 4 miles north of Corbridge.

Claire Murray
Queens Head Inn
Great Whittington,
Newcastle-upon-Tyne NE19 2HP

Tel +44 (0)1434 672267

Entry 420 Map 12

Barrasford Arms
Barrasford

Chef/landlord Tony Binks is slowly upgrading this substantial inn with a sheltered garden close to Hadrian's Wall. Expect a mix of locals (the marrow club meet here) and a robust atmosphere, with beers from nearby High House Farm and Allendale Breweries on hand pump. The bar has a high ceiling, deep velour upholstery, various stuffed animals and antlers, local photographs and dark varnished wood. Tony's passion for real food is evident: each week he buys a rare-breed pig locally; the shoulder for sausages and the legs for Sunday lunch (with sublime crackling) – even the pickled onions and eggs are local. Try chilli beetroot risotto with a glass of spicy Primitivo del Tarantino Masseria dei Trullan. You eat in one of three dining rooms, popular with farmers and fishermen; you are a stone's throw from the rushing north Tyne.

Meals	Lunch £5-£9.50. Dinner £9.50-£16.50. Sunday lunch £14 & £16.50. Not Sunday eve.
Closed	2.30pm-6pm & Mon lunch.
Directions	5 miles north of Hexham, signposted off A6079.

Tony Binks
Barrasford Arms
Barrasford,
Hexham NE48 4AA

Tel +44 (0)1434 681237
Web www.barrasfordarms.co.uk

Entry 421 Map 14

Northumberland

The Ship Inn
Low Newton-by-the-Sea

An authentic coastal inn with tongue and groove boarding, old settles, scrubbed tables and a solid-fuel stove. Step in and step back a hundred years. Landlady Christine Forsyth fell in love with the simplicity of the place and gives you provender to match. The tip-top home-brewed beer (Dolly Daydream, Sandcastles at Dawn) and fairtrade coffee and chocolate blend with a menu built around the best local produce – simple, fresh, satisfying. Local hand-picked crab rolls, lobster from over the way, Craster kippers from two miles down the coast, ploughman's with local unpasteurised cheddar and Turnbulls free-range ham. In the evenings there's often a choice (venison, smoked haddock, sirloin steak) but do book first. Park on a compulsory plot back from the beach and take the short walk to the sand, green and pub. Worth every step.

Meals	Lunch & dinner £7-£22.
Closed	See website for details.
Directions	From Alnwick B1340 for Seahouses for 8 miles to crossroads; straight over, follow signs.

Christine Forsyth
The Ship Inn, The Square,
Low Newton-by-the-Sea,
Alnwick NE66 3EL

Tel +44 (0)1665 576262
Web www.shipinnnewton.co.uk

Entry 422 Map 14

The Olde Ship
Seahouses

The Glen dynasty has been at the helm of this nautical gem for a century and their enthusiasm for this coastal gem remains undimmed. The inn sparkles with maritime memorabilia to remind you of Seahouses' fine heritage and the days when Grace Darling rowed through huge seas to rescue stricken souls. Settle into the atmospheric main bar by the glowing fire with a decent pint – there are eight ales to choose from – and gaze across the harbour to the Farne Islands; later, take the ferry. In the smaller 'cabin' bar you can get stuck into the likes of ham hock terrine, chicken and mushroom casserole, fish chowder and bosun's fish stew, ginger trifle... and coffee and mints in the lounge. The place positively creaks with history – retreat here after a bracing coastal walk to Bamburgh Castle.

Meals	Lunch from £8. Bar meals & dinner from £10. Sunday lunch, 3 courses, £10.50.
Closed	Open all day.
Directions	B1340 off A1 8 miles north of Alnwick; inn above harbour.

A & J Glen, D Swan & J Glen
The Olde Ship
7-9 Main Street,
Seahouses NE68 7RD
Tel +44 (0)1665 720200
Web www.seahouses.co.uk

Entry 423 Map 14

Martin's Arms
Colston Bassett

An Elizabethan farmhouse that became an ale house around 1700, and an inn 100 years later. Today it is a deeply civilised pub. The front room exudes so much country-house charm – scatter cushions on sofas and settles, crackling logs in Jacobean fireplaces, 18th-century prints – that the bar seems almost an intrusion. Fresh, seasonal menus change daily. Bar snacks include special sandwiches and splendid ploughman's lunches with Colston Bassett stilton from the dairy up the road (do visit). In the restaurant, highlights include Park Farm Estate game shot by Salvatore, classic jugged hare, turbot with chorizo and pea risotto, and Sunday roast beef. Polish it all off with warm Bakewell tart with cinnamon anglaise. Behind the bar is an impressive range of well-kept real ales, cognacs, wines and malts from Adnams. Superb.

Meals	Lunch £5.95-£13.50; dinner £16.50-£24.95.
Closed	3pm-6pm in winter.
Directions	Off A46, east of Nottingham. Take Owthorpe turning.

Lynne Strafford Bryan
& Salvatore Inguanta
Martin's Arms, School Lane,
Colston Bassett, Nottingham NG12 3FD
Tel +44 (0)1949 81361
Web www.themartinsarms.co.uk

Entry 424 Map 9

The Prince Rupert
Newark

Now sympathetically restored, this 15th-century town-centre local creaks with history and has a deliciously pubby atmosphere inside. It's just the kind of place you hope to chance upon – not grand, not scruffy, just right, where locals pile in for pints of locally sourced ales (as much thought goes into the beers here as the wines). The entrance opens to a series of small rooms where, in among dark beams and polished wood, warmth and cosiness emanate from an open fire and maybe a spot snug enough for two. But upstairs is where the biggest treat lies: two rooms revealing the full glory of this ancient building, all beamed ceilings, timbered walls and an ancient skylight exposed during the renovation. The regularly changing menu reveals further simple enticements: stone-baked pizzas; ham, eggs and sauté potatoes; beef lasagne.

Meals	Lunch & dinner from £6.95. Not Sunday.
Closed	Open all day.
Directions	Centre of Newark, walking distance from castle and market square.

Tony & Heidi Yale
The Prince Rupert
46 Stodman Street,
Newark NG24 1AW

Tel +44 (0)1636 918121
Web www.theprincerupert.co.uk

Entry 425 Map 9

Nottinghamshire

Caunton Beck
Caunton

Having hatched the successful Wig & Mitre in Lincoln, the Hopes looked for a rural equivalent and found one in Caunton. The pub was lovingly reconstructed from the skeleton of the 16th-century Hole Arms and then renamed. A decade on and it is a hugely popular pub-restaurant, opening at 8am for breakfast – orange juice, espresso, scrambled eggs. Later, there are sandwiches, mussels with pickled ginger and coriander laksa and pot-roasted guinea fowl; the puddings are fabulous. It's all very relaxed and civilised, the sort of place where newspapers and magazines take precedence over piped music and electronic wizardry. Come for country chairs at scrubbed pine tables, rag-rolled walls and a fire in winter, parasols on the terrace in summer. Well-managed ales are on hand pump, and the village is pretty.

Meals	Lunch & dinner £9.50–£19.95.
Closed	Open all day.
Directions	6 miles NW of Newark past sugar factory on A616.

Michael & Valerie Hope
Caunton Beck
Main Street, Caunton,
Newark NG23 6AB

Tel +44 (0)1636 636793
Web www.wigandmitre.com

Entry 426 Map 9

The Full Moon
Morton

Determination and innovation have created wonders at the Full Moon – thanks to landlords William and Rebecca. This red-brick, sleepy-Morton pub has become the village hub. They do takeaway fish and chips, breakfast from 10am, have a Sunday Roast Club for locals and run the Nippie Chippie, a local-events fish and chip van; there's even an annual Scarecrow Trail with a fish and chip supper for every entrant. Families flock (note the toys, the garden play equipment, the fresh children's menu), while foodies beat a path for delicious local ingredients; try beef and ale pie, monkfish in pancetta, apple and blackberry crumble. The cosy, smartly updated interior combines exposed old beams and brick walls with soothing colours and an eclectic mix of reclaimed tables and chairs. A great little find – you can even get married here.

Meals	Lunch £5.50-£12. Dinner £11-£18.50. Sunday lunch, 2 course, £16.
Closed	Open all day.
Directions	Follow signs for Fiskerton off A612 south east of Southwell, then Morton & pub signs; in village centre.

Community pub

William & Rebecca White
The Full Moon
Main Street, Morton,
Southwell NG25 0UT

Tel +44 (0)1636 830251
Web www.thefullmoonmorton.co.uk

Entry 427 Map 9

Nottinghamshire

The Victoria
Beeston

A large picture of Queen Victoria rules the main bar of this unpretentious and bustling city-suburb pub. It's an ex-Victorian railway hotel with bags of character, and its awesome raft of ales, wines by the glass and malt whiskies pulls in a crowd. The civilised main bar, with fire, newspapers on racks and etched windows, sets the tone for the other rooms, all plainly painted in magnolia with woodblock flooring and scrubbed dark-wood or brass-topped tables. Blackboards give the food and booze headlines. You get Sicilian pork, cottage pie and veggie dishes to delight even non-vegetarians (pasta with goat's cheese and rocket pesto). At the back, there's a heated marquee area for cooler summer nights; dine as the trains go by. Service is efficient and friendly. Try to catch the summer festival of ale, food and music.

Meals	Lunch & dinner £7.50-£12.95.
Closed	Open all day.
Directions	Off A6005 at the bottom of Dovecote Lane. Follow signs to Beeston station.

Neil Kelso & Graham Smith
The Victoria
85 Dovecote Lane, Beeston,
Nottingham NG9 1JG

Tel +44 (0)1159 254049
Web www.victoriabeeston.co.uk

Entry 428 Map 8

The Kingham Plough

Kingham

Overlooking a pretty green, the perfect Cotswold pub. What's more, the food is exemplary modern British and much of what you eat comes from within ten miles. Scan the chalkboards if you're after a snack: a hand-raised pork pie with chutney, perhaps, simple and delicious with a pint of Hook Norton or a glass of Weston's pear cider. Up a few steps and you're into the beamed and vaulted dining area, for rustic platefuls of warm pork belly and watercress salad, slow-cooked haunch of venison with port and chestnut sauce, spicy pears poached in mulled wine. Chef-patron Emily Watkins, once sous-chef at the Fat Duck, is another young cook who has swapped the glamour of Michelin stars for her own kitchen in the country – "come here for the gold standard", says food critic A A Gill. Everything is done with simplicity and integrity and that includes the interior of slate, brick and wood floors, exposed stone walls, beams, open fires and wooden tables. Bedrooms (four large, three small) are as comfy as can be – in one is a magnificent claw-foot bath – while white linen, digital screens and homemade biscuits add to the treats.

Price	£90-£130. Singles from £75.
Rooms	7 twins/doubles.
Meals	Lunch from £15. Bar meals from £5. Dinner, 3 courses, about £30. Sunday lunch from £17.
Closed	Open all day.
Directions	In village, off B4450, between Chipping Norton & Stow-on-the-Wold.

Emily Watkins & Miles Lampson
The Kingham Plough
The Green, Kingham,
Chipping Norton OX7 6YD
Tel +44 (0)1608 658327
Web www.thekinghamplough.co.uk

Kings Arms Hotel
Woodstock

Standing proud in historic Woodstock – estate village to Blenheim Palace, one of the country's architectural gems – is the Kings Arms, a refuge from town bustle. David and Sara's passion for this Georgian building has seen it restored to former glory; old and new combine as airy open-plan interiors drift from one room to another. Tradition can be found downstairs in the classic bar – all boarded floors and leather banquettes – then it's through to the chic, atrium-style dining room with chequered floor, open fire, high-backed leather chairs and huge gilded mirrors. Equally up-to-date are the menus, a typical meal reeling in scallops with pork belly and parsnip purée, pot-roasted leg of lamb, ginger brûlée with mulled plums. Lovely bedrooms of all sizes ramble over two floors and have a cosy, contemporary feel following gentle refurbishment. Be spoiled by solid-wood beds with down duvets and richly coloured throws, leather bucket chairs, modern artwork and new tiled bathrooms featuring Molton Brown potions. The staff are great and the locals love it.

Price	£140-£150. Singles from £75. No under 12's overnight.
Rooms	15: 14 doubles, 1 twin.
Meals	Lunch from £8.75. Dinner, 3 courses, about £30.
Closed	Open all day.
Directions	In Woodstock on A44 at corner of Market Street in town centre.

David & Sara Sykes
Kings Arms Hotel
19 Market Street,
Woodstock OX20 1SU
Tel +44 (0)1993 813636
Web www.kingshotelwoodstock.co.uk

The Kings Head Inn
Bledington

About as Doctor Dolittle-esque as it gets. Achingly pretty Cotswold stone cottages around a village green with quacking ducks, a pond and a perfect pub with a cobbled courtyard. Archie is young, affable and charming with locals and guests, but Nic is his greatest asset – a milliner, she has done up the bedrooms and they look fabulous. All are different, most have a stunning view, some family furniture mixed in with 'bits' she's picked up, painted wood, great colours and lush fabrics. The bar is lively – not with music but with talk – so choose rooms over the courtyard if you prefer a quiet evening. The pretty flagstoned dining room (exposed stone walls, Farrow & Ball paints, pale wood tables) is inviting, there are lovely unpompous touches like jugs of cow parsley in the loo, and you can lunch by the fire in the bar – on devilled kidneys, sausage and mash, local Dexter beef and Guinness pie. There's a brilliant new chef and they do homemade puds and serious cheeses, too, and breakfasts are huge! Loads to do round these parts: antiques in Stow, walking and riding in gorgeous countryside, even a music festival in June.

Price	£90-£125. Singles from £70.
Rooms	12: 10 doubles, 2 twins/doubles.
Meals	Lunch from £7.50. Bar meals from £5. Dinner from £9.50. Sunday lunch, 3 courses, £30.
Closed	Open all day.
Directions	East out of Stow-on-the-Wold on A436, then right onto B4450 for Bledington. Pub in village on green.

Archie & Nicola Orr-Ewing
The Kings Head Inn
The Green, Bledington,
Chipping Norton OX7 6XQ

Tel +44 (0)1608 658365
Web www.kingsheadinn.net

The Feathered Nest Country Inn
Nether Westcote

The village is tiny, the view is fantastic, the bar is lively, the rooms are a treat. This 300-year-old malthouse recently had a facelift and now shines. Interiors mix all the old originals – stone walls, timber frames, beamed ceilings, open fires – with a contemporary, rustic style. The net result is an extremely attractive country inn, one of the best in the south. Downstairs, one room flows into another. You get beautiful bay windows, roaring fires, saddled bar stools, green leather armchairs. Everywhere you go something lovely catches the eye, not least the view – the best in the Cotswolds; it will draw you to the terrace where your eyes drift off over quilted fields to a distant ridge. There are beds of lavender, swathes of lawn, a vegetable garden that serves the kitchen. Bedrooms upstairs are gorgeous. One is enormous, two have the view, beds are dressed in crisp linen. Most have power showers, one has a claw-foot bath, all have robes. There are coffee machines and iPod docks, too. Brilliant food waits downstairs: Old Spot terrine, Fairford chicken, rhubarb and champagne jelly.

Price	£130-£165. Suite £180.
Rooms	4: 1 double, 1 twin, 1 family, 1 suite.
Meals	Lunch & dinner £6.50-£30. Not Sun eves.
Closed	Monday (except bank hols).
Directions	North from Burford on A424 for Stow-on-the-Wold. After 4 miles right for Nether Westcote. In village.

Tony & Amanda Timmer
The Feathered Nest Country Inn
Nether Westcote,
Chipping Norton OX7 6SD
Tel +44 (0)1993 833030
Web www.thefeatherednestinn.co.uk

The Swan
Swinbrook

This ancient pub sits in glorious country with the river Windrush passing yards from the front door and a cricket pitch waiting beyond. It started life as a water mill and stands on the Devonshire estate (the Duchess advised on its restoration). Outside, wisteria wanders along stone walls and creepers blush red in the autumn sun. Interiors come laden with period charm: beautiful windows, open fires, warm colours, the odd beam. Over the years thirsty feet have worn grooves into 400-year-old flagstones, so follow in their footsteps and stop for a pint of Hook Norton at the bar, then eat from a seasonal menu that brims with local produce: deep-fried Windrush goat's cheese, Foxbury Farm chargrilled steak, rich chocolate tart with orange sorbet. Fires roar in winter while doors in the conservatory restaurant open onto a pretty garden in good weather. Bedrooms in the old forge are the most recent addition. Expect 15th-century walls and 21st-century interior design. You get pastel colours to soak up the light, smart white linen on comfy beds and a pink chaise longue in the suite.

Price	£120-£180. Singles from £70.
Rooms	6: 4 doubles, 1 twin, 1 suite.
Meals	Lunch & bar meals from £7.50. Dinner from £12. Sunday lunch, 3 courses, £30.
Closed	Open all day.
Directions	West from Oxford on A40 for Cheltenham/Burford. Past Witney and village signed right at 1st r'bout.

Archie & Nicola Orr-Ewing
The Swan
Swinbrook,
Burford OX18 4DY
Tel +44 (0)1993 823339
Web www.theswanswinbrook.co.uk

Old Swan
Minster Lovell

Having transformed Babbacombe Beach's Cary Arms into a chic coastal bolthole, owner Lana de Savary has woven her understated magic at this 15th-century beauty, a half-timbered riverside inn of great charm. In the rambling bar and the residents' snug are gnarled beams and timbers, bright kilims and stone-flagged floors, and crisp checked armchairs by big beautiful fireplaces – aromatic with logs in winter. In perfect sympathy with the mood, traditional British food is cooked with a modern approach; ingredients are the best and the vegetables are home-grown. Try ham hock terrine, bream with tiger prawn ravioli, rib-eye steak with horseradish mayonnaise... and for pud, old-fashioned Eton mess. Upstairs, wonky floors lead to stunning bedrooms that combine solid darkwood antiques with every modern comfort – laundered linen and fine down, big beds, cafetières of coffee, decanters of sloe gin, bathrobes in lovely bathrooms. The rooms in the modern Minster Mill across the road are smaller and more contemporary, but overlook gorgeous gardens. Heaven in the Cotswolds, and Oxford and Burford close.

Price	£160-£325.
Rooms	16: 15 doubles, 1 suite.
Meals	Lunch from £8.25. Bar meals from £8.25. Dinner from £13.95. Sunday lunch, 3 courses, £30.
Closed	3pm-6.30pm.
Directions	Minster Lovell is signed off A40 between Oxford and Burford.

Shelley Pearse
Old Swan
Old Minster Lovell, Minster Lovell,
Witney OX29 0RN
Tel +44 (0)1993 774441
Web www.oldswanandminstermill.com

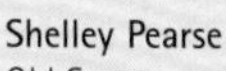

The Fleece

Witney

If you need to be in Oxford, staying at the Fleece is an attractive alternative (a cheaper one, too!). This is the first outpost of what has become the hugely successful Peach Pub Company. Expect a sparkling gastropub interior – wooden floors, plum walls, squashy sofas, low tables – and continental opening hours that start with coffee and bacon sarnies at 8.30am. It's a humdinger of a place, and moving the bar to the front has worked wonders, drawing in casual drinkers for pints of Greene King. Thumbs up too for the regularly changing wine list at sensible prices, and for the all-day sandwiches, salads and deli-board menu. Starters of cheese, charcuterie, fish, olive tapenade, marinated chillies, and delicious dishes like braised shoulder of lamb with roasted winter roots are ferried to packed tables by an enthusiastic and attentive staff. Crisp modern bedrooms are big enough to hold an armchair or two and beds are extremely comfortable; if you fancy peace and quiet, take a room at the front, overlooking Witney's church and green. Breakfasts set you up for Cotswolds' forays and are brilliant.

Price	£80-£100.
Rooms	10: 8 doubles, 1 twin, 1 family room.
Meals	Lunch from £7. Bar meals from £5. Dinner from £11. Sunday lunch £13.50.
Closed	Open all day.
Directions	Witney is off A40 between Oxford and Burford; pub on green, near church.

Helen Sprason
The Fleece
11 Church Green,
Witney OX28 4AZ

Tel +44 (0)1993 892270
Web www.fleecewitney.co.uk

The Trout at Tadpole Bridge

Buckland Marsh

A 17th-century Cotswold inn on the banks of the Thames, so pick up a pint, drift into the garden and watch life float by. The Trout is a drinking fisherman's paradise, walls are busy with bendy rods, children are liked and dogs can doze in the flagstoned bars. The downstairs is open plan and timber-framed, there are gilt mirrors and logs piled high in alcoves. Gareth and Helen have cast their fairy dust into every corner: super bedrooms, fabulous modern food (fish chowder, Kelmscott pork belly with cider jus, pear frangipane tart), a relaxed style. Bedrooms at the back are away from the crowd and three open onto a small courtyard – but you may prefer to stay put in your room and indulge in funky fabrics, monsoon showers (one room has a claw-foot bath), DVD players, a library of films. Sleigh beds, brass beds, upholstered armchairs… one even has a roof terrace. You can watch boats pass from the breakfast table, feast on local sausages, tuck into homemade marmalade courtesy of Helen's mum. Food is as local as possible, and there are maps for walkers to keep you thin. Bliss!

Price	£130. Suite £160. Singles from £85.
Rooms	6: 2 doubles, 3 twins/doubles, 1 suite.
Meals	Lunch & dinner £10.95-£19. Sunday lunch from £11.95.
Closed	3.30pm-6pm (Sat & Sun).
Directions	A420 southwest from Oxford for Swindon. After 13 miles right for Tadpole Bridge. Pub on right by bridge.

Gareth & Helen Pugh
The Trout at Tadpole Bridge
Buckland Marsh,
Faringdon SN7 8RF

Tel	+44 (0)1367 870382
Web	www.trout-inn.co.uk

The Lamb at Buckland

Buckland

Follow the signs through picture-perfect Buckland to the 18th-century Lamb, a Cotswold-stone building tucked into a cul-de-sac on a tranquil estate village. The combined talents and enthusiasms of Shelley, chef Richard and business partner Chris have restored this old pub's fortunes. Step into the simple, spruced up bar to find crackling logs, low beams, fat candles, old dining tables and leather wing chairs – and, behind the bar, local Loose Canon ales and homemade sloe gin. Beyond is the more refined dining room, where modern seasonal menus champion local suppliers (Kelmscott pork, home-grown vegetables, game from Chris's farm). Tuck into ham hock terrine with homemade piccalilli, hearty braised ox cheek with red wine jus, chocolate and walnut brownie with cream. Choose from the great value week day set menu, or fish and chips to take away, and stay: this trio of bedrooms is delightful. Find crisp cotton, down duvets and colourful throws, a mix of pine and painted furniture, iPod-radios, and bathrooms fresh and simple. The Thames Path, William Morris's Kelmscott Manor and Oxford are close by.

Price	£80-£90.
Rooms	3 doubles.
Meals	Lunch from £9.50. Bar meals from £6. Dinner from £12.95. Sunday lunch, 3 courses, from £12.
Closed	3pm-6pm. Sun eves & all day Mon (except bank hols lunch)
Directions	Off A420 midway between Oxford & Swindon, 3 miles east of Faringdon.

Chris Green, Richard & Shelley Terry
The Lamb at Buckland
Lamb Lane, Buckland,
Faringdon SN7 8QN

Tel +44 (0)1367 870484
Web www.lambatbuckland.co.uk

The Fat Fox Inn
Watlington

A stone's throw from the big smoke yet wonderfully rural. You are on the edge of the Chiltern Hills, red kites wheel above beech woods and the Ridgeway runs through historic Watlington. The 17th-century building has been part pub, butchers, bakery and shop in its day but is now an inn to the core. The bronze buddha on the bar gazes serenely over pumps with Brakspear Bitter and Oxford Gold, the carpeted bar is cosy and simple, there's a wood-burner, sofas and a piano in the lobby and an elegant separate dining room with oriental rugs, panelling, calm terracotta walls and a medley of tables and chairs. The cassoulet of pork shoulder, goose and smoked Red Lion farm shop sausage would have a Frenchman singing 'la Marseillaise': follow it with apple clafoutis, chocolate pot and chantilly cream – a tribute to chef Leon Bugler and quite simply divine. Staff and owner are delightful and the whole place hums along on this team's super-friendly and engaging manner. Set well behind the bustle in several old barns are a variety of bedrooms – some with signature beds and trappings, all with antiques, beams and small tidy bathrooms.

Price	£79-£109.
Rooms	9: 5 doubles, 4 twins.
Meals	Lunch from £12. Bar meals from £5. Dinner from £27. Sunday lunch, 2-3 courses, £20-£25.
Closed	Open all day.
Directions	Sent on booking.

John Riddell
The Fat Fox Inn
13 Shirburn Street,
Watlington OX49 5BU

Tel +44 (0)1491 613040
Web www.thefatfoxinn.co.uk

The Boar's Head
Ardington

A dapper estate village with a church, a pub and a post office, the pub being the home of the village cricket club. It's a civilised place populated by locals and barbour-clad walkers who come for open fires, the daily papers, local ales, upmarket food. Sunday lunch can roll on to six and the bar is lively most evenings, making it the smart spruce hub of this small community. Gilt mirrors and old oils hang on the walls. There are big oak tables in the restaurant and doors onto a terrace for al fresco summer suppers. And the bedrooms upstairs are unmistakably smart. The small double has a beamed ceiling, the big double comes with a claw-foot bath, the suite has a sofa for kids and views over the village. All have good beds, crisp linen and piles of cushions. Much enthusiasm in the kitchen and the food is popular as a result. Everything is homemade: bread, pasta, pastries, ice cream... try scallops with black pudding and roasted foie gras, sea bass with mussels and girolles, Tulwick lamb with garlic confit and mustard sauce, and bread, butter and vanilla pudding.

Price	£95-£140. Singles £85-£95. Check in before 3pm or after 6pm by arrangement.
Rooms	3: 2 doubles, 1 suite.
Meals	Lunch & dinner £13.95-£16.95. Bar meals £7.95-£14.95. Sunday lunch, 3 courses, £23.50.
Closed	3pm-6.30pm (7pm Sun).
Directions	A417 west from Didcot for Wantage. Through West Hendred & turn left to Ardington. In village, left by bus stop; on left.

Bruce & Kay Buchan
The Boar's Head
Church Street, Ardington,
Wantage OX12 8QA

Tel	+44 (0)1235 833254
Web	www.boarsheadardington.co.uk

The Eyston Arms
East Hendred

The Eyston family have owned this pub at the foot of the Ridgeway since 1443! A renovation by the Daileys has brought a mix of the traditional and the new so step in to find Cotswold flagstone floors and an original water pump, fresh flowers and chunky wooden tables. It's a well-loved local, and the most regular regulars are immortalised in sketches on the dining room's papered walls. Come for happy chatter, a pint of London Pride, and first-class food. Chef Maria Jaremchuck earned her stripes here, left and has returned: the meat is properly hung for thick grilled steaks with triple-cooked chips, and rump of lamb with gratin dauphinoise, and desserts are just as good – try the lemon and saffron panna cotta. Daily specials are chalked up; ask partner Daisy Barton behind the bar for a suggestion. They look after you well here.

Meals: Lunch & dinner £11-£16.95. Sunday lunch £14.
Closed: 3pm-6pm (from 7pm Sun).
Directions: East Hendred is just off A417 between Wantage and Rowstock, 2 miles west of A34; pub in village centre.

George Dailey & Daisy Barton
The Eyston Arms
High Street, East Hendred,
Wantage OX12 8JY
Tel: +44 (0)1235 833320
Web: www.eystonarms.co.uk

Entry 440 Map 4

Oxfordshire

The Lord Nelson
Brightwell Baldwin

The back-lane setting of Brightwell Baldwin lives up to expectations: cottages tumbling down the hill, a church perched on a bank, a rambling inn festooned with flowers, flags on Trafalgar Day. The creamy façade and front veranda entice you into a civilised and charming interior, wonky beams, logs fires and cosy corners; antiques, fine old prints and Nelson memorabilia keep the eye entertained. Most come to dine and dine well you can, on scallops with lime and coriander dressing, rack of lamb with red wine sauce, and sea bass on crab mash with tomato and black olive tapenade. Retire to the snug (deep sofas, table lamps, a country-house feel) for coffee and a little doze. And there's more – Brakspear on tap, 20 wines by the glass, friendly, smiley service and a wonderful rear terrace for summer sipping.

Meals: Lunch & dinner £10.50-£18.95. Bar meals £10.
Closed: 3pm-6pm. Open all day Sun.
Directions: Village signed off B4009 between Benson & Watlington.

Roger & Carole Shippey
The Lord Nelson
Brightwell Baldwin,
Watlington OX49 5NP
Tel: +44 (0)1491 612497
Web: www.lordnelson-inn.co.uk

Entry 441 Map 4

The Crooked Billet
Stoke Row

Dick Turpin apparently courted the landlord's daughter and Kate Winslet held her wedding breakfast here. Pints of Brakspear are drawn direct from the cask (there is no bar!) and the rusticity of the place charms all who manage to find it: beams and inglenooks, old pine, walls lined with bottles and baskets of spent corks. In the larger room, red walls display old photographs and mirrors; shelves are stacked with books... by candlelight it's irresistible. It's more restaurant than pub, so the menu is modern, eclectic and long: salt and pepper squid with chilli jam, Moroccan spiced lamb rump, Bakewell tart and custard. The food is founded on well-sourced raw materials (allotment holders are encouraged!) and bolstered by a satisfying wine list. Weekly music, too, and a big garden bordering the beech woods where children can roam.

Meals	Lunch & dinner £12.50-£20.
Closed	2.30pm-7pm. Open all day Sat & Sun.
Directions	5 miles west of Henley, off B481 Reading to Nettlebed road.

Paul Clerehugh
The Crooked Billet
Newlands Lane, Stoke Row,
Henley-on-Thames RG9 5PU
Tel +44 (0)1491 681048
Web www.thecrookedbillet.co.uk

Oxfordshire

The Lamb at Satwell
Satwell

The fortunes of this 16th-century beamed cottage were revived by Chris & Nick Gross following a period of closure in 2009. Enter a gorgeously low-beamed bar: scrubbed pine tables on tiled floors, logs crackling in the grate, local ales on hand pump (try the exclusively-brewed Leaping Lamb). Arrive early to bag a seat by the fire or settle into the cosy dining room next door; be treated to Yorkshire style fish and chips or daily changing pies from the bar menu. Look to the carte for Brixham crab tart, pan-fried foie gras with spiced pears, braised ox cheeks with fondant potatoes, cauliflower purée and thyme jus. Finish with poached pears with blackberry and raspberry syrup or coconut panna cotta with lime. Don't miss the Sunday roasts. There's a secluded garden and roaming chickens, too. Close to watery Henley-on-Thames.

Meals	Lunch & dinner £4.95-£18.95. Sunday lunch, 3 courses, £21.95.
Closed	3pm-6pm. Open all day Fri-Sun.
Directions	A4130 north from Henley; 3 miles; 1st exit at r'bout near Nettlebed onto B481 to Highmoor; thro' village; 1 mile to Satwell, left at 'Shepherd's Green' sign.

Chris Smith & Nick Gross
The Lamb at Satwell
Satwell,
Henley-on-Thames RG9 4QZ
Tel +44 (0)1491 628482
Web www.thelambpub.net

The Bull & Butcher
Turville

Landlords Carlos and Joy ensure this little pub quenches the thirsts of all who come to visit one of the most bucolic film locations in Britain. The Vicar of Dibley has strutted Turville's streets, suspects from *Midsomer Murders* have propped up the bar. There's bags of atmosphere here, style too, in cream walls, latched doors, fresh flowers. It's a jolly place in which to down a pint of Brakspear's finest and indulge is some good pub food: game stew with thyme dumplings, fish and chips, sausages and mash, homemade pies. No fruit machines, no pubby paraphernalia, just fine 17th-century beams, working log fires, a unique function room, and friendly people. Get there early at weekends when Londoners descend. There's a garden to spill into and great walks through the Chiltern beech woods.

Meals	Lunch & dinner £10-£14. Bar meals £6-£10.
Closed	Open all day.
Directions	M40 junc. 5; through Ibstone; for Turville at T-junction.

Carlos Maidana & Joy Roberts
The Bull & Butcher
Turville,
Henley-on-Thames RG9 6QU
Tel +44 (0)1491 638283
Web www.thebullandbutcher.com

Entry 444 Map 4

Oxfordshire

The Frog
Skirmett

By the village lane, deep in the beautiful Hambledon valley, the spruced up 18th-century coaching inn is surrounded by open meadows and glorious walks. Head for the secluded garden, pint of Marlow Rebellion in hand, gaze across the valley and watch the red kites wheel. Or retreat inside, mingle with the walkers and the foodies, and bag a deep sofa by the log fire. Wood floors, warm colours, bold mirrors and an eclectic mix of tables and chairs fill the pretty dining areas. Seasonal menus feature pub classics like steak, Guinness and mushroom pie alongside chicken, tarragon and tomato risotto, and roast Hambledon Estate venison with juniper sauce. Don't miss the sticky toffee pudding – or the once-a-month pub 'shop' selling Noelle's luscious savoury pastries, cakes and chutneys.

Meals	Lunch & bar meals from £6.95. Dinner from £9.95. Not Sunday eve Nov-April.
Closed	3pm-6pm. Open all day Sun (except Sun eves in winter).
Directions	Take Hambleden road off A4155 north east of Henley and follow valley road to Skirmett.

Jim Crowe & Noelle Greene
The Frog
Skirmett,
Henley-on-Thames RG9 6TG
Tel +44 (0)1491 638996
Web www.thefrogatskirmett.co.uk

Entry 445 Map 4

The Mole Inn
Toot Baldon

The Mole Inn continues to wow Oxford foodies – it is packed most days. Expect an impeccable stone exterior, a landscaped garden and a ravishing bar. There are stripped beams and chunky walls, black leather sofas, logs in the grate and a dresser that groans with breads and olive jars. Chic rusticity proceeds into three dining areas: fat candles on blond wooden tables, thick terracotta floors and the sun angling in on a fresh plateful of beef casserole with garlic and bacon dauphinoise. Daily specials point to a menu that trawls the globe for inspiration, and whether you go for light salad and pasta bowl lunches or monkfish and king prawn stir fry with egg noodles and sweet chilli, you'll eat well. Scrumptious ice creams, British cheeses, good wines, local Hook Norton ale and polite staff complete the picture.

Meals: Lunch & dinner £12.95-£18. Bar meals £5.95-£9.95.
Closed: Open all day.
Directions: From A4074, 5 miles south of Oxford; turn at Nuneham Courtenay for Marsh Baldon & Toot Baldon. 10 minutes from junc. 7 of M40.

Gary Witchalls
The Mole Inn
Toot Baldon,
Oxford OX44 9NG
Tel +44 (0)1865 340001
Web www.moleinntootbaldon.co.uk

Entry 446 Map 8

Oxfordshire

The White Hart
Fyfield

Incredible to think that when Henry VIII came to the throne this building was already 70 years old. Stone mullioned windows, huge oak timbers and a magnificent arch-braced roof are the backdrop for oak settles, wrought-iron candle holders, white linen napkins and delicious food cooked by Mark. The menu is modern, British and changes from day to day depending upon what is fresh and seasonal: baked, caramelised garlic custard with wild mushroom toastie, roast local duck and black pudding hotpot with sprout tops and chestnuts, apple and calvados mousse with coconut praline. Suppliers are mostly local and mentioned on the menu so you can see where everything comes from. Enjoy four real ales and Cheddar valley cider, and staff who are capable and knowledgeable (they were all taken to Hook Norton to see how the beer was brewed).

Meals: Lunch £13-£20. Bar meals £6-£20. Dinner £13-£20. Sunday lunch, 3 courses, £24. Not Sunday eve.
Closed: 3pm-5.30pm & Mon all day (except bank hols). Open all day Sat & Sun.
Directions: Fyfield is just off A420 Oxford to Swindon road, 6 miles south west of Oxford; pub in village centre.

Mark & Kay Chandler
The White Hart
Main Road, Fyfield,
Abingdon OX13 5LW
Tel +44 (0)1865 390585
Web www.whitehart-fyfield.com

Entry 447 Map 8

The Magdalen Arms
Oxford

Suburban Oxford is not the most obvious setting for some of Britain's best pub food. But Anchor & Hope graduates Florence Fowler and Tony Abarno have created a hostelry worthy of foodie acclaim. Those fretting over another local hijacked for elaborate gastropubbery need not: half this pub's not inconsiderable space is cutlery free and, thanks to a billiards table, four well-kept real ales and cocktails that ooze class, drinkers will find much to like; plus a chop house-chic interior of advertising posters, scuffed wooden floor, mish mash wooden tables and bright streams of bunting – the antithesis of fine dining. Equally unpretentious is the food: gutsy, produce-led fare, as affordable as it is likeable. Knuckle down to Hereford beef with duck fat potato cake and béarnaise; braised shank of wild boar with polenta; boozy cherries and buttermilk pudding.

Meals	Lunch £15. Dinner from £25. Sunday lunch, 3 courses, £30.
Closed	Mon & Tues lunch.
Directions	A4142 from A40 or A34; A4158 towards Oxford town centre.

Florence Fowler & Tony Abarno
The Magdalen Arms
Iffley Road,
Oxford OX4 1SJ
Tel +44 (0)1865 243159

Entry 448 Map 8

The Fishes
North Hinksey

Location, location, location – The Fishes has it all. Three acres of gardens, minutes from the A34, and walking distance from the dreaming spires. It's run by Peach Pubs, the most innovative small pub group in the land; where else can you borrow a rug for the garden, order a Pimm's and a picnic basket for two and spread out by a river? Just arrive early on fine days. Order (by midweek) a family roast beef platter for the weekend, on Sunday sit down to it on the veranda. The successful Peach food formula is reproduced here: the deli board selection, the starters of sautéed squid linguini with chilli, lemon and parsley, or goat's cheese and spinach risotto, the main dishes of venison with bubble and squeak, sea bream with cider cream sauce, and sausage and mash. Greene King ales, decent wines by the glass and a passion for locally sourced produce complete this very rosy picture.

Meals	Lunch from £7. Bar meals from £5. Dinner from £11. Sunday lunch £13.50.
Closed	Open all day.
Directions	North on A34; left junction after Botley Interchange, signed to Rugby Club. From south, exit A34 at Botley & return to A34 south; then as above.

Chris Amey
The Fishes
North Hinksey,
Oxford OX2 0NA
Tel +44 (0)1865 249796
Web www.fishesoxford.co.uk

Entry 449 Map 8

The Anchor Inn
Oxford

Residential North Oxford is an unlikely setting for one of the city's best food pubs, but Jamie and Charlotte have defied the odds, and turned a somewhat unattractive Art Deco-styled building into a brilliant dining pub. Weekend walkers escape the city via the canal – the towpath's over the road – while the well-heeled folk of Walton Manor regularly drop by. In two high-ceilinged bars, each embellished with period furnishings and fireplaces, ex-Harvey Nicks chef Jamie delivers seasonal British food using fresh and local ingredients. So there's game terrine, rack of Wytham Wood Farm lamb and treacle tart with ginger cream. Wadworth ales on tap, good house wines by the glass, local book club meetings, quizzes, sport on the big screen and a 'breakfast club' for mums each Friday ensure, along with the fabulous food, the Anchor's survival.

Meals: Lunch & dinner £9.50-£16. Bar meals £4-£7.85.
Closed: Open all day.
Directions: A34 ring road north; exit Peartree r'bout, on Woodstock Road for city centre, 1.5 miles; right at Polstead Road. Pub on right.

Jamie & Charlotte King
The Anchor Inn
2 Hayfield Road, Walton Manoir,
Oxford OX2 6TT
Tel: +44 (0)1865 510282
Web: www.theanchoroxford.com

Entry 450 Map 8

Oxfordshire

The Pheasant
Brill

Perched on the hillside of Brill village, a quaint microcosm of bell ringers, cricket team and rambling society, the Pheasant has mesmerising views over five counties and a restored 17th-century windmill. In spite of the timeless setting, inside is surprisingly modern and glossy, with a slate tiled floor, invitingly puffy seating, smart carpets and pristine cream walls, partly mirrored. From inside the windmill glimpses are sadly restricted but a raised terrace of smart pine boards and wicker seats is a virtual viewing platform come summer. Three ales rotate at the bar, while food is a please-all selection of pub standards, from tiger prawns, garlic and chilli to Loch Duart salmon and tomato sauce, or Jamaican lamb curry with coconut and pepper. Functional stuff to be sure, but generously filled rolls score highly with the regulars – deservedly so.

Meals: Lunch £7-£16. Dinner £12-£16.
Closed: See website for details.
Directions: M40 to Bicester, then B4011 to Oakley and left onto Brill Road; pub in village centre.

Marilyn Glover
The Pheasant
39 Windmill Street, Brill,
Thame HP18 9TG
Tel: +44 (0)1844 239370
Web: www.thepheasant.co.uk

Entry 451 Map 8

Nut Tree Inn
Murcott

The menu reads like a Michelin-starred restaurant's – which indeed this is. But you can get bar food and a good value midweek set menu and there are pigs out the back. Imogen and Mike are friendly and fun and operate their own version of 'The Good Life', here in this idyllic whitewashed thatched pub; they grow a lot of their own food. The bar is soothing, relaxing, with its open fire, white linen, stripped oak beams, stone walls and leather chesterfields. Choose from delicious bar food (smoked salmon with scrambled eggs, artisan cheeses) or take a look at the specials board: tea-smoked wild goose with mango purée and pickled ginger salad; chopped venison steak; wild mushroom risotto; hot pistachio soufflé. There's real ale, draught cider, a long wine list and a pretty rear terrace for summer days with views over the smallholding.

Meals	Lunch & dinner £17-£27. Bar meals £5.50-£10. Sunday lunch from £15.50. Set menu, 2 courses, £18. Tasting menu £55. Not Sunday eve or Monday.
Closed	Sun eves & Mon.
Directions	Murcott 5 miles south of Bicester, signed off A41 towards Aylesbury.

Michael & Imogen North
Nut Tree Inn
Murcott,
Kidlington OX5 2RE
Tel +44 (0)1865 331253
Web www.nuttreeinn.co.uk

Entry 452 Map 8

Oxfordshire

The Oxford Arms
Kirtlington

A robust 19th-century dining pub tucked away down a lane in a village eight miles from Oxford – the coat of arms above the door shows an ox walking through a ford. Pretty windows are painted pale green grey and window boxes are coloured with geraniums. The main bar faces south, the floors are flagged and boarded, wood smoke tinges the air; the perfect place to decide what to eat while you sip a half of Hooky Bitter or something from the excellent wine list. To one side is a candlelit dining area with large tables and comfy sofas, the other is more pubby and informal with bar stools and farmhouse chairs. Wherever you decide to eat there will be the convivial rumble of chat in the background and the food is a treat: splash out on potted shrimps with toast, then confit duck leg or roast pork belly with black pudding.

Meals	Lunch from £10. Bar meals from £6.50. Dinner from £12. Sunday lunch, 3 courses, £26.
Closed	3pm-6pm. Sun eves.
Directions	On A4095 between A44 south of Woodstock & Bicester.

Bryn Jones
The Oxford Arms
Troy Lane, Kirtlington,
Kidlington OX5 3HA
Tel +44 (0)1869 350208
Web www.oxford-arms.co.uk

Entry 453 Map 8

Royal Oak
Ramsden

Blazing winter fires, piles of magazines and well-thumbed books by the inglenook make this the perfect place for a pint of real ale, so tuck into a corner filled with plump scatter cushions, or join the band of locals at the bar. Some good food can be had in the pubby bar – open-stone walls, cream and soft green windows – as well as in the extension beyond, where glass doors open to a pretty terrace with wrought-iron chairs and outdoor heaters for chilly evenings. Dishes such as confit duck with puy lentils and garlic potatoes, homemade burgers, and calves' liver with Madeira should put a smile on your face; in winter, there's lots of game. Well-behaved children and dogs are welcome, the staff are delightful, the village is a stunner and the local walks are wonderful. You won't hear a bad word said about this place.

Meals	Lunch & dinner £11-£22.95. Bar meals from £5. Sunday lunch, 3 courses, £21.95.
Closed	3pm-6.30pm.
Directions	On B4022, 3 miles north of Witney.

Jon Oldham
Royal Oak
High Street, Ramsden,
Chipping Norton OX7 3AU
Tel +44 (0)1993 868213
Web www.royaloakramsden.com

Entry 454 Map 8

Oxfordshire

The Rose & Crown
Shilton

Small, cosy, friendly and run with panache. In a mellow Cotswold stone village, the pub's setting could not be more idyllic. The 16th-century Rose & Crown holds just two rooms: the bar room itself, simple and unadorned, and a fractionally larger extension built in 1701. There's an open fire in the inglenook and a medley of kitchen tables and chairs, making the once rundown local a most atmospheric and civilised public house. Be charmed by low beams, exposed stone walls, a terracotta floor, fresh flowers, Old Hooky on tap, and good food. You'll find a happy crowd sitting down to venison terrine, roast partridge with blackberries, or good steak, ale and mushroom pie, and bread and butter pudding. This is a gorgeous, sheltered spot and there's a garden you can drift into on warm days.

Meals	Lunch £8.50-£15.50. Dinner £9-£15.50. Sunday lunch, 3 courses, £21.
Closed	3pm-6pm. Open all day Fri-Sun & bank hols.
Directions	Shilton is signed off B4020, 2 miles SE of A40 at Burford.

Martin Coldicott
The Rose & Crown
Shilton,
Burford OX18 4AB
Tel +44 (0)1993 842280
Web www.roseandcrownshilton.com

Entry 455 Map 8

The Highway Inn
Burford

You can sit out on the high street under the shade of a parasol in summer and watch the shoppers haul their bounty up the hill, but this lovely inn comes complete with a small medieval courtyard where honeysuckle and orange blossom roam. The building itself goes back to 1480, with rather lovely interiors where all the architectural gems are to hand: mind-your-head beams, nooks and stairs, ancient flags. Tally and Scott, both locals, spent their wedding night here, then returned to renovate, thus rescuing the inn from years of neglect. They have kept the mood warmly traditional so expect padded window seats, stripped boards, open fires, a good pint and hearty pub food in the bar or private dining room – fishcakes with tartare sauce, Cotswold rib-eye steak with béarnaise, apple and blackberry crumble. This is a very friendly base.

Meals	Lunch & dinner £9.95-£15.95. Bar meals from £4.50.
Closed	Open all day.
Directions	A40 west from Oxford to Burford. On right in town, halfway down hill.

Tally & Scott Nelson
The Highway Inn
117 High Street,
Burford OX18 4RG
Tel +44 (0)1993 823661
Web www.thehighwayinn.co.uk

Entry 456 Map 8

Oxfordshire

The Carpenters Arms
Fulbrook

Some pubs put a smile on your face the moment you walk in. Funky animal paintings on exposed stone walls, a red Gaggia coffee machine at a white wood bar, chunky wooden tables on reclaimed boards, assorted cushions on painted pews. And, at the far end – this is a big place – a generous hearth with a wood-burner. Order a pint of Greene King, or Staropramen from Prague, on tap for hot days. The family-run Carpenters Arms is a family-friendly roadside dining pub that serves top-quality British pub food with an awareness of seasonality: chilli squid salad, partridge with game jus and blackberry jelly, steak and ale pie with creamy mash, sticky toffee pudding. The kitchen has a light easy touch, there are good lunch deals to be had, and a huge garden at the back away, well from the road.

Meals	Lunch & dinner £11-£20. Not Sunday eve.
Closed	3pm-6.30pm. Sun from 4pm.
Directions	On A361 2 miles north of Burford.

Adrian & Bridgett Howard
The Carpenters Arms
Fulbrook Hill, Fulbrook,
Burford OX18 4BH
Tel +44 (0)1993 823275
Web www.carpentersarmsfulbrook.com

Entry 457 Map 8

Lamb Inn
Shipton-under-Wychwood

A gorgeously done-up dining pub tucked down a quiet lane in an idyllic Cotswold village. Centuries-old, with mellow stone walls under a stone-tiled roof, it draws you in to its as-immaculate beamed bar. Tracey and Paul have spruced up the stone-walled bar, injecting a horse racing theme with jockey colours and Cheltenham photos. The polished wooden floor, roaring log fire and scrubbed tables make it a fine setting for homemade food: a steak and mustard mayonnaise sandwich, a cottage pie, or something from the antipasto board. Opt for the cosy dining room at night – chunky candles, log fire in inglenook, local artwork on stone walls – for Kelmscott pork belly, a fine sirloin steak, a rhubarb crème brûlée. And there's a super terrace for a pint of real ale or one of 18 wines by the glass.

Meals	Lunch from £4.95. Bar meals from £8.95. Dinner from £10.95. Sunday lunch, 3 courses, £21.
Closed	Open all day.
Directions	In village centre, off A361 between Chipping Norton and Burford.

Tracey & Paul Hunt
Lamb Inn, High Street,
Shipton-under-Wychwood,
Chipping Norton OX7 6DQ
Tel +44 (0)1993 830465
Web www.shiptonlamb.com

Oxfordshire

The Chequers
Churchill

Eye-catching with an immaculate stone frontage, the 18th-century Chequers stands smartly on the village lane. The Goldings took it on in 2003 and months of refurbishment followed before the reincarnation was unveiled. Prepare for a dramatic, airy and open-plan interior of bare boards and pine tables, cleverly partitioned dining areas, stone walls, roaring wood-burner and stacked logs, and chunky tables topped with candles and flowers. Soaring rafters and a vast dresser racked with wine bottles create an impression in the dining extension. No music, just a buzz when busy, and excellent food – red snapper and shrimp bouillabaisse, rib-eye steak with red wine sauce, lemon and raspberry posset. Book for the crispy duck night (Thursday) and roast Sunday lunches. Upstairs are a lounge and a private dining area.

Meals	Lunch & dinner £4-£16.50.
Closed	Open all day.
Directions	Churchill on B4450 between Chipping Norton & Stow-on-the-Wold.

Peter & Assumpta Golding
The Chequers
Church Road,
Churchill,
Chipping Norton OX7 6NJ
Tel +44 (0)1608 659393

Falkland Arms
Great Tew

Five hundred years on and the logs still glow in the stone-flagged bar under a low-slung timbered ceiling that drips with tankards and jugs. Tradition runs deep: the hop is treated with reverence, ales are changed weekly, old pump clips hang from the bar and they stock tins of snuff with great names like Irish High Toast and Crumbs of Comfort. In summer Morris Men jingle in the lane outside and life spills out onto the terrace at the front and into the lovely big garden behind. Dig into a homemade burger and ploughman's in front of the fire or hop next door to the tiny beamed dining room for home-cooked delights – try Guinness-baked ham hock with leek and sweetcorn champ. It's all blissfully short on modern trappings: mobile phones meet with swift and decisive action. Perfect pub, perfect village: archetypal Cotswolds.

Meals	Lunch from £7.95. Bar meals from £4.95. Dinner from £8.95. Sunday lunch, 3 courses, £17.95.
Closed	Open all day.
Directions	North from Chipping Norton on A361, then right onto B4022, signed Great Tew. Inn by village green.

Kathryn Partridge & Richard Bennett
Falkland Arms
19-21 The Green, Great Tew,
Chipping Norton OX7 4DB
Tel +44 (0)1608 683653
Web www.falklandarms.co.uk

Entry 460 Map 8

Oxfordshire

The George at Brailes
Lower Brailes

The old coaching inn has been serving the community since the 14th century and that is still its credo, now under the eye of Bill and Charmaine. The bar is as traditional and lively as a bar can be with regular events for all to bond over, so grab a well-kept pint of Hooky and get with the gossip, enter a quiz or try a turn of dominoes. If you're here to eat, and it would be a shame not to, head to the restaurant with its great inglenook, stone mullion windows and historic wood panels. Bill has worked with Marco Pierre White and Gordon Ramsay and delivers his own take on classic dishes: try shoulder of lamb with olives, capers and rosemary jus, gratin dauphinoise and glazed carrots, or a fillet of bream with artichokes, olives and a fennel and gazpacho sauce. There's a big garden, and glorious countryside to spin off in.

Meals	Lunch & bar meals from £4. Dinner from £7. Take away available.
Closed	Open all day.
Directions	See website.

Bill & Charmaine Leadbeater
The George at Brailes
High Street, Lower Brailes,
Banbury OX15 5HN
Tel +44 (0)1608 685223
Web www.thegeorgeatbrailes.co.uk

Entry 461 Map 8

George & Dragon
Shutford

A typical Cotswold sandstone pub, overshadowed by the church, and well worth roaring down to for good food, real ale, and now a rather lively social calendar. Paul encourages darts, a quiz team and robust participation in the celebration of national days. Lean back on high oak settles and enjoy the heat from the roaring fire with its huge grate and dragons' heads made locally – here you can choose bar snacks (very good value) and try the drink the regulars like as a chaser to their Hooky bitter – Dragon's Blood (that's Navy rum, sloe and spices). The restaurant is quieter with exposed cream and brick walls, a low beamed ceiling and a toothsome British food menu: silver mullet with red onion and parsley salsa to start; confit shoulder of pork with braised savoy cabbage; and a simple lemon tart or homemade ice cream for pudding.

Meals	Lunch & dinner £9-£19. Bar meals from £3.
Closed	2.30pm-5.30pm & Mon all day (except bank hols). Open all day Sat & Sun.
Directions	Village is located off A422, 4 miles west of Banbury.

Paul Stanley
George & Dragon
Church Lane, Shutford,
Banbury OX15 6PG

Tel	+44 (0)1295 780320
Web	www.thegeorgeanddragon.com

Oxfordshire

Wykham Arms
Sibford Gower

Gordon Ramsay got his first job here. Later, under the name The Moody Cow, it lost some of its popularity; now the listed free house is a thoroughly modern inn. Having seen the Cotswold village, you'd be forgiven for expecting cushions and chintz; instead you get creams and deep reds, flagged floors and farmhouse furnishings. The menu, served through a warren of connected rooms, spills over with local and seasonal produce; flavours are strong, clean and uncomplicated. So tuck into Cornish scallops with celeriac remoulade, salmon with beetroot and marinated artichoke salad, and wild boar and apple sausages with beer mustard mash. Lots of wines by the glass, from a list that is excellent and affordable, and families and dog owners are made very welcome. For summer there's a big patio and a wooded garden.

Meals	Lunch from £10. Bar meals from £8.50. Dinner from £25. Sunday lunch, 3 courses, £20. Not Sunday eve.
Closed	3pm-6pm. Monday.
Directions	Between Brailes & Swalcliffe; on B4035, follow signs to Sibford Gower.

Damian & Deborah Bradley
Wykham Arms
Temple Mill Road, Sibford Gower,
Banbury OX15 5RX

Tel	+44 (0)1295 788808
Web	www.wykhamarms.co.uk

The Finch's Arms
Hambleton

In the idyllic Hambleton village on the Rutland Water peninsula, The Finch's Arms has the greatest of views; Colin Crawford could have sat back and twiddled his thumbs and people would still have poured in. But he has not been idle: he has spruced up the interior, added four new bedrooms, and has created a terrific kitchen team led by talented Mark Gough, ex-Hambleton Hall. Décor in the Garden Room is ultra-elegant, with seasonal food to match; choose from peppered hare loin with mulled figs, sea bream with basil mash and chorizo, and rack of Egleton lamb. Round off with glazed rice pudding... the bar and restaurant menus change daily, and look out for Mark's delicious winter game dinners. There's a cracking rustic bar with stripped boards and log fires, a fine selection of local ale and a great wine list. Both the hillside terrace, perfect for summer sipping, and four of the 10 swish modern bedrooms, one with its own private balcony, have wonderful watery views. Rooms are minimalist rustic-chic with white rugs on wood floors, sleigh beds and flat-screen TVs, and classy bathrooms with huge walk-in showers and roll top baths.

Price	£95-£125. Singles from £75.
Rooms	10 doubles.
Meals	Lunch & dinner £10.50-£18. Sunday lunch, 3 courses, £19.95.
Closed	Open all day.
Directions	Off A606, east of Oakham.

Colin & Celia Crawford
The Finch's Arms
Oakham Road, Hambleton,
Oakham LE15 8TL
Tel +44 (0)1572 756575
Web www.finchsarms.co.uk

The Olive Branch
Clipsham

This is not your usual chi-chi ex-boozer in a sleepy village; a relaxed pub personality is pinned here to a Michelin star. The casual mood is created by old beams, exposed stone walls, loosely arranged tables and a warm medley of books, furniture and roaring log fire – a rustic-chic informality rules (a perfect backdrop for a rhubarb cocktail!). Chalk boards on tables in the restaurant reveal the names of the evening's diners, while the English food – cauliflower soup, roast rib of beef, caramelised lemon tart – is the greatest treat. So are the hampers of terrine, cheese and homemade pies that you can whisk away for picnics in the country. Bedrooms in Beech House across the lane are impeccable. Three have terraces, one has a free-standing bath, all come with crisp linen, pretty beds, Roberts radios, real coffee. Super breakfasts – smoothies, boiled eggs and soldiers, the full cooked works – are served in a smartly renovated barn, with flames leaping in the wood-burner. The front garden fills in summer, the sloe gin comes from local berries, and bridle paths lead out across peaceful fields.

Price	£115-£195. Suite £175-£260. Singles from £97.50.
Rooms	6: 5 doubles, 1 family suite.
Meals	Bar meals £10.50. Dinner £14.50. Sunday lunch £24.95.
Closed	3pm-6pm. Open all day Sat & Sun.
Directions	A1 five miles north of Stamford, then exit onto B668. Right and right again for Clipsham. In village (Beech House across the road from The Olive Branch).

Ben Jones & Sean Hope
The Olive Branch
Main Street, Clipsham,
Oakham LE15 7SH
Tel +44 (0)1780 410355
Web www.theolivebranchpub.com

The Golden Cross Hotel
Shrewsbury

In an ancient hilltop town setting, with the Lady Chapel of Old St Chad's opposite, is a 600-year-old pub – marvellous. All beams, passageways and tunnels, this was once a Royalist meeting place and sacristy. Fortunately today's buzz is more about delicious food and wine than war. Of course delightful Gareth clears tables for those in search of a pint (Salopian Shropshire Gold, Hobson's Twisted Spire) but the emphasis here is on food. The interior has a sumptuous theatrical feel – exotic tablecloths, Venetian masks, quirky chandeliers – and is great fun. But eat one must and Theresa oversees the kitchen with the motto "a good stock is the elixir of all cooking". For proof of this try the duck cooked two ways: a confit leg and seared breast with fondant potato, butternut squash purée, spiced red cabbage and calvados jus – heaven on a plate. Wines from Bibendum and Tanners seal the deal. And if you thought it couldn't get any better, skip upstairs: the suite is sheer indulgence and the attic bathroom is a showstopper. The suite is more contemporary; the two compact doubles have all you need.

Price	£75-£150.
Rooms	4: 2 doubles, 1 twin, 1 suite.
Meals	Lunch & dinner £10.50-£18.50. Sunday lunch, 3 courses, £16.50.
Closed	Open all day.
Directions	From High Street, first left into Milk Street and right into Princess Street. Pub on right.

Gareth & Theresa Reece
The Golden Cross Hotel
14 Princess Street,
Shrewsbury SY1 1LP
Tel +44 (0)1743 362507
Web www.goldencrosshotel.co.uk

The Lion & Pheasant
Shrewsbury

Old meets new in this stunning transformation of a town centre inn, with exposed beams, roaring log fire and minimalist-rustic décor. Have a crack at Wood Shropshire Lad or Salopian Shropshire Gold while you peek at the menu, created by chef Matthew Strefford. Game terrine with toasted sourdough, Scottish salmon on blinis, fillet of sea bass with basil mash and chorizo, slow-cooked lamb shank with braised onions: this is food to linger over. The wine list is long and includes a dazzling array of dessert wines, port and different fizzes. Staff are young, friendly and deeply efficient. When you've had enough to eat and drink, wind up the twisting staircase to smart bedrooms above the bar (perhaps not for early retirers). The rooms are packed with character and atmosphere: some with a myriad of beams, all with soft lighting, uncluttered décor, feathery duvets, plump pillows and glamorous touches. Bathrooms have bath tubs or capacious showers and the loft suite is particularly exciting with its hip bath on a raised level and a separate room with drenching shower.

Price	£95-£175.
Rooms	22: 21 twins/doubles, 1 suite.
Meals	Lunch & dinner £4.95-£17.95. Bar meals from £6.50.
Closed	Open all day.
Directions	On the Wyle Cop street in centre of Shrewsbury.

Jim Littler
The Lion & Pheasant
50 Wyle Cop,
Shrewsbury SY1 1XJ

Tel	+44 (0)1743 770345
Web	www.lionandpheasant.co.uk

Riverside Inn
Cound

There's a great buzz in this large comfortable huntin', shootin' and fishin' inn – standing on a magnificent bend of the Severn, looking gloriously out to the Wrekin and beyond. It's worth seeking out for its crackling wood-burner in winter and its dining conservatory with views all year round. In summer there's a pretty garden smartly furnished, and you can fish from the bank for salmon and trout. The seasonal monthly menu might start with winter vegetable and lentil broth and move on to roast pork belly with apricot and sage sauce or beef and Guinness pie with shortcrust pastry. There's port to accompany your cheese, and lovely Salopian beers and homemade puddings – try the raspberry and thyme crème brûlée. It's all good value and comfortingly traditional. And, there's no need to hurry home: upstairs are seven well-proportioned and comfortable Georgian bedrooms. 'Executive' rooms have river views from sash windows and all are in excellent order. The service, as in every good pub, is both relaxed and efficient.

Price	£65-£75. Singles £50.
Rooms	7: 6 doubles, 1 twin.
Meals	Lunch & dinner £7.75-£14.
Closed	3pm-6pm. Open all day Sat & Sun May-Sept.
Directions	South from Shrewsbury on A458, through Cross Houses to Cressage; pub on left.

Peter Stanford Davis
Riverside Inn
Cound,
Shrewsbury SY5 6AF

Tel	+44 (0)1952 510900
Web	www.theriversideinn.net

The Clive Bar & Restaurant with Rooms
Bromfield

It doesn't really matter whether you're in the mood for old or new; this pub does both. Inside the old redbrick farmhouse on the Ludlow-Shrewsbury road you discover a chic restaurant on one side and a bar on the other. The bar starts life all chrome tables and blonde wood floors, then turns a corner and changes mood, becoming an elegant collection of antique chairs, rugs and pictures dotted around a huge old stone fireplace. The food remains resolutely modern. Prime ingredients, from Corvedale lamb to Mortimer Forest venison, are the star players in a menu glittering with talent and clever combinations. It's not just fancy footwork though – the food is terrific, be it wild mushroom, borlotti and pinto bean tagliatelle with roast garlic, basil and gorgonzola, or seared fillet of Woofferton beef with rösti potato, roasted shallots and red wine jus. And then there are the bedrooms in converted outbuildings, all of them stylish and impeccable visions of unfussy modern comfort within a framework of solid oak beams. Bathrooms are white and pristine, the furniture contemporary, the outlook blissfully rural.

Price	£90-£115. Family suite £115-£210.
Rooms	14: 13 twins/doubles, 1 family suite.
Meals	Lunch from £9.95. Bar meals from £5.95. Dinner from £15.95.
Closed	Open all day.
Directions	2 miles north of Ludlow on A49.

Paul Brooks
The Clive Bar & Restaurant with Rooms
Bromfield,
Ludlow SY8 2JR
Tel +44 (0)1584 856565
Web www.theclive.co.uk

Baron at Bucknell
Bucknell

A stone's throw from Ludlow yet in the midst of the Shropshire Hills, the Baron sits at the base of Bucknell Mynd in a tranquil village by the Teme Valley. Peace reigns supreme and a flurry of super walks lead from the door: guides are behind the bar. Phil and Debbie have worked wonders on the bedrooms; all five are well-groomed and tasteful with oak furniture, contemporary wallpaper, stylish lighting and fat mattresses to induce deep asleep; one has a Juliet balcony, all have country views. Bathrooms are modern and white, one with a double-ended whirlpool bath. Ales from Hobson and Wye Valley await in the simple bar with its traditional carpet and wooden seating. Homemade pub food is the mantra here, uncomplicated and cooked to order. Start with glazed goat's cheese and beetroot salad with rocket, pine nuts and crusty bread, move on to slow-braised lamb shank with a fruity minty couscous. Eat in the restaurant beside a large millstone and grinding wheel and a huge wooden cider press dated 1770, or in the conservatory that overlooks the garden with boules pitches. You can camp, too!

Price	£90-£130.
Rooms	5: 3 doubles, 2 twins/doubles.
Meals	Lunch & bar meals from £4.95. Dinner from £8.95. Sunday lunch, 2-3 courses, £14.20-£19.15. Not Sun eves or Mon lunch (except bank hols).
Closed	Sun eves & Mon lunch (except bank hols).
Directions	Sent on booking.

Phil & Debbie Wright
Baron at Bucknell
Bucknell,
Ludlow SY7 0AH
Tel +44 (0)1547 530549
Web www.baronatbucknell.co.uk

The Hundred House Hotel

Norton

The Phillips family has been at the helm for 25 years and Henry is an innkeeper with humour. As for the inn, having begun its life in the 14th century, it rambles charmingly inside as well as out. Enter a world of blazing log fires, soft brick walls, oak panelling and quarry-tiled floors. Dried flowers hang from beams, herbs sit in vases, and blackboard menus trumpet Hundred House fish pie, roast rack of Shropshire lamb and double chocolate mousse with orange anglaise. You are surrounded by Sylvia's wild and wonderful collage art, which hangs on the walls, and the fun continues in riotously patterned and floral bedrooms upstairs. Just go easy on the ale before you open the door: most have a swing hanging from the oak beams with a colourful velvet seat! Lounge on antique beds – large, comfortable and wrapped in lavender-scented sheets. Wander out with a pint of Ironbridge Brewery and share a quiet moment with a few stone lions in the beautiful garden, a real flight of fancy full of herbaceous plants and a herb garden with over 100 varieties – a real summer treat. And you can tie the knot in the restored Tithe Barn.

Price	From £65. Singles from £55.
Rooms	9: 8 doubles, 1 twin/double.
Meals	Lunch form £4.95. Dinner & bar meals from £8.95. Sunday lunch, 2 courses, £16.95.
Closed	Never.
Directions	In village of Norton, midway between Bridgnorth & Telford on A442.

The Phillips Family
The Hundred House Hotel
Bridgnorth Road, Norton,
Shifnal TF11 9EE

Tel +44 (0)1952 580240
Web www.hundredhouse.co.uk

All Nations
Madeley

The old Victorian pub, spruce and white, could be an extension of the Victorian open air museum on the other side of the bridge. Step across the threshold and you're into timeworn-tavern territory – cast-iron tables, leatherette benches, coal fire at one end, log fire at the other. Old photographs of Ironbridge strew the walls, secondhand paperbacks ask to be taken home (donations to charity accepted), dogs doze and spotless loos await outside. It's a chatty, friendly, ex-miners' ale house and some of the locals could have been here forever. Drink is own-brew, well-kept, low-cost Dabley from the hatch plus three others and a cider, while the menu encompasses several sorts of roll – black pudding perhaps, or cheese and onion, with tomato on request. Catch it before it's gone.

Meals	Filled rolls £1.90-£3.
Closed	Open all day.
Directions	Off Legges Way, near entrance to Blists Hill Victorian museum.

Jim Birtwistle
All Nations
20 Coalport Road,
Madeley,
Telford TF7 5DP
Tel +44 (0)1952 585747

Entry 472 Map 8

Shropshire

The Fox
Newport

As you wander from room to room you realise just how vast this 1920s pub is. Yet there are plenty of nooks to be private in. Fires crackle in magnificent fireplaces, heavy cast-iron radiators add warmth, Turkish rugs are scattered on stained-wood floors and summer promises a great big garden with rolling views. Pews, solid oak tables and chairs – there's a happy mix of furniture and a bistro feel. It's a grown-ups' pub and attracts a civilised crowd, appreciative of the good selection of wines by the glass and the six regularly changing guest ales. Choose a table, then browse that day's menu: there might be crab linguini with ginger, red chilli and coriander, braised shoulder of lamb with minted gravy, steak and kidney pie, ham, egg and chips, fig and frangipane tart with Greek yoghurt and honey, and very good coffee.

Meals	Lunch & dinner £7.95-£19.95.
Closed	Open all day.
Directions	Just off A41 south of Newport.

Samantha Forrest
The Fox
Pave Lane,
Newport TF10 9LQ
Tel +44 (0)1952 815940
Web www.brunningandprice.co.uk

Entry 473 Map 8

New Inn

Baschurch

Outside, jolly hanging baskets and a plain, whitewashed frontage. Inside, a sensitive stripping back to old brick and beams and an open fire. There are comfortable sofas at one end, scrubbed oak dining chairs and tables at the other and a big traditional bar in between. In spite of the 48 covers, a well-placed wall and brick fireplace give the dining areas a certain intimacy; outside, sun shades and decking invite summer drinkers and diners. Five ales on the pump and good house wines are served by Jenny Bean and her charming staff. In the kitchen, Marcus prepares such delights as ham hock and parsley terrine with cheese scone and spiced apple chutney; roast duck breast with sweet plum and star anise jus; white chocolate and mascarpone cheesecake, all locally sourced and delicious. All villages should have a pub like this.

Meals	Lunch & dinner £9.50-£16.95. Bar meals £4.95-£8.50. Sunday lunch £14 & £17. Not Sunday eve.
Closed	3pm-6pm. Open all day Sat & Sun.
Directions	Pub just off B5067 in Baschurch, 5 miles north west of Shrewsbury.

Marcus & Jenny Bean
New Inn
Church Road, Baschurch,
Shrewsbury SY4 2EF

Tel +44 (0)1939 260335
Web www.thenewinnbaschurch.co.uk

Entry 474 Map 7

Shropshire

The Inn at Grinshill

Grinshill

A ridge of pine soars high above the very pretty village; bring the boots and take to Shropshire's wild hills. Down at the inn, a top-to-toe renovation that still shines. Wander at will and you find an 18th-century panelled family room with rugs and games, a 19th-century bar with glass shelves, tiled floors, a crackling fire, and a 21st-century dining room, serene in cream, flooded with light courtesy of glazed coach-house arches. Ambrosial delights pour from the kitchen – try pan-fried pheasant with honeyed root vegetable and red wine glaze, or chicken on a tomato and asparagus salad. A baby grand piano gets played occasionally and life spills out into the garden in summer. Church bells peal, roses ramble, and the Shropshire Way passes by outside. Don't miss the magical follies at Hawkstone Park.

Meals	Lunch from £4.50. Sunday lunch from £13.95. Dinner (not Sun/Mon) £25-£35.
Closed	3pm-6pm (Sun from 4pm) & Mon.
Directions	A49 north from Shrewsbury. Grinshill signed left after 5 miles, just past Hadnall.

Kevin & Victoria Brazier
The Inn at Grinshill
High Street, Grinshill,
Shrewsbury SY4 3BL

Tel +44 (0)1939 220410
Web www.theinnatgrinshill.co.uk

Entry 475 Map 7

The Three Tuns
Bishops Castle

Beer deliveries are a cinch for the Three Tuns. There's been a licensed brewery next door in a listed Victorian tower since 1642 (the oldest brewing license in the UK). Pub and brewery are now under separate ownership but the pub still sells up to four of their beers at any one time, and very good they are too. The place has an unassuming air, like the rest of this time-warp town. The separate snug, public bar and lounge have been simply redecorated with pale green paintwork, scrubbed tables, leather booths and old oak flooring. (In contrast to some impressive marble loos...) A more recent addition is the oak-framed, conservatory dining room where tasty dishes appear, hot-smoked organic salmon with avocado, tomato and dill salad. A great mix of regulars, from suits to bohemians, a real fire in the stone fireplace, and live music at weekends.

Meals	Lunch from £5.10. Dinner from £8.95. Sunday lunch £9.15. Not Sunday eve.
Closed	Open all day.
Directions	Town on B4385 off A488 12 miles north of Knighton; pub in town centre at top of the hill.

Tim & Catherine Curtis-Evans
The Three Tuns
Salop Street,
Bishops Castle SY9 5BW

Tel +44 (0)1588 638797
Web www.thethreetunsinn.co.uk

Entry 476 Map 7

The Crown Country Inn
Munslow

Richard and Jane Arnold bought this listed Tudor inn in a parlous state. A courtroom, a doctor's surgery and a jail in its previous lives, it is now a happier place. While locals gather for a chat and a pint of Holden's Golden Glow at dark polished tables in the winter-cosy, log-stoved bar, the secret of the inn's success is revealed on its walls, adorned with food awards and a map of suppliers. Proprietor and chef Richard is passionate about local produce and the menu is stuffed with it. Try crostini ('little toasts') of local black pudding with Wenlock Edge Farm bacon, lamb tagine, and roast smoked chicken with mustard creamed leeks. As for the cheese board, it's a treat of lesser-known British cheeses – including the hop-rolled Hereford Hop. And there's a super sun-trap terrace for summer drinking.

Meals	Lunch & dinner £11.95-£16.95. Bar meals £4.95-£11.50.
Closed	2.30pm-6.45pm. Sun from 3pm & Mon all day.
Directions	On B4368 to Bridgnorth, at extreme western end of Munslow.

Richard & Jane Arnold
The Crown Country Inn
Munslow,
Craven Arms SY7 9ET

Tel +44 (0)1584 841205
Web www.crowncountryinn.co.uk

Entry 477 Map 7

Fighting Cocks
Stottesdon

As you tail tractors and horses on the lane to get here, you pass the farm that supplies the kitchen with its excellent meat. Sandra Jefferies wears multiple hats: jolly landlady, enthusiastic chef, manager of the great little shop next door. So step into the bar and choose a velour-topped seat or a settle or a sofa by the fire. The décor is haphazard, the carpet patterned, the piano strewn with newspapers and guides (Shropshire's ancient hills beckon) and the copper-topped bar hung with tankards. Up steps is a room for darts, dominoes and TV; outside, a beer garden. The dining room is as unpretentious as can be and a match for the cooking; you'll love the gamey (and spicy) casseroles, the organic salmon, scrumptious pies and tempting nursery puddings. A true community pub, with a welcome that embraces outsiders.

Meals	Lunch & dinner £8-£17.
Closed	Mon-Fri lunch. Open all day Sat & Sun.
Directions	Village signed off A4117 & B4363 east of Ludlow at Cleobury Mortimer.

Sandra Jefferies
Fighting Cocks
1 High Street, Stottesdon,
Kidderminster DY14 8TZ
Tel +44 (0)1746 718270

Shropshire

The Unicorn
Ludlow

Ludlow, full of timber-framed houses and artisan shops, looks and tastes delicious. As for The Unicorn, it hides at the bottom end of town on the east bank of the river as you approach the Shrewsbury road and, unlike its more distinguished restaurant neighbours, does not have to be booked weeks in advance. Along with well-priced bar snacks there's proper food and plenty of it (own-recipe sausages with bubble and squeak, chicken roulade with sweet and sour sauce, syrup sponge and custard). You eat at scrubbed tables in the dining rooms or in the beer garden by the stream, or, best of all, before log fires in the panelled, beamed bar where floor and ceiling slope drastically. Ceremony here is about as out-of-place as Formula One tyres on a family Ford and the beer is expertly kept: no wonder it remains popular.

Meals	Lunch & dinner £6.75-£12.95. Sunday lunch from £7.95.
Closed	Open all day.
Directions	From A49, B4361 to Ludlow. After lights & bridge, bear right; bear left up hill. Next right after lights at bottom of hill. 50 yds on left.

Graham Moore
The Unicorn
66 Corve Street,
Ludlow SY8 1DU
Tel +44 (0)1584 873555

The Royal Oak Inn
Luxborough

Five miles south of Minehead, as the pheasant flies, is Luxborough, tucked under the lip of Exmoor's Brendon hills. This is hunting country, and from September to January the bar hums with the sound of gamekeepers, beaters, drivers and picker-uppers from the nearby Chargot shoot. Often they stay to dine, very well: on potted ham hock, fish from St Mawes, vegetables from local growers, and beef, lamb and venison that's almost walked off the hills. Two low-beamed, log-fired, dog-dozed bars (with locals' own table) lead to a warren of dining rooms kitted out with polished dining tables and hunting prints on deep green walls. (In spate, the river Washford has been known to take a detour!) A shelf heaves with walking books and maps; James and Siân lend them freely, all are returned. The village is small but people have been coming here all their lives, for a pint and a chat over cribbage, backgammon, scrabble. For those lucky enough to stay, bedrooms ramble around the first floor (one below has a private terrace) and are individual, peaceful, homely and great value.

Price	£75-£100. Singles from £65.
Rooms	10: 7 doubles, 3 twins/doubles.
Meals	Bar meals from £4.95. Dinner, 3 courses, £25-£30.
Closed	2.30pm-6pm Oct-May. Open all day Sat & Sun.
Directions	M5 junc. 25, A358 north, B3224 west. Village signed right, midway between Brendon Hill and Wheddon Cross.

James & Siân Waller
The Royal Oak Inn
Luxborough, Watchet TA23 0SH
Tel +44 (0)1984 640319
Web www.theroyaloakinnluxborough.co.uk

The Rock Inn
Waterrow

Perambulating along the Somerset and Devon borderlands in search of country cooking and a comfortable bed, you'd feel lucky to chance upon this coaching inn. Lost along the back road between Taunton and South Molton, built into the rockface by the river in a green valley, it is run by a mother and son team. Joanna (chef) and Matt (ex Hotel du Vin) have restored the fortunes of the old timbered inn. Good home-cooked food, served at pine tables in the rustic bar or the bistro-style dining room, draws the farmers from the hills and taps into a network of quality suppliers: free-range pork, craft cheeses, local lamb. So tuck into steak and kidney pie; Brixham fish; Exmoor venison steak with port and berry sauce; and pear and almond tart with chocolate ice cream. Local extends to the ales: very well-kept Otter, Cotleigh Tawny and Exmoor Gold. Homely bedrooms are warm and comfortable, with crisp cotton sheets on old pine or brass beds, and flatscreen TVs; the largest has a leather sofa and a wood-burning stove, a treat on a winter's night. A wonderful place.

Price	£85. Singles £60.
Rooms	8 twins/doubles.
Meals	Lunch & dinner £7.50-£15.95.
Closed	3pm-6pm.
Directions	On B3227 between Bampton & Wiveliscombe.

Matt Harvey & Joanna Oldman
The Rock Inn
Waterrow,
Taunton TA4 2AX
Tel +44 (0)1984 623293
Web www.rockinn.co.uk

The Bower Inn

Bridgwater

This pretty red-brick inn was once a farm and there are still peaceful fields all around – even though it's near the M5 and on the edge of Bridgwater. New owners have been busy and it is uplifting to find a pub refurbished with such character. A wooden tiger and spotty dog greet you on the way in and ample floor space unfolds before the bar; sofas and coffee tables wait expectantly and a wood-burner glows in a double sided fireplace. Pints of Doom Bar or Otter can be enjoyed in the comfort of padded windsor chairs at round wooden tables or outside in the pretty garden. Unfussy menus feature homemade local produce and offer great value: pork loin steak on creamed potato with vegetables and a cider and black pepper sauce or creamy chicken and leek pie with puff pastry topping, mashed potatoes and garden peas. Bedrooms have that 'je ne sais quoi' touch to them and one show-stealer has French Art Deco furniture in maple veneer and a bateau bath – mon dieu! All are deeply comfortable with Japanese prints, duck down duvets, well chosen antiques and smart bathrooms. Terrific – and they cater for weddings.

Price	£90. Singles £70.
Rooms	5: 3 doubles, 1 twin, 1 twin/double.
Meals	Lunch from £6. Bar meals from £6.50. Dinner from £9.50. Not Mon lunch.
Closed	Open all day.
Directions	Sent on booking.

Candida Leaver & Peter Starling
The Bower Inn
Bower lane, East Bower,
Bridgwater TA6 4TY
Tel +44 (0)1278 422926
Web www.thebowerinn.co.uk

Lord Poulett Arms
Hinton St George

In a ravishing village, a ravishing inn, French at heart and quietly groovy. Part pub, part country house, with walls painted in reds and greens and old rugs covering flagged floors, it fuses classical design with earthy rusticity. A fire burns on both sides of the chimney in the dining room; on one side you can sink into leather armchairs, on the other you can eat under beams at antique oak tables while candles flicker. Take refuge with the daily papers on the sofa in the locals' bar or head past a pile of logs at the back door and discover an informal French garden of box and bay trees, with a piste for boules, a creeper-shaded terrace, a hammock. Bedrooms upstairs come in funky country-house style, with fancy flock wallpaper, perhaps crushed velvet curtains, a small chandelier or a carved-wood bed. Two rooms have slipper baths behind screens in the room; two have claw-foot baths in bathrooms one step across the landing; Roberts radios add to the fun. Brilliant food includes summer barbecues, Sunday roasts and the full works at breakfast. Great value and friendly to all – dogs included.

Price	£85-£95. Singles £60-£65.
Rooms	4: 2 doubles en suite; 2 doubles, each with separate bath.
Meals	Lunch & dinner £10-£20.
Closed	Open all day.
Directions	A303, then A356 south for Crewkerne. Right for West Chinnock. Through village, 1st left for Hinton St George. Pub on right in village.

Steve & Michelle Hill
Lord Poulett Arms
High Street,
Hinton St George TA17 8SE
Tel +44 (0)1460 73149
Web www.lordpoulettarms.com

The Masons Arms
Odcombe

The old thatched cider house serves its very own Odcombe Ales; try Spring or A Winter's Tail. All are brewed by Drew, just 20 feet behind the bar; now that's local. Inside all is carpeted cosiness, matched by beams and a former inglenook, now a mini-snug (fires and thatch don't mix!). Owner Paula ferries plates of modern pub food, often with an Asian twist, through the lively crowd who throng here. Try free-range pork loin with dauphinoise potatoes and a cider cream sauce, or game casserole with herb dumplings. The à la carte changes daily, the blackboard specials follow the seasons and you're treated to the best from the markets and the producers nearby. If the sun is out, head to the long, sheltered garden replete with tidy thatched dining hut; views reach over the vegetable plot to pretty fields and pub campsite beyond. Behind the pub, in a single-storey annexe alongside the garden, are six contemporary bedrooms smartly furnished with pale-oak beds and all you might need for business or pleasure. The Masons is a simple, unpretentious pub with a community vibe.

Price	£85-£105. Singles £55.
Rooms	6: 4 twins/doubles, 1 single, 1 family room.
Meals	Lunch from £5.50. Bar meals from £7. Dinner from £11.50. Sunday lunch, 3 courses, £21.75.
Closed	3pm-6pm.
Directions	Odcombe signed off A30 and A3088 just west of Yeovil, then follow signs for Lower Odcombe.

Paula Tennyson & Drew Read
The Masons Arms
41 Lower Odcombe, Odcombe,
Yeovil BA22 8TX
Tel +44 (0)1935 862591
Web www.masonsarmsodcombe.co.uk

The Devonshire Arms

Long Sutton

A lively English village with a well-kept green; the old school house stands to the south, the church to the east and the post office to the west. The inn (due north) is 400 years old and was once a hunting lodge for the Dukes of Devonshire; a rather smart pillared porch survives at the front. These days open-plan interiors are warmly contemporary with high ceilings, shiny blond floorboards and fresh flowers everywhere. Hop onto brown leather stools at the bar and order a pint of Moor Revival, or sink into sofas in front of the fire and crack open a bottle of wine. In summer, life spills onto the terrace at the front, the courtyard at the back and the lawned garden beyond. Upstairs, a flurry of large, light and absolutely fabulous bedrooms, with low-slung wooden beds, seagrass matting and crisp white linen. The hosts are engaging and the food's a joy; choose from ploughman's with homemade chutney or game burger and chips, linger over lamb rump with roast vegetables and puy lentils, dive into dark chocolate fondant. Then take to the nearby Somerset Levels and walk off your indulgence in style.

Price	£85-£130. Singles from £75.
Rooms	9: 8 doubles, 1 twin.
Meals	Lunch from £6.50. Dinner £10.95-£18.95.
Closed	3pm-6pm.
Directions	A303, then north on B3165, through Martock to Long Sutton. On village green.

Philip & Sheila Mepham
The Devonshire Arms
Long Sutton,
Langport TA10 9LP
Tel +44 (0)1458 241271
Web www.thedevonshirearms.com

Kings Arms
Charlton Horethorne

With three dining pubs and a thriving food company behind them, Tony and Sarah have returned to the world of pubbery – and how! A serious restoration project saw the old boarded-up Kings Arms rise from the ashes in 2009, its original and striking façade opening to a contemporary-chic interior. Step in to wood and stone floors, bold-red and green walls, vintage dining tables, a cheery wood-burner, squashy leather sofas and four real ales in the front bar. The restaurant has a more civilised, less funky feel – a coir-matted floor, arched mirrors, local artwork, and terrace views. From Sarah's daily-changing lunch and dinner menus find roasted pork belly with apple terrine; lamb rump with rosemary jus; butternut squash and ricotta ravioli with marjoram butter sauce; apple and calvados trifle. Delicious food for children too. Named after gem stones, each with its own style, are ten bedrooms in the new extension sporting distinctive wallpapers, big beds and marble and mosaic bathrooms with bathrobes, posh smellies and walk-in showers. A class act – and good value, too.

Price	£110.
Rooms	10 twins/doubles.
Meals	Lunch & dinner £8.95-£16.50. Sunday lunch £11.50.
Closed	Open all day.
Directions	On the B3145, in centre of Charlton Horethorne, between Sherbourne & Wincanton, 3 miles from A303.

Tony & Sarah Lethbridge
Kings Arms
Charlton Horethorne,
Sherborne DT9 4NL
Tel +44 (0)1963 220281
Web www.thekingsarms.co.uk

The Queen's Arms
Corton Denham

Stride across rolling fields, feast on Corton Denham lamb, retire to a perfect room. Buried down several Dorset/Somerset borders lanes, Gordon and Jeanette Reid's 18th-century stone pub has an elegant exterior – more country gentleman's house than pub. The bar, with its rug-strewn flagstones and bare boards, pew benches, deep sofas and crackling fire, is most charming. In the dining room – big mirrors on terracotta walls, new china on old tables – robust British dishes are distinguished by fresh ingredients from local suppliers. Try pheasant, pigeon and black pudding terrine, follow with monkfish with chive velouté… then make room for a comforting crumble. Bedrooms are beautifully designed in soothing colours, and all have lovely views over the village and surrounding hills. New coach house rooms are super, too: underfloor heating, crisp linen and down duvets, brass and sleigh beds, iPod docks and immaculate wet rooms. Expect Moor Queen's Revival on tap, homemade pork pies on the bar, Black Spot bacon at breakfast, and stunning walks from the front door.

Price	£85-£120. Singles from £75. Dogs welcome in ground floor bedroom.
Rooms	8: 5 doubles, 1 twin,1 twin/double, 1 four-poster.
Meals	Lunch from £6.50. Dinner, 3 courses £25-£30.
Closed	3pm-6pm. Open all day Sat & Sun.
Directions	From A303 take Chapel Crosse turning. Through South Cadbury then next left & follow signs to Corton Denham. Pub at end of village on right.

Gordon & Jeanette Reid
The Queen's Arms
Corton Denham,
Sherborne DT9 4LR
Tel +44 (0)1963 220317
Web www.thequeensarms.com

Kingsdon Inn
Kingsdon

If you're beetling down the A303 to Cornwall, in need of a bite or a bed, this achingly pretty thatched inn, minutes from the Podimore roundabout, is as perfect a refuge as you'll find. What could be better than a home-cooked meal, a pint of Butcombe and a cosy bed? With new enthusiastic landlords in 2011, chef Adam and restaurant manager Cinzia, the Kingsdon Inn, a flower-edged path leading to its cottage door, has a charming single bar with bending beams, an inglenook with a winter fire, and farmhouse chairs at pine tables. At lunch you could tuck into creamy leek and chestnut soup, or roast tarragon chicken with chive mash. At dinner, ham hock terrine with poached egg and mustard dressing and homemade Cornish fishcakes perhaps, or look to the chalkboard for one of Adam's more elaborate specials. Right under the thatch, reached via a novel rooftop walkway, are three gleaming bedrooms behind pine doors, simply kitted out with crisp linen, down duvets, colourful throws on big sleigh beds, painted furniture and smart, slate-floored bathrooms with walk-in showers. Beats the faceless hotel/services at Podimore any day!

Price	£95. Singles £65.
Rooms	3 doubles.
Meals	Lunch & dinner, 2 courses, from £14. Sunday lunch, 3 courses, £17.50.
Closed	3pm-6pm (7pm Sun).
Directions	Kingsdon is signed off A372 Langport road, 1/2 mile from A303 at Podimore.

Adam Cain & Cinzia Iezzi
Kingsdon Inn
Kingsdon,
Somerton TA11 7LG
Tel +44 (0)1935 840543
Web www.kingsdoninn.co.uk

The Three Horseshoes Inn
Batcombe

A magnificent spot, England at its best. You get the full works here: a beautiful valley lost to the world, an English village impeccably preserved, a great little inn that sits in the shade of an ancient church tower. Inside, fires burn at both ends of the bar, there are low ceilings, window seats and a warm mix of traditional and contemporary design. Rustic food hits the spot perfectly. Westcombe Cheddar sandwiches come with a real ale chutney, but if you want something more substantial, you can have it: pan-fried quail with ginger purée, tiger prawns in an Asian broth, Dorset mussels with lemongrass and chilli. In summer you slip outside and take your choice from a pretty courtyard where walls are clad in wisteria or a lush lawn, where you can sip your pint while church bells chime. Back inside, three bedrooms wait for those wise enough to linger. Two are decidedly snug, one is open to the rafters, all have crisp linen, comfy beds and attractive prices. Kids are very welcome, there's a locals' bar for a game of darts and great walks start from the front door. Glastonbury is close.

Price	£70-£85. Singles from £65.
Rooms	3 doubles.
Meals	Lunch from £6. Dinner, 3 courses, £25-£30. Sunday lunch from £11.50.
Closed	3pm-6pm. Open all day Sat & Sun.
Directions	Off A359 between Frome & Bruton, 7 miles south west of Frome, 4 miles east of Royal Bath & West Showground.

Kaveh Javvi
The Three Horseshoes Inn
Batcombe,
Frome BA4 6HE

Tel +44 (0)1749 850359
Web www.thethreehorseshoesinn.com

Archangel
Frome

In lovely old Frome: a coaching inn that opened its doors in 1311. Its recent renovation is exceptional, the old bones of the building brought back to life, then dressed gracefully with 21st-century design. The restaurant is magnificent – ancient walls embrace a floating glass mezzanine cube – while French windows open onto a courtyard in summer, and beds of lavender give the feel of Provence. Back inside, you find a couple of sitting-room bars at the front, so sink into sofas for cocktails in front of the fire. Exposed stone mixes with deep purples, there are cowhide rugs, a zinc-topped bar, and vast Renaissance murals. Bedrooms are a steal. Some are open to the rafters, most have zinc bathtubs in the room, all come with golden beds, crisp white linen, and speakers in bathroom ceilings. In the restaurant, some seriously good food, perhaps mussels with coconut and coriander broth; spiced pork belly with black pudding mash and red wine jus; chocolate fondant with pistachio ice cream. Bath, Longleat and Stonehenge are within striking distance, but you may just choose to linger.

Price	£120. Singles £80.
Rooms	6: 5 doubles, 1 single.
Meals	Lunch from £12.95. Dinner from £16. Sunday lunch, 2 courses, £16.
Closed	Open all day.
Directions	In centre of Frome, from A362, onto Bath Street (B3090), then right onto King Street.

Lisa Penny
Archangel
1 King Street,
Frome BA11 1BH
Tel +44 (0)1373 456111
Web www.archangelfrome.com

The Swan
Wedmore

Wedmore's dying Swan has been resuscitated: welcome to a revived village inn! Now locals throng in the open-plan bar, happy as Larry with the big mirrors and the crackling fires, the cosy corners, battered leather sofas, vintage rugs on flagged floors, and fine Cheddar Ales on tap. It buzzes from breakfast to afternoon tea (china cups and cake) and dinner from 6pm, when the restaurant fills with foodies eager to try Tom Blake's (ex-River Cottage) seasonal menus. Starting with the bar snacks – crab on toast, potted pig with mustard salsa – he delivers some memorable dishes; try Old Spot pork belly with braised red cabbage, baked whiting with salsa verde, dark chocolate trifle. Look forward to organic Chew Valley beef, Wedmore pork, and breads and cakes fresh from the kitchen. Bedrooms are equally contemporary and sleek. Expect stone-grey hues, colourful throws on deep beds, vintage French furniture. Power showers drench, and smaller rooms have a quirky 60s vibe while two rooms have roll top baths in the rooms themselves. Mendip walks, bird-rich nature reserves and New Age Glastonbury are close. Fabulous.

Price	From £85.
Rooms	6 doubles.
Meals	Lunch & dinner £10-£19. Bar meals from £4.50. Sunday lunch £14. Sun eve, bar meals only.
Closed	Open all day.
Directions	Wedmore is on B3151 between Glastonbury & Cheddar, 4 miles south of Cheddar; pub in village centre.

Duncan Zvonek-Little
The Swan
Cheddar Road,
Wedmore BS28 4EQ
Tel +44 (0)1934 710337
Web www.theswanwedmore.com

The George

Wedmore

Wedmore's striking 15th-century coaching inn was lost in a time warp, until Gordon Stevens took over in 2009. His passion and vision for the vast stone building has breathed new life into its labyrinth of rooms; all now ooze character and charm. Wooden floors, half-panelled walls, stone fireplaces, old prints, warm greens and terracottas and wax-encrusted candlesticks on scrubbed dining tables set the scene for happy pints of Potholer or heady Orchard Pig cider. Food is hearty and locally sourced, and the eclectic menu ranges from crab sandwiches and afternoon teacakes with jams to rack of Mendip lamb, beef and vegetable stew, a spicy pork curry. There's a cracking locals' bar and skittle alley, a pizza/pasta restaurant next door (in a section that dates from 1760), and the restoration of the bedrooms upstairs is well under way.

Meals	Lunch from £7. Bar meals £5. Dinner from £12. Sunday lunch, 2 courses, £18. Not Sun eves.
Closed	Open all day.
Directions	Village centre.

Gordon Stevens
The George
Church Street, Wedmore,
Cheddar BS28 4AB
Tel +44 (0)1934 712124
Web www.thegeorgewedmore.co.uk

Entry 492 Map 3

Somerset

Wookey Hole Inn

Wookey Hole

On the edge of the Mendip hills: a traditional façade, a funky décor, excellent food and no end of choice behind the funky-kitsch bar. The whole place throngs, particularly in summer when the big walled garden (replete with quirky sculptures) comes into its own. It's also relaxed and properly child-friendly with toys and wax crayons for doodling on paper tablecloths. Terracotta tiles, open fires, stripped boards and wooden panelling, splashes of strong colour, arty lamps, photos and interesting objets. The atmosphere is laid-back and the food seriously tasty, imaginative and locally sourced: wild boar burger, smoked haddock and saffron risotto, lamb rump with dauphinoise, red onion tarte tatin and carrot purée. The desserts are seductive, too – we loved the date and pecan pudding.

Meals	Lunch from £5.75. Dinner from £14. Sunday lunch £16.95 (2 courses) & £19.95 (3 courses).
Closed	Sun eves.
Directions	Follow brown tourist signs for Wookey Hole off A371 or A39 in Wells.

Richard Davey
Wookey Hole Inn
Wookey Hole,
Wells BA5 1BP
Tel +44 (0)1749 676677
Web www.wookeyholeinn.com

Entry 493 Map 3

The Talbot Inn at Mells

Mells

Even in fog the village is lovely. Huge oak doors open to a cobbled courtyard and rough-boarded tithe barn bar on one side, and dining rooms on the other. Inside, a warren of passageways, low doorways, nooks, crannies and beams – all you'd hope for from a 15th-century inn. Butcombe Bitter flows from the cask and there are wines galore including five by the glass; it's a great drinking pub and, with a garden with views, a big draw for tourists in summer. Soak up any excess with battered cod and chips, chargrilled rib-eye steak with roasted red pepper and chilli butter, or local ham, eggs and chips, then head down to the brook and converse with the ducks. Dinner under the hop-strewn rafters highlights fresh Brixham fish such as brill fillets in nut-brown butter. The effortless hospitality is a further plus.

Meals	Lunch & dinner £11.95-£17.95. Sunday lunch, 2 courses, £12.95.
Closed	2.30pm-6.30pm (3pm-7pm Sun).
Directions	From Frome A362 for Radstock; left signed Mells.

Rob Rowlands
The Talbot Inn at Mells
Selwood Street, Mells,
Frome BA11 3PN

Tel +44 (0)1373 812254
Web www.talbotinn.com

Entry 494 Map 3

Somerset

The Black Horse

Clapton-in-Gordano

The Snug Bar once doubled as the village lock-up and, if it weren't for the electric lights and the cars outside, you'd be hard pushed to remember you were in the 21st century. With flagstones and dark moody wood, the main room bears the scuffs of centuries of drinking. Settles and old tables sit around the walls; cottage windows with wobbly shutters let a little of the outside in. The fire roars in its vast hearth beneath a fine set of antique guns – so pull off your muddy boots and settle in. Sepia prints of parish cricket teams and steam tractors clutter the walls and cask ales pour from the stone ledge behind the hatch bar. The food is unfancy bar fodder, with daily specials. Ale takes pride of place; beneath a chalkboard six jacketed casks squat above drip pans. There are fine wines too, and plenty of garden.

Meals	Lunch & dinner £3.50-£6.95.
Closed	Open all day.
Directions	M5 junc. 19 for Portbury & Clapton. Left into Clevedon Lane.

Nicholas Evans
The Black Horse, Clevedon Lane,
Clapton-in-Gordano,
Bristol BS20 7RH

Tel +44 (0)1275 842105
Web www.thekicker.co.uk

Entry 495 Map 3

The Crown

Churchill

Once a coaching stop between Bristol and Exeter, then the village grocer's, now an unspoilt pub. Modern makeovers have passed it by and beer reigns supreme, with up to ten ales tapped from the barrel. For years landlord Tim Rogers has resisted piped music and electronic games; who needs them in these beamed and flagstoned bars? The rustic surroundings and the jolly atmosphere draw both locals and walkers treading the Mendip hills. Find a seat by the log fire, cradle a pint of Butcombe or RCH PG Steam bitter, be lulled by the hum of regulars at the bar. If you're here at lunchtime you'll find a short, traditional, blackboard menu: warming bowls of soup, thick-cut rare roast beef sandwiches, winter casseroles, treacle pud. Evenings are reserved for the serious art of ale drinking, and it's packed at weekends.

Meals	Lunch & bar meals from £4.85. No food in evenings.
Closed	Open all day.
Directions	From Bristol A38 to Churchill, right for Weston-super-Mare. Immed. left in front of Nelson Pub, up Skinners Lane, pub on bend.

Tim Rogers
The Crown
The Batch,
Churchill,
Congresbury BS25 5PP
Tel +44 (0)1934 852995

Entry 496 Map 3

Somerset

The Apple Tree Inn

West Pennard

The energy, enthusiasm and talent of chef-patrons Lee and Ally Evans (ex The Wheatsheaf, Combe Hay) have transformed this run-down roadside inn into a foodie haven, firmly on the Somerset culinary map ever since their arrival in early 2011. In the main bar, original boards and flagstones have been revealed and big sofas front the blazing wood-burner. Arrive early to soak up the heat and enjoy the menu with a pint of Bristol's Best. Menus trawl the local seasonal larder; dishes are presented with flair and an element of surprise. Try the cheese burger with chips, chutney and pickles, or push the boat out for venison and blackberry pie, braised blade of beef with roast shallots and mash, dark chocolate fondant with fig and mascarpone ice cream. With work still to be done the Apple Tree can only get better.

Meals	Lunch & dinner £9.95-£19.95. Bar meals from £5.50. Sunday lunch £11.95 & 19.95.
Closed	Sun eves & Mon.
Directions	On A361 between Glastonbury and Pilton.

Lee & Ally Evans
The Apple Tree Inn
West Pennard,
Glastonbury BA6 8ND
Tel +44 (0)1749 890060
Web www.appletreeglastonbury.co.uk

Entry 497 Map 3

The Montague Inn

Shepton Montague

The O'Callaghans' 17th-century public house has been a stables, livery, grocery; now it is an inn in the true sense of the word. All remains beautiful, with Bath Ales and regional guests that may come from Butcombe and Blindman's Brewery, two wood-burners in the bar, candles on stripped pine tables and organic produce from neighbouring farms. Head chef Matt Dean's food is simple yet imaginative. There are lunchtime ploughman's of local cheeses while daily specials could mean a hotpot on Tuesday and fresh fish in beer batter and chips on Friday. And then there's grilled local goat's cheese in a celery, apple and walnut salad, and seared fillet of local beef with garlic cream mash, bacon and lentil jus – all of it brilliant. The restaurant and rear terrace have bosky views to Redlynch and Alfred's Tower.

Meals	Lunch from £4.95. Bar meals from £4.95. Dinner from £11.95. Sunday lunch, 3 courses £21.50. Not Sunday eve.
Closed	3pm-6pm & Sun from 3pm.
Directions	A303 to Wincanton, turn off A359 2 miles east of Castle Cary, towards Bruton.

Sean & Suzy O'Callaghan
The Montague Inn
Shepton Montague,
Wincanton BA9 8JW

Tel +44 (0)1749 813213
Web www.themontagueinn.co.uk

Entry 498 Map 3

Somerset

The Old Inn

Holton

Old indeed – 1650 to be precise. And a gem. This whitewashed pub sits in the middle of a peaceful village and is now owned by a local farmer, who, generous fellow, has not merely refurbished the inn but built a delightful restaurant to go with it. This marriage of old and new works a treat: flagstones, a wood-burner and smart leather benches in the bar, then high ceilings, exposed wood and lots of glass in the restaurant. You get good ales and old world wines, then delicious fish and meat, some of the latter reared on the owner's farm; try mussels in white wine, rack of local lamb, sticky toffee pudding with butterscotch sauce. There are tables outside on a gravelled terrace or a small lawned garden tucked away at the back. The A303 passes silently within a mile, making this a great stop for locals and travellers alike.

Meals	Lunch & bar meals from £7.80. Dinner from £13.50.
Closed	Open all day.
Directions	From Wincanton B3081, 2nd exit on to A371. Right at Anchor Hill, left on Holton Street.

Steve Woodward
The Old Inn
Holton,
Wincanton BA9 8AR

Tel +44 (0)1963 32002
Web www.theoldinnrestaurant.co.uk

Entry 499 Map 3

Red Lion

Babcary

The Red Lion is a Somerset revival that combines the best of pub tradition with excellent food. There is a single central bar with a locals' snug behind dispensing Glastonbury Hedge Monkey ale, local cider and house wines from France and Oz. To one side, hair-cord carpets, sofas and the cast-iron stove give a welcome to the bright bar/lounge, while to the far right a dozen well-spaced country dining tables plainly set out on original flagstone flooring are part of an immaculate reconstruction. Daily menus offer as little or as much as you'd like, from wild boar terrine with red cabbage chutney or wild mushroom soup to pork and herb sausages with mash and mustard jus, chicken with Tuscan bean stew and chorizo, and braised lamb shank. Best to book at weekends.

Meals	Lunch from £6.80. Bar meals from £5.95. Dinner from £8.50. Sunday lunch, 3 courses, £22.50.
Closed	2.30pm-6pm.
Directions	Off A37 & A303 7 miles north of Yeovil.

Clare & Charles Garrard
Red Lion
Babcary,
Somerton TA11 7ED
Tel +44 (0)1458 223230
Web www.redlionbabcary.co.uk

Entry 500 Map 3

Somerset

Halfway House

Pitney Hill

Somerset's mecca for beer and cider aficionados. No music or electronic wizardry to distract you from the serious business of sampling up to ten ales tapped straight from the cask, heady Hecks' ciders and bottled beers from around the globe. Local clubs gather for chess, music, hockey, golf. In the two simple and homely rooms is a friendly, conversational buzz: there are old benches and pews, scrubbed tables, stone-slabbed floors, three crackling log fires and the daily papers to nod off over. A quick lunchtime pint can swiftly turn into two hours of beer-fuelled bliss – so blot up the alcohol with a ploughman's or a salmon steak straight from the pub's smokery. In the evenings the Halfway's revered homemade curries are gorgeous and go down very nicely with pints of Butcombe, Branscombe and Hop Back ales.

Meals	Lunch & dinner £4.50-£10.95.
Closed	3pm-5.30pm. Open all day Sun.
Directions	Beside B3153, midway between Langport & Somerton.

Mark Phillips
Halfway House
Pitney Hill,
Langport TA10 9AB
Tel +44 (0)1458 252513
Web www.thehalfwayhouse.co.uk

Entry 501 Map 3

Rose & Crown Inn (Eli's)

Huish Episcopi

Quirky, unspoilt and in the family for over 140 years. The layout has evolved, gradually taking over the family home. There's no bar as such – you choose from the casks – but who cares when the locals are so lovely, the cider so rough and the beer (Glastonbury Mystery Tor) so tasty. Walk in and you step back to the Fifties. There are worn flagstones and aged panelling in five low parlours radiating off a central tap room. The 'gentleman's kitchen' is the oldest, the pool and juke box room the largest and newest. They do folk music nights and occasional quiz nights and Morris dancers drop by in summer. The food is brilliant value: creamy winter vegetable soup, a tasty pork, apple and cider cobbler, chicken breast with tarragon, chocolate torte. Everyone's happy and children like the little play area outside.

Meals — Lunch & dinner £6.95-£7.95.
Closed — 2.30pm-5.30pm Mon-Thurs. Open all day Fri-Sun.
Directions — 300 yards from St Mary's Church. On left hand side towards Wincanton on leaving Huish.

Steve & Maureen Pittard & Patricia O'Malley
Rose & Crown Inn (Eli's)
Huish Episcopi,
Langport TA10 9QT
Tel +44 (0)1458 250494

Entry 502 Map 3

The Helyar Arms

East Coker

Mathieu Eke's gastropub is worth leaving the A30 for – for the atmosphere, the food (lots of produce from local suppliers) and the handsome village it lives in. Daily-updated boards of tasty dishes express the enterprising style: cauliflower soup (when in season, naturally); shin of beef and Guinness stew with thyme dumplings; Somerset pork belly with sage and cider jus; sticky toffee pudding. Real ales, Somerset cider and global wines are well priced. For ploughman's there might be local cheeses, such as Montgomery cheddar served with homemade chutney. Low beams, sofas by the crackling log fire, pictures crowding the walls, flickering candles on old tables, daily papers and board games in the bar, a raftered restaurant in the apple loft, a garden and skittles – this is a great all-round village pub.

Meals — Lunch & dinner £8.50-£16. Sunday lunch from £9.
Closed — 3pm-6pm.
Directions — A37, A30 signs to East Coker.

Mathieu Eke
The Helyar Arms
Moor Lane, East Coker,
Yeovil BA22 9JR
Tel +44 (0)1935 862332
Web www.helyar-arms.com

Entry 503 Map 3

The Candlelight Inn

Bishopswood

Aptly named, this 17th-century flint built pub shines in the heart of the Blackdown Hills. Inside and out are polished woods of all hues, exposed stonework and brick with timber framing, bar skittles and a log fire. Stone flags border the bar behind which a rack holds eight gravity-fed casks of Otter Bitter, and guests such as Sharp's or Exmoor, all lovingly looked after by Tom. And there's Sheppy's Farmhouse cider and Bolhayes Perry, perfect for washing down the contents of the sandwich board. Hot dishes? Chef Barry delivers a great steak and kidney suet pudding, and a chargrilled rump steak with their own recipe herb butter. It's all homemade bar the ice cream. A former skittle alley makes a super light dining area with views to the pretty garden; its fishpond and covered barbecue look over the river Yarty.

Meals	Lunch from £9.50. Bar meals from £4. Dinner from £12. Sunday lunch, set menu, £11-£20.
Closed	3pm-6pm. Monday.
Directions	From A303 between Ilminster and Honiton; signed Bishopswood. In village on right hand side.

Debbie Lush
The Candlelight Inn
Bishopswood,
Chard TA20 3RS
Tel +44 (0)1460 234476
Web www.candlelight-inn.co.uk

Entry 504 Map 2

Somerset

The Rising Sun Inn

Bagborough

Ten years ago the Sun rose from the ashes of a fire and shines more brightly than ever in the hands of the ambitious Brinkmans. It sits in sleepy West Bagborough on the flanks of the Quantock Hills. Constructed around the original 16th-century cob walls and magnificent door, its reincarnation is bold and craftsman-led, with 80 tons of solid oak timbers and windows and a slate-floored bar. Add Art Nouveau features, spotlighting and swagged drapery and you find one very smart pub. There's Exmoor, Proper Job and Butcombe to sample and, high in the rafters, a dining room with views that unfurl to Exmoor and the Blackdown Hills. It's an impressive setting for impressive food: goat's cheese on a walnut and plum salad; fillet of beef with peppercorn sauce; lemon sole with crayfish tails; bread and butter pudding. Worth walking down the hill for.

Meals	Lunch from £9.50. Bar meals from £5.95. Dinner from £11.
Closed	3pm-6pm.
Directions	Off A358 Taunton-Minehead road, 8 miles north west of Taunton.

Jon & Christine Brinkman
The Rising Sun Inn
Bagborough,
Taunton TA4 3EF
Tel +44 (0)1823 432575
Web www.risingsuninn.info

Entry 505 Map 2

Woods Bar & Dining Room

Dulverton

It hasn't been a pub for ever – indeed, it used to specialise in tea and cakes – but it is in the centre of a lively village, and wine buffs and foodies have much to be grateful for. Landlords Sally and Paddy are friendly and welcome families and dogs. A stable-like partition divides the space up into two intimate seating areas, beyond which is a smart, soft-lit, deeply cosy bar: two wood-burners, lots of pine, a few barrel tables and exposed stone walls. Ales include Exmoor Gold, Otter and St Austell, but the wines are the thing, and many come by the glass. Expect fine modern British dishes, with an emphasis on sourcing and food in season. There's roast tomato soup with serrano ham, roast Exmoor lamb with confit garlic and rosemary sauce, rich chocolate brownie. Or munch on a stilton and onion marmalade baguette.

Meals	Lunch & dinner £8.50-£16.50. Bar meals from £5.
Closed	3pm-6pm (7pm Sun).
Directions	From Tiverton, A396 north; left on B3222 for Dulverton; near church & bank.

Sally & Paddy Groves
Woods Bar & Dining Room
4 Bank Square,
Dulverton TA22 9BU

Tel	+44 (0)1398 324007
Web	www.woodsdulverton.co.uk

Entry 506 Map 2

Somerset

Tarr Farm Inn

Dulverton

Come for rare peace – no traffic lights, no mobile signals, not for miles. Tucked into the Barle valley, a short hop from the ancient clapper bridge at Tarr Steps, this well-established 16th-century inn is surrounded by beautiful woodland above the hauntingly high spaces of Exmoor National Park. The blue-carpeted, low-beamed main bar has plenty of comfy window seats and gleaming black leather sofas; Exmoor Ale and Mayner's cider flow as easily as the conversation. To fill the gap after a bracing walk the menu draws heavily on local game – hunting and shooting are big sports here – so you get venison and rabbit casserole, pan-roasted partridge and a hundred French and New World wines. The garden views are sublime; where better to try the best West Country cheeses followed by perfect coffee?

Meals	Lunch from £8. Bar meals from £6. Dinner from £13. Sunday lunch, 3 courses, £17.50.
Closed	Open all day.
Directions	From Dulverton, take B3223 north, left to Tarr Steps & inn is signed.

Judy Carless & Richard Benn
Tarr Farm Inn
Tarr Steps,
Dulverton TA22 9PY

Tel	+44 (0)1643 851507
Web	www.tarrfarm.co.uk

Entry 507 Map 2

The George

Alstonefield

A green sward ripples endlessly in this remote limestone village with its old church, perched on a plateau between the remarkable gorges of the rivers Dove and Manifold. Set amidst this verdant Eden, the handsome George is an ultra-reliable local, in the family for four decades and lovingly managed by Emily. As you walk into the small, timeless rooms of old beams, gleaming quarry tiles and crackling log fire, you know you're in safe hands. It's an unhurried place, where everyone knows everyone else (or soon will), ramblers cram the benches and tables out front and time passes slowly. The 18th-century coaching house is perfect for private parties. The welcome is warm, the beer's on song and the food is fab. Young chefs are creative with seasonal produce, so there's Devon crab, steak and red ale pie, and treacle tart.

Meals	Lunch £9-£30. Bar meals £5.50-£16. Dinner £11-£30.
Closed	3pm-6pm. Open all day Fri, Sat & Sun.
Directions	Village signed off A515, 7 miles north of Ashbourne.

Emily Hammond
The George
Alstonefield,
Ashbourne DE6 2FX

Tel +44 (0)1335 310205
Web www.thegeorgeatalstonefield.com

Entry 508 Map 8

Staffordshire

The Riverbank

Rushington

The approach, down winding country lanes, is best viewed from the driving seat of a classic motorcar. This charming establishment has seen a number of different owners over the years but its future is now secure thanks to a generous benefactor from the Hall up the road. Locals can be a vicious bunch (feuds are common with rival pub 'The Pickled Weasel') but can usually be found propping up the bar, swapping yarns over a pint of Tanglefoot. The menu is ever changing and the ingredients are seasonal, having travelled mere minutes before landing on your plate. Try deep-fried damsonfly followed by brown trout with watercress and dandelion salad; finish up with 'picnic plunder'. As the afternoon wears on, borrow a boat, explore the neighbourhood, mind the weir – and don't stand up!

Price	£1/14/11d per lb of catch. Watercress on the house.
Meals	When the fishing's good.
Closed	Open all day.
Directions	Through the meadows, left at the willows, straight on to the hole in the bank.

Ken Grahame
The Riverbank
Willow Lane,
Rushington SP1 8SH

Tel +44 (0)1256 499578
Web www.lazyriverdays.co.uk

Entry 509 Map 8

Old Cannon Brewery

Bury St Edmunds

Tricky to find down Bury's back streets but well worth the effort, the Old Cannon is an admirable revitalisation of a Victorian brewhouse-pub. Bare boards clatter, wooden tables are simple and plain, the décor is light and airy with splashes of bold colour, and a huge mirror vies with two gleaming stainless-steel brewing vessels smack beside the bar. The atmosphere is youthful, friendly and enlivened by foaming pints of own-brew Gunner's Daughter (5.5%), Blonde Bombshell (4.2%), and a seasonal autumn brew like Rusty Gun (4%). On the chalkboard menu: Elveden Estate venison, mushroom and vegetable stew, steak, kidney and ale pie, local sausages with colcannon and onion gravy, cod in beer batter, and lunchtime cheese ploughman's; good hearty food. A cobbled courtyard beyond the old coach arch has swish tables and chairs for summer sipping; in the former brewhouse are seven light, modern and freshly refurbished bedrooms, replete with good-sized shower rooms, curtains at Victorian windows and TVs. And you are a five-minute walk from Bury, hub of East Anglia – and its treasures.

Price	£110. Singles £85.
Rooms	7: 6 doubles, 1 twin.
Meals	Lunch & dinner £9.75-£14.95. Bar meals from £4.95. Sunday lunch from £10.95.
Closed	3pm-5pm (7pm Sun).
Directions	From A14, Bury exit, for centre, left at r'bout to Northgate St; right at Cadney Lane & into Cannon St.

Garry & Hannah Clark
Old Cannon Brewery
86 Cannon Street,
Bury St Edmunds IP33 1JR

Tel +44 (0)1284 768769
Web www.oldcannonbrewery.co.uk

The Crown

Stoke-by-Nayland

A slick operation in a smart new-build behind the pub, find rather posh bedrooms with elegant wallpapers, brass beds with superb mattresses and uncluttered bathrooms with storm showers and fluffy towels. All are toasty warm with underfloor heating, thick new carpets (three have French doors leading to a terrace) and country views. Back in the pub, low-ceilinged but rambling rooms are decked in muted colours, and the mood is warm, appealing and refreshingly music-free. There's space to prop up the bar and down a pint from Suffolk brewers Adnams, while the seasonal menu is a sympathetic combination of traditional and contemporary. Chefs dispatch exuberant renditions of wild Norfolk mussels with bacon and parsley on toast, and locally shot pheasant with bacon, prunes and leeks – topped off with steamed sticky quince and ginger pudding or a plate of five British cheeses. The wine list is outstanding, with wines matched to the food and bottles to take home from the shop. Head to the terrace on sunny days: the views are as fabulous as all the rest.

Price	£120-£200. Suite £175-£220. Singles from £90.
Rooms	11: 10 doubles, 1 suite.
Meals	Lunch & dinner £5-£19.95.
Closed	Open all day.
Directions	North from Colchester on A134, then B1087 east into Stoke-by-Nayland. Right at T-junction; pub on left.

Richard Sunderland
The Crown
Park Street, Stoke-by-Nayland,
Colchester CO6 4SE

Tel +44 (0)1206 262001
Web www.crowninn.net

The Crown at Woodbridge

Woodbridge

Everyone loves Woodbridge's Crown, from its pastel façade to its cool laid-back interiors and humorous touches: beneath a sloping glass roof an immaculate wooden skiff is suspended. Welcome to a 400-year-old pub with great food and a long granite-topped bar, urbane bedrooms and a cosmopolitan air. In intimate dining rooms, chef-patron Stephen David's menu trawls Europe for inspiration and draws as much as it can on Suffolk's natural larder. Look forward to hearty dishes full of flavour and some amazing taste combinations: lamb sweetbreads with celeriac purée and minted apple crème fraîche; chilli fried squid, spaghetti, lime tomato dressing and spinach; Pimm's jelly. Wash it all down with Adnams or Meantime beers or delve into the impressive list of wines. Cosseting bedrooms decorated in chic, Nantucket style and themed in white and grey are a further attraction. There are big beds, quirky touches and a host of extras, from fruit, fresh coffee and homemade shortbread to soft bathrobes and heated bathroom floors. As for the staff, nothing is too much trouble for them. A welcoming Suffolk bolthole – unmissable!

Price	£125-£180. Singles from £95.
Rooms	10: 8 twins/doubles, 2 family rooms.
Meals	Lunch & dinner £9.50-£30. Sunday lunch from £12.50.
Closed	Open all day.
Directions	A12 north from Ipswich, then B1438 into town. Pass station and left into Quay St. On right.

Stephen David
The Crown at Woodbridge
Thoroughfare,
Woodbridge IP12 1AD

Tel	+44 (0)1394 384242
Web	www.thecrownatwoodbridge.co.uk

Sibton White Horse

Sibton

Step through the door of an unassuming pub and prepare for a surprise. The heart of this thriving village local is 16th-century and the bar is steeped in character: old pews, huge inglenook, horsebrasses on blackened beams, wonky walls, a fire in winter. Ale drinkers will note the gleaming brass beer engines on the old oak servery and settle in for pints of Adnams and Woodforde's, or a weekly-changing guest beer. (Take a peek through the window panel into the cellar to see a reclaimed Roman floor.) Food is fresh, seasonal, with local game, meat from the next village, vegetables from the kitchen garden. Try chicken, tomato and herb terrine with tomato chutney; roast breast and confit leg of duck with wild mushroom jus; sticky toffee pudding. The bread is homemade, it's all delicious, and on sunny days you can spill onto the lawns. Thoroughly modern annexe bedrooms are furnished in old and new pine; beds are comfy; bathrooms spotless; views are to open countryside. You are 20 minutes from Aldeburgh and charming Southwold: enjoy beach cricket, a pint of prawns, a dip in the North Sea.

Price	£80-£90. Singles £65.
Rooms	6: 5 twins/doubles, 1 single.
Meals	Lunch from £8.75. Dinner from £10.50. Sunday lunch £12.95
Closed	3pm-6pm.
Directions	A1120 off A12 at Yoxford; at Peasenhall, turn right opposite Creasey's butchers; pub signed.

Neil & Gill Mason
Sibton White Horse
Halesworth Road, Sibton,
Saxmundham IP17 2JJ

Tel	+44 (0)1728 660337
Web	www.sibtonwhitehorseinn.co.uk

The Westleton Crown

Westleton

This is one of England's oldest coaching inns, with 800 years of continuous service under its belt. It stands in a village two miles inland from the sea at Dunwich, with Westleton Heath running east towards Minsmere Bird Sanctuary. Inside, you find the best of old and new. A refurbishment has introduced Farrow & Ball colours, leather sofas and a tongue-and-groove bar, while the panelled walls, stripped floors, ancient beams and spindle-back chairs remain. Weave around and find nooks and crannies in which to hide, flames flickering in open fires, a huge map on the wall for walkers. You can eat wherever you want, and the Garden Room restaurant opens onto charming terraced gardens for summer barbecues. Fish comes straight off the boats at Lowestoft, local butchers provide local meat. Modern bedrooms – some in annexes – come in cool lime white with comfy beds, crisp cotton, sofas, fresh coffee, homemade biscuits. Super bathrooms are fitted out in Fired Earth and the stunning new suites have claw-foot baths and walk-in showers. Aldeburgh and Southwold are close by.

Price	£90-£215. Singles from £80.
Rooms	34: 26 doubles, 2 twins, 3 family rooms, 2 suites, 1 single.
Meals	Lunch & bar meals from £5.50. Dinner from £11.95. Sunday lunch £26.
Closed	Open all day.
Directions	A12 north from Ipswich. Right at Yoxford onto B1122, then left for Westleton on B1125. On right in village.

Gareth Clarke
The Westleton Crown
The Street, Westleton,
Saxmundham IP17 3AD
Tel +44 (0)1728 648777
Web www.westletoncrown.co.uk

The Ship

Dunwich

Once a great port, Dunwich is now a tiny (but famous) village, gradually sinking into the sea. Its well-loved smugglers' inn, almost on the beach, overlooks the saltmarsh and sea and pulls in wind-blown walkers and birdwatchers from the Minsmere Reserve. In the old-fashioned bar – nautical bric-a-brac, flagged floors, simple furnishings and a stove that belts out the heat – you can tuck into legendary hake and chips washed down with a pint of Adnams. There's also a more modern dining room where hearty food combines with traditional dishes: glorious big platefuls of ham, egg and chips, Blythburgh pork belly and ham hock terrine, and lamb cutlets served with an individual shepherd's pie. Up the fine Victorian staircase are spruced up bedrooms – simple, uncluttered – with period features, cord carpets, brass beds, old pine, little shower rooms. Rooms at the front have glorious salt marsh views, two new rooms overlook the garden, courtyard rooms are cosy with pine, and the family room under the eaves is fabulous: single beds, a big futon-style bean bag, and a flat-screen for the kids.

Price	£95-£125. Special midweek rates off season.
Rooms	15: 11 doubles, 1 twin, 3 family rooms.
Meals	Lunch from £6.95. Bar meals from £9.75. Dinner from £9.95. Sunday lunch £11.95.
Closed	Open all day.
Directions	Village signed off B1125 between A12 at Blythburgh and Westleton.

Matt Goodwin
The Ship
St James's Street, Dunwich,
Saxmundham IP17 3DT
Tel +44 (0)1728 648219
Web www.shipatdunwich.co.uk

The Anchor

Walberswick

Seeking sea air, beer guru Mark and wife Sophie are doing wonders at this well-loved pub. To the sound of the sea crashing on the beach beyond, the vast lawn hosts summer soirées and barbecues, and the wild flower meadow is perfect for picnics. Inside, sand, stone and aqua tones are redolent of the ocean and open skies and add a contemporary touch, while Sophie's menus overflow with produce sourced from a rich vein of organic farms and top local butchers. Fresh food is definitely on the menu; the allotment at the back has doubled in size. Their "Extra Special" wine list is very impressive and seasonal food is matched to beer and wine: try game terrine with Flying Dog IPA or roast cod, lentils and chorizo with a glass of Pouilly Fumé. Tempura rock oysters with a draught wheat beer are a summer treat, out on the sun terrace overlooking allotments, beach huts and distant sea. Verdant borders festooned with beach-loving plants front the six spruced up chalet rooms. Now cedar-clad, they have smart new bathrooms, comfortable beds and soft Farrow & Ball hues; three have terraces for savouring the sunrise. Dogs are welcome too.

Price	£110-£140.
Rooms	10: 9 doubles, 1 single/double.
Meals	Lunch from £6. Dinner from £13.25. Sunday lunch, 2 courses, £20.
Closed	Open all day.
Directions	From A12 south of Southwold, B1387 to Walberswick.

Mark & Sophie Dorber
The Anchor
Main Street, Walberswick,
Southwold IP18 6UA
Tel +44 (0)1502 722112
Web www.anchoratwalberswick.com

Duke's Head

Somerleyton

The shabby-chic gastropub overlooks the Somerleyton Estate; visit the grand hall, explore the glorious grounds. This 17th-century village inn has been restored in a simple, understated style with a laid-back feel: bare boards and beams, roaring log fire, warmly cosy bar. Next door, in the rambling, simply adorned dining area, good, gutsy, seasonal food is served. Daily menus use produce grown and shot on the estate, ranging from brie and fruit chutney sandwiches to pigeon breast with beetroot relish and Duke burgers with hand-cut chips. Delicious desserts include traditional ginger cake with toffee sauce; at Sunday lunch, listen to live music while tucking into estate-bred roast beef served with all the trimmings. The Duke's Head is great in summer, too, so plonk yourself down on a rustic al fresco bench and relish the views.

Meals: Lunch & dinner £8.50-£12.50.
Closed: Open all day.
Directions: Village & pub signed off B1074, 5 miles north west of Lowestoft.

Andrew Rogers
Duke's Head
Slugs Lane, Somerleyton,
Lowestoft NR32 5QR
Tel +44 (0)1502 730281
Web www.dukesheadsomerleyton.co.uk

Entry 517 Map 10

Suffolk

The Crown

Southwold

Well-heeled weekenders flock to Southwold most of the year but outside the silly season it's a gem. The chic Crown, stalwart of the dining pub world, oozes metropolitan sophistication. Ceilings are elegantly beamed, walls are colourwashed and uncluttered, the bar is large and laid-back. Adnams, famed for its beers countrywide, is on home turf here, and you would struggle to find a smarter brewery tap. The wood-panelled rear snug is the province of hard-core traditionalists, the brasserie wine bar at the front is beloved of the urbane crowd. Expect fresh, local, seasonal produce – perhaps roast Suffolk partridge, with truffled polenta, free-range pork fillet with homemade black pudding, bramble and Bramley knickerbocker glory. Don't just stick to the palate-quenching ales: the unpretentiously serious Adnams wine list is oenophiles' heaven.

Meals: Lunch from £8.95. Dinner from £12.95. Sunday lunch, 3 courses, £18.95.
Closed: 3pm-6.30pm Mon-Fri in winter. Open all day in summer.
Directions: From A12, A1095 to Southwold. Inn on High Street.

Jenny Knights
The Crown
90 High Street,
Southwold IP18 6DP
Tel +44 (0)1502 722275
Web www.adnams.co.uk/hotels

Entry 518 Map 10

The King's Head

Laxfield

Known locally as the Low House because it lies in a dip below the churchyard, the 600-year-old pub is one of Suffolk's treasures. Little has changed in the last 100 years and the four rooms creak with character – all narrow passageways, low ceilings, wood panelling and tiny fires for cold nights. The simple parlour is dominated by a three-sided, high-backed settle and there's no bar – far too new-fangled a concept for this place. Instead, Adnams ales are served from barrels in the tap room. In keeping with the authenticity, the food is rustic, hearty and homemade, the short blackboard menu listing soup, sandwiches, hot dishes and puddings. It's the sort of place where folk music starts up spontaneously, while summer brings Morris men. The lovely garden overlooking the brook at the back was once a bowling green.

Meals: Lunch & dinner £6.50-£9.50. Bar meals £4.25-£6.
Closed: 3pm-6pm. Open all day in summer.
Directions: From Laxfield church, left down hill for 50 yards. Left; pub on right.

Robert Wilson
The King's Head
Gorams Mill Lane, Laxfield,
Woodbridge IP13 8DW
Tel: +44 (0)1986 798395
Web: www.laxfieldkingshead.co.uk

Entry 519 Map 10

Suffolk

The Dennington Queen

Dennington

Traditional 16th-century features blend with contemporary touches at this beautifully refurbished Tudor inn next to the church in Dennington. If you're heading east to the coast, or west to Framlingham Castle, then head for the family-friendly Queen for a pint of Adnams ale and some great value food. Sink into a leather sofa by the fire with the papers and a coffee, or dine at scrubbed tables in the beamed, timbered and wood-floored dining room. There's lots of good things on the menu: cheddar and chutney ciabattas, salmon fishcakes with grain mustard mayonnaise, roast pork belly with spiced apple sauce, sea bass with smoked garlic, red onion risotto, a nicely gooey treacle tart. Rustic benches in the front garden overlook the church – perfect for summer.

Meals: Lunch & dinner £7.50-£12.50.
Closed: 3pm-6pm.
Directions: On A1120 between Earl Soham and Yoxford, 2 miles north of Framlingham.

Martin Royal
The Dennington Queen
Dennington,
Woodbridge IP13 3AB
Tel: +44 (0)1728 638241

Entry 520 Map 10

Station Hotel

Framlingham

The railway disappeared long ago, the old buildings are now business units, but the 'hotel' continues to thrive. Cask ales (a classic Victorian bitter, a sweet, wintry porter) are perfect accompaniments for gutsy cooking. Who would imagine, chalked up on the board on the edge of a market town somewhere in Suffolk, roast squash, chilli and ginger soup, confit duck leg or whole sea bass with chorizo, pepper and spinach casserole? Or lemongrass and ginger crème for pudding? Lunch is quiet but it bustles at night, helped along by the master of the kitchen, Mike Jones, and his friendly, laid-back team. The building is pretty in a shabby-boho way, the interior is charming. Expect blackened stripped boards, cream papered walls, a stuffed head, and bone-handled knives partnering paper serviettes – a characterful mix.

Meals	Lunch & dinner £4-£15.75. Bar meals £3.25-£11.
Closed	2.30pm-5pm (7pm Sun).
Directions	From Wickham Market, 10 min off the A12.

Mike Jones
Station Hotel
Station Road, Framlingham,
Woodbridge IP13 9EE
Tel +44 (0)1728 723455
Web www.thestationhotel.net

Suffolk

Eels Foot Inn

East Bridge

The sign depicts an eel wriggling out of an old boot, and this plain-looking and oddly named backwater village pub lives up to its slightly eccentric reputation. It's a twitchers' pub where you will find watchers and wardens from Minsmere RSPB Reserve swapping stories with walkers, cyclists and holidaymakers. All are drawn to this local for pints of tip-top Adnams ale (the full range is on tap), and hearty food (beer battered cod, steak and ale pie, treacle tart) served in a cosy wood-floored bar, replete with log fire and simple furnishings; there's a homely upper dining area, too. Don't miss the craic on music nights – every Thursday is Squit Night (a folk, country and blues jamming session) and the last Sunday night of the month is folk night. Note – the place is mobbed in summer! Camping facilities available.

Meals	Lunch & dinner £5-£13.
Closed	3pm-6pm. Open all day Sat & Sun.
Directions	Off B1122 between Yoxford & Leiston.

Corinne Webber
Eels Foot Inn
East Bridge,
Leiston IP16 4SN
Tel +44 (0)1728 830154
Web www.theeelsfootinn.co.uk

The Froize

Chillesford

Impassioned by local produce years before it became fashionable, David Grimwood lives in chef's whites or shooting tweeds – a Suffolk countryman too chivalrous to accept his reputation as East Anglia's best game cook. Off the beaten track, the path to these once charmingly remote 18th-century keepers' cottages is well worn by regulars. Blythburgh pork, Orford and Lowestoft fish, bags of local game (much of it retrieved by the landlord's black labs) combined with retro rustic cooking reflect the 'field, forest and foreshore' landscape The Froize sits in. A perfect joint always stands alongside reworked classics such as devilled kidneys, stuffed skate wing or cider-braised rabbit and prunes, and the homemade puddings are legendary. Ales are the county's best, mostly Adnams, and there's Aspall's cider, too.

Meals	Lunch & dinner from £13.50.
Closed	Monday (except bank hols).
Directions	On B1084 between Woodbridge and Orford.

	David Grimwood The Froize The Street, Chillesford, Woodbridge IP12 3PU
Tel	+44 (0)1394 450282
Web	www.froize.co.uk

The King's Head Inn

Orford

Standing in the shadow of the village church and windswept graveyard, the 12th-century King's Head is steeped in smuggling history: Orford's ancient quay is a stroll away. Adrian and Susan Searing have breathed new life into the place. This is no gastropub, however, but a proper, no-nonsense village local: children and dogs are welcome. A winter fire warms the beamed and carpeted traditional bar, and there are old scrubbed tables on a rug-strewn wooden floor in the rustic-chic dining room next door. Expect classic pub food – sourced entirely from locally sourced ingredients – from fish pie with sautéed French beans and moules and frites to Suffolk ham ploughman's, treacle tart and traditional Sunday roasts. Or drop by for a glass of prosecco or cracking pint of Adnams Broadside – itself a meal in a glass.

Meals	Lunch & dinner from £8.95. Bar meals £3.95-£10.95. Sunday lunch £12.95.
Closed	3pm-6pm (Mon-Fri).
Directions	Leave A12 at Woodbridge; A1152 & B1084 to Orford; pub on main square.

	Susan & Adrian Searing The King's Head Inn Front Street, Orford, Woodbridge IP12 2LW
Tel	+44 (0)1394 450271
Web	www.thekingsheadorford.co.uk

The British Larder

Bromeswell

Keen to give her phenomenally successful recipe blog a physical and spiritual base, Madalene (ex-Gordon Ramsay) has transformed this run-down Suffolk pub into a British Larder – and you can come and taste the food! Her philosophy is based on fresh seasonal ingredients sourced from farmers and producers in and around Suffolk – and that includes ales from Adnams and ciders from Aspall. The exciting daily menu brims with creativity and treats, from Dingley Dell pork and Orford-landed John Dory to Mr Atkinson's roasted squash, and there's a delicious local game-tasting board, too: venison scotch eggs, rabbit rillette, partridge, prune and bacon sausages, game terrine. Find a wood-burner in the bar, chunky tables in the informal dining room, a garden for fine weather... this place has the seasons covered.

Meals	Lunch from £7.50. Dinner from £12.50. Set lunch £15 & £18.
Closed	Open all day.
Directions	On A1152 3 miles east of Woodbridge and A12.

Madalene Bonvini-Hamel
The British Larder
Orford Road, Bromeswell,
Woodbridge IP12 2PU
Tel +44 (0)1394 460310
Web www.britishlarder.co.uk

Entry 525 Map 10

The Ship

Levington

The owners have changed at this 14th-century beauty overlooking the River Orwell, but thankfully they've kept its character intact. The low-ceilinged bar and flower-festooned terrace continue to attract yachting types, locals and tourists, and in the series of warm, welcoming little rooms nautical memorabilia still reaches into every corner. Beers are from Adnams – Bitter tapped from the cask, Ghost Ship and Broadside on handpump – and fish features strongly on the menu, perhaps fish pie glazed with cheddar cheese, or sea bass with risotto verde and white wine cream. Elsewhere there could be steak and mushroom pie, liver and bacon with lyonnaise potatoes, Eton mess with pavlova meringue. This is a unique local's favourite, with welcoming, friendly staff and wonderful riverside walks straight from the door.

Meals	Lunch & dinner £8.95-£15.95. Not Sun eves (Nov-Feb).
Closed	2.30pm-6pm. Open all day Sat & Sun. Open all day June-Sept.
Directions	A12/A14 junction to Woodbridge; follow signs for Levington.

Adrian & Susan Searing
The Ship
Church Lane, Levington,
Ipswich IP10 0LQ
Tel +44 (0)1473 659573
Web www.theshipinnlevington.co.uk

Entry 526 Map 10

Anchor Inn

Nayland

The Bunting family, like many farmers, have had to diversify: they bought the pub next to their land. And they take huge pride in the produce that appears on the menus – pheasant, duck and rabbit from farm shoots, eggs from their bantams, lamb from their fields, vegetables from their kitchen garden. Not only that, the smokehouse at the back produces game, fish and treacle bacon – unmissable! When it came to updating the building they sensibly kept things simple. This pretty butter-coloured pub successfully features soft modern colours in traditional small rooms with open fires; and there's a good big restaurant upstairs. Another draw is the setting, right beside the river Stour with summer barbecues bringing out the best of the garden. At the Buntings Heritage Farm behind, rare Suffolk Punch horses plough the fields in the old way; check their website for times.

Meals — Lunch & dinner £9.50-£16.50. Sunday lunch £9.95.
Closed — See website for details.
Directions — From Colchester A134 on Essex & Suffolk border. 300m off the A134 where road crosses River Stour.

Hector Bunting
Anchor Inn
26 Court Street, Nayland,
Colchester CO6 4JL
Tel +44 (0)1206 262313
Web www.anchornayland.co.uk

Entry 527 Map 10

Suffolk

The Lindsey Rose

Lindsey

The Lindsey Rose has long been known as a food haunt between Hadleigh and Lavenham. And the atmospheric feel of the 15th-century Suffolk hall house remains – in open beamed partitions, rich red décor, scrubbed wooden tables and bare planked floors. Things have become decidedly posher of late, thanks to the introduction of a retro grill – though the simplicity of the menu belies the quality of the cooking. Choose your own cut and weight of their slow-reared, well-hung estate beef at the meat counter, cooked to your taste along with some rather good trimmings. For fish-lovers and vegetarians there are Colchester oysters and beer-battered cod, garlic mushrooms with Suffolk Blue cheese, and pasta with roasted vegetables and pesto, unfussily presented and extremely tasty. Puddings, too, are excellent.

Meals — Lunch & dinner £8-£16.
Closed — 3pm-5.30pm. Open all day Sun.
Directions — Lindsey is signed south off A1141, between Hadleigh & Lavenham.

James Buckle
The Lindsey Rose
Lindsey,
Ipswich IP7 6PP
Tel +44 (0)1449 741424
Web www.redroseinn.co.uk

Entry 528 Map 10

The Swan

Monks Eleigh

The polished, wooden floored interior is not unlike that of a bistro, but Nigel and Carol's 16th-century thatched Swan is still a pub at heart. There's a large bar, Adnams on hand pump and a good line in wines by the glass. The modernised interior is invitingly open with recessed ceiling lights, soft sage tones and a winter log fire. Nigel has created a blackboard menu to please both the traditionalist and the adventurer, so wintry offerings may include potted pork rillettes with apple and sultana chutney, whole roast partridge with braised lentils, bacon and onions, and a fabulously sticky toffee pudding with butterscotch and mascarpone. Fish can be relied upon to be beautifully fresh. Service, by Carol, is a lesson in how these things should be done: efficient, knowledgeable, cheerful and charming.

Meals	Lunch & dinner £10-£16.75. Bar meals £4.25-£7.
Closed	3pm-7pm. Sun eves & Mon all day.
Directions	On B1115 between Lavenham & Hadleigh.

Nigel & Carol Ramsbottom
The Swan
The Street, Monks Eleigh,
Ipswich IP7 7AU
Tel +44 (0)1449 741391
Web www.monkseleigh.com

Entry 529 Map 10

Suffolk

The Bildeston Crown

Bildeston

There are flagstones in the bar, warm reds on the walls and sweet-smelling logs smouldering in open fires. The inn dates from 1529, the interior design from 2005. Not that the feel is overly contemporary; ancient beams have been reclaimed and varnished wood floors shine like honey. There are gilded mirrors and oils on the walls, candles in the fireplace, smart locals at the bar. An airy open-plan feel runs throughout, with lots of space in the dining room and smart leather chairs tucked under hand-made oak tables. They're proud of their food here and it ranges from roast Suffolk beef sandwiches with mustard mayo to a theatrically, chic-ly presented eight-course tasting menu in the evening. There are flowers in the courtyard and Suffolk beers to quench your thirst.

Meals	Lunch & dinner £24-£50. Bar meals from £5. Sunday lunch £25.
Closed	Open all day.
Directions	A12 junc. 31, then B1070 to Hadleigh. A1141 north, then B1115 into village & on right.

Hayley Lee
The Bildeston Crown
104 High Street, Bildeston,
Ipswich IP7 7EB
Tel +44 (0)1449 740510
Web www.thebildestoncrown.co.uk

Entry 530 Map 10

The White Horse

Whepstead

Built in 1640, with an early 19th century addition, this rural beauty is worth more than a passing nod. For here Gary and Di Kingshott are continuing the modus operandi that made their previous pub, The Beehive at Horinger, such a favourite with the local country lifers. Stock in trade are real ales from Adnams, a reasonably priced wine list, cosy fires, and a chatty, informal beamed bar. Comfortable dining areas come decorated with fresh, contemporary colours – one doubles as an art gallery with regularly changing exhibits – in which to enjoy the blackboard menu. Fried duck egg on toast with a sauté of wild mushrooms, traditional beef bourguignon and treacle tart are unpretentious and strong on flavour. Fun, friendly and charismatic, it is hard to believe that this grand cru of a pub was picked up in a distress sale.

Meals	Lunch & dinner from £9.95. Bar meals from £8.95. Sunday lunch, 3 courses, £24.45.
Closed	Sunday evenings.
Directions	5 miles south of Bury St Edmunds; signposted off the A143 or the B1066.

Gary & Diane Kingshott
The White Horse
Rede Road, Whepstead,
Bury St Edmunds IP29 4SS
Tel +44 (0)1284 735760
Web www.whitehorsewhepstead.co.uk

Entry 531 Map 10

Suffolk

The Fox Inn

Bury St Edmunds

Town centre inns don't get much better than The Fox – a stunning 15th-century building opposite the Abbey Gardens, a stroll from the famous cathedral. Refurbished with style and panache by passionate owners, it draws a small but loyal drinking crowd for tip-top Greene King ales, and foodies for seasonal dishes that champion local produce: free-range farm meats, Bury-baked bread, organic milk and eggs, cheese from Norfolk. Escape the shops and bag a table by the fire in the Green Room, replete with fine Jacobean panelling, painted Lloyd Loom chairs and fresh flowers. There's duck liver and tarragon parfait, Old Spot pork loin with cider cream sauce, haddock with beetroot and caper relish; or relax over a roast leg of lamb with fresh mint stuffing for Sunday lunch. Delicious.

Meals	Lunch from £5.25. Bar meals from £5.95. Dinner from £10.95. Sunday lunch £22.50.
Closed	Open all day.
Directions	Adjacent to Abbey Gardens in town centre.

Ron & Sheila Blackmore
The Fox Inn
1 Eastgate Street,
Bury St Edmunds IP33 1XX
Tel +44 (0)1284 705562
Web www.thefoxinnbury.co.uk

Entry 532 Map 10

The Stag on the River

Eashing

Once through Eashing is a small bridge with a warning that heavy loads might lead to its demise. We trust this won't happen, as the pretty stone structure built by 13th-century monks forms an essential link to the spruced-up Stag on the River. With a lease dating back to 1771, this is an attractive and an atmospheric place to discover good home cooking, real ale and a happy buzz. Produce is local – meats are sourced from Osney Lodge Farm at Godstone – and in season. Try lamb rump with bean cassoulet and red wine jus or winter vegetable tagine; finish with a warm chocolate and walnut brownie. In spring and summer the teak-furnished terrace by the water makes a languorous spot for supping a pint of Surrey Hills Shere Drop. In winter you can seek out a cosy corner in one of several rambling rooms, where wood and brick floors and open fires blend with modern tables and trendy armchairs. Immaculate new bedrooms are warm, contemporary and stylish, one with wall timbers and wonky floors; all with designer wall coverings, coffee machines, goose down duvets and walk-in showers.

Price	£65-£95.
Rooms	3: 2 doubles, 1 family room.
Meals	Lunch & dinner £10.75-£22.95.
Closed	Open all day.
Directions	A3 south; 5 miles after Guildford, Eashing signed left at services. Left at garage; over bridge; on right.

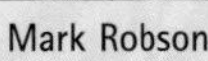

Mark Robson
The Stag on the River
Lower Eashing Lane, Eashing,
Godalming GU7 2QG
Tel +44 (0)1483 421568
Web www.stagontherivereashing.co.uk

The Crown Inn

Chiddingfold

Beautifully restored in 2008, the Crown is a contender for the oldest hostelry in the country. Thirteenth-century bowed brick walls, warped weathered timbers, plaster ceilings and lattice windows... think yourself back in the days of the highwaymen. The bar's stained-glass leaded lights – for which charming Chiddingfold was once famous – tell of 'the Lion and the Unicorn's fight for the Crown', while the pattern-carpeted main bar holds a very fine stone fireplace from 1619 and a crackling fire. It's a fascinating place so, pint of Sharp's Doom in hand, take a wander and a gander at the small glass case of coins that date back to 1558. In keeping, the menu lists classic dishes – coq au vin, game pie, fish and chips, apple and rhubarb crumble – prepared from excellent ingredients. Historic charm extends upstairs to cosy rooms with wonky walls and madly sloping floors, antique chests and polished wardrobes, carved wooden four-posters (three in all) and beds dressed in crisp cotton. Mod cons include iPod radios, posh tellys, and elegant Ren smellies in smart bathrooms.

Price	£125-£165. Suite £200. Singles £100.
Rooms	8: 3 doubles, 3 four-posters, 1 single, 1 suite.
Meals	Lunch & dinner £10-£20.
Closed	Open all day.
Directions	On A283 between Guildford and Petworth.

Marcus Tapping
The Crown Inn
The Green, Chiddingfold,
Godalming GU8 4TX
Tel +44 (0)1428 682255
Web www.thecrownchiddingfold.com

The Swan Inn

Chiddingfold

After 20 years at Knightsbridge's revered Swag & Tails, Annemaria and Stuart escaped to the country to revive an old Surrey bolthole. What you find now are sparkling dining areas and a cool bar, wooden floors, blazing log fires, chunky tables and bags of style. It may be more classy eatery than traditional pub, but there's artisan ale from Surrey Hills Brewery, big smiles from attentive staff, and proper homemade burgers for those in for a bite. And more: beer-battered haddock with fries and pea purée, chargrilled rib-eye steak with caramelised shallots and béarnaise sauce, scallops with black pudding and smoked bacon risotto cake, braised beef cheeks with horseradish mash and curly kale – unpretentious dishes that juggle popular with modern. If you're staying, contemporary bedrooms are warm and cosy, with excellent linen and downy duvets, big beds and flat-screen TVs, sofas in spacious suites, and trendy bathrooms with power showers and toiletries. Outside: a super landscaped garden for summer socialising. In short, the Swan represents a relaxed revival of an old inn in a rather fetching village.

Price	£100-£180.
Rooms	10: 8 doubles, 1 suite, 1 family room.
Meals	Lunch & dinner £7.50-19.95. Bar meals from £7.50. Sunday lunch, 3 courses, £26-£28.
Closed	Open all day.
Directions	South of village green beside A283 between Guildford & Petworth.

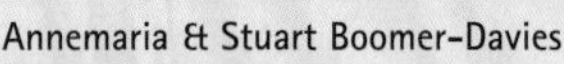

Annemaria & Stuart Boomer-Davies
The Swan Inn
Petworth Road, Chiddingfold,
Godalming GU8 4TY

Tel +44 (0)1428 684688
Web www.theswaninnchiddingfold.com

The Richard Onslow

Cranleigh

A spruced-up Surrey outpost for the innovative Peach Pubs. Since John Taylor revamped the old tile-hung inn (named after the Onslows of Clandon Park) it has become the hub of Cranleigh. Period features blend beautifully with a contemporary feel to create a super-relaxed background for monthly quiz and movie nights, and enjoyable all-day dining. Call in for breakfast from 7.30am; share a deli board heaped with cheeses and cold cuts; tuck into a daily roast. There's linguine with squid, clams, cockles, lemon and parsley, and lamb shank with tomato ragout, available for both lunch and dinner. You can choose between the laid-back bars or the retro dining room, a high-ceilinged space with huge mirrors and lampshades, upholstered banquettes and old tables. Period fireplaces, ancient beams and low doorways – the building goes back to the 16th century – were rediscovered during the refurbishment of the bedrooms. Those at the back overlooking the patio ooze historic charm while the stylish rest face the street; all have contemporary fabrics, British-made beds, iPod docks and bathrooms with walk-in showers.

Price	£95.
Rooms	10 doubles.
Meals	Lunch from £7. Bar meals from £5. Dinner from £11. Sunday lunch £13.50.
Closed	Open all day.
Directions	In the centre of Cranleigh village.

John Taylor
The Richard Onslow
113-117 High Street,
Cranleigh GU6 8AU
Tel +44 (0)1483 274922
Web www.therichardonslow.co.uk

Dog & Pheasant

Brook

Safe in the hands of the two Davids, this popular old roadside inn oozes bonhomie. And, though the food is the driving force, the small bar heaves with upmarket locals in for a pint of Adnams Broadside or a glass of pinot noir. Smart and cosy it is, with black wood ceiling beams, striking wall timbers and warming winter fires; service is both friendly and upbeat. Chef Remi Ravaux's lengthy repertoire should please all with classic and modern dishes, and seafood a speciality. Blackboard specials like pan-fried fillet of rainbow trout with curly kale and roasted garlic sauce complement a main menu that covers all. Wednesday 'Grill Night' is not to be missed and sees Remi cooking all the meats in the inglenook fireplace at the centre of the pub. A front terrace, a big garden and a private dining room upstairs complete the happy picture.

Meals	Lunch & dinner £8-£17.
Closed	Open all day.
Directions	On the Haslemere Road (A287) between Godalming and Haslemere.

David Gough & David Hall
Dog & Pheasant
Haslemere Road, Brook,
Godalming GU8 5UJ

Tel	+44 (0)1428 682763
Web	www.dogandpheasant.com

Entry 537 Map 4

Surrey

The Hare & Hounds

Lingfield

Eric and Tracy Payet have changed little since taking over this striking pub close to Lingfield Racecourse. It's still an idiosyncratic place whose quirky collectables and bold paintings fill every corner and wall. Bar bustle can be surveyed from old cinema seats or one of a pair of throne-like chairs, while cushion-laden banquettes make a cosy spot from which to view Eric's (ex-Club Gascon, London) menus. Look to the chalkboard for daily dishes: rabbit stew with mustard sauce; roast hake with confit fennel. On the printed menu are aged parmesan and pea risotto; honey-glazed pork chop with black pudding and caramelised apple; roast pear clafoutis. Diners are as happy among the hop garlands and the greenery of the main bar as beneath the artwork in the lovely dining room. Nurse a summer pint of Abbot Ale in the partly decked garden.

Meals	Lunch & dinner £7.95-£18.95.
Closed	Open all day (closed Sun from 7pm).
Directions	From A22 towards Lingfield Racecourse into Common Road.

Eric & Tracy Payet
The Hare & Hounds
Common Road,
Lingfield RH7 6BZ

Tel	+44 (0)1342 832351
Web	www.hareandhoundspublichouse.co.uk

Entry 538 Map 4

The Parrot

Forest Green

Having left her mini-empire of London pubs for a livestock farm in the Surrey hills, Linda Gotto also runs this rambling, 17th-century pub overlooking the village green and cricket pitch. She is passionate about food, its provenance and quality, and The Parrot showcases meats reared on the farm – Shorthorn cattle, Middlewhite pigs, and mutton – both on the short, imaginative menu and in the unique new farm shop next to the pub. Surely one of few pubs where you can tuck into game pie, lamb rump with minted pea purée and roast belly pork with mash and braised cabbage, and then buy the produce to take home (farm meats, free-range eggs, sausages, pickles, cheeses, pies). Elsewhere, beams, flagstones and lovely bits and bobs, old settles and blazing fires, London Pride on tap and 16 wines by the glass. The value is outstanding.

Meals	Lunch & dinner £9.50-£18. Bar meals from £5.50. Sunday lunch, 3 courses, £25. Not Sunday eve.
Closed	Open all day.
Directions	Opposite the village green, off B2127 just west of junction with B2126, 5 miles south west of Dorking.

Linda Gotto
The Parrot
Forest Green,
Dorking RH5 5RZ

Tel +44 (0)1306 621339
Web www.theparrot.co.uk

Entry 539 Map 4

Surrey

The Inn

West End

Wine importer Gerry Price draws them in from all over Surrey. Stylishly revamped dining areas are light and modern with wooden floors and fine fabrics. The feeling is relaxed and friendly – quiz nights, film club, boules, barbecues; the homely bar has hand-pumped ale from Fuller's and Young's and the list of wines is long, with a nod to Portuguese shores. Monthly menus have modern British choices ranging from salmon and dill fishcakes with tartare sauce to pot-roasted pork with cabbage and dauphinoise potatoes – and partridge, pheasant, woodcock and teal in winter. A pastry chef masterminds a select choice of desserts; cheeses are farmhouse best. Add good-value set lunches, lunchtime wine-tasting sessions, an alfresco wood oven and popular wine dinners, and you have a superbly run place.

Meals	Lunch & dinner £5.25-£32.50. Sunday lunch £24.95.
Closed	3pm-5pm. Open all day Sat & Sun.
Directions	On A322 towards Guildford, 2 miles from M3 junc. 3.

Gerry & Ann Price
The Inn
42 Guildford Road, West End,
Woking GU24 9PW

Tel +44 (0)1276 858652
Web www.the-inn.co.uk

Entry 540 Map 4

The Crab & Lobster

Sidlesham

Backing directly onto Pagham Harbour and the bird-rich marshes, The Crab flaunts an inglenook fireplace and ancient flagstones that blend effortlessly with upholstered banquettes, ornate mirrors and vintage photos on white walls. This fabulous proper pub is managed by Sam but is often driven by the locals; Burns Night and wine evenings are popular events. Windows offer endless sea views and there's a fishy focus to the menu, as you'd expect – crab and lobster ravioli, organic sea trout with niçoise salad, Cornish sardines with black olive butter. Carnivores can tuck into the likes of lamb cutlets with roasted garlic and thyme jus, and all is served on cool white plates. Enjoy a pint of local Sussex and choose a seat on the back terrace for views of sheep-grazed meadows and marshes. Bedrooms are for birdwatchers, particularly Room 4 with its perfectly perched telescope... find handmade beds, planked floors and walk-in storm showers, heritage colours, fresh coffee and beautiful bathrooms sporting Ren toiletries. And there's Crab Cottage, a seaside hobbit house, an opulent gem.

Price	From £140. Cottage from £220.
Rooms	4 + 1: 4 doubles. Self-catering cottage for 4.
Meals	Lunch from £10.50. Bar meals from £6.50. Dinner from £16.95. Sunday lunch, 2-3 courses, £24-£35.
Closed	Open all day.
Directions	Mill Lane is off B2145 Chichester to Selsey road, just south of Sidlesham. Pub close to Pagham Harbour.

Sam Bakose
The Crab & Lobster
Mill Lane, Sidlesham,
Chichester PO20 7NB
Tel +44 (0)1243 641233
Web www.crab-lobster.co.uk

The Foresters Arms

Graffham

Set in somnolent, wooded countryside below the South Downs, the Foresters is as English as they come. Dating back to the 17th century, the front is bright with hanging baskets in summer, while inside glows; the big inglenook with crackling logs enough to cheer the heart of the chilliest walker. Grab a pint of Harvey's and settle into the most comfortable and comforting of surroundings. Old beams, timbers and walls of exposed brick, along with Windsor chairs and cottagey pews are softened by lamps and coordinated curtains and cushions. The cooking is honest British too, with an occasional nod to the Med; so tuck into some ale-battered smoked haddock, or spaghetti with tiger prawns, chorizo and baby squid. Sunday roasts are the business – try the goose fat roast potatoes. If you're planning to stay the night, cosy bedrooms in the adjoining annexe, small but perfectly formed, are full of light and dressed in pastel shades. Expect chunky wooden beds, trim carpets, good quality linen and bijou bathrooms with showers. The Sussex breakfasts are worth setting the alarm for.

Price	£70-£99. Singles £60-£99.
Rooms	3 doubles.
Meals	Lunch from £5. Bar meals from £8.95. Dinner from £9.95. Sunday lunch, 3 courses, £18.
Closed	3pm-6pm. Open all day Sat & Sun (Jul-Aug).
Directions	From Midhurst, 2 miles south on A286, then left for Heyshott/Graffham. Straight ahead, left at T-junction in village; pub on right.

The Foresters Arms
The Street, Graffham,
Petworth GU28 0QA

Tel +44 (0)1798 867202
Web www.forestersgraffham.co.uk

The Horse Guards Inn

Tillington

After a visit to Petworth House, head for the 300-year-old inn on the park's western edge. Up from the tiny lane, opposite the church, serene views sweep towards the South Downs from the pub's hammock'd garden. Inside, a series of rambling and intimate rooms with a *Country Living* feel: old prints, quirky pieces, fresh flowers, wonky beams, brick floors, painted panelling, old pine tables and four log fires – one in an old back range. Sam and Misa love this pub and their passion is reflected in the homemade goodies on sale and their promotion of local food; chalkboards champion the farmers and producers that supply the kitchen. Great dishes include potted rabbit, blade of beef with red wine sauce, a rich and delicious fish pie, washed down – why not? – with a pint of Harvey's Sussex. Then a perfect ricotta on baked damsons. Our pick of the three simple, characterful and contemporary bedrooms is the big brass bedded double upstairs, with thick beams, sloping floor, a view of the church. Hand-made chocolates are on the house; the bathroom has locally made treats. Fantastic.

Price	From £80.
Rooms	3 twins/doubles.
Meals	Lunch & dinner from £10. Bar meals from £6.
Closed	Open all day.
Directions	Just off A272 1 mile west of Petworth. Pub opposite the church.

Sam & Misha Beard
The Horse Guards Inn
Tillington,
Petworth GU28 9AF
Tel +44 (0)1798 342332
Web www.thehorseguardsinn.co.uk

The Bull

Ditchling

In a picturesque village, a pretty inn, dark and cosy and warmed by cheery fires and candlelight. The rambling and atmospheric bar hasn't changed for years, there are four ales on tap including Dark Star, and the other areas have been stylishly transformed, with pine and parquet and modern art on mellow walls. And there's some rather upmarket food to match, like filo-encrusted cannon of lamb stuffed with apricots and cumin. Even the ciabattas are filled with locally smoked salmon and horseradish cream: all of the produce can be traced back to local farms, and the game comes from the Balcombe estate. Similar treats can be found on the separate children's menu, and you can eat or drink wherever you like, including the snug at the back, for as long as you wish. Bring wellies or bikes and try out the high-level trails on the South Downs, return to bedrooms where new and old blend successfully. Expect rain showers, comfortable beds, crisp linen sheets and a bit of noise from below until closing time. This year, there's a new kitchen, an extended restaurant and big new rooms in the converted barn out back too.

Price	£80-£120.
Rooms	4: 3 doubles, 1 twin/double.
Meals	Lunch & dinner from £10.
Closed	Open all day.
Directions	Leave A23 just north of Brighton for Pyecombe. North on A273, then west for Ditchling on B2112. In centre of village at crossroads.

Dominic Worrall
The Bull
2 High Street, Ditchling,
Hassocks BN6 8TA
Tel +44 (0)1273 843147
Web www.thebullditchling.com

The Ram Inn

Firle

The road runs out once it reaches Firle village nestling beneath the South Downs... hard to believe now, but this quiet backwater was once a staging post. Built of brick and flint, the inn reveals a fascinating history – the Georgian part was once a courthouse and the kitchen goes back 500 years. Rescued from closure in 2006, the Ram Inn is once again thriving. Its three rooms have been decorated in rustic-chic style – bare boards and parquet, coal fires in old brick fireplaces, chunky candles on darkwood tables. Walkers stomp in from the Downs for pints of Harveys Sussex and hot steak sandwiches; foodies flock after dark for great fresh food, perhaps ham and pea broth, rump of Hankham Farm organic lamb with red wine jus, and sticky toffee pudding. Retire upstairs to quirky, individual rooms with bold colours, exposed beams, super comfortable beds, fluffy bathrobes in tiled bathrooms, and dreamy village or South Downs views. And there's a splendid flint-walled garden for peaceful summer supping. Handy for Charleston Farmhouse, country home to the Bloomsbury set.

Price	£90-£145. Singles £60-£80.
Rooms	4: 2 doubles, 2 twins/doubles.
Meals	Lunch & dinner £9.95-£16.95. Sunday lunch £11.95.
Closed	Open all day.
Directions	Pub & village signed off A27 east of Lewes.

Hayley Bayes
The Ram Inn
The Street, Firle,
Lewes BN8 6NS
Tel +44 (0)1273 858222
Web www.raminn.co.uk

The Griffin Inn

Fletching

A proper inn, one of the best, a community local that draws a well-heeled and devoted crowd. The occasional touch of scruffiness makes it almost perfect; fancy designers need not apply. The Pullan family run it with huge passion. You get cosy open fires, 400-year-old beams, oak panelling, settles, red carpets, prints on the walls... it's aged well. There's a lively bar, a small club room for racing on Saturdays and two cricket teams play in summer. Bedrooms are tremendous value for money and full of uncluttered country-inn elegance: uneven floors above the bar, lovely old furniture, soft coloured walls, free-standing Victorian baths, huge shower heads, crisp linen, fluffy bathrobes, handmade soaps. Rooms in the coach house are quieter, those in next-door Griffin House quieter still. Smart menus based on the finest seasonal produce include fresh fish from Rye and Fletching lamb; both food and beers are as local as can be. There's a wood oven on the terrace and, on summer Sundays, a spit-roast barbecue – accompanied by ten-mile views stretching across Sheffield Park to the South Downs.

Price	£85-£145. Singles £60-£80 (Sun-Thur).
Rooms	13: 6 doubles, 7 four-posters.
Meals	Lunch from £11. Dinner, 3 courses, £30-£40.
Closed	Open all day.
Directions	From East Grinstead A22 south, right at Nutley for Fletching. On for 2 miles into village.

Nigel & James Pullan
The Griffin Inn
Fletching,
Uckfield TN22 3SS

Tel	+44 (0)1825 722890
Web	www.thegriffininn.co.uk

The Cat

West Hoathly

Owner Andrew swapped grand Gravetye Manor for the buzzy, pubby atmosphere of The Cat in 2009; he hasn't looked back. The 16th-century building, a fine medieval hall house with a Victorian extension, has been comfortably modernised without losing its character. Inside are beamed ceilings and panelling, planked floors, splendid inglenooks, and an airy room that leads to a garden at the back, furnished with teak and posh brollies. Harvey's Ale and some top-notch pub food, passionately put together from fresh local ingredients by chef Max Leonard, attract a solid, old-fashioned crowd: retired locals, foodies and walkers. Tuck into rare roast beef and horseradish sandwiches, Rye Bay sea bass with brown shrimp and caper butter, South Downs lamb chops with dauphinoise (and leave room for treacle tart!). The setting is idyllic, in a pretty village opposite a 12th-century church – best viewed from two of four bright and comfortable bedrooms. Crisp linen on big beds, rich fabrics, fawn carpets, fresh bathrooms and antique touches illustrate the style. A sweet retreat in a charming village backwater.

Price	£100-£140.
Rooms	4 doubles.
Meals	Lunch from £12. Bar meals from £6. Dinner from £12. Sunday lunch, 3 courses, £26. Not Sunday eve.
Closed	3pm-6pm. Sun eves from 5pm.
Directions	Village signed off B2028 6 miles north of Haywards Heath.

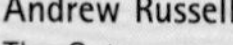

Andrew Russell
The Cat
Queen's Square, West Hoathly,
East Grinstead RH19 4PP
Tel +44 (0)1342 810369
Web www.catinn.co.uk

The Tiger Inn

East Dean

Following investment by the Davies-Gilbert family, the celebrated estate-owned Tiger roared back into life in 2010. New kitchen, new loos, extra dining space and five beautiful bedrooms have transformed this downland treasure into one classy inn, without losing any of the charm and character. Other than a lick of paint, little has changed in the atmospheric bar, all low beams, stone floors, ancient settles and crackling fire; delightful to wash up here after a blustery walk on Beachy Head. Beside a cottage-lined green in a fold of the South Downs, the Tiger Inn is a supporter of the community: find estate-brewed ales like Legless Rambler and organic meat from estate farms. There are traditional sandwiches, ploughman's and stews at lunch time, while sausage and mash rub shoulders with salmon and spicy chorizo cassoulet in the evening. Bolthole bedrooms ooze style: calming colours, feather down bedding, an eclectic mix of pretty old pine and antique furnishings, fine beds, fresh bathrooms. Book 'Minnie' for views of the green and the Downs. Mobbed in summer, the old Tiger is a refuge in winter.

Price	£95.
Rooms	5: 4 doubles, 1 twin.
Meals	Lunch from £8.95. Bar meals from £2.75. Dinner from £8.95. Sunday lunch, 3 courses, £25.
Closed	Open all day.
Directions	West from Eastbourne on A259. Left in village and on right.

Jacques Pienaar
The Tiger Inn
The Green, East Dean,
Eastbourne BN20 0DA

Tel	+44 (0)1323 423209
Web	www.beachyhead.org.uk

The George in Rye

Rye

Ancient Rye has a big history. It's a reclaimed island, a wealthy cinque port which once had its own army yet regularly fell into French hands. Henry James lived here, and the oldest working church clock in England chimes in a gracious square at the top of the hill. As for The George, it stands serenely on the cobbled high street. It was built in 1575 from reclaimed ships' timbers and its exposed beams and joists remain on display to this day. A contemporary revamp in classical style trumpets airy interiors, stripped floors, panelled walls and open fires – Jane Austen in the 21st century. There's a huge leather sofa in the bar by the fire, screen prints of the Beatles on the walls in reception, voile curtains and parquet floors in the restaurant. Divine bedrooms, including ten recent additions, come in all shapes and sizes, but fabulous fabrics, Frette linen, flat-screen TVs and Vi-Spring mattresses are standard, as are Ren potions by the bath and cashmere covers on hot water bottles. Superb food in the smart new Grill restaurant – Rye Bay lobster, Romney Marsh lamb – can be washed down by local English wines. Exceptional.

Price	£135-£195. Suites £295. Singles from £95.
Rooms	34: 8 doubles, 21 twins/doubles, 5 suites.
Meals	Lunch & dinner from £12.95.
Closed	Open all day.
Directions	Follow signs up hill into town centre. Through arch; hotel on left, below church. Parking at foot of hill.

Alex & Katie Clarke
The George in Rye
98 High Street,
Rye TN31 7JT
Tel +44 (0)1797 222114
Web www.thegeorgeinrye.com

The Ship Inn

Rye

The 16th-century smuggler's warehouse stands by the quay at the bottom of cobbled Mermaid Street. Climb the church tower for stunning coast and marsh views, then retreat to the laid-back warmth of the Ship's rustic bars. Cosy nooks, ancient timbers, blazing fires and a quirky delicious décor characterise this place; there are battered leather sofas, simple café-style chairs, old pine tables and good paintings and prints. Quaff a pint of Harvey's Sussex or local farm cider, leaf through the daily papers, play one of the board games – there are heaps. Lunch and dinner menus are short and imaginative and make good use of local ingredients, so tuck into confit duck with grilled aubergine and saffron yogurt, roast sea bream with buttered samphire, warm salad of squid, fennel and chorizo, and fresh Rye Bay fish. The relaxed funky feel extends to bright and beachy bedrooms upstairs: find painted wooden floors, jazzy wall coverings, comfortable beds, splashes of colour. Quirky extras include Roberts radios, sticks of rock, and rubber ducks in simple bathrooms. And they love dogs!

Price	£90-£100.
Rooms	10 doubles.
Meals	Lunch & dinner £11.75-£18.50.
Closed	Open all day.
Directions	Close to the Quay at the bottom of cobbled Mermaid Street.

Karen Northcote & Theo Bekker
The Ship Inn
The Strand,
Rye TN31 7DB

Tel +44 (0)1797 222233
Web www.theshipinnrye.co.uk

The Star Inn

Old Heathfield

Built as an inn for pilgrims in the 14th century, with a rough honey-stone façade, The Star has gained a few creepers over the centuries and its atmospheric interior has mellowed nicely. Low-beamed ceilings, wall settles and panelling, huge log-fuelled inglenook – it's cosy, candlelit and hugely inviting. The appeal in summer is the peaceful award-winning garden, bright with flowers and characterful with hand-crafted furniture; the view 15 miles to the South Downs coast was once painted by Turner. The chalkboard lists game pie, venison (from Heathfield Park), shoulder of lamb with garlic potatoes and rosemary gravy, fish and chips, warm treacle tart. To drink, try Harveys Sussex Bitter from Lewes. And visit the impressive church with its fine early-English tower – it's right next door.

Meals	Lunch & dinner £9.50-£17.35.
Closed	Open all day.
Directions	From A265 east of Heathfield, left onto B2096, then 2nd right.

Mike & Sue Chappell
The Star Inn
Church Street, Old Heathfield,
Heathfield TN21 9AH

Tel +44 (0)1435 863570
Web www.starinnoldheathfield.co.uk

Entry 551 Map 5

Sussex

The Brewers Arms

Vines Cross

Not the most inspiring of buildings – or positions, opposite the village petrol station. But step inside the brick-built Brewers and you'll find a cracking country local. Expect the unexpected: rustic little rooms oozing character, rugs on old boards, dark walls – green and terracotta – lined with paintings, simple benches, plain settles, wax-encrusted candelabras, fat candles on old tables, and blazing winter fires. The food too comes as a surprise. Tim makes the bread, the pâtés and the ice creams, while blackboards announce pumpkin ravioli with parmesan and sage butter, roast partridge with wilted spinach and rösti potato, and treacle and almond tart. Bar dishes include salt and pepper squid and pork and herb sausages. Comedy nights, live bands and opera evenings complete the picture – of a much-loved, passionately run Sussex treasure.

Meals	Lunch & dinner from £9.
Closed	3pm-6pm (Mon-Thurs in winter).
Directions	Village signed off B2203 I mile east of Horam.

Tim Earley
The Brewers Arms
Vines Cross,
Heathfield TN21 9EN

Tel +44 (0)1435 812288
Web www.brewersarmsvinescross.co.uk

Entry 552 Map 5

The Gun

Gun Hill

Winding lanes lead to this 16th-century tiled and timbered farmhouse with glorious views across rolling countryside. Its name originates from the cannon foundries that were located at Gun Hill. Expect a neat open-plan interior with comfortably furnished alcoves, several log fires and an old Aga in the cosy main bar. Plank floors, thick candles on scrubbed tables, fresh flowers and bold artwork create a civilised feel, traditional menus champion local produce and every dish is freshly prepared. Kick off with a game terrine with red onion compote, follow with Speldhurst sausages with onion gravy, or pan-fried halibut with tarragon sauce, and finish with a warm chocolate fondant. Worth hunting down in all seasons, it has a terrace and lawn for lazy summer days. Pick up the 'Gun Walk' leaflet and explore the surrounding footpaths.

Meals	Lunch & dinner £8.95-£17.20.
Closed	3pm-6pm in winter. Open all day Sat & Sun & in summer.
Directions	From A267 south of Horam, right after 0.25 miles for Gun Hill; pub after 0.5 miles.

Martial Chaussy
The Gun
Gun Hill,
Heathfield TN21 0JU

Tel +44 (0)1825 872361
Web www.thegunhouse.co.uk

Entry 553 Map 5

Sussex

The Lamb Inn

Wartling

Rob and Alison's rural dining pub continues to draw the crowds for good, homemade food, good beer and good cheer. There's a bar with a wood-burner, a beamy snug with chunky candles and fresh flowers, a dining room in the stables, and a lounge with comfy sofas and log fires… no music, no pool, just chatter. Specialising in fresh fish and local produce from Chilley Farm, the menu announces rib-eye of local Limousin beef with garlic and parsley butter; pancake of creamy garlic mushrooms glazed with stilton; fish pie. A good selection of cheeses will follow, along with temptations such as plum and blackberry sponge with cinnamon custard. Make a mental note of this secluded pub if you are planning a visit to Herstmonceux Castle: the drive across the Pevensey Levels is worth it.

Meals	Lunch & dinner £8.95-£17.95. Bar meals £5.75-£12.95. Sunday lunch, 3 courses, £15.50.
Closed	3pm-6pm. Sun eves & Mon.
Directions	A259 to Polegate & Pevensey; 1st exit for Wartling; on right after 3 miles.

Robert & Alison Farncombe
The Lamb Inn
Wartling,
Hailsham BN27 1RY

Tel +44 (0)1323 832116
Web www.lambinnwartling.co.uk

Entry 554 Map 5

George Inn
Alfriston

You can't miss the ancient façade of The George as you stroll down Alfriston's pretty little High Street. Step inside the creaky old inn, first licensed in 1397, and things become even more historic, thanks to worn planked floors, head-cracking beams, thick standing timbers, a huge inglenook with a crackling winter fire, and hop bines strewn above the bar. It is the cosiest possible setting for some tasty pub food and a foaming pint of Greene King. Share a rustic board for two laden with charcuterie and breads, roasted garlic and warm olive oil, or tuck into a brie and bacon sandwich. Then there are hearty steaks, daily risottos, and, in the evening, dishes such as rump of lamb from Ashmore farm. Lunch in the flint-walled garden, explore the village, hike the South Downs Way.

Meals	Lunch & bar meals from £4.95. Dinner from £10.95. Sunday lunch, 3 courses, £21.
Closed	Open all day.
Directions	Alfriston is signed off A27 between Polgate & Lewes, 4 miles west of Polegate.

Roland & Cate Couch
George Inn
High Street, Alfriston,
Polegate BN26 5SY
Tel +44 (0)1323 870319
Web www.thegeorge-alfriston.com

Entry 555 Map 5

Giants Rest
Wilmington

Most East Sussex pubs are supporters of Harveys brewery in Lewes and this is no exception; local produce is on the menu, too. Adrian's wife Rebecca is chef, and her wild rabbit and bacon pie, home-cooked ham, sausages with bubble-and-squeak and fruit crumbles are just the ticket. It's not old by rural standards, but the high ceilings, the black and cream wallpaper, the pine dressers and the candlelight make a very respectable backdrop for a plate of devilish homemade chocolate brownie or meringue glace, served in front of a log fire. There are pews and pine tables at the long bar, and puzzles and games on the tables. Monthly quiz nights are held for charity. Work up an appetite with a brisk stroll to view the impressive Long Man figure carved into the South Downs: it's no distance at all.

Meals	Lunch £10.50-£16.50. Bar meals £4-£8.50. Sunday lunch £11.
Closed	3pm-6pm. Open all day Sat & Sun.
Directions	On A27 just past Drusilla's roundabout.

Adrian & Rebecca Hillman
Giants Rest
The Street, Wilmington,
Polegate BN26 5SQ
Tel +44 (0)1323 870207
Web www.giantsrest.co.uk

Entry 556 Map 5

The Cricketers Arms

Berwick

Walkers seek refuge from the breezy South Downs; so do visitors to Berwick Church and Charleston Farmhouse. The 500-year-old, brick and flint, creeper-clad pub is utterly unspoilt outside and in. An ale house for the past 200 years, it has three delightfully unpretentious rooms with beams and half-panelled walls dotted with cricket bats. Blazing log fires, scrubbed tables and wall benches on worn, quarry-tiled floors add to the pleasure of being here; all feels friendly and unhurried. Harveys ales are tapped from the cask in a back room and the food is perfectly straightforward pub grub, perhaps gammon steak and egg or a seafood platter. Try your luck at playing the Sussex coin game, Toad-In-Ye-Hole. Surrounded by a cottage garden resplendent with foxgloves and roses, The Cricketers is equally charming in summer.

Meals	Lunch from £5.25. Bar meals from £8.95. Dinner from £6.50. Sunday lunch, 3 courses, £20.
Closed	3pm-6pm in winter. Open all day Sat & Sun.
Directions	Just off A27 Lewes to Polegate road near Berwick church.

Peter Brown
The Cricketers Arms
Berwick,
Polegate BN26 6SP

Tel	+44 (0)1323 870469
Web	www.cricketersberwick.co.uk

Entry 557 Map 5

Sussex

The Sussex Ox

Milton Street

Tucked below the Downs, The Sussex Ox is a popular retreat with ramblers and A27 travellers – time it right and you'll catch a South Downs sunset from the garden. David and Suzanne have invested well in refurbishing the rambling old place, so expect a clean, uncluttered and civilised feel: creamy walls, wonky timbers, wood and worn-brick floors, painted panelling, big vases overflowing with lilies. Bag a cushioned pew at a scrubbed pine table in the Garden Room for the best of those long sweeping views. The chalkboard above the wood-burning stove lists the day's locally sourced choices – lunchtime sandwiches, warming soups, beef, ale and mushroom pie, white chocolate cheesecake, artisan cheeses. Ales come from the Dark Star and Harveys breweries, to be enjoyed in summer on the decked terrace.

Meals	Lunch & dinner £8.75-£15.
Closed	3pm-6pm.
Directions	Village & pub signed off A27, 3 miles west of Polegate.

David & Suzanne Pritchard
The Sussex Ox
Milton Street,
Polegate BN26 5RL

Tel	+44 (0)1323 870840
Web	www.thesussexox.co.uk

Entry 558 Map 5

The Jolly Sportsman

East Chiltington

Deep in Sussex, a little place with a passion for beers, food and wine. Brewery mats pinned above the bar demonstrate Bruce Wass's support of small breweries, while the food has been described as "robust, savoury, skilled and unpretentious". In the stylish restaurant, where oak tables are decorated with flowers and candles, plates are filled with mussel, prawn and herb risotto, marinated Ditchling lamb rump, peppered red deer fillet. In the bar, dogs doze, the fire glows and there are winter snifters from Bruce's impressive whisky collection to try, including rarities bought at auction. A new garden room houses Moroccan-tiled patio tables made by a previous employee. Outside, ancient trees give shade to rustic tables and the idyllic garden has a play area for children. A team of talented enthusiasts runs this pub.

Meals	Lunch from £13. Bar meals from £9.75. Dinner, 2 courses, from £19.50. Sunday lunch, 3 courses, £25.
Closed	Sunday evenings in winter.
Directions	From Lewes A275; B2166; 2nd right Novington Lane; 1st left Chapel Lane.

Bruce Wass
The Jolly Sportsman
Chapel Lane, East Chiltington,
Lewes BN7 3BA
Tel +44 (0)1273 890400
Web www.thejollysportsman.com

Entry 559 Map 4

The New Inn

Hurstpierpoint

On the High Street and not that new (parts go back 500 years), the New Inn is the sister pub to the Bull Inn in Ditchling. Push open the door, leave bustle behind and step into a cosy, stone-flagged and timbered bar. A pint of Harvey's, a decent coffee, a crackling fire – lovely. There's a rustic-chic feel throughout, with old pine tables and cushioned pews, heritage hues on wonky walls, stacked logs and fat church candles... and dark panelling and leather chesterfields in the intimate snug beyond. Linger over a beef and horseradish sandwich or a 'small plate' of Thai salmon fishcakes with sweet chilli sauce; dig into a chicken and ham pie or a garlic and rosemary beefburger with chips. Leave room for spiced plum tart or a plate of Sussex cheeses. Modern art, a quirky eclectic décor and a secluded terrace complete the scene.

Meals	Lunch & dinner from £10.
Closed	Open all day.
Directions	From A23 exit on to B2118. Follow signs for Hurstpierpoint on B2116 for 1.5 miles, pub on right after mini r'bout.

Dominic Worrall
The New Inn
76 High Street, Hurstpierpoint,
Brighton BN6 9RQ
Tel +44 (0)1273 834608
Web www.thenewinnhurst.com

Entry 560 Map 4

The Ginger Fox

Albourne

This pretty country pub looks splendidly traditional, its thatch crowned by a fox stalking a pheasant. The second of Ben McKeller's pubs (the first is Hove's Ginger Pig) again adds a contemporary zing. Both the aim (to serve modern British dishes made of fine produce) and the look (armchairs and banquettes, stone and wood floors, open fires) are close to the Hove original, resulting in a cool uncluttered style that blends beautifully with the old. Chalked-up menus are short and to the point: roast breast of pheasant with braised-leg cottage pie; fillet of sea bass with confit shallot potatoes and salsify; tomato risotto with parmesan crisps and pea shoots. There's even Welsh rarebit as an alternative to puddings like chocolate jaffa brûlée; team it with a pint of Harveys Sussex Best. Service is friendly and smartly dressed.

Meals	Lunch & dinner £10.50-£16.50.
Closed	Open all day.
Directions	From A23 (London Road) take A281; take a right onto Muddleswood Road (towards Crawley) the pub is immediately on the right.

Ben McKeller
The Ginger Fox
Muddleswood Road, Albourne,
Hassocks BN6 9EA
Tel +44 (0)1273 857888
Web www.gingermanrestaurants.com

Entry 561 Map 4

Sussex

Royal Oak

Wineham

The part-tiled, part-timbered cottage almost lost down a country road is six centuries old and has been refreshing locals for two. It is unspoilt in every way. In the charming bar and tiny rear room are brick and boarded floors, a huge inglenook with log fires and sturdy rustic furniture, while antique corkscrews, pottery jugs and aged artefacts hang from low-slung beams and walls. Michael and Sharon Bailey have changed little since taking over in 2007, drawing Harveys Best straight from the cask (no pumps) and, in keeping with ale house tradition, delivering a menu of good, freshly made pub food using locally sourced produce; you can expect an updated full menu as well as a light lunches: sandwiches, ploughman's and hearty soups. No music or electronic hubbub, just traditional pub games. A heart-warming rural survivor.

Meals	Lunch & dinner £8.95-£15.95.
Closed	2.30pm-5.30pm (3.30pm-6pm Sat, 4pm-7pm Sun).
Directions	Off A272 between Cowfold & Bolney.

Michael & Sharon Bailey
Royal Oak
Wineham Lane,
Wineham,
Henfield BN5 9AY
Tel +44 (0)1444 881252

Entry 562 Map 4

The Coach & Horses

Danehill

With ale on tap from Harveys in Lewes, fresh fish from Seaford and lamb from the field opposite, this is one fine pub. The central bar is its throbbing hub, original wooden panelling and open fires accompanying the gentle pleasure of mulled wine in winter-cosy rooms. During the rest of the year the big raised garden comes into its own; spread yourselves on the terrace under the boughs of a spreading maple. Whatever the weather, the food attracts folk from far and wide. In the stable block restaurant a changing seasonal menu from chef Dan Hockaday places the emphasis on quality rather than quantity, in butterbean and garlic soup, spicy crab and saffron risotto, roast pork belly with salsa verde. Pub classics include chicken and leek pie and lamb stew, and don't miss the summer Sunday barbecues. A lovely rural pub, and a true local.

Meals	Lunch & dinner £10.50-£19.95. Bar meals £6.75-£10.50 (lunch only).
Closed	3pm-6pm. Open all day Sat & Sun.
Directions	From Danehill (A275) take School Lane towards Chelwood Common; pub on left 0.25 miles.

Ian & Catherine Philpots
The Coach & Horses
Coach & Horses Lane, Danehill,
Haywards Heath RH17 7JF
Tel +44 (0)1825 740369
Web www.coachandhorses.danehill.biz

Entry 563 Map 4

Sussex

The Crabtree

Lower Beeding

Welcome to a former haunt of Hillaire Belloc, who'd sit in the garden munching bread and Sussex cheese. You can do the same today, on benches topped with fleeces. This country pub has it all: a vast inglenook stacked with logs, lots of cosy flagstone'd corners, a daily menu that supports local producers, and a very stylish wine list. Pop in for a pint and a pie, a scrumptious snack (Scotch egg and curried mayo, red pepper hummus with spiced flatbread) or a beautifully presented three courses. There are great Sunday lunches too, and a kids' menu that will delight. Get chatty in the open bar, filled with light from the big sash window; find a wicker chair in the sunshiney Garden Room, where a dresser overflows with biscotti and crabapple jellies (homemade). There are local events on Fridays, sweet Sussex views and the staff are totally on the ball.

Meals	Lunch from £10. Dinner from £12. Sunday lunch, 2 courses, £16.
Closed	Open all day.
Directions	See website.

Simon Hope
The Crabtree
Brighton Road, Lower Beeding,
Horsham RH13 6PT
Tel +44 (0)1403 892666
Web www.crabtreesussex.co.uk

Entry 564 Map 4

The Stag

Balls Cross

The quintessential Sussex pub – some might say (and often do), the best pub in the world. Under 16th-century beams by a crackling fire – or in the garden in summer – riders, walkers and locals enjoy a natter over well-kept Badger and Sussex Bitter. Wholesome home-cooked food is another draw, the traditional pies (steak and kidney) being a severe temptation; try too the mutton and pearl barley broth. A sweet shop in a former life, this little inn still pulls the children in: in a set-aside room they may play undisturbed. There is also lots for adults: their own darts team, jazz nights in summer and the travelling Mummers at Christmas. There's a 17th-century stone-floored bar, a large old clock that ticks above the inglenook and the dining room is carpeted and cosy. There's also a tethering post should you drop by with your horse.

Meals	Lunch & dinner £7.50-£18. Bar meals £6-£18. Not Sun eve or Mon.
Closed	Open all day.
Directions	2 miles from Petworth on Kirdford road.

Authentic pub

Reuben Waller
The Stag
Balls Cross,
Petworth GU28 9JP

Tel +44 (0)1403 820241
Web www.staginn-ballscross.co.uk

Entry 565 Map 4

Sussex

Welldiggers Arms

Petworth

Once occupied by well-diggers, this rustic 300-year-old roadside cottage has little immediate appeal. But enter and you are greeted by Ted Whitcomb, landlord and larger-than-life persona, pulling pints of Young's and cracking jokes behind the bar for 50-odd years. Surprisingly, this is a dining-orientated pub, its low-ceilinged bar and snug packed with happy eaters at long settles and huge oak tables. Come for classic British food: king prawns in garlic, fresh mussels, whole Dover sole, and properly hung T-bone steaks. Alternatives may include braised oxtail and dumplings, steak, Guinness and stilton pie, black pudding and mash, seasonal game – and magnificent Sunday roasts. Popular with enthusiasts of racing (Goodwood), shooting and polo (Cowdray Park), so be sure to book. At the back is a garden with views over the South Downs.

Meals	Lunch from £10. Bar meals from £5.95. Dinner from £20. Sunday lunch, 3 courses, £26.
Closed	3.30pm-6pm. Sun, Tues & Wed eves. Mon.
Directions	Beside A283 Pulborough road, 1 mile east of Petworth.

Ted Whitcomb
Welldiggers Arms
Pulborough Road,
Petworth GU28 0HG

Tel +44 (0)1798 342287

Entry 566 Map 4

The White Horse Inn

Sutton

Squirrelled away in the South Downs, in the smart village of Sutton, the White Horse Inn is not easy to find. But find it you must! Stylishly revived, the old pub combines an unexpected modernity with a lovely warm feel. More gastropub than local, it sets much store by its food – regional, seasonal and delicious. Find Sussex Down rump of lamb served with roasted vegetables, sautéed potatoes and rosemary jus; chunky Sussex cheddar and pickle sandwiches; hearty mixed-game casserole, good for walkers. All go down a treat with local hand-pump ales such as Harveys Sussex Bitter. The smart, light, opened-up interior is decorated in pleasing neutral tones that blend harmoniously with Indonesian teak furniture, long gleaming wood bar and polished floorboards. Stunning walks start from the door and Goodwood is nearby – visit house and horses.

Meals	Lunch & dinner £9.50-£17. Bar meals £4.50-£10.
Closed	3pm-6pm (7pm Sun). Sun & Mon eves.
Directions	Sutton is signed off A286 south of Petworth and A29 south of Pulborough; pub in village centre.

Mr & Mrs Hajigeorgiou
The White Horse Inn
The Street, Sutton,
Pulborough RH20 1PS
Tel +44 (0)1798 869221
Web www.whitehorse-sutton.co.uk

Entry 567 Map 4

Sussex

The Fox Goes Free

Charlton

King William III may have stopped off here to refresh his royal hunting parties but this 400-year-old flint pub, secreted away in the South Downs, is now home to some fine ales from small local breweries. Settle down by a big blazing fire under beamed ceilings for a pint of Ballards Best and the pub's own Fox Goes Free; in summer there's a garden with sweeping farmland views. The traditional bar food suits the surroundings, so sit at scrubbed tables and choir chairs for fresh butcher's sausages with mash, onion gravy and veg, followed by a comforting treacle sponge with custard. In the dining room – once a stable for race horses – are less familiar creations, perhaps chicken breast stuffed with banana, curry sauce and basmati rice. Goodwood racecourse is just up the hill and there are downland walks from the door.

Meals	Lunch & dinner £9.50-£19.50. Bar meals £9.50-£11.95. Sunday lunch £10.95-£12.95.
Closed	Open all day.
Directions	From Chichester follow A286 towards Midhurst. At Singleton right to Charlton.

David Coxon
The Fox Goes Free
Charlton,
Chichester PO18 0HU
Tel +44 (0)1243 811461
Web www.thefoxgoesfree.com

Entry 568 Map 4

Anglesey Arms at Halnaker

Halnaker

Laid back, relaxed, free of airs and graces, a Georgian brick pub in an affluent part of West Sussex. It's not a pie-and-a-pint pub or a chips-with-everything roadside diner, just a cracking local run by George and Jools Jackson, genuinely committed to keeping it charming and old-fashioned. Expect varnished and stripped pine, flagstones, beams and panelling, crackling log fires, locals downing pints at the bar, and a cosier, smarter dining room. Food is fresh and home-cooked using great local produce – crab and lobster from Selsey, traceable meats (organic South Downs lamb and pork, well-hung beef from the Goodwood estate), venison and game from local shoots. Even the ciders, wines and spirits are organic. A great little local, with inter-pub cricket, golf and quizzes and regular 'moules and boules' events in the two-acre garden.

Meals	Lunch from £8.50. Dinner from £10.50. Sunday lunch £13.
Closed	3pm-5.30pm. Open all day Sun.
Directions	On A285, 4 miles north east of Chichester.

George & Jools Jackson
Anglesey Arms at Halnaker
Halnaker,
Chichester PO18 0NQ
Tel +44 (0)1243 773474
Web www.angleseyarms.co.uk

Entry 569 Map 4

Sussex

The Earl of March

Lavant

Having been taken over by ex-Ritz executive head chef Giles Thompson, it's no surprise this is a snappy performer, from its upbeat remodelling to the simple handling of excellent ingredients that tick all the right local and seasonal boxes. There are views over the South Downs from terrace and dining area, and lots of sepia prints of old racing cars and aircraft. It's a clean-lined, fashionable space with a positively cosmopolitan vibe; modern leather seating in the bar quarter and high-backed suede chairs in the dining area. Bolstered by specials (there's also a separate bar and terrace menu – delicious sausage, mash and onion gravy) the up-tempo dining roster delivers the likes of seasonal game, or fresh seafood in the summer Champagne and Seafood menu – dressed Selsey crab salad, king prawns with mayonnaise, whole smoked mackerel with saffron rouille.

Meals	Lunch from £12.50. Bar meals from £10.50. Dinner from £18.50. Sunday lunch, 3 courses, £21.50.
Closed	Open all day.
Directions	On A286 Chichester to Midhurst road, 2 miles north of Chichester.

Giles Thompson
The Earl of March
Lavant,
Chichester PO18 0BQ
Tel +44 (0)1243 533993
Web www.theearlofmarch.com

Entry 570 Map 4

The Royal Oak Inn

East Lavant

There's a cheery wine-bar feel to the Royal Oak; locals and young professionals come with their children and it's as countrified as can be. Inside, a modern-rustic look with traditional touches prevails: stripped floors, exposed brickwork, dark leather sofas, open fires and racing pictures on the walls: this was once part of the Goodwood estate. The dining area is big, light and airy, with a conservatory from which you can amble out onto a terrace that's warmed by outdoor lamps on summer nights. At scrubbed-top tables you can tuck into delicious trio of Barbary duck, seared scallops on pumpkin purée, fig tart with pistachio ice cream. Staff are attentive, a secret garden looks over cornfields, and you're well-placed for Chichester Theatre and the boats at pretty Bosham.

Meals	Lunch from £6.25. Dinner, 3 courses, £30-£35.
Closed	Open all day.
Directions	From Chichester A286 for Midhurst. First right at first mini roundabout into E. Lavant. Down hill, pass village green, over bridge, pub 200 yds on left. Car park opposite.

Charles Ullmann
The Royal Oak Inn
Pook Lane, East Lavant,
Chichester PO18 0AX
Tel +44 (0)1243 527434
Web www.royaloakeastlavant.co.uk

Entry 571 Map 4

Sussex

The Partridge Inn

Singleton

It's a genteel, traditional affair, this 17th-century inn in a quintessential English village on the Goodwood Estate. Now it's in the hands of a former Ritz chef. Giles Thompson also owns the more foodie-styled Earl of March pub in nearby Lavant, and is a man with the Midas touch. While the food matters, the pubby atmosphere is the thing: the Partridge is a local, and a family-friendly one at that. There's heaps of character in old beams, timbers and log fires across a series of rooms. Enjoy Harvey's Sussex Best with a traditional ploughman's in the bar, or one of several accomplished dishes; beer-battered haddock and chips wrapped in newspaper, or pan-fried lamb's liver and bacon with onion gravy. Desserts are the best of old British: treacle sponge, spotted dick. The lovely big garden attracts a crowd in summer.

Meals	Lunch & dinner £9.50-£19.95.
Closed	3pm-5.30pm. Open all day Sat & Sun.
Directions	On A286 midway between Midhurst and Chichester. In Singleton village.

Giles Thompson
The Partridge Inn
Singleton,
Chichester PO18 0EY
Tel +44 (0)1243 811251
Web www.thepartridgeinn.co.uk

Entry 572 Map 4

The Star & Garter

East Dean

If fresh fish and seafood appeal then follow the winding Sussex lanes to this 18th-century brick-and-flint pub. Hidden in the folds of the South Downs, with miles of breezy walks from the front door, the old ale house now draws the well-shod from Goodwood and Midhurst. Seafood platters spill over with whole Selsey lobster and crabs, scallops, wild salmon, crevettes and prawns. There are big bowls of mussels, whole baked bass, venison pie and, in season, a mouthwatering game grill, with partridge from West Dean, pigeon from East Dean and local wild boar sausages. Drink fine Sussex ales straight from the cellar in the open-plan, wooden floored room, where hops adorn stripped beams, old village photographs line bare-brick walls and daily papers fill the rack by the door. In summer, head for the sun-trap patio or lawned gardens.

Meals	Lunch & dinner £11-£21. Bar meals £7.50-£9.50. Sunday lunch £12.
Closed	3pm-6pm. Open all day Sat & Sun.
Directions	Village signed off A286 between Midhurst & Chichester at Singleton.

Oliver Ligertwood
The Star & Garter
East Dean,
Chichester PO18 0JG

Tel +44 (0)1243 811318
Web www.thestarandgarter.co.uk

Entry 573 Map 4

Sussex

The Three Horseshoes

Elsted

Low beams, latched doors, red tile or brick floors, high settles, deep-cream bowed walls, big log fires and home-cooked food: all that you'd hope for, and more. Built in 1540 as a drovers' ale house, it has no cellar, so staff pull ales from the barrel instead. The lower bar was formerly a butcher's shop and still has the ceiling hooks. Local seafood, meat and game appear on a tempting country menu – Selsey sea bass, cottage pie, venison goulash, or steak and kidney in Guinness pie – and are served in snug rooms. The main dining room is smarter and less rustic and also comes with its wood-burning stove. In summer sit in the glorious garden and enjoy golden pints and the cracking views over the South Downs. Landlady Sue will look after you here.

Meals	Lunch & dinner £8.95-£17.95. Bar meals £6.95-£9.95.
Closed	2.30pm-6pm (3pm-7pm Sun).
Directions	Elsted is signed off A272 between Midhurst and Petersfield, 2 miles east of Midhurst.

Sue Beavis & Michael Newton
The Three Horseshoes
Elsted,
Midhurst GU29 0JY

Tel +44 (0)1730 825746

Entry 574 Map 4

The Duke of Cumberland Arms

Henley

In the spring the Duke looks divine, its brick and stone cottage walls engulfed by flowering wisteria. Beyond is the tiered garden, with babbling pools and huge Weald views. Latch doors lead to two tiny bars that creak with character – painted tongue-and-groove walls, low ceilings, scrubbed tables, log fires in the grate. Choose a pint of Hip Hop or Goodwood Organic Blonde straight from the cask. Rescued from closure by a local a few years back, the Duke has Simon Goodman as chef-landlord (2010 Pub Chef of the Year), and the new dining room – a light, modern, country confection – is a show-stopper, with a big fire, an al fresco terrace and marvellous views. Popular daily menus rely on fresh local produce, including Goodwood organic rib-eye steak, estate venison, South Downs lamb; delectable Sunday roasts are brought as a joint to the table. It's a treasure.

Meals	Lunch £7.25-£17.95. Dinner £14.95-£21.95
Closed	3pm-5pm in winter. Open all day in summer.
Directions	From Fernhurst towards Midhurst; pass pub on right; next left to Henley; follow road, on right.

Simon Goodman
The Duke of Cumberland Arms
Henley,
Haslemere GU27 3HQ

Tel +44 (0)1428 652280
Web www.dukeofcumberland.com

Entry 575 Map 4

Sussex

Noah's Ark

Lurgashall

In an idyllic setting – beside village pond and churchyard, overlooking the cricket green – the Ark would restore anyone's faith in the well-being of the English country pub. In this couple's hands, the old village boozer has become a pub of charm; no more darts, but a surprise at every turn. From bar to cosy dining areas – and one barn-like room – are beams, floorboards, winter fires, traditional country furniture and a sprinkling of modern leather. The kitchen's insistence on good-quality local seasonal produce results in a roll-call of British dishes, and the simple lunchtime bar menu is bolstered come evening by the likes of pan-fried wood pigeon breasts with sautéed savoy cabbage and crispy pancetta. A cottagey garden to the side and picnic tables out front complete the upbeat package.

Meals	Lunch & dinner £10.95-£18.95. Bar meals from £6. Sunday lunch, 3 courses, £23.
Closed	3.45pm-5.30pm. Sun eves.
Directions	From Haslemere take B2131. From Chichester follow the A285. From London follow the A3 and exit onto the A283 towards Petworth. Follow signs to Lurgashall.

Henry Coghlan & Amy Whitmore
Noah's Ark
Lurgashall,
Petworth GU28 9ET

Tel +44 (0)1428 707346
Web www.noahsarkinn.co.uk

Entry 576 Map 4

The Rose & Crown

Warwick

Peach Pubs' flagship Rose and Crown opens with bacon sarnies for breakfast (rather good ones) and stays open all day. Enter a cheery, airy, wooden-floored front bar with red and white walls, big leather sofas, low tables and a crackling winter fire. To the back is the big and bustling eating area and a private room that can be booked for parties. The food is scrummy and children can enjoy downsized versions from the main menu. Served all day, the tapas-style portions of cheeses, hams, marinated anchovies, mixed olives and rustic breads slip down easily with a pint of Purity Gold or a glass of pinot, while hot dishes are modern British with a Mediterranean slant. On the menu may be baked sea trout; lemon and thyme couscous with chilli oil; pork loin with rhubarb confit, apple and cider jus. Lovely contemporary bedrooms right above have a large bath and shower; two rooms overlook the square, filled on warm summer nights with a merry throng. It's young and fun and conveniently central for Warwick, which has history in spades. Visit Warwick Castle, too.

Price	£70-£80.
Rooms	5: 2 doubles, 3 triples.
Meals	Lunch from £7. Bar meals £5. Dinner from £11. Sunday lunch £13.50.
Closed	Open all day.
Directions	In Warwick centre, on market place. Ask about parking.

Jeremy Kynaston
The Rose & Crown
30 Market Place,
Warwick CV34 4SH
Tel +44 (0)1926 411117
Web www.roseandcrownwarwick.co.uk

The Bell

Alderminster

Big changes have been rung at this old coaching inn where you're spoilt for sitting areas: leather armchairs by the fire or country divans, reading room or conservatory – and candles galore. The walls display vintage sepia canvases of the Alscot Estate – they own the pub and provide some of the produce – while Wye Valley HPA backs up the Alscot ale. For those in a hurry the grazing boards, sandwiches and baguettes are ideal but for those with time the three-course supper deal is great value. You could start with smoked chicken and pancetta salad with a dolce latte dressing, move on to confit duck with sweet and sour sauce and crushed new potatoes, and finish up with white chocolate crunch cheesecake with blueberry vodka soaked apricots: marvellous. The wine list has grapes to suit all. Charming staff see that it ticks along nicely and if you think downstairs is good, upstairs is even better. Four rooms await, each different, each fabulous, from the proudly patriotic to the boldly opulent, all utterly spoiling. A stylish summer garden makes this special from start to finish.

Price	From £115. Singles from £75.
Rooms	4 doubles.
Meals	Lunch from £13. Bar meals from £6. Dinner from £13. Sunday lunch, 3 courses, £25. Not Sunday eve (except bank hols).
Closed	3pm-6pm. Sun eves & Mon in winter. Open all day Fri & Sat, Sun in summer & bank hols.
Directions	On A3400 in Alderminster.

Martin Devereux
The Bell
Shipston Road, Alderminster,
Stratford-upon-Avon CV37 8NY
Tel +44 (0)1789 450414
Web www.thebellald.co.uk

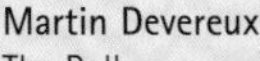

The Howard Arms

Ilmington

The Howard buzzes with good-humoured babble as well-kept beer flows from the flagstoned bar. Logs crackle contentedly in a vast open fire; a blackboard menu scales the wall above; a dining room at the far end has unexpected elegance, with great swathes of bold colour and some noble paintings. Gorgeous bedrooms are set discreetly apart from the joyful throng, mixing period style and modern luxury beautifully: one with a painted antique headboard and bleached beams, another more folksy, while five garden rooms come in elegant contemporary style with fancy bathrooms. All are individual, all huge by pub standards. The village is a surprise, too, literally tucked under a lone hill, with an unusual church surrounded by orchards and an extended village green. Round off an idyllic walk amid buzzing bees and fragrant wild flowers with a meal at the inn, perhaps salmon trio with celeriac remoulade and orange dressing, then beef, ale and mustard pie, finally spiced pear and apple flapjack crumble. From a blackboard menu, the food is inventive, upmarket and very good.

Price	£125-£155. Singles £85.
Rooms	8: 5 doubles, 3 twins/doubles.
Meals	Lunch from £4.50. Dinner from £10.50.
Closed	Open all day.
Directions	From south take A429 Fosse Way through Moreton-in-Marsh. After 5 miles left to Ilmington.

Emma O'Connell
The Howard Arms
Lower Green, Ilmington,
Shipston-on-Stour CV36 4LT
Tel +44 (0)1608 682226
Web www.howardarms.com

The Red Lion

Long Compton

Dogs are welcome in this ancient warren of a pub and canine sketches adorn the walls. The pub's own Cocoa – 'The Landlady' – is often around. But that doesn't mean the whiff of wet canine. Instead you get the mouthwatering aroma of excellent, imaginative cooking from Sarah Keightley, co-manager and chef. Crispy-battered cod and chips with caper berries and mushy peas are served here on *The Red Lion Times* while pork tenderloin comes wrapped in pancetta with apple purée, black pudding and Dijon mustard sauce. A meltingly warm pear and ginger pudding with toffee sauce will round it all off nicely. And you can stay, in five bedrooms that reflect the unfussy approach. With natural colours and crisp ginghams, their comfort and quality make up for their size; in a place that goes back 250 years, bedrooms are not likely to be huge. Downstairs is space for everyone, from the pool room to the restaurant to the beautiful flagged bar area warmed by a real fire and a wood-burning stove. A smart but sensitive refurb has not cost this village pub its character, nor its sense of community.

Price	£85-£185. Singles £55-£75.
Rooms	5: 2 doubles, 1 twin, 1 single, 1 family room.
Meals	Lunch & dinner £11.95-£18.95.
Closed	2.30pm-6pm Mon-Thurs. Open all day Fri-Sun & Mon bank hols.
Directions	Beside A3400 between Chipping Norton & Shipston-on-Stour.

Lisa Phipps & Sarah Keightley
The Red Lion
Main Street, Long Compton,
Shipston-on-Stour CV36 5JS
Tel +44 (0)1608 684221
Web www.redlion-longcompton.co.uk

The Fox & Hounds Inn

Great Wolford

The gorgeous, honey-coloured pub has been trading since 1540 and dozes contentedly in a tiny community on the edge of the Cotswold hills. On entering the bar through a low oak door the pub opens out, captivatingly, before you. Bunches of dried hops are tucked into ancient beams, there are candlelit tables on flagstoned floors, polished oak settles and a huge stone fireplace that crackles with logs in winter. Flames flicker in the copper bar counter as you order a pint of Hook Norton and study the blackboard menu announcing such treats as roast garlic and potato soup and whole partridge with braised puy lentils and home-cured bacon, treacle tart with vanilla ice cream. The menu is kept short and fresh and changes each day. It couldn't be cosier, or more welcoming – a perfect country pub. And there's also a good terrace for summer.

Meals	Lunch & dinner £12-£20.
Closed	2.30pm-6pm & Mon.
Directions	Off A3400 between Shipston-on-Stour & Long Compton.

Gill & Jamie Tarbox
& Sioned Rowland
The Fox & Hounds Inn, Great Wolford,
Shipston-on-Stour CV36 5NQ

Tel	+44 (0)1608 674220
Web	www.thefoxandhoundsinn.com

Warwickshire

The Chequers Inn

Ettington

New life has been breathed into this north Cotswold pub by Kirstin and James – and how! A bold style of classic British meets country French thanks to rich tapestries, gilt mirrors, padded chairs, round tables and aged wooden flooring throughout. There is a proper glowing wood bar too with St Austell Tribute and London Pride on tap; plus Stowford Press cider, an impressive wine selection and several varieties of fizz for special occasions. The calm, elegant Provençal dining area at the back overlooks a well-planted and sheltered garden which also hides the chef's veg patch. Start with honey-glazed crispy duck salad with hoisin dressing and cashew nuts, move on to brill with buttered mash and gremolata. The puds will also tempt, and then there's freshly ground coffee. Different, slightly decadent, and definitely worth a visit.

Meals	Lunch & bar meals from £4.50. Dinner £9.50-£16.95. Sunday lunch, 3 courses, £23.45.
Closed	3pm-5pm. Sun eves & Mon.
Directions	Off A429 11 miles south of Warwick, onto A422 east; pub at far end of village on left.

James & Kirstin Viggers
The Chequers Inn
91 Banbury Road, Ettington,
Stratford-upon-Avon CV37 7SR

Tel	+44 (0)1789 740387
Web	www.the-chequers-ettington.co.uk

The One Elm

Stratford-upon-Avon

Stratford has a reputation for great pubs and drama – and was the birthplace of the first Slug and Lettuce. In the narrow building that The Slug once occupied stands The One Elm. Owned by Peach Pubs (of Warwick's Rose and Crown), it, too, is a cracker. The bar is light, airy and wooden-floored and the décor modern and stylish, with leather sofas, a real fire and a vibrant feel. In the bar are good beers and great wines; outside, an attractive, sheltered terrace; at the back, the restaurant, with a private, secluded mezzanine and a short but mouthwatering menu. There's a chargrill section, a 'roast of the day' and a variety of deli boards that are available all day (fish, cheeses, meats). Being slightly off the tourist trail this attracts a local crowd, and the friendly staff are on tap from breakfast until closing time.

Meals	Lunch & bar meals from £5. Dinner from £10.
Closed	Open all day.
Directions	In town centre on corner of Guild Street & Shakespeare Street.

Nathan Nock
The One Elm
1 Guild Street,
Stratford-upon-Avon CV37 6QZ
Tel +44 (0)1789 404919
Web www.oneelmstratford.co.uk

Entry 583 Map 8

Warwickshire

Bell Inn

Welford-on-Avon

If things Elizabethan and Shakespearian entrance and inspire you, then the Bell will not disappoint, running alongside the village high street, set amongst the black and white timbered houses. There is a richness about the natural oak beams and settles, the stone floors partially covered with Persian rugs and the dog-grates cradling glowing embers. This is very much a historic village inn serving top-quality, locally sourced food, whether it be a simple pub favourite such as pork loin with sausage and bean cassoulet or beef bourguignon with mash. Don't miss Tuesday's fish and chips night, or the Indian-inspired Fridays. If you're into food provenance, every supplier is listed on the back of the menu and they are almost all small independents (a pub farm shop is planned for 2012). A thriving traditional English pub.

Meals	Lunch & dinner £9.95-£18.50. Bar meals from £5. Sunday lunch £12.95-£13.75.
Closed	3pm-6pm. Open all day Sat & Sun.
Directions	Leave A3400 south west of Stratford on B439; continue to Welford; Bell on right through village.

Colin & Teresa Ombler
Bell Inn
Binton Road, Welford-on-Avon,
Stratford-upon-Avon CV37 8EB
Tel +44 (0)1789 750353
Web www.thebellwelford.co.uk

Entry 584 Map 8

The King's Head
Aston Cantlow

It is said that Shakespeare's parents had their wedding reception at The King's Head. One can imagine the scene at this long, low, rambling country inn with its small leaded windows, flagged floors and inglenook crackling with logs; perhaps they even tucked into the famous Duck Supper, a house speciality and diner's favourite. More up-to-date delicacies join the menu today, and all is tasty, from the crayfish, smoked salmon and cream cheese baguette to sea bream with lemon velouté, lamb steak with rosemary mash and red wine jus, and the King's Head beef burger. Arrive early for Sunday roast beef (from Ragley Estate) with all the trimmings. In the bar, stylish with limewashed beams, scrubbed pine and painted brick walls, are real ale and good wines. There's a small garden for summer and the walks start from the door.

Meals	Lunch & dinner £10-£17. Bar meals £5-£10. Sunday lunch, 3 courses, £25.
Closed	3pm-5.30pm. Sun eves after 7.30pm. Open all day Sat.
Directions	Off A46 for Aston Cantlow.

Peter & Louise Sadler
The King's Head
21 Bearley Road,
Aston Cantlow B95 6HY
Tel +44 (0)1789 488242
Web www.thekh.co.uk

Entry 585 Map 8

Warwickshire

The Crabmill
Preston Bagot

The lovely, rambling building, with tiny leaded windows and wonderfully wonky beams, once contained a cider press. Later a pub, now it's a busy gastro haven with a dining room for every mood – one stone and scented with lilies, another brown, its walls hung with risqué drawings of nudes, and third a candlelit mushroom-cream. There's a steely bar with sandblasted glass panels, great flagstones and a winter fire. At the back, a split-level lounge with wooden floors, elegant tubs chairs and a garden that heads off into open countryside. For summer there's stylish paved area outside. The food is popular and the dishes imaginative and colourful, from simple soup or ploughman's with pork pie and pickles to roast pork belly with black pudding, cauliflower purée and apple sauce or smoked haddock fishcake with poached egg and hollandaise.

Meals	Lunch & dinner £5.95-£18.95. Sunday lunch £12.75.
Closed	Open all day. Closed Sun eves from 6pm.
Directions	From Henley-in-Arden on A4189 towards Claverdon.

Sally Coll
The Crabmill
Preston Bagot,
Henley-in-Arden B95 5EE
Tel +44 (0)1926 843342
Web www.thecrabmill.co.uk

Entry 586 Map 8

The Bluebell

Henley-in-Arden

Leigh and Duncan Taylor went to town updating this 500-year-old coaching inn, creating one of the most distinctive bistro-style pubs in the country. A clever combination of country casual and urban chic means atmosphere and style are delivered in spades: bold colours and striking furniture blend with ancient beams, flagstones and a big fireplace. Real ales, wines and an irresistible menu draw keen diners from far and near, ingredients are sourced with care and vegetables are grown on the owners' allotment. The menu combines colourful modern dishes – seared black pepper venison with rocket and parmesan, or open-style Scotch fillet steak Wellington with sautéed white truffle chard – with old favourites like steak and kidney pie; fishcakes; battered haddock with chips. In summer, lunch on the decked area is sublime.

Meals	Lunch & dinner £13-£19. Set menu £15 & £18. Sunday lunch £13.95.
Closed	Mon lunch (except bank hols).
Directions	M40 junc. 16, follow A3400 south for 3 miles to Henley-in-Arden; pub in village centre.

Duncan & Leigh Taylor
The Bluebell
93 High Street,
Henley-in-Arden B95 5AT
Tel +44 (0)1564 793049
Web www.bluebellhenley.co.uk

Entry 587 Map 8

Warwickshire

The Case is Altered

Hatton

No food, no mobiles and a Sopwith Pup propeller suspended from the ceiling. This is a Warwickshire treasure. There's even a vintage bar billiards machine, operated by sixpences from behind the bar. In the main room are terracotta tiles, leather-covered settles and walls covered in yellowing posters offering beverages at a penny a pint. Jackie does not open her arms to children or dogs; this is a place for adult conversation and liquid refreshment. Devotees travel some distance for the fabulous pork scratchings and the expertly kept beer. The sign used to show lawyers arguing but the name has nothing to do with the law; it used to be called, simply, 'The Case' and was so small that it was not eligible for a spirit licence. It was made larger, the name was changed, and everyone was happy. They've been that way ever since.

Meals	No food served.
Closed	2.30pm-6pm (2.15pm-7pm Sun).
Directions	Follow Rowington off A4177/A4141 Five Ways junction, north of Warwick. First right into Case Lane.

Jackie & Charlie Willacy
The Case is Altered
Case Lane, Five Ways,
Hatton,
Warwick CV35 7JD
Tel +44 (0)1926 484206

Entry 588 Map 8

Red Lion
Hunningham

The 150 sandbags in the car park are a gentle reminder that the 17th-century Red Lion has been flooded twice in the past decade – but then it does stand next to the river Leam (with ancient bridge) and the river runs past the end of the garden. Owner Sam Cornwall-Jones originally wanted to be an illustrator and his passion for classic comics is evident from the walls, plastered with vintage copies of Fantastic Four, Batman and Supergirl. The food is honest, unfussy and sourced locally, perhaps a starter of caramelised red onion and water buffalo cheese tart with poached local duck egg, olive and walnut dressing, followed by slow roast Buttercross Farm belly pork and apple sauce. The old pub may be hard to find but you'll love it for its open fires, cheery bar staff, real ales and Sunday papers, guaranteed to put a smile on your face.

Meals	Lunch from £8.95. Bar meals from £4.95. Dinner from £9.50. Sunday lunch, 3 courses, £22.85.
Closed	Open all day.
Directions	Off B4455 (Fosse Way) between Eathorpe and Offchurch east of Leamington Spa; pub is beside the River Leam.

Sam Cornwall-Jones
Red Lion
Main Street, Hunningham,
Leamington Spa CV33 9DY
Tel +44 (0)1926 632715
Web www.redlionhunningham.co.uk

Entry 589 Map 8

Warwickshire

The Orange Tree
Chadwick End

The flagship pub of the Classic Country Pubs group has a striking interior. Be seduced by earthy colours, low limewashed beams, open log fires, big lamps, deep sofas around low tables and chunky lightwood furniture in airy eating rooms. A gorgeous Italian-style deli counter shows off breads, cheeses and vintage oils. This tastefully rustic décor – Mediterranean with oriental touches – is matched by an ambitious, Italian-inspired menu. Food-lovers descend in droves for authentic fired pizzas and robust, full-flavoured meat dishes cooked on the on-view rotisserie spit. There are also homemade pasta dishes, delicious warm salads and fishy specials. All this plus great wines by the bottle or glass, real ales, a heated patio dotted with stylish teak tables and all-day opening hours.

Meals	Lunch & bar meals from £5.95. Dinner £7.95-£25.95. Sunday lunch from £12.95. Not Sun eves.
Closed	Open all day.
Directions	On A4141 between Warwick & Solihull. On edge of village, 5 miles south of M42 junc. 5.

Paul Hales
The Orange Tree
Warwick Road, Chadwick End,
Solihull B93 0BN
Tel +44 (0)1564 785364
Web www.theorangetreepub.co.uk

Entry 590 Map 8

The Almanack

Kenilworth

The clever Peach Pubs people continue to reinvent the gastropub. This, their tenth venture, is a swish new-build beneath apartments in Kenilworth town centre. It opened in 2009 and business has boomed since. Although more trendy bar-restaurant than pub, there's a vast island bar, lots of spacious informal seating and local Purity ales on tap. Expect a cool retro feel, with vintage 60s and 70s armchairs and sofas and a colourfully eclectic décor throughout. Pop in for breakfast or coffee and cake and settle down to free WiFi – or graze from a modern pub menu. In the all-day, open-to-view kitchen, corned beef hash and BLT sandwiches are created, along with substantial lunches and suppers: a daily roast, coq au vin with creamy mash, a fish deli-board, duck with redcurrant jus. Young and fun.

Meals	Lunch from £6. Bar meals from £5. Dinner from £11. Sunday lunch £13.50.
Closed	Open all day.
Directions	On Abbey End, in front of Abbey End car park, next to the Clock Tower r'bout.

Suzie Ayling
The Almanack
Abbey End North,
Kenilworth CV8 1QJ
Tel +44 (0)1993 892270
Web www.thealmanack-kenilworth.co.uk

Warwickshire

The Boot Inn

Lapworth

The Boot was here long before the canal that runs past the back garden. With its exposed timbers, quarry floors, open fires and daily papers it combines old-fashioned charm with rustic chic. Under the guidance of Paul Salisbury and James Elliot, the down-at-heel boozer became one of the first gastropubs of the Midlands more than a decade ago, and has been pulling foodies in ever since. Menus have a distinct touch of Mediterranean and Pacific rim: fresh tian of spiced crab, Asian five spice duck breast, dukka spiced rack of lamb, great Greek sharing plates topped with olives. Ingredients are as fresh as can be and seafood dishes are a speciality. Eat in the lounge or in the stylishly revamped dining room upstairs, and in summer go a lfresco: there's a lovely terrace to the side.

Meals	Lunch from £6. Dinner from £9. Sunday lunch £12.95.
Closed	Open all day.
Directions	Off M42 junc. 4 for Hockley Heath; Lapworth signed.

Paul Salisbury & James Elliot
The Boot Inn
Old Warwick Road, Lapworth,
Solihull B94 6JU
Tel +44 (0)1564 782464
Web www.lovelypubs.co.uk

The Punchbowl

Lapworth

The Punchbowl looks pubby enough from the outside, and functions as such with a big fire and beamed bar dispensing Timothy Taylor's Landlord. So it's a surprise to discover that the building is new – the original burnt down 13 years ago. James Feeney has a flair for design, and from simple materials has created contemporary opulence: candelabra on long wooden tables, modern canvasses and ornate mirrors on bare brick, windows swept by crushed velvet. Food is a strength, menus are printed daily on paper and the cooking embraces many ideas: cumin-crusted tuna with sweet potato purée; spinach and tomato fondue; Thai red prawn curry; classic sirloin of beef with mushroom sauce. There's comfort food, too, in fish and chips and rack of lamb. And the glassed-in patio area has a conservatory feel.

Meals	Lunch from £5.95. Dinner from £9.95.
Closed	Open all day.
Directions	Lapworth off B4439; pub near station.

James Feeney
The Punchbowl
Mill Lane, Lapworth,
Solihull B94 6HR

Tel +44 (0)1564 784564
Web www.thepunchbowllapworth.com

Entry 593 Map 8

The Malt Shovel at Barston

Barston

No surprise that the car park holds some swanky motors. This is a smart, food-driven place that knows its market and caters to it well. Gastropubs may come and go but this is a favourite. Whether you're ensconced in the smart cream-and-green bar, on the trellis-shaded terrace or in the country-rustic restaurant, the food is to savour and the well-kept ales (Tribute, Old Speckled Hen) are matched by some decent wines. The menu covers global as well as pubby treats – Aberdeenshire rump steak, fishcakes, slow roast pork belly with plum and lemongrass sauce – and executes both with aplomb. The culinary innovation extends to the vegetarian options, perhaps a filo tart of crushed carrot topped with a poached egg, courgette strips and rocket pesto. A slick operation out in the country, that's also friendly and relaxed.

Meals	Lunch & dinner £10.95-£17.95.
Closed	Open all day.
Directions	Off A452; 1 mile beyond village.

Helen Somerfield
The Malt Shovel at Barston
Barston Lane, Barston,
Solihull B92 0JP

Tel +44 (0)1675 443223
Web www.themaltshovelatbarston.com

Entry 594 Map 8

The Red Lion Inn
Cricklade

A stroll from the ancient North Meadow, famous for its spring show of wild fritillaries, the rambling old coaching inn lies off the Thames path. Specialising in seasonal, locally sourced and often organic food, it combines contemporary features with a charming 16th-century fabric and extends its welcome to all (and that includes your dog). In the red-carpeted bar, all low beams, stone walls, ancient settles and log fires, treat yourself to a pint of ale; the choice is mind-boggling, from Arbor Moteuka to Butcombe Bitter. Lunches involve the best of English classics: real burgers with triple-cooked chips; chicken and locally foraged wild mushroom pie; delicious homemade bread and a beer to match each dish. Evening dishes, served at reclaimed wooden tables in the elegant restaurant, include tea-smoked salmon, roast local pork with crispy potatoes, black pudding and sprouting broccoli, rhubarb and ginger crumble. The pick of the bedrooms are the two in the old stables with their stone walls and tiled floors, chunky, hand-crafted beds, crisp linen, and bathrooms that sparkle. Marvellous.

Price	£75.
Rooms	5: 3 doubles, 2 twins/doubles.
Meals	Lunch & bar meals from £6. Dinner from £9. Sunday lunch, 3 courses, £19.95.
Closed	Sunday evenings.
Directions	Cricklade is off A419 between Swindon and Cirencester; pub at lower end of High Street.

Tom Gee
The Red Lion Inn
74 High Street,
Cricklade SN6 6DD
Tel +44 (0)1793 750776
Web www.theredlioncricklade.co.uk

The Bell at Ramsbury

Ramsbury

New owners have snapped up The Bell, creating a classy new-wave inn and one that showcases the top-notch estate produce. Come for Ramsbury beers, kitchen garden fruit and veg, and seasonal game. Completing this pleasing picture are nine stunning bedrooms named after game birds and fish. Cosy lodgings for fishermen, and for visitors exploring the glorious Marlborough Downs, they come with soothing Farrow & Ball colours, rich fabrics, down duvets, big beds and vintage books, while bathrooms are delightful with heated slate floors, rain showers and White Company lotions. Back downstairs, enjoy a pint of Gold with fish and chips in the smart, hop-adorned bar, or bag the sofa in the library-style lounge and peruse a copy of *The Field*. Or treat yourself to assiette of spring lamb, followed by lemon ice mousse, at a clothed table in the stylish restaurant. There's also a wonderful little café (Café Bella) at the back serving teas, coffee and cakes during the day. As for the village, it's really pretty; the pub, on the main square, is 100 yards from the river bank.

Price	£110-£175.
Rooms	9 doubles.
Meals	Lunch £20-£25. Bar meals £7-£17. Dinner £30-£45. Sunday lunch, 2 courses, £21.50.
Closed	3pm-6pm.
Directions	Ramsbury is off B4192, 6 miles east of Marlborough, 5 miles west of Hungerford. Between junctions 14 & 15 of M4.

Ramsbury Estates
The Bell at Ramsbury
The Square, Ramsbury,
Marlborough SN8 2PE

Tel +44 (0)1672 520230
Web www.thebellramsbury.com

The White Horse Inn

Compton Bassett

Whitewashed walls echo the chalk horse that gave its name to this very handsome village inn. Inside all is as neat as a new pin. Lovingly polished parquet glows beneath scrubbed wooden tables, while padded bar stools and assorted chairs – some antique and carved – are well spaced around the reclaimed oak bar, a beautiful piece of recycling. Having been a grocer's shop, a bakery and an inn during its long life the pub now focuses on what it does best: providing great food and drink to villagers and visitors. Eat by the sturdy wood-burner in the bar or in the elegant terracotta dining area with its beams and mullioned windows. Lunches are relaxed affairs of sandwiches and pub classics (homemade sausages and creamy mash, dried smoked bacon and red wine shallot jus). Dinner lists pork and game from the pub's own farm in season – and children are well looked after. In the old stable lie eight simple but comfortable rooms, with pine furniture and pretty fabrics. Many have views to paddocks, sheep and geese, all are blissfully peaceful at night. A super pub from start to finish – very friendly, too.

Price	£75-£85. Singles £65. Family room £85.
Rooms	8: 6 doubles, 1 single, 1 family room.
Meals	Lunch from £9.65. Bar meals from £5.95. Dinner from £11.95. Sunday lunch from £9.95.
Closed	Sunday eves & Monday.
Directions	Sent on booking.

Danny & Tara Adams
The White Horse Inn
Compton Bassett,
Calne SN11 8RG

Tel +44 (0)1249 813118
Web www.whitehorse-comptonbassett.co.uk

The George & Dragon

Rowde

Behind the whitewashed exterior hides a low-ceilinged bar, its stone fireplace ablaze in winter, its half-panelled walls lined with old paintings, its antique clock ticking away the hours. Furnishings are authentically period, there are wooden boards in the dining room, painted walls and plenty of dark timber. The kitchen's chutneys and preserves are for sale, international bottled beers and organic ciders line the shelves and hand-pumped Butcombe Bitter announces itself on the bar. Experienced owners are maintaining the pub's reputation for fish delivered fresh from Cornwall – with the odd concession to meat eaters. There are puddings to diet for, and specials such as delectable chargrilled scallops with black pudding brochettes or whole grilled mackerel with anchovy butter. Rooms are charming and individual – Country, Classic or Funky – with wall timbers and wonky floors, contemporary wall coverings, White Company duvets and linen on wooden or brass beds; bathrooms are the business. Great value, and a treat to come back to after a long walk along the Kennet & Avon Canal.

Price	£55-£115.
Rooms	3: 2 doubles, 1 family room.
Meals	Lunch & dinner £9.95-£18.50. Sunday lunch £19.50.
Closed	Sunday evenings.
Directions	On A342, 2 miles west of Devizes.

Chris Day & Michelle & Philip Hale
The George & Dragon
High Street, Rowde,
Devizes SN10 2PN

Tel +44 (0)1380 723053
Web www.thegeorgeanddragonrowde.co.uk

The Old House at Home

Burton

If you're headed for Castle Combe or the Badminton Horse Trials, why not drop by the Old House at Home, a great little place for dinner and a bed? This traditional ivy-clad pub is no more than a five-minute drive away. The Warburton family have been at its helm for 28 years, with Mark and Matthew now driving the family business (which includes The Northey at Box) with passion and verve. Each of the six bedrooms, built from local stone in the hillside garden at the back, is named after a wine from around the world and, although compact, is cosy and stylishly kitted out. Find wooden floors, rich fabrics, fashionable wallpapers, opulent throws, top-notch beds, coffee machines, plasma screens and fancy wet rooms. In contrast, tradition reigns supreme in the old pub, distinguished by ancient beams, old dining tables and crackling logs in a lovely open fireplace. Expect Wadworth 6X on tap and a wide-ranging menu that combines classics like ham, egg and chips with... tiger prawn and monkfish linguine, beef fillet flamed in cognac, infused with garlic, mushrooms and red wine, and orange and lime tart.

Price	£89-£140.
Rooms	6: 5 double, 1 twin.
Meals	Lunch & bar meals from £6. Dinner from £11. Sunday lunch, 3 courses, £16.
Closed	Open all day.
Directions	On B4039 north west of Chippenham; 2 miles from Castle Combe.

Mark Warburton
The Old House at Home
Burton,
Chippenham SN14 7LT
Tel +44 (0)1454 218227
Web www.ohhcompany.co.uk

Methuen Arms Hotel

Corsham

Built around the remains of a 14th-century nunnery, converted into a brewery and coaching inn in 1608, and with an impressive Georgian façade, the Methuen has history in spades. Restyled as a boutique inn following a sympathetic restoration, its doors swung open in 2010 to reveal a stunning interior. From a grand tiled hallway a sweeping staircase leads to a dozen ultra-stylish rooms, those in the former nunnery oozing character with wonky beams and other fascinating features. All have colourful headboards on big beds, wonderfully upholstered armchairs, funky colourful rugs and some rather swish bathrooms, the best with roll top tubs and walk-in showers. Back downstairs are rugs on stone and wood floors, crackling logs in old stone fireplaces, glowing candles on tables and vintage photos of Corsham; the traditional bar and informal dining rooms are truly inviting. A seasonal modern British menu is a further enticement, so tuck into pasta with game ragout, fish pie, or lamb marinated in oregano and garlic. This grand almost Tardis-like inn promises more rooms in 2012.

Price £120-£160. Singles from £85.
Rooms 10: 9 doubles, 1 twin/double.
Meals Lunch from £5.95.
Dinner, 3 courses, about £30.
Sunday lunch £16.50-£19.50.
Closed Open all day.
Directions M4 junc. 17, then A350 south & A4 west. B3353 south into Corsham. On left.

Martin & Debbie Still
Methuen Arms Hotel
2 High Street,
Corsham SN13 0HB
Tel +44 (0)1249 717060
Web www.themethuenarms.com

The Northey

Box

The former Box Station Hotel owes its architecture to Brunel. The glory for its refurbishment rests on the shoulders of Sally Warburton – an undeniable modernity now sashays down the corridors. Where Noel Coward once entertained with a song there is cool jazz from Ella or Frank so settle into the leather lounge area with a 6X or one of the many excellent wines on offer and get in the swing. Michelin-recognised menus specialise in fresh fish but you can also dig into hearty pub food, and sandwiches, ciabatta, salads and snacks. Eat in the large boldly decorated dining area at chunky wooden tables or, in summer, out in the pretty garden beneath a pair of giant pines. Those staying the night will be royally spoilt as bedrooms sport pieces of one-off furniture, sculpture and art – and flowers, period fireplaces, and beds super comfortable with dazzling white linen and thick mattresses. Bathrooms are a tribute to the textures and colours of travertine marble, slate and stone and are spaces to wallow in – super thick robes and towels and Molton Brown toiletries. Prepare to pamper!

Price	£89-£145.
Rooms	5 doubles.
Meals	Lunch & bar meals from £6. Dinner from £11.
Closed	Open all day.
Directions	On A4 north east of Bath; between junctions 17 &18 of M4.

Mark Warburton
The Northey
Bath Road, Box,
Corsham SN13 8AE
Tel +44 (0)1225 742333
Web www.ohhcompany.co.uk

The Tollgate Inn

Holt

All would pay the toll – were there one – to sample the delights of The Tollgate Inn. In a warm and convivial bar and lounge, lovely leather sofas, a log-burning stove, planked pine tables, newspapers and magazines encourage you to linger over a hand-pumped pint of Exmoor or a glass of sauvignon. The two dining areas have distinct personalities; the smaller off the bar with a traditional appeal, the upper, in the former chapel of the weavers who worked below, smart with high black rafters, open fire and an eclectic décor. Chef Alexander Venables' pedigree shines through in dishes that make the most of local produce (suppliers are named with the menu) and daily fish from Brixham. Light bites include omelette Arnold Bennett and set lunch is a snip at £12.50; try roast saddle of venison with stilton mash and port jus. Country-style bedrooms are in excellent order: oak beams, smart linen, lovely beds. For country views of goats and fields ask for one at the back. Breakfasts are as superb as all the rest, and there's a new deli and farm shop (Seasons) in the renovated barn out back.

Price	£90-£110. Singles £70-£110.
Rooms	4 doubles.
Meals	Lunch & bar meals from £7.50. Dinner 3 courses, £19.95. Sunday lunch, 3 courses, £17.95.
Closed	3pm-5.30pm. Sun eves & Mon.
Directions	On B3107 between Bradford-on-Avon & Melksham.

Alison Ward-Baptiste & Alexander Venables
The Tollgate Inn
Ham Green, Holt BA14 6PX
Tel +44 (0)1225 782326
Web www.tollgateholt.co.uk

The Castle Inn

Bradford-on-Avon

On top of the hill that dips down to the mellow heart of Bradford-on-Avon, this heart-warming renovation of a neglected Bath stone inn is the work of Flatcappers, who, in their first foray into the world of real pubs, have struck gold. Enter a warren of planked rooms – one large, three small – in muted greys, reds and greens, lovingly and imaginatively restored. Imagine solid stone walls and little log fires, recycled chairs and long farmhouse tables, a leather sofa to sink into, books on the shelves and prints on the walls. Six ales from local breweries dominate the bar as locals pop in for a pint and the papers, and muted jazz plays. An Anglo-Saxon take on tapas stands alongside British pub classics, the specials are special (rabbit ragout with handmade pappardelle) and our Sunday sirloin with Yorkshire pud was heaven. Above, four equally characterful bedrooms have modish wallpapers and stylish hues, wonky door frames and period fireplaces, stunning walk-in bathrooms and wide-reaching views – of the church, or the White Horse on the Wiltshire hills. Great fun.

Price	£100-£140.
Rooms	4: 3 doubles, 1 family room.
Meals	Lunch & dinner £7.95-£18.95.
Closed	Open all day.
Directions	Entering Bradford-on-Avon on A363, pub is on mini-r'bout before turning for town centre.

Pierre Woodford
The Castle Inn
Mount Pleasant,
Bradford-on-Avon BA15 1SJ

Tel	+44 (0)1225 865657
Web	www.flatcappers.co.uk

The Bath Arms at Longleat

Horningsham

A 17th-century coaching inn on the Longleat estate in a village lost in the country; geese swim in the river, cows munch the fields. At the front, a dozen pollarded lime trees shade a gravelled garden; at the back, two stone terraces soak up the sun. Inside are the best of old and new: flagstones and boarded floors, a stainless steel bar and Farrow & Ball colours. The feel is smart and airy, with a skittle alley that doubles as a sitting room (they show movies here) and shimmering Cole & Son walls in the lovely intimate dining room. Stop for crab bisque, pork belly with Irish cabbage and parsnip purée, lemon panna cotta. They grow veg, keep pigs: produce makes its short way to the kitchen; young guests may be given a small selection of vegetables to take home. Flashman, English Eccentric, Geisha... each of the splendid bedrooms lives up to its name, some in the main house, others in the barn. The Kama Sutra room is heavily influenced by Lord Bath's own series of murals, and there's a spacious lodge overlooking Longleat House, nicely private for a small family. The walk down to Longleat is majestic.

Price	£145-£185. Singles from £135. Half-board from £97.50 p.p. Lodge £150 for 2-4.
Rooms	15 + 1: 13 doubles, 2 twins. Self-catering lodge for 4.
Meals	Lunch from £5. Dinner, 2 courses, £25.
Closed	Open all day.
Directions	A303, then A350 north to Longbridge Deverill. Left for Maiden Bradley; right for Horningsham. Through village, on right.

Peter Stevens
The Bath Arms at Longleat
Horningsham,
Warminster BA12 7LY

Tel	+44 (0)1985 844308
Web	www.batharms.co.uk

The Bath Arms Crockerton

Crockerton

The rambling old pub stands on the Longleat Estate, minutes from Shearwater Lake and woodland walks, and draws an eclectic crowd: ramblers, tourists, foodies. With a culinary background that ranges from country-house hotels to The Ivy, Dean Carr presents a pub menu that's a cut above the norm. So expect wild sea bass with chorizo risotto alongside gammon and poached eggs, and rump steak with rocket pesto alongside shepherd's pie, all with a modern twist. There are classy baguettes too, like steak and horseradish, and nursery favourites like sticky toffee pudding. The setting is homely and traditional, the open-plan bar and dining area displaying beams, brasses and plain pine tables; arrive early to bag a bench by the lovely log fire and a pint of local Crockerton Classic. The bedrooms, just two, 'Left' and 'Right', are a big surprise; both are huge with a contemporary yet sumptuous feel. Be cheered by crisp linen on wooden sleigh beds, leather sofas, vast plasma screens, bold modern paintings and bathrooms combining 'wet room' showers with Gilchrist & Soames.

Price	£80-£110.
Rooms	2 doubles.
Meals	Lunch & bar meals from £6.95. Dinner from £10.95. Sunday lunch, 3 courses, £22.85.
Closed	3pm-6pm. Open all day Sat & Sun in summer.
Directions	2 miles south of Warminster off A350 towards Shaftesbury.

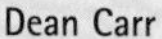

Dean Carr
The Bath Arms Crockerton
Crockerton,
Warminster BA12 8AJ
Tel +44 (0)1985 212262
Web www.batharmscrockerton.co.uk

The Lamb at Hindon

Hindon

The Lamb has been serving ale on Hindon's high street for 800 years. It is a yard of England's finest cloth, a place where shooting parties come for lunch, where farmers meet to chew the cud. Find huge oak settles, heavy old beams, deep red walls and roaring fires. A clipped Georgian country elegance lingers; you almost expect Mr Darcy to walk in, give a tormented sigh, then turn on his heels and vanish. There are flagstone floors and stripped wooden boards, window seats and gilded mirrors; old oils entwined in willow hang on the walls, a bookshelf is stuffed with aged tomes of poetry. At night, candles come out, as do some serious whiskies, and in the restaurant you can feast on ham hock and foie gras ballotine, game pie or Dover sole, then local cheeses. Revamped bedrooms come with mahogany furniture, rich colours, tartan throws, the odd four-poster, and some rather smart bathrooms. Splash out and stay in one of the cosy new rooms in the converted coach house. Fishing can be arranged, or you can shoot off to Stonehenge, Stourhead, Salisbury or Bath.

Price	From £75. Four-posters from £85. Suites from £100.
Rooms	19: 10 doubles, 2 twins/doubles, 4 four-posters, 3 suites.
Meals	Lunch & dinner £5-£25.
Closed	Open all day.
Directions	M3, A303 & signed left at bottom of steep hill two miles east of junction with A350.

Merle Crampton
The Lamb at Hindon
High Street, Hindon,
Salisbury SP3 6DP
Tel +44 (0)1747 820573
Web www.lambathindon.co.uk

The Beckford Arms

Tisbury

Wash up at this country-house inn and expect to be seduced; after a severe fire it has risen, phoenix-like, from the ashes. And you arrive in style: a sweep though the Fonthill estate and under the Triumphal Arch. The half-acre garden is ridiculously pretty – hammocks in the trees, parasols on the terrace, church spire soaring to the heavens – but this Georgian house is equally sublime, an inn for all seasons. Inside: a drawing room where facing sofas are warmed by a roaring fire; a restaurant with a wall of glass that opens onto the terrace; a bar with parquet flooring for an excellent local pint. Follow your nose and chance upon the odd chandelier, roaming wisteria, logs piled high inside and out and a rather grand mahogany table in the private dining room. Bedrooms are small but perfectly formed: white walls, sisal matting, wonderful bathrooms and pretty new attic rooms perfect for a family. As for the food, there's much to please, perhaps marrow fritters with lemon mayo, local partridge with bread sauce, chocolate bread and butter pudding. There are film nights most Sundays, the cricket team comes to celebrate.

Price	£95-£120.
Rooms	8: 7 doubles, 1 twin/double.
Meals	Lunch & dinner £5-£30. Sunday lunch from £11.50.
Closed	Open all day.
Directions	On the road between Tisbury and Hindon, three miles south of A303 (Fonthill exit).

Daniel Brod & Charlie Luxton
The Beckford Arms
Fonthill Gifford, Tisbury,
Salisbury SP3 6PX
Tel +44 (0)1747 870385
Web www.beckfordarms.com

Pub with rooms

The Compasses Inn

Tisbury

In the middle of a lovely village of thatched and timber-framed cottages, this inn seems so content with its lot it could almost be a figment of your imagination. Over the years, 14th-century foundations have gradually sunk into the ground. Its thatched roof is like a sombrero, shielding bedroom windows that peer sleepily over the lawn. Duck instinctively into the sudden darkness of the bar and experience a wave of nostalgia as your eyes adjust to a long wooden room, with flagstones and cosy booths divided by farmyard salvage: a cartwheel here, some horse tack there; at one end is a piano, at the other, a brick hearth. The pub crackles with Alan and Susie's enthusiasm and their hospitality is a big draw. People come for the food as well: Lyme Bay scallops on black pudding with crispy bacon, or Wiltshire venison steak, dauphinoise potatoes and red wine and juniper jus. Bedrooms are at the top of stone stairs outside the front door and have the same effortless charm; thick walls, wonky windows, spotless bathrooms. And the sweet serenity of Wiltshire lies just down the lane.

Price	£85. Singles from £65. Cottage £100-£130.
Rooms	4 + 1: 3 doubles, 1 twin/double. Self-catering cottage for 4.
Meals	Lunch from £5.50. Dinner from £15.
Closed	Monday (Jan-Mar).
Directions	From Salisbury A30 west. 3rd right after Fovant, signed Lower Chicksgrove, then 1st left down single track lane to village.

Alan & Susie Stoneham
The Compasses Inn
Lower Chicksgrove, Tisbury,
Salisbury SP3 6NB

Tel +44 (0)1722 714318
Web www.thecompassesinn.com

The Horseshoe Inn

Ebbesbourne Wake

The Ebble Valley and Ebbesbourne Wake have escaped the intrusions of modern-day life, dozing down tiny lanes close to the Dorset border. A bucolic charm pervades the village inn that has been run as a "proper country pub" by the Bath family for over 30 years. Climbing roses cling to the 17th-century brick façade, while the traditional layout of two bars around a central servery still survives. Old farming implements and country bygones fill every available cranny and a mix of rustic furniture is arranged around the crackling winter fire. Beer is tapped straight from the cask and food is hearty and wholesome, prepared by Pat Bath using local meat and vegetables, and game from local shoots. Tuck into steak and kidney pie, fresh fish bake, nursery pud, three roasts on Sundays (do book). Benches and flowers fill the garden.

Meals	Lunch & dinner £9.95-£17. Bar meals £4.95-£12.95. Sunday lunch from £9.50.
Closed	3pm-6.30pm. Sun from 4pm & Mon until 7pm.
Directions	A354 south of Salisbury, right at Coombe Bissett; follow valley road for 8 miles.

Anthony & Patricia Bath
The Horseshoe Inn
The Cross,
Ebbesbourne Wake,
Salisbury SP5 5JF
Tel +44 (0)1722 780474

Entry 609 Map 3

Wiltshire

The Forester Inn

Donhead St Andrew

Tiny lanes frothing with cowparsley twist down to this fine little pub in Donhead St Andrew. The revitalised 600-year-old inn sports rustic walls, black beams, a log fire in the inglenook and planked floors; colours are muted, there's not an ounce of flounce and locals still prop up the bar of a late weekday lunchtime. Foodies come from far for chef Andrew Kilburn's cooking – rib-eye steak with béarnaise, 'a trio of lamb chops' with bubble-and-squeak, goat's cheese omelette, tomato tarte tatin – and fine puddings cooked to order, slowly. Andrew uses local Rushmore venison, Old Spot pork and specialises in fresh Cornish seafood – brill with shellfish bisque and mussels, skate wing with brown butter and capers. Lucky dogs get delicious gravy bones, the garden terrace has views, there are three ales on tap, Westons' Organic cider and ten gorgeous wines by the glass.

Meals	Lunch from £7.50. Bar meals from £7. Dinner from £12.50. Sunday lunch, 3 courses, £25.50. Not Sun eves.
Closed	3pm-6.30pm. Sun from 4pm.
Directions	A30 between Shaftesbury & Salisbury. Through Ludwell then left for Donhead; pub on right in 1.2 miles.

Chris & Lizzie Matthews
The Forester Inn
Lower Street, Donhead St Andrew,
Shaftesbury SP7 9EE
Tel +44 (0)1747 828038
Web www.theforesterdonheadstandrew.co.uk

Entry 610 Map 3

Fox & Hounds

East Knoyle

If you love beech trees and high ridges, make time for a walk with views over the vale before you land at the 17th-century thatched pub on the green. Enter to discover two areas: one bright and conservatory-like, with a great view, the other older and cosier, its fireplace flanked by small red leather sofas. There are warming ales from Palmers and Butcombe, and the inimitable Summer Lightning, and a well-presented wine card that tells you exactly what you'll get – which is what you'd expect from a no-nonsense landlord. Being a New Zealander, he cooks in an eclectic, untypical gastro style. Tuck into chorizo, bean and red pepper casserole in red wine with belly pork or sweet onion, ricotta and parmesan tart; follow with melting chocolate fondant and mascarpone cream... you'll stay till the pub closes, no hardship at all!

Meals	Lunch & dinner £9-£17.
Closed	3pm-5.30pm.
Directions	Off A303 onto A350 to Blandford; right to East Knoyle; right onto Wise Lane (opposite the playground), keep going - it's further than you think!

Murray Seator
Fox & Hounds
The Green, East Knoyle,
Salisbury SP3 6BN

Tel +44 (0)1747 830573
Web www.foxandhounds-eastknoyle.co.uk

Entry 611 Map 3

Wiltshire

The Spread Eagle

Stourton

While Stourhead Gardens "echo with references to the heroes and gods of ancient Rome", this proper inn makes more than a passing nod to Bacchus. Mellow and old-fashioned it may appear but peep inside and you find slate or coir floors, Farrow & Ball colours and lovely jugs of garden flowers on old pine tables. In the bar a wood-burning stove is merry and the seats are comfy; you can eat here or in the restaurant that doubles as a sitting room. Red walls, large modern paintings, old prints, the odd game of scrabble create a mood that is cosy and warm. Food is English and locally supplied: Wiltshire ham with sweet mustard, West Country fish soup, griddled organic salmon salad with anchovy mayonnaise. As for the estate: you can pretend that this stupendous example of a landscape garden with lake and follies is all yours.

Meals	Lunch & dinner £8.50-£16. Bar meals from £5.50.
Closed	Open all day.
Directions	Turn off B3092 signed Stourhead Gardens. Spread Eagle is below main car park on left at entrance to garden. Private car park for inn.

Andrew & Angela Wilson
The Spread Eagle
Church Lawn, Stourton,
Warminster BA12 6QE

Tel +44 (0)1747 840587
Web www.spreadeagleinn.com

Entry 612 Map 3

The Malet Arms

Newton Tony

Formerly a bakehouse for a long-lost manor, the old flintstone pub draws walkers from miles. Expect cracking local ales, robust country cooking and a cheerful welcome from the Cardews. The low-beamed bar, cosy with rustic furnishings, blazing logs, old pictures and interesting bits and pieces, would be a nice spot for a pint of Stonehenge Heelstone. Hearty food, listed on boards above the fireplaces, reflects the rural setting, with local game (shot by Noel) a winter favourite. Fill your boots with a rich stew of pheasant and pigeon in Guinness, proper fish and chips or a local beefburger, and follow with Annie's speciality: an old English pudding (try the walnut and date tart). The pub cricket team play on the field opposite and there's a summer music festival in the paddock at the back – a true community pub.

Meals	Lunch & dinner £8.50-£15.
Closed	3pm-6pm (7pm Sun).
Directions	Off A338, 6 miles north of Salisbury, 3 miles south of A303.

Noel & Annie Cardew
The Malet Arms
Newton Tony,
Salisbury SP4 0HF
Tel +44 (0)1980 629279
Web www.maletarms.com

Entry 613 Map 3

Wiltshire

The Red Lion

East Chisenbury

Unless you found yourself lost on Salisbury Plain, chances are you wouldn't stumble upon the Red Lion. You'd be missing much: this smart thatched village inn is both a local serving ale from Wiltshire microbreweries and a restaurant drawing food lovers from far and wide. Owner-chefs Guy and Brittany Manning arrived with something of a star-spangled CV. Guy worked for three years at the Chez Bruce in London, both worked under Thomas Keller at the breathtaking Per Se in New York. The couple apply cutting-edge cookery techniques to simple rustic dishes and the results are very special. The menu changes every day – sometimes twice – so expect the likes of pheasant and ham hock terrine, mushroom tortellini, roast pollock with olive oil mash and New England cheesecake with rhubarb. The Sunday roasts are superb!

Meals	Lunch & dinner £10-£18. Bar meals from £7. Sunday lunch, 2 courses, £18.
Closed	3pm-6pm weekdays.
Directions	East Chisenbury is off A345/Salisbury Road.

Guy & Brittany Manning
The Red Lion
East Chisenbury,
Pewsey SN9 6AQ
Tel +44 (0)1980 671124
Web www.redlionfreehouse.com

Entry 614 Map 3

The Angel Inn

Upton Scudamore

A blaze of summer colour on the smart, sheltered decked area that faces south west; beams and a huge log burner in the bare-boarded bar; contemporary art and sofas in the split-level restaurant. It's a comfortable and sophisticated environment for Tony and Carol Coates' menu and specials board that delivers straightforward modern food. Informality and decent sized portions are among the attractions, the menu changes frequently and the produce is sourced locally. Fish dishes star, in the form of roast halibut with haricot beans and vanilla, and smoked haddock with chive butter. A surprisingly light sticky toffee pudding makes a satisfying finish. There are Wadworth 6X and Butcombe on tap. Round off the treats with a visit to Longleat, Salisbury or Bath.

Meals	Lunch & dinner £12-£22.
Closed	3pm-6pm.
Directions	Village signed off A350 Warminster to Westbury road & off A36.

Tony & Carol Coates
The Angel Inn
Upton Scudamore,
Warminster BA12 0AG
Tel +44 (0)1985 213225
Web www.theangelinn.co.uk

The Three Daggers

Edington

Restored, renamed and rejuvenated in 2010, The Three Daggers thrives as a village local – and as a stop-off for top-notch British food. It's been spruced up with style but hasn't lost the feel of a classic country pub, so there are stripped beams, a slate-tiled floor, Farrow & Ball walls, fat church candles on old dining tables, chapel chairs, cushioned wall benches and a blazing log fire. And a posh new conservatory for dining. Come to peruse the papers with a pint of Butcombe or to sample Adrian's seasonal food. Tuck into a sharing board laden with game goodies, enjoy a lamb shank shepherd's pie or pork belly with a cider and thyme sauce: it's all delicious, and it would be a shame not to leave room for sticky toffee pudding. Walk it off in invigorating countryside, and don't miss Edington's magnificent Priory Church.

Meals	Lunch & dinner £8.50-£18.95. Not Sun eves.
Closed	3pm-5pm. Open all day Sat, Sun & everyday (Apr-Sept).
Directions	On B3098 4 miles east of A350 at Westbury; pub in village centre.

Adrian Jenkins & Jackie Cosens
The Three Daggers
Westbury Road, Edington,
Westbury BA13 4PG
Tel +44 (0)1380 830940
Web www.threedaggers.co.uk

The Somerset Arms

Semington

The bricks and mortar of this listed coaching inn go back to 1694; the interior design is rather more recent. The inn stands in the middle of a cul-de-sac village, assuring peace at all times, though contented diners hum their approval in the restaurant and ale aficionados keep the bar busy. Outside are picnic tables on the terrace; inside is an airy world of painted beams, whitewashed walls, open fires and exposed red brick. Cask ales are treated with reverence and 80 guests have featured in 18 months, so expect a good pint; they also have beer festivals throughout the year (May, August and November). English classics sit on the menu: game terrine with a juniper compote, beef Wellington, apple crumble with vanilla ice cream. Bath is close for culture and you can walk your socks off in the local hills.

Meals	Bar meals from £5.75. Dinner from £9.50. Sunday lunch, 3 courses, £18.95.
Closed	Open all day.
Directions	From A361, exit for Semington.

James Galton
The Somerset Arms
High Street, Semington,
Devizes BA14 6JR
Tel +44 (0)1380 870067
Web www.somersetarmssemington.co.uk

Entry 617 Map 3

The Fox

Broughton Gifford

You are in good hands here, along with the wire fox in the window. An amphitheatre of leather sofas and armchairs is a delightful backdrop to a dazzling array of beverages: great ales such as Gem, Otter and Butcombe, ciders from Bounders and Ashton Press, a score of malts, numerous high end spirits and some seriously good wines. But eat you must and the best is yet to come. Alex and his team are passionate about using seasonal and regional produce, and raise their own pigs to produce sausages, charcuterie, air- and wet-cured hams, and bacon – a smoke house is planned. As for the pork chops, they're the stuff of legend, and much of the bread is home-baked; you'll be joining the queue at the door. Behind is a garden flanked by pines and willows, tubs of herbs and vegetables; further back are the pigs and the hens. Prepare to unwind!

Meals	Lunch & bar meals from £8.50. Dinner from £11.95. Sunday lunch, 3 courses, £27.95. Not Sun eves or Mon lunch.
Closed	Open all day.
Directions	See website.

Local, organic & seasonal produce

Alex Geneen
The Fox
The Street, Broughton Gifford,
Melksham SN12 8PN
Tel +44 (0)1225 782949
Web www.thefox-broughtongifford.co.uk

Entry 618 Map 3

Quarrymans Arms

Box

A fine old pub lost in pretty hills with views that stretch across lush country. As the name suggests, it once served the miners from the local quarry and fascinating maps and pictures adorn the walls, as do some lethal-looking stonecutting equipment. Outside, you can watch farmers and walkers weave through the hamlet from a tiny terrace at the front, but it's the big garden at the back where the faithful gather in good weather – and where better to wash down a plate of rare roast beef with a pint of Butcombe on a Sunday in summer? Traditional interiors fit the bill (old beams, exposed stone, an open fire), while tasty rustic food offers homemade pies, Wiltshire ham, perhaps lemon sole or roast spatchcock. A great fuel stop for cyclists, walkers and potholers; some of the mines are accessible to all and tours can be arranged.

Meals: Lunch from £4.50.
Bar meals from £2.95.
Dinner from £7.95.
Sunday lunch, 3 courses, £16.

Closed: Open all day.

Directions: Just off A4, on hillside to right of village; phone for directions.

John & Ginny Arundel
Quarrymans Arms
Box Hill, Box,
Corsham SN13 8HN
Tel +44 (0)1225 743569
Web www.quarrymans-arms.co.uk

Entry 619 Map 3

Wiltshire

The Rattlebone Inn

Sherston

It was built in the late 17th-century and named after Saxon warrior John Rattlebone – when bones doubled up for armour! The village bar is all flagstones, beams and wood furniture with friendly Rob distributing Young's Bitter or St Austell Tribute. Behind, another carpeted area leads to numerous nooks and crannies from which to delve into the snack and main menus: homemade shepherd's pie; medallions of pork (with stilton sauce and spring onion mash and toasted cashews) plus interesting wines to go with your choice, as well as good cheeses and desserts. A wood-burner keeps it toasty in winter, there's a long, calm dining area for cosy meals, and outside, just off the High Street, two patio areas, two boules pistes and a skittle alley. On certain days you can even try Mangold hurling – an old West Country sport.

Meals: Lunch, bar meals & dinner, all from £4.75.

Closed: 3pm-5pm. Open all day Sat & Sun.

Directions: On B4040 west of Malmesbury; pub in village centre.

Jason Read
The Rattlebone Inn
Church Street, Sherston,
Malmesbury SN16 0LR
Tel +44 (0)1666 840871
Web www.therattlebone.co.uk

Entry 620 Map 3

The Vine Tree

Norton

With a fine store of ales and over 40 wines by the glass the old watermill is a watering hole in every sense. It may be hidden away but the faithful return, for the food and the beer. On Sundays, memorable roast sirloin of beef from the neighbour's farm is served with all the trimmings. There's plenty of fresh fish, too, and local game in season, sautéed scallops with wild mushroom risotto, and rack of Cotswold lamb. Service is young and friendly and surroundings are inviting: deep red walls, candlelight and beams, a wood-burning stove; tables in the minuscule upstairs room are super-cosy. In summer, relax and gaze on the immaculate terrace – a delicious spot with urns of flowers and a fountain. This Vine Tree has a rich harvest for guests – and their dogs – to reap; no wonder Clementine the lab looks so content.

Meals	Lunch from £8.95. Dinner from £13.95. Bar meals from £4.95. Sun eves (Sept-March).
Closed	3pm-5.45pm. Open all day Sun in summer.
Directions	From M4 junc. 17 take A429 for Cirencester. After 1.5 miles left for Norton. There, right for Foxley. Follow road; on left.

Charles Walker & Tiggi Wood
The Vine Tree
Foxley Road, Norton,
Malmesbury SN16 0JP
Tel +44 (0)1666 837654
Web www.thevinetree.co.uk

Entry 621 Map 3

Wiltshire

The Horse & Groom Inn

Charlton

The solidly elegant Cotswold stone house fronted by a tree-shaded lawn stands well back from the road. Its long history as a coaching inn is documented in the framed prints that adorn the spruced up 17th-century interior. Choose between the rustically atmospheric main bar, all exposed stone, scrubbed tables and roaring fire, or one of two smart dining areas – gleaming tables, polished glasses. Food on well-priced menus champions both the classics and innovative pub dishes; try pea and rocket risotto; lamb rump with garlic mash, rosemary and red wine jus; ham, egg and hand-cut chips; homemade burger with spicy tomato relish; orange and cinnamon panna cotta. Decent sandwiches are served throughout the day, and there's a secret walled garden for civilised summer drinking.

Meals	Lunch from £5.50. Sunday lunch from £10. Dinner, 3 courses, about £30.
Closed	Open all day.
Directions	M4 junc. 17, then A429 north for Cirencester. Right onto B4040 after 5 miles. On left in village after 1 mile.

Keith Meris
The Horse & Groom Inn
The Street, Charlton,
Malmesbury SN16 9DL
Tel +44 (0)1666 823904
Web www.bespokehotels.com/horseandgroom

Entry 622 Map 3

The Potting Shed Pub

Crudwell

Jonathan and Julian, owners of the Rectory Hotel across the road, have transformed the village inn. As well as the open fireplaces and the stylish kilim sofas, you'll note a light fitting fashioned from a wheelbarrow, door handles from trowels, hand pumps from fork handles and old butchers' block tables; the large, airy dining room displays mix 'n' match antiques. As for the food, it is exuberantly British, from the rabbit terrine to the battered hake and lamb hotpot. Two acres of lawns and an apple orchard at the back have been turned into an organic vegetable patch, while local ales, ploughman's lunches and dog biscuits on the bar further reflect the focus on real-pub values and unpretentiousness. There's an excellent children's menu, and puds to warm your heart; try the spiced rice pudding. It's 21st-century pub heaven.

Meals	Lunch from £5.50. Dinner from £11.95.
Closed	Open all day.
Directions	In village centre on A429 between Cirencester & M4 junc. 17.

Jonathan Barry & Julian Muggridge
The Potting Shed Pub
Crudwell, Malmesbury SN16 9EW
Tel +44 (0)1666 577833
Web www.thepottingshedpub.com

Wiltshire

The Wheatsheaf

Oaksey

Ancient on the outside, inglenooked inside – the archetypal English country pub. Local drinkers are welcome, but, with cooking like this, it would be silly to come merely to booze. Peep around the corner from the bar and tradition ends – the dining room has pale wood and sisal floors, dark red walls and modern prints, and good-looking food served on big white plates. Chef-patron Tony Robson-Burrell's imaginative country dishes reflect current trends, so whether you choose a pub classic like Hereford rump steak with parmesan and pesto salad and fat chips, or roast monkfish with gnocchi and braised leeks, you'll eat well (while dessert-lovers will relish the baked hot chocolate fondant with rum and raisin ice cream or dark chocolate pot with hazelnut cookie). Real ales include Bath ales and Sharp's Doom Bar, children and dogs are welcome.

Meals	Lunch & dinner £12-£19. Bar meals £5-£12. Sunday lunch, 3 courses, £24. Not Sunday eve or Monday lunch.
Closed	3pm-6pm. Sun eves & Mon lunch. Open all day Sat.
Directions	Oaksey signed off A429 at Crudwell, 5 miles north of Malmesbury.

Tony Robson-Burrell
The Wheatsheaf
Wheatsheaf Lane, Oaksey,
Malmesbury SN16 9TB
Tel +44 (0)1666 577348
Web www.thewheatsheafatoaksey.co.uk

Wiltshire

The Royal Oak
Bishopstone

Passionately organic, delightfully unpreachy. In 2005 the simple pub in the idyllic village was taken on by farmer Helen Browning and has been flying the flag ever since. There's food bartering with locals, a wild garden with barbecues (they provide the ingredients, you do the rest) and open days with hay bales for kids to romp on: all part of the commitment to be a full-on local. The planked open-plan bar has a lovely feel with roaring fire and beams and the staff are friendly, but best of all is the menu that changes twice daily: crayfish from the Thames served with Bishopstone watercress, home-cured bacon from home-reared pigs, asparagus from Lotmead down the road, fish from day boats out of Newlyn, gooseberries from the garden. Perfect ingredients, perfect food, beer from Arkells and six wines by the glass.

Meals	Lunch & dinner £8-£20. Bar meals £3.95-£6.50. Sunday lunch from £12.50.
Closed	3pm-6pm. Open all day Sat & Sun.
Directions	Bishopstone is 8 miles east of Swindon, take minor road off A419 just north of M4 junc. 15. Left onto Cues Lane; 50 yards on right. Car park at back.

Helen Browning
The Royal Oak
Bishopstone,
Swindon SN6 8PP

Tel +44 (0)1793 790481
Web www.royaloakbishopstone.co.uk

Entry 625 Map 3

Worcestershire

The Fleece
Bretforton

"No potato crisps to be sold in the bar." So ordered Lola Taplin when The Fleece was bequeathed to the National Trust after 500 years in her family. It's the sort of tradition that thrives in the Pewter Room where you pitch up for fresh local food, ales from Uley and Fleece Folly cider. Local sausages with red onion marmalade and red wine gravy and locally culled rhubarb in pies and crumbles may tempt you but there is so much more: the Asparagus Festival commences in the courtyard, with an auction on the last Sunday in May, summer festivals twirl with Morris dancers and the original farmyard is a gorgeous setting for hog roasts and live theatre. The black-and-white timbered building is as stuffed as a museum with historical artefacts, stone flagged floors, big log fires, ancient beams and a wonderful collection of pewter.

Meals	Lunch from £8.75. Bar meals from £5.50. Dinner from £8.75.
Closed	3pm-6pm Mon & Tues (Sept-May).
Directions	B4035 from Evesham for Chipping Campden. In Bretforton bear right into village. Opp. church in square.

Nigel Smith
The Fleece
The Cross, Bretforton,
Evesham WR11 7JE

Tel +44 (0)1386 831173
Web www.thefleeceinn.co.uk

Entry 626 Map 8

Butcher's Arms

Eldersfield

A two-room pub for Slow Foodies – with a lovely big garden and a cottage for let in the car park! But the Butcher's is still a place for regulars popping in for pints of Wye Valley Bitter from the cask, and for Herefordshire cider. As for the Michelin-starred food, James has a hands-on philosophy and cooks single-handedly for just 18 covers a time; and Elizabeth does friendly front of house. He used to work with Alastair Little and his gutsy British dishes, listed on a sensibly short menu, use local produce from named suppliers. Try loin and shoulder of lamb with braised lentils and leek and bacon mash – or be adventurous and tuck into that old English delicacy Bath chap, served with potato scone and grain mustard. The finale? Seville orange marmalade pudding with Drambuie custard, if you fancy. A marvellous little place for 'nose to tail' dining.

Meals	Lunch & dinner £16-£24. Bookings only at lunch. Not Sun eve or Tues lunch.
Closed	2.30pm-7pm. Monday all day.
Directions	From Tewkesbury, A438 west towards Ledbury; left on B4211 & follow signs for Eldersfield & Lime Street.

James & Elizabeth Winter
Butcher's Arms
Lime Street, Eldersfield,
Gloucester GL19 4NX

Tel +44 (0)1452 840381
Web www.thebutchersarms.net

Entry 627 Map 8

The Inn at Welland

Welland

David and Gillian have created a 'contemporary traditional' style that flows together effortlessly. Those who just want to sup their Butty Bach or Otter bitter can retire to comfy leather armchairs with trunk tables or cushioned park style benches. The main sweep has gorgeous Limestone tile flooring and a mix of tables and chairs: a bleached wooden sideboard hosts food items for sale and beside it a stack of wine cases filled with bin end bottles – for later perhaps? The kitchen team serve up a proper gastro medley all of great provenance and with artisan bread baked on the premises. Enjoy Pan fried Cornish scallops, pea mint purée, crisp lardons and tomato oil followed by crisp belly pork, garlic mash, pak choi, orange and ginger jus. here are log fires and the garden has views of the nearby Malvern Hills. Welcome back!

Meals	Lunch & dinner from £11. Bar meals from £6.50. Sunday lunch, 2-3 courses £19.50-£24.50.
Closed	Mon & Sun eves.
Directions	See website.

David & Gillian Pinchbeck
The Inn at Welland
Drake Street, Welland,
Malvern WR13 6LN

Tel +44 (0)1684 592317
Web www.theinnatwelland.co.uk

Entry 628 Map 8

Nag's Head
Malvern

No beauty competition winner perhaps, but this low-slung white pub, converted from what was once a row of cottages, and with a timber-clad restaurant that was once a boxing gym, is worth seeking out. Tucked away in the side streets of lovely Malvern is a paradise for fans of whisky or real ale (fans of both tipples may have to be stretcher'd off). There are 25 single malts on offer and 18 beers, three of which are made at the pub's own brewery at Callow End. No wonder the homely bar with its deep-pink walls and living-room feel gets packed. This is a pub's pub. Stick to the bric-a-brac-strewn dining room for food, where ambitious restaurant-style fare (homemade chicken liver pâté, whole lemon sole) is proffered, and let the serious drinkers hog the bar. A great find.

Meals	Lunch & dinner £10.50-£17.50.
Closed	Open all day.
Directions	At the bottom of Bank Street.

Claire Willetts
Nag's Head
Bank Street,
Malvern WR14 2JG
Tel +44 (0)1684 574373
Web www.nagsheadmalvern.co.uk

Entry 629 Map 8

Worcestershire

The Live & Let Live
Bringsty Common

Well off the beaten track and reached down a stone road this 300-year-old thatched pub sits in splendid isolation. It was rescued by owner Sue Dovey after it had lain closed and unloved for 11 years; she spent an age restoring it, and restoring it beautifully – even the thatch is new. The single-room bar is a refuge for locals and walkers and is quaint with pale gnarled beams, flagstones, dusky pink walls, stoneware bottles and a wonderfully big fireplace. Upstairs is a dear little restaurant open all week, bookings allowing. On sunny days, outside is best – a pretty little garden with superb views of the ancient common. Wherever you perch you can tuck into delicious beer, cider and perry from nearby, and good grub – Bringsty lamb chops, ham, egg and chips, steak and kidney pie, and, more surprisingly, Hungarian goulash.

Meals	Lunch & dinner £9.95-£18.95.
Closed	2.30pm-5pm & Mon (except bank hols). Open all day Fri-Sun.
Directions	Bringsty Common is signposted off A44 between Knightwick and Bromyard. Look for cat and mouse on pub sign.

Sue Dovey
The Live & Let Live
Bringsty Common,
Bringsty WR6 5UW
Tel +44 (0)1886 821462
Web www.liveandletlive-bringsty.co.uk

Entry 630 Map 8

The Talbot
Knightwick

It's run by Annie and her extended family, owners with a dedication to all things self-sufficient. Hops for their microbrewery are grown locally; organic produce comes from the farmers' market they host the second Sunday of every month. Their infectious commitment to using fresh local food pulls a crowd; the crab bisque, raised pies and spotted dick are legendary. Fresh fish comes from Cornwall and scallop beignets are wrapped in nori seaweed (not local, but delicious). The pot-roast lamb recipe is from Alnwick Castle in Northumberland, and the wild duck – drizzled with meat juices, a little grand marnier and served over mashed potato – suggests a touch of genius. Out of the way, on the bank of the Teme (you may fish with a permit): a superb place, well-run, and with a fire in the comfortable bar.

Meals	Lunch & dinner £10-£20. Bar meals £5-£16. Sunday lunch, 3 courses, £27.
Closed	Open all day.
Directions	From Worcester A44 for Leominster; 8 miles on, through Cotheridge & Broadwas; right on B4197; on left.

Annie Clift
The Talbot
Bromyard Road, Knightwick,
Worcester WR6 5PH
Tel +44 (0)1886 821235
Web www.the-talbot.co.uk

Entry 631 Map 8

Worcestershire

The Chequers
Cutnall Green

On the site of an ancient coaching inn, The Chequers was rebuilt in the 1930s. You'd never know: its open fires, comfy sofas and snug little booths have evolved as smoothly as its menu. While the thirsty gather round the church-panel bar with pints of Timothy Taylor's, the hungry head for the dining room – cosy and candlelit with deep cranberry walls, pale exposed beams and a huge display of wines. Make the most of a vibrant 'mod Brit' menu from award-winning chef Roger Narbett: the food bursts with flavour and local products. There's chicken liver parfait with plum compote, pot-roasted belly pork with crackling and duck fat potatoes, and apple tarte tatin. And if the liqueur coffees catch your fancy, slip off and savour one in the Players' Lounge, a small room that has photos of Roger's Football Chef days.

Meals	Lunch & dinner £9.25-£16.25. Bar meals £4.95-£11.95.
Closed	3pm-6pm (3.30pm-6pm Sun).
Directions	3 miles north of Droitwich Spa on A442 towards Kidderminster. M5 exit 5.

Roger & Jo Narbett
The Chequers
Kidderminster Road, Cutnall Green,
Droitwich WR9 0PJ
Tel +44 (0)1299 851292
Web www.chequerscutnallgreen.co.uk

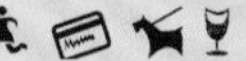

Entry 632 Map 8

Colliers Arms

Clows Top

Stocking up on local, seasonal food is easy here – they just nip into the garden. This pretty patch of Worcestershire countryside provides so much for the busy pub kitchen; even hazelnuts and artichokes are close to hand. There's still plenty of outdoor space for visitors too, with a pretty south-facing terrace and beer garden providing glorious views. Feast your eyes on Rock Church (largest Norman church in England), the local gallop – or just your plate. They aim high in this friendly yet unassuming place – all is pristine and traditional inside – and it works. Try aspirational stuff such as scallops, crab and chilli risotto or stick to fish and chips or beef stroganoff: it's all great. There are a couple of good cask ales to go with it – or even a local white wine (Astley Vineyard) if you fancy. A real find.

Meals	Lunch & dinner £8.95-£15.95.
Closed	3pm-6pm. From 5pm Sun. Open all day Sat.
Directions	Beside A456 between Kidderminster & Tenbury Wells.

Michael Claydon
Colliers Arms
Tenbury Road, Clows Top,
Kidderminster DY14 9HA

Tel +44 (0)1299 832242
Web www.colliersarms.com

Entry 633 Map 8

Bell & Cross Inn

Clent

No cavernous interior here but a network of small, cosy rooms that reveal not just the roots of this 19th-century pub but the determination of its successive owners to maintain its integrity. And those cosy rooms decked in smart modern hues are usually full of happy diners; try excellent grilled sea bass with prawns and rocket or a lightly tweaked 'pub classic', faggots with cheese mash. Owner Roger Narbett – busy now at his other pub, The Chequers – was chef to the England football team and footie memorabilia decorates the corridors. Wife Jo runs a brisk yet friendly service; co-owner Paul Mohan is also a classically trained chef. It's still a place for the locals though, and they crowd into the snug bar with its four real ales and open fire. At the foot of the Clent hills yet close to Birmingham – and a nice big garden and patio, too.

Meals	Lunch & dinner £8.50-£15.50. Sunday lunch £13.50.
Closed	3pm-6pm. Open all day Sun.
Directions	Off A491 south-east of Hagley. On Holy Cross Green.

Roger & Jo Narbett
Bell & Cross Inn
Bromsgrove Road, Clent,
Stourbridge DY9 9QL

Tel +44 (0)1562 730319
Web www.bellandcrossclent.co.uk

Entry 634 Map 8

The Wheatsheaf Inn

Egton

Unlike many pubs in this area, the family-run Wheatsheaf has avoided expansion and held on to its character. Indeed, it sits so modestly back from the village's wide main street you could pass it by. The first entrance brings you into the main bar, all low beams and cushioned settles, but the main treat is the bar with the original Yorkshire range – aglow most of the year. This drinkers' den takes 16 at a push and is a favourite of walkers, fishermen and dogs. (The river Esk at the foot of the steep hill is famous for fly-fishing, hence the angling memorabilia.) A range of cask ales ensures the chat flows, while the food sustains walkers: finnan haddock kedgeree, oxtail soup, local partridge in season, steaks from local farmers. Three quiet, cosy bedrooms have been freshly spruced up, so why not stay? After a day's yomp on the moors you can look forward to a soak in a Victorian roll top bath: two rooms have them. Fine cotton linen and sumptuous silk cushion top French cast-iron beds, oak furniture glows with the patina of age, and the views over the village to the hills are lovely.

Price	From £85.
Rooms	3 twins/doubles.
Meals	Lunch & dinner £8.50-£17.95. Bar meals from £8.50. Sunday lunch £15.
Closed	2.30pm-5.30pm & Mon lunch. Open all day Sat & Sun.
Directions	Off A171; 6 miles west of Whitby.

Nigel & Elaine Pulling
The Wheatsheaf Inn
High Street, Egton,
Whitby YO21 1TZ
Tel +44 (0)1947 895271
Web www.wheatsheafegton.com

The Fox & Hounds

Sinnington

The 18th-century coaching inn sits handsomely on the main street in sleepy Sinnington, on the edge of the North Yorkshire moors; the mounting block by the front door hints at its past. Somehow you feel embraced by the place the moment you walk in: Andrew and Catherine have been welcoming folk for many years and they have hospitality down to a fine art. The feel is utterly traditional, all oak settles, open fires, prints on dark green walls and hops hanging from beams; relax with a pint of Copper Dragon while choosing your lunch. Slow-cooked belly pork, squash purée, apple risotto, scrumpy reduction makes a mouthwatering starter; follow with the fish platter: crab cake, seared smoked salmon, little fish pie, mini fish and chips. If you can find room – portions are generous – the assiette of puddings is perfect for sharing: coconut crème brûlée, chocolate truffle torte, apple and berry crumble, Eton mess and mulled wine sorbet should not be missed. There are ten comfy, homely, spotless bedrooms, four of them on the ground floor, all with crisp linen, most with modern bathrooms. Lovely.

Price	£80-£130.
Rooms	10: 8 doubles, 2 twins.
Meals	Light lunch & early supper £8.25. Dinner £9.95-£22.95. Sunday lunch, 3 courses, £20.50.
Closed	Open all day.
Directions	In village just off A170 between Pickering and Kirkbymoorside.

Andrew & Catherine Stephens
The Fox & Hounds
Main Street, Sinnington,
York YO62 6SQ
Tel +44 (0)1751 431577
Web www.thefoxandhoundsinn.co.uk

Pipe & Glass Inn

South Dalton

In the elegant estate village of South Dalton, rejoicing in one of the highest church spires in the Wolds, is this 16th-century inn. The front garden has classic parkland vistas, the back is lushly lawned, the polished interiors glow with well-being. Turn right for a pubby pint, left for a leather sofa by the log-stacked fire. Eating and lounging areas are woody and stylish, window seats have chocolate cushions, customers cluck with pleasure as they head to their tables. Kate does front of house while James, the chef, creates food attune to the very best of seasonal, regional and humanely reared. Adventurous combinations include wild rabbit rissoles, braised lamb, mutton and kidney faggots – the website shares the recipes and the wines are from small producers. Overlooking woods and fields, two immaculately and plushly designed suites trumpet every modern thing. Be seduced by state of the art media systems, fabulously decadent bathrooms, huge sleigh beds, fat mattresses, quirky dressing tables. Breakfast is top class and brought to your door. We loved it all.

Price	£160.
Rooms	2 suites.
Meals	Lunch & dinner £9.95-£24.95. Sunday lunch £13.95. Not Sunday eve or Mondays (except bank hols).
Closed	Monday (except bank hols).
Directions	Village signed off A164 & B1248, 5 miles north west of Beverley.

James & Kate Mackenzie
Pipe & Glass Inn
West End, South Dalton,
Beverley HU17 7PN

Tel +44 (0)1430 810246
Web www.pipeandglass.co.uk

The Durham Ox

Crayke

At the picturesque top of the Grand Old Duke of York's hill is an L-shaped bar of flagstones and rose walls, worn leather armchairs, carved panelling and big fires. There are two more bars to either side, a new wood floored extension with exposed brickwork and a dapper wine-themed restaurant that draws all and sundry. Chalkboards above the stone fireplace and seasonal menus list game terrine with homemade chutney, prime Yorkshire rib-eye steak, frites with béarnaise sauce and rich sunken chocolate tart. The Bar Bites menu and the Sunday roasts are inevitably popular. There's a coffee shop serving homemade truffles, and a garden with a marquee for summer frivolity. No need to drive home: the delightfully quirky rooms in the old farmworkers' cottages have been renovated in contemporary, country-house style. Expect original quarry-tile floors, warmly painted walls, beams and revamped bathrooms. A smart new room, The Studio, is in the main pub with its own outside staircase. The far-reaching views across the valley are stunning; in summer, flowers burst from stone troughs. Such peacefulness 20 minutes outside York.

Price	£100-£180. Singles £80.
Rooms	5 doubles.
Meals	Lunch & dinner £8.95-£26.95. Bar meals from £6.95. Sunday lunch from £14.95.
Closed	3pm-5.30pm. Open all day Sat & Sun.
Directions	Exit right off A19 York to Thirsk road. Through Easingwold to Crayke.

Michael Ibbotson
The Durham Ox
Westway, Crayke,
York YO61 4TE
Tel +44 (0)1347 821506
Web www.thedurhamox.com

The Oak Tree Inn

Helperby

Helperby is a historic spot and this new village pub is the jewel in its crown. The mellow brick exterior has scrubbed up nicely and a big paved area at the back is a great place to eat out on a sunny day. Inside, the old snug remains, complete with its open fire, oak floors and beams. Two bright and airy dining spaces, one by the rather sophisticated bar, strike a more clubby note: tartan check wool on wing chairs, ruby-red walls, dark elegant tables. An impressive line of brews beckon, including Timothy Taylor and Theakstons, so enjoy a pint by the fire while you choose your food. Souped-up pub classics are chalked on boards: home-cured salmon with capers, shallots and lemon dressing perhaps, followed by local venison with sautéed wild mushrooms and red wine sauce. Upstairs, soak any aches and pains away in a deep bath bubbling with L'Occitane treats. The six sumptuous bedrooms have funky wine-glass chandeliers, huge beds and fine linen, generously padded headboards and monster mirrors. After a spot of retail therapy in nearby Thirsk, Knaresborough or York, the Oak Tree is a pleasure to come home to.

Price	£120-£150.
Rooms	6: 5 doubles, 1 twin/double.
Meals	Lunch from £9.95. Dinner from £14.95. Sunday lunch, 3 courses, £19.95.
Closed	Open all day.
Directions	Sent on booking.

Sally Ford
The Oak Tree Inn
Raskelf Road, Helperby,
York YO61 2PH

Tel	+44 (0)1423 789189
Web	www.theoaktreehelperby.com

Crown Inn

Roecliffe

Is Roecliffe the prettiest village in Yorkshire? One of Roecliffe's greatest treasures stands alongside its immaculate green: a handsome window-box-tumbled coaching inn. Inside are stone-flagged floors, beams and crackling fires, comfy gingham chairs and gleaming old oak; you almost feel you've stumbled into the home of a rather smart country couple who happen to have a bar in the sitting room. Above the pub, four elegant bedrooms await, each with its own character, though all have sumptuous beds, white duvets and polished antiques both authentic and retro; pristine modern bathrooms sport L'Occitane soaps and free-standing baths. Back downstairs there's good food too, the kitchen turning out the likes of Scarborough lemon sole fillet with crayfish mousse and crab velouté, and Red Lincoln jugged beef shin with tarragon forcemeat and Wensleydale mash. You can eat in the bar or the charming olive-green side room, or in the more formal dining room. Or settle in the window with the paper and a hand-pulled pint of Old Speckled Hen – and take in that sweet village view.

Price	£90-£120.
Rooms	4 doubles.
Meals	Lunch & dinner £14.95-£17.95. Bar meals £9.95-£17.95. Sunday lunch, 2 courses, £15.95.
Closed	3pm-5pm.
Directions	By village green, 2 miles west of Boroughbridge and 5 mins from A1M (junc. 48).

Karl & Amanda Mainey
Crown Inn
Roecliffe,
York YO51 9LY

Tel	+44 (0)1423 322300
Web	www.crowninnroecliffe.co.uk

The General Tarleton

Ferrensby

Chef-patron John and wife Claire run the old coaching inn with an easy charm. The rambling, low-beamed, nooked and crannied brasserie-bar has been stylishly updated and mixes rough stone walls with smooth ones; there are leather chairs, muted heritage colours and a roaring fire. You have Black Sheep Bitter on hand pump, 12 well-chosen wines by the glass and unfussy dishes based on the finest local produce. Here the menu ranges from roast Dales lamb to grilled haunch of venison with madeira sauce, roast wood pigeon with pickled figs and brilliant fish and chips. There's baked custard tart for grown-ups, homemade ice cream for kids, delightful staff and a big buzz. The cosy-chic dining room, formerly a stables, comes with white napery; for warm days there's a super terraced garden. If you're tempted to stay, comfortable, well-equipped bedrooms are in a purpose-built extension and flaunt the best of contemporary... along with soft feather pillows, homemade biscuits and Molton Brown oils. But the food is the thing – it's fabulous – including the breakfasts.

Price	From £129.
Rooms	13 twins/doubles.
Meals	Lunch & dinner from £12 (brasserie). Dinner, 3 courses, £25. Sunday lunch £16-£18.50.
Closed	3pm-5.30pm.
Directions	From A1 junction 48; A6055 for Knaresborough; pub on right in Ferrensby.

John Topham
The General Tarleton
Boroughbridge Road, Ferrensby,
Knaresborough HG5 0PZ

Tel	+44 (0)1423 340284
Web	www.generaltarleton.co.uk

Ye Old Sun Inn

Colton

A pretty, low-lying Yorkshire village, and a spick and span, 18th-century pub with a welcoming porch. Young enthusiastic owners have kept the bones – rustic beams and red-brick fireplaces – but sprinkled a bit of bling here and there in sumptuous fabrics and tapestry cushions. There's an admirable dedication to good, local ingredients, too; rabbit from the Ledston estate finds itself in a pie (like poor Peter's father) with thyme, ginger and wild mushrooms, while trio of local Yorkshire pork might be crisp belly with red cabbage, toad in the hole, and pork fillet wrapped in smoked ham. There's a brand new dining space, a cosy snug to sit in and thumb through the papers, and a rambling garden with views across open fields. The energetic McCarthys have turned the handsome Georgian house next door into a smart B&B with three bright bedrooms; snooze in a huge leather sleigh bed with faux fur throws and cushions, admire the well-lit 'hidden' dressing area, splash about in the swanky bathroom. In the summer, a huge hot tub in the leafy, private back garden is yours – perfect for lovers.

Price	£100-£120. Singles £100.
Rooms	3: 2 doubles; 1 double with separate bathroom.
Meals	Lunch from £5.50. Dinner from £11.95. Sunday lunch from £10. Not Sun eves.
Closed	Open all day.
Directions	A64 towards York; follow signs to Colton.

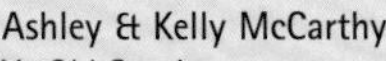

Ashley & Kelly McCarthy
Ye Old Sun Inn
Main Street, Colton,
Tadcaster LS24 8EP

Tel +44 (0)1904 744261
Web www.yeoldsuninn.co.uk

The Shibden Mill Inn

Shibden

There's still a pubby feel to this rambling old inn – although it's known for its restaurant. Shibden Bitter, Theakstons and three rotating bitters keep beer drinkers happy in front of several open fires, the deep green valley setting within sound of the mill stream makes for idyllic summer drinking and the wine list is very impressive. An unstuffy integrity lies behind this venture, from the front-of-house warmth – the staff really are lovely – to the modern British kitchen from which delicious dishes flow: Yorkshire wood pigeon pithivier; pan-fried guinea fowl; home-beetroot-cured wild Loch Duart salmon, lambs leaf and horseradish mayo; sticky toffee pudding (what better to come home to after a brisk valley walk?). There are cosy gate-leg tables and sofas in the bars, crisp white napery and candelabra in the restaurant, and most of the fruit and vegetables come from local suppliers. A monthly tasting menu boasts the best of that season's spoils. As for the bedrooms, all of which have been renovated, they are carpeted, comfortable, individual and equipped with everything. The Pink Room and the suite are huge fun.

Price	£105-£166. Singles £85-£140.
Rooms	11: 10 doubles, 1 suite.
Meals	Lunch & dinner £9.95-£18.95. Sunday lunch £12.50.
Closed	2.30pm-5.30pm. Open all day Sat & Sun.
Directions	Off A58 Halifax to Leeds, near A6036 junction.

Simon Heaton
The Shibden Mill Inn
Shibden Mill Fold, Shibden,
Halifax HX3 7UL
Tel +44 (0)1422 365840
Web www.shibdenmillinn.com

The Wheatley Arms

Ben Rhydding

New life has been breathed into this fine old stone inn – and how! Oak floors, open fires, comfortable chairs… and it feels as if it's been like this for years. A labyrinth of rooms are linked by a vivid décor; bold textiles, original prints, clusters of mini-collections – something interesting at every turn. A wide range of well-kept ale will please the beer lovers, whilst a confident menu should please the rest. Smoked duck with orange and pomegranate and a balsamic glaze makes a robust start, followed by scampi in a basket (yes, it's back!). Puddings are impossible to resist; the apricot and cinnamon beignets with lemon and pine nut parfait is divine. The same flair and care has been lavished on 12 sumptuous bedrooms, some with private roof terraces and wet rooms. All have luxurious beds, funky furniture, fabulous fabrics and high-spec audio technology. Statement wallpapers – a different one for each room – continue the film-set vibe. Bathrooms match the glamour: marble tiles, huge white vintage sinks, L'Occitane treats. Refreshingly unpompous. Prepare to be wowed.

Price	£89.99-£135. Singles from £79.99.
Rooms	12 twins/doubles.
Meals	Lunch & dinner from £10.95. Sunday lunch, 3 courses, from £19.95.
Closed	Open all day.
Directions	A65 from Leeds to Ilkley, left onto Wheatley Lane to Ben Rhydding.

Michael Baravelli
The Wheatley Arms
Wheatley Lane, Ben Rhydding,
Ilkley LS29 8PP
Tel +44 (0)1943 816496
Web www.wheatleyarms.co.uk

The Crescent Inn

Ilkley

The handsome Victorian building wrapped round a corner on the high street in Ilkley has been restored to its former glory – and it feels as though it's always been this way. Smooth walls are a vibrant blue, reflected in upholstered settles and checked wool curtains at tall windows; floors are in old oak and a glorious fire at the end of the comfortable bar belts out the heat. Choose from an impressive list of speciality beers and ciders, seven cask ales and wines by the glass. The value-for-money menu includes a gourmet British beef burger with skinny fries and a ploughman's platter that positively groans under the weight of local pork pie, ham off the bone and scrumptious Yorkshire cheeses. Pub classics are chalked up on boards, so tuck in to steak, ale and mushroom pie or fish and chips. At the top of an elegant curved staircase 11 peaceful, high-ceilinged, boutiquey bedrooms await, some in the French country style, all with sumptuous linen, fat mattresses and sleek state of the art bathrooms. In short, the perfect spot in which to relax after a bracing yomp on the moors (or round Ilkley's fabulous shops!).

Price	£70-£120.
Rooms	11 doubles.
Meals	Lunch from £9.95. Bar meals from £5.95. Dinner from £13.90. Sunday lunch £11.95-£13.95.
Closed	Open all day.
Directions	Sent on booking.

Mark Barbour
The Crescent Inn
Brook Street, Ilkley LS29 8DG

Tel +44 (0)1943 811250
Web www.thecrescentinn.co.uk

The Timble Inn

Timble

Dick Turpin stayed here on his fateful journey between London and York. True or not, the story perfectly suits this charming, stone-built, listed pub in postcard-perfect Timble, a quick hop from Harrogate. Following a sympathetic makeover inside, the old flag floors are topped with oak settles covered in hunting jacket tweed and the exposed brick walls decorated with glass sconces and gothic gilt-framed mirrors. Locals prop up the bar with a pint of Theakstons, while those who are hungry can choose from a pub grub menu of local-pork pies with mushy peas and mint sauce, steak and kidney pies cooked in beer, and fruit crumbles; judging by the number of piping hot pies flowing from the kitchen, they're going down a storm. Seven bedrooms have had the same eye for detail passed over them – thanks to Marie, interior designer turned landlady. Imagine big beds with fat mattresses, fabulous fabrics, high-tech audio/visual systems and cutting-edge bathrooms. Most rooms have long views over the delightful Washburn Valley, and the peace is a balm to the soul. A big treat.

Price	£99-£150. Well-behaved dogs welcome.
Rooms	8 twins/doubles.
Meals	Lunch & dinner £8.95-£12.95. Sunday lunch, 3 courses, from £24.
Closed	Mon & Tues.
Directions	From Harrogate, A59 towards Skipton. Turn left at signs for Swinoty Reservoir, then Timble.

Paul Radcliffe & Marie Cooper
The Timble Inn
Timble, Otley LS21 2NN
Tel +44 (0)1943 880530
Web www.thetimbleinn.co.uk

The Tempest Arms

Elslack

A 16th-century ale house with great prices, friendly staff and an easy style. Inside you find stone walls and old beams, settles and plump cushions, Yorkshire ales on tap and a smart beamed restaurant. An airy open-plan feel runs throughout with sofas and armchairs strategically placed in front of a fire that burns on both sides. Delicious traditional food is a big draw – the inn was packed for lunch on a Tuesday in April. You can eat wherever you want, so grab a seat and dig into Yorkshire puddings with a rich onion gravy, raised pork pie with homemade piccalilli, treacle tart with pink grapefruit sorbet. Bedrooms are just as good. Those in the main house are slightly simpler, but most are ten paces beyond in two newly built stone houses: rather swish with private terraces or balconies overlooking a babbling stream. They have hand-crafted furniture and L'Occitane toiletries, slate bathrooms and flat-screen TVs; a couple have decks with hot tubs to soak in and those at the back have views of the fells. Walkers pile in: the Dales are on the doorstep.

Price	£85. Suites £100-£140. Singles from £62.50.
Rooms	21: 9 twins/doubles, 12 suites.
Meals	Lunch & bar meals from £8.95. Dinner from £14.95.
Closed	Open all day.
Directions	A56 west from Skipton. Signed left after two miles.

Martin & Veronica Clarkson
The Tempest Arms
Elslack, Skipton BD23 3AY
Tel +44 (0)1282 842450
Web www.tempestarms.co.uk

The Lister Arms at Malham

Malham

You'll be hard pushed to find a better looking pub in a more gorgeous village. The National Trust's Malham is a favourite with potholers – this part of Yorkshire is riddled with caverns – but there are many surface pleasures to be had. Sitting on the edge of the village green, the 17th-century coaching inn was once home to the first Lord of Ribblesdale; very grand it looks too. But don't stand on ceremony; inside are flagged floors, wood-burning stoves and well-kept local ales. Terry and Kirsty have also put an interesting menu together using mostly local produce. Start with potted Malham pork with sticky apples, herbs and crackling... push the boat out and order slow-cooked shoulder of lamb served with pan juice gravy and pumpkin purée; then, if you still have room, finish off with rhubarb and ginger crème brûlée. Upstairs are comfortable bedrooms with calm colours, lovely linen and immaculate bathrooms; most have views over the village green to the lush hills beyond. A perfect place to park yourself for a few days above ground.

Price	£80-£130. Singles £59-£79.
Rooms	9: 5 doubles, 3 family, 1 twin.
Meals	Lunch & dinner from £10.50. Bar meals from £6.95. Sunday lunch, 3 courses, £15.50.
Closed	Open all day.
Directions	A65 west from Skipton, then north for Malham. In village, over bridge & on left.

Terry Quinn & Kirsty Urwin
The Lister Arms at Malham
Malham, Skipton BD23 4DB
Tel +44 (0)1729 830330
Web www.listerarms.co.uk

The Lion at Settle

Settle

Generations of travellers have enjoyed the welcome at this grand 17th-century coaching inn; following a recent renovation its doors are open to all. Original features have been saved, including smooth oak floors, a fabulous inglenook fireplace in the grand entrance hall and the graceful sweeping staircase; comfortable sofas and chairs are upholstered in checked tartan wool. Locally sourced ingredients dominate a menu which places its emphasis on comfort: try Settle Pudding (tender braised beef with a suet lid) and homemade Scotch egg with thick-cut chips, and, if you can find room, Phillipa's sticky toffee pudding is a must. The elegant but cosy dining room with its pleasingly mismatched furniture, panelled walls and old photos buzzes with friendly chat. If you're a Three Peaks bagger, a devotee of the stunning Settle to Carlisle railway or simply want to get away from it all you can stay in characterful bedrooms with five-star mattresses, white cotton bed linen, immaculate bathrooms, plasma screens and fresh milk for your morning cuppa. The historic town is worth exploring: lose yourself in its cobbled alleyways.

Price	£75-£90. Family room from £100.
Rooms	14 twins/doubles.
Meals	Lunch from £6.95. Bar meals from £5.95. Dinner from £8.95.
Closed	Open all day.
Directions	Signed for Settle. Lion on main road through town.

Ian Pilcher
The Lion at Settle
Duke Street,
Settle BD24 9DU
Tel +44 (0)1729 822203
Web www.thelionsettle.co.uk

Sandpiper Inn

Leyburn

Malt whisky lovers will eye the 100 bottles behind the bar appreciatively. In 1999, former Roux Scholar Jonathan Harrison swapped a slick city kitchen for an old stone pub in the Yorkshire Dales. In cosy alcoves beneath low black beams, locals and walkers put the world to rights over pints of Black Sheep, Copper Dragon and Theakston ale opposite chalkboards listing Jonathan's daily menus: fishcakes with herb sauce, club sandwiches, fish and chips in beer batter, braised beef in Guinness. Cooking moves up a gear in the simple stylish dining room as in-season game, Wensleydale heifer beef and home-grown herbs and veg come into play. Loosen belts before delving into Sunday lunch, which could be roast rib-eye of beef with Yorkshire pudding or Moroccan-spiced chicken with couscous – all of ours delicious, including the sticky toffee pudding with butterscotch sauce. Up a twisting stair at the back, two simple but charming bedrooms lie – fresh, warm and cosy to come back to after you've walked the legs off the dogs. Visit the falls at West Burton – or Middleham for the horses on the gallops.

Price	£85-£90.
Rooms	2 doubles.
Meals	Lunch from £8.50. Bar meals from £5. Dinner from £10.95. Sunday lunch, 3 courses, £25.20.
Closed	3pm-6.30pm (7pm Sun). Mon & Tues in winter.
Directions	From A1, A684 for Bedale; on for 12 miles; pub at edge of market place.

Jonathan & Janine Harrison
Sandpiper Inn
Railway Street,
Leyburn DL8 5AT
Tel +44 (0)1969 622206
Web www.sandpiperinn.co.uk

The Black Horse

Kirkby Fleetham

Kirkby Fleetham: a tranquil village with old oak trees on a classic green edged with Georgian houses. The old boozer has been brought back to life; wooden settles, 'distressed' in pastel colours, are boldly upholstered, candy-stripe curtains and grandfather clocks add quaint touches, stone fireplaces, old beams and a snug with darts remain intact. Pub as hub, and dashes of humour too (the cushions embroidered "Be nice to your children: they choose your nursing home!"). And good things are happening in the kitchen, with head chef Adrian Knowles from The Crab & Lobster at the helm. Try local wild rabbit terrine, spiced pear purée and toasted brioche followed by baked monkfish with parma ham, butternut squash risotto and chive butter sauce. A reworked classic of strawberry knickerbocker glory – with cookies and marshmallows to finish – is irresistible. As for the bedrooms, they will charm you with their muted colours, oak floored bathrooms and picnic-hamper breakfasts. The two-room family suite sports cast-iron beds and Cath Kidston fabrics, fat floral eiderdowns and gingham-topped chairs.

Price	£60-£100. Family suite £60-£120.
Rooms	7: 5 doubles, 1 twin, 1 family suite for 2-4.
Meals	Lunch from £6.95. Dinner from £10.95. Sunday lunch, 2-3 courses, £13.95-£17.95.
Closed	Open all day.
Directions	Village signed off A1.

Jackie Gardner
The Black Horse
7 Lumley Lane, Kirkby Fleetham,
Northallerton DL7 0SH
Tel +44 (0)1609 749010
Web www.blackhorsekirkbyfleetham.com

Golden Lion

Osmotherley

Bustling with walkers doing the Coast to Coast in the day, humming with well-dressed diners at night, the old stone inn overlooking the green is run by young hands-on owners and friendly staff. Arrive early to bag a pew in the brown-wood bar with its open fire and flickering candles; what a sanctuary after a day tramping the moors! Order a pint of local bitter – or a first-class wine – as you choose from a refreshingly simple menu. The chef has a modern take on retro dishes here – chicken Kiev, coq au vin, poached pear in wine with hot chocolate sauce; each stands the test of time. More contemporary dishes are free of flourish and fuss. There's also a fabulous gluten-free menu: from fish soup to calves' liver with onions and mash. Upstairs are five stylish and comfortable bedrooms with soft wool carpets, calm colours, lovely linen and chic bathrooms. Beautiful hand-crafted furnishings are the icing on the cake and the effect is stunning. The freshness of approach means you'll leave smiling, and the village is as unspoilt as any in the North Yorkshire Moors National Park.

Price	£95. Singles £65.
Rooms	5 twins/doubles.
Meals	Lunch & bar meals from £9.95. Dinner £9.95-£20.95. Not Monday or Tuesday lunch.
Closed	3pm-6pm. Open all day Sat & Sun.
Directions	Off A19 10 miles north of Thirsk & Northallerton.

Christie Connelly
Golden Lion
6 West End, Osmotherley,
Northallerton DL6 3AA
Tel +44 (0)1609 883526
Web www.goldenlionosmotherley.co.uk

The White Bear Hotel

Masham

Minutes from the bustle of an ancient and quaint market square stands the Theakston family's face-lifted flagship inn. In the handsome public bar, an open fire throws golden light on old oak floors, whilst gleaming brass platters jostle for space with huge jugs of fresh flowers, newspapers and local magazines. Sit with a pint of Theakston's Best Bitter in the cosy tap room complete with dart board and cribbage, or wander through to the elegant dining room, where local and seasonal ingredients have prominence. Go for homemade steak and ale pie, or rolled fillet of plaice with a cream dill sauce. To finish, banana butterscotch pancakes will fuel an afternoon tramp up into the heart of Wensleydale. On your return, 14 luxurious bedrooms await across the yard in what was once the Lightfoot brewery, but don't expect nostalgia here; the style is contemporary, with top-class textiles, huge sumptuous beds and cutting edge bathrooms, warm tones and splashes of colour; some have lovely views across town. As a special treat, book the vast top floor penthouse suite with a raftered ceiling and a swish bathroom.

Price	£98.50. Suite £185.
Rooms	14: 13 twins/doubles, 1 suite.
Meals	Lunch from £4.95. Dinner, 3 courses, about £30.
Closed	Open all day.
Directions	North from Ripon on A6108. In Masham up hill (for Leyburn). Right at crest of hill. Signed.

Sue Thomas
The White Bear Hotel
Wellgarth, Masham, Ripon HG4 4EN

Tel +44 (0)1765 689319
Web www.thewhitebearhotel.co.uk

The Oak Tree Inn

Hutton Magna

A tiny cottage at the end of a row, masquerading as a pub, the Oak Tree was snapped up by the Rosses, ready to swap London for the Dales. Alastair trained at The Savoy and together they have created a gem. The front bar has old wooden panelling and whitewashed stone, an attractive medley of tables, chairs and pews, newspapers, fresh flowers and an open fire. The dark green dining area at the back is softly lit, its tables separated by pews. All is delightful and informal. Locally shot game appears on the menu in season and the produce is as fresh as can be. Expect blue cheese and pear with beetroot and truffle honey, fillet of stone bass with scallops, tenderstem broccoli, capers and herbs; orange mascarpone and pistachio semi-freddo with orange sorbet and caramelised raspberries. Booking is recommended.

Meals	Lunch & dinner £18.50-£22.50. Dinner from £30.
Closed	Tues-Sun lunch & Mon.
Directions	Off A66, 6.5 miles west of Scotch Corner.

Alastair & Claire Ross
The Oak Tree Inn
Hutton Magna,
Richmond DL11 7HH
Tel +44 (0)1833 627371

Entry 654 Map 12

Yorkshire

The Punch Bowl Inn

Low Row

The hamlet of Low Row clings to the hillside high above the Swale. The front of the pub is a sun-trap, the views to the moors are superb and Gunnerside, Muker and Keld are a walk away. Inside, a contemporary-cum-traditional style is the order of the day, with regard to both food and décor. Walls are plain, interspersed with the odd tasteful picture or cream panelling, and scrubbed pine tables are married with matching chairs. It's not hugely pubby but it's spotless and stylish and feels pretty cosy when the fires are lit. There are real ales and good wines but the food is the draw and the menu is written on the mirror; try crab fishcakes served with a basket of warm bread, local lamb with homemade black pudding, and Yorkshire parkin with plum compote to finish... excellent fodder for walkers and shooters.

Meals	Lunch & dinner £10-£15. Sunday lunch £9.95.
Closed	Open all day.
Directions	From A1 take exit at Scotch Corner; A6108 to Richmond, then B6270 to Reeth; Low Row, 25m from main road on right.

Charles Cody
The Punch Bowl Inn
Low Row, Arkengarthdale,
Richmond DL11 6PF
Tel +44 (0)1748 886233
Web www.pbinn.co.uk

Entry 655 Map 12

The Old Hill Inn

Chapel-le-Dale

A proper, wild-country tavern with terrific beer and food. It used to be a farmhouse, then a doss-house for potholers; now it's a comfortable old inn, a warm, safe haven in a countryside of crags, waterfalls and moors. Enter the unpretentious bar – a large, comfortable room with open-stone walls, wood floors, old pine tables and big log fire. Six pumps deliver ales in top condition – Black Sheep Bitter, Dent Aviator – while food is served in the candlelit intimacy of the diminutive dining rooms. From the family of chefs comes butternut squash risotto, lamb shank with dauphinoise potatoes and a rich lamb gravy, duck with prune, port and orange sauce, and homemade bread; from master confectioner Colin, warm chocolate pudding and lemon tart. His sugar sculptures alone are worth the trip.

Meals: Lunch & dinner £10.95-£25. Bar meals £5.25-£10.

Closed: 3.30pm-6.30pm (from 4pm Sun) & all day Mon (except bank hols). Open all day Sat.

Directions: On the B6255 between Ingleton & Ribblehead.

Sabena Martin
The Old Hill Inn
Chapel-le-Dale,
Ingleton LA6 3AR

Tel: +44 (0)1524 241256
Web: www.oldhillinn.co.uk

Entry 656 Map 12

Yorkshire

The Falcon Inn

Arncliffe

Tucked into the top corner of Arncliffe in Littondale, one of the most remote and unspoilt of Yorkshire's dales. Several generations of Millers have been licensees here and they have preserved an inn and a way of life almost lost. The fine bay-windowed and ivy-clad building looks more like a private house than a village local... expect few frills and old-fashioned hospitality. The entrance passageway leads to a small hallway at the foot of the stairs – there's a tiny bar counter facing you, a small, simple lounge, a log fire and sporting prints on the walls. A sunny back room looks out across the garden to open fells. Beer is served, as ever, straight from the cask in a large jug, then dispensed into pint glasses at the bar. At lunchtime, call in for pie and peas, sandwiches and ploughman's lunches.

Meals: Bar meals £2.50-£6 (lunchtime only).

Closed: 3pm-7pm. Reduced winter opening times, phone to check.

Directions: Off B6160 16 miles north of Skipton.

Robin Miller
The Falcon Inn
Arncliffe,
Skipton BD23 5QE

Tel: +44 (0)1756 770205
Web: www.thefalconinn.com

Entry 657 Map 12

The Wensleydale Heifer Inn
West Witton

Be lulled into a false sense of 'leather armchair by the fire' and 'mine's a pint of Black Sheep' security as you step off the street. Enter the Fish Bar and you're met with wall-to-wall seagrass and modish-naff touches. But the welcome is warm, and the food is sensational. Choose dressed crab with potato, capers and chive salad or Cornish fish stew with new potatoes, parsley and olive oil. As for the Whitby cod in crispy Black Sheep Bitter batter with peas and fat chips – it's the best fish and chips this side of Whitby's Magpie Café. Chef David Moss has achieved the impossible: a great fish restaurant as far from the sea as you can get. There's a shiny, slightly more formal but still kitted-out-with-joke-crockery dining room, a garden for summer sipping and a cosy whisky lounge – all guaranteed to put a smile on your face.

Meals	Lunch from £12.75. Dinner from £17.50. Bar meals from £3.50. Sunday lunch, 3 courses, £22.50.
Closed	Open all day.
Directions	On A684 between Leyburn & Hawes.

David Moss
The Wensleydale Heifer Inn
Main Street, West Witton,
Leyburn DL8 4LS
Tel +44 (0)1969 622322
Web www.wensleydaleheifer.co.uk

Entry 658 Map 12

Yorkshire

The Blue Lion
East Witton

The Blue Lion has a big reputation locally; so big it followed our inspector round Yorkshire. Paul and Helen have mixed the traditions of a country pub with the elegance of a country house. This is a bustling place that serves superlative food and no one seems in a hurry to leave. Polished beer taps dispensing Yorkshire ale, stone-flagged floors, open fires, newspapers on poles, big settles, huge bunches of dried flowers hanging from beams, splashes of fresh ones. The two restaurants have boarded floors and shuttered Georgian windows, two coal fires and candles everywhere. Food is robust and heart-warming; local game, chargrilled beef fillet with shiraz sauce, braised marsala mutton with cumin sweet potato. East Witton has an interesting plague tale, Jervaulx Abbey is a mile away and there's an enclosed garden at the back.

Meals	Lunch & dinner £10.50-£27.50.
Closed	Open all day.
Directions	From Leyburn, A6108 for 3 miles to East Witton.

Paul & Helen Klein
The Blue Lion
East Witton,
Leyburn DL8 4SN
Tel +44 (0)1969 624273
Web www.thebluelion.co.uk

Entry 659 Map 12

Black Sheep Brewery

Masham

Masham is a hugely appealing market town in Wensleydale, and has the added attraction of being the home of the Black Sheep Brewery. The visitor centre and bistro are integral here, at this handsome stone shrine to good ale. The guided tour is fascinating, and you may whet your appetite with a glass or two of bitter before settling down to lunch in the restaurant. Food is straightforward and tasty, perhaps pork medallions with black pudding, sausages and mash or braised lamb shank with root vegetables in beer. The coffee and snacks are delicious and there's a 'pub', of course, with old oak floors and all your favourite Black Sheep beers on tap. The spacious dining area on its mezzanine level has fabulous far-reaching views over the town to the hills beyond.

Meals	Lunch from £4.50. Dinner from £9.95. Sunday lunch, 3 courses, £16.95.
Closed	Sun-Wed eves.
Directions	Centre of Masham on A6108 between Ripon & Leyburn.

Jess Burns
Black Sheep Brewery
Wellgarth, Masham,
Ripon HG4 4EN
Tel +44 (0)1765 680101
Web www.blacksheepbrewery.co.uk

The Bruce Arms

West Tanfield

This handsome stone pub has experienced a chequered past but has recently been rescued by cheerful ex-Yorke Arms chef Hugh Carruthers, who, with business partner David Stead, is creating a stir in this corner of Yorks. The bar is a pleasingly open-plan arrangement, with a stone flagged area by the pumps, dark grey walls and a wood-burning stove in the corner; in the airy carpeted dining room find a squishy sofa for loafing in front of the open fire. Traditional meets contemporary with David's eye-catching artworks everywhere. Hugh's kitchen credentials are top-notch, as you'd expect: try chicken liver and foie gras parfait followed by Moroccan spiced gurnard with chickpeas, chorizo and piquillo peppers, or pork loin with mash, spring greens and mustard. A cracking Dales pit-stop close to Ripon and Fountains Abbey.

Meals	Lunch & bar meals from £7.95. Dinner from £12.95. Sunday lunch, 2 courses, £12.50.
Closed	Sun eves & Mon.
Directions	On A6108 between Ripon and Masham.

Hugh Carruthers
The Bruce Arms
Main Street,
West Tanfield,
Ripon HG4 5JJ
Tel +44 (0)1677 470325

The George At Wath

Wath

The handsome Georgian pub in sleepy Wath has been renovated by a local couple determined to breathe new life into old stones. Its former sorry state is impossible to imagine now. Oak floors gleam, checked wool chairs beckon, a wood stove chucks out the heat and the welcome is as genuine as it gets. Behind the bar are Theakstons and Rudgate Brewery cask ales or a glass of prosecco to treat yourself to as you address the menu. Talented young chef Gavin Swift cooks up a storm: crispy hen's egg, wild mushrooms, truffle and tender stem broccoli as a starter, and slow-cooked belly pork with kale, Yukon Gold Medal mash and mulled cider jus as a main. And there's steak and ale pie for the traditionalists. Pub as hub – conveniently close to the A1.

Meals	Lunch from £5.95. Bar meals from £9. Dinner £12-£35. Sunday lunch, 2 courses, £13. Not Sun eves.
Closed	Mon & Tues lunch.
Directions	See website.

Gavin Swift, Mandy Hall, Richard & Amanda Bennington
The George At Wath
Main Street, Wath, Ripon HG4 5EN

Tel +44 (0)1765 641324
Web www.thegeorgeatwath.co.uk

Entry 662 Map 12

Yorkshire

Freemason's Arms

Nosterfield

The Freemason's whitewashed exterior may suggest an ordinary village pub but over the years an unusual assemblage of items has been added to the traditional décor: 1900s enamel advertisements, agricultural implements, Union flags, miners' lamps, a piano, and beams littered with old bank notes. It's a low-beamed place with interconnecting rooms, some flagged floors, two open fires, pew seating, soft lighting, candlelight – traditional, unspoilt, cosy and intriguing. It's also a darn good pub, with four local cask ales on offer and a blackboard to tantalise the hungry: partridge in rowan berry sauce, pink liver and onions with bacon. Kris Stephenson enjoys buying locally and delivers with flair. Eat in the bar, or at one of the bigger tables in the far room, perfect for dining. Just the spot after a day at the Ripon races.

Meals	Lunch from £8. Dinner from £10.
Closed	3pm-5pm. Mon. Open all day Sun.
Directions	On B6267 for Masham, 2 miles off A1.

Kristian Stephenson
Freemason's Arms
Nosterfield,
Bedale DL8 2QP

Tel +44 (0)1677 470548

Entry 663 Map 12

The Fox & Hounds

Carthorpe

Part of this 200-year-old pub was once the village blacksmith's, serving the A1; now it draws those in search of good food. Vincent and Helen have taken over from her parents, who first put this humble local on the culinary map. The L-shaped bar remains comfortably plush and cosy, with its warm red carpet, soothing classical music and glowing log fires, while the high-raftered dining room displays an interesting array of old smithy implements. Menus champion traditional British dishes cooked with skill and flair, with contemporary touches. There are scallops with crab and Pernod risotto, local hare casserole with parsley root mash, seafood platter... and a bread and butter pudding served with custard and vanilla ice cream. Black Sheep Bitter is on tap and there are decent wines by the glass.

Meals	Lunch & dinner £10-£17.50. Bar meals from £5.25.
Closed	3pm-7pm. Monday.
Directions	Carthorpe is 4 miles south of Bedale & 1 mile west of the A1.

Vincent & Helen Taylor
The Fox & Hounds
Carthorpe,
Bedale DL8 2LG
Tel +44 (0)1845 567433
Web www.foxandhoundscarthorpe.co.uk

Entry 664 Map 12

The Carpenters Arms

Felixkirk

This steady old village pub has undergone quite a transformation; Michael and Sasha of the Durham Ox have worked their considerable magic while keeping period detail, and it paid off handsomely in 'Best Freehouse Pub in Great Britain 2011'. Beneath the beamed apex at one end of the building is a very pleasant place to lunch; find too a wood stove, red walls and a chandelier made of wine glasses. Elsewhere, stone floors, comfy old furniture and open fires. Prawn cocktail – a kitsch classic – comes in a tall glass with homemade brown bread. Slow cooked lamb shank with rosemary mashed potato, curly kale and rustic vegetable jus is heaven on a chilly day or there's rib-eye steak with dauphinoise potatoes and madeira reduction. There's a proper tap room for drinkers, a good wine list, and the staff are local and lovely.

Meals	Lunch & dinner £9.95-£18.95. Sunday lunch from £12.95.
Closed	3pm-5pm. Open all day Sat & Sun.
Directions	From Thirsk A170 to Sutton Bank; 1st left for Felixkirk. Pub 2 miles.

Michael Ibbotson
The Carpenters Arms
Felixkirk,
Thirsk YO7 2DP
Tel +44 (0)1845 537369
Web www.thecarpentersarmsfelixkirk.com

Entry 665 Map 12

The Black Swan at Oldstead

Oldstead

In glorious isolation, tucked back from the road, the Black Swan goes back some 400 years. The Banks family has farmed for almost as long, and they've pulled off a marvellous transformation. Open fires, stone flags and beams, candelabra and oak furniture: it's a cheerful and comforting space. The food, served off slate place mats on antique tables, is refined too, truly delicious, with much from the nearby farms. Enjoy rabbit cannelloni, cauliflower, spinach and piccalilli; venison saddle with crushed potatoes and mulled-wine salsify; apple crumble crème brûlée with blackberries. A growing collection of awards confirms the attention to detail from chef Adam Jackson and his team. Take a pint of Copper Dragon to the blossom trees and gaze on the hills; don boots and set off from the door. A classic in the making.

Meals	Lunch from £8.95. Dinner, 3 courses, £37.50-£47. Tasting menu £49.95. No lunch Mon-Wed.
Closed	3pm-6pm. Mon-Weds lunch. Open all day Sat & Sun.
Directions	A19 from Thirsk; left to Thirkleby & Coxwold, then left for Byland Abbey; follow signs left for Oldstead.

The Banks Family
The Black Swan at Oldstead
Oldstead,
York YO61 4BL
Tel +44 (0)1347 868387
Web www.blackswanoldstead.co.uk

Entry 666 Map 12

Yorkshire

The Hare

Scawton

If you've braved the vertical ascent of the infamous Sutton Bank and are in need of sustenance, come to The Hare. This absurdly pretty 13th-century pub is lovely outside and in. On sunny days, sit in the garden on cream wrought-iron French chairs and admire the distant view of Riveaulx Abbey; on damp ones, feel embraced by big fires, red walls and ancient beams. Chef/patron Geoff Smith thoughtfully sources his ingredients and presents them temptingly on the plate: the twice-baked cheese soufflé is exemplary, the risotto of Portland crab with parmesan is creamy, the roast rack of Sutton Bank lamb with tarragon is earthy and rich; and there's a great cheese selection, so save some space. Business partner Jan pulls a well-kept pint and chats to you like you're an old friend... brilliant after the North Yorkshire Moors.

Meals	Lunch & dinner £6.75-£19.50.
Closed	3pm-6pm. Sun eves & Mon.
Directions	Village signed off A170, 7 miles east of Thirsk.

Geoff & Jan Smith
The Hare
Scawton,
Thirsk YO7 2HG
Tel +44 (0)1845 597769
Web www.thehareinn.co.uk

Entry 667 Map 12

The Blacksmith's Arms

Lastingham

Low black beams, glowing fires, timeworn saddles, a ghost called Ella and a pint of Copper Dragon. For country-lovers it's a dream. You almost slide down to the lovely little village, so deeply is it sunk into the valley. This low, rambling, dimly-lit pub has provided shelter and comfort to monks, shepherds and travellers since 1693; now it is visited by gamekeepers, walkers and church enthusiasts; St Mary's (1030) sits next door and, rumour has it, a secret tunnel runs between the two. Once an impoverished priest with 13 children ran both the pub and church, to the dismay of the bishop; the current landlord is approved by all. The little dining rooms are not quite as atmospheric as the bar with its lit range, but this is a great place for a gossip, a pint and hearty traditional food like game casserole and lamb and mint pie.

Meals Lunch & dinner £8.95-£14.95.
Closed Tues lunch.
Directions Left off A170 Kirkbymoorside to Pickering road.

Peter & Hilary Trafford
The Blacksmith's Arms
Front Street, Lastingham,
York YO62 6TL
Tel +44 (0)1751 417247
Web www.blacksmithslastingham.co.uk

Entry 668 Map 13

Yorkshire

The Horseshoe Inn

Levisham

A drive down the beautiful bowl-shaped valley to the station where the steam train passes through is a must. But you don't have to be a train spotter to appreciate the lovely old village of Levisham. Typical of this part of Yorkshire, the wide main street is flanked by old stone houses with pantile roofs, the 19th-century Horseshoe Inn standing proudly at the head. Step in to find oak floors, beams, chalkboard menu and roaring open fires, and a really lovely welcome. Yorkshire Warrior and Black Sheep are on tap, and honest, good value food (prepare for big Yorkshire portions) flows from the kitchen: Whitby crab and prawn risotto, smoked salmon and orange salad, shortcrust steak and ale pie and fat hand-cut chips – perfect fodder for walkers. Then it's a brisk trot from the door onto the stunning North York Moors.

Meals Lunch from £4.95.
Bar meals from £5.95.
Dinner from £10.50.
Sunday lunch, 3 courses, £20.
Closed See website for details.
Directions 5 miles from Pickering towards Whitby, off A169 through Lockton to Levisham.

Charles & Toby Wood
The Horseshoe Inn
Main Street, Levisham,
Pickering YO18 7NL
Tel +44 (0)1751 460240
Web www.horseshoelevisham.co.uk

Entry 669 Map 13

The Postgate Inn

Egton Bridge

This neck of the woods is best known for its 'Heartbeat' celebrity. Indeed, the Victorian stone pub sitting so handsomely at the bottom of the leafy Esk Valley – right by to the historic train line – is Heartbeat's 'Black Dog'. There's every reason to take the short trip inland from Whitby – for the big welcome, the homely feel (stone floors, beams, open fires) and the locally sourced ingredients brought together with such skill. Lamb noisettes with minted pea mash and a redcurrant and heather honey sauce are dense and toothsome; Whitby haddock and crab with gin crème sauce and white asparagus make the very best of the local catch. A terraced garden takes advantage of the views, making this a brilliant spot for lunch before stepping onto the steam train and rolling across the famous moors to Pickering.

Meals	Lunch & dinner £10.95-£18.95.
Closed	3.30pm-6.30pm (5.30pm in summer).
Directions	Off A171 east of Whitby; go through Egton to reach Egton Bridge in the Esk Valley.

Mark & Shelley Powell
The Postgate Inn
Egton Bridge,
Whitby YO21 1UX

Tel +44 (0)1947 895241
Web www.postgateinn.com

The Birch Hall

Beck Hole

Two small bars with a shop in between, unaltered for 70 years. Steep wooded hillsides and a stone bridge straddling the rushing river and, inside, a glimpse of life before World War II. The Big Bar has been beautifully repapered and has a little open fire, dominoes, darts and service from a hatch; benches come from the station waiting room at Beck Hole. The shop (postcards, traditional sweets) has its original fittings, as does the Little Bar with its handpumps for three cask ales. The original 19th-century enamel sign hangs above the door. Food is simple and authentic: local pies, baked stotties or baps, homemade scones and delicious beer cake. Steep steps take you to the terraced garden that looks over the inn and across the valley. Parking is scarce so show patience and courtesy in this old-fashioned place.

Meals	Sandwiches & pies from £1.90.
Closed	3pm-7.30pm. Mon eves & Tues in winter. Open all day in summer.
Directions	9 miles from Whitby towards Pickering.

Glenys & Neil Crampton
The Birch Hall
Beck Hole,
Whitby YO22 5LE

Tel +44 (0)1947 896245
Web www.beckhole.info

The Anvil Inn

Sawdon

The fact that this village is not on a bus route tells you one of two things; either you're in the back of beyond, or public transport is in a poor state. Whichever; beat a path to this welcoming door, even if you have to hitch a lift. The Anvil was a working forge until the mid 1980s, the building is over 200 years old and the blacksmith's workshop – now the bar – forms a unusual centrepiece to a great little pub. Partner-chefs Mark and Alexandra have pulled the place up by its bootstraps and have created an environment you'll linger long in. Sit on an old oak pew or lounge in a leather tub chair with a pint of Daleside or Copper Dragon, and scan the tempting menu. Invention without pretension is the philosophy here, and thoughtfully executed, locally sourced food flows from the kitchen. A classic in the making.

Meals	Lunch £7.50-£15.45. Dinner £9.50-£15.45. Sunday lunch £11.50.
Closed	2.30pm-6.30pm & all day Mon & Tues.
Directions	Sawdon is signed north off A170 Thirsk road, 7 miles west of Scarborough.

Mark Wilson & Alexandra Warricker
The Anvil Inn
Main Street, Sawdon,
Scarborough YO13 9DY
Tel +44 (0)1723 859896
Web www.theanvilinnsawdon.co.uk

Entry 672 Map 13

Yorkshire

The White Swan Inn

Pickering

Victor swapped the City for the North Yorkshire Moors and this old coaching inn; the place oozes comfort and style. Personality too: duck in through the front door to a tiny, cosy, panelled tap room serving real Yorkshire ales, with smart country furniture, fine wines and eager young staff. Best of all is the dining room: you'll find heaven on a plate when you dig into supper. Try seared, hand-dived king scallops with air-dried ham, Levisham mutton with Irish cabbage, poached rhubarb on toasted brioche and homemade ice cream. Menus change monthly and 80% of the ingredients are locally sourced, with meat coming from Levisham's celebrated Ginger Pig. Don't miss the beamed club room for roaring fire, board games and an honesty bar. Castle Howard is nearby, the moors are wild and the steam railway is great fun.

Meals	Lunch from £5.25. Dinner £25-£45. Sunday lunch £22.50.
Closed	Open all day.
Directions	From North A170 to Pickering. Entering town left at traffic lights, then 1st right into Market Place. On left.

Victor & Marion Buchanan
The White Swan Inn
Market Place,
Pickering YO18 7AA
Tel +44 (0)1751 472288
Web www.white-swan.co.uk

Entry 673 Map 13

The Star Inn

Harome

You know you've hit the jackpot as soon as you walk into The Star – low ceilings, flagged floors, gleaming oak, a flickering fire. Andrew and Jacquie arrived in 1996 and the Michelin star in 2002. It's been a formidable turnaround for the 14th-century inn yet the brochure simply says: "He cooks, and she looks after you"... and how! Andrew's food is rooted in Yorkshire tradition, refined with French flair and written in plain English on ever-changing menus that brim with local produce (do book). Risotto of partridge with black trumpet mushrooms, mutton and caper suet pudding, gutsy desserts and a 'cheese board of the week'. There's a bar with a Sunday papers-and-pint feel, a coffee loft in the eaves, and their own deli across the road... even the schnapps is homemade. Exceptional.

Meals	Lunch & dinner £16-£24.
Closed	Mon lunch.
Directions	From Thirsk, A170 towards Scarborough. Through Helmsley, then right, signed Harome. Inn in village.

Andrew & Jacquie Pern
The Star Inn
High Street, Harome,
Helmsley YO62 5JE

Tel	+44 (0)1439 770397
Web	www.thestaratharome.co.uk

Entry 674 Map 13

The Grapes Inn

Great Habton

In an unremarkable Yorkshire village, an unremarkable pub. Take heart, step inside. Adam and Katie have plans, when cash allows, to spruce up the exterior; in the meantime, enjoy what they've achieved in the short time they've been here. They deserve support in breathing life so beautifully into an old boozer in a sleepy village. Now there's dominoes, cricket, darts, a crackling fire to greet you, and exposed stone walls and fresh flowers to cheer up the old swirly carpets and retro moquette upholstery. And then there's Adam's cooking, which is modern and inventive. Meat, fish and vegetables are regionally sourced, and everything is made from scratch. May breast of pigeon on truffle mash with sloe gin jus inspire you! Add well-kept Ringwood Best Bitter and Jennings Bitter, and you know you've struck gold.

Meals	Lunch & dinner £8.50-£19.95. Bar meals from £8.25. Sunday lunch, 3 courses, £13.50.
Closed	3pm-6pm. Mon. Open all day Sun.
Directions	Village signed off B1257 Malton to Helmsley road & A169 between Malton & Pickering.

Adam & Katie Myers
The Grapes Inn
Great Habton,
Malton YO17 6TU

Tel	+44 (0)1653 669166
Web	www.thegrapes-inn.co.uk

Entry 675 Map 13

The Bay Tree

Stillington

The sorry old boozer has been transformed into this pub as hub, and with style. In the bar are stone floors, beams, open fires, and settles covered in ticking and candy striped cushions. Slightly raised at one end is a private dining area with twinkling tea lights and striped linen upholstered chairs. A further dining room has a seagrass carpet and bedouin-like tented ceiling, and French windows opening to a fabulous garden with shabby chic furniture and shady spots for a hot day. The menu has something for everyone; grilled mackerel with onion and beetroot salad is as fresh as fresh as can be; Nidderdale chicken breast 'French housewife style' comes with red wine, bacon and shallots. Enjoy a pint of Copper Dragon, read the papers, smile at the homespun epithets chalked on the walls; 'cheese, wine and friends must be old to be good'. Indeed.

Meals	Lunch & dinner £10.95-£17.95. Sunday lunch, 3 courses, £15.95.
Closed	See website for details.
Directions	On B1363, in the centre of Stillington.

Pablo Bouza-Causier
The Bay Tree
Main Street, Stillington,
York YO61 1JU
Tel +44 (0)1347 811394
Web www.baytreestillington.com

Bay Horse Inn

Burythorpe

Long, low and inviting, the old Bay Horse is the flagship of Real Yorkshire Pubs, and visitors and locals beat a path to the door for the food. Honest, wholesome English dishes are the order of the day, so expect whitebait with lemon mayonnaise, rump steak with hand-cut chips and all the trimmings fish pie, treacle sponge with toffee sauce, a local cheese board with apple oatcakes and cracking Sunday roasts. Meats and cheese are from local farms, fish is from Whitby and Hartlepool – all suppliers feature on the menu map. Walls have been warmly Farrow & Ball'd, scrubbed pine tables are matched with comfortable leather dining chairs, and smart light oak floors merge into fine stone flags. A small fire burns in the alcove by the door and there are books and newspapers to browse. It's friendly, young and civilised.

Meals	Lunch from £8.95. Bar meals from £5.95. Dinner from £9.95. Sunday lunch, 3 courses, £12.95. Not Monday.
Closed	3pm-6pm. Mon. Open all day Sun.
Directions	Kirkham Priory on right, sharp left towards Langton; 3 miles; signs for Burythorpe for 1.25 miles.

Dawn Pickering
Bay Horse Inn
Main Streeet, Burythorpe,
Malton YO17 9LJ
Tel +44 (0)1653 658302
Web www.bayhorseburythorpe.co.uk

The White Horse Inn (Nellie's)

Beverley

You could pass the White Horse by: its brick front and old pub sign do not stand out on busy Hengate. Inside is more beguiling – be transported back 200 years. (The building itself is even older.) Known as 'Nellie's', it's a wonderfully atmospheric little place; your eyes will take a while to become accustomed, so dim are the gas-lit passages. Little has changed in these small rooms with their old quarry tiles, bare boards, smoke-stained walls and open fires. Furniture is a mix of high-backed settles, padded benches, marble-topped cast-iron tables, old pictures and a gas-lit, pulley-controlled chandelier. Food is straightforward and good value: sandwiches, bangers and mash, steak and ale pie, spotted dick with custard. The only concession to the modern age is the games room at the back with a pool table and darts.

Meals	Lunch & dinner £3-£6.
Closed	Open all day.
Directions	Off North Bar, close to St Mary's Church.

Peter Hardy
The White Horse Inn (Nellie's)
22 Hengate,
Beverley HU17 8BN

Tel	+44 (0)1482 861973
Web	www.nellies.co.uk

Entry 678 Map 13

Yorkshire

The Star at Sancton

Sancton

There was a time when every farming village in the Yorkshire Wolds had a pub that was the beating heart of the community. By the time Ben and Lindsey Cox bought the 800-year-old building its heart had stopped. But youth and enthusiasm prevailed, and now the welcome is warm, the fires are lit and the comfortable, laid-back vibe gives barely a nod to the pub's sorry past. It's still very much a place for locals to pop in for a pint – beer is from the Copper Dragon and Great Newsome Breweries – but you must stay to eat. Ben is making a name for himself and the menu is tempting. Try homemade tagliatelle with parsley and grain mustard cream; Yorkshire pheasant breast with little venison suet pudding and mulled pear and red beet salad. Much of the produce comes from their allotment and orchard – a real treat.

Meals	Lunch & dinner £13.95-£19.95. Bar meals £4.95-£10.95. Set lunch £15 & £18.
Closed	Monday.
Directions	See website.

Ben & Lindsey Cox
The Star at Sancton
Sancton,
Market Weighton YO43 4QP

Tel	+44 (0)1430 827269
Web	www.thestaratsancton.co.uk

Entry 679 Map 13

St Vincent Arms

Sutton-upon-Derwent

Humming with happy chat, the traditional public bar is the heart of the place, sporting panelled walls lined with brass plates, warm red curtains, tartan carpeting. There are up to eight cask beers and no background music or electronic gadgetry – just an old radiogram. To the left of the lobby is a smaller, snugger bar decorated in pale green with matching tartan; this leads into several attractive small eating areas. Food ranges from crab sandwiches to chorizo and scallop risotto (delicious), steak, ale and mushroom pie, lobster with garlic butter, and sticky toffee pudding. And if you're not into ale there are several excellent wines by the glass. The St Vincent Arms is a great little local and the staff seem to enjoy themselves as much as the customers – you can't ask for more.

Meals	Lunch & dinner £8.50-£18.50.
Closed	3pm-6pm (6.30pm Sun).
Directions	On B1228, 8 miles south east of York.

Simon, Philip & Adrian Hopwood
St Vincent Arms
Main Street, Sutton-upon-Derwent,
York YO41 4BN
Tel +44 (0)1904 608349
Web www.stvincentarms.co.uk

Entry 680 Map 13

The Blue Bell

York

Unlike most city pubs, The Blue Bell is as it's always been – a timeless classic, a mecca for real ale fans. Its narrow brick frontage on Fossgate, not far from The Shambles, is easy to miss, but once you've found the old place, you enter a corridor that leads to the back. On the right, a tiny bar with red-tiled floor and high ceilings, panelling, Edwardian stained glass, a cast-iron and tiled fireplace, settle seating on two sides and iron-leg tables. 'Ladies only' were confined to the narrow back lounge; now the red carpet is trod on by all. Original fireplaces, polished panelling, interesting old pictures, ticking clocks and general clutter… all this and a terrific range of cask beers, at least seven, and wines too. No hot food but hearty sandwiches at lunchtime. Don't miss the annual beer festival in November.

Meals	Sandwiches from £2.
Closed	Open all day.
Directions	In York city centre.

Jim Hardie
The Blue Bell
53 Fossgate,
York YO1 9TF
Tel +44 (0)1904 654904

Entry 681 Map 13

Dawnay Arms
Newton on Ouse

The script on the lintel reads 1778. This stately Georgian building has been rescued from dereliction by Kerry and Martel Smith, who have taken one step sideways from their Leeds brasserie. Now the old boozer in the picture-postcard village is a shrine to modernity. Stone flagged floors and massive fireplaces have been kept, and chunky tables (constructed from timber pilfered from a post office in Durham) and old church pews sit stylishly in a pale palette, broken by splashes of colour from funky cushions and modern art in chubby rococo frames. Faultless food scrupulously sourced flows from a kitchen run by maestro Martel – perhaps steak and kidney pudding with root vegetables and ale sauce, and treacle tart with butterscotch ice cream. There's a glorious riverside garden for lazy summer days.

Meals	Lunch from £7.95-£14.95. Dinner from £9.95-£16.95. Sunday lunch, 3 courses, £17.95.
Closed	3pm-6pm. Mon. Open all day Sat & Sun.
Directions	A19 from York towards Thirsk; left at Shipton following signs to Beningbrough Hall.

Kerry Smith
Dawnay Arms
Newton on Ouse,
York YO30 2BR

Tel +44 (0)1347 848345
Web www.thedawnayatnewton.co.uk

Entry 682 Map 12

Yorkshire

The Crown Inn
Great Ouseburn

No longer does this handsome village pub stable circus animals for Blackpool Pleasure Beach! Today an enthusiastic team oversees a merry mix of locals, drinkers, cyclists, families and anyone up for a good meal. Yorkshire bonhomie is woven into the fabric of this gloriously revamped place; Liz and Paul have uncovered old fireplaces and stripped back beams to bring it all back to its original splendour. In the bar: candles and fresh flowers on mismatched tables, old pictures, soft-lit corners and a large open fire; to the back, a strikingly modern dining room, ideal for celebrations. Food is generous and a good notch above the norm, whether you're here for the celeriac gnocchi (with tomato coulis and watercress cream) or the North Yorkshire wild rabbit 'three ways'. Crown Blonde on tap, open fires, a tiny deli at the back – all is delightful.

Meals	Lunch from £7.25. Dinner from £11.50. Sunday lunch, 2 courses, £14.95.
Closed	Tuesdays. Monday lunchtime. Open all day weekends
Directions	On B6265 midway between Boroughbridge & Green Hammerton, exit towards Great Ouseburn.

Community pub

Paul & Liz Jackson
The Crown Inn
Main Street, Great Ouseburn,
York YO26 9RF

Tel +44 (0)1423 330013
Web www.thecrown-inn.com

Entry 683 Map 12

The Aldwark Arms

Aldwark

There's something reassuring about this solid mock-Tudor pub in the middle of the sleepy village. Find Jags in the car park and a feature wagon wheel inside – plus banquettes, a brick fireplace and happy chaps drinking Tim Taylors at the bar. But don't be fooled by the pubbiness: some serious cooking is happening here. Chris Hill's credentials are gold-plated; he's cheffed at Hambleton Hall, the Drunken Duck and the restaurant at Harvey Nicks, so expect dots and smears and stylish amuse-bouches alongside the pub staples. Crispy fried Alne Hen's egg, caramelised pork belly and mustard dressing with dandelion leaf salad makes a (very good) small meal on a large plate, while the three types of lamb with fondant potato, pumpkin purée and braised red cabbage is more substantial. The formal dining room at the back is somewhat less atmospheric.

Meals	Lunch & bar meals from £8.95. Dinner from £13.95. Sunday lunch, 3 courses, £23.
Closed	Monday (except bank hols).
Directions	Aldwark is signposted off the A19 and B6265 (between A59 at Green Hammerton and A1 at Boroughbridge) north west of York.

Chris Hill
The Aldwark Arms
Aldwark, York YO61 1UB
Tel +44 (0)1347 838324
Web www.aldwarkarms.co.uk

Entry 684 Map 12

Yorkshire

The Malt Shovel

Brearton

The Bleikers of smoked fish fame took on this pretty 16th-century pub in 2006, a warm family atmosphere permeates this carefully restored building. Stone floors, open fires and beamed ceilings abound. Choose from three eating spaces – the bar with its salvaged church panelling and candles, the dining room stuffed with vintage finds, the conservatory complete with piano... regular opera nights are a unique treat, dinner has been accompanied by many prominent opera singers. Local ingredients are put to ambitious use in a long menu including home-cured pancetta; the Kiln Platter with plenty of home-smoked fish; chocolate and lime chilli tart with raspberry coulis. There are several gruyère dishes on the bistro menu, while oxtail and kidney pudding is a winner on a damp Yorkshire day. Ales are well-kept, the wines are a cut above the norm.

Meals	Lunch & dinner from £12.95. Bar meals from £7.95. Sunday lunch, 3 courses, £18.95.
Closed	3pm-6pm. Sun eves.
Directions	Village signposted off A61, 5 miles north of Harrogate.

Jurg & Jane Bleiker
The Malt Shovel
Main Street, Brearton, Harrogate
HG3 3BX
Tel +44 (0)1423 862929
Web www.themaltshovelbrearton.co.uk

Entry 685 Map 12

Fountaine Inn

Linton

Imagine a village green with a tiny stone bridge, dabbling ducks and a babbling stream – such is the setting for this 17th-century inn. In spite of some serious sprucing up, the Fountaine remains a classic Yorkshire village pub of interconnecting rooms with glowing coal fires, slate floors, curved settles, old beams and cosy nooks. Weekend walkers arrive in droves for local Litton ales, all day thick-cut sandwiches and traditional burgers with relish and pickles. Wish to linger longer? Then settle into the dining room for crab and courgette risotto, slow-cooked Linton lamb with redcurrant and mint gravy, or mixed fish grill with garlic mayonnaise, followed by a fabulous chocolate fudge brownie. The green is well used in summer; for a seat and shade bag one of the smart benches and brollies out front.

Meals	Lunch & dinner £7.50-£14.
Closed	Open all day.
Directions	Village signed off B6265 south of Grassington.

Chris Gregson
Fountaine Inn
Linton, Skipton BD23 5HJ
Tel +44 (0)1756 752210
Web www.fountaineinnatlinton.co.uk

Entry 686 Map 12

Yorkshire

The Angel Inn

Hetton

The old drovers' inn remains staunchly, reassuringly traditional – but comes with a stylish restaurant and wines that have come, over the years, to rival the hand-pumped Yorkshire ales. There's even a 'cave' for functions and private-party tastings. There are nooks, crannies, beams and crackling fires, and thought has gone into every detail, from the antique furniture in the timbered rooms (one with a magnificent oak-panelled bar) to the fabrics and the colours. Menus change with each season and include dishes ranging from filo 'moneybags' of seafood in lobster sauce – the fish comes fresh from Fleetwood – to their own Yorkshire twist on tapas (known as 'Yapas'!). Vegetarians are well looked after and the sticky toffee pudding is legendary. The glorious up-hill-and-down-dale drive to get here is part of the charm. Best to book.

Meals	Lunch from £11.50. Dinner £15.95-£38.50. Sunday lunch £26.
Closed	3pm-6pm. Open all day Fri-Sat (reduced choice menu).
Directions	North from Skipton on B6265. Left at Rylstone for Hetton. In village.

Juliet Watkins
The Angel Inn
Hetton, Skipton BD23 6LT
Tel +44 (0)1756 730263
Web www.angelhetton.co.uk

Entry 687 Map 12

Craven Arms

Appletreewick

Authentically restored, this ancient rustic, creeper-clad pub (built in 1548) stands among gorgeous hills overlooking Wharfedale. It's a favourite with walkers so you could end up chin-wagging with them alongside the glowing cast-iron range in the classic stone-flagged bar. Just plain settles, panelled walls, thick beams, nothing more; beyond, a snug with simple benches and valley views, and a homely dining room. The final treat are the Wharfedale ales – Folly Gold, Executioner. Head out back to the loo to take a peek at the amazing function room housed in a replica medieval barn; back in the bar, free of music and flashing games, there are hot sandwiches to be tucked into, and the legendary slow-roasted and minted lamb shoulder. Just the job after a blustery hike or cycle ride across the moors.

Meals Lunch & dinner £8.95-£15.25.
Bar meals £7.50-£10.50.

Closed Open all day.

Directions A59 Skipton to Leeds; B6160 at Bolton Abbey towards Grassington; Appletreewick signed right.

Mark Cooper
Craven Arms
Appletreewick,
Skipton BD23 6DA
Tel +44 (0)1756 720270
Web www.craven-cruckbarn.co.uk

Entry 688 Map 12

Ilkley Moor Vaults

Ilkley

A stone's throw from the centre of genteel, elegant, bustling Ilkley town is an establishment known for years as 'the Taps'. Though Joe McDermott and his loyal team have spruced it up you can still whet your whistle with a good pint of local ale; but there's so much more to enjoy. Joining the stone flagged floors, the scrubbed pine tables and the crackling fires are kitschy standard lamps with tasselled shades and a menu that promises robust dishes with a twist – and delivers. Out back is a smoker and kitchen garden, so air miles don't exist. Homemade smoked sausage, pickled peppers and mustard made a gorgeous starter plate, served with a slice of the sublime sourdough bread that Joe's wife Elizabeth makes daily; rhubarb and buttermilk pudding creates a silky-smooth finale. The vibe is young but completely inclusive. Don't hesitate, just go.

Meals Lunch & dinner £8.90-£15.50.
Bar meals from £4.50.
Sunday lunch £10.90.

Closed 3pm-5pm. Mon.
Open all day Sat & Sun.

Directions Just off A65 towards Skipton; 5 mins walk from the town centre.

Joe McDermott
Ilkley Moor Vaults
Stockeld Road,
Ilkley LS29 9HD
Tel +44 (0)1943 607012
Web www.ilkleymoorvaults.co.uk

Entry 689 Map 12

The Shoulder of Mutton

Kirkby Overblow

A few miles south of Harrogate, this handsome old inn has far-reaching views over the rolling hills towards the lovely Wharfe Valley; David and Kate having been here since 2004, and the pub is the hub of village life. Outside: a child-friendly garden and ancient trees for shade on a sunny day. Inside: a proper 'pubby' vibe, with oak floors and beams, wood-burning stoves and old prints on rough plaster walls. David's passion for beer is evident; guest ales feature week by week. There's dedication in the kitchen too, with pub classics updated for modern times; homemade chicken liver pâté comes with warm sodabread and red onion chutney, and haunch of venison with celeriac dauphinoise and mixed berry jus. This enterprising couple have also opened a shop next door, selling store cupboard staples alongside their own produce, including scrumptious pies and cakes.

Meals	Lunch & dinner £9.95-£17.50. Sunday lunch, 3 courses, £18.95.
Closed	3pm-6pm. Monday.
Directions	Village signed off A61 & A658 3 miles south of Harrogate.

David & Kate Deacon
The Shoulder of Mutton
Main Street, Kirkby Overblow,
Harrogate HG3 1HD
Tel +44 (0)1423 871205
Web www.shoulderofmuttonharrogate.co.uk

Entry 690 Map 12

Yorkshire

The Chequers Inn

Ledsham

Fires glow, horse brasses gleam… this honey-stone village inn could be in the Dales. In fact, you're a couple of miles from the A1. The panelled, carpeted rooms radiating off the central bar are cosy with log fires and plush red upholstery; faded sepia photographs are a reminder of an earlier age. Rare hand-pumped ales from the Brown Cow Brewery at Selby do justice to good English food of Yorkshire proportions: steaming platefuls of loin of venison and red cabbage, wild boar with onion confit and sweet potato mash… and just when you think you're replete, along comes a chocolate torte with cream. The pub has been welcoming travellers since the 18th century and still closes on Sundays; the tradition started in 1832 when the lady of Ledsham Hall, confronting a drunken farmer on her way to church, insisted they close on the Sabbath.

Meals	Lunch & dinner £5.50-£19.95.
Closed	Sun.
Directions	From A1(M) at junc. 42, follow A63 Leeds to Selby road. Turn left & follow signs for Ledsham, 1 mile.

Chris Wraith
The Chequers Inn
Claypit Lane, Ledsham,
Leeds LS25 5LP
Tel +44 (0)1977 683135
Web www.thechequersinn.com

Entry 691 Map 12

The Old White Beare

Norwood Geen

Originally a farmhouse on the packhorse track, this handsome whitewashed pub in a pretty Pennine village was rebuilt following a fire in 1593 – using timbers from one of the 'Great Ships' in the Elizabeth I's fleet. Fast forward a few hundred years and the comfort quotient has improved! The place is instantly inviting, with its flagged floors, glowing oak settles and a roaring fire in the ancient snug, lovely in winter when Jack Frost is nipping at your nose; the beamed dining room bedecked with nautical ephemera is slightly more formal. Ales include Timothy Taylor's and Thwaites and the wine list is thorough, with lots by the glass. Homemade steak and ale pie vies with rack of three-Dales lamb and Lishman's black pudding in the food stakes; jam roly poly with crème anglaise and apple tarte tatin bring up the rear.

Meals Lunch & dinner £8.95-£18.50.
Closed Open all day.
Directions M62 junc. 26, take A58 towards Halifax, 3 miles to Norwood vllage.

Andrew Krawec & Chris Blood
The Old White Beare
Village Street, Norwood Geen,
Halifax HX3 8QG
Tel +44 (0)1274 676645
Web www.oldwhitebeare.com

Entry 692 Map 12

Yorkshire

The Pack Horse

Widdop

This old whitewashed inn sags beneath weathered gritstone tiles in a gloriously remote spot. Once, water engineers had a whale of a time constructing reservoirs to slake the thirst of the local textile industry – the pub's stone walls sport old plans and photos of their endeavours. Today's thirsts are those of ramblers on the Pennine Way and riders on the Pennine Bridleway, which briefly meet right behind the pub. Four or five real ales to enjoy alongside whopping portions of crispy roast duck, rack of lamb and a whole side of grilled plaice ensure this is a popular spot. Two thickly beamed rooms off a passageway bar, with cavernous log fires, horsey ephemera and a comfy rag-tag of furnishings, invite you to unwind over a drink; this is a great pub with grand food, not a dining pub with good beer.

Meals Lunch & dinner £5.95-£12.95.
Closed Mon (except bank hols) & weekday lunch Oct-Easter. Open all day Sun.
Directions From A646 in Hebden Bridge take the road at the Fox & Goose, signed for Heptonstall & Slack. In Slack fork right for Widdop.

Andrew Hollinrake
The Pack Horse
Widdop,
Hebden Bridge HX7 7AT
Tel +44 (0)1422 842803

Entry 693 Map 12

Alma Inn & Fresco Italian Restaurant

Four Lane End

High on the heather-clad moors this old boozer has a few surprises up its sleeve. The stone paved terrace is large and lovely and the bar is cosy and warm – all flagged floors, stone walls, glowing fires, pine tables, old settles. Timothy Taylor's Golden Best and Landlord are on tap, along with 75 Belgian beers. More surprising, the food is Italian, and fabulous. Vegetables come from the market, local meat is brought in on the bone and every last bit used in stocks and gravy. So tuck into *gamberoni all'aglio e burro* – prawns in garlic butter – or fillet steak, monkfish with pancetta, partridge with Parma ham, and big thin-crust pizzas from a wood-burning oven. Eat in the bar or in the fresh airy dining room, with its sophisticated look and open kitchen.

Meals	Lunch & dinner £7.95-£15.95.
Closed	Open all day.
Directions	A58 at Triangle Inn signed Cottonstones/Millbank - pub 1.5 miles from Triangle.

David Giffen
Alma Inn & Fresco Italian Restaurant
Alma Lane, Four Lane End,
Sowerby Bridge HX6 4NS

Tel +44 (0)1422 823334
Web www.almainn.com

Entry 694 Map 12

The Old Bridge Inn

Ripponden

An ancient packhorse bridge and a little low inn… such is the setting. Family involvement over several decades has resulted in a thoroughly civilised, unspoilt little local; a friendly one, too. Three carpeted, oak-panelled, split-level rooms – suitably dimly lit – are furnished with old oak settles and rush-seated chairs. The small, green-walled snug at the top is atmospheric; the bar has a lofty ceiling with exposed timbers and a huge fireplace with log-burning stove; the lower room is good for dining. The buffet lunches are as popular as ever, while the evening menu announces sound English cooking (venison steak with spiced red cabbage, Yorkshire cheese selection) featuring local produce and a modern slant. The bar is well used by local folk who come for Timothy Taylor's Best Bitter, Landlord and Golden Best; wines are good too.

Meals	Lunch from £3.95. Dinner from £9. Salad or sandwiches only on weekday lunch. Not Sun eves.
Closed	3pm-5.30pm. Open all day Fri-Sun.
Directions	4 miles from junc. 22 M62 in Ripponden.

Tim & Lindsay Eaton Walker
The Old Bridge Inn
Priest Lane,
Ripponden HX6 4DF

Tel +44 (0)1422 822595
Web www.theoldbridgeinn.co.uk

Entry 695 Map 12

The Sair Inn

Linthwaite

Clinging to the side of the valley, The Sair oozes character with a warren of small rooms. Floors of rippling flagstone and scuffed boards carry tables, pews and chairs from The Ark. Massive winter fires ensure that Vulcan would feel at home; Pandora would be delighted by the artefacts and oddments. It's a Yorkshire treasure, enhanced by locals and traditional pub games; in the old pub Joanna allows impromptu entertainment, side rooms allow escape from the hubbub. Beers? – to die for, created in the brewhouse behind the pub; any or all of eight and more. Patrons flock from afar to soak up the atmosphere of this iconic idyll, so concerns about catering are the last thing on anyone's mind. It's uncompromising, not one for shrinking violets, 'grand' in the Wallace and Grommit sense, brilliant value and welcoming to all.

Meals	No food served.
Closed	Mon-Fri lunch. Open all day Sat & Sun.
Directions	Off A62 in Linthwaite; up steep Hoyle Ing 400 yds.

Ron Crabtree
The Sair Inn
139 Lane Top,
Linthwaite,
Huddersfield HD7 5SG

Tel +44 (0)1484 842370

Entry 696 Map 12

Yorkshire

Butcher's Arms

Hepworth

From the top of the hill in Hepworth you can almost see Norah Batty's wrinkled stockings in Holmfirth – this is the land of *Last of the Summer Wine*. But there's nothing quaint about Tim Bilton's refurbished pub on the windswept moors; he trained with Raymond Blanc, then ran the immensely popular Bibis in Leeds. Step into an interior of stone floors, beams and log fires – and if you think this is a typical Pennine boozer, just take a look at the menu, rooted in Yorkshire simplicity. Not only is there pot roast pheasant with braised red cabbage, air-dried bacon and pear purée but 'plate of pig' too: milk-fed belly of suckling pig cooked with its own sausage toad-in-the-hole style, and a pan-seared pork fillet with windfall apple sauce. You can bring the dog, sup a pint of well-kept Timothy Taylor's, read the papers.

Meals	Lunch & dinner £13.95-£17.95.
Closed	Mon lunch.
Directions	7.5 miles south of Huddersfield; off A616 Sheffiled Road.

Tim Bilton
Butcher's Arms
38 Towngate, Hepworth,
Holmfirth HD9 1TF

Tel +44 (0)1484 682361
Web www.thebutchersarmshepworth.co.uk

Entry 697 Map 12

King's Arms

Heath

Enter Heath and step back years. A string of wool merchants' houses, 100 acres of heathland, a couple of tethered ponies... who'd guess Wakefield was down the road? In the heart of Yorkshire's most unspoilt village is the equally unspoiled King's Arms. In a dark, rich network of tap rooms and snugs, softly hissing gas lamps cast an amber glow on oak-panelled walls, yellowed ceilings and low beams, while a magnificent Yorkshire range is the best of several open coal fires. It's no museum – just a superbly old-fashioned pub that serves Clarks Classic Blond, and Stella for non-believers. Traditional pub grub includes filled Yorkshire puddings and beef and ale pie. Attached is a serviceable restaurant, at the back is a conservatory that breaks the spell. The gardens have gentle moorland views.

Meals	Lunch & dinner £8.95-£17.95.
Closed	3pm-5pm in winter. Open all day weekends & in summer.
Directions	Heath signed off A655.

Andrew & Renata Shepherd
King's Arms
Heath,
Wakefield WF1 5SL
Tel +44 (0)1924 377527
Web www.kingsarmswakefield.co.uk

Entry 698 Map 12

The Milestone

Kelham Island

A shining beacon in Sheffield's post-industrial back streets, this Victorian gastropub is full of pizzazz. Food is elevated to dizzying heights with a mix of forgotten cooking techniques, the freshest ingredients and an insistence on making as much as possible on site. A glowing pine floor provides an anchor for a medley of modern farmhouse tables and chairs. Light pours onto walls hung with archive photos and there's more seating upstairs under an exposed roof. In the bar you can sup beer from Kelham Island – old industrial area up the road – along with speciality lagers, spirits and exciting wines, before diving into pork liver parfait with fig and red wine reduction, sausage casserole with puy lentils, paprika and crispy back fat, and wine-poached pear with vanilla panna cotta and lemon balm ice cream. A milestone indeed. Put it on your foodie map.

Meals	Lunch from £9.50. Dinner from £13.95. Sunday lunch £9.95.
Closed	Open all day.
Directions	Off A61 ring road, near Kelham Island Museum, opposite Shalesmoor tram stop.

Marc Sheldon & Matt Bigland
The Milestone
84 Green Lane at Ball Street,
Kelham Island, Sheffield S3 8SE
Tel +44 (0)1142 728327
Web www.the-milestone.co.uk

Entry 699 Map 12

The Inn at Troway

Troway

High on a hill with rolling country views sits this large 1930s mock Tudor pub with an arms-open-to-all approach. Inside, polished wood and terracotta tiles sweep you towards a bar primed with Thornbridge Wild Swan and Jaipur alongside Black Sheep and Cocker Hoop ales. To either side are open-plan areas with red leather sofas, padded bench seats, period fireplaces and modern cartoon prints on walls. Enthusiastic staff settle you in and blackboards list the great meal offers for families, from grills, fish and chips and sandwiches to menus announcing modern pub classics such as Yorkshire pheasant with parsnip purée and buttered vegetables. Great homemade desserts as well, and pork crackling with apple sauce – the real deal. There's a smart separate games room, masses of fresh flowers and treats for children on arrival.

Meals	Lunch & dinner from £8. Bar meals from £2. Sunday lunch from £10.
Closed	Open all day.
Directions	On B6056 east of A61 to the south of Sheffield.

Richard Smith
The Inn at Troway
Snowdon Lane, Troway,
Sheffield S21 5RU
Tel +44 (0)1246 417666
Web www.relaxeatanddrink.com

Yorkshire

The Cricket Inn

Totley

'Children, dogs, muddy boots welcome!' is the legend over the door of this old stone pub, next to the cricket pitch in a leafy Sheffield suburb; the feel is rural. Local restaurateurs Richard and Victoria Smith have joined forces with Thornbridge Brewery to create a laid-back, welcoming pub with stone floors, tongue-and-groove walls, open fires and wholesome, value-for-money food flowing from the kitchen. Crispy breadcrumbed belly pork with black pudding mash, sweet and sour cabbage and sage and scrumpy reduction is a signature dish – along with steamed 'snake and pigmy' pudding, roast carrots and creamy mash. After a walk in the woods, pop in here, put up your feet by the fire and pick up the paper and a pint of specially brewed Jaipur. Or take a ringside seat by the pitch in summer. Marvellous.

Meals	Lunch & dinner £12-£20; sandwiches from £5. Set menu £25. Sunday roast from £13.50.
Closed	Open all day.
Directions	On A621 south from Sheffield; in Totley take Hillfoot Road; left into Penny Lane; pub on right.

Richard Smith
The Cricket Inn
Penny Lane, Totley,
Sheffield S17 3AZ
Tel +44 (0)1246 417666
Web www.relaxeatanddrink.com

Wales

Photo: istockphoto.com
annthphoto

The Seacroft

Trearddur Bay

Big skies, sandy beaches, wheeling gulls, spectacular sunsets – that's what you find at the top of Anglesey. The Seacroft is wonderfully positioned 200 metres inland, its whitewashed walls sparkling in the summer sun. It's a very happy place, a pub to some (Tuesday night is quiz night) and a restaurant to others (beer-battered haddock, pizzas, steaks, Anglesey lamb, mussels from the Menai Strait). Outside is a vast decked terrace overlooking the lane; inside, New England interiors give an airy seaside feel. Conran lampshades hang above cool little dining booths, pints of Timothy Taylor wait at the American oak bar, dining tables circle a wood-burner that burns on both sides. As for the bedrooms, they are pretty, cosy and warm. Two have decked balconies, all come in blues and creams with excellent bathrooms and crisp linen on smart wooden beds. Spin outside to explore the island and the wide sands of Trearddur Bay, the coastal path, the sailing school... you could catch a ferry to Dublin, day trips are easy. There's links golf at the end of the road, and picnic hampers can be arranged.

Price	£98-£108. Singles from £75.
Rooms	6: 5 doubles, 1 twin.
Meals	Lunch & dinner £7.95-£15.95.
Closed	Open all day.
Directions	A55 north onto Anglesey for Holyhead. Exit at junc. 2, B4545 into village. Ravenspoint Road signed right after Spar. On right.

Patrick Flynn
The Seacroft
Ravenspoint Road, Trearddur Bay,
Holyhead LL65 2YU
Tel +44 (0)1407 860348
Web www.theseacroft.com

Ship Inn

Red Wharf Bay

The boatmen still walk across from the estuary with their catch. Inside the Ship, fires roar in several fireplaces and bars share nautical bits and bobs. There are pews and benches and bare stone walls, and huge blackboards where the daily specials change almost by the hour. At night, the menu proffers Welsh seafood based on the best the boats have brought in: grilled turbot served with lemon and seasonal vegetables; dressed crab. But the old Ship is so much more – a family-friendly public house where, for 30 years, regulars and visitors have been enjoying great ales and freshly prepared food, from 'brechdanau' – sandwiches – to 'pwdin'. Fine Welsh cheeses, too. These lovely people are as proud of their hospitality as they are of their language – and the vast sea and sand views from the front terraces are inspiring.

Meals	Lunch & dinner £11.50-£16.95.
Closed	Open all day.
Directions	Off B5025, north of Pentraeth.

Neil Kenneally
Ship Inn
Red Wharf Bay,
Pentraeth LL75 8RJ

Tel +44 (0)1248 852568
Web www.shipinnredwharfbay.co.uk

Entry 703 Map 6

Anglesey

Ye Olde Bulls Head Inn

Beaumaris

This was a favourite haunt of Samuel Johnson and Charles Dickens and now attracts drinkers and foodies like bees to clover. In the rambling, snug-alcoved bar there's draught Bass on offer, while in the modern brasserie in the stables you have a choice of ten wines by the glass to match your Moroccan fish stew or confit duck leg. Spot the ancient weaponry and old ducking stool, which contrasts with the sophisticated remodelling of the intimate Loft Restaurant upstairs. Here, Welsh dishes are designed around seafood from the Menai Strait, and as much beef, lamb and game as the chefs can find on the island. The results: lamb loin rolled in thyme and garlic with coriander jus, and wild turbot with braised pigs cheeks, fondant potato and glazed vegetables, seasoned as required with Anglesey sea salt. Service comes with warmth and charm.

Meals	Lunch & dinner in brasserie £5-£30. Dinner in restaurant, 3 courses, £41 (Tue-Sat evenings only).
Closed	Open all day.
Directions	A55 onto Anglesey, then A545 to Beaumaris. On left at far end of main street.

David Robertson
Ye Olde Bulls Head Inn
Castle Street,
Beaumaris LL58 8AP

Tel +44 (0)1248 810329
Web www.bullsheadinn.co.uk

Entry 704 Map 6

Y Polyn

Nantgaredig

The pub sits by a fork in the roads, one leading to Aberglasney, the other to the National Botanic Garden of Wales. This lot know their onions – Susan was head chef at the Worshipful Company of Innholders, Maryann chef-patron at the Four Seasons in Nantgaredig – and have jollied up the interior with bold colours, herringbone matting, local art, fresh flowers and candles. A wicker sofa and armchairs by the fire encourage you to loll, while the restaurant has a happy mix of tables and chairs. The short menu is pleasingly simple: fresh local ingredients well put together. Start with duck and ham hock terrine with piccalilli, move onto crispy roast pork belly with caramelised apples or Welsh lamb hotpot, finish with plum and frangipane tart or rhubarb fool. You are equally welcome to just pop in for a drink.

The open-all-day 'pantry pub' is a delicious new trend. Check out the Hampshire Hog in Hammersmith, London and the Bell in Wiltshire – keeping young mums happy...

Meals	Lunch & dinner £9.50-£29.50. Sunday lunch, 2 courses, £17.50.
Closed	4pm-7pm. Sun eves & Mon.
Directions	Off junction of B4300 & B4310 between A48 & A40 east of Carmarthen.

Mark & Susan Manson
Y Polyn
Nantgaredig,
Carmarthen SA32 7LH

Tel +44 (0)1267 290000
Web www.ypolynrestaurant.co.uk

Harbourmaster

Aberaeron

Lobster boats at lunch, twinkling harbour lights at dinner, real ale, well-chosen wines and dazzling service. The old harbourmaster's residence has become decidedly chic with an inspirational restaurant and bar. Step in to find a space that's cosy but cool: soft shades, blocked-oak tables. In the celebrated bistro, daily menus are studded with the best local produce and the dishes delight: Carlingford oysters, sea bass with roast pepper, anchovies and ratatouille, rack of Welsh lamb, chocolate fondant. In the bar tuck into local crab linguini with chilli and lime. The Heulyns' dedication to all that is best about Wales shines forth. If you're staying, wind up the staircase to super little bedrooms that come with shuttered windows, loads of colour and quietly funky bathrooms, or eat at one of the large, swish doubles in the adjoining converted warehouse. You get Frette linen, Welsh wool blankets and a hot water bottle in winter... cosy, characterful, contemporary, they're a pleasure to return to. There are even bikes to borrow: cycle tracks spin off into the hills, coastal paths lead north and south.

Price	£110-£195. Suites £150-£250. Singles £65. Half-board from £80 p.p.
Rooms	13: 11 doubles, 2 singles.
Meals	Lunch & bar meals from £9.50. Dinner from £16. Sunday lunch, 3 courses, £21.
Closed	Open all day.
Directions	A487 south from Aberystwyth. In Aberaeron right for the harbour. Hotel on waterfront.

Glyn & Menna Heulyn
Harbourmaster
Pen Cei, Aberaeron SA46 0BT

Tel +44 (0)1545 570755
Web www.harbour-master.com

The Queen's Head

Glanwydden

The old wheelwright's cottage has gone up in the world. Now there are low beams, polished tables, walls strewn with maps and a roaring fire in the bar. The food is good, the portions generous and you can see the cooks at work through the open hatch. This is home-cooked pub food with a modern twist that in summer might include fresh Conwy crab and Great Orme lobster. Friendly, smartly turned-out staff serve starters of crispy duck leg or Conwy fish soup, and mains of salmon and coriander fishcakes or Welsh rump steak with garlic butter; desserts might include bara brith bread-and-butter pudding. Robert and Sally Cureton have been here for 28 years, nurturing a country local that puts those of Llandudno to shame. Complete the treat by booking a night in the old parish storehouse across the road, a sweet retreat for two, recently revamped. A gallery bedroom under white-painted eaves, a bathroom lavishly tiled, a small private garden for breakfast coffee and fresh croissants – it's the perfect set up for a romantic break.

Price	£100-£150. Self-catering option also available.
Rooms	Cottage for 2.
Meals	Lunch & dinner £9.95-£21.95. Sunday lunch £10.25.
Closed	3pm-6pm. Open all day Sat & Sun.
Directions	From A55; A470; right at 3rd r'bout for Penrhyn Bay; 2nd right to Glanwydden after 1.5 miles.

Robert & Sally Cureton
The Queen's Head
Glanwydden,
Llandudno Junction LL31 9JP

Tel	+44 (0)1492 546570
Web	www.queensheadglanwydden.co.uk

The Kinmel Arms

St George

In a tiny hamlet- yet easily reachable from the A55 – the Kinmel Arms shines like a culinary beacon. Lynn and Tim arrived a decade ago and the place continues to delight. Walk in to an open-plan space of cool neutral colours, hardwood floors and a central bar with stained-glass above; then through to a conservatory-style restaurant, painted a cheery yellow and decorated with Tim's photographs. Seasonal brasserie-style menus champion local producers – try Welsh beef fillet with Penderyn whisky sauce, or Asian-spiced sea bass with crispy squid in a coconut and lentil cream. The slate-topped bar dispenses top quality local ales and great value bin-end wines. Behind this striking stone building are four gorgeous suites, each with wide French windows to a decked seating area facing east to catch the morning sun. You could breakfast out here in summer; goodies are left the night before in your fridge. Big beds are topped with crisp linen, walls are fresh yellow, towels are vast. You're a hop from the stunning North Wales coast, and Snowdonia. Great walks start from the door.

Price	£115-£175. No children or dogs overnight.
Rooms	4 suites.
Meals	Lunch £6.95-£17.50. Dinner £14.95-£24.95.
Closed	3pm-6pm. Sun & Mon all day.
Directions	A55, junc. 24a from Chester, left up Primrose Hill to village; or junc. 24 from Conwy, 1st exit at r'bout onto A547; 1st right towards St George; right onto Primrose Hill.

Tim Watson & Lynn Cunnah-Watson
The Kinmel Arms
The Village, St George,
Abergele LL22 9BP
Tel +44 (0)1745 832207
Web www.thekinmelarms.co.uk

The Lion Inn

Gwytherin

A simple 300-year-old inn lost in the hills of North Wales – you're more likely to hear birdsong, bleating sheep or a tractor than a car. In summer you can sit at colourful tables on the pavement and watch buzzards circle high in the sky, in winter you can sip your Welsh whisky by a fire that burns on both sides in the bar. All year round you tuck into delicious food: fish soup, rack of lamb with rosemary and cider jus, bread and butter pudding. Downstairs there are paintings by local artists decorating stone walls. Upstairs, bedrooms are an unexpected tonic, warm and cosy, nicely stylish and super value for money. Find Farrow & Ball paints on old stone walls and Canadian pitch pine furniture, rustic wooden beds made up with excellent linen and Welsh woollen throws, spotless bathrooms, DVDs for wintery nights. Big breakfasts set you up for the day – porridge, toast from homemade bread, free-range eggs – so burn off the excess on Snowdon or ride your bike through local forests. The mobile reception is useless, the hospitality is magnificent and Portmerion and Anglesey are close.

Price	£90-£95. Singles £65. Family room from £115. Children over 7 welcome.
Rooms	6: 3 doubles, 1 twin, 1 single, 1 family room.
Meals	Dinner £13.95-£27.
Closed	Mon & Tues (except bank hols; Jul & Aug). Open from 7pm Wed-Sun.
Directions	A55 to Abergele; A544 south to Llansannan; B5384 west to Gwytherin. In village.

Tim & Fiona Hughes
The Lion Inn
Gwytherin,
Llanrwst LL22 8UU
Tel +44 (0)1745 860123
Web www.thelioninn.net

Bryn Tyrch

Capel Curig

Bang in the heart of Snowdonia National Park: a very comfortable mountain retreat for walkers and climbers. Its interior has been gently renovated, its style is laid-back and there's a great big blackboard over the fire displaying seasonal food from a team of talented chefs: try pressed ham hock terrine with apple and pistachio jelly, mature Welsh Black sirloin steak, fresh fish from Anglesey, local sausages and homemade cakes and bread. Picture windows run the length of the main bar with carefully placed tables making the most of the views (Siabod and Snowdon), and there are big brown chesterfields by the fire where you can sip something from the wine menu or down a pint of Purple Moose's Snowdonia. Bedrooms, most now revamped with local slate and natural oak, are not huge but are perfectly formed: super-comfy beds, big gleaming baths and showers, views worth waking up for; catch the mountains in snow and you'll imagine yourself skiing. For hikers there are now two very smart four-person bunk rooms with super showers; friendly staff know the best hikes and climbs. You can go to cookery school here, too.

Price	£55-£110. Singles from £35.
Rooms	12: 10 twins/doubles, 2 bunk rooms.
Meals	Lunch from £6.95. Bar meals & dinner from £9.95. Sunday lunch, 2 courses, £12.95.
Closed	Mon-Thurs lunch Nov-Mar. Open all day Fri-Sun.
Directions	On A5 near Plas-y-Brenin Mountain Centre, 5 miles west of Betws-y-Coed.

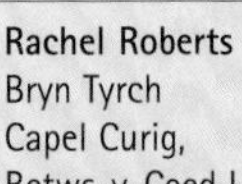

Rachel Roberts
Bryn Tyrch
Capel Curig,
Betws-y-Coed LL24 0EL
Tel +44 (0)1690 720223
Web www.bryntyrchinn.co.uk

The Groes Inn

Ty'n-y-Groes

The first licensed house in Wales (1573) is splendidly old-fashioned, with rambling bars, nooks and crannies, and low beams and doorways that demand heads be bowed. Painted stonework is hung with local prints and pictures, there are displays of teacups and Victorian postcards, a red carpet, a polished Welsh dresser, a wood-burner to keep things toasty. Our pint of Orme's Best – brewed by Justin's cousin – went down a treat, as did the prime-beef burger in its great toasted bap, with crisp mixed salad and delicious hand-cut chips. In the more elegant restaurant, 32 wines accompany award-winning dishes: baked field mushrooms, Conway crab and Anglesey oysters, sweet Welsh lamb with rich rosemary jus, chocolate-scented pancakes with sumptuous ice cream. For summer: a pretty garden with lovely mountain views. Excellent all round.

Meals: Lunch & dinner from £13.25. Bar meals from £9.65.
Closed: 3pm-6pm.
Directions: A55 to Conwy, then B5106 south for 1.5 miles; hotel on right.

Dawn & Justin Humphreys
The Groes Inn
Ty'n-y-Groes,
Conwy LL32 8TN
Tel: +44 (0)1492 650545
Web: www.groesinn.com

Entry 711 Map 7

Pen-y-Bryn

Colwyn Bay

The interior shines like a film set: oak floors and bookcases, open fires and polished furniture – the make-believe world of Brunning & Price. No wonder the locals have taken to Pen-y-Bryn like ducks to water. Staff are well-informed and never too busy to share their knowledge of the food and its provenance. Menus are enticing and generously priced. Pan-fried squid is served with butterbean and chorizo; warming leek and potato soup comes with crusty bread. Pork and lamb is local, cheeses fly the Principality's flag and luscious mussels come from down the coast. You're high up on Colwyn Heights here but a few glasses of Orme Brewery's Cambria will soon warm your toes. Sturdy wooden furniture in the garden fits in well with the neighbourhood's residential air... but inside is best.

Meals: Lunch & dinner £6.25-£16.95. Bar meals £4.50-£9.25. Sunday lunch £10.25.
Closed: Open all day.
Directions: Follow B5113 south west of Colwyn Bay for 1 mile.

Andrew Grant
Pen-y-Bryn
Wentworth Avenue,
Colwyn Bay LL29 6DD
Tel: +44 (0)1352 750500
Web: www.penybryn-colwynbay.co.uk

Entry 712 Map 7

The Hand at Llanarmon

Llanarmon Dyffryn Ceiriog

Single-track lanes plunge you into the middle of nowhere, lush valleys rise and fall – pull on the boots and scale a mountain. Back at the inn, once frequented by 16th-century drovers, the pleasures of a country local are hard to miss. A coal fire burns on the range in reception, a fire crackles under brass in the front bar and a wood-burner warms the lofty dining room. There are exposed stone walls, low beamed ceilings, old pine settles and candles on the mantelpiece, a games room for darts and pool, a quiet sitting room for maps and books. Delicious food is popular with locals, so grab a table and enjoy seasonal menus – perhaps chicken liver parfait with fruit chutney and toasted homemade bread, duck with pancetta, black pudding and red wine, and autumn berry pudding. Stay and you'll get a lovely cooked Welsh breakfast. Bedrooms are just as they should be: not too fancy, cosy and warm, with crisp white linen and scrupulously clean. A very friendly place: Martin and Gaynor are full of passionate enthusiasm and have made their home warmly welcoming. Everyone loves this place.

Price	£90-£125. Singles from £52.50.
Rooms	13: 8 doubles, 4 twins, 1 suite.
Meals	Lunch from £6. Sunday lunch £20. Dinner £12-£20.
Closed	Open all day.
Directions	Leave A5 south of Chirk for B4500. Llanarmon 11 miles on.

Gaynor & Martin De Luchi
The Hand at Llanarmon
Llanarmon Dyffryn Ceiriog,
Llangollen LL20 7LD
Tel +44 (0)1691 600666
Web www.thehandhotel.co.uk

The Corn Mill

Llangollen

The 18th century has been left far behind in this renovated corn mill beside the swiftly flowing Dee. Not only is the interior light, airy and well-designed but the busy menu is laced with contemporary ideas. There are also gorgeous views onto the river whether you're quaffing your pint of Phoenix in the fabulous bar, or settling down to eat in one of the upper-floor dining areas. The decked veranda-cum-walkway is stunning, built out over the cascading rapids with a gangway overhanging one end beyond the revolving water wheel. Watch dippers and wagtails as you tuck into smoked haddock and mozzarella rarebit, Welsh pork sausages with spring onion mash, king prawn salad with chilli dressing. The Brunning & Price formula is known for its 'something-for-everyone' appeal, and the setting is supreme.

Meals	Lunch & dinner £8.95-£16.50.
Closed	Open all day.
Directions	Off Castle Street (A539) just south of the river bridge.

Andrew Barker
The Corn Mill
Castle Street,
Llangollen LL20 8PN
Tel +44 (0)1978 869555
Web www.cornmill-llangollen.co.uk

Entry 714 Map 7

Denbighshire

Pant-yr-Ochain

Gresford

A long drive snakes through landscaped parkland to a magnificent multi-gabled country house sheltered by trees. To one side a huge conservatory opens up views across terraces to the estate lake; inside, a jigsaw of richly panelled rooms and drinking areas lures those who come to dine and those in search of the hop: note the nine real ales. There are intimate corners, comfy alcoves and private snugs, open fires, quarry tiles and bare boards below an eccentric ceiling-line. Everywhere, a cornucopia of bric-a-brac: penny slots and cases of clay pipes, caricatures and prints. It sounds OTT but it fits comfortably here, while the ever-reliable Brunning & Price menus feature the likes of venison with sloe gin and cherry sauce, and smoked haddock and salmon fishcakes. Outside is a flower-filled, lakeside garden.

Meals	Lunch & dinner £5.75-£16.95.
Closed	Open all day.
Directions	Gresford signed off A483 Wrexham bypass.

James Meakin
Pant-yr-Ochain
Old Wrexham Road, Gresford,
Wrexham LL12 8TY
Tel +44 (0)1978 853525
Web www.pantyrochain-gresford.co.uk

Entry 715 Map 7

Glasfryn

Sychdyn

Drawing a hugely varied crowd, this solid red brick pub – a former judges' residence with an Arts & Crafts pedigree – sits on a south-facing slope with views over the town to the Clwydian range. A stunning makeover has led to acres of oak flooring, Indian rugs, book-lined walls and locally themed pictures and prints. Real ale aficionados will thrill to eight cask ales; Purple Moose's Snowdonia ale delivers a crisp, citrus beer whilst Flowers Original is, quite literally, brewing heritage in a glass. Foodies are not forgotten and can feast on mint-braised shoulder of lamb with mustard mash and broccoli or minced beef and onion pie with chips and peas. There are nearly 80 malts, every spirit imaginable and an Italian makes the coffee – need we say more? Yes, it's abuzz – and the staff couldn't be more helpful.

Meals	Lunch & dinner £8.50-£15.95.
Closed	Open all day.
Directions	Leave Mold on A5119, turn left to the theatre, pub on left.

Andrew Grant
Glasfryn
Raikes Lane, Sychdyn,
Mold CH7 6LR

Tel +44 (0)1352 750500
Web www.glasfryn-mold.co.uk

Entry 716 Map 7

Flintshire

Stables Bar

Sychdyn

The approach towards Soughton Hall, a former Bishop's Palace, is worth the visit alone. The listed stables to one side have been startlingly transformed but preserve the memory of the racing occupants; now the cobbles are varnished and carry oriental rugs, the huge old blacksmith's bellows have become a fireside table, and a Beecher's Brook of a bar is fronted with metal bar stools. Honey Pot and Wizard's Wonder are beers not horses, and the posh pub grub flourishes local and seasonal specialities. Upstairs, through the impressive wine shop where South African bottles reign, is a restaurant with exposed brick walls under a huge raftered roof. Try pan-fried loin of venison served with crushed celeriac, crispy pancetta, and pommes Anna with a blackberry caramel. Super staff and fountain'd gardens make this a winner.

Meals	Lunch from £7.50. Dinner from £10.
Closed	Open all day.
Directions	Follow Northop sign from A55; A5119 through village; brown signs for Soughton Hall.

John & Rosemary Rodenhurst
Stables Bar
Sychdyn,
Mold CH7 6AB

Tel +44 (0)1352 840577
Web www.soughtonhall.co.uk

Entry 717 Map 7

Cross Foxes

Brithdir

Nicol and Dewi have worked wonders breathing new life into this stone built former farmhouse. A steel and glass entrance leads through to a modern bar where flagstones, exposed stonework and beams mingle with contemporary sofas, designer bar stools and sleek lighting. In summer, sup Purple Moose's Snowdonia Ale on the terrace and gaze up at lofty Cadair Idris – a giant's seat indeed. Food from the open kitchen comes with impeccable local credentials and the char-grill compliments the meats perfectly. What could be more local than Conwy mussels, leeks and cream followed by confit leg of Welsh lamb, rosemary and honey gravy, potatoes and seasonal vegetables? There are great Sunday roasts too, light bites, and afternoon teas. Upstairs the comfort factor scales new heights as natural stone, beams and antiques blend with a crisp modernity; there are beds for dreaming in and mountain views through windows. Gorgeous bathrooms, with Thierry Mugler lotions and thick robes, soothe those who have stretched their muscles in the surrounding hills. A 15-minute drive brings you to delightful Barmouth and the coast.

Price	£90-£135.
Rooms	6: 2 doubles, 2 twins/doubles, 2 suites.
Meals	Lunch from £4.95. Dinner & bar meals from £9.95. Sunday lunch, 2 courses, £12.95.
Closed	Open all day.
Directions	See website.

SPECIAL AWARD
see pages 14 - 15

Pub with rooms

Nicol Gwynne
Cross Foxes
Brithdir,
Dolgellau LL40 2SG
Tel +44 (0)1341 421001
Web www.crossfoxes.co.uk

Newbridge On Usk

Tredunnock

As darkness falls, the old stone bridge is floodlit, its arches reflected in the waters of the Usk. The setting is seductive, the garden runs down to the river bank, salmon leap in the eddying river outside and the views from the window are stunning. This is what a gastropub should be; warm, inviting and beautifully turned out. In several rooms on several levels, pots of flowers or collections of squashes reflect the seasons, big leather sofas invite you to sit, and the interior reveals the naked beauty of floorboards and beams. You don't have to eat here but you should and the set lunch is a steal. Ingredients are sourced from around the UK and with care; try woodland mushroom and white truffle risotto, Brecon venison wrapped in smoked bacon, a wicked sticky toffee pudding. Groups can sit down to an indulgent feasting menu in an atmospheric wine store. Avoid the dark, windy roads and stay in one of the six inviting purpose-built rooms set away from the pub; rustically styled with solid oak furniture and heavenly bathrooms. Go up a level for a four-poster and a view.

Price	£94-£135.
Rooms	6: 5 doubles, 1 four-poster.
Meals	Set lunch, 2 courses, £19.95. Dinner, 3 courses, from £30.
Closed	Open all day.
Directions	From Usk A449 towards Caerleon; 2 miles after Llangibby, left for Tredunnock; thro' village, down hill; inn beside river.

James Lewis
Newbridge On Usk
Tredunnock,
Usk NP15 1LY
Tel +44 (0)1633 410262
Web www.newbridgeonusk.co.uk

The Hardwick

Abergavenny

After tuning his skills in the kitchens of Paris, St Tropez and Marco Pierre White, Stephen Terry left London to create his own special place near Abergavenny. As you might expect, the fashionably back-to-basics interior is a modest background for some seriously fine wines and some astonishingly good food. While some of the ingredients are imported from Italy, most originate from closer to home (including the Welsh beers on draught). The lengthy menu incorporates Blumenthalian marvels such as thrice-cooked chips; swoon over comforting classics like Herefordshire beef and onion suet pudding with mashed potato and winter greens, or, more exotically, local pigeon breast with chorizo, sherry vinegar and crème fraîche. A sleek stylish bar and function room have been successfully added and, in a separate annexe, eight superb rooms. Revel in designer furniture, contemporary art, king-size beds, Welsh wool throws, bathrooms with mosaics tiles and heated slate floors, and wood and granite washstands stocked with thick towels and organic aromatics. A delight from top to toe.

Price	£145-£165. Singles from £95. Half-board from £99.50 p.p.
Rooms	8: 7 doubles, 1 twin/double.
Meals	Lunch from £21.50. Dinner, 3 courses, £30-£35. Sunday lunch, 3 courses, £28.
Closed	3pm-6pm. Sun eves & Mon.
Directions	One mile south-east of Abergavenny on B4598.

Stephen & Jo Terry
The Hardwick
Raglan Road, Hardwick,
Abergavenny NP7 9AA
Tel +44 (0)1873 854220
Web www.thehardwick.co.uk

The Bell at Skenfrith

Skenfrith

The Bell stands by an ancient stone bridge in a little-known valley with hugely beautiful hills rising behind and a Norman castle paddling in the river a hundred yards from the front door. A sublime spot – and the inn is as good. It dates to the 17th century, but its crisply designed interiors ooze a cool country chic. In the locals' bar you find slate floors, open fires, plump-cushioned armchairs and polished oak. In summer, doors fly open and life decants onto the terrace at the back; priceless views of wood and hill are interrupted only by the odd chef pottering past on his way to a rather impressive kitchen garden. Stripped boards in the restaurant give an airy feel, so stop for delicious food served by young, attentive staff, perhaps roasted red pepper soup, breast of local duck, and fig tarte tatin with lemon and thyme ice cream. Finish with a fine cognac – the list is long. Bedrooms above are as you'd expect: dressed in fine fabrics, uncluttered and elegant, brimming with light, some beamed, others overlooking the river. Circular walks start from the front door and sweep you into blissful hills.

Price	£110-£170. Four-posters £195-£220. Singles from £75.
Rooms	11: 6 doubles, 2 twins, 3 four-posters.
Meals	Lunch from £14. Sunday lunch £25. Dinner, 3 courses, around £33.
Closed	Open all day. Closed Tues Nov-Mar.
Directions	From Monmouth B4233 to Rockfield; B4347 north for 5 miles; right on B4521; Skenfrith 1 mile.

William & Janet Hutchings
The Bell at Skenfrith
Skenfrith,
Abergavenny NP7 8UH
Tel +44 (0)1600 750235
Web www.skenfrith.co.uk

Hunter's Moon Inn

Llangattock Lingoed

Haydn Jones and his partner Jana run this deep-country inn just off Offa's Dyke with enthusiasm and passion. The original building, with its low ceilings and 1217-flagged floors, was constructed by stonemasons establishing a place to stay before building the neighbouring church. Book ahead; the 'table for the evening' policy ensures much care is taken with the locally sourced food. Specials may include 28-day aged beef, shank of lamb, or pork cooked in a sage, cream and apple sauce. The local and guest ales are well-kept, the wine list well chosen, there's Leffe on draught and a range of bottled ciders. In summer you sit out – under parasols overlooking the churchyard or in the beer garden – and the famous Puskins (their in-house moggy) may make an appearance. There's a drying room for walkers, too.

Meals	Lunch & dinner £8-£20.
Closed	Mon. Tues-Fri lunch, 3pm-6.30pm Sat (7pm Sun).
Directions	A465 Abergavenny to Hereford; for Skenfrith on B4521 thro' Llanvetherine. Signed left to Llangattock Lingoed.

Haydn Jones
Hunter's Moon Inn
Llangattock Lingoed,
Abergavenny NP7 8RR
Tel +44 (0)1873 821499
Web www.hunters-moon-inn.co.uk

Monmouthshire

Clytha Arms

Clytha

The inn stands on the old coaching route into border country, in gorgeous surroundings. Sit outside in fine weather and enjoy cockles, crab sandwiches, tapas and a ploughman's with three local cheeses. Inside, two bars: one with button-back sofas and low tables, the other more rustic, with high ceiling, stripped floors and bar games; both have cheery fires. The restaurant is smart and homely with marbled walls, new stone floor, and white linen tablecloths. In the kitchen is Andrew Canning, your host and cook who rustles up grilled tuna Sicilian style, herb-crusted hake, and steak and oyster pie. The monthly set menu is full of temptations such as lamb mixed grill with garlic jus and seafood stew. The wine list (11 by the glass) and the range of beers and cider are impressive, and there's homemade perry for the bibulously curious.

Meals	Lunch & dinner £14-£20.
Closed	3pm-6pm. Mon lunch. Open all day Fri-Sun.
Directions	6 miles east of Abergavenny off old Abergavenny to Raglan road.

Andrew & Beverley Canning
Clytha Arms
Clytha,
Abergavenny NP7 9BW
Tel +44 (0)1873 840206
Web www.clytha-arms.com

The Charthouse

Llanvihangel Gobion

New owner and head chef Wesley Harris has honed his culinary skills in London and Ireland as well as locally – notably at the nearby Hardwick under Stephen Terry – and is now embarking on his first solo venture. The new refurbishment is crisp and modern; smart padded oak stools front the bar and sofas and wooden chairs beg a pre-dinner drink. There are wooden floors throughout and two dining areas with stylish table sets beneath contemporary art on pale walls. Menus are a mix of individual and regional dishes using fresh and seasonal ingredients, many of which are locally sourced; try fillet of wild sea bass and steamed mussels with saffron and anchovy risotto; make space for dark chocolate and granb marnier brûlée with orange shortbread. On Friday and Saturday evenings there are food-and-wine match menus using their 37 bins.

Meals	Lunch & dinner from £11.95.
Closed	Mon lunch & Sun.
Directions	Village is on B4598 between Abergavenny & Usk, just south of A40.

Wesley Harris
The Charthouse
Llanvihangel Gobion,
Abergavenny NP7 9AY

Tel	+44 (0)1873 840414
Web	www.thecharthouse-abergavenny.co.uk

Entry 724 Map 7

Monmouthshire

Raglan Arms

Llandenny

An effortless combination of village local and excellent place to eat. In a bright, spacious bar with slate underfoot, anticipation mounts as you peruse the menu from leather sofas arranged around a log fire. The landlord Giles prepares fairly priced dishes showcasing produce from the area. Savour chicken liver and pistachio parfait, brill with linguini, local samphire, mussels and chilli, or an upmarket open sandwich: slow-roasted shoulder of Gloucester Old Spot with apple sauce. To finish: pear and almond tart, a selection of cheeses. You can eat al fresco on the smart raised deck area, replete with planters and parasols, when the sun shines. Butty Bach is the only real ale; if this doesn't appeal, console yourself with the well-chosen modern wine list. It's worth the small detour to get here.

Meals	Lunch £6-£12. Dinner £10-£19. Sunday lunch, 3 courses, £22.
Closed	3pm-6pm. Sun eves & Mon.
Directions	In the centre of Llandenny.

Giles Cunliffe
Raglan Arms
Llandenny,
Usk NP15 1DL

Tel	+44 (0)1291 690800
Web	www.theraglanarms.co.uk

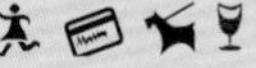

Entry 725 Map 7

Stackpole Inn
Stackpole

In the lovely Stackpole National Park, a jolly, thriving, dining pub with owners who are infectiously enthusiastic and a chef with great local food connections: as much as possible is Welsh and all is cooked from scratch. Ramble through several rustic rooms with a mix of exposed beams and stonework, carpets and slate floors, all warmed with wood-burners, freshly painted, softly lit and cosy. Daily specials (fresh sea bass, Welsh Black beef) compete with a sensibly priced menu: try Welsh blue cheese pots with crusty bread and local pork in an apple and cider cream sauce. There are several good single-malt whiskies to choose from, wine is plentiful by the glass and real ales include Rev James and Double Dragon. Bedrooms, in a separate building, are light, airy, beachy, with a wonderfully fresh feel; family rooms are excellent value. This is perfect for walking the coastal path, climbing cliff and rock faces, fishing from beach or boat, surfing those tricky beaches; each room has a locker downstairs for outdoor equipment and there's a cycle rack.

Price	£90. Singles from £60.
Rooms	4: 2 twins/doubles, 2 family rooms.
Meals	Lunch from £5. Dinner, 3 courses, £25-£30 (not Sun Oct-Mar). Sunday lunch, 3 courses, 17.95.
Closed	3pm-6pm & Sun eves in winter. Open all day Sat & Sun in summer.
Directions	B4319 south of Pembroke for 3 miles, then left for Stackpole. Through Stackpole Cheriton, up hill, right at T-junction. On right.

Gary & Becky Evans
Stackpole Inn
Stackpole,
Pembroke SA71 5DF

Tel	+44 (0)1646 672324
Web	www.stackpoleinn.co.uk

The Old Point House Inn

Angle

Lonely, windswept, so close to the sea they're cut off at spring tide. Weary fishermen have beaten a path to the old inn's door for centuries; part-built with shipwreck timbers, it started life as a bakehouse for the ships' biscuits. The tiny, low-beamed bar, its bare walls papered with old navigation charts, is utterly authentic, the restaurant is cosy by night, and in fine weather you may sit out and devour vast prawn sandwiches. Everyone is welcome here, from weathered regulars meeting over pints of Felinfoel to families in for Sunday lunch. Naturally, menus favours fish, with local Milford cod, sea bass, and a delicious, peppery fish chowder chalked up on the board. Other crowd-pleasers include a pint of prawns and rib-eye steak with red wine sauce with piles of chips.

Meals	Lunch & dinner £4.50-£12.75.
Closed	3pm-6pm. Closed Tues in winter. Open all day in summer.
Directions	From Pembroke follow signs for Angle. There, from Lifeboat Trust, cross beach to pub.

John Noble
The Old Point House Inn
Angle Village, Angle,
Pembroke SA71 5AS
Tel +44 (0)1646 641205

Entry 727 Map 6

Pembrokeshire

The Swan Inn

Little Haven

Little Haven is jumbled into the seaward end of a narrow valley with glorious views across St Bride's Bay… trek up the cobbled path to reach the lovely old Swan, whose fabric and fortunes have been restored by Paul Morris. Original features abound in the uncluttered but snug side room and warm blue-painted dining room; imagine bare boards and stone, simple wooden furnishings and glowing stoves for wild winter days. Equally warming is the delicious food: at lunch, homemade sodabread topped with smoked salmon or traditional Welsh cawl with local Caerfai cheese; in the evening, pan fried scallops with chorizo, whole roasted sea bass with caper butter and samphire. For summer there's a broad wall to lounge on and a tiny terrace, so settle in for the day with a foaming pint of Bass and enjoy the views – they're stupendous.

Meals	Lunch from £5.50. Dinner from £11.50.
Closed	Open all day.
Directions	By the beach in the village centre.

Paul & Tracey Morris
The Swan Inn
Point Road, Little Haven,
Haverfordwest SA62 3UL
Tel +44 (0)1437 781880
Web www.theswanlittlehaven.co.uk

Entry 728 Map 6

The Sloop

Porthgain

Perfectly in keeping with its seawashed setting, The Sloop has been welcoming fisherfolk since 1743. The village remains a fishing harbour – the landlord catches his own lobster, mackerel and crab and dives for scallops – but, until the Thirties, Porthgain was more famous for bricks and granite. Weatherbeaten on the outside, with a little seating area at the front, the old Sloop is surprisingly cosy within. Expect bare beams, some bare boards, a happy mêlée of furniture, a canoe suspended from the ceiling and a board announcing daily specials. Tuck into homemade mackerel pâté, lobster thermidor or Welsh Black steak; breakfast too (open to all) sounds a treat. Holidaymakers descend in summer but the rest of the year this is a community pub, with a proper games room and real fires.

Meals	Lunch & dinner £5.35-£18.
Closed	Open all day.
Directions	Village signed off A487 at Croesgoch between Fishguard & St Davids.

Matthew Blakiston
The Sloop
Porthgain,
Haverfordwest SA62 5BN

Tel +44 (0)1348 831449
Web www.sloop.co.uk

Entry 729 Map 6

Pembrokeshire

Dyffryn Arms

Pontfaen

Miss the small sign peeping out of Bessie's well-tended garden and you'll miss the pub – which would be a shame, because it's a treasure. Bessie has been here half a century and nothing has changed in that time, including the outside loos. A trooper possessed of a dry wit she shows no sign of tiring, keeps the place spotless and serves from a hatch in the wall seven days a week. The bar has the proportions of a domestic front room so you'll fall into easy conversation with the locals: farmers, hunters and the like. Old quarry tiles on the floor, fresh flowers on the window sill, peanuts, crisps and Bass from the barrel – it's perfect. To the left of the pub is a garden with a bench under Bessie's washing line from which you may drink in the peace and the view: of the verdant little valley below, threaded by a silver river.

Meals	No food served.
Closed	Open all day.
Directions	Pontfaen is on the Gwaun Valley road off the B4313 east of Fishguard, second on left.

Bessie Davies
Dyffryn Arms
Cwm Gwaun,
Pontfaen,
Fishguard SA65 9SG

Tel +44 (0)1348 881305

Entry 730 Map 6

Tafarn Sinc

Rosebush

The highest pub in Pembrokeshire is the quirkiest pub in the world – a corrugated crimson shed. It was speedily erected in 1876 as a hotel on the GWR railway; now this huge zinc building with a panorama of the Preseli Hills oversees a tiny railway platform complete with mannequin-travellers and a Victorian pram. It is beautifully tended outside and in, with a profusion of planters and picnic sets outside and an arresting Alpine-panelled bar within. Hams and lamps hang from the ceiling, there's sawdust on the floors and two big wood-burners that belch out heat. It's warm and welcoming and full of merry walkers. Hafwen the perfect landlady, and husband Brian, oversee the cosy constant buzz and serve a solidly traditional menu (Preseli lamb burgers, faggots with onion gravy), and their own excellent beer. No further introduction is needed – just a visit.

Meals	Lunch & dinner £9.80-£16.50. Sunday lunch, 3 courses, £12.95.
Closed	Open all day. Closed Mon in winter.
Directions	Rosebush is on the B4329 Haverfordwest to Cardigan road.

Brian & Hafwen Davies
Tafarn Sinc
Rosebush,
Clynderwen SA66 7QT
Tel +44 (0)1437 532214
Web www.tafarnsinc.com

Pembrokeshire

Nag's Head Inn

Abercych

Behind the vibrant orange exterior is a feast of bare wood and stone. The lighting is soft and warm, there's a rustic chicken-wire sideboard crammed with old beer bottles, a glass cabinet displaying the famous 'rat' of Abercych (a stuffed coypu) and a photo of old Emrys, the treasured regular after whom the home-brewed beer is named. The Nag's Head has a simple, tasteful charm, is full of old tales, curios and quirkery and serves the best kind of hearty pub food, from whitebait and fresh soups to steak and kidney pudding, treacle tart, and delicious Sunday roasts. Come with the family and explore the pushchair-friendly Clynfyw sculpture trail – it starts from here. There's a play area too, in the long, lovely riverside garden. By a bridge on the river bank, at the bottom of a steep hill, the setting alone is worth the trip.

Meals	Lunch & dinner £8-£15. Sunday lunch, 3 course, £13.95.
Closed	3pm-6pm. Open all day Sun.
Directions	Off A4332 between Cenarth & Boncath.

Sam Jamieson
Nag's Head Inn
Abercych,
Boncath SA37 0HJ
Tel +44 (0)1239 841200

The Felin Fach Griffin

Felin Fach

It's quirky, homespun, utterly intoxicating and thrives on a mix of relaxed informality and colourful style. The timber-framed bar resembles the sitting room of a small hip country house, with sofas in front of a fire that burns on both sides and backgammon waiting to be played. Painted stone walls throughout come in blocks of colour. An open-plan feel sweeps you through to the restaurant, where stock pots simmer on an Aga; try hake fillet with pernod cream, pheasant rillette, Eve's pudding with cinnamon custard, all of it delicious. Bedrooms above are warmly simple with comfy beds wrapped in crisp linen, making this a must for those in search of a welcoming billet close to the mountains. There are framed photographs on the walls, the odd piece of mahogany furniture, good books, no TVs (unless you ask). Breakfast is served in the dining room; wallow with the papers and make your toast on the Aga. A road passes outside, quietly at night, lanes lead into the hills, and a small organic kitchen garden provides much for the table. The Beacons are close, so walk, ride, bike, canoe – or head to Hay for books galore.

Price	£115-£155. Singles from £80. Half-board from £82.50 p.p.
Rooms	7: 2 doubles, 2 twins/doubles, 3 four-posters.
Meals	Lunch from £18.50. Dinner £27.50. Sunday lunch, 3 courses, £23.50
Closed	Open all day.
Directions	From Brecon A470 north to Felin Fach (4.5 miles). On left.

Charles & Edmund Inkin, Julie Bell
The Felin Fach Griffin
Felin Fach,
Brecon LD3 0UB
Tel +44 (0)1874 620111
Web www.felinfachgriffin.co.uk

The White Swan

Llanfrynach

The front resembles the row of cottages this once was but the cavernous interior has been remodelled and its central bar is a split-level zone, making bar staff appear unnaturally tall as they serve Brains Bitter and other fine ales. The specials board majors in fish, so there could be bouillabaisse with aïoli and sea bass with tomato and artichoke mash – alongside confit shoulder and best end of local mutton with roasted shallots. The restaurant menu may include Hereford beef, Brecon lamb, local pheasant; the cheeses are Welsh and the ice creams and puddings homemade. There are farmhouse tables, leather sofas, big wood-burners and a trellised patio at the back – gorgeous in summer. You're spoilt for walks here, so stride off into the Brecon Beacons for the day. Or potter along the towpath of the Monmouthshire & Brecon canal.

Meals	Lunch & dinner £10.95-£17.95.
Closed	3pm-6.30pm. Mon.
Directions	Signed from A40 3 miles east of Brecon on Crickhowell road.

Richard Griffiths
The White Swan
Llanfrynach,
Brecon LD3 7BZ

Tel +44 (0)1874 665276
Web www.the-white-swan.com

Entry 734 Map 7

Powys

Nantyffin Cider Mill Inn

Crickhowell

Diners pour in here for menus that spotlight pork, lamb, duck, guinea fowl, beef – exuberantly casseroled in farmhouse cider. A network of small suppliers provides the rest, while autumn brings mushrooms and game from a nearby estate. It started life in the 15th century as a drovers' inn and an old cider press occupies one end of the impressive, high-raftered restaurant in the old mill room. You can also sit in one of two intimate bars and choose from a bar menu and a specials board that is chalked up daily. Expect country cooking concocted with minimum fuss and maximum flavour – lamb with colcannon mash and rosemary garlic sauce, fish casserole – plus ales and ciders on tap, delicious wines by the glass, hot punch in winter and luscious lemonade in summer.

Meals	Lunch from £9.50. Bar meals from £6.95. Dinner from £10.95. Sunday lunch, 3 courses, £20.50. Not Sunday eve (October-March).
Closed	3pm-6pm (7pm Sun). Sun eves in winter & all day Mon (except bank hols).
Directions	1 mile outside Crickhowell on the A40 to Brecon, at junc. with A479.

Vic, Ann & Sharon Williams
Nantyffin Cider Mill Inn
Brecon Road,
Crickhowell NP8 1SG

Tel +44 (0)1873 810775
Web www.cidermill.co.uk

Entry 735 Map 7

Bear Hotel

Crickhowell

Viewed from the square of this small market town, the 15th-century frontage of the old coaching inn looks modest. Behind the cobbles and the summer flowers, it is a warren of surprises and mild eccentricity – bars and brasserie at the front, nooks and crannies carved at the back – behind which is the family- and dog-friendly garden. The beamy lounge has parquet, plush seating and a mighty fire; settle in and savour their good beers, wines, whiskies and ports. There are two dining areas where at night you can feast on Welsh Black beef, Usk salmon, Brecon venison and locally grown seasonal vegetables and regional farmhouse cheeses. Homemade ice creams, mousses and puddings are equally sumptuous. We've never seen the place empty and Mrs Hindmarsh is still firmly in charge of an operation that rarely comes off the rails.

Meals	Lunch & dinner £5.95-£20.
Closed	3pm-6pm (7pm Sun).
Directions	In centre of Crickhowell, on A40 between Abergavenny & Brecon.

Judy Hindmarsh
Bear Hotel
High Street,
Crickhowell NP8 1BW

Tel +44 (0)1873 810408
Web www.bearhotel.co.uk

Entry 736 Map 7

The Harp

Old Radnor

Chris Ireland and Angela Lyne have recently taken over this ancient Welsh longhouse tucked up a dead-end lane near the parish church and there are no plans to change this deep-country gem. The wonderful interior is spick-and-span timeless: 14th-century slate flooring in the bar, tongue-and-groove in a tiny room that seats a dozen diners, crannies crammed with memorabilia, an ancient curved settle, an antique reader's chair, two fires and a happy crowd. Enjoy a pint of Wye Valley or Three Tuns bitter with a Welsh Black rump steak with chips and roasted root vegetables, or sea bass with salsa verde. Or take a ploughman's to a seat under the sycamore and gaze upon the spectacular Radnor Valley for total tranquillity. Life in this tiny village, like its glorious pub, remains delightfully unchanged.

Meals	Lunch from £5. Dinner from £10. Sunday lunch, 3 courses, from £17. Not Monday or Tuesday-Friday lunch.
Closed	Tues-Fri lunch. 3pm-6pm Sat & Sun & Mon all day.
Directions	From Kington A44 towards Rhyader; after 3 miles left for Old Radnor (follow brown signs).

Chris Ireland & Angela Lyne
The Harp
Old Radnor,
Presteigne LD8 2RH

Tel +44 (0)1544 350655
Web www.harpinnradnor.co.uk

Entry 737 Map 7

The Talkhouse

Pontdolgoch

What was once a typical pub now serves 'niche boutique' wines. Stephen and Jacqueline have a winning formula in their 17th-century drovers' rest, combining attentive service with marvellous food. The first room you come into is a sitting room with comfy armchairs and sofa – just the place for pre-lunch drinks or after-dinner coffee. The bar has beams, log fire and sumptuous sofas; the claret-and-cream dining room has French windows that open to the garden in summer: dine outside. Classical, seasonal cooking – the lightest sweet potato and butternut soup; beef fillet with steak and kidney pudding and horseradish rösti; delicately cooked Welsh lamb – is a treat, the daily changing menu using the finest local produce. A small, perfect find in the rolling wilderness of mid-Wales. Booking is essential.

Meals	Lunch & dinner £11.95-£19.95.
Closed	Tues-Sat lunch. Sun eves & Mon all day.
Directions	On A470 1 mile west of Caersws & 5 miles from Newtown.

Stephen & Jacqueline Garratt
The Talkhouse
Pontdolgoch,
Caersws SY17 5JE
Tel +44 (0)1686 688919
Web www.talkhouse.co.uk

Entry 738 Map 7

Powys

Wynnstay Hotel

Machynlleth

In the quaint first capital of Wales, you'll be charmed to discover this rambling old coaching inn. It's rather more hotel than pub, but there's a cracking bar with traditional oak floors, low beams, scrubbed tables and candlelight. Bag a seat by the log fire in winter and peruse Gareth Johns's menus over a pint of fine Welsh ale. He applies his skills to fine local produce: Conwy mussels, Borth lobster, salmon and sewin from the river Dyfi, Welsh Black beef and lamb from the valley. Salt duck terrine with homemade chutney may precede hake with roasted vegetables and herb oil, or rib-eye of beef with chips; finish with Welsh cheeses. There are some wonderful wines from small producers and, surprisingly, a traditional pizzeria at the back. Walk off any excess with a glorious countryside stroll.

Meals	Lunch £7.95-£15.95. Dinner from £11.95. Sunday lunch, 3 courses, £16.50.
Closed	2.30pm-6pm (bar only).
Directions	In the centre of Machynlleth. Car park via Bank Lane.

Gareth & Paul Johns
Wynnstay Hotel
Heol Maengwyn,
Machynlleth SY20 8AE
Tel +44 (0)1654 702941
Web www.wynnstay-hotel.com

Entry 739 Map 7

The Brigands Inn

Mallwyd

The Cambrian Mountains loom like vast waves over the Dovey valley and this big old coaching inn on an ancient drovers' path has been offering sustenance to travellers since the 15th century. The recent renovation has retained the integrity of the rambling building and as you step in to the big oak bar with its polished flagstones and waxed beams you feel that you've entered a well-run ship. Food is a mix of contemporary and classic Welsh cuisine. Best end of local Welsh lamb with baby veg, fondant potato and redcurrant jus stand alongside pan-fried fillet of bream with ratatouille, a sweet red pepper dressing and baby clams; make your choice as you sip a pint of Clogwyn Gold or Rev James. There's also a pretty view-filled garden, and a sofa'd snug in which to peruse the (rather tempting) wines.

Meals	Lunch & dinner £8.50-£16.50.
Closed	Open all day.
Directions	On r'bout where A470 meets A458, 10 miles east of Dolgellau.

Dawn Davies
The Brigands Inn
Mallwyd,
Machynlleth SY20 9HJ

Tel +44 (0)1650 511999
Web www.brigandsinn.com

Entry 740 Map 7

Pen y Cae Inn

Pen-y-Cae

Everything about the Pen y Cae is pristine, from the multi-levelled garden at the back to the claret leather sofas and wood-burner in the bar. They've even created a new upper floor, reached by a wooden staircase, supported by chunky beams. It's an exceptionally lovely interior, the best of old and new, and you feast under rafters. French windows open to the Brecon Beacons in summer, informed staff are delightful and there's food to match, from classic pub grub at lunch to liver with crispy pancetta on creamed potatoes at dinner. And local Welsh Black rib-eye steak with dauphinoise potatoes (fabulous), and rump of Breconshire lamb with chive mash and roasted vegetables (delicious). Wash it all down with a bottled beer from Tomos Watkin, Wales's fastest growing brewery, and trundle off home – charmed, well-fed and happy.

Meals	Lunch, bar meals & dinner £4.95. Sunday lunch from £9.95.
Closed	3pm-6pm. Sun eves & Mon. Open all day Sat.
Directions	On A4067 north of Abercraf, midway between Brecon & Swansea; near Dan-Yr-Ogof show caves.

Anthony Christopher
Pen y Cae Inn
Brecon Road, Pen-y-Cae,
Swansea SA9 1FA

Tel +44 (0)1639 730100
Web www.pen-y-caeinn.com

Entry 741 Map 7

The Blue Anchor

East Aberthaw

Inglenooks and open log fires, stories of smugglers and derring-do – it's rich in atmosphere. Inside is a warm warren of little rooms and doorways less than five feet high. The Colemans have nurtured this 700-year-old place for 66 years and restored the pub to its former glory following a fire in 2004. Dine in winter on pheasant from their local shoot, in summer on sewin from Swansea Bay and salads from the vegetable garden. Pop in for a bowl of mussels and a moreish pint of Wye Valley – or dip into the chef's selection of regional cheeses. Under the eaves of a classic thatched roof, the restaurant delivers hake with chorizo and roasted red pepper risotto, duck with savoy cabbage, pancetta and redcurrant jus, lemon and sultana cheesecake, Sunday roasts (do book). It's pubby, good looking and wonderful at doing what it knows best.

Meals	Lunch £8.95-£10.95. Dinner £12.50-£17.85.
Closed	Open all day.
Directions	2 miles west of Cardiff Airport just off B4265.

Jeremy Coleman
The Blue Anchor
East Aberthaw,
Barry CF62 3DD

Tel +44 (0)1446 750329
Web www.blueanchoraberthaw.com

Entry 742 Map 2

Vale of Glamorgan

Plough & Harrow

Monknash

Originally part of a monastic grange, and well off the beaten track, today's Plough & Harrow is hugely convivial. Ancient, low white walls lead you to the front door, then you dip into two dim-lit, low-ceilinged, character-oozing rooms, their rustic fireplaces filled with church candles or crackling logs. There are cheerful yellow walls, original floors, church pews, smiling staff and a small bar area with a big array of handpumps – up to 11 ales are served. Traditionalists will be relieved to see gammon and chips on the lunch menu while the more adventurous may plump for summer crab salad, moules marinière and roast belly pork with mustard mash and sweet cider sauce. A brilliant atmosphere, a great find, the kind of pub you wish was your local – and it is as friendly to single drinkers as it is to groups.

Meals	Lunch & dinner £6.95-£13.95.
Closed	Open all day.
Directions	Village signed off B4265, between St Brides Major & Llantwit Major, 6 miles south west of Cowbridge.

Janine Gorman
Plough & Harrow
Monknash,
Cowbridge CF71 7QQ

Tel +44 (0)1656 890209
Web www.theploughmonknash.com

Entry 743 Map 2

The Cross Foxes

Erbistock

It's set on a travellers' crossroads, as the highway crosses the waters of the Dee and both man and fish move in either direction, depending on the season. Rest on the terrace with a pint of Marston's Burton Bitter or Ringwood's Huffkin and soak up the views from this timeless spot. Inside, a log fire throws light on a well-carved bar front, polished wood tables and quarry tiles, while on the shelves glows one of the best whisky and armagnac collections for many a mile: cockle-warming stuff. The big blackboard at the end of the bar is scrawled with good things to eat, from Cumberland sausage with black pudding mash and onion gravy to venison and pheasant meat loaf with red cabbage and juniper sauce. Settle into the wood-panelled area, the fireside snug or the conservatory, and enjoy a genuine classic.

Sunday roasts account for one-fifth of pub meals. At the Three Mariners in Kent and the Crooked Well in Camberwell the entire roast is ferried to your table – enjoy!

Meals	Lunch & dinner £9.50-£16.95. Bar meals from £4.75.
Closed	Open all day.
Directions	On A528 beside Overton Bridge, 7 miles south of Wrexham.

Ian Pritchard-Jones
The Cross Foxes
Erbistock, Wrexham LL13 0DR

Tel +44 (0)1978 780380
Web www.crossfoxes-erbistock.co.uk

England

Bath & N.E. Somerset

745 Gascoyne Place 1 Sawclose, Bath BA1 1EY +44 (0)1225 445854

Bang opposite the Theatre Royal, Gascoyne Place, steeped in history, is now a thoroughly contemporary place. Food is modern, British and based around produce from local farms – and there are 90 wines to have fun with! Map: 3

746 The Salamander 3 John Street, Bath BA1 2JL +44 (0)1225 428889

A fine Bath Ales pub without the spittle. The main bar, like a Victorian apothecary, is stacked with bottles on a Welsh dresser and hand pumps gleam under glass fluted lights. Head upstairs for traditional dishes from an open kitchen. Map: 3

747 The Chequers 50 River Street, Bath BA1 2QA +44 (0)1225 360017

The team behind the thriving Marlborough Tavern took this on in 2010 and haven't looked back. Call in for a Bath-central pint of Butcombe and a classic pub dish in the bar; there's more serious dining upstairs. Reports welcome. Map: 3

748 Wheelwrights Arms Church Lane, Monkton Combe, Bath BA2 7HB +44 (0)1225 722287

Grab the table in the wonderful snug or plonk yourself by the fire and tuck into delicious food – or take a pint and a paper to the garden. A two-mile walk from Bath, near the canal. Map: 3

749 The Hop Pole 7 Albion Buildings, Upper Bristol Road, Bath BA1 3AR +44 (0)1225 446327

Gently sophisticated boozer with a polished feel, a verdant summer courtyard and a modern British menu. An easy pedal from the Bristol-Bath cycle path for tip-top Bath ales. Map: 3

Berkshire

750 The Dundas Arms 53 Station Road, Kintbury RG17 9UT +44 (0)1488 658263

At the junction of the Kennet river and canal, dabbling ducks entertain diners while narrowboats glide by and summer crowds fill the patio. New owners in early 2012 so expect big changes to this traditional inn, once family-owned for 40 years. Map: 3

Brighton & Hove

751 The Dorset 28 North Road, Brighton BN1 1YB +44 (0)1273 605423

A friendly, kooky, heart-of-Brighton pub ten minutes from the pier in the pedestrianised North Laines. Bare boards, scrubbed tables, eclectic music, decent ales and very tasty, very well-priced food. On the pavement or inside, a lovely vibe. Map: 4

752 The Preston Park Tavern 88 Havelock Road, Brighton BN1 6GF +44 (0)1273 542271

The locals of Preston must love this spruced-up boozer. More gastro than pub, under than same ownership as the nearby Chimney House, the open kitchen delivers no-nonsense food prepared from very fine produce. Map: 4

Bristol

753 Old Duke 45 King Street, Bristol BS1 4ER +44 (0)117 9277137

There's a New Orleans speakeasy, British-pub feel to this shrine to jazz and blues not far from Bristol Old Vic. Music is served up nightly along with the occasional curry or stew. Map: 3

754 The King's Head 60 Victoria Street, Bristol BS1 6DE +44 (0)117 9277860
In Bristol's heart, untouched Victorian inside, 1660 out. A rare period narrow bar and an entirely panelled rear snug, a splendid mirrored back bar, photos of old Bristol and gallons of Smiles. Map: 3

755 The Merchants Arms 5 Merchants Rd, Hotwells, Bristol BS8 4PZ +44 (0)117 9073047
Bare-boarded and real, done-up without a whiff of modern pretension. Simple, friendly, civilised and Bath Ales-owned, with excellent beers and good snacks. Map: 3

756 The Albion Boyces Avenue, Clifton, Bristol BS8 4AA +44 (0)117 9733522
Clifton village is Georgian to the core. Inside, a long stylish bar serving Butcombe and monthly guest ales, a winter log fire and a discreet wooden staircase leading to a restaurant that feels like a private room. Map: 3

757 White Hart Littleton-on-Severn, Bristol BS35 1NR +44 (0)1454 412275
Hops hang from old beams; chairs, tables and a cushioned settle are scattered across flagged floors; fires blaze in grand fireplaces in this 16th-century former farmhouse. Lovely garden, peaceful views, Youngs beers and traditional pub food complete the picture. Map: 3

Buckinghamshire

758 The Swan 2 Wavendon Road, Salford, Milton Keynes MK17 8BD +44 (0)1908 281008
Innovative Peach Pubs have revamped this ordinary village boozer with style and panache; escape the M1 for great antipasti nibbles and enjoyable modern pub food, served all day. Map: 9

Cambridgeshire

759 Cambridge Blue 85 Gwydir Street, Cambridge CB1 2LG +44 (0)1223 471680
Away from the centre, this simple local has a warm atmosphere, stacks of breweriana and a large garden. A wide choice of ales, ciders and world beers, and straightforward pub grub. Map: 9

760 The Old Bridge Hotel 1 High Street, Huntingdon PE29 3TQ +44 (0)1480 424300
A smart hotel with battalions of devoted locals who come for the informal pubby bar (good local ales), the food (delicious), the wines (exceptional) and the hugely comfortable interiors. Map: 9

Cheshire

761 The Old Harp 19 Quayside, Little Neston, Neston CH64 0TB +44 (0)1513 366980
Small and unassuming in a stunning spot on the edge of the Dee Marshes. Watch marsh harriers or little egrets as you down real ales and gaze over the estuary to North Wales. Map: 7

762 Old Harkers Arms Russell Street, Chester CH3 5AL +44 (0)1244 344525
A buzzy atmosphere and a great range of microbrewery ales at this beautifully converted warehouse down by the canal. Run by Brunning & Price pubs, so expect good modern pub food. Map: 7

763 The Boot Inn Boothsdale, Willington, Tarporley CW6 0NH +44 (0)1829 751375
A prettily ivy-strewn row of country cottages turned pub, with views towards the Welsh Hills and south over the Cheshire Plain. Old quarry tiles, some panelling, characterful beams and a log-burning stove pull in the walkers and talkers for popular food and local Weetwood Ales. Map: 7

764 Dusty Miller Cholmondeley Rd, Wrenbury, Nantwich CW5 8HG +44 (0)1270 780537
Hugely popular pub in a beautifully converted watermill beside the Shropshire Union Canal. Local food is ever-present on the imaginative menus. Super alfresco areas. Map: 7

765 The Buffet Bar Stalybridge Station, Rassbottom Street, Stalybridge SK15 1RF +44 (0)1613 030007
Only a handful of these charming Victorian establishments survive – this extraordinary, narrow little bar is an integral part of the busy Stalybridge Station. Renowned for its choice of real ale, pies and puddings. Map: 12

Cornwall

766 The Maltsters Arms Chaple Amble, Wadebridge PL27 6EU +44 (0)1208 812473
Away from the busy beaches around Rock is this inviting 16th-century pub, with fun and funky eating areas and a good all-round menu including excellent fresh-fish specials. Reports please. Map: 1

767 The Cornish Arms Churchtown, St Merryn, Padstow PL28 8ND +44 (0)1841 520288
Local lad Rick Stein has added a pub to his eaterie empire. The ancient St Austell boozer remains a traditional village local with slate floors, log fires and classic pub food (scampi and chips, steak and Tribute pie) cooked from the best local produce. Map: 1

768 The Dock Inn 17 Quay Street, Penzance TR18 4BD +44 (0)1736 362833
A cosy little inn down by the water where good pub food flies from the kitchen: meat from Cornwall and fish from the Newlyn boats. The ferry for the Scillies leaves from across the road. Map: 1

769 Cadgwith Cove Inn Cadgwith, Ruan Minor, Helston TR12 7JX +44 (0)1326 290513
Smack on the coastal path, in a thatched fishing hamlet, sits this old smugglers' inn. Decked with seafaring mementos, there's a fishy menu and five ales on tap. Views reach across the cove from the sun-trap terrace. Map: 1

770 Seven Stars The Moor, Falmouth TR11 3QA +44 (0)1326 312111
Unchanging, unspoilt and rather quirky town-centre pub with splendid narrow tap room, racked Sharp's and Skinner's ales and snug back bar. Map: 1

771 The Rashleigh Inn Polkerris, St Austell PL24 2TL +44 (0)1726 813991
A pub *on* the beach, in a tiny cove! The old coastguard station is cosy in winter, unbeatable in summer, so down a pint of real ale and watch the sun set across St Austell Bay. Map: 1

772 The Blue Peter Quay Road, Polperro, Looe PL13 2QZ +44 (0)1503 272743
Unspoilt little fishing pub built into the cliffside by Polperro's harbour. Dark and cosy wood-floored bar with hidden corners, nautical artefacts, tip-top Cornish ales, and sea views. Map: 1

Cumbria

773 The Cross Keys Inn Carleton, Penrith CA11 8TP +44 (0)1768 865588
Donald Newton and son Paul, owners of the successful Highland Drove in Great Salkeld, have refurbished this 16th-century roadside inn close to Penrith. It has a super terrace and fine views. Map: 11

774 The Pheasant Bassenthwaite Lake, Cockermouth CA13 9YE +44 (0)1768 776234
The wonderful snug has a ceiling coloured by 300 years of tobacco and polish, there are open fires, good bar food and cracking Jennings beers on tap. A country-cottage garden, too. Map: 11

775 The Three Shires Little Langdale, Ambleside CA13 0RU +44 (0)15394 37215
Walkers love this friendly pub – for its stunning Lakeland setting, and hearty snacks in the slate-walled public bar or carpeted lounge. Worth calling in after journeying over the high Wrynose and Hardknott passes. Map: 11

776 The Wasdale Head Inn Wasdale Head, Gosforth CA20 1EX +44 (0)19467 26229
At the head of Wasdale, in a setting of romantic grandeur – the steep slope of Scafell its dramatic backdrop – is this legendary mountain pub beloved of walkers and climbers. Refurbishment is planned under new owners. Reports please! Map: 11

777 Old Dungeon Ghyll Great Langdale, Ambleside LA22 9JY +44 (0)15394 37272
To hikers ruddy from the day's exertions, the infamous, barn-like Walkers' Bar serves decent grub, mugs of tea, and God's own beer, Yates. The atmosphere is infectious. Map: 11

778 The Sun Hotel & Inn Coniston LA21 8HQ +44 (0)15394 41248
A no-nonsense little pub at the back of an Edwardian hotel, with stone flags and walls, old settles, local ales from the cask and hearty pub food. Great views from the garden. Map: 11

779 Manor Arms The Square, Broughton-in-Furness LA20 6HY +44 (0)1229 716286
A modest 18th-century pub in Broughton's Georgian square that draws ale-lovers for pints of Yates, Copper Dragon, Roosters and more from eight handpumps. Traditional bar snacks all day. Map: 11

780 Hole in t'Wall Lowside, Bowness-on-Windermere LA23 3DH +44 (0)15394 43488
A good old-fashioned tavern, not plain but not plush, packed with tourists in season and prepared for walkers all year round. Hearty food and a flagged front terrace that's a suntrap in summer. Map: 11

781 The Watermill Inn Ings, Kendal LA8 9PY +44 (0)1539 821309
The draw of this converted old wood mill in prime Windermere country is the mind-boggling range of 16 real ales, including cracking beers brewed in the pub's own microbrewery visible from the bar. Heady farm ciders and 50 malt whiskies, too. Map: 11

Derbyshire

782 The Plough Leadmill, Hathersage, Hope Valley S32 1BA +44 (0)1433 650319
The isolated 16th-century inn, once a corn mill, stands in super gardens on the banks of the Derwent, with stunning views to rolling hills. Cosy, plush interior with old beams and log fires, and a posh printed menu with traditional food. Map: 8

783 The Samuel Fox Country Inn Bradwell, Hope Valley S33 9JT +44 (0)1433 621562
A traditional exterior hides a bistro interior with a combined restaurant and bar. Modern wicker mixes with country, Deco and foxy prints, and their own bitter from Tower Brewery. Menus promise modern and traditional dishes with the emphasis on homemade. Map: 8

784 The Barley Mow Main Street, Kirk Ireton, Ashbourne DE6 3JP +44 (0)1335 370306
In a gem of a village, a gem of a Jacobean pub. The tiled tap room floor is framed by wall benches, dotted with old stools and barrels of ale are racked behind the bar; it is austere, dimly lit, sheer delight for drinkers, ramblers and historians. Tuck into a lunchtime cob. Map: 8

Devon

785 Rose & Crown Market Street, Yealmpton, Plymouth PL8 2EB +44 (0)1752 880223
Delicious smells tempt you the moment you enter this big, open-plan pub; people travel miles for the food. Traditional bar meals and roasts on Sunday complete the picture. Glorious and delicious. Map: 2

786 Fortescue Arms East Allington, Totnes TQ9 7RA +44 (0)1548 521215
A small country inn with views from the garden that climb to the church. Inside: chalkboard menus (perhaps potted Brixham crab) and open fires. The coast is close and the walking is majestic. Map: 2

787 Cricket Inn Beesands, Kingsbridge TQ7 2EN +44 (0)1548 580215
Bang on the water this inn is a blessed relief for walkers in search of sustenance. There's Otter ale or champagne by the glass, then the freshest fish on the menu: crab soup, fish pie, half a lobster. Map: 2

788 The Start Bay Inn Torcross, Kingsbridge TQ7 2TQ +44 (0)1548 580553
Packed the minute it opens (arrive late at your peril), this modest 14th-century beachside inn serves the best fresh fish and chips in Devon. Dressed crab too. Arrive hungry. Map: 2

789 The Peter Tavy Inn Peter Tavy, Tavistock PL19 9NN +44 (0)1822 810348
Atmospheric 15th-century inn on the flanks of desolate Dartmoor. Masses of charm in black beams, polished slate, long pine tables and wood-burners in huge hearths. Cracking beer and walks from the door. Map: 2

790 The Drewe Arms Drewsteignton, Devon EX6 6QN +44 (0)1647 281224
Long, low and thatched, an unpretentious and well-loved local in a pretty square by the church. Local ales still served from hatchways, and home cooking for walkers. Castle Drogo is nearby. Map: 2

791 The Turf Hotel Exminster, Exeter EX6 8EE +44 (0)1392 833128
Reached only on foot (20-min walk), by bike or by boat, a unique, rambling old pub overlooking the estuary mudflats. Bareboard bar with big bay windows for winter wader-watching and top-notch Otter Ales. Closed Dec-Feb. Map: 2

792 The Blue Ball Sandygate, Exeter EX2 7JL +44 (0)1392 873401
Handy for the motorway, the thatched, roadside inn offers a welcoming respite. Good, traditional pub food in a contemporary interior, and beams, flagstones and log fires in the rustic bar. New owners. Map: 2

793 The Fountain Head Branscombe, Seaton EX12 3BG +44 (0)1297 680359
Be charmed by big flagstones, wood-clad walls, dim-lit corners, good pub grub and village-brewed beers. No fruit machines, just local babble and possibly a snoozing dog – walking country by the sea. Map: 2

794 The Masons Arms Knowstone, South Molton EX36 4RY +44 (0)1398 341231
Arrive through fern or twisting lane to reach Mark Dodson's celebrated 13th-century pub-restaurant. Call in for a pint in the beamed, flagged bar or come for food fit for kings – classic French and British dishes cooked with flair and with prices to match. Map: 2

795 Poltimore Arms South Molton EX36 3HA +44 (0)1598 710381
An isolated old coaching inn, high on the edge of Exmoor with great views. Very rustic with flagstones, lit with a generator, it attracts farmers and huntsmen with its traditional food and ales. Map: 2

Dorset

796 The New Inn Stoke Abbott, Beaminster DT8 3JW +44 (0)1308 868333
Local chef George Marsh is cooking up a storm at this homely village pub hidden down Dorset lanes... worth finding for pints of Palmers and inventive pub cooking. Local fish, seasonal meats and game and 50 varieties of vegetables, salads and herbs harvested from the pub's kitchen garden. Map: 3

797 The Anchor Inn Seatown, Chideock, Bridport DT6 6JU +44 (0)1297 489215
A terrific coastal path watering-hole below Golden Cap. The big sun terrace and clifftop gardens overlook a pebbly beach. Open fires, pints of Palmers, crab sandwiches. Map: 3

798 The New Inn Cerne Abbas 14 Long Street, Cerne Abbas DT2 7JF +44 (0)1300 341274
Mullioned windows, open fires, Palmers ales and good food await at a handsome old coaching inn in a picture-book village deep in Dorset downland. Reopened in 2012 following refurbishment, it now has smart new bedrooms – reports welcome. Map: 3

799 Crown Inn Ibberton, Blandford Forum DT11 0EN +44 (0)1258 817448
True old Dorset local in a sleepy village under Bulbarrow Hill. Kick off your hiking boots in the lovely garden, savour local ciders and real ales, refuel on fabulous, well-priced food. Map: 3

800 Vine Inn Vine Hill, Pamphill, Wimborne BH21 4EE +44 (0)1292 882259
Former bakehouse run by the Sweatland family for generations, now owned by the National Trust. Two timeless bars, London Pride on tap and sandwiches for sustenance. Close to Kingston Lacy House. Map: 3

Essex

801 The Cricketers Clavering, Saffron Walden CB11 4QT +44 (0)1799 550442
The family home and training ground of Jamie Oliver. As such, this rambling 16th-century inn draws fans and foodies from afar and handles its glory with good humour. Booking essential. Map: 9

802 The Swan at Felsted Station Road, Felsted, Dumnow CM6 3DG +44 (0)1371 820245
An imposing Edwardian public house transformed into a sophisticated dining pub by Jono and Jane Clarke of The Compasses at Pattiswick. A well-designed interior and imaginative food. Map: 9

803 The Blue Boar Silver Street, Maldon CM9 4QE +44 (0)1621 855888
Old coaching inn, now a hotel, with a smart but pubby bar. Its own microbrewery turns out Farmers Ale, Blue Boar Bitter and Hotel Porter stout, tapped from the cask. Map: 10

Gloucestershire

804 The Eight Bells Church Street, Chipping Campden GL55 6JG +44 (0)1386 840371

Tiny Cotswold pub in popular Chipping Campden, with 14th-century beams, flagstones and priest's hole. Walkers in socks wolf down sandwiches and Hooky by the fire. Enjoyable hot dishes too, in the bar, the more formal restaurant or the sun-trap patio. Tricky parking. Map: 8

805 Woolpack Inn Slad Road, Slad, Stroud GL6 7QA +44 (0)1452 813429

Packed with rusticity and charm, a perfect pitstop for walkers, a friendly no-frills pub where the ale from the Uley brewery is as important as the 'nose-to-tail' bar menu. Tuck into the simple best – no wonder it heaves at weekends. Map: 8

806 The Red Hart Blaisdon, Gloucester GL17 0AH +44 (0)1452 830477

A lively little village pub, often packed with locals and wet walkers quaffing pints of Hooky by the fire in the stone-flagged bar. Expect a traditional feel with hop-hung beams, solid, hearty cooking, good value Sunday roasts and a character landlord. Map: 8

807 The Gumstool Inn Calcot Manor, Calcot, Tetbury GL8 8YJ +44 (0)1666 890391

Quietly civilised bar/brasserie attached to the Calcot Manor Hotel. Cosy up by the log fire in the elegant bar; take your pick of local ales, good wines and imaginative food. Westonbirt Arboretum is up the road. Map: 3

Hampshire

808 The Plough Inn Longparish, Andover SP11 6PB +44 (0)1264 720358

New owners are settling in at this long-established Test Valley local in pretty Longparish. Expect a rustic-chic makeover, local ales and promising modern pub food. Reports please. Map: 3

809 The Mayfly Chilbolton, Stockbridge SO20 6AX +44 (0)1264 860283

Unrivalled river scenes draw summer crowds to this beamed old farmhouse on the banks of the fast-flowing Test. Comfortable bar, good food, splendid riverside terrace. Arrive on foot (or bike) via the Test Way. Map: 3

810 Yew Tree Inn Hollington Cross, Highclere, Newbury RG20 9SE +44 (0)1635 253360

A contemporary and sympathetic makeover stitches the elegant dining room into the old fabric and character of this building with its inglenooks, timbers and light uncluttered walls. This is more restaurant than pub, but expect the best of British food. Map: 4

811 The Northbrook Arms East Stratton, Winchester SO21 3DU +44 (0)1962 774150

Tim Gray, landlord of the Yew Tree at Lower Wield (also in Hants), took over this classic estate village pub in 2009 and has kept things simple. Enjoy a homely, traditional feel, Hampshire ales and hearty home-cooked food. Skittle alley out back. Map: 4

812 The Plough Inn Sparsholt, Winchester SO21 2NW +44 (0)1962 776353

Walkers drop by for Wadworth ales on draught and children frolic in the flowery garden's wooden chalet and play fort. After 17 years at the helm, Richard and Kathryn continue to run this busy pub with enthusiasm and good humour. Map: 4

813 No 5 Bridge Street Bridge Street, Winchester SO23 0HN +44 (0)1962 863838
A Winchester opening from the team behind the White Star Tavern, Southampton – in a great spot close to the river Itchen, a short walk from the cathedral. Expect a vibrant, lively and informal bar, classic British food and plans for six boutique bedrooms. Reports welcome. Map: 4

814 Selborne Arms High Street, Selborne, Alton GU34 3JR +44 (0)1420 511247
In a charming village and handy for the zig-zag climb up to the Selborne Hill viewpoint . Fires, hoppy beams and hearty food that cranks up a gear in the evenings. Makes good use of local produce. Map: 4

815 The White Horse Inn Monkey Lane, Priors Dean, Petersfield GU32 1DA +44 (0)1420 588387
This isolated downland pub may be fiendish to find but it's worth the effort. Candlit Jacobean charm (log fires, old tables, ticking clocks) and a mind-boggling choice of eight real ales. Blissfully cosy in winter, and in summer you can sprawl in the garden. Map: 4

816 The Trooper Inn Froxfield, Petersfield GU32 1BD +44 (0)1730 827293
Rustic and remote downland inn with a laid-back atmosphere made up of candlelit wood-floored bars, cracking real ale and solidly good, daily changing menus. Map: 4

817 Hampshire Bowman Dundridge Lane, Bishops Waltham SO32 1GD +44 (0)1489 892940
Secreted-away country local on a winding lane. Draws an eclectic crowd for farm cider and Hampshire ales tapped from the barrel in the time-worn bar, hearty home cooking, and orchard garden. Map: 4

818 Brushmakers Arms Shoe Lane, Upham, Bishops Waltham SO32 1JJ +44 (0)1489 860231
It's tricky to find but that's half the joy. A friendly, time-worn pub where pints of beer are as important as food and namesake brushes hang from walls and beams. Food comes in hearty portions (hare in cider, fish and chips) and there's a garden out the back. Map: 4

819 The Jolly Sailor Lands End Rd, Bursledon, Southampton SO31 8DN +44 (0)23 8040 5557
Reached via 45 steps or by boat, this former shipbuilder's house overlooks the river Hamble. Watch all things nautical from the terrace and from big windows in the newly furbished bars. Map: 4

Herefordshire

820 The Cottage of Content Carey, Hereford HR2 6NG +44 (0)1432 840242
With the Wye Valley on the doorstep and miles and miles of footpaths, you are in fine walking country. The main bar oozes authenticity and the name says it all – come and settle in for a couple of hours. You'll be well cared for here. Map: 7

821 Three Tuns 4 Broad Street, Hay-on-Wye HR3 5DB +44 (0)1497 821855
Beautifully restored with slate floors, oak beams and exposed stone, following a devastating fire in 2005. Hay's oldest pub (16th-century) draws locals and tourist in for exceptional Wye Valley beers and interesting fresh food. We look forward to your reports. Map: 7

822 The Tram Eardisley, Hereford HR3 6PG +44 (0)1544 327251
Find a perfect combination of styles at this 16th-century half-timbered freehouse, where a quarry tiled and beamed bar dispenses Dorothy Goodbody and Reverend James and a large plush dining room serves delicious meals. New genial owners, a great garden and a family-friendly feel. Map: 7

823 The Boot Orleton, Ludlow SY8 4HN +44 (0)1568 780228
A 16th-century timbered pub with a rich history, once a cobbler's, a cider house and a butchers. Cracking quarry-tiled bar with vast open fire and a super garden. Map: 7

Hertfordshire

824 The Rusty Gun London Road, St Ippolyts, Hitchin SG4 7PG +44 (0)1462 432653
Rejuvenated pub with a food shop in a converted barn, run by a small innovative pub company with a passion for regional, seasonal food. Expect a colourful, funky rustic feel throughout and hearty dishes on monthly menus. Map: 9

825 The Valiant Trooper Trooper Road, Aldbury, Tring HP23 5RW +44 (0)1442 851203
Blazing log fires, old-fashioned comfort and a good garden. Serving ale since 1752, this dear little brick and tiled cottage high in the Chiltern Hills draws booted ramblers, families and diners escaping town. Map: 9

826 The Old Mill London Road, Berkhamsted HP4 2NB +44 (0)1442 879590
A beautifully restored old mill, with natural oak furnishings and deep sofas in classy rooms, and menus to match – a class act from vibrant Peach Pubs. Great canal-side terrace. Map: 9

827 The Holly Bush Potters Crouch, St Albans AL2 3NN +44 (0)1727 851792
An immaculate 17th-century country pub elegantly furnished with antiques and big oak tables candlelit at night. Fabulous Fuller's ales, straightforward food, nice garden. Map: 9

Isle of Wight

828 The Boat House Springvale Road, Isle of Wight PO34 5AW +44 (0)1983 810616
The sister pub to Martin Bullock's renowned New Inn is on the coast. Expect a contemporary beachy feel throughout, Island-brewed ales on tap, and a specials board for local fish and seafood. Map: 4

Kent

829 Spotted Dog Smarts Hill, Penshurst, Tonbridge TN11 8EP +44 (0)1892 870253
Ancient, low-beamed, panelled, nooked, crannied and rambling – everyone loves this country pub and the glorious views from its back terrace. Map: 5

830 Nevill Crest & Gun Eridge, Tunbridge Wells TN3 9JR +44 (0)1892 864209
Brunning & Price have lavished time and money on restoring and rejuvenating this 500-year-old tile-hung pub on the Eridge Estate. Their winning formula has been replicated so innovative food is served all day, alongside a raft of ales and wines and a laid-back vibe. Map: 5

831 The Great House Gills Green, Cranbrook TN18 5EJ +44 (0)1580 753119
Former Elizabethan cottages with an alluring mix of beams, furnishings and open fires in the rambling bar or cool Orangery dining room. Fresh brasserie food best enjoyed on the terrace. Map: 5

832 The Black Pig Moor Hill, Hawkhurst TN18 4PF +44 (0)1580 752306
Buoyed by the success of The Bull at Benenden, the Barron-Reids have worked their magic at this newly spruced-up local in nearby Hawkhurst. Find fat candles on scrubbed tables, ales locally brewed and delicious food, best enjoyed in the glorious garden. Map: 5

833 The Royal Oak High Street, Brookland, Romney Marsh TN29 9QR +44 (0)1797 344215
Crossing the breezy, mysterious Romney Marsh and in need of a break? Stop-off at this spick-and-span 18th-century village inn. Good ales, interesting food and a cheery welcome await – and don't miss the the historic church next door. Reports appreciated. Map: 5

834 The Bell Inn Smarden, Ashford TN27 8PW +44 (0)1233 770283
In the pretty village of Smarden, a lovely old Kentish inn – candlelit rooms with rosy brick floors ramble round the Cellar Bar. Come for heady Biddenden scrumpy and hearty homemade food, and a secluded garden where barbecues reign in summer. Map: 5

835 The Tiger Stowting, Ashford TN25 6BA +44 (0)1303 862130
Hard-to-find, civilised country pub with friendly locals, rugs on bare boards, candles on scrubbed tables, roaring winter fire, real ales and splendid live jazz on Monday evenings. Map: 5

836 The Dirty Habit The Pilgrims Way, Upper Street, Hollingbourne, Maidstone ME17 1UW +44 (0)1622 880880
The latest addition to Martial Chaussy's select Elite pubs stands beside the Pilgrim's Way below the North Downs. Crackling fires in beamed bars, scrumptious food and pints of Harvey's entice walkers and foodies. Reports welcome. Map: 5

837 The Pepperbox Inn Windmill Hill, Harrietsham, Maidstone ME17 1LP +44 (0)1622 842558
The 15th-century smugglers' haunt has views across the Kentish Weald from a glorious decked terrace. Dining areas ramble round the cosy, carpeted central bar with its sofa-fronted inglenook and a log fire; tuck into a big bowl of chilli or monkfish in garlic butter. Map: 5

838 The Anchor Inn 52 Abbey Street, Faversham ME13 7BP +44 (0)1795 533633
Thriving Shepherd Neame local run by Claire Houlihan (ex-Three Mariners at Oare). Come for pints of Spitfire, live music and hearty food – potted goose, fish stew, rib-eye steak. Map: 5

839 Shipwright's Arms Hollowshore, Faversham ME13 7TU +44 (0)1795 590088
Full of character and quirkiness, pub and boatyard are surrounded by salt marshes – a wonderful isolation. Plain and simple are the three tiny bar rooms, warmed by open fires or stoves. Beers from Kent brewers are expertly kept, basic food sustains walkers on the Saxon Shore Way. Map: 5

840 The Gate Inn Church Lane, Chislet, Canterbury CT3 4EB +44 (0)1227 860498
A charming rural local with two small, well-worn bars, old leather sofas fronting the log fire, Shepherd Neame tapped from the cask, and simple hearty food. The glorious cottage garden borders a stream. Map: 5

Lancashire

841 The Parkers Arms Newton-in-Bowland, Clitheroe BB7 3DY +44 (0)1200 446236
Travelling that scenic rollercoaster of a road (the B6478) through the Trough of Bowland just north of Clitheroe is a sturdy stone pub in a lovely spot by the river. A useful pit-stop for warming fires, Bowland ales and locally sourced food. Map: 12

Leicestershire

842 The Cow & Plough Stoughton Grange Farm, Gartree Rd, Leicester LE2 2FB +44 (0)116 2720852
In the former milking sheds of a working farm, founded in 1989 and filled with good beer and brewery memorabilia, it's a great spot for shooting lunches – and a pint of their own Steamin' Billy ale. Map: 8

London

843 Fox and Grapes 9 Camp Rd, Wimbledon Common, London SW19 4UN +44 (0)20 8619 1300
Michelin-starred chef Claude Bosi and brother Cedric took on the old-fashioned boozer in 2011. A contemporary dining pub, with a menu brimful of simple British dishes and a raft of wines by the glass, it feels like a country pub: rustic tables, real ales, Wimbledon Common outside the door. Map: 4

844 Prince of Wales 138 Upper Richmond Rd, Putney, London SW15 2SP +44 (0)20 8788 1552
Gastropub conversion of a Victorian Putney boozer that keeps its pubby feel in the small, traditional front bar: dark green walls, wooden floors, leather chesterfields, Adnams on tap. The appealing modern British menu draws a local crowd. Map: 15

845 The Fox & Hounds 66 Latchmere Rd, Battersea, London SW11 2JU +44 (0)20 7924 5483
A bright little corner pub, a foodie destination and a shrine to the golden brew. Mediterranean-style dishes flow from the open-to-view kitchen; a great atmosphere, and a garden for summer. Map: 15

846 The White Horse 1-3 Parson's Green, Fulham, London SW6 4UL +44 (0)20 7731 2183
'The Sloany Pony' may be a hotbed of Fulhamites but it's also reputed to have the best-kept beers in Europe. Comfy sofas, log fires, slatted blinds, a big terrace, and a menu that suggests the best accompanying liquor. Map: 15

847 The Atlas 16 Seagrave Road, Fulham, London SW6 1RX +44 (0)20 7385 9129
A great little place at the un-posh end of Fulham in which to delve into more modern brews, and 24 wines by the glass. Tasty dishes change twice a day – grilled sardines, Tuscan sausages – and doors lead to a walled beer garden where folk flock under the rain cover. Map: 15

848 Fox and Anchor 115 Charterhouse St, Smithfield, London EC1M 6AA +44 (0)20 7250 1300
The former dawn-drinking hole for Smithfield market has become a gastropub with rather stylish bedrooms and robust English dishes (duck egg with Welsh rarebit soldiers, steak and oyster pie). Ale comes in tankards in the unspoilt Victorian bar. Map: 15

849 The Eagle 159 Farringdon Road, Clerkenwell, London EC1R 3AL +44 (0)20 7837 1353
No tablecloths, no reservations, scuffed floors, worn leather chairs, and Mediterranean food – gutsy, delicious – ordered from the bar. With its real ales and decent choice of wines, the appeal is as much for drinkers as for diners. One of the Clerkenwell gastropub originals. Map: 15

850 The Peasant 240 St John Street, Islington, London EC1V 4PH +44 (0)20 7336 7726
A Victorian gin palace with a reputation for splendid food, wines, beers and cocktails. Tapas, mezze and the daily papers downstairs; pretty restaurant up. Brilliantly positioned for antique shops, the Design Centre and Sadler's Wells. Map: 15

851 The Albion 10 Thornhill Road, Islington, London N1 1HW +44 (0)20 7607 7450
Hidden in leafy, well-to-do Islington, this wisteria-clad Georgian jewel has winter fires, period detail and dark woods... and a wonderful big walled garden. The food is wonderful and Sunday lunch is what Sundays were made for. Don't miss the Yorkshire puds. Map: 15

852 The Junction Tavern 101 Fortess Roadd, Kentish Town, London NW5 1AG +44 (0)20 7485 9400
From the open-to-view kitchen flows food that is modern European and wide-ranging. While half the pub is restaurant, the rest is old-fashioned bar, serving over ten real ales a week. A great Saturday brunch, and kid-friendly too. A joy in laid-back Kentish Town. Map: 15

853 The Narrow 44 Narrow Street, Limehouse, London E14 8DJ +44 (0)20 7592 7950
Gordon Ramsay's first pub, in an Edwardian dockmaster's house on a gorgeous bend of the Thames. Good range of real ales and ciders and predictably modern British food, with barbecues at weekends. The setting is the thing. Map: 15

Manchester

854 Marble Arch 73 Rochdale Road, Manchester M4 4HY +44 (0)1618 325914
Marvellous tiled interior, with mosaic friezes high up in the vaulted roof and a deceptively sloping floor. A microbrewery at the rear produces an enticing array of organic vegan beers. Map: 12

855 Circus Tavern 86 Portland Street, Manchester M1 4GX +44 (0)1612 365818
In the city centre, one of Britain's smallest pubs, thrice as deep as wide, with a tiny under-stairs bar and two magnificent, panelled roomettes. Twenty punters (supping Tetleys Bitter) is a crowd here. Map: 12

856 Arden Arms 23 Millgate, Stockport SK1 2LX +44 (0)1614 802185
A superb tiled lobby bar, hidden snug, real fires and sublime Edwardian wood and glass bar, in the shadow of ASDA. The lunchtime food is of restaurant quality. Map: 12

857 The Swan 1 The Square, Dobcross, Oldham OL3 5AA +44 (0)1457 873451
Slabbed stone floors and colourwashed ceilings pitch like a dinghy in a storm; rooms warmed by fires hive off in all directions from the lobby bar at this Moors pub on a lovely village square. Map: 12

Norfolk

858 The Lifeboat Inn Ship Lane, Thornham, Hunstanton PE36 6LT +44 (0)1485 512236
Glowing lamps and open fires in this bags-of-character inn. It's been an ale house since the 16th century and they still serve a decent pint, but food and dining room are due a makeover following the arrival of Marco Pierre White. The sea is a brisk walk across fields. Map: 9

859 The Lord Nelson Walsingham Rd, Burnham Thorpe, King's Lynn PE31 8HN +44 (0)1328 738241
Ancient benches and settles, worn brick, tile floors, and a serving hatch instead of a bar distinguish this marvellous place. Be tempted by a tot of Nelson's Blood or a pint of Woodforde's. Family-friendly garden. Map: 10

860 The George Cley, Holt NR25 7RN +44 (0)1263 740652
The Norfolk Naturalists Trust was formed at this rambling inn overlooking the saltmarshes. Dan Goff (of the White Horse in Blakeney) has completed the refurbishment and menus champion local produce. Reports please. Map: 10

861 The Walpole Arms The Common, Itteringham, Norwich NR11 7AR +44 (0)1263 587258
New owners have taken over this renowned Norfolk food pub in rolling countryside close to the National Trust's Blickling Estate – expect big changes. You have a glorious vine-covered terrace for summer, and great walks from the door. Map: 10

862 Fat Cat 49 West End Street, Norwich NR2 4NA +44 (0)1603 624364
Victorian corner pub and beer drinkers' heaven: 30 real ales with some on hand pump, others tapped from cask. The owners proudly keep this a traditional and simple drinking pub. Map: 10

863 The White Hart Hotel 3 Market Place, Hingham, Norwich NR9 4AF +44 (0)1953 850214
The latest Flying Kiwi Inn overlooks the market square in Georgian Hingham, near Norwich. Welcome to a contemporary makeover (rugs on wooden floors, fat lamps, books and a relaxed feel), simple pub cooking that champions local producers, and an immaculate garden. Rooms to follow – watch this space. Map: 10

Northamptonshire

864 The Falcon Fotheringhay, Peterborough PE8 5HZ +44 (0)1832 226254
Discreetly modernised with a conservatory addition, it keeps its pubby feel – darts in the tap bar, an open fire, Digfield Fools Nook on hand pump. Cooking is stylishly simple and wines are as good, with a surprising 24 by the glass. Map: 9

865 The Red Lion East Haddon, Northampton NN6 8BU +44 (0)1604 770223
A posh country inn close to Northampton with a serious approach to cooking great British food; Adam Gray's innovative menu champions local seasonal produce. It may have a Cookery School in the grounds but it's still the village local – three real ales on tap in the cosy bar. Map: 8

Northumberland

866 The Manor House Inn Shotley Bridge, Carterway Heads, Consett DH8 9LX +44 (0)1207 255268
Cheerful landlords, tasty food, a good bar with local cask ales and a cask cider, a raft of malts. Take your pint of Nels Best into the garden in summer where the eye sweeps over to the moors. Map: 12

867 Dipton Mill Dipton Mill Road, Hexham NE46 1YA +44 (0)1434 606577
Former 18th-century mill house in a deep hollow next to a babbling brook a short drive south of Hexham. Squeeze into the single panelled bar for blazing log fires, top-notch Hexhamshire ales (the pub is the brewery tap), and warming home-cooked food. Super summer garden. Map: 12

868 The Ship Marygate, Holy Island, Berwick-upon-Tweed TD15 2SJ +44 (0)1289 389311
Rustic bare boards and beamed bars – a spotless little pub that sits in a terrace of cottages on a fascinating tidal island. Hadrian and Border ales and good seafood. Map: 14

Nottinghamshire

869 Ye Olde Trip to Jerusalem 1 Brewhouse Yard, Nottingham NG1 6AD +44 (0)1159 473171
An amazing place carved into solid rock on which the castle sits, with rickety staircases and an aptly named Rock Lounge… plus a courtyard for those who choose daylight. The Trip serves a mixed crowd – locals, tourists, students – and the food is standard pub grub. Map: 8

870 Larwood and Voce Fox Road, West Bridgford, Nottingham NG2 6AJ +44 (0)1159 819960
Thriving town-centre 'pub and kitchen' next to Trent Bridge cricket ground. Come for the modern bar, cricket on the screen, live jazz and superb gastropub food. On match days the bar throngs. Map: 8

871 Black Horse 29 Main Street, Caythorpe, Nottingham NG14 7ED +44 (0)1159 663520
A tiny, carpeted bar where Sharron Andrews sells beer brewed on the premises and the fish menu is so popular that booking is essential. Dick Turpin once hid in the gents, apparently. Map: 8

872 Bottle & Glass High Street, Harby, Newark NG23 7EB +44 (0)1522 703438
Quirky village pub owned by the Hope family from Lincoln's famous Wig & Mitre. Victorian features blend with soft furnishings and chalkboard menus list soup to Sevruga caviar, all-day breakfast and 38 wines by the glass. Map: 9

Oxfordshire

873 Olde Reindeer Inn 47 Parsons Street, Banbury OX16 5NA +44 (0)1295 264031
Banbury's oldest pub has a reputation for good value, home-cooked lunches and cracking Hook Norton ale, in a cosy bar with polished boards and a magnificent carved fireplace. Don't miss the panelled Globe Room. Map: 8

874 The Bird in Hand Whiteoak Green, Hailey, Witney OX29 9XP +44 (0)1993 868321
A mellow stone Cotswolds' inn with a stylish bar (leather bucket seats, baskets of logs) and predominantly British food. The gentle hum of chatter, two real ales and an interesting wine list tempt you to linger – by the fires or on the terrace. Map: 8

875 Rose & Crown 14 North Parade Avenue, Oxford OX2 6LX +44 (0)1865 510551
A characterful, three-room Victorian pub in North Oxford – great ales, traditional lunchtime food, a heated back yard, interesting clientele and no music or mobile phones. Map: 8

876 The Bear 6 Alfred Street, Oxford OX1 4EH +44 (0)1865 728164
Oxford's oldest boozer, popular with town and gown, has a miniscule and shambolic interior, many years' worth of framed, frayed ties (it's a long story), tasty hamburgers and cracking ale. Map: 8

877 Fox and Hounds Christmas Common, Watlington OX49 5HL +44 (0)1491 612599
Known as the 'Top Fox', this 15th-century cottage stands high in the Chilterns. A timeless bar with a vast inglenook, a restaurant with an open-to-view kitchen, glorious walks from the door. Map: 4

878 King William IV Hailey, Wallingford OX10 6AD +44 (0)1491 681845
Take an OS map to locate this rural treat tucked down single-track lanes in the Chilterns. Spick-and-span traditional interior, the full range of Brakspear ales, grassy front garden with peaceful views – super after a hike in the hills. Map: 4

879 The Sweet Olive at The Chequers Inn Baker St, Aston Tirrold, Didcot OX11 9DD +44 (0)1235 851272
A homely village local close to the Ridgeway Path, with first-class French country cooking (plus a hint of North Africa) in the rustic bistro. The blackboard menu changes daily with small portions for kids – and the coffee is perfect. Map: 4

880 Black Horse Checkendon, Reading RG8 0TE +44 (0)1491 680418
Persevere up the pitted lane to this old-fashioned country local and enter another age. The pub has been run by the same family for 104 years; come for local ales from the cask, filled rolls, pickled eggs and a peaceful garden. Map: 4

881 Stag & Huntsman Hambleden, Henley-on-Thames RG9 6RP +44 (0)1491 571227
The setting's the thing and the picture-book village is popular with film crews. Now the pub is the star attraction following a revamp by Hillbrooke Hotels. Expect a quirky luxury throughout bar and bedrooms, and modern British fodder. Walks into the Chilterns lead from the door. Map: 4

Rutland

882 The Wheatsheaf 1 Stretton Road, Greetham, Oakham LE15 7NP +44 (0)1572 812325
Locals pile in for portions of good value pub food at this large, unpretentious pub just off the A1. Game sausages or beef and mushroom pie fit the bill – and in summer you can drink beside a stream complete with ducks and duck house! Map: 9

Shropshire

883 The Royal Oak Cardington, Church Stretton SY6 7JZ +44 (0)1694 771266
At the foot of Caer Caradoc, a 500-year-old pub loved by muddy-booted ramblers who come for its dependable range of real ales, cider and inexpensive daily specials from local suppliers. Map: 7

Somerset

884 The Bridge Inn 20 Bridge Street, Dulverton TA22 9HJ +44 (0)1398 324130
On the edge of a popular Exmoor village, you're greeted with good food and cask ales. Sip drinks on the terrace or warm up in front of the fire; dig into homemade pies or a good ploughmans. Map: 2

885 Three Horseshoes Langley Marsh, Wiveliscombe, Taunton TA4 2UL +44 (0)1984 623763
A real traditional local and proud of it. Come for Otter and Cotleigh beers tapped from the cask and good food (fish and game from Exmoor, locally reared beef) best enjoyed in the timeless and bustling front room. Map: 2

886 The Blue Ball Inn Triscombe, Bishops Lydeard, Taunton TA4 3HE +44 (0)1823 430921
Old thatched buildings and ancient stables were restored some while ago to create the Blue Ball, now a thriving food pub on a dead-lane below the Quantock Hills. Follow cracking pub food in high-raftered dining rooms with wonderful walks from the door. Map: 2

887 Cat Head Inn Cat St, Chiselborough, Stoke-sub-Hamdon TA14 6TT +44 (0)1935 881231
Striking hamstone pub in countryside close to Montacute. Spotless flagstoned rooms, fresh imaginative food, Otter bitter on tap and attractive gardens with views over the village. Map: 3

888 The Hunters' Lodge Priddy, Wells BA5 3AR +44 (0)1749 672275
On the windswept crossroads, a stark little treasure. Mr Dors is its proudest fixture, administering ale and just-made bowls of chilli to cavers, pot-holers, hikers and the odd local. An unpretentious treat. Map: 3

889 Tucker's Grave Inn Faulkland, Radstock BA3 5XF +44 (0)1373 834230
An unassuming, almost-unsigned 17th-century stone building, Tucker's is a treasure. Few frills, no bar, just four beer casks and containers of local heady cider in the bay, and a stack of crisp boxes against the wall. Defiantly informal. Map: 3

890 Ring O'Bells Hinton Blewett, Bristol BS39 5AN +44 (0)1761 452239
Snug and cosy village local tucked away by the old church and brimming with cheer and hospitality. Come for cracking Bath ales and honest home-cooked food. Map: 3

891 Carpenter's Arms Stanton Wick, Pensford, Bristol BS39 4BX +44 (0)1761 490202
Beams and stone walls are jazzed up by a tartan carpet, and the gleaming country style bar bristles with beverages at this classy inn set above the Chew Valley. Good food and fine wines, too. Map: 3

Suffolk

892 Star Inn The Street, Lidgate, Newmarket CB8 9PP +44 (0)1638 500275
The pretty Star was built in 1588. Fire blaze in winter, the garden glows in summer and the rich (French/Spanish) aromas that greet you are delicious all year round. Greene King on hand pump, and Newmarket close by. New owners in the offing. Map: 9

893 Queens Head Hawkedon, Bury St Edmunds IP29 4NN +44 (0)1284 789218
A true community pub lost down lanes amid unspoilt Suffolk farmland. The draw is the unpretentious atmosphere, the huge inglenook that glows in winter, the excellent country cooking (own butcher's shop and livestock) and the six changing regional ales. Don't miss the July beer festival. Map: 10

894 Butt & Oyster Pin Mill, Ipswich IP9 1JW +44 (0)1473 780764
In a charmingly untouristy sailing village, an old estuary pub with settles, tiled floors, summer terrace with barbecue and Adnams tapped from the cask. Arrive early if you want a window seat. Map: 10

895 The Ramsholt Arms Ramsholt, Woodbridge IP12 3AB +44 (0)1394 411229
Idyllic – on the shore of the river Deben. Down a pint of Nethergate on the terrace, listen to the calls of the curlew. Cosy fires, game in season and great fish and chips. Map: 10

896 The Crown Inn Bridge Road, Snape, Saxmundham IP17 1SL +44 (0)1728 688324
Garry, forager and lover of the 'good life', shares this Adnam's inn and smallholding with partner Teresa. A timeless interior, roaring log fires and a rare Suffolk settle combine with dayboat fish and their own meats. Families and dogs are encouraged. Map: 10

897 The Golden Key Priory Road, Snape, Saxmundham IP17 1SQ +44 (0)1728 688510
Young owners have taken on this civilised little cottage-style pub close to Snape Maltings. The classic beamed bar has quarry tiles and an ancient curved settle fronting the inglenook, there's well-kept Adnams on tap, good food using local produce and two terraces for summer supping. Map: 10

898 Victoria The Street, Earl Soham, Woodbridge IP13 7RL +44 (0)1728 685758
Inauspicious whitewashed village local by the green, famous for its home-brewed beers (Earl Soham Brewery). Few frills in the main bar but hearty pub food and a proper pint of Victoria Ale. Map: 10

899 The Queens Head The Street, Bramfield, Halesworth IP19 9HT +44 (0)1986 784214
Chef-landlord Mark Corcoran is passionate about provenance and his menus are filled with local farm meats and vegetables, served in a high-raftered bar with dark timbered walls, scrubbed pine tables and a blazing log fire. Lovely terraced courtyard and Adnams on tap. Map: 10

900 The Randolph Hotel 41 Wangford Rd, Reydon, Southwold IP18 6PZ +44 (0)1502 723603
As good for a quick bite and a pint of Adnams as for a three-course meal that takes in local fish and game. This Victorian pub-hotel has sleek modern good looks – and gardens for summer. Map: 10

Surrey

901 The Spotted Cow at Lower Bourne Bourne Grove, Lower Bourne, Farnham GU10 3QT +44 (0)1252 726541
The hidden setting is the prize: an idyllic wooded valley south of Farnham. Savour a pint of Hogs Back TEA and traditional pub food in the dog- and child-friendly four-acre garden. Map: 4

902 Stephan Langton Friday St, Abinger Common, Dorking RH5 6JR +44 (0)1306 730775
Secluded country pub at the bottom of leafy Leith Hill, with a handful of cottages and a hammer pond for company. Great refuelling spot after exploring Surrey's finest walks. Reports please. Map: 4

903 The Jolly Farmers Reigate Road, Betchworth, Reigate RH3 7BG +44 (0)1737 221355
On the A25, and thriving, is Jon and Paula Briscoe's gastropub. Find flagstones, timbers and brown leather sofas in bar and café; tuck into fresh food from meticulously sourced produce: coffee and cakes, lunches, dinners, local wines and superb ales. Map: 4

904 The Inn on the Pond Nutfield Marsh Rd, Nutfield, Redhill RH1 4EU +44 (0)1737 643000
Smartly renovated sister pub to The Ostrich in Colnbrook, tucked away by the village cricket pitch and overlooking Nutfield Marsh. Come for local Horsham ales, fresh food, logs fires in eclectic rooms, and a super terrace. Map: 4

905 Red Barn Tandridge Lane, Lingfield RH7 6LL +44 (0)1342 830820
Geronimo Inns has transformed this rambling, former Brewer's Fayre pub. Eat enjoyably at scrubbed tables in the high-raftered barn with its central fire. Reports please. Map: 4

Sussex

906 The Keepers Arms Trotton, Petersfield GU31 5ER +44 (0)1730 813724
High above the road, with a front terrace and views, it is pleasing outside and in. There's a warm friendly bar, food is good and draws a local crowd and you eat at candlelit tables in the dining room next to the bar. Map: 4

907 Black Jug 31 North Street, Horsham RH12 1RJ +44 (0)1403 253526
Victorian town centre pub owned and revamped by Brunning & Price. Expect classic wooden panelling, wooden floors, trademark bookcases and modern pub food served all day. Map: 4

908 The Half Moon The Street, Warninglid, Horsham RH17 5TR +44 (0)1444 461227
Unpretentious brick and stone 18th-century pub just off the A23 south of Crawley – drop off for excellent modern pub food, Harvey's ales, decent wines, and a super summer garden. Map: 4

909 The Fountain Inn Ashurst, Steyning BN44 3AP +44 (0)1403 710219
Paul McCartney's *Wonderful Christmas Time* was filmed in the flagstoned candlelit bar, aromatic with woodsmoke from a 16th-century inglenook. Raised decking overlooks the garden pond for a summery pint of Harveys Sussex. Foodie owners took over in 2011 – reports welcome. Map: 4

910 The Royal Oak Inn The Street, Poynings, Brighton BN45 7AQ +44 (0)1273 857389
A pretty village location below the South Downs for Paul Day's revamped pub. Come for the lovely summer garden, the local Harveys bitter and the ambitious menus brimming with local foods. Map: 4

911 The Hatch Inn Colemans Hatch TN7 4EJ +44 (0)1342 822363
Tiny 15th-century weatherboarded cottage hidden down lanes on the edge of the Ashdown Forest. Worth seeking out for tip-top Larkins' ales, blazing log fires and a big summer garden. Food is hearty and home-cooked; arrive early – the beamed bar fills quickly. Map: 4

912 Rose Cottage Inn Alciston, Polegate BN26 6UW +44 (0)1323 870377
Close to the South Downs Way, this wisteria-clad pub is on a quiet lane to nowhere. Run by the Lewis family since 1960, it's a bolthole for foodies in search of cosy bars, cushioned pews, a decent pint and fresh fish and game. Map: 5

913 Six Bells The Street, Chiddingly, Lewes BN8 6HE +44 (0)1825 872227
Gary Glitter, Led Zeppelin and Leo Sayer all played in this quirky little boozer renowned for its music and atmosphere. Log fires, Harveys on hand pump, boules in the garden, great value food. Map: 5

914 The Queen's Head Parsonage Lane, Icklesham, Rye TN36 4BL +44 (0)1424 814552
Arrive early to bag a rustic garden bench in summer; in winter retreat to the beamed bar for pints of Dark Star or heady Biddenden cider. Traditional pub food too at this tile-hung 17th-century pub, set on a ridge with spectacular views across the Brede Valley to Rye. Map: 5

915 The Bell High Street, Ticehurst TN5 7AS +44 (0)1580 200234
The Bell opened its spruced-up doors in 2011 following a £2m refurbishment. Find cool quirky design details throughout, good country cooking and local produce, funky bedrooms with birch trees and iPads (yes, really!) and American Airstreams in the garden. Map: 5

Wiltshire

916 The Neeld Arms The Street, Grittleton, Chippenham SN14 6AP +44 (0)1249 782470
True country boozer with friendly locals, two glowing inglenooks, fresh tasty food, good beers and drinkable wines. Four-poster beds upstairs, breakfast feasts. Map: 3

917 Rising Sun 32 Bowden Hill, Lacock, Chippenham SN15 2PP +44 (0)1249 730363
Unpretentious pub high on a hill above Lacock. Escape the crowds for the terrace and unrivalled views, sup a pint of Moles as hot-air balloons drift across the sky on summer evenings. Map: 3

918 The Barge Inn Honeystreet, Pewsey SN9 5PS +44 (0)1672 851705
The famous canalside pub thrives again. Now community-owned and supported by the BBC Village SOS project, it's become the village hub. This crop-circle enthusiasts' HQ has camping facilities, live music (don't miss Honeyfest), local beers, food and a wonderful laid-back vibe. Map: 3

919 The Boot High Street, Berwick St James, Salisbury SP3 4TN +44 (0)1722 790243
Lush gardens, great Wadworth beers and proper pub food (come for Sunday lunch) draw locals and walkers to this ex-cobbler's in the Wylye Valley. Map: 3

920 Red Lion Inn Kilmington, Warminster BA12 6RP +44 (0)1985 844263
The four-centuries-old farmhouse has become a quiet, traditional local. Accompany a great-value homemade cottage pie with a pint of Butcombe Bitter and a fabulous view of the South Wiltshire Downs. Map: 3

Worcestershire

921 The Swan Worcester Road, Hanley Swan, Worcester WR8 0EA +44 (0)1684 311870
Worth noting if heading for the Malvern Hills – a smartly revamped local overlooking the village green and pond. Contemporary layout and décor, three ales on tap and modern pub food. Map: 8

922 Plough & Harrow Rhydd Road, Guarlford, Malvern WR13 6NY +44 (0)1684 310453
Nice buzzy atmosphere and impressive upmarket menus with an emphasis on home-grown and local produce, in this rambling 18th-century pub in the wilds outside Malvern. Map: 8

923 The Monkey House Defford, Upton-on-Severn WR8 9BW +44 (0)1386 750234
One of the last four cider houses in England – a curiosity. No signs guide you to the thatched house set back from the road but the locals will. Try Westons First Quality or Woodmancote Dry cider served through the hatch, and sit outside; there's a shed if the weather's bad. Map: 8

Yorkshire

924 The Fox & Rabbit Lockton, Pickering YO18 7NQ +44 (0)1751 460213
This friendly family-run roadside inn is worth stopping for. Look forward to open fires, a series of small rooms and an interesting menu: figs with Parma ham alongside pub classics like gammon and homemade chips and steak and ale pie. Map: 13

925 The Coachman Inn Pickering Road West, Snainton, Scarborough YO13 9PL
+44 (0)1723 859231
It's been an inn since 1776, and was the last staging post for the York mail coach before Scarborough. There's warmth in the Yorkshire welcome from the landlady and you are perfectly placed for striding into the Yorkshire Moors. Map: 13

926 The Alice Hawthorn Nun Monkton, York YO26 8EW +44 (0)1423 330303
Handsome outside, warm and pubby within, all open fires, beams and leather wing chairs. The menu is steadfastly English (but new owners in 2012), the pumps are Black Sheep and Timothy Taylor's, and the area is a haven for walkers – bring your canine chum. Map: 12

927 Ye Olde Punch Bowl Marton, Marton-cum-Grafton, York YO51 9QY
+44 (0)1423 322519
Cosy up by one of the roaring log fires in this 16th-century whitewashed pub. Packed full of character with deep red walls and vintage motor racing pictures, it's perfect for meeting up with a group of friends. Just north of York. Map: 12

928 Whitelocks Turks Head Yard, Leeds LS1 6HB +44 (0)1132 453950
In Leeds' centre, an interior barely changed since Victorian times: old button-backed leather banquettes with panelled mirrored dividers in a tiny narrow bar. Come for the history not the food, and the Deuchars. Map: 12

929 The Fat Cat 23 Alma Street, Sheffield S3 8SA +44 (0)1142 494801
In Sheffield and desperate for a pint? Follow signs to the Kelham Island Museum and this bustling backstreet boozer. Great home-brewed beers and guest ales await. Good value pub grub. Map: 12

930 The Lord Nelson 15 High Street, Luddenden, Halifax HX2 6PX
+44 (0)1422 882176
Opposite a churchyard and a gurgling beck, this 17th-century pub was once a meeting place for artists and writers. Timothy Taylor's is on tap today along with an extensive pub menu. Outside are two stunning levels of garden with views over the village to the hills. Map: 12

931 Queens Arms Litton, Skipton BD23 5QJ +44 (0)1756 770208
Glorious walks onto the moors and along the river from this homely 16th-century Dales inn. Head here for warming fires, home-brewed ales, hot food, stunning views. Map: 12

932 The George Kirk Gill, Hubberholme, Skipton BD23 SEJ +44 (0)1756 760223
Sympathetically updated but still fairly basic Dales pub with good beer and traditional pub food. J B Priestley's favourite watering hole – he's buried in the church opposite. Map: 12

933 The Moorcock Inn Garsdale Head, Sedbergh LA10 5PU +44 (0)1969 667488
Wild and remote in an isolated moorland spot at the top end of Wensleydale. There's a quirky stylishness that is striking in such an unworldly setting; plus local ales and homemade pub grub. Map: 12

934 Charles Bathurst Inn Richmond DL11 6EN +44 (0)1748 884567
Retreat after a bracing walk to the Codys' wonderful inn tucked high above Swaledale. Rustic pine-furnished interiors; hearty dishes of local produce; pints of Black Sheep. Map: 12

Wales

Carmarthenshire

935 White Hart Thatched Inn & Brewery Llanddarog, Carmarthen SA32 8NT
+44 (0)1267 275395
An oddity for west Wales, a thatched pub whose low-beamed rooms ooze fairytale charm. Real log fires, real homemade pies and real beers (home brewed) – worth leaving the A40 for. Map: 6

Conwy

936 The Lord Newborough Conway Rd, Dolgarrog, Conwy LL32 8JX +44 (0)1492 660549
On the quiet side of the valley, yards from the river, this sky-blue-painted inn was a hunting lodge. Step in to an upbeat bar with yellowy hues, real fires and great-value homemade pub food. Great walks from the front door. Map: 7

Gwynedd

937 Penhelig Arms 27-29 Terrace Road, Aberdyfi LL35 0LT +44 (0)1654 767215
It's small, friendly and rather smart, and village life pours through. Local art adorns the walls in the restaurant and a fire burns in the bar; along the quay come the fishermen, butchers, bakers and smallholders who deliver daily to the kitchen. Map: 6

938 Ty Coch Inn Porthdinllaen, Morfa Nefyn, Pwllheli LL53 6DB +44 (0)1758 720498
Find time to walk along the beach to the tiny beachside hamlet and this spectacularly sited pub – sup a pint of Isallt Purple Moose with your feet in the sea. A Welsh welcome and simple food await – lovely. Phone for winter opening times. Map: 6

939 Pen-y-Gwryd Hotel Nant Gwynant, Caernarfon LL55 4NT +44 (0)1286 870211
Snowdonia's ex-Mountain Rescue HQ and training base for the 1953 Everest expedition. Spot their boots in the bar and eat by candlelight. A treasure. Map: 6

940 Castell 33 Y Maes, Caernarfon LL55 2NN +44 (0)1286 677970
Smack in the Market Square, a stone's throw from Caernarfon Castle, this old Georgian hotel is undergoing some ambitious reworking. Get ready for bold artwork on vibrant walls and an eclectic modern menu. Bedrooms are planned. Map: 6

Monmouthshire

941 Llanthony Priory Llanthony, Abergavenny NP7 7NN +44 (0)1873 890487
Once only walkers knew Llanthony was here, now the abbot's cellar holds an atmospheric hotchpotch of tables and high-backed pews. Simple food, pints of Felinfoel, proper espresso, romantic views. Map: 7

942 The Crown at Pantygelli Pantygelli, Abergavenny NP7 7HR +44 (0)1873 853314
Handsome 16th-century pub with glorious country views towards the Skirrid. A true community pub with farmers at the bar, local ales on tap and good food sourced from surrounding farms. Map: 7

Pembrokeshire

943 Cresselly Arms Cresswell Quay, Kilgetty SA68 0TE +44 (0)1646 651210
The walls of this timeless old pub are hung with wisteria; pick an outside table and gaze onto the estuary and the woods. Inside, ale is poured from a jug – there's no truck with modern innovation here. Authentically plain. Map: 6

Vale of Glamorgan

944 The Bush St Hilary, Cowbridge CF71 7DP +44 (0)1446 772745
Beautifully restored after a disastrous fire this wonderful thatched pub stands in gentle countryside. A cul-de-sac setting opposite the church makes outside benches very popular. For winter: a roaring fire, hearty food, pints of Hancocks – reports please. Map: 2

For many years Alastair Sawday Publishing has been 'greening' the business in different ways. Our aim is to reduce our environmental footprint as far as possible and with almost everything we do we have environmental implications in mind. In recognition of our efforts we won a Business Commitment to the Environment Award in 2005, a Queen's Award for Enterprise in the Sustainable Development category in 2006, and the Independent Publishers Guild Environmental Award in 2008.

The buildings

Beautiful as they were, our old offices leaked heat, used electricity to heat water and rooms, flooded spaces with light to illuminate one person, and were not ours to alter.

So in 2005 we created our own eco offices by converting some old barns to create a low-emissions building. Heating and lighting the building, which houses over 30 employees, now produces only 0.28 tonnes of carbon dioxide per year – a reduction of 35%. Not bad when you compare this with the six tonnes emitted by the average UK household. We achieved this through a variety of innovative and energy-saving building techniques, some of which are described below.

Insulation By laying insulating board 90mm thick immediately under the roof tiles and on the floor, and lining the inside of the building with plastic sheeting, we are now insulated even for Arctic weather, and almost totally air-tight.

Heating We installed a wood pellet boiler from Austria in order to be largely fossil-fuel free. The heat is conveyed by water to all corners of the building via an underfloor system.

Water We installed a 6,000-litre tank to collect rainwater from the roofs. This is pumped back, via an ultra-violet filter, to lavatories, shower and basins. There are also two solar thermal panels on the roof providing heat to the one hot-water cylinder.

Lighting We have a mix of low-energy lighting – task lighting and up lighting – and have installed three sun pipes.

Electricity Our electricity has long come from the Good Energy Company and is 100% renewable.

Photo top: Tom Germain
Photo right: Jackie King

Materials Virtually all materials are non-toxic or natural, and our carpets are made from (80%) Herdwick sheep wool from National Trust farms in the Lake District.

Doors and windows Outside doors and new windows are wooden, double-glazed and beautifully constructed in Norway. Old windows have been double-glazed.

More greenery

Besides having a building we are proud of, and which is pretty impressive visually, too, we work in a number of other ways to reduce the company's overall environmental footprint.

- office travel is logged as part of a carbon sequestration programme, and money for compensatory tree planting donated to SCAD in India for a tree-planting and development project
- we avoid flying and take the train for business trips wherever possible
- car sharing and the use of a company pool car (LPG fuelled) are part of company policy
- organic and Fair Trade basic provisions are used in the staff kitchen and organic and/or local food is provided by the company at all in-house events
- green cleaning products are used throughout
- kitchen waste is composted on our allotment
- the allotment is part of a community garden – alongside which we keep a small family of pigs and hens

However, becoming 'green' is a journey and, although we began long before most companies, we realise we still have a long way to go.

Alastair Sawday has been publishing books since 1994 finding Special Places to Stay in Britain and abroad. All our properties are inspected by us and are chosen for their charm and individuality and now with 25 titles to choose from there are plenty of places to explore. You can buy any of our books direct at a reader discount of 25%* on the RRP.

www.sawdays.co.uk/bookshop

List of titles:	RRP	Discount price
British Bed & Breakfast	£15.99	£11.99
British Bed & Breakfast for Garden Lovers	£19.99	£14.99
British Hotels and Inns	£15.99	£11.99
Pubs & Inns of England & Wales	£15.99	£11.99
Venues	£11.99	£8.99
Cotswolds	£9.99	£7.49
Devon & Cornwall	£9.99	£7.49
Wales	£9.99	£7.49
Dog-friendly Breaks in Britain	£14.99	£11.24
Ireland	£12.99	£9.74
French Bed & Breakfast	£15.99	£11.99
French Self-catering	£14.99	£11.24
French Châteaux & Hotels	£15.99	£11.99
French Vineyards	£19.99	£14.99
Paris	£9.99	£7.49
Green Europe	£11.99	£8.99
Italy	£15.99	£11.99
Portugal	£12.99	£9.74
Spain	£15.99	£11.99
Morocco	£9.99	£7.49
India	£11.99	£8.99
Go Slow England & Wales	£19.99	£14.99
Go Slow France	£19.99	£14.99
Go Slow Italy	£19.99	£14.99
Eat Slow Britain	£19.99	£14.99

*postage and packaging is added to each order

How to order:

You can order online at: **www.sawdays.co.uk/bookshop/**

or call: **+44(0)1275 395431**

Dorset 

2 ## The Chetnole Inn

3 Chetnole

4 A cream-painted pub reached by leafy lanes south of Sherborne, half an hour from the wonderful Dorset coast. Opposite the parish church, the updated inn has not lost touch with its roots; there's a snug bar area with a wood-burning stove; a stone-floored, hop-hung lounge bar; a restaurant beyond, similarly attractive; and a beer garden with giant rabbits. Dishes range from straightforward, for children, to imaginative, and Mike sources ingredients as locally as possible. A memorable meal might include pan-fried breast of pigeon with puy lentils, black pudding and pancetta followed by duo of duck with red cabbage and redcurrant jus, and an orange and cardamom crème brûlée to round things off. If staying over you'll be comfortable in one of the smart, pale-carpeted bedrooms; all look towards the church, all are prettily dressed. Beds are inviting with thick duvets and feather pillows, so too are the homemade biscuits, the real coffee and the magazines. Gleaming bathrooms have bathrobes and Molton Brown treats. As winner twice of the Best Dining Pub in the Taste of Dorset Awards, the Chetnole is hard to fault!

5	Price	From £95. Singles £70.
6	Rooms	3: 2 doubles, 1 twin/double.
7	Meals	Lunch & dinner £9-£16. Bar meals from £5. Sunday lunch from £9.50.
8	Closed	3pm-6.30pm. Sun eves & Mon (Oct-Apr).
9	Directions	Chetnole is signed off A37 between Yeovil and Dorchester, 7 miles south of Yeovil, 7 miles south west of Sherborne.

Mike Lewin
The Chetnole Inn
Chetnole,
Sherborne DT9 6NU

Tel +44 (0)1935 872337
Web www.thechetnoleinn.co.uk

 10

Entry 180 Map 3 11